SEVENTH EDITION

CUSTOMER SERVICE

SKILLS FOR SUCCESS

Robert W. Lucas

Principal, Robert W. Lucas Enterprises

McGraw Hill Education

CUSTOMER SERVICE: SKILLS FOR SUCCESS, SEVENTH EDITION

Published by McGraw-Hill Education, 2 Penn Plaza, New York, NY 10121. Copyright © 2019 by Robert W. Lucas. All rights reserved. Printed in the United States of America. Previous editions © 2015, 2012, and 2009. No part of this publication may be reproduced or distributed in any form or by any means, or stored in a database or retrieval system, without the prior written consent of McGraw-Hill Education, including, but not limited to, in any network or other electronic storage or transmission, or broadcast for distance learning.

Some ancillaries, including electronic and print components, may not be available to customers outside the United States.

This book is printed on acid-free paper.

1 2 3 4 5 6 7 8 9 LMN 21 20 19 18

ISBN   978-1-259-95407-8
MHID   1-259-95407-2

Executive Brand Manager: *Meredith Fossel*
Lead Product Developer: *Kelly Delso*
Marketing Manager: *Elizabeth Schonagen*
Content Project Managers: *Melissa M. Leick, Bruce Gin*
Buyer: *Sandy Ludovissy*
Design: *Matt Diamond*
Content Licensing Specialist: *Deanna Dausener*
Cover Image: © *Getty Images/Vetta*
Compositor: *Lumina Datamatics, Inc.*

All credits appearing on page or at the end of the book are considered to be an extension of the copyright page.

Library of Congress Cataloging-in-Publication Data

Names: Lucas, Robert W., author.
  Title: Customer service : skills for success / Robert W. Lucas, Principal, Robert W. Lucas Enterprises.
  Description: Seventh Edition | Dubuque, IA : McGraw-Hill Education, [2017] |
  Revised edition of the author's Customer service, 2015. Includes bibliographical references and index.
  Identifiers: LCCN 2017020710| ISBN 9781259954078 (alk. paper)
  ISBN 1259954072 (alk. paper)
  Subjects: LCSH: Customer services.
  Classification: LCC HF5415.5 .L83 2017 | DDC 658.8/12—dc23
  LC record available at https://lccn.loc.gov/2017020710

The Internet addresses listed in the text were accurate at the time of publication. The inclusion of a website does not indicate an endorsement by the authors or McGraw-Hill Education, and McGraw-Hill Education does not guarantee the accuracy of the information presented at these sites.

mheducation.com/highered

ROBERT (BOB) W. LUCAS is an internationally known award-winning author and learning and performance expert who specializes in workplace performance-based training and consulting services. He is the principal of Robert W. Lucas Enterprises and owner of Success Skills Press.

For over four decades, Bob has shared his knowledge and expertise as a coach and consultant. He has facilitated training sessions for thousands of workplace professionals in a variety of industries from national and international organizations. He also taught for over 15 years as an adjunct professor in the Human Resource Development Master of Arts program at Webster University and regularly presents educational sessions to various local and national groups. In addition, Bob has led or served on the boards of the Central Florida Chapter of the Association for Talent Development, the Florida Safety Council, Leadership Seminole, and the Florida Authors and Publishers Association.

In recent years, Bob has dedicated much of his time to self-publishing books on a variety of skills topics and writing three blogs (Customer Service Skills, Creative Training, and Nonfiction Writing). His areas of expertise include customer service, creative training and management program development, presentation skills, interpersonal communication, adult learning, and diversity. Listed in *Who's Who in the World, Who's Who in America,* and *Who's Who in the South & Southeast*, he is an avid writer. In addition to this book, he has written and contributed to 37 books and has published over 1,000 articles. Some of his other titles are *Please Every Customer: Delivering Stellar Customer Service Across Cultures* and *How to Be Great Call Center Representative*.

Bob earned a Bachelor of Science degree in Law Enforcement from the University of Maryland, an M.A. degree with a focus in Human Resources Development from George Mason University in Fairfax, Virginia, and a second M.A. degree in Management and Leadership from Webster University in Orlando, Florida.

 **connect**®

McGraw-Hill Connect® is a highly reliable, easy-to-use homework and learning management solution that utilizes learning science and award-winning adaptive tools to improve student results.

Homework and Adaptive Learning

- Connect's assignments help students contextualize what they've learned through application, so they can better understand the material and think critically.

- Connect will create a personalized study path customized to individual student needs through SmartBook®.

- SmartBook helps students study more efficiently by delivering an interactive reading experience through adaptive highlighting and review.

Over **7 billion questions** have been answered, making McGraw-Hill Education products more intelligent, reliable, and precise.

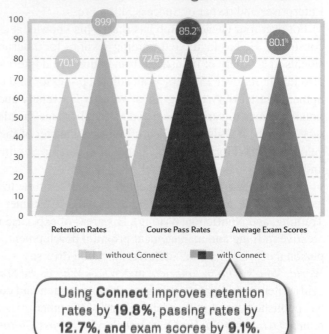

Connect's Impact on Retention Rates, Pass Rates, and Average Exam Scores

Retention Rates: 70.1% without Connect, 89.9% with Connect
Course Pass Rates: 72.5% without Connect, 85.2% with Connect
Average Exam Scores: 71.0% without Connect, 80.1% with Connect

without Connect — with Connect

Using **Connect** improves retention rates by **19.8%**, passing rates by **12.7%**, and exam scores by **9.1%**.

73% of instructors who use **Connect** require it; instructor satisfaction **increases** by 28% when **Connect** is required.

Quality Content and Learning Resources

- Connect content is authored by the world's best subject matter experts, and is available to your class through a simple and intuitive interface.

- The Connect eBook makes it easy for students to access their reading material on smartphones and tablets. They can study on the go and don't need internet access to use the eBook as a reference, with full functionality.

- Multimedia content such as videos, simulations, and games drive student engagement and critical thinking skills.

©McGraw-Hill Education

Robust Analytics and Reporting

©Hero Images/Getty Images

- Connect Insight® generates easy-to-read reports on individual students, the class as a whole, and on specific assignments.

- The Connect Insight dashboard delivers data on performance, study behavior, and effort. Instructors can quickly identify students who struggle and focus on material that the class has yet to master.

- Connect automatically grades assignments and quizzes, providing easy-to-read reports on individual and class performance.

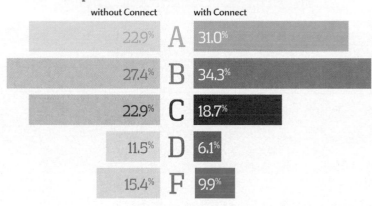

Impact on Final Course Grade Distribution

without Connect		with Connect
22.9%	A	31.0%
27.4%	B	34.3%
22.9%	C	18.7%
11.5%	D	6.1%
15.4%	F	9.9%

More students earn **As** and **Bs** when they use **Connect**.

Trusted Service and Support

- Connect integrates with your LMS to provide single sign-on and automatic syncing of grades. Integration with Blackboard®, D2L®, and Canvas also provides automatic syncing of the course calendar and assignment-level linking.

- Connect offers comprehensive service, support, and training throughout every phase of your implementation.

- If you're looking for some guidance on how to use Connect, or want to learn tips and tricks from super users, you can find tutorials as you work. Our Digital Faculty Consultants and Student Ambassadors offer insight into how to achieve the results you want with Connect.

BRIEF CONTENTS

PART ONE

THE PROFESSION 2

1 The World of Customer Service 4

2 Contributing to the Service Culture 50

PART TWO

SKILLS FOR SUCCESS 94

3 Verbal Communication Skills 96

4 Nonverbal Communication Skills 134

5 Listening to the Customer 172

PART THREE

BUILDING AND MAINTAINING RELATIONSHIPS 206

6 Customer Service and Behavior 208

7 Service Breakdowns and Recovery 240

8 Customer Service in a Diverse World 290

9 Customer Service via Technology 330

PART FOUR

RETAINING CUSTOMERS 384

10 Encouraging Customer Loyalty 386

Glossary 435

Notes 443

Bibliography 445

Index 446

CONTENTS

Preface xi

Acknowledgments xix

PART ONE
THE PROFESSION 2
Customer Service Interview: Barbara Tanzer, Owner, TBS Group

---

1 The World of Customer Service 4

In the Real World: (Retail)—Amazon.com Inc. 5

LO 1-1 Defining Customer Service 6
The Concept of Customer Service 9
Post–World War II Service in the United States 11
The Shift to Service 11

LO 1-2 Growth of the Service Sector 12
Impact of the Economy 13

LO 1-3 Societal Factors Affecting Customer Service 19
Shifts in Consumer Needs, Wants, and Expectations 19
Global Economic Shifts 20
Shifts in the Population and Labor Force 22
Increased Efficiency in Technology 24
Deregulation of Many Industries 27
Geopolitical Changes 27
Changing Values 28
More Women Entering the Workforce 30
A More Racially and Ethnically Diverse Population is Entering the Workforce 30
More Older Workers Entering the Workforce 31
Growth of E-Commerce 32

LO 1-4 Consumer Behavior Shifts 33
Different Mindset 33
Expectation of Quality Service 34
Enhanced Consumer Preparation 35

LO 1-5 The Customer Service Environment 35
Components of a Customer Service Environment 36
The Customer 36
Organizational Culture 39

Human Resources 39
Deliverables 42
Delivery Systems 43
Service 43

LO 1-6 Addressing the Changes 44
Small Business Perspective 45

---

2 Contributing to the Service Culture 50

In the Real World: (Delivery Services)—FedEx 51

LO 2-1 Defining a Service Culture 53
Service Philosophy or Mission 55
Employee Roles and Expectations 57
Policies and Procedures 63
Products and Services 65
Motivators and Rewards 66
Management Support 68
Employee Empowerment 71
Training 71

LO 2-2 Establishing a Service Strategy 72

LO 2-3 Customer-Friendly Systems 73
Typical System Components 74
Service Delivery Systems 74
Tools for Service Measurement 78

LO 2-4 Eleven Strategies for Promoting a Positive Service Culture 80

LO 2-5 Separating Average Companies from Excellent Companies 85

LO 2-6 What Customers Want 86
Small Business Perspective 88

PART TWO   SKILLS FOR SUCCESS   94
Customer Service Interview: Ginger Marks, CEO, Calomar, LLC

3 Verbal Communication Skills 96

In the Real World: Insurance—State Farm Insurance 97

LO 3-1 The Importance of Effective Communication 98

LO 3-2 Ensuring Two-Way Communication 100
Interpersonal Communication Model 101

LO 3-3 Communicating Positively 104
Prepare for Positive Customer Interactions 105
Let Your Customers Know They Are Important 107
Address Your Customer's Expectations Positively 109
Nurture a Continuing Relationship 114

LO 3-4 Providing Feedback Effectively 117
Verbal Feedback 118
Nonverbal Feedback 118

LO 3-5 Avoiding Negative Communication 119

LO 3-6 Dealing Assertively with Customers 122

LO 3-7 Assertive versus Aggressive Service 124
Small Business Perspective 128

4 Nonverbal Communication Skills 134

In the Real World: (Financial Services)—American Express 135

LO 4-1 What Is Nonverbal Communication? 137

LO 4-2 The Scope of Nonverbal Behavior 137
Body Language 138
Vocal Cues 143
Appearance and Grooming 146
Spatial Cues 149
Environmental Cues 150
Miscellaneous Cues 151

LO 4-3 The Role of Gender in Nonverbal Communication 155

LO 4-4 The Impact of Culture on Nonverbal Communication 157

LO 4-5 Negative Nonverbal Behaviors 158
Unprofessional Handshake 158
Fidgeting 159
Pointing a Finger or Other Object 159
Raising an Eyebrow 160
Peering over Top of Eyeglasses 160
Crossing Arms or Putting Hands on Hips 160
Holding Hands Near Mouth 160

LO 4-6 Strategies for Improving Nonverbal Communication 160
Seek out Nonverbal Cues 161
Confirm Your Perceptions 161
Seek Clarifying Feedback 162
Analyze Your Interpretations of Nonverbal Cues 162

LO 4-7 Customer-Focused Behavior 163
Small Business Perspective 166

5 Listening to the Customer 172

In the Real World: Retail—Nordstrom 173

LO 5-1 Why Is Listening So Important? 174

LO 5-2 What Is Listening? 175
Hearing and Receiving the Message 176
Attending 177
Comprehending or Assigning Meaning 177
Responding 177

LO 5-3 Characteristics of a Good Listener 179

LO 5-4 Causes of Listening Breakdown 181
Personal Obstacles 181
Listening Skill Level 185
External Obstacles 187
Additional Obstacles to Effective Listening 190

LO 5-5 Strategies for Improved Listening 191
Stop Talking! 191
Prepare Yourself 192
Listen Actively 192
Show a Willingness to Listen 194
Show Empathy 194
Listen for Concepts 194
Listen Openly 194
Send Positive Nonverbal Cues 195
Do Not Argue 195
Take Notes, If Necessary 195

LO 5-6 Information-Gathering Techniques 196
Open-End Questions 196
Closed-End Questions 198

LO 5-7 Additional Question Guidelines 200
Avoid Criticism 200
Ask Only Positively Phrased Questions 200
Ask Direct Questions 200
Ask Customers How You Can Better Serve 201
Small Business Perspective 201

PART THREE BUILDING AND MAINTAINING RELATIONSHIPS   206
Customer Service Interview: Venkatesh P. Nagalapadi, President, CFP Physicians Group

6 Customer Service and Behavior   208

In the Real World: Supermarket—Trader Joe's   209

LO 6-1 What Are Behavioral Styles?   211

LO 6-2 Identifying Behavioral Styles   212
R: Rational   216
I: Inquisitive   217
D: Decisive   218
E: Expressive   219

LO 6-3 Communicating with Each Style   220

LO 6-4 Building Stronger Relationships   223
Discover Customer Needs   224
Say "Yes"   226
Seek Opportunities for Service   227
Focus on Process Improvement   228
Make Customers Feel Special   229
Be Culturally Aware   229
Know Your Products and Services   231

LO 6-5 Dealing with Perceptions   232
Perceptions and Stereotypes   233
Small Business Perspective   235

7 Service Breakdowns and Recovery   240

In the Real World: Retail/Manufacturing—Coca-Cola   241

LO 7-1 What Is a Service Breakdown?   243

LO 7-2 The Role of Behavioral Style   245

LO 7-3 Difficult Customers   246
Demanding or Domineering Customers   248
Indecisive Customers   249
Dissatisfied and Angry Customers   251
Rude or Inconsiderate Customers   253
Talkative Customers   254

LO 7-4 Handling Emotions with the Emotion-Reducing Model   255

LO 7-5 Reasons for Customer Defection   257

LO 7-6 Working with Internal Customers (Coworkers)   258
Stay Connected   259
Meet All Commitments   260
Do Not Sit on Your Emotions   261
Build a Professional Reputation   261
Adopt a Good-Neighbor Policy   261

LO 7-7 Strategies for Preventing Dissatisfaction and Problem Solving   263
Make Positive Initial Contact   263
Think Like the Customer   263

Pamper the Customer   264
Respect the Customer   264
Exceed Expectations   266
Responding to Conflict   267
Causes of Conflict   267
Salvaging Relationships after Conflict   269

LO 7-8 The Problem-Solving Process   272
1. Identify the Problem   272
2. Compile and Analyze the Data   274
3. Identify the Alternatives   274
4. Evaluate the Alternatives   274
5. Make a Decision   275
6. Monitor the Results   275

LO 7-9 Implementing a Service Recovery Strategy   275
1. Apologize, Apologize, and Apologize Again   276
2. Take Immediate Action   277
3. Show Compassion   280
4. Provide Compensation   280
5. Conduct Follow-Up   281

LO 7-10 Disaster Planning Initiatives in the Service Recovery Process   281
Small Business Perspective   283

8 Customer Service in a Diverse World   290

In the Real World: Restaurant Franchise—Subway   291

LO 8-1 The Impact of Diversity   292

LO 8-2 Defining Diversity   294

LO 8-3 Customer Awareness   295

LO 8-4 The Impact of Cultural Values   296
Modesty   298
Expectations of Privacy   298
Forms of Address   299
Respect for Elders   301
Importance of Relationships   301
Gender Roles   303
Attitude toward Conflict   303
The Concept of Time   304
Ownership of Property   305

LO 8-5 Providing Quality Service to Diverse Customer Groups   307
Customers with Language Differences   307
Customers with Disabilities   312
Elderly Customers   317
Younger Customers   319

LO 8-6 Communicating with Diverse Customers   322

Small Business Perspective   324

9 Customer Service via Technology   330

In the Real World: Technology—Microsoft   331

LO 9-1 The Role of Technology in Customer Service   333

LO 9-2 The Customer Contact/Call Center or Help Desk   337

Call Center Technology   338

Traditional Call Center Technology   338

LO 9-3 Tapping into Web-Based and Mobile Technologies   345

Websites   345

Social Media   347

Advantages and Disadvantages of Technology   355

LO 9-4 Technology Etiquette and Strategies   361

E-Mail   361

Facsimile   364

LO 9-5 The Telephone in Customer Service   366

Communication Skills for Success   367

Tips for Creating a Positive Telephone Image   369

Effective Telephone Usage   371

Voice Mail and Answering Machines or Services   373

Taking Messages Professionally   375

General Advice for Communicating by Telephone   376

Small Business Perspective   377

PART FOUR   RETAINING CUSTOMERS   384
Customer Service Interview: Richard Ulrych, Partner, Waterways Car Spa

10 Encouraging Customer Loyalty   386

In the Real World: Wholesale—Costco   387

LO 10-1 Customer Loyalty   389

LO 10-2 The Role of Trust   392

Communicate Effectively and Convincingly   395

Display Caring and Concern   395

Be Fair   396

Admit Errors or Lack of Knowledge   396

Trust Your Customers   398

Keep Your Word   398

Provide Peace of Mind   399

Be Responsible for Your Customer Relationships   399

Personalize Your Approach   399

Keep an Open Mind   400

Individualize Service   400

Show Respect   401

Elicit Customer Input   401

LO 10-3 The Importance of Customer Relationship Management   403

Benefits of Customer Relationship Management   406

LO 10-4 The Role of Channel Partner Relationships on Customer Loyalty   408

Three Types of Channel Partners   408

LO 10-5 Provider Characteristics Affecting Customer Loyalty   409

Responsiveness   409

Adaptability   411

Communication Skills   411

Decisiveness   413

Enthusiasm   413

Ethical Behavior   413

Initiative   415

Knowledge   416

Perceptiveness   416

Planning Ability   417

Problem-Solving Ability   419

Professionalism   419

LO 10-6 Making the Customer Number One   420

Establish Rapport   421

Identify and Satisfy Customer Needs Quickly   422

Exceed Expectations   422

Follow-Up   423

LO 10-7 Enhancing Customer Satisfaction as a Strategy for Retaining Customers   424

Pay Attention   424

Deal with One Customer at a Time   425

Know Your Customers   425

Give Customers Special Treatment   425

Service Each Customer Adequately   425

Do the Unexpected   425

Handle Complaints Effectively   426

Sell Benefits, Not Features   426

Know Your Competition   427

Cost of Dissatisfied Customers   427

LO 10-8 Strive for Quality   428

Small Business Perspective   428

Glossary   435

Notes   443

Bibliography   445

Index   446

New to This Edition

Every Chapter

- New *Customer Service interviews* with service
- Updated research and statistics throughout text
- New *Words to Live By* quotes at the end of the *Quick Preview* section of each chapter
- Updated and addition of *Trending Now* sections in many chapters

Chapter 1

- Interview by customer service industry professional
- New *In the Real World* chapter opening case study (Amazon.com)
- New *Think About It*
- Updated research and statistics throughout chapter
- New section *Key Developments That Impacted Customer Service Profession*
- Expanded definitions of service-related terminology
- New *Trending Now* segments added
- Updated discussion of *Global Economic Shifts* impacting customer service
- Additional *Work It Out* section
- Addition of section on *Shifts in Consumer Needs, Wants, and Expectations*
- Addition of suggestions for dealing more effectively with *Internal Customers*
- Additional *Customer Service Tips*
- Expanded discussion of small business trends and customer service
- Additional *Search It Out* resources

Chapter 2

- Updated *In the Real World* chapter opening case study (FedEx)
- New *Think About It*
- Updated research and statistics
- Inclusion of sample mission statements
- Additional *Trending Now* segments
- Expanded definitions related to service terminology
- New *Customer Service Success Tip* added
- *Updated 11 Strategies for Promoting a Positive Service Culture* section
- Additional *Search It Out* resources
- Additional *Collaborative Learning Activity*

Chapter 3

- New *In the Real World* chapter opening case study (State Farm Insurance)
- New *Think About It*
- Addition of *Words to Live By* quote
- Expanded definitions related to service terminology
- Additional *Customer Service Tips*
- Additional *Trending Now* segments
- Updated research and statistics
- Expanded *Importance of Effective Communication* section
- Updated section on *Assertive vs. Aggressive Customer Service*
- Entire section on conflict moved to Chapter 7
- *Small Business Perspective* segment expanded and updated
- Additional *Search It Out* activity resources
- Additional resources to *Collaborative Learning Activity* section

Chapter 4

- Interview by customer service industry professional
- New *In the Real World* chapter opening case study (American Express)
- Updated *Think About It*
- Addition of *Words to Live By* quote
- Expanded definitions related to service terminology
- Additional *Customer Service Tips*
- Additional *Trending Now* segments
- Updated *Work It Out* segment
- Updated research and statistics
- Additional *Search It Out* activity resources

Chapter 5

- New *In the Real World* chapter opening case study (Nordstrom)
- New *Think About It*
- Addition of *Words to Live By* quote
- Expanded definitions related to service terminology
- Additional *Customer Service Tips*
- Additional *Trending Now* segments
- Additional *Search It Out* activity resources
- Additional resources to *Collaborative Learning Activities* section

Chapter 6

- Addition of *Words to Live By* quote
- Expanded *What Are Behavioral Styles?* section
- Expanded *Identifying Behavioral Styles* section
- Revised *Work It Out 6.1*
- Additional *Trending Now* segments
- Additional *Search It Out* activity resources

Chapter 7

- Interview by customer service industry professional
- Updated *In the Real World* chapter opening case study (Coca-Cola)
- Addition of *Words to Live By* quote
- Expanded definitions related to service terminology
- Updated section on *Demanding or Domineering Customers*
- Updated section on *Indecisive Customers*
- Updated section on *Dissatisfied or Angry Customers*
- Additional *Customer Service Tips*
- Expanded *Reasons for Customer Defection* section
- Expanded *Strategies for Preventing Dissatisfaction and Problem Solving* section
- Addition of *Conflict* sections from that moved from Chapter 4 of the sixth edition
- Addition of *Work It Out 7.8—Recovering from Policy Restrictions* activity
- Expanded *Disaster Planning Initiatives in the Service Recovery Process* section
- Additional *Search It Out* activity resources
- Additional resources to *Collaborative Learning Activities* section

Chapter 8

- New *In the Real World* chapter opening case study (Subway)
- New *Think About It*
- Addition of *Words to Live By* quote
- New *Work It Out 8.1—Encountering Diversity* added
- Expanded *Importance of Relationships* section
- Updated research and statistics
- Additional *Search It Out* activity resources

Chapter 9

- Updated *In the Real World* chapter opening case study (Microsoft)
- Updated *Think About It*
- Addition of *Words to Live By* quote
- Updated research and statistics
- Additional *Trending Now* segments
- Updated *The Customer Contact/Call Center or Help Desk* segment
- Enhanced *Traditional Call Center technology* segment
- Expanded definitions related to service terminology
- Updated *Social Media* section
- Additional *Customer Service Tips*
- Expanded *Technology Etiquette and Strategies*
- Expanded *The Telephone and Customer Service* segment
- Additional *Search It Out* activity resources

Chapter 10

- Interview by customer service industry professional
- Updated *In the Real World* chapter opening case study (COSTCO)

- New *Think About It*
- Addition of *Words to Live By* quote
- Expanded definitions related to service terminology
- Updated research and statistics
- Additional *Trending Now* segments
- Expanded information on ethics in customer service
- Updated section on *Channel Partners*
- Updated *Small Business Perspective* section
- Additional *Search It Out* activity resources
- Additional resources to *Collaborative Learning Activities* section

An Update on a Trusted Customer Service Textbook Resource

Welcome to a brand new look for the top-selling customer service textbook in the United States. This book has been the top-selling customer service textbook in the United States for over a decade and won the 2017 Textbook Excellence Award from the Textbook and Academic Authors Association (TAA). In this edition, we have updated, expanded, and reformatted much of the content.

Customer Service: Skills for Success addresses real-world customer service issues and provides a variety of revised resources, activities, examples, and tips from the author and active customer service professionals in the industry. We did this to help gain and hold readers' interest while providing additional insights into the concepts and skills related to customer service. The text begins with a macro view of the history of customer service and what the profession involves today. It also provides projections for the future, and then focuses on specific skills and related topics to aid service practitioners.

The seventh edition of *Customer Service: Skills for Success* contains 10 chapters divided into three parts, plus the Appendix, Glossary, and Bibliography. These parts focus on different aspects of customer service: (1) The Profession, (2) Skills for Success, and (3) Building and Maintaining Relationships. Along with valuable ideas, guidance, and perspectives, readers will also encounter interviews of real-world service providers who offer advice for current and aspiring service professionals. Readers will also discover tips for implementing proven customer service strategies, case study scenarios, and activities to help you apply concepts learned to real-world situations in order to challenge your thinking on the issues presented. For users of previous editions, you will note the addition of several new information elements and a tie-in to today's technology throughout the chapters. In the Instructor Resources in Connect, you will find various individual and small group activities, case studies, and other support material. These can be used to engage readers and enhance content found in the book.

Each chapter begins with behavioral-based **Learning Outcomes** to direct students' focus and to measure end-of-chapter success in grasping the concepts presented. Students will also find a **quote** from a famous person to prompt their thinking related to the chapter topic and text focus. Throughout the book, the abbreviation LO indicates the Learning Outcome that applies to that section.

As students explore the chapter material, they will find many helpful tools to enhance their learning experience and assist them in transferring their new knowledge to the workplace. Throughout the chapters, students are asked key questions in the form of a **Knowledge Check**. This allows students to consider what they have just read and test themselves to help ensure that they have grasped the concepts covered in each chapter.

Every chapter opens with **In The Real World.** These candid snapshots offer a view into a variety of well-known businesses, industries, and organizations and are designed to provide insight into how customer service leads to success in a highly competitive global world. To support the scenarios, students are asked to do an Internet search on the featured organization and answer the questions provided in the **Thinking About It** section that follows.

Self-assessments listed as **Quick Previews** allow students to pretest their knowledge on a range of topics, and prime them to watch for specific content as they read the chapter. Answers to the questions are also provided at the end of each chapter.

Throughout the chapter, **Work It Out** activities challenge students' knowledge and provide an opportunity for individual and/or small group work on a specific topic or issue. The **Street Talk** tips are offered by customer service professionals currently working in various organizations and industries provide a glimpse of real-world insights into strategies and techniques that professionals are using every day in their interactions with customers to enhance their service delivery. Also threaded throughout every chapter, **Trending Now** highlights new and innovative strategies being put into practice in companies and industries to enhance the service experience for current and potential customers.

There are also number of activities in every chapter that encourage students to engage with common customer service problems. **Ethical Dilemmas** present a difficult scenario and ask readers how they might appropriately handle the situation. Potential solutions or best practices are provided at the end of each chapter. **Small Business Perspective** activities discuss situations that a small business may be faced with, and present students with information that makes for great in-class discussion.

At the end of each chapter is a **Summary** with **Review Questions**, which bring together the key elements and issues covered throughout the chapter. While the summaries encapsulate and reinforce key themes, the review questions test students' retention of the content and highlight areas for remedial study to promote mastery of the chapter topics. Students also are encouraged to use the Internet to research chapter-related skills and obtain a variety of customer service facts, figures, and related information to use in group activities, presentations, or discussions through **Search It Out** activities.

Collaborative Learning Activities encourage role-playing. In these activities students are given a variety of scenarios they can act out with an instructor or a peer in order to engage with real customer service issues, practice their skills, and reinforce their knowledge of the chapter topic, while **Face-to-Face** exercises provide students with a detailed background narrative of a specific employee and allow them to identify with that employee by using the information to determine how they might handle a similar customer service issue if faced with it on the job. Additionally, the **Planning to Serve** activities provide a roadmap for students to identify techniques and strategies from the book to provide superior customer service in their future.

The Reader Satisfaction Survey, found in the Instructor's resources in CONNECT, can be used to provide the author with feedback. This brief survey can be provided to students by the instructor. For completing the survey, students will receive a free publication (*Communicating One-To-One*) on interpersonal communication written by this book's author (Robert W. Lucas).

The Customer Service Text That Gives You More

ADDITIONAL RESOURCES

Author's Customer Service Skills blog   There are hundreds of articles on various customer service-related topics to supplement information in this book on the author's blog that can be used as references or as discussion starters for classroom and online. To access the blog, please visit the instructor resources www.customerserviceskillsbook .com within Connect.

INSTRUCTOR RESOURCES

Instructor's Manual   The Instructor's Manual outlines course materials, additional in-class activities, and support for classroom use of the text. It has been organized to give instructors not only a basic outline of the chapter, but to assist in all facets of instruction. For every question posed in the text, the IM provides a viable answer. The text page numbers provide easy reference for instructors. In addition, the Instructor's Manual guides instructors through the process of integrating supplementary materials into lessons and assignments. It also includes sample syllabi and video notes. Ultimately, this will be an instructor's greatest advantage in using all materials to reach all learners.

Test Bank   Every chapter provides a series of test questions, available in our Test Bank. Questions are organized by learning outcome and Bloom's Taxonomy. A Test Table aligns questions with the content and makes it easy for you to determine the questions you want to include on tests and quizzes.

Connect Matrix   We know that instructors' time is valuable. To help you prepare, we have created a Connect Matrix that organized by chapter, learning outcome, Bloom's and Level of Difficulty autogradable assessments are available for you to assign in Connect. Visit the Instructor Resources within Connect to preview how the Connect Matrix can help!

PowerPoints   PowerPoint slides, created specifically for instructors, include additional teaching notes and are tied directly to learning outcomes. Each slide is provided in a format that offers alt descriptions, screen reader capability, and a color palette that will accommodate for students requiring accommodations.

Create   Instructors can now tailor their teaching resources to match the way they teach! With McGraw-Hill Create, www.mcgrawhillcreate.com, instructors can easily rearrange chapters, combine material from other content sources, and quickly upload and integrate their own content, such as course syllabi or teaching notes. For those instructors needing additional information on customer service skills of stress and time management and communicating with customers in writing, there are three additional chapters available in Create. Find the right content in Create by searching through thousands of leading McGraw-Hill textbooks. Arrange the material to fit your teaching style. Order a Create book and receive a complimentary print review copy in three to five business days or a complimentary electronic review copy via e-mail within one hour. Go to www.mcgrawhillcreate.com_today and register.

Basis for Content

In the past, some students have commented that the content in this book is common sense. Certainly, that might be true if you have experience and education related to dealing with a variety of other people. However, my experience is that "common sense" is not so common for many people. If that were true, every service provider would be effective at offering stellar customer service to every one of his or her customers. When has that happened to you as a customer?

Since customer service spans all organizations and involves internal customers (employees) and those outside the organization, I encourage you to keep an open mind as you read the content in these pages. Objectively assess your current knowledge and skills against what you find. Do you have the knowledge and skills addressed herein? If you sincerely know all there is to know about customer service, then I applaud you. I am sure you will make a fine CEO for a service organization someday. In the meantime, I encourage you to think about what you find in the text, discuss ways to improve with your instructor and classmates, and make notes of potential areas for improvement as you go through the semester. Never forget that customer service is the pivotal role in any organization. Everyone from the CEO down to frontline employees must embrace positive customer service skills and work to gain and retain customers. Without customers, there is no need for any position in a company.

This book draws from my more than four-plus decades of real-world experience in customer service environments, management, and human resource development. My background includes positions serving as a frontline employee and managing or overseeing entire companies. I have worked in sales, retail management, and service functions for a number of organizations; owned and run all phases of operation and management for an online retail business for over 19 years; was a partner in a human resource performance consulting firm working with client organizations around the world; and taught at numerous colleges and universities from undergraduate through Master's level for over two decades. Currently, I am an author, a presenter, and the principal of Robert W. Lucas Enterprises, where I consult, write, publish, and promote my own books through Success Skills Press. Part of my role involves negotiating and contracting with other businesses and organizations and providing a variety of services to them. I deal with customer issues and needs every day and know that the techniques described in this book will work because I, and other service professionals cited in the book, have used them effectively. While there are some research and theoretical sections in the chapters, much of the information is derived from personal experience, research, and reflections of actual customer service encounters experienced by others.

Whether you are new to the service profession and have no base of customer service knowledge, or are more experienced and wish to enhance your knowledge and skills, *Customer Service: Skills for Success* and accompanying ancillary materials can provide a catalyst for your success. I encourage you to visit CONNECT to access and review ancillary materials designed to assist you in your quest for customer service expertise.

I am confident that this book will assist you in reaching your goal to become a better service provider.

Bob Lucas

ACKNOWLEDGMENTS

Throughout the years, my wife, friend, and life partner, M.J., and my mother, Rosie, have sacrificed much as I have dedicated time and effort to developing tools such as this book to help others grow. Their support and love have been an invaluable asset in helping me reach my goals and are much appreciated.

A special note of appreciation also goes to Susan Gouijnstook, Meredith Fossel, Elizabeth Schonagan, Kerry Shanahan, Christian Lyon, Kelly Delso, Mark Christianson, Melissa Leick, Bruce Gin, Matt Diamond, Deanna Dausener, Sandy Ludovissy, and the entire McGraw-Hill team, for their expert guidance and support. Their efforts were essential in helping to create this book and add many new features to enhance its value.

Preparing any project of the length and depth of this book requires much assistance. No one person can bring together all the necessary knowledge, expertise, and insights to capture the essence of a topic.

Special thanks to the following service experts who provided *Street Talk* suggestions throughout the book:

Patricia Charpentier

Gary Goldberg

Jennifer Harper

Anne Hinkle

Stacey Oliver-Knappe

Sharon Massen

Barry Nadler

Tony Petrovich

Leilani Poland

Wendy Richard

Barbara Tanzer

Anne Wilkinson

Teri Yanovich

I also want to thank the four service experts who provided their knowledge and expertise in the *Customer Service Interviews* at the beginning of several of the chapters:

Ginger Marks

Dr. Venkatesh Nagalapadi

Barbara Tanzer

Richard Ulrych

It is with deepest gratitude that I thank to all of the following experts who took the time to read through many draft pages of the manuscript for this edition of *Customer Service: Skills for Success* and provide valuable insights, guidance, and suggestions for improvement. Without them, the final product would have proven to be of far less value to its users.

W. Russell Brown, *Navarro College Yun Chu, Robert Morris University*

Toni L. Clough, *Umpqua Community College*

Gary Corona, *Florida State College at Jacksonville Ivan Franklin Harber, Jr., Indian River State College*

Christopher Ross, *Trident Technical College*

Ronald N. Scott, *Trident Technical College*

Lydia Tisdale, *Horry Georgetown Technical College*

We would also like to thank those who contributed to previous edition reviews.

De Lena Aungst, *Sinclair Community College*

Mark P. Bader, *MBA, CMPE, Ivy Tech Community College*

Ed Cerny, *Horry-Georgetown Tech*

Toni Clough, *Umpqua Community College*

Diana Joy Colarusso, *Daytona State College*

Dan Creed, *Normandale Community College*

Yvonne Drake, *Pensacola State College*

Kelly Garland, *Tallahassee Community College*

Pearl M. Ivey, *Central Maine Community College*

Diane Kosharek, *Madison Area Technical College*

John Maier, *Northeast Wisconsin Technical College*

Todd Price, *Montcalm Community College*

Catherine Rogers, *Laramie County Community College*

Linda Rose, *Westwood College Online*

Joan Seichter, *Moraine Park Technical College*

Maria Stanko, *Ivy Tech Community College, East Chicago, Indiana*

Donna M. Testa, *Herkimer County Community College*

Nancy Warren, *Highline Community College*

Nancy Yates, *Butler County Community College*

We would like to thank the reviewers who contributed by providing useful insight into the Supplements and Connect offering for this edition.

Rebecca Lamers, *Northeast Wisconsin Technical College*

Miranda Kato, *Bellevue College*

Brenda T. Anthony, *Tallahassee Community College*

Lydia Tisdale, *Horry Georgetown Technical College*

Barbara A. Rodriguez, *Pensacola State College*

Kathryn K. Trachte, *Mid-State Technical College*

Christopher Ross, *Trident Technical College*

Diana Carmel, *Golden West College*

I would also like to thank all of those reviewers who contributed by providing feedback and insightful suggestions for previous editions of the text.

Jorjia Clinger, *McCann School of Business and Technology*

Gary M. Corona, *Florida State College at Jacksonville, Kent Campus*

Michael Discello, *Pittsburgh Technical Institute*

Gordie Dodson, *Remington College Cleveland East*

Fran Green, *Everest University*

Toni R. Hartley, *Laurel Business Institute*

Richard S. Janowski, *The Butler Business School/The Sawyer School*

Diane Lolli, *Cambridge College*

Barbara VanSyckle, *Jackson Community College*

Scott Warman, *ECPI Technical College*

Joel Whitehouse, *McCann School of Business and Technology*

Special thanks also to the following educators who reviewed previous editions and offered suggestions, critique, and guidance in the refinement of the book content and format.

SEVENTH EDITION

CUSTOMER SERVICE

SKILLS FOR SUCCESS

Mc
Graw
Hill
Education

©Robert W. Lucas

PART ONE

THE PROFESSION

1 The World of Customer Service

2 Contributing to the Service Culture

Barbara Tanzer

Title/Position: *Small business owner, the TBS Group (travel agency, manufacturing, insurance agency, small business consulting) Total years' experience providing service to internal and external customers: 30+*

Website: *http://www.OurCruiseAgent.com*

d.   **Subject Matter Knowledge.** If you do not know how to speak intelligently about the concern or need of the customers, research and get back to them if needed—do not ad lib.

1 **What are the personal qualities that you believe are essential for anyone working with customers in a service environment?**

a.   **Communication.** The ability to gather information from customers while being sensitive to their emotions, strengths, and weaknesses. Keep your voice low and speak clearly.

b.   **Listening Skills.** Knowing when to stop the communication and listen without anticipation of your response.

c.   **Patience.** Everyone is not comfortable identifying and sharing a problem. Use your skills in A and B above to help him or her have a successful conversation.

2 **What do you see as the most rewarding part of working with customers? Why?**

Problem solving, especially helping them come to a solution on their own. What seems overwhelming to many can often be resolved with another set of eyes and ears and years of experience. Start with a soft voice, really good listening skills, and note taking. Before you know it, there is a smile and relief. I love it!

3 **What do you believe the biggest challenges are in working with customers?**

Some of the biggest challenges are the customer's urgency and limited organizational resources readily available to resolve an issue.

2

4 **What have you done or could you do to help overcome the challenges you indicated in order to deliver better customer service?**

a.   In every situation, you have to gather the facts, be compassionate, and do all you can to resolve the issue.

b.   If you have an opportunity to identify the situation prior to your initial contact, you might be able to gather some facts prior to meeting with the customer.

c.   When that cannot happen, make sure you take good notes and provide the customer with YOUR contact information. This demonstrates your commitment to owning the problem and continuing communication while remaining reachable so that he or she does not have to start over for any follow-up communication.

d.   If you are going to contact him or her, choose a time and date to which the customer agrees and that is reasonable for you to be ready for that follow up.

5 **What changes have you seen in the customer service profession since you took your first service provider position?**

a.   Because of technology, customers have access to more information through the Internet. This can create challenges because they often come with unrealistic, preconceived ideas about compensation due when something goes wrong. For example, if a client is booked in a cruise stateroom that is in need of mechanical repair, he or she is not satisfied with just being moved to a comparable stateroom. He or she feels an upgrade or refund of the cruise is warranted. In effect, he or she is looking to receive benefits in excess of the inconvenience experienced, rather than simply being made whole.

b.   Customer service representatives—I have seen very angry customers leave with a smile when an experienced, well-trained CSR is involved. It is a beautiful thing.

c.   Inadequate service resources—Often, there is frustration and lack of resolution when a customer service department is understaffed or CSRs are undertrained. The results cannot be the same when employees are working under stress.

d.   Technology has helped and hurt customer service.

-   When there is a toll-free number to call customer service and you have to go through a menu of questions to identify the correct person to help you—this is not good service. The customer explains the situation and any follow up is often with a different CSR. If good notes were not included in the customer's file, he or she has to explain again to a new representative. I would rather see a direct number provided on the product documentation so that customers could directly contact the department representative who has the authority to implement a resolution.

-   The fact that technology allows help to be available 24/7/365 is a good thing. It is important that all customer service personnel be able to speak clearly, exhibit good listening skills, and have product knowledge in order to effect an appropriate resolution.

6 **What future issues do you see evolving in your industry/organization related to dealing with customers and why do you think these are important?**

The ever-changing dynamics of all industries and a company's ability to stay on track with its objectives will be a future issue. For example, the insurance industry is unsettled. The coverage and premium available to you today could be gone tomorrow. Additionally, in travel, our world is challenged by unsettled and competing forces. Customers want to experience as much as they can. Often, without proper guidance from their agent, they are unaware of differences in the cultures and environments where they want to travel.

7 **What advice related to customer service do you have for anyone seeking or continuing a career in a customer service environment?**

I believe customer service is a challenging and rewarding career. You will not have the same questions, concerns, or results with each customer. This is not a "learn the task—do the job—get the optimum results" type of job. Your patience will be challenged every day. You are in a unique career that can impact so many. You get to improve their day, resolve their problem, and secure loyal customers for the company or organization. Unlike being a doctor/lawyer/engineer, you do not get to study, perfect, and apply what you have learned in line with the law or guidelines. In the customer service profession, you continue to learn every day from every situation and the knowledge you have is a database to draw upon. You have to know what solution applies to each situation.

Application to Customer Service

After reading Barbara's comments, think about how what she said relates to your organization and the customer service profession as a whole and respond to the following:

a.   Do you believe that the qualities and skills that Barbara described are applicable to both small and large businesses? Why or why not?

b.   In addition to the solutions to challenges that Barbara identified, what other strategies would you recommend for customer service professionals?

c.   In addition to the changes in the customer service profession mentioned by Barbara, what other changes have you experienced or read about and how do they impact service delivery in an organization?

d.   In addition to the advice that Barbara provides for people entering the customer service profession, what tips would you add?

Courtesy of Barbara Tanzer

The World of Customer Service

"Treat every customer as if they sign your paycheck, because they do."
—UNKNOWN

©ttatty/123RF RF

LEARNING OUTCOMES

After completing this chapter, you will be able to:

1-1 Define customer service.

1-2 Describe factors that have impacted the growth of the service sector in the United States.

1-3 Identify societal factors that have influenced customer service.

1-4 Recognize the changes in consumer behavior that are impacting service.

1-5 List the six major components of a customer-focused environment.

1-6 Explain how some companies are addressing the changes impacting the service sector.

Use SmartBook to help you read, study, and retain what you have learned. Access SmartBook in your Instructor's Connect course, or go to connect.mheducation.com for help. ▤ SMARTBOOK™

IN THE REAL WORLD (RETAIL)—AMAZON.COM INC.

Mission Statement: "Amazon's vision is to be earth's most customer-centric company; to build a place where people can come to find and discover anything they might want to buy online."

Source: Amazon Inc., Mission statement.

Jeff Bezos founded his company in 1994 as "Cadabra.com" and launched Amazon.com out of his garage in 1995. By 2016, Bezos boasted that the company was the fastest to ever reach the $100 billion sales mark. Forbes magazine listed Bezos as the third richest person in the world on its 2017 list of wealthiest people in the world. In deciding on his business model, he observed predictions that online commerce would grow dramatically in coming years and then decided on five product lines that would sell well. Of the five, he focused on books since there is a universal demand for knowledge. As the company's capabilities and reputation grew, so did its product line. Today, the online behemoth carries music CDs, DVDs, MP3s, electronics (e.g., Kindle e-readers, Fire tablet, Echo, and Fire TV), computer software, video games, furniture, toys, cosmetics, and many other commercial items.

Based in Seattle, Washington, and often referred to as Amazon, this mighty retail operation stands out among others for many reasons. As the world's largest Internet retailer, the company dominates e-commerce through superior electronic and cloud computing sales and marketing. In recent years, it has moved into land-based retail ventures by opening brick-and-mortar bookstores. Amazon has now surpassed many publicly traded companies in market value. For example, in 2016, the company was ranked fourth in *Financial Times*'s Global 500 rankings. In doing so, it surpassed many well-known brands (e.g., Facebook, Johnson & Johnson, Exxon, Wells Fargo, and General Electric).

Since its inception, Amazon has continued to be a retail innovator by using strategies such as an associate program to allow affiliates to place Amazon banner links on their own websites. These direct potential buyers who click them to Amazon.com. If the prospect purchases any item, the associate receives a sales commission. Additional success strategies have included the following:

1. Opening websites in numerous foreign countries

2. Opening retail sites for products such as, apparel, groceries, health and personal care, sporting goods, and kitchenware

3. Acquiring established catalog businesses (e.g., www.Abebooks.com, www.Zappos.com, www.audible.com, and www.Shopbop.com) to tap established business lines and customer bases

4. Establishing geographically dispersed fulfillment centers to speed up processing and shipping to customers

5. Patenting 1-Click checkout to allow customers to purchase an item with a single click on the website

6. Forming corporate relationships with retail giants such as Toys "R" Us and Target

7. Offering free shipping on orders over $25.00

8. Setting up a textbook trade-in program for students

9. Introducing cloud technology that supports multiple consumer needs

10. Establishing its International Mobile App Distribution portal

These initiatives have been focused at driving up revenue while providing a seamless shopping experience for a diverse customer base with varying needs, wants, and expectations.

Learn more about Amazon by visiting www.amazon.com. You can scroll to its retail offerings at the bottom of its website and to its Leadership Principles that begin with "Customer Obsession" at the Jobs/Principles portions of the site, https://www.amazon.jobs/principles. You can also search the Internet for books, articles, and additional information.

Think About It

1. What have you heard or experienced related to Amazon's approach to customer service?

2. From a service perspective, how does this company differ from other online businesses that you have dealt with or heard of?

3. What do you believe to be this company's customer service-related strengths and weaknesses? Why do you feel this way?

4. What role do you think Jeff Bezos plays in the service culture of this organization? Explain your answer.

5. As a consumer, would you consider using Amazon's services in the future? Why or why not?

Quick Preview

Before reviewing the content of the chapter, respond to the following statements by placing a "T" for true or an "F" for false on the rules. Use any questions you miss as a checklist of material to which you will pay particular attention as you read the chapter. For those you get right, give yourself a pat on the back, but review the sections they address in order to learn additional details about the topics.

_____ 1. The concept of customer service evolved from the practice of selling wares in small general stores, off the back of wagons, or out of the home.

_____ 2. The migration from other occupations to the service industry is a recent trend and started in the late 1970s.

_____ 3. One reason for the shift from a manufacturing to a customer service–dominated society is more stringent government regulations.

_____ 4. As more women have entered the workforce, the demand for personal services has increased.

_____ 5. Advances in technology have created a need for more employees in manufacturing businesses.

_____ 6. Because of increasing income related to their employment, women often now have more disposable income as consumers than they did in the past.

_____ 7. As a result of deregulation in a variety of industries, competition has slowed.

_____ 8. Quality customer service organizations seek to actively recruit, select, and train qualified people.

_____ 9. Luckily, the worldwide recession had little impact on the service industry.

_____ 10. To determine whether delivery needs are being met, organizations must examine industry standards, customer expectations, capabilities, costs, and current and projected requirements.

_____ 11. There are two customer types with which service representatives must interact.

_____ 12. An organization's "culture" is what the customer experiences.

Answers to Quick Preview are located at the end of the chapter.

---

customer service The ability of knowledgeable, capable, and enthusiastic employees to deliver products and services to their internal and external customers in a manner that satisfies identified and unidentified needs and ultimately results in positive word-of-mouth publicity and return business.

service industry A term used to describe businesses and organizations that are engaged primarily in service delivery. _Service sector_ is a more accurate term, since many organizations provide some form of service to their customers even though they are primarily engaged in research, development, and manufacture of products.

Words to Live By

"The Customers perception is your reality."

— **SOURCE: KATE ZABRISKIE**

LO 1-1 Defining Customer Service

CONCEPT **Customer-focused organizations determine and meet the needs of their internal and external customers. Their focus is to treat everyone with respect and as if they were special.**

There have been many attempts to define the term **customer service**. However, depending on an organization's focus, such as retailing, medical, dental, industry, manufacturing, or repair services, the goals of providing customer service may vary. In fact, we often use the term **service industry** as if it were a separate occupational field unto itself. In reality, most organizations provide some degree of customer service. For the purposes of this text, we will define _customer service_ as the ability of knowledgeable,

capable, and enthusiastic employees to deliver **products** and services to their internal and external customers in a manner that satisfies their identified and unidentified needs and ultimately results in positive word-of-mouth publicity and return business. By doing these things, organizations can truly become **customer-focused organizations** (see Figure 1.1).

Many organizations specialize in providing only services. Examples of this category are as follows:

Associations

Banks and credit unions

Consulting firms

Internet service providers

Utility companies

Waste management services

County tax collectors

Call centers

Brokerage firms

Libraries

Laundries

Plumbing and electrical companies

Transportation companies

Medical or dental facilities

Other organizations provide both products and services. Examples are businesses such as car dealerships, bricks and mortar (physical buildings), online retail stores,

product Something produced or an output by an individual or organization. In the service environment, products are created to satisfy customer needs or wants.

customer-focused organization A company that spends energy and effort on satisfying internal and external customers by first identifying customer needs, and then establishing policies, procedures, and management and reward systems to support excellence in service delivery.

Some common characteristics for leading-edge customer-focused organizations are as follows:

- They have and support internal customers (e.g., peers, coworkers, bosses, subordinates, people from other areas of their organization) and/or external customers (e.g., vendors, suppliers, various telephone callers, walk-in customers, other organizations, others not from within the organization).

- Their focus is on determining and meeting the needs of customers while treating everyone with respect and as if he or she is special.

- Information, products, and services are easily accessible by customers.

- Policies are in place to allow employees to make decisions in order to serve customers better.

- Management and systems support and appropriately reward employee efforts to serve customers.

- Reevaluation and quantitative measurement of the way business is conducted is ongoing and results in necessary changes and upgrades to deliver timely quality service to the customer.

- Continual benchmarking or comparison with competitors and related organizations helps maintain an acute awareness and implementation of best service practices by the organization.

- The latest technology is used to connect with and provide service to customers, vendors, or suppliers and to support business operations.

- They build relationships through **customer relationship management (CRM)** programs.

FIGURE 1.1

Customer-Focused Organizations

customer relationship management (CRM) Concept of identifying customer needs: understanding and influencing customer behavior through ongoing communication strategies in an effort to acquire, retain, and satisfy the customer. The ultimate goal is customer loyalty.

Before distribution systems were modernized, peddlers went from house to house, particularly in rural areas, to deliver merchandise or services. Doctors often went to the sick person's home for patient visits. *How do these methods of delivery differ from those used today? Do you think the ones used today are better? Why or why not?*

internal customers People within the organization who either require support and service or provide information, products, and services to service providers who interact with external customers. Such customers include peers, coworkers, bosses, subordinates, and people from other areas of the organization.

external customers Those people outside the organization who purchase or lease products and services. This group includes vendors, suppliers, people on the telephone or Internet, and others not from the organization.

service sector Refers to organizations and individuals involved in delivering service as a primary product.

publishers, and manufacturers that have support services for their products, supermarkets, theaters, and restaurants.

Take a moment to consider all the organizations with which you have dealt with in the past or do so currently. Which one of them does not have a customer service component? Cannot think of one? That is because customer service is an intricate component of any business or organization. All companies and organizations (e.g. private, public, government or military) have **internal** or **external** customers, or both. No matter what type of organization you work in, it is crucial for you to remember that when dealing with customers, it is not about you. Your purpose and goal should be to assist customers in meeting their needs whenever possible. Be proactive and positive and strive to do the best you can by taking ownership of a customer contact situation. You have a vested interest to prevail since your success and that of your organization depend on it.

The term **service sector** as used by the Census Bureau and the Bureau of Labor Statistics in their reports and projections typically includes the following:

Transportation, communication, and utilities

Wholesale trade

Retail trade

Finance, insurance, and real estate

Other services (including businesses such as legal firms, barbershops and beauty salons, personal services, housekeeping, and accounting)

Federal government

State and local governments

In addition, there are people who are self-employed and provide various types of services to their customers and clients.

THE CONCEPT OF CUSTOMER SERVICE

The concept or practice of customer service is not new throughout the world. Over the years, it has evolved from a meager beginning into a multibillion-dollar, worldwide endeavor. In the past when many people worked on farms, small artisans and business owners provided customer service to their neighbors. No multinational chain stores existed. Many small towns and villages had their own blacksmith, general store, feed store, boardinghouse (hotel), restaurant, tavern, barber/dentist, doctor, and similar service-oriented establishments owned and operated by people living in the town (often the place of business was also the residence of the owner). People bought materials at the general store to make their own repairs to clothing, equipment, and household items. Further, to supplement their income, many people made and sold or bartered products from their homes in what came to be known as **cottage industries**. For people living in more rural areas, peddlers with wagons of kitchenware, medicine, and other goods made their way from one location to another to serve their customers and distribute various products. As trains, wagons, carriages, and stagecoaches began to cross the United States, Europe, Asia, and other parts of the world, they carried vendors and supplies in addition to providing transportation. During that whole era, customer service differed from what it is today by the fact that the owners were also the chief executive officers (CEOs) and motivated frontline employees working face-to-face with their customers. They had a vested interest in providing good service and in succeeding.

cottage industries The term adopted in the early days of customer service when many people started small businesses in their homes or cottages and bartered products or services with neighbors.

(continued)

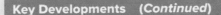

Key Developments   (Continued)

1886   R.W. Sears Watch Company (the forerunner of Sears, Roebuck & Company) began selling watches via mail order. After several restructures, the catalog expanded to include a variety of clothing, household goods, appliances, and other products.

1913   The U.S. Postal Service began a parcel post delivery system, speeding delivery while reducing costs.

1913   Merchants Parcel Delivery (today's United Parcel Service [UPS]) started.

1913   Ford Motor Company began using the automobile assembly line that provided a steady stream of affordable cars to the world.

1925   The Air Mail Act was passed allowing the U.S. Post Office to contract with private airlines to deliver mail, thus improving delivery times and service.

1938   The Civil Aeronautics Act established the Civil Aeronautics Board that regulated airfares. That forced airlines to improve service in order to beat competition.

1952   Bell Laboratories began developing primitive versions of interactive voice technology that has led to a wide variety of speech recognition tools in cars, and on computers, wired telephones, smartphones, and other devices. Ultimately, it was incorporated into call center technology that has been used since the 1970s.

1960s   Electronic mail was developed and by the 1970s morphed into the format we now recognize as e-mail.

Mid-1960s   Private automated branch exchanges (PABX) were used as a replacement for manually having to handle incoming calls into an organization.

1962   Walmart, Kmart, and Target opened stores and offered low prices and self-service, changing the way consumers in the United States viewed shopping.

1964   First personal computer (Programma 101) was introduced at the New York World's Fair.

1967   AT&T introduced toll-free (1-800) number calling services.

1968   Graphical user interface (GUI) invented by Douglas Englebart allows use of computer mouse, icons, and other technology elements to interact and perform tasks for users.

1971   FedEx started operations.

1978   The U.S. Congress passed the Airline Deregulation Act that allowed airlines to establish their own fares and routes and compete more aggressively.

1980   Tim Berners-Lee began work on a project that would result in the birth of the World Wide Web that really took hold in the 1990s and continues today.

1981   First mass-produced portable microprocessor-based computer was released.

1983   Mobile phones released by Motorola led the way for the mobile technology that is commonplace today.

1990s   The number of companies with an online presence skyrocketed.

1993   Smartphones became available to the general public.

1997   Wireless Fidelity (Wi-Fi) standards were developed, which led to a wide array of wireless technology and increased access to organizations and customer service.

1997   SixDegrees.com social network was launched, followed by MySpace, Facebook, and other social media platforms. Many social networks are now being used by businesses as customer communication and service platforms.

Early 2000s   Software companies worked to develop and refine customer service technology with the result being modern-day CRM systems.

2000s   Many companies began to outsource their customer call/care centers abroad.

2000s   Companies began employing customer service applications (apps) and websites that allow customers to access service options remotely and participate in self-service options for orders and information.

When industry, manufacturing, and larger cities started to grow, the service industry really started to gain ground. In the late 1800s, societal and technological changes occurred that set the stage for what would become the customer service profession of today. In rural areas, the population grew and expanded westward, and service providers followed.

POST–WORLD WAR II SERVICE IN THE UNITED STATES

After World War II, the desire, and in some cases need, to obtain products and services started to grow throughout much of the world. In the United States, there was a continuing rise in the number of people in service occupations. According to an article published on www.minnpost.com,

> Before World War II, the service sector grew because we got richer. Think about it: From domestic servants to waiters, blacksmiths to cobblers, and barbers to bankers, Americans have always been engaged in a variety of service activities. And, as the American economy grew and average incomes increase[d], Americans increased their demand for meals, repairs, grooming and financial services. Thus, more and more workers were *pulled* into the service sector by this increasing demand.[1]

THE SHIFT TO SERVICE

Today, businesses have changed dramatically as the economy has shifted from a dependence on manufacturing to a focus on providing timely quality service. The age of the **service economy** has been alive and strong for some time now. Tied to this trend has been the development of international quality standards by which service effectiveness is measured in many multinational organizations. Organizations such as the International Council of Customer Service Organizations (www.iccso.org) work to help develop and promote service and professional excellence standards throughout the world. This is being done by setting internationally acceptable standards and certifications to create a global atmosphere of service. For example, quality standards, such as ISO 9000 and ISO 10002:2004, were developed and overseen by the International Organization for Standardization (www.iso.org). These are globally accepted guidelines for quality in the area of product and customer service excellence. They were designed to help enhance the customer experience in affiliated organizations. In addition, to help attract and maintain a more loyal customer base, many customer-centric organizations are stepping up their enthusiasm and support for such standards. To project a more service-oriented posture, they are adding executive-level positions such as chief customer officer (CCO), or similar presti-

service economy A term used to describe the trend in which businesses have shifted from primarily production and manufacturing to more service delivery. As part of this evolution, many organizations have developed specifically to provide services to customers.

KNOWLEDGE CHECK

1. Why is "service sector" a more appropriate term than "service industry" when describing customer service?

2. What are common characteristics of leading-edge customer-focused organizations?

3. How has the concept of customer service evolved since its origin?

FIGURE 1.2

From Pre–World War II
Occupations to Service
Occupations

Typical Former Occupations	Typical Service Occupations
Farmer	Salesperson
Ranch worker	Insurance agent
Machinist	Food service
Engineer	Administrative assistant
Steelworker	Flight attendant
Homemaker	Call center representative (CSR)
Factory worker	Repair person
Miner	Travel professional
Tradesperson (e.g., watchmaker)	Child care provider
Railroad worker	Security guard

gious titles, to their hierarchy. CCOs are responsible for all operational functions that influence or relate to customer relations and add a new dimension to the customer service career path.

As shown in Figure 1.2, since the end of World War II, people have moved from other occupations to join the rapidly growing ranks of service professionals.

LO 1-2 Growth of the Service Sector

CONCEPT Technology has affected jobs in the following ways: quantity of jobs created, distribution of jobs, and quality of jobs. The service sector is projected to have the largest job growth.

According to the U.S. Bureau of Labor Statistics, "Although customer service representatives are employed in nearly every industry, many work in telephone call centers, credit and insurance agencies, banks, and retail stores. About 1 in 5 worked part time in 2014. The median hourly wage for customer service representatives was $15.25 in May 2015. Employment of customer service representatives is projected to grow 10 percent from 2014 to 2024, faster than the average for all occupations. Overall job opportunities should be good. Candidates with good customer-service skills and who have experience using computer software applications should have the best job prospects."[2] Other great news from recent summaries is that customer service representative and other types of service jobs are projected to have the most job growth between 2014 and 2024. For more statistics on customer service job opportunities by state, visit http://www.bls.gov,oes/current/oes434051.htm#st. Other Bureau of Labor Statistics predictions are that "Service-providing sectors are projected to capture 94.6 percent of all the jobs added between 2014 and 2024. Of these 9.3 million new service sector jobs, 3.8 million will be added to the health care and social assistance major sector." Further, "The health care and social assistance major sector is expected to become the largest employing major sector during the projections decade, overtaking the state and local government major sector and the professional and business services major sector. Health care and social assistance is projected to increase its employment share from 12.0 percent in 2014 to 13.6 percent in 2024."[3] Among other factors, the latter increase is likely being fueled by the aging society and future need for medical care and assistance (see Figure 1.3).

Street Talk Adopt an internal client mentality

One company I used to work with instilled in me the mentality that my hiring managers were my internal candidates, thus making me treat them as a customer. This does not mean they walked all over me or got everything they wanted. Focusing on others in your organization as customers helps make you more responsive. I remember a manager who had a very detail-oriented spreadsheet that he wanted completed on a weekly basis . . . much to my chagrin and that of his other direct reports. One such manager asked me if it drove me crazy to always have to update the form. My response to him was, "He's my manager and if he wants it, he will get it."

COURTESY OF ANNE WILKINSON

EMPLOYMENT BY INDUSTRY SECTOR—SERVICE OCCUPATIONS

	2014	2024
Service-providing occupations (total in thousands)	110,646.9	129,904.6
Utilities	563.8	505.1
Wholesale trade	5,663.0	6,151.4
Retail trade	15,058.2	16,129.1
Transportation and warehousing	4,248.6	4,776.9
Information	3,118.3	2,712.6
Financial activities	8,105.1	8486.7
Professional and business services	16,394.9	20,985.5
Educational services; private	2,762.5	3,756.1
Health care and social assistance	14,429.8	21,852.2
Leisure and hospitality	12,493.1	15,651.2
Other services	6,188.3	6,662.0
Federal government	2,730.0	2,345.6
State and local government	18,891.3	19,890.1

Source: Bureau of Labor Statistics Employment by Major Industry Sector, http://www.bls.gov/news.release/ecopro.t02.htm.

FIGURE 1.3

Employment by Major Industry Sector

The impact of these numbers can be seen as technology replaces many production line workers and increasing numbers of service jobs are created. This comes about because, as greater numbers and greater varieties of goods are produced, more service people, salespeople, managers, and other professionals are needed to design and market service delivery systems that support those products. Technology-related service jobs such as those of database administrators, computer support specialists, computer scientists, computer engineers, and systems analysts are expected to continue to grow at a rapid pace.

IMPACT OF THE ECONOMY

According to leading economists, today's economy is affecting jobs in three ways: (1) overall quantity of jobs created; (2) the distribution of jobs among industries, occupations, geographic areas, and organizations of different sizes; and (3) the quality of jobs, measured by wages, job security, and opportunities for development.

Quantity of Jobs Being Created

A variety of factors, including prevailing interest rates and consumer demand, typically cause companies to evaluate how many people they need and which jobs will be established or maintained. In addition, the advent of technology has brought with it the need for people with many new technical skills in the areas of computer hardware and software operation and maintenance. At the same time, technology has created an opportunity for organizations to transfer to automation tasks previously performed by employees.

According to the U.S. Department of Labor, the 30 detailed occupations that are projected to add the most new jobs by 2022 are expected to account for almost half of all new jobs (see Figure 1.4).

FIGURE 1.4 Employment and Wages of Occupations with the Largest Numeric Projected Growth in Jobs, Projected 2012–2022 (Numbers in Thousands)

2012 National Employment Matrix Title	Employment		Projected Change, 2012–2022		Median Annual Wage, May 2012[4]$	Typical Education Needed for Entry
	2012	**2022**	**Number**	**Percentage (%)**		
Total, all occupations	145,355.8	160,983.7	15,628.0	10.8%	$34,750	—
Personal care aides	1,190.6	1,771.4	580.8	48.8	19,910	Less than high school
Registered nurses	2,711.5	3,238.4	526.8	19.4	65,470	Associate's degree
Retail salespersons	4,447.0	4,881.7	434.7	9.8	21,110	Less than high school
Home health aides	875.1	1,299.3	424.2	48.5	20,820	Less than high school
Combined food preparation and serving workers, including fast food	2,969.3	3,391.2	421.9	14.2	18,260	Less than high school
Nursing assistants	1,479.8	1,792.0	312.2	21.1	24,420	Postsecondary nondegree award
Secretaries and administrative assistants, except legal, medical, and executive	2,324.4	2,632.3	307.8	13.2	32,410	High school diploma or equivalent
Customer service representatives (CSRs)	2,362.8	2,661.4	298.7	12.6	30,580	High school diploma or equivalent
Janitors and cleaners, except maids and housekeeping cleaners	2,324.0	2,604.0	280.0	12.1	22,320	Less than high school
Construction laborers	1,071.1	1,331.0	259.8	24.3	29,990	Less than high school
General and operations managers	1,972.7	2,216.8	244.1	12.4	95,440	Bachelor's degree
Laborers and freight, stock, and material movers, hand	2,197.3	2,439.2	241.9	11.0	23,890	Less than high school
Carpenters	901.2	1,119.4	218.2	24.2	39,940	High school diploma or equivalent
Bookkeeping, accounting, and auditing clerks	1,799.8	2,004.5	204.6	11.4	35,170	High school diploma or equivalent
Heavy and tractor-trailer truck drivers	1,701.5	1,894.1	192.6	11.3	38,200	Postsecondary nondegree award

2012 National Employment Matrix Title	Employment		Projected Change, 2012–2022		Median Annual Wage, May 2012[4]$	Typical Education Needed for Entry
	2012	2022	Number	Percentage (%)		
Medical secretaries	525.6	714.9	189.2	36.0	31,350	High school diploma or equivalent
Child care workers	1,312.7	1,496.8	184.1	14.0	19,510	High school diploma or equivalent
Office clerks, general	2,983.5	3,167.6	184.1	6.2	27,470	High school diploma or equivalent
Maids and housekeeping cleaners	1,434.6	1,618.0	183.4	12.8	19,570	Less than high school
Licensed practical and licensed vocational nurses	738.4	921.3	182.9	24.8	41,540	Postsecondary nondegree award
First-line supervisors of office and administrative support workers	1,418.1	1,589.6	171.5	12.1	49,330	High school diploma or equivalent
Elementary school teachers, except special education	1,361.2	1,529.1	167.9	12.3	53,400	Bachelor's degree
Accountants and auditors	1,275.4	1,442.2	166.7	13.1	63,550	Bachelor's degree
Medical assistants	560.8	723.7	162.9	29.0	29,370	Postsecondary nondegree award
Cooks, restaurant	1,024.1	1,174.2	150.1	14.7	22,030	Less than high school
Software developers, applications	613.0	752.9	139.9	22.8	90,060	Bachelor's degree
Landscaping and groundskeeping workers	1,124.9	1,264.0	139.2	12.4	23,570	Less than high school
Receptionists and information clerks	1,006.7	1,142.6	135.9	13.5	25,990	High school diploma or equivalent
Management analysts	718.7	852.5	133.8	18.6	78,600	Bachelor's degree
Sales representatives, wholesale and manufacturing, except technical and scientific products	1,480.7	1,612.8	132.0	8.9	54,230	High school diploma or equivalent

Source: Bureau of Labor Statistics, Monthly Labor Review, Occupational employment projections to 2022, December 2013, www.bls.gov.

Today, many employees work from their homes all or part of the time. Telecommuting, as this is called, is used frequently by companies in large cities, such as Los Angeles, to decrease travel time. *Do you think you would need different skills or abilities to telecommute? Why or why not?*

©Martin Novak/123RF RF

telecommuting A trend seen in many congested metropolitan areas and government offices. To reduce traffic and pollution and save resources (e.g., rent, telephone, and technology systems), many organizations allow employees to set up home offices and from there electronically communicate and forward information to their corporate offices.

telework Similar to telecommuting (working from home rather than going to a designated workplace), this term applies to people who work in an office but also conduct work from a remote location.

broadband Internet access Refers to a very fast connection to the Internet that is made possible by technology that can communicate much more data or information than was possible with the old phone dial-up Internet connections. With broadband, users can download images, video clips, and music; send e-mail; and perform other functions at a much faster speed.

Skype Refers to a software application that is a division of Microsoft® and provides free or paid service that allows people to connect with other Skype subscribers via the Internet anywhere in the world with voice, videos, or text messages.

Distribution of Jobs

Two parallel trends in job development are occurring. The first comes about from the need for employees to be able to have regular access to personal and professional networks and to engage in collaborative exchanges. This trend means that more jobs are likely to develop in major metropolitan areas, where ease of interaction with peers and suppliers, high customer density, and access to the most current business practices exist. Training and technology resources are also available in these areas. Access to technology resources helps ensure continued learning and growth of employees. It also aids organizations in achieving their goals and objectives.

The second trend in job development arises from the ease of transmission and exchange of information by means of technology. It is called either **telework** or **telecommuting** and various other terms to describe it (e.g., e-work and work shifting). The practice does not include people who are self-employed. With enhanced phone technology, **broadband Internet access** facilitates more personal communication with customers, suppliers, distributors, and colleagues. With visual imaging and collaboration software like **Skype** and GoToMeeting, **instant messaging**, **social media**, e-mail, text chat, and other technology, employees can now work from their homes or satellite office locations worldwide. Government agencies, technology-focused organizations, and many companies with large staffs in major metropolitan areas that experience traffic congestion (e.g., Los Angeles, Boston, Chicago, and Washington, DC) have used telework and telecommuting for a number of years to eliminate the need for employees to travel to work each day. They also use the practices to reduce corporate overhead, such as office space and technology, utility, and equipment costs.

Small businesses are also using the telecommuting strategy as a way to hold down costs of hiring full-time employees. They are using a network of people from remote locations who have the specialized skills that are needed to provide service to customers. For example, the author of this book has run several small businesses and worked from a home office since 1999. During that time, he has often contracted with bookkeepers, webmasters, marketing and graphics associates, and product suppliers in other parts of the country. He stays connected with them almost exclusively through technology. In fact, he only met a former webmaster one time face-to-face during a 10-year association. As a performance consultant, he typically saw his business partner one or two times a week and conducted a majority of their business via technology. Similarly, much of the contact he has had with publishers, editors, customers, and clients has been through technology.

Even though many organizations have experienced savings in terms of time and money and increases in productivity, some companies (e.g., Yahoo) have reversed their use of telecommuters and brought their employees back to the organizational worksite after indicating discontent with the results of the efforts to have people work independently. Some pundits think that the lack of success experienced by Yahoo might have been the result of a poorly instituted telecommuting policy rather than a shortcoming in the process itself.

From an industry perspective, workers employed in professional and business services, in financial activities, and in education and health services are among the most likely to work at home. Technology, such as the telephone, fax, smartphone, and computer, makes it possible to provide services from almost any remote location. For example, telephone sales and product support services can easily be handled from an employee's home if the right equipment is used and adequate employee selection and training are provided. To accomplish this, a customer calls a designated toll-free number and a switching device at the company dispatches the call to an employee working at home or even in another country. This is seamless to the customer, who receives the service needed and has no idea from where the call was answered. This also makes it easier for many companies to outsource some functions, thus saving money by relocating those jobs to geographical areas worldwide where wages and benefits may be less competitive.

instant messaging Refers to a form of Internet communication where users can transmit text messages or chat in real time via the Internet to one or more people. More advanced forms allow voice calling, video chat, and hyperlinks to various media.

social media Websites through which users come together as "communities" of friends, relatives, and like-minded individuals for social networking and microblogging (blogging) and to share ideas, content (e.g., videos or images), and personal and other information. Examples of social media include Facebook, Twitter, Tumblr, Instagram, Pinterest, LinkedIn, Google Plus, Dribble, and Reddit.

Customer Service Success Tip

Make yourself indispensable to your employer by building a strong internal network of associates within the organization in order to reduce your chances of layoff during **downsizing**. This will help you share information and resources and add to your personal power base because you will have information that coworkers potentially do not have. Also, become thoroughly educated on the products and services that your organization provides and continually volunteer ideas and assistance to improve the organization.

downsizing Term applied to the situation in which employees are terminated or empty positions are left unfilled once someone leaves an organization.

Quality of Service Jobs

The last decade of the twentieth century saw increasing economic growth, low interest rates, and new job opportunities. Unemployment rates reached a historic low in 1999, and then rose dramatically as the worst recession (2007–2009) or downturn in the economy since the Great Depression occurred and resulted in unemployment rates of 6 to 14 percent or more in most areas of the United States and around the world. As many people continue to struggle to find meaningful employment, social and workplace demographics continue to shift and people move around in a more mobile society. A major result is that job security has been affected and it is likely that competition for desired prime service jobs will continue to become much more intense into the foreseeable future in many sectors. However, because of changing workplace demographics where more millennials are entering the workplace and boomers are retiring or moving into part-time positions, the future might not be so bleak after all.

networking The active process of building relationships and sharing resources.

Employees who do obtain and maintain the better customer service jobs that provide good working conditions, security, and benefits will be the ones who are better educated, trained, and prepared. They will also be the ones who understand and have tapped into the concept of professional **networking**. This is the active process of building relationships inside and outside the organization through meetings, interpersonal interactions (face-to-face or via technology), and activities that lead to sound relationships and sharing of resources. Practices such as joining and becoming actively involved in committees and boards of governors or directors for professional associations or groups that support your industry will prove to be invaluable. Additionally, creating and maintaining an ongoing professional social media presence is crucial in finding jobs and developing links to other service providers and workplace professionals. Many good books have been published on the subject of networking. The Internet—for example, Amazon (http://amzn.to/2u3YSj6) and Barnes & Noble (http://www.barnesandnoble.com/s/personal+networking_requestid=690621)—can provide such resources. Additionally, an abundance of technology (e.g., smartphones, wireless communication devices, and computers) can allow access, organization, and storing of information and provide a gateway to social networking sites like Facebook, Twitter, Google+, and LinkedIn. All of this will enhance the job search process and provide valuable information and opportunities for those attempting to prepare and position themselves for key jobs in the service sector.

 WORK IT OUT 1.1

Improving Service Quality

Take a moment to list some of the changes related to service that you have personally witnessed in the business world during your lifetime. Are these changes for better or worse? Why do you believe this to be true? With these changes in mind, what do you—or would you—do to improve service quality as a customer service professional in your own chosen industry or position?

Customer Service Success Tip

Social media can be a powerful tool in your effort to find a new job. Unfortunately, some people fail to realize that, just as technology can be an asset, it can also be a detriment if users fail to act responsibly, post unprofessional-sounding comments that are laden with profanity, or post inappropriate comments about peers, supervisors, and their organizations. Many job recruiters and employers actively scour Facebook, LinkedIn, and other social networking sites to see what they can find about candidates and current employees. There are many stories on the Internet about people who were turned down or lost jobs because of their poor judgment in posting comments or images. Also, keep in mind that your customers also use social media and may see what you post.

LO 1-3 Societal Factors Affecting Customer Service

CONCEPT Many factors caused the economic shift from manufacturing to service. Increased technology, globalization of the economy, deregulation, and many government programs are a few factors. You will read about these and others in the following paragraphs.

The economies of North America and many other geographic areas are being dramatically changed by the forces that are shaping the world. Shifts in consumer needs, wants and expectations, declining economic conditions in some areas, demographic shifts in population, constant technological change, globalization, deregulation of industries, geopolitical changes, increases in the number of white-collar workers, socioeconomic program development, and more women entering the workplace are some of the major shifts that continue to occur each year around the world.

You may wonder what factors have impacted the service industry. Some of the more important elements are identified in the following sections.

SHIFTS IN CONSUMER NEEDS, WANTS, AND EXPECTATIONS

Consumer behavior continues to shift. That is why car manufacturers, clothing designers, homebuilders, restaurants, and others continually change the appearance and functionality of their products and services. Organizations and service providers that effectively prepare for and predict coming needs, wants, and expectations can improve their profit margin. They can do so by reducing or eliminating waste and better preparing to serve their customer base. Companies that monitor societal changes, such as ones outlined in this chapter, are more adept and effective at preparing for their future. They are also less likely to fail when trends negatively impact all of society.

For years, economists have used **demand curves** to illustrate shifts in consumer behavior in a particular market. Through graphs, they can show trends or movements at different points and see upward or downward deviations in spending habits. Managers can use similar tools to monitor the purchase or use of particular products and service categories so that they can modify as necessary. This is particularly helpful for small business owners who normally have fewer resources than their larger chain competitors. By anticipating changes, they can move revenue or personnel to areas where more customer activity is likely to occur.

Many of the shifts that are evident in today's business world are tied directly to the demographic shifts discussed in this chapter. For example, the aging population creates a need for a variety of services, such as medical care and assistance, vacation planning, transportation, recreational activities, and delivery services for purchases made. Younger consumers often seek out technology-based products, trendy clothing

demand curves Graphic representations of expected behavior in the real world that economists and business people can use to predict coming trends or shifts in consumer needs, wants, or expectations.

Consumer desires drive organizational offerings and performance. That is why recent years have produced services not imagined in past decades for the service industry. The changes being introduced by many companies are designed to capture market share and stay a step ahead of competition. More importantly, companies are trying to anticipate and meet the ever-changing needs, wants, and expectations of consumers.

Some recent trends include ways of providing transportation for commuters to ease traffic congestion and take some of the cost and stress out of moving about a city. Many metropolitan cities throughout the world have seen a growth in bicycle rental stations, car sharing, Uber drivers as an alternative to taxicabs, and toll roads in the center of major highways to allow faster commutes. Other shifts involve house swapping to lower the cost of vacations, UberEats that uses its people movers to deliver meals for restaurants, Google Express that has partnered with retailers (e.g., Walgreens, Costco Wholesale, PetSmart, and Whole Foods Market) to provide a quick-delivery service, and Amazon Restaurants that provides eatery-to-door delivery from restaurants to its prime subscribers. Amazon has also started opening retail bookstores.

and accessories, activities that involve group engagement and recreation, and entertainment. People who immigrate into a country often bring needs, wants, and expectations based on their background, beliefs, and values. In many cases, in addition to wanting to access products and services from their new culture to better understand and assimilate into society, many prefer a desire to access food, clothing, television/radio programming, and other products and services familiar to them.

GLOBAL ECONOMIC SHIFTS

Not since the 1980s have economic indicators (e.g., stock trades, home sales, purchases, international transactions, and construction) been in such turmoil worldwide. Many people have lost jobs, personal savings are dwindling, people are losing their homes, and spending is down greatly around the world. As the economy took a downward spiral in the latter part of the first decade of the twenty-first century, consumer confidence shifted, many organizations struggled to provide quality service levels with reduced staff, and budgets and revenue from products and services slipped for most organizations as consumers held onto precious cash. The problem was compounded by a worldwide recession from late 2007 to mid-2009. The negative impact on people and businesses are still being felt in many areas.

The latest log on this fire of economic change was the decision by citizens of the United Kingdom to exit the European Union in June 2016 in what was billed a BREXIT (British Exit). Assuming all the predicted consequences occur from the split, the impact of the break will be seen for years. An example of this occurred when financial markets worldwide plunged at the news and estimates of the economic and social impact are still being regularly recalculated. The move will have immediate economic implications in the United Kingdom and throughout the rest of the European communities in the European Union. Trade between partnering countries and restrictions on freedom of movement for citizens of the United Kingdom within the European community are possible outcomes of the change. That latter impact alone will potentially have some effect on businesses throughout the European Union that benefit from a flow of revenue from travelers. Ultimately, the economic repercussions could extend to the United States since EU members are a large market for U.S. businesses and consumers. Financial markets (e.g., banking and stocks) are also impacted by actions in Europe. Consumers often pull back on spending when there are economic changes and uncertainty. That means that businesses see lost revenue and have to impose their own cuts in inventory, services, and employment-related areas. Ultimately, such reductions can have a negative impact on employee morale that is passed on to customers.

In addition to governmental policy and economic changes, new legislation impacting health care and taxes, job elimination in the government sector, and shifts in consumer spending can significantly affect many organizations, forcing downsizings and in many cases closures. This is especially true in small businesses that benefit in strong economies where consumers have more disposable income and are willing to make more purchases of products and services. In such instances, small businesses hire more people to serve customers, invest in equipment and space, and often increase product and service offerings. However, when the economic picture is not so positive, the opposite is true and many small business owners are forced to downsize or even close their doors.

Overall, consumers do business as never before. Large numbers of customers search and do their homework for products and services online and often use retail outlets as a showroom to physically examine things they are interested in potentially purchasing. The result is that sales in brick-and-mortar stores are down for many retailers and suppliers. Best Buy instituted a price-matching strategy in March 2013 to combat this shop-around practice. The company decided to match prices for all product categories against all local retail competitors and major online operations such as Apple.com, Dell.com, homedepot.com, Lowes.com, and other highly recognized retailers.

Another important factor related to the changes in the economic environment that have occurred in recent years is that many companies have made dramatic shifts in the way they do business and attempt to attract and hold customers. The approach to customer service in many instances is no longer "business as usual." Instead of viewing it as something that should be done well, most organizations now see it as something that must be done.

Because of the financial meltdown that occurred during the high point of the recession, many organizations that have been household names for decades and had international presence have cut back severely on the size of their workforce and inventory and sold off, merged, or closed operations. This can easily be witnessed by walking into major mall department stores and looking at how much space they now have between

Growth of Small Businesses

- The 28 million small businesses in America account for 54% of all U.S. sales.
- Small businesses provide 55% of all jobs and 66% of all net new jobs since the 1970s.
- The 600,000 plus franchised small businesses in the U.S. account for 40% of all retail sales and provide jobs for some 8 million people.
- The small business sector in America occupies 30-50% of all commercial space, an estimated 20-34 billion square feet.

Furthermore, the small business sector is growing rapidly. While corporate America has been "downsizing," the rate of small business "start-ups" has grown, and the rate for small business failures has declined.

- The number of small businesses in the United States has increased 49% since 1982.
- Since 1990, as big business eliminated 4 million jobs, small businesses added 8 million new jobs.

Source: U.S. Small Business Administration, Small Business Trends, Small Business, Big Impact!

clothing racks. Organizations have also taken dramatic steps to attract and keep custom-ers. Companies like Chrysler, General Motors, Citigroup, Goldman Sachs, and Ameri-can Express received funds through the Emergency Economic Stabilization Act of 2008 from the U.S. federal government to remain financially solvent. In addition, companies struggled (and still do in many instances) to find a balance between profitability and providing quality service. For example, companies like Sears, Macy's, JCPenney, Best Buy, Dell, Borders Books, and other notable companies have continually juggled their retail and service policies since 2010 in an effort to remain competitive and stay in busi-ness. Some succeeded while others did not. All of this turmoil and change has had an adverse impact on the economy, the service industry, and ultimately employees and potential employees. Radio Shack, Borders Books, Blockbuster, and Circuit City have closed and other well-known organizations are likely to disappear in the near future. These include:

- Time Warner
- DirectTV
- Shutterfly
- Russell Stover
- HHGregg
- Hillshire Farm
- RIM (Blackberry)
- Eastman Kodak

SHIFTS IN THE POPULATION AND LABOR FORCE

There are a number of important factors impacting the future of the labor force in the United States. Today's labor force is older, more racially and ethnically diverse, and composed of more women than in the past. Additionally, it is expected to grow at a slightly slower rate than in previous decades. Figure 1.5 shows projections of labor force participation by sex and age.

"During the 1970s and 1980s, the labor force grew vigorously as women's labor force participation rates surged and the baby-boom generation entered the labor market. However, the dynamic demographic, economic, and social forces that once spurred the level, growth, and composition of the labor force have changed and are now damping labor force growth. The labor force participation rate of women, which peaked in 1999, has been on a declining trend. In addi-tion, instead of entering the labor force, baby boomers are retiring in large numbers and exiting the workforce. In the first 12 years of the 21st century, the growth of the population has slowed and labor force participation rates gener-ally have declined. As a result, labor force growth also has slowed. The Bureau of Labor Statistics (BLS) projects that the next 10 years will bring about an aging labor force that is growing slowly, a declining overall labor force partici-pation rate, and more diversity in the racial and ethnic composition of the labor force. Overall, the U.S. labor force is projected to reach 163.5 million in 2022. The labor force is anticipated to grow by 8.5 million, an annual growth rate of 0.5 percent, over the 2012–2022 period. The growth in the labor force during 2012–2022 is projected to be smaller than in the previous 10-year period, 2002–2012, when the labor force grew by 10.1 million, a 0.7-percent annual growth rate."[5]

FIGURE 1.5

Labor Force Participation by Age and Sex, 2015–2024

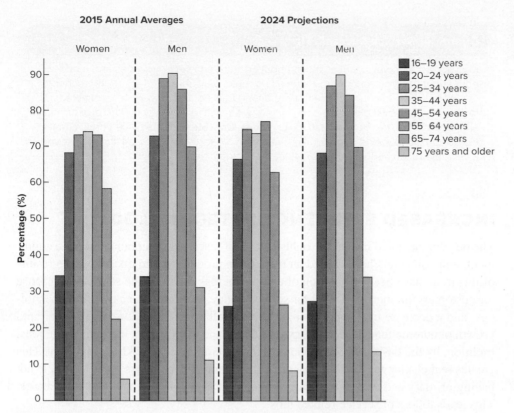

Source: 2015 Current Population Survey and 2024 Employment Projections, U.S. Bureau of Labor Statistics Graph by the Women's Bureau, U.S. Department of Labour.

According to U.S. Census data, "the U.S. population is projected to increase from 319 million to 417 million, between 2014 and 2060, reaching 400 million in 2051. By 2030, one in five Americans is projected to be 65 and over; by 2044, more than half of all Americans are projected to belong to a minority group (any group other than non-Hispanic White alone); and by 2060, nearly one in five of the nation's total population is projected to be foreign born."[6]

The upside of this growing, evolving, and aging population is that there will be a need for more consumer goods and services to provide for the needs and expectations of diverse customers. This will also lead to an expansion of jobs to fill the positions needed to produce products and serve customers.

An interesting side note to the aging issue in the United States is that even as experienced workers age out, there is a fairly steady stream of younger skilled workers coming in due to immigration. Unlike many other countries in Europe, Japan, Korea, and China, where some analysts project the age of those populations to range as high as 40 percent by 2060, the United States is not facing such a dire shortage of future employees. The result is that there will be a pool of workers to provide needed services.

For more information on the projected U.S. population, visit U.S. Census 2012 National Population Projections: Summary Tables (http://www.census.gov/population /data/national/2012/summarytables.html).

Since the size of the labor force is the most important factor related to the size and makeup of the available pool of workers, organizations that hire service representatives will have to make some adaptations related to the way they recruit and hire in order to obtain quality candidates for open positions. This may include seeking viable candidates from other geographic areas if qualified ones cannot be found locally.

INCREASED EFFICIENCY IN TECHNOLOGY

The development and increased sophistication of machines, telephones, service equipment, and computers have caused an increase in production and quality. Three results of this trend have been acquisition of equipment that enhances the service experience for customers, an increased need for service organizations to take care of the technology, and a decrease in manufacturing and blue-collar jobs. The downside of the rapid growth or automation and technology throughout the world is that manufacturing jobs, traditionally the basis of most economies for generations, is quickly going away. This creates real challenges from an economic standpoint since job loss leads to people not having primary and disposable sources of cash to pay their bills and make purchases. This leads to loss of service-related jobs.

One reason for the ongoing shift to replace manual labor with technology is that machines and equipment can work 24 hours, 7 days a week with few lapses in quality, with no need for breaks, and without increases in salary and benefits. They also potentially enhance the ease of service delivery and provide faster processing. For example, instead of having to direct customers to a cash register or central customer service desk in a store where they often required to stand in long lines to check out, individual sales representative can be given a portable data collection device that looks similar to an iPad screen and that they can carry with them. When a customer is ready to make a purchase, the sales representative simply scans the product bar code, takes the customer's credit card and swipes the magnetic strip through the device, and then has the customer sign the screen with his or her fingertip. If the customer desires a receipt, it can be sent to an e-mail address the customer enters into the device. When customers get to their computers, their receipt is waiting for them. The author of this book uses an alternative method to process book sales at the back of the room at his presentations. He uses a Wi-Fi-connected iPad or smartphone with a small portable scanner called the Square, which plugs into the top of the device. Inventory items are already entered into the iPad, so once the appropriate item is selected on the screen, the customer's credit card is scanned, he or she signs on the display screen, and the transaction is completed much the same as described above.

Another example of technology efficiency is that customers can now access information via a website with either a computer or a mobile device, place orders, print receipts, and track delivery schedules. They can do this from anywhere if there is a secure Wi-Fi Internet connection. If there is a question or problem, they can typically interact with a customer care or information technology specialist via a telephone or text chat. These options add convenience while meeting the needs, wants, and expectations of a diverse and technically savvy customer base.

All of this makes technology extremely attractive to profit-minded business and corporate shareholders and managers who are concerned with service delivery and how it impacts sales. Similarly, service and nonprofit organizations are looking to available technology as a way to communicate with and provide services to their clients and members. Although technology can lead to the loss of some jobs, technological advances in the computer and telecommunications industry alone have created hundreds of service opportunities for people who install, monitor, and run the machines and automated services. Everything from point-of-sale transactions, toll-free numbers, and telemarketing or teleselling to shopping and service via the Internet, television, telephone, and mobile devices have evolved and continues to expand.

Statistics from Internet World Stats indicates that as of June 30, 2016, there were an estimated 7,340,094,096 people in the world. Of that number, 3,675,824,813 use the Internet. That is a 50.1 percent penetration level and a 918.3 percent growth rate since 2000.[7] Of these totals, 91,245,000 households use the Internet at home, according to a 2012 U.S. Census survey.[8]

While many areas of the world have little or no effective Internet services, efforts are under way to help reduce that gap. The U.S. government passed the Recovery Act in 2009 with money allocated for expanding nationwide Internet access to rural areas and into schools, libraries, public safety offices, and other community buildings. Other governments have also invested in their own systems. Additionally, private businesses are investing in the growth of the Internet. SpaceEx partnered with Fidelity and Google to raise money for a fleet of low Earth-orbit satellites to expand worldwide Internet service. Facebook and Google had already been working on strategies to help expand services. Google announced a plan to spend almost $1 billion to create a network of satellites, balloons, and drones that could connect far-reaching areas of the world and provide Internet services.

An impact of expanded Internet access is that more people will have access to products and services via computers, smartphones, iPads, and similar devices. They can shop, search for information, and buy from the convenience of their home and other locations without ever visiting retail organizations. This means the need for fewer sales associates and other in-house service providers but opens the door for more customer care representatives, call centers, and technology support people.

Globalization of the Economy

Beginning in the 1960s, when worldwide trade barriers started to come down, a variety of factors have contributed to expanded international cooperation and competition. This trend has been termed **globalization**, with many companies focusing on **business-to-business (B2B)** initiatives, as well as individual consumers. Since the 1960s, advances in technology, communication, and transportation have opened new markets and allowed decentralized worldwide access for production, sales, and service. To

globalization The term applies to an ongoing trend of information, knowledge, and resource sharing around the world. As a result of a more mobile society and easier access to transportation and technology, more people are traveling and accessing products and services from international sources than ever before.

business-to-business (B2B) Refers to business-to-business customer service.

Trending NOW

Many organizations have discovered the power of using social media in their marketing and sales initiatives. Not only can they receive and give customer feedback quickly, but also they can send out information about pertinent products, services, and events and do it a lot cheaper than through traditional marketing and advertisement initiatives cost. Some organizations also use social media to look for new employees. Major companies like Whole Foods and Nike (both with over 4 million Twitter followers), Walmart (with over 34 million Facebook fans), Starbucks, T-Mobile, and other multinational organizations have successfully tapped into the social media craze. In many cases, the companies have created separate Twitter accounts on which they engage customers.

For many customer service jobs, skill in using technology will increase your value as a source of information for current and future customers. *How can you keep abreast of changes in technology?*

offshoring Refers to the relocation of business services by an organization from one country to another (e.g., services, production, and manufacturing). The work may be kept in another entity of the organization that is located in another country or contracted (outsourced) to a third party. Typically, this is done to cut costs with cheaper worker salaries and/or tax savings.

outsourcing Refers to the practice of contracting with third-party companies or vendors outside the organization (often in another country) to deliver products and services to customers or to produce products.

insourcing The opposite of outsourcing, this occurs when organizations decide to have internal employees assume functions and perform work instead of contracting it out to third parties or outsourcing it.

survive and hold onto current market share while opening new gateways, U.S. firms need to hone the service skills of their employees, strengthen their quality, enhance their use of technology, and look for new ways of demonstrating that they can not only meet but also exceed the expectations of customers. All of this means more competition and the evolution of new rules and procedures that they have not been able to obtain in the past. Sometimes the deciding factor for the customer on whether to purchase a foreign or domestic product will be the service you provide.

At some point, many companies make staffing and/or production decisions based on bottom-line figures. When this happens, companies can, because of recent changes in the law, take their production or call center functions "offshore" (**offshoring**) to other countries (Mexico, India, etc.). In doing so, companies often save money on costs such as production, wages, and benefits. This is becoming more and more common in technology-oriented companies. Unfortunately, in some industries (e.g., high-tech, manufacturing, and telecommunications), there are simply not enough qualified job candidates to fill positions. For that reason, businesses look to alternate sources overseas. One point to remember about offshoring is that while many politicians and citizens demean offshoring as detrimental to the economy, the reality is that it is just one of the strategic decisions that help to keep companies that participate in the practice profitable and can actually add to the economy by generating profits for investors. In turn, they might put some of that money into other companies and ventures, create alternative products and services to offer, and buy products that further stimulate the economy. These choices can lead to a need for more service providers. Like any other corporate decision, there are pros and cons with the practice of offshoring.

In addition to offshoring, many organizations are also **outsourcing** job functions that have been traditionally handled internally (e.g., recruiting, payroll, benefits, training, marketing, manufacturing, and distribution) to third-party companies that specialize in these areas.

An advantage of outsourcing jobs, especially to other geographic locations where salaries are not as high, is that it can help keep costs low, increase profit margins, and aid companies in their efforts to be globally competitive. A major disadvantage is that the practice potentially takes jobs away from local workers.

According to research done by business and accounting firm BDO USA, manufacturing is leading the change overseas, as the most heavily outsourced function for more than 60 percent of U.S. technology firms. Research and development, distribution, and IT services and programming are the other company functions outsourced most frequently. In spite of supply chain interruptions that plagued the region over the past few years, Southeast Asia is the leading outsourcing destination for U.S. tech companies. The businesses are also moving parts of their operations to India, Eastern Europe, and Russia.[9]

Related to offshoring and outsourcing, **insourcing** is an interesting trend started in recent years after many countries suffered severe unemployment and drops in their economies. With a glut of skilled employees available in the job market, organizations have been able to recruit highly talented candidates for relatively lower salaries and benefit packages. In some cases, this has negated the need for companies to seek cheaper alternatives overseas while bolstering their image in their home countries because they appear to be supporting local workers. While this has not reversed the offshoring or outsourcing initiatives of some major companies, it does hold potential promise for some skilled unemployed workers seeking new opportunities in the production and service industries on a local level.

DEREGULATION OF MANY INDUSTRIES

Over the years, the United States has witnessed the deregulation of a number of industries (e.g., airline, telephone, railroads, and the utility industries from the later 1970s to the early 2000s). **Deregulation** is the removal of government restrictions on an industry. The continuing deregulation of major U.S. public services has caused competition to flourish. However, deregulation has also brought major industry shakeups, sometimes leading to breakdowns in service quality in many companies and, in some instances, closure or restructuring of the company. An example of this was the breakup of AT&T ("Ma Bell") into many smaller communication companies ("Baby Bells") in 1984.

For more information on deregulation, check out the article "10 Effects of Deregulation" at http://money.howstuffworks.com.

These events have created opportunities for newly established companies to step in with improvements and innovations to close the gaps and better serve customers. For example, smaller low-cost carriers (e.g., Southwest Airlines and Jet Blue) came into existence and provided cheaper fares to cities not traditionally covered by larger carriers or where demand is not normally as great. They even challenged the traditional internationally known airlines (United, USAir, and Delta) on traditional routes to larger cities in the United States.

deregulation Occurs when governments remove legislative or regulatory guidelines that inhibit and control an industry (e.g., transportation, natural gas, and telecommunications).

GEOPOLITICAL CHANGES

Events such as economic embargoes, political unrest, and conflicts and wars involving various countries have reduced U.S. business access and competition within some areas of the world (e.g., Vietnam, Iran, Iraq, Myanmar, and Venezuela) while companies from some countries have free access in those areas. These circumstances not only limit access to product, manufacturing, and distribution channels, but also reduce the markets to which U.S. businesses can offer products and services. In effect, every closed port or country border has a negative effect on some manufacturers and other businesses—for example, travel industry professionals, such as reservationists, air transport and manufacturing employees, cruise operators, tour guides, suppliers, and related service and retail businesses.

Other positive and negative historical changes have occurred that—like it or not—have affected the way companies do business and will continue to do so into the twenty-first century. The passage of the **North American Free Trade Agreement (NAFTA)**, which was a trade agreement between the United States, Canada, and Mexico that eliminated a number of trade and investment barriers between the three countries, made it easier for many U.S.-based companies to relocate and send jobs across borders (offshoring) in order to find less-expensive labor forces, increase profits, and avoid unions and federal taxes. Like many such political arrangements, there are pros and cons to this agreement that impact a number of industries. These

North American Free Trade Agreement (NAFTA) A trade agreement entered into by the United States, Canada, and Mexico to help, among other things, eliminate barriers to trade, promote conditions of fair trade across borders, increase investment opportunities, and promote and protect intellectual property rights.

agreements were a subject of major political disagreement and campaigning in the 2016 U.S. presidential election.

Further events such as trade agreements with China and the thawing of relations with Vietnam and Myanmar in recent years have provided the potential for opening new political and economic doors. The shift in relations with Iran, Iraq, Afghanistan, and several other nations as the result of human rights violations, violence, terrorism, and military-related actions has created obstacles to international trade and commerce in a variety of ways in areas of the Middle East, Asia, and South America.

Geopolitical event shifts such as these typically lead to more multinational mergers and partnerships and a need for better understanding of diversity-related issues by all employees and managers. To better adapt and succeed as changes around the world occur, all service providers must take responsibility for researching and educating themselves on world events and the cultures of others. Such actions can lead to better understanding and relationships with customers. Failure to do so can lead to breakdowns in customer communication and ultimately the loss of business. From a personal standpoint, this could also limit chances to travel internationally and secure meaningful employment in the service industry and be offered workplace opportunities such as training, pay, or enhanced benefits from an employer.

With increased ease of transportation and communication in today's business world, companies cannot afford to ignore international competitors. For years, North American firms viewed Japan as their chief economic and business rival. Now other countries have challenged and surpassed Japan (e.g., Taiwan, South Korea, Vietnam, Pakistan, China, and India) as global suppliers and have become firmly entrenched in the marketplace. An example of this was the introduction of the South Korea–made Kia car line into the U.S. market in the 1990s. Initially, many people did not view that company as a significant economic threat and the car was sometimes called the "poor person's automobile." Kias were even compared to the ill-fated Russian Yugo that was manufactured in Yugoslavia in the mid-1980s and introduced into the U.S. market. That brand quickly faded from existence due to its terrible quality and service support. To the surprise of many, Kia has turned its reputation around and has built a series of vehicles that now rival the quality of many U.S. and foreign manufacturers. Some of its models now win national awards and recognition from major car reviewers.

Another geopolitical event that has impacted many organizations was the formation of the European Union. This alliance of neighboring countries formed an economic market made up of 28 states that subscribe to a standardized system of laws that ensure free movement of people, goods, services, and capital. The majority of member states adopted the euro as a common currency and accepted it at a standard exchange rate. They also eliminated the requirement for a passport from the people of member countries traveling throughout the Union. The last step has positive economic implications because it encourages more use of travel-related services.

CHANGING VALUES

Values are internalized and a result of individual life experiences and societal mores. As the world changes so do individual values in some instances. Such changes can have an impact on what people view as valuable and important, what they want and desire, and how they approach relationships with others around them. For example, many people in the United States value such things as personal control, equality, individualism, action, and competition. People from other parts of the world might value traditionalism, group cohesiveness, societal ownership, and acceptance of hierarchy, status, and birthright.

Throughout the world, there has been a tremendous amount of dynamic change in recent decades due to economic instability, quickly expanding and enhanced technology, global mobility where people move quickly and frequently, and other factors outlined in this chapter. The result has been a gradual shift in what many consumers hold near and dear.

Because different societies view what is important from different perspectives, clashes can sometimes result when service providers encounter customers who have values that are different from their own. The important thing to remember in such situations is that neither the customer nor the provider has the "right" set of values; they are simply different and each must respect and honor those of the other party if a positive customer–provider relationship is to occur.

As a result of societal values, companies often change their approach to doing business. They focus on finding ways to attract and hold customers. This often includes shifting the way they do business, the products that they deliver, and their manner in which service is delivered. For example, instead of offering only telephone support for their company and website, they might integrate mobile apps, text chats, auto-response phone systems that provide information, and e-mail contact options. This approach can appeal to a broader range of customer preferences and values.

Because many consumers are now cost-conscious, are ecologically aware, and value sustainability, many automobile manufacturers are developing vehicles that are more energy efficient, use ecologically sensitive fuels and electric power systems, and cost less. Examples of this trend are the Chevrolet Volt, Toyota Prius, and Nissan Leaf. Another example involving service enhancement is a move by the fast-food chain McDonald's. After seeing its market share slip to Subway, Wendy's, and other competitors, executives met with franchisee owners to discuss ways to enhance and speed up slipping service time and efficiency. They had found that one in five complaints from customers involved "friendliness" of service providers. To address this and other issues, the organization decided to focus on customer service as the real driver for branding the organization and increasing sales. To counter negative consumer perceptions related to service, McDonald's examined ways to increase staffing at crucial periods of the day. It also rolled out a "dual point" ordering system nationwide to select locations in order to personalize service. Under it, a customer places an order at the register and receives a receipt with a number. Once that number shows up on a screen indicating the order is complete, the customer picks it up at the other end of the counter from a "runner." That person's sole purpose is to hand out cups, condiments, and other items to customers and thank them for coming into the store, thus freeing up cashiers to take orders correctly. Some stores also deliver food to customer tables once they order and are seated.

WORK IT OUT 1.2

Personal Exposure to the Global Trend

To help you recognize the impact this global trend has on you and your family as consumers, think about all the products you own (e.g.,, car, clothing, microwave oven, television, portable electronic devices, game systems, computer). List five major products that you or your family members own, along with their country of origin (you can find this on the warranty plate along with the product's serial number, usually on the back or bottom of the product).

Self-service kiosks are becoming standard in many business locations. In addition to traditional financial institution ATMs, customers can now order food in the lobby of some McDonald's locations, then pick up their food at the counter once it has been prepared instead of standing in line to deal with a cashier. In theaters, patrons can order their theater tickets and bypass the long lines that are traditional during peak periods. Additionally, many supermarket and "big box" retailers are using kiosks to allow people with only a few items to use self-checkout and avoid waiting behind those customers with baskets full of products.

MORE WOMEN ENTERING THE WORKFORCE

The fact that more women are in the workplace means that many of their traditional roles in society have shifted, out of necessity or convenience, to service providers such as cleaners, cooks, and child care providers. The tasks previously handled by the stay-at-home wife and mother are now being handled by the employees of various service companies. In many cases, these more traditional tasks are being assumed by a stay-at-home spouse or partner.

The Department of Labor has published statistics showing that the number of women in the workforce will reach 92 million (48 percent of the workforce) by 2050[10] in many different occupations. As women have become a larger part of the workforce, they have slowly seen their income levels rise compared to those of their male counterparts, but have not yet reached equality in workplace compensation. Even so, the direct impact of increasing income related to service is that many women often now have more disposable income as consumers than they did in the past. Also, many research studies on consumer buying habits find that women either make or heavily influence buying decisions in a home. As service providers, they are in a good position to recognize needs and recommend appropriate products and services, especially those related to the home and family.

For more information about women in business, visit the U.S. Department of Labor, Women's Bureau, Data & Statistics (https://www.dol.gov/wb/stats/latest_annual_data.htm#part).

A MORE RACIALLY AND ETHNICALLY DIVERSE POPULATION IS ENTERING THE WORKFORCE

As with the entrance of women into the workforce, the increase in numbers of people from different cultures entering the workforce will have a profound impact on the business environment. Members of this expanded worker category bring with them new ideas, values, expectations, needs, and levels of knowledge, experience, and ability. As consumers themselves, they also bring a better understanding of the needs of the various groups that they represent.

By 2022, the U.S. civilian labor force age 16 and over is expected to number 163.5 million. Among the major race and ethnicity groups, labor force participation rates according to race are projected to be whites, 61.7 percent; blacks, 59.8 percent; and Asians, 63.2 percent. People of Hispanic origin are expected to account for 31.2 million workers by 2022 because of their younger population, higher fertility rates, and increased immigration.[11]

MORE OLDER WORKERS ENTERING THE WORKFORCE

Think about the last time you went to a fast-food restaurant or traditional restaurant, or a retail store like McDonald's, Wendy's, Burger King, Bob Evans, Walmart or Target. Did you notice the number of people serving and assisting you who seemed to be older than people you usually see in those roles? This evolving phenomenon is the result of a variety of social factors. The most significant factor is that the median age of people in the United States is rising because of the aging of the "baby-boom" generation (those born between 1946 and 1964).

From a workplace perspective, this means that more of the people in this age group will stay in the workplace or return after they leave (see Figure 1.6). This may be caused by pure economic necessity, since many people may have not prepared adequately for retirement and cannot be certain that the Social Security system will support them. Some

---

Ethical Dilemma 1.1

With all the competition for customer service jobs in your organization, you are concerned that you might not be able to get a promotion that you feel you deserve. You have heard that there are three other employees being considered for a job opening for which you want to apply. You know all three people and their work habits. Each has a "skeleton in the closet" related to performance issues in the past of which you are aware, but your supervisor is not. Your supervisor will be screening applicants soon.

1. Should you inform your supervisor of what you know to ensure that she makes an educated choice based on qualifications? Why or why not?

2. What could be the potential result of any action that you take about this issue?

See possible responses at the end of the chapter.

Customer Service Success Tip

Diversity is here to stay. Network with people from different cultures; visit ethnic restaurants; travel to other countries; read books and articles about different countries; learn a second language; and explore research on the Internet about different cultures, gender issues, age groups, religions, ability issues, and other factors that each person brings to the workplace. All this will help you more effectively interact with and maximize the potential of others while enhancing your opportunities for success as a customer service professional.

In 2020, baby boomers will be age 56 to 74 years, and this age group will be the largest age group in the workforce, comprising 25.2 percent. Other age groups comprise the remainder of the workforce in the following percentages:

45–54 years = 20.1

35–44 years = 21.4

25–24 years = 22.2

16–24 years = 11.2

FIGURE 1.6

2010–2020 Workforce Percentage of Labor Force by Age

Source: Bureau of Labor Statistics Division of Industry Employment Projections, www.bls.gov/ooh/About/Projections-Overview.htm.

people return to the workplace for social reasons—they miss the work and/or the opportunity to interact with others and feel useful. Whatever the reason for the desire or willingness of older workers to reenter the workforce, many organizations have realized that they often have an admirable work ethic. Also, since there are not enough entry-level people in the traditional pool of younger workers (because of lower birthrates during the 1970s), companies are actively recruiting older workers and those from other countries.

GROWTH OF E-COMMERCE

e-commerce Refers to the entire spectrum of companies that market products and services on the Internet and through other technology and the process of accessing them by consumers.

The past two decades have been witness to unimagined use of the personal computer and the Internet by the average person. As an example of the impact of **e-commerce**, the retail trade sector (e.g., motor vehicles and parts, furniture, electronics, food, sporting goods, and mail order houses) had sales of nearly $1,209 billion in the second quarter of 2016. Nearly $97.3 billion of that amount was in e-commerce sales.[12] Almost any product or service is available at the click of a mouse, press of a key, or voice command. Consumers regularly "surf the net" for values in products and services without ever leaving their homes or offices. For example, many people do business with others all over the world without ever meeting them face-to-face or even talking to them on the telephone. Entire business-to-business customer relationships occur every day between people who are strangers but who provide key products and services to their customers electronically (e.g., computer programmers, accountants, book editors, graphic artists, and website designers). This new way of accessing goods and services through technology has been termed e-commerce.

Armed with a password, site addresses, and credit cards, shoppers use this virtual marketplace to satisfy needs or wants that they likely did not know they had before logging onto their computer and connecting with the Internet. With so many options available for just a small investment of time, they can comparison-shop simply by changing screens. No wonder the twentieth century saw the establishment of more millionaires and billionaires than any of its predecessors.

The creators and owners of the most innovative sites and products can provide products, services, and information worldwide without ever physically coming into contact with a customer, and yet can amass huge reserves of money. Examples of these success stories and popularity are eBay (an online auction service), Craig's List (an online listing of items for sales, services, personal announcements, local classifieds, and forums for jobs, housing, and events), Microsoft (software products), and Amazon.com (an online book and product seller and auction line), which have become household names and are used by millions of shoppers yearly.

> ### Street Talk We all have customers
>
> Even if you do not directly serve external customers, you always have them. You probably serve an internal client. It could be co-workers, a manager, another team, or even another division within your organization. Learn as much as you can about those customers and identify the service you actually provide to them. Learn how you fill their needs. That helps you better identify the skills you need to improve, the industry knowledge you need to have, and potentially other ways you can support these clients. Enhancing these skills will create a stronger value for you as a team member.
>
> **COURTESY OF BARRY NADLER**

KNOWLEDGE CHECK

1. Of the 11 societal factors that have affected customer service, which do you think has the biggest impact? Why?

2. What other societal factors do you believe have affected the customer service sector? Why?

LO 1-4 Consumer Behavior Shifts

CONCEPT Many people in different parts of the world are still struggling to make ends meet financially due to some of the worst economic conditions in recent memory. They are looking for ways to maintain their desired standard of living without too many sacrifices. The result has been a shift in the ways people approach buying and obtaining the necessities and desired products and services.

DIFFERENT MINDSET

In the past, many consumers took a "money is no object" approach to shopping because, if they did not have cash readily available, they had several pieces of plastic in their wallet that allowed them to spend (often beyond their means). This was possible because financial institutions were doling out these instruments of commerce in a very haphazard manner to virtually all who looked like they could potentially repay what they spent. Unfortunately, that practice proved to be highly flawed. As a result, the financial institutions that let credit practices run rampant fell like proverbial dominos and took along the world's economy with them. In the aftermath of this economic carnage, many consumers have had a reality check and have learned that prudence is an important element of commerce. Plainly speaking, if you do not have the money, do not spend it!

A majority of consumers who formerly acted on impulse and bought whatever they desired are now taking a very cautious approach. Initially, the shock of having credit severely curtailed or cut off totally by their banks and credit unions sent many people into panic mode. As jobs disappeared, savings and bank accounts dwindled, and many people became homeless, a sense of panic spread throughout the United States and the world.

Economic reports are now indicating that people have begun to shift from a "cutting back" mentality to a slightly more optimistic "cautious spending" approach. Part of their new strategy is to reevaluate their paradigm, or the way they look at products. Where they might have only gone for the nationally known brand or reputation in the past, they now evaluate and consider generic or store brands with comparable options and services offered by local providers. They are also being more conscientious about their spending and instead of seeking chic, top-of-the line products, they are shopping at discounters like Ross, TJMaxx, dollar stores, and BIG Lots; comparison-shopping more; bargaining with retailers; bartering; and renting versus buying items. The sales advertisements and coupons that they overlooked in the past are often sought out and acted upon. Online, they frequent www.eBay.com and similar auction sites or product clearance sites like www.overstock.com. Sites like www.pricegrabber.com that allow online product and price comparison are also very popular.

Trending NOW

An increasing trend related to product ownership is that many consumers of all ages are opting to rent rather than buy items such as books, homes, cars, furniture, tires and hubcaps, and even clothes. With the advances in mobile and other electronic technology, it is easy for consumers to scour the Internet for companies offering various items that were not previously rented. This trend is especially strong with younger consumers who are often very technically savvy, have more limited budgets, and may not care to amass a large cache of personal belongings that impede personal mobility.

Another interesting outcome of the recession and massive job losses is that many consumers, especially younger ones, want to have less financial obligation in the event something traumatic happens in their life related to employment and financial security. Many are already dealing with heavy student loan debt and struggle to find meaningful employment. This has led many millennials to forego fancy cars, mortgages, large furnishing purchases, and to abandon the shopping patterns of their parents. An article on www.Bloomberg.com emphasized how companies are moving to address this trend toward temporary usage versus ownership.

> Enterprise Holdings Inc. and Hertz Global Holdings Inc....are expanding in what the Santa Monica, California–based research firm IBISWorld estimates to be the $1.8 billion hourly car-rental business, a segment dominated by younger drivers.... Startups such as Rent the Runway Inc. are supplying high-fashion apparel to satisfy those who want to rent, not own. CORT, a unit of Warren Buffet's Berkshire Hathaway Inc...., is increasing its furniture-rental marketing efforts to college students and fledgling households.[13].

Today's consumers are also looking to save money in other ways. Instead of jumping in their car and driving around to numerous stores to compare sale prices and products, they often sit at their computer and do their research and buying there. They also look to consolidate trips in order to save on the amount of gas they expend. This is why Walmart, Costco, Sam's, BJs, and Target Super Stores have become so popular and powerful.

Customer Service Success Tip

If your goal is to ultimately have your own service-oriented business, start planning today. Take college courses on business-related topics, network with others in your industry through professional groups like the International Customer Service Association (http://ic-satoday.org/), and conduct research on how to start a small business effectively through the Small Business Association (SBA; https://www.sba.gov/). Many community colleges have relationships with SBA and SCORE (Service Corps of Retired Executives) and some states sponsor incubator programs for new businesses to help them get started.

EXPECTATION OF QUALITY SERVICE

Most customers expect that if they pay a fair dollar, in return they will receive a quality product or service. If their expectations are not met, they simply call or visit a competing company where they can receive what they think they paid for.

An even more powerful example of a new trend where consumers are getting what they want via technological means was highlighted in an article on www.trendwatching.com. It discusses the fact that when consumers or others band together to send a message online, the results can be powerful and businesses line up to compete. Examples of the outcome of combined buying power that many people have come to use and trust are www.priceline.com and www.hotwire.com. The site dubbed the trend "crowd clout." An example of the full potential of such collaboration or clout was seen in the efforts to get Barack Obama elected as the 44th president of the United States.

The expectation of quality service that most consumers have also creates a need for better-trained and better-educated customer service professionals. Not only do service professionals need up-to-date product information in order to be at the top of their game when interacting with customers, but they also need to be abreast of current organizational policies and procedures, what the competition offers, and the latest techniques in customer service and satisfaction. Companies recognize that if they do not meet the service expectations of customers, they lose business and revenue. Thus, the superior service providers invest large amounts of money in training and empowering employees, providing the latest service technology, and building a supervisory team that has the knowledge and skill to effectively coach and support employees in order to achieve peak performance.

ENHANCED CONSUMER PREPARATION

Customers today are not only more highly educated than in the past, they are also well informed about the price, quality, and value of products and services. This has occurred in part through the advertising and publicity by companies competing for market share and by the activities of consumer information and advocacy groups that have surfaced. With the advent of the Internet, consumers are really in a power position when it comes to dealing with organizations providing products and services that they want. For example, in the past, car buying was a painful experience for most customers, who were literally at the mercy of car salespeople who had all the knowledge about the industry, sales process, inventory, and pricing data. That has all changed for people who are Internet savvy and take the time to do their homework. Now, sites such as www.edmunds.com, www.kelleybluebook.com, www. usaa.com, and others have all sorts of pricing tools, interest calculators, invoice information, and articles on how to effectively shop for, negotiate, and buy a new or used car. Having the same information and tools salespeople have available evens the playing field.

Armed with knowledge about what they should receive for their money, consumers make it extremely difficult for less-than-reputable businesspeople to prosper or survive in today's world. With consumers now on the defensive and ready to fight back, all business owners find that they have to continually prove the worth of their products and services. They must provide **customer satisfaction** or face losing customers to competitors. In addition, they face the potential of negative publicity through social media and sites like yelp.com where customers can immediately post comments about the level of service and product quality that they receive.

customer satisfaction The feeling of a person whose needs have been met by an organization.

KNOWLEDGE CHECK

1. What are the societal factors affecting customer service?

2. In what ways have recent worldwide economic events caused a shift in consumer behavior?

LO 1-5 The Customer Service Environment

CONCEPT   In this section, the six components that make up a service environment and contribute to customer service delivery are discussed. Use these factors to ensure that a viable customer service environment is the responsibility of every employee of the organization—not just the customer service representatives.

COMPONENTS OF A CUSTOMER SERVICE ENVIRONMENT

customer service environment An environment made up of and influenced by various elements of an organization. The key components are the customer, organizational culture, human resources, products, delivery systems, and service.

Let's take time to examine the six key components of a **customer service environment**, which will illustrate many factors that contribute to customer service delivery:

1. The customer
2. Organizational culture
3. Human resources
4. Products/deliverables
5. Delivery systems
6. Service

Many factors affect your customers and what they perceive as quality service. With the exception of the customer, all of these factors are under the control of the service provider and staff.

THE CUSTOMER

As shown in Figure 1.7, the central component in a customer-focused environment is the customer. Customers are the "star" of the show and should be the central focus of all workplace efforts. By striving to identify the specific needs of each individual customer, and then acting to satisfy him or her, employees can help ensure his or her loyalty, satisfaction, and positive word-of-mouth publicity. By remembering that all aspects of the service organization revolve around that crucial entity and that without the customer, there is no reason for any organization to exist, service professionals help ensure personal and business success.

One crucial point to keep in mind is that all employees have two types of customers with whom they must regularly interact: internal and external. A continuing consciousness of the need to provide exceptional, enthusiastic customer service is the only way to outpace the competition. As Karl Albrecht and Ron Zemke say in their classic book on customer service, *Service America*, "If you're not serving the customer, you'd better be serving someone who is." This is true because if you are not providing stellar support and service to internal customers, external customers usually suffer. And, if you are not providing exceptional service to your external customers, your internal customers will suffer because revenue for salaries, benefits, training, equipment, and other important elements required to function will shrink.

External Customers

External customers may be current or potential customers or clients. They are the ones who actively seek out; research; and buy, rent, or lease products or services offered by your organization. This group can sometimes involve business customers

FIGURE 1.7

Components of a Customer-Focused Environment

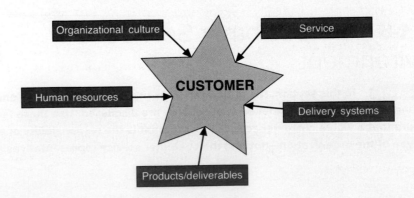

who purchase your product to include with their own for resale. It can also involve an organization that acts as a franchise or distributor. Such an organization buys your products to resell or uses them to represent your company in its geographic area.

Internal Customers

Unless you own your own business as a sole proprietor, you have internal customers. Many employees in the workplace will tell you that they do not have "customers." They are wrong. Everyone in an organization, from the CEO to the frontline employee, has customers. They may not be traditional customers who contact a service professional to buy or use products or services. Instead, they are internal customers who are coworkers, employees of other departments or branches, and other people who work within the same organization. The interesting thing about internal customers is that there is typically a symbiotic relationship between employees. That is because, on any given day, employees from different areas of an organization depend on others for information, products, and services. This allows each person in the organization to have the tools needed to better serve external customers.

Unfortunately, many employees neglect their internal customers for a variety of reasons. Typically, that is because they do not recognize others as their internal customer or realize their importance in allowing employees to support their external customers. One way to improve internal customer service is to shift thinking of other employees as "coworkers" and refer to them as "customers."

The following are suggestions for building stronger relationships and better serving internal customers:

- **Be reliable.** When you commit to something, follow through by delivering as promised. This includes meeting deadlines for information needed by others. In many cases, someone might request material or products to serve an external customer. If that is not received in a timely manner, the external customer becomes dissatisfied, the requesting internal customer becomes dissatisfied and may be dinged for poor performance, and the organization ultimately might lose revenue, business, and suffer ill effects from negative publicity.

- **Develop positive relationships.** Make an effort to greet others pleasantly each day and display common courtesies such as saying "please" and "thank you."

- **Take time to get to know more about others.** Possibly take breaks or go to lunch or talk before or after work to get to know internal customers on a more personal level. Learn about your customer's background and about the job that he or she does. This can lead to a better understanding about what they might have to offer and how you might be able to assist them and make their job easier. People are more likely to provide better internal customer service when they like the person they are serving.

- **Listen objectively.** When another employee has an idea, especially when it involves ways to better serve external customers, take the time to listen and discuss it. Consider the merits of what is offered before responding.

- **Acknowledge the contributions of others.** Always give credit for work done by others and never claim it as your own. The latter can lead to resentment and actually get you fired.

- **Show appreciation for help provided by others.** If someone goes out of his or her way to assist you, take the time to acknowledge it. This could be a text or e-mail message, or, more powerfully, a handwritten note. Depending on the effort of the person, perhaps give a small reward. For example, give a hand-baked jumbo cookie along with a note.

- **Avoid office politics and gossip.** One of the quickest ways to get a bad workplace reputation is to become the person who acts like a pollinator by moving from one person to another sharing stories he or she has collected about things that are going on in the office or with another employee. Not only do these actions cause loss of productivity time that you can use to serve external customers, but also it can gain you a reputation as someone who is not trustworthy.

- **Help others.** Even if it means you have to put out extra effort, take the time to assist your internal customers. If you cannot do so immediately, negotiate when you can help. People remember your generosity and willingness to assist them when the time comes where you need help.

- **Respect diversity.** In a world where people of all shapes, sizes, abilities, and backgrounds come together, all employees must learn about and appreciate others in order to appreciate their views, values, and beliefs. This pertains to external customers and certainly to internal ones. Since employees spend the major part of their life interacting with others in workplace and job situations, they can benefit from better understanding people. Just because someone might look or act differently, have an accent, or does not have the same knowledge or abilities as a service provider does not mean there is something wrong with him or her. Diversity must be embraced and respected for the benefit of all internal and external customers.

Examples of internal customers include the following:

Cafeteria workers. You are their customer because they provide products and services to you and they depend on you to buy food and drinks that they prepare or sell, thus providing them employment.

Human Resources (HR) staff. Managers and other employees depend on HR staff to support hiring and staff management functions and to manage employee benefits. The HR staff also depend on the managers and others to provide them with information and feedback in the form of employee surveys, updated job descriptions, forms, and other job-related information that they use to manage the HR function.

Information Technology (IT) staff. Think of how much you depend on your computer and related technology to serve your internal and external customers on any given day. What would happen if your computer crashed at 8:00 a.m. as you are just beginning your workday. What implications would that have for you and your customers? Your first call would likely be to the IT staff. Recognize and show appreciation for their efforts in making your job easier and in many cases possible. As a customer, you provide them a reason to exist inside the organization.

Print shop employees. These are the employees who provide printed and promotional materials used by various departments to support and market to their customers. They depend on department staff to provide them with business that keeps them employed.

⚙ WORK IT OUT 1.3

Who Are My Internal Customers?

Take a few minutes to think about your current organization or select any organization with which you have been associated and create two lists: one of your internal customers and another of your suppliers. Then compare your lists to see which customers also act as suppliers and help you better serve the external customers of your organization. Next, choose the ones that you interact with regularly and make a list of ways that you can enhance your relationship with them.

Security personnel. These are the employees to whom all other employees depend upon to oversee safety and look out for their well-being. They depend on the other employees to provide feedback on how they are doing their job, to report hazards and safety or security violations, and to use their services (e.g., escorting employees to their cars in dark areas of the property after dark).

Recognizing this formidable group of customers is important and crucial to everyone in the organization for on-the-job success. That is because, in the internal customer chain, an employee is sometimes a customer and at other times a supplier. At times, you may call a coworker in another department for information. Later that same day, this coworker may call you for a similar reason. Only when both parties are acutely aware of their role in this customer–supplier relationship can the organization effectively prosper and grow to full potential.

The important point to remember related to your internal customers is that you must take care of them, just as you do your external customers. They must be serviced effectively and treated with respect in order to allow them to provide exceptional service to their customers. Without the information, products, and services that you provide them, they do not have the tools needed to do their job.

ORGANIZATIONAL CULTURE

Without the mechanisms and atmosphere to support frontline service, the other components of the business environment cannot succeed. Put simply, **organizational culture** is what the customer experiences. This culture is made up of a collection of subcomponents, each of which contributes to the overall service environment. Typically, culture includes the dynamic nature of the organization and encompasses the values and beliefs that are important to the organization and its employees and managers. The experiences, attitudes, and norms cherished and upheld by employees and teams within the organization set the tone for the manner in which service is delivered and how service providers interact with both internal and external customers.

organizational culture Includes any element of an organization that a customer encounters.

HUMAN RESOURCES

To make the culture work, an organization must take great care in recruiting, selecting, training, and retaining qualified people—its **human resources**. That is why, when you apply (or applied) for a job as a customer service professional, a thorough screening process will be (or was) likely used to identify your skills, knowledge, and aptitudes. Without motivated, competent workers, any planning, policy, and procedure change or systems adaptation will not make a difference in customer service.

human resources Refers to employees of an organization.

Many organizations go to great lengths to obtain and retain the "right" employees who possess the knowledge, skills, and competencies to professionally serve customers (see Figure 1.8). This includes thorough background checks, reference checking, and reviewing social media channels to discover the type of online

WORK IT OUT 1.4

Types of Service

Take a minute to think about customer service. In what ways do organizations typically provide service to external customers?

persona applicants possess. For example, does the person post personal information and images that paint a picture of his or her personality, likes, dislikes, values, and beliefs about others, organizations, the government, and society? Companies go to these lengths because job candidates who are skilled, motivated, and enthusiastic about providing service excellence and who possess all or a majority of the requisite skills needed to perform required job responsibilities are often hard to find, expensive to recruit, and appreciated by employers and customers. As noted earlier, organizations now rely on all employees to provide service excellence to customers; however, they also maintain specially trained "elite" groups of employees who perform specific customer-related functions. Depending on their organization's focus, these individuals have a variety of titles (e.g., a customer service representative in a retail organization's customer care center might be called a *member counselor* in an association, but these employees often perform similar service functions).

A challenge for many organizations is finding a way to attract and keep qualified employees. In years past, it was not unusual for someone to spend an entire career with one or two employers. Times have changed for many reasons. One of the biggest reasons is that there is often no loyalty toward the organization by employees or vice versa by the organization toward employees. One U.S. Bureau of Labor Statistics study found the following:

> "In January 2016, median employee tenure (the point at which half of all workers had more tenure and half had less tenure) for men was 4.2 years, down from 4.6 percent in January 2014. For women, median tenure was 4.60 years, down from 4.5 years in January 2014. Among men, 29 percent of wage and salary workers had 10 years or more of tenure with their current employer; among women, the figure was 28 percent.

FIGURE 1.8 Typical Titles and Functions Performed by Customer Service Personnel in Organizations (Median Incomes in the United States)

Receptionist/Front Desk Clerk

Salary average: $9.90 per hour

Employees performing this function in organizations have the primary role of meeting, greeting, and offering initial assistance to customers and visitors. This is a crucial role that starts setting the tone for how others view the organization. Whether in a doctor's or attorney's office, gym, car dealership, homeless shelter, or office building, these frontline service representatives are the standard bearer for an organization and should be adequately trained and empowered to assist those with whom they come into contact.

Customer Service (CS)/Member Support Clerk

Salary average: $13.46 per hour

This is typically an entry-level position requiring strong organizational ability; an ability to follow instructions, listen, and manage time; and a desire to help. A key function is clerical support, which includes filing, researching information, typing, and similar assignments. They deal with customers via telephone, e-mail, correspondence, and face-to-face.

Customer Service (CS) Representative/Member Counselor

Salary average: $13.23 per hour

This position is an entry-level position into the customer service field (although many people have years of experience in the job). Since these employees interact directly with customers and potential customers, they need strong interpersonal (communication, conflict management, listening) skills as well as a desire to help others, a fondness for working with people, a knowledge of organizational products and services, and a thorough understanding of what a CS representative does. Key functions include interacting face-to-face or over the telephone with customers, receiving and processing orders or requests for information and services, responding to customer inquiries, handling complaints, and performing associated customer contact assignments.

Data Entry/Order Clerk I

Salary average: $15.37 per hour

The data entry/order clerk is an entry-level position requiring knowledge of personal computers and software, ability to work on repetitive tasks for long periods of time, and an eye for accuracy. Key functions include verifying and batching orders received from customer service representatives for input by computer personnel. In organizations that have personal computer systems connected by networks, data entry/order clerks enter data and generate and maintain reports.

Senior Customer Service (CS) Representative/Member Counselor

Salary average: $27.40 per hour

This position is usually staffed by personnel with experience as a CS representative. A position like this one requires a person with a sound understanding of basic supervisory skills, since job duties may include providing feedback, training, and support and administering performance appraisals to other representatives or counselors.

Service Technician or Professional

Salary range varies by specialty and training. For example, an average auto service technician/mechanic earns in the area of $19.23 per hour.

This group provides many different types of services and carries a variety of titles (e.g., air-conditioning technologist, plumber, automotive specialist, office equipment technician, law enforcement officer, firefighter, or sanitation worker). Each specialized area requires specific knowledge and skills.

Inbound/Outbound Call Center Representative

Salary range: $12.03–$14.02 per hour

Customer service representatives may perform some or all of the functions of this job, but often specially hired or trained employees fill the position. They make and receive phone calls with the intent of promoting or selling company products or services. In many organizations, these employees are full-time or part-time sales personnel whose job is to use the telephone to call customers or potential customers or receive orders or questions from customers. Employees in these positions need strong self-confidence because of the number of rejections to offers and irate calls they receive, sound verbal communication and listening skills, a positive attitude, good knowledge of sales techniques, an ability to handle people who are upset, and a desire to help others through identification and satisfaction of needs. Key functions include placing and/or receiving calls, responding to inquiries with product and service information, asking for and recording orders, and following up on leads and requests for information.

Help Desk Computer Analyst

Salary average: $23.52 per hour

Typically, these employees are responsible for providing hardware or software support via an automatic call distributor (ACD) system (see Chapter 9) or e-mail to callers in various geographic locations for their desktop PCs, laptops, and peripheral devices. They answer calls, log all incidents into their call-tracking database, and provide technical assistance.

Counter and Rental Clerk

Salary average: $15.65 per hour

These employees work in a variety of organizations receiving orders for services such as repairs, car and equipment rentals, dry cleaning, and storage. They are typically responsible for estimating costs, accepting payments, and, in some cases, completion of rental agreements.

Other Service-Related Functions

In addition to these positions, many organizations have supervisory, manager, director, and vice president positions in most of the job areas indicated or in the service area as a whole. The existence of higher-level positions provides opportunities for upward advancement and learning as experience is gained.

Note: Salaries vary greatly in any occupation and industry and are often dictated by an employee's experience, education, knowledge, initiative, and ability to quickly assume more responsibility or perform at a higher level. Salary examples shown here are from www.monster.com. To get an idea of salaries for various types of service jobs in your area, visit www.payscale.com, www1.salary.com, and www.glassdoor.com.

The median tenure for 55 percent of employees between the age of 55–64 was 10.1 years in January 2016, over three times the tenure for workers age 25 to 34 (2.8 years). Among workers age 60–64, 55 percent were employed for at least 10 years with their current employer in January 2016, compared with 13 percent of workers age 30 to 34.

Among the major race and ethnicity groups, 22 percent of Hispanics had been with their current employer for 10 years or more in January 2016, compared with 30 percent of whites, 25 percent of blacks and Asians.… The shorter tenure among Hispanics can be explained, in part, by their relative youth. 44 percent of Hispanic workers were between the ages of 16 and 34; by comparison, the proportions for Whites (36 percent), Blacks (40 percent), and Asians (36 percent) were smaller.

Among the major occupations, workers in management, professional, and related occupations had the highest median tenure (5.1 years) in January 2016. Within this group, employees with jobs in management occupations (6.3 years), architecture and engineering occupations (5.5 years), and legal occupations (5.5 years) had the longest tenure. Workers in service occupations, who are generally younger than persons employed in management, professional, and related occupations, had the lowest median tenure (2.9 years). Among employees working in service occupations, food service workers had the lowest median tenure, at 1.9 years."[14]

Figure 1.9 lists some common competencies needed by successful customer service professionals.

DELIVERABLES

deliverables Products or services provided by an organization.

The fourth component of a service environment is the **deliverables** offered by an organization. A deliverable may be a tangible item manufactured or distributed by the company, such as a piece of furniture, or a service available to the customer, such as pest extermination. In either case, there are two potential areas of customer satisfaction or dissatisfaction—quality and quantity. If your customers receive what they perceive as a quality product or service to the level that they expected, and in the time frame promised or viewed as acceptable, they will likely be happy. On the other hand, if customers believe that they were sold an inferior product or given an inferior service or one that does not match their expectations, they will likely be dissatisfied and could

FIGURE 1.9

Competencies of Customer Service Professionals

There are many things that make one successful in the service profession and life. Many skills and competencies that someone possesses can carry over into other situations throughout life. The following are some general competencies or qualities that can make you successful when interacting with internal and external customers:

Adaptable	Good communicator: oral, listening, and written	Good judgment	Reliable
Detail-oriented		Ability to negotiate	Resilient
Good business acumen	Lifelong learner	Solid organizational knowledge	Self-aware
Compassionate	Creative thinker		Service-oriented
Collaborative	Diversity-aware	Problem-solving skills	Technically oriented
	Result-oriented	Professional	Good time manager
	Takes initiative	Quality-oriented	

WORK IT OUT 1.5

Attracting and Training Employees

Think about organizational strategies aimed at recruiting and training service employees. What are some things you have heard or read about that companies are doing to attract, hire, and keep qualified service employees?

take their business elsewhere. They may also provide negative word-of-mouth advertising for the organization.

DELIVERY SYSTEMS

The fifth component of an effective service environment is the method(s) by which the product or service is delivered. In deciding on **delivery systems**, organizations examine the following factors:

delivery system The method(s) used by an organization to provide services and products to its customers.

> *Industry standards:* How is the competition currently delivering? Are current organizational delivery standards in line with those of competitors?
>
> *Customer expectations:* Do customers expect delivery to occur in a certain manner within a specified time frame? Are alternatives acceptable?
>
> *Capabilities:* Do existing or available systems within the organization and industry allow for a variety of delivery methods? Do our systems match customer expectations?
>
> *Costs:* Will providing a variety of techniques add real or perceived value at an acceptable cost? If there are additional costs, will consumers be willing to absorb them?
>
> *Current and projected requirements:* Are existing methods of delivery, such as mail, phone, and face-to-face service, meeting the needs of the customer and will they continue to do so in the future? If not, what must be adjusted to remain competitive?

SERVICE

Stated simply, service is the manner in which you and other employees treat your customers and each other as you deliver your company's deliverables. Effective use of the techniques and strategies outlined later in this book is required in order to satisfy the needs of your customers.

KNOWLEDGE CHECK

1. What are the six components of a customer service environment?
2. Which customer service environment element do you believe is most important? Why?
3. Do you believe that there should be a difference in the way you deal with internal and external customers? Explain.

learning organizations A term used by Peter Senge in his book *The Fifth Discipline* (www.amazon.com) to describe organizations that value knowledge, education, and employee training. They also learn from their competition, industry trends, and other sources, and they develop systems to support continued growth and development in order to remain competitive.

LO 1-6 Addressing the Changes

> **CONCEPT** All customer-based organizations must provide excellence in service and an environment in which customer needs are identified and satisfied.

With all the changes, developing strategies for providing premium service that will attract and hold loyal customers has become a priority for most organizations. All customer-based organizations have one focus in common: they must provide service excellence and an environment in which customer needs are identified and satisfied—or perish.

To this end, organizations must become **learning organizations**. Basically, a learning organization is one that uses knowledge as a basis for competitive advantage. This means providing ongoing training and development opportunities to employees so that they can gain and maintain cutting-edge skills and knowledge while projecting a positive can-do customer-focused attitude. A learning organization also ensures that there are systems that can adequately compensate and reward employees on the basis of their performance. In such an organization, systems and processes are continuously examined and updated. Learning from mistakes, and adapting accordingly, is crucial.

In the past, organizations took a reactive approach to service by waiting for customers to ask for something or by trying to recover after a service breakdown. Often, a small customer service staff dealt with customer dissatisfaction or attempted to fix problems after they occurred. In today's economy, a proactive approach of anticipating customer needs is necessary and becoming common. With the advent of technology, accessing customer needs, wants, and expectations has been simplified. Through social media websites such as surveymonkey.com, even small businesses can tap into customer opinions and gather information on which they base business decisions quickly and often inexpensively.

To excel, organizations must train all employees to spot problems and deal with them before the customer becomes aware that they exist. Every employee must take personal responsibility for customer care. If all employees assume ownership for continuous product and service quality improvement, their organization can flourish.

service recovery The process of correcting something that has gone wrong involving provision of a product or service to a customer. The concept involves not only replacing defective products, but also going the extra step of providing compensation for the customer's inconvenience.

If a service breakdown does occur, managers in truly customer-focused organizations should empower employees at all levels to do whatever is necessary to satisfy the customer. For this to happen, management must educate and train staff members on the techniques and policies available to help serve the customer. They must then give employees the authority to act without asking first for management intervention in order to resolve customer issues. This concept is known as **service recovery**.

KNOWLEDGE CHECK

1. What are the six components of a customer service environment?
2. What is a learning environment and what role does it play in helping create a competitive advantage?

Small Business Perspective

Men and women of different backgrounds and ages are starting businesses in record numbers. Many of these are in the service industry. Some examples are lawn, pool, automobile, and home care; health care and assistance; dog grooming; accounting; consulting; training and educational services; and transportation. Among other things, the impetus for much of this entrepreneur initiative addresses factors such as loss of jobs in various industries; lack of job opportunities for recent college graduates; frustration with workplace policies, practices, and politics; and personal desire to be the boss and independently make meaningful decisions.

In addition to adequate education and knowledge of how to create and run a successful business, a key factor in owner success is to create a customer-centric organization. In such an environment, everyone involved in the company strives to identify customer needs, wants, and expectations and fulfill them. Customer service is equally or more important in small businesses because those organizations do not have the deep pockets possessed by their multinational competitors. Because of limited staff and resources, these organizations must excel at quickly identifying and addressing the needs of current and potential customers. They must then depend on every employee to put forth 110 percent effort to help satisfy customer needs and expectations. Smaller companies do not have the luxury of a large human resource team to support employees. The owners must get creative to figure out ways to effectively train staff in order to provide them with the knowledge, skills, and attitudes needed to excel and to aid employee retention. With the multitude of free and inexpensive resources such as customer service professional organizations, youtube.com, Small Business Administration, customer service blogs, Internet articles, local colleges, and trade schools, enhancing employee knowledge and skills has become easier.

The law defines a small business as "one that is independently owned and operated and is not dominant in its field of operation." According to the **Small Business Administration (SBA)**, small business is big business in the United States. This is because of the following:

- The 28 million small businesses in America account for 54 percent of all U.S. sales.
- Small businesses have provided 55 percent of all jobs and 66 percent of all net new jobs since the 1970s.
- The 600,000 plus franchised small businesses in the United States account for 40 percent of all retail sales and provide jobs for some 8 million people.
- The small business sector in America occupies 30 to 50 percent of all commercial space, an estimated 20–34 billion square feet.

Furthermore, the small business sector is growing rapidly. While corporate America has been "downsizing," the rate of small business "start-ups" has grown, and the rate for small business failures has declined.

- The number of small businesses in the United States has increased 49 percent since 1982.
- Since 1990, as big business eliminated 4 million jobs, small businesses added 8 million new jobs.[15]

Nationally, these small businesses make up more than 70 percent of all businesses. They may be run by one or more individuals, can range from home-based businesses to corner stores or construction contractors, and often are part-time ventures with owners operating more than one business at a time.

According to the National Women's Business Council, in 2012, women owned 9,878,397 million small businesses in the United States. Of nonfarm and privately held businesses, women owned 36.3 percent; 88.3 percent of those businesses were sole proprietorships

Small Business Administration (SBA) U.S. governmental agency established to assist small business owners.

(*continued*)

and 89.5 percent had no employees other than the owner. The remaining 10.5 percent employed 8,431.614 million employees, paid employees $263.7 billion in salary, and generated $1.2 trillion in receipts.[16] Figure 1.10 shows the percentage of women-owned businesses by age and race/ethnicity as of 2012. The numbers have increased since then.

FIGURE 1.10

National Women's Business Council, Women-Owned Businesses, by Age and Race/Ethnicity, 2012

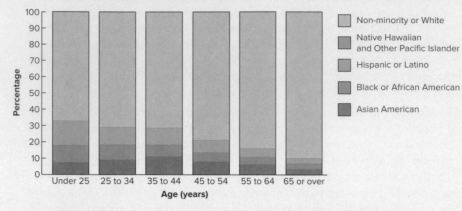

Source: https://www.nwbc.gov/sites/default/files/NWBC_FS_Age_Final_lr.pdf.

Impact on Service

Based on your experience and what you just read, answer the following questions.

1. What level of customer service have you experienced from small businesses in your local area? Explain.

2. In what ways have you seen service providers in small businesses excel from a service standpoint?

3. In what ways have you seen service providers in small businesses fail from a service standpoint?

4. If you were a small business owner, what are five things that you would do to ensure that your customer needs are met?

⬛︎ISMARTBOOK™   **Use SmartBook to help you read, study, and retain what you have learned. Access SmartBook in your Instructor's Connect course, or go to connect.mheducation. com for help.**

Key Terms

broadband Internet access

business-to-business (B2B)

cottage industries

customer-focused organization

customer relationship management (CRM)

customer satisfaction

customer service

customer service environment

deliverables

delivery system

deregulation

downsizing

e-commerce

external customers

globalization

human resources

insourcing

instant messaging

internal customers

learning organizations

networking

North American Free Trade Agreement (NAFTA)

offshoring

organizational culture

outsourcing

product

service economy

service industry

service recovery

service sector

Skype

Small Business Administration (SBA)

social media

telecommuting

telework

Summary

As many organizations move toward a more quality-oriented, customer-focused environment, developing and fine-tuning policies, procedures, and systems to better identify customer needs and meet their expectations will be crucial. Through a concerted effort to perfect service delivery, organizations will be able to survive and compete in a global economy. More emphasis must be placed on better understanding a continually shifting and diverse customer base and finding out what consumers expect, then going beyond those expectations. Total customer satisfaction is not just a buzz phrase; it is a way of life that companies are adopting in order to gain and maintain market share. As a customer service professional, it is your job to help foster a customer-oriented service environment. By better educating and training yourself in some of the areas addressed in this chapter, you set yourself above other less motivated customer service professionals. You also position yourself for opportunities to succeed and ultimately reap the benefits and satisfaction of a job well done.

Review Questions

Either on your own or in discussion with someone else review what you have learned in this chapter by responding to the following questions:

1. What is service?
2. Describe some of the earliest forms of customer service.
3. What are some of the factors that have facilitated the shift to a service economy?
4. What have been some of the causes of the changing business environment in recent decades?
5. Describe the impact of a company's culture on its success in a customer-focused business environment. Discuss why each is important.
6. What role does the human resources element of the customer service environment play in customer satisfaction?
7. What two factors related to an organization's products or deliverables can lead to customer satisfaction or dissatisfaction?
8. When organizations select a delivery method for products or services, where do they get information on the best approach to take?
9. What are the six key components of a customer service environment and how does each directly impact customer loyalty and satisfaction?
10. Why are many organizations changing to learning organizations?

Search It Out

1. To learn more about the history, background, and components of customer service occupations, select one of the topics below, log on to the Internet, and gather additional research data. One valuable site is the U.S. Department of Labor at http://stats.bls.gov. You can also type in the term "salaries" on a search engine to identify other sources of income information. Report your findings to your work team members, peers, or students, depending on the setting in which you are using this book.

   Research the projected salaries and benefits for customer service providers in your industry or in one that interests you.

   Search for information on organizational behavior and organizational culture and share your findings with the class. Discuss how behavior and culture impact service delivery.

   Develop a bibliographic listing of books and other publications on topics introduced in this chapter. The resources should be less than five years old. You can do this by going to sites such as:

   http://www.amazon.com

   http://www.barnesandnoble.com

   http//www.mhprofessional.com

   Find the websites of at least three companies that you believe have adopted a positive customer service attitude and are benefiting as a result. Select any issue raised in this chapter and research it further.

2. For additional articles and information on the customer service profession and job of CSRs, visit the author's Customer Service Skills Blog http://www.customerserviceskillsbook.com to search "Customer Service Representatives" and related topics addressed in this chapter. Also, search www.youtube.com to watch short videos on the customer service profession.

3. Search Ted Talks for videos on customer service topics discussed in this chapter. Here is a starting point— https://binged.it/2gs2Z10.

Collaborative Learning Activities

Emphasizing Education

1. Team up with several other people to form a discussion group. Spend some time talking about what you believe the role of schools is today and how well they are preparing young people for the work world related to customer service. Share specific personal examples from your own educational background or that of someone you know.

2. Form groups of three to five members and discuss the impact of study results obtained by the Gallup organization survey that identified the "Top 14 Issues Facing Americans." Because of time constraints, each group might be assigned several different issues to discuss.

Top 14 Issues Facing Americans

A study by the Gallup research organization found that the following issues were of "great concern" to a large percentage of Americans. They worried about each to lesser degrees.
Economy—71%
Federal spending and budget deficit—64%
Availability and affordability of health care—58%
Unemployment—57%
Social Security system—51%
Size and power of federal government—48%
Availability and affordability of energy—46%
Crime and violence—44%
Illegal immigration—42%
Hunger and homelessness—41%
Possibility of future terrorist attacks in the United States—40%
Drug use—40%
Quality of the environment—34%
Race relations—16%
Source: Gallup Poll, March 21, 2011.

As a group, discuss the following questions and be prepared to share your views with the rest of the class.
Based on what you read in this chapter, what factors might be affecting survey recipients?
How does each factor listed in this study analysis potentially negatively impact service organizations and professionals?
How do you see these responses personally impacting you, as a consumer and service professional, in the future?

3. Form small groups and revisit the competencies list in Figure 1.9. What additional competencies do you feel are necessary to be successful when working with customers? Do you believe each of these competencies is crucial or not? Discuss your beliefs.

4. In small teams, review the list of "Key Developments That Have Impacted the Customer Service Profession" and pick the one that you believe has most affected customer service in your lifetime and tell why you believe that to be true. In your opinion, has this change been a positive one? Why or why not?

Face-to-Face

Getting Ready for New Employee Orientation at PackAll

Background

PackAll is a packing and storage company headquartered in Minneapolis, Minnesota, with franchises located in 21 cities throughout the United States. Since opening its first franchise in Minneapolis in 1987, the company has shown great market potential, ending its first year with a profit and growing every year since.

The primary services of the organization are packaging and preparing nonperishable items for shipment and mailing via parcel post. Air-conditioned spaces for short-term storage of personal items and post office boxes are also available to customers.

To ensure consistency of service at all locations, specific standards for employee training and service delivery have been developed and implemented. Before owners or operators can hang up their PackAll sign, they must sign an agreement to comply with standards and must successfully complete a rigorous eight-week management training program. The program focuses on the key management and business skills necessary to run a successful business and educates employees on corporate philosophy and culture. In addition, management offers tips for guiding employee development. At intervals of three and six months after opening their operation, owners or operators are required to participate in a retreat during which they share best practices, receive additional management training, and have an opportunity to ask questions in a structured setting.

Your Role

Today, you joined a PackAll franchise in Orlando, Florida, as a customer service representative. New-employee orientation will be held tomorrow. At that time, you will learn about the service culture, policies and procedures, techniques for handling customers, and specific job skills and requirements.

Before being hired, you were told that your primary duties would be to service customers, provide information about services offered, write up customer orders, collect payments, and package and label orders.

Critical Thinking Questions

1. What interpersonal skills do you currently have that will allow you to be successful in your new position?

2. What general questions about handling customers do you have for your supervisor?

3. If a customer asks for a service that PackAll does not provide, how will you handle the situation? Exactly what will you say?

Planning to Serve

Working alone or with others, create a list of the major issues facing the service industry or your organization (if you are working) and that directly impact you. Also, list strategies that you can implement to personally address these issues.

To do this, draw a line down the center of a sheet of blank paper. On the left side, write the word "Issues" and on the right side, the word "Strategies."

Here is an example of one issue with strategies to address it:

Issue	Strategies
Service industry is growing quickly.	Do Internet research to gather statistics on an occupation that I am currently in or in which I am interested. Identify geographic areas of opportunity, possible salary and benefits, and specific targeted employers.

Quick Preview Answers

1. F	3. F	5. T	7. T	9. F	11. T
2. T	4. F	6. T	8. T	10. T	

Ethical Dilemma Summary

Ethical Dilemma 1.1 Possible Answers

1. Should you inform your supervisor of what you know to ensure that she makes an educated choice based on qualifications? Why or why not?

   This is a touchy issue. If a candidate's performance (or lack of it) is affecting you, other employees, the organization, and customers, then you should probably approach your supervisor in a confidential manner to inform her of what is going on. The downside of taking such action is that your supervisor might question your timing and motives for doing so, especially since there are three different people involved and you have not come forward earlier.

2. What could be the potential result of any action that you take about this issue?

   In such situations, when you witness inappropriate activities or behavior of others that impacts the organization, you should discreetly point it out to them, and, if necessary, to someone in charge. It is unwise to save such information for an opportune time when you can use it in retaliation or to gain personally. This could affect how they, your supervisor, and peers view you and could impact trust in the future, thus negatively affecting your future opportunities. (See also customer service environment related to dealing with internal customers.)

Contributing to the Service Culture

Your earning ability today is largely dependent upon your knowledge, skill and your ability to combine that knowledge and skill in such a way that you contribute value for which customers are going to pay.
—BRIAN TRACY

©Kevin Griffin/123RF RF

LEARNING OUTCOMES

After completing this chapter, you will be able to:

2-1 Explain the elements of a successful service culture.

2-2 Define a service strategy.

2-3 Recognize customer-friendly systems.

2-4 Implement strategies for promoting a positive service culture.

2-5 Separate average companies from exceptional companies.

2-6 Identify what customers want.

Use SmartBook to help you read, study, and retain what you have learned. Access SmartBook in your Instructor's Connect course, or go to connect.mheducation.com for help. ▤ SMARTBOOK™

IN THE REAL WORLD (DELIVERY SERVICES)—FEDEX

Mission Statement: "FedEx Corporation will produce superior financial returns for its share-owners by providing high value-added logistics, transportation and related business services through focused operating companies. Customer requirements will be met in the highest quality manner appropriate to each market segment served. FedEx will strive to develop mutually rewarding relationships with its employees, partners and suppliers. Safety will be the first consideration in all operations. Corporate activities will be conducted to the highest ethical and professional standards."

Source: FedEx Mission statement.

For over four decades, FedEx has been a leader in the air, ground, and sea shipping and delivery services industry in the United States and overseas. Since its founding in 1973, FedEx has grown rapidly. By 1983, the corporation had reached $1 billion in revenue. That was a first for any U.S. company without going through a merger or acquisition. By 1989, the company had branched out from the United States with deliveries to Europe. As a customer-oriented business, the company continually strives to provide the state-of-the art and quality service. One of its first major efforts to add to customer satisfaction was a transportation website in 1994 that allowed customers to track their shipment delivery status. In 1996, FedEx introduced an online system to allow customers to process their shipping orders without having to go to a FedEx shipping center. Since then, the company has implemented other automated and innovative advances to help customers maximize its overnight and standard deliveries.

In addition to innovation, the company has received recognition for advancements and has gained a variety of international certifications. An example of this was receipt of the ISO 9001 International Quality Management certification. Progressive and service-focused companies adhere to this standard in order to help ensure that they are doing the right things related to customer service and delivery of customer satisfaction.

Since its founding, FedEx has acquired numerous international shipping businesses to extend its reach globally. In recent years, FedEx has expanded its scope of operations further. Through traditional two to three days express and international shipping services, its 400,000-plus employees serve individuals and businesses in over 220 countries. To help accomplish this, FedEx has collaborated with other organizations to expand its market share. Through a network of over 1,800 local service centers, the company provides packing supplies and assistance. It also now offers small business-related support services. For example, in addition to delivery services, customers can access print services (e.g., flyers, resumes, promotional materials, banners, magnetic signs, posters, and many other products).

As a customer-centric organization, FedEx is very ecologically focused. For its efforts in reducing pollutants in the world, the company has received accolades around the world. In 2008, its UK operation received the ISO 14001 certification after successfully complying with rigorous environmental management standards. In this decade, FedEx has invested large sums of revenue to aid the environment and cut its environmental footprint on the earth. Examples of this include opening its largest solar-powered, state-of-the-art hub at the Cologne/Bonn airport in 2010 to serve customers in Central and Eastern Europe. In 2011, the company launched an electronically assisted bicycle delivery and collection service in the Paris, France vicinity. In 2012, it became the first transportation company to launch free carbon-neutral shipping for all FedEx envelopes globally.

Since opening its doors in the 1970s, the organization has received many accolades. In 2011, Great Places to Work Institute named FedEx as one of the Top 5 "World's Best Multinational Workplaces."

Think About It

Visit http://about.van.fedex.com/, search the Internet, and visit local libraries to learn more about FedEx and its business operations. Read articles and books about this highly successful global company. Based on what you read above and learn through your research, answer the following questions and be prepared to discuss your responses in the class.

1. Do you have personal experience with this company? If so, describe your impressions as a customer.

2. How does this organization differ from other successful service organizations of which you are aware?

3. Related to providing quality customer service, what do you think are some of the strengths of FedEx?

4. As a current or potential customer, what do you think the company might do to improve customer service and satisfaction?

5. Would you want to work for this company? Why or why not?

Quick Preview

Before reviewing the chapter content, respond to the following questions by placing a "T" for true or an "F" for false on the rules. Use any questions you miss as a checklist of material to which you will pay particular attention as you read the chapter. For those you get right, give yourself a pat on the back, but review the sections they address in order to learn additional details about the topic.

_____ 1. Service cultures include such things as policies and procedures.

_____ 2. To remain competitive, organizations must continually monitor and evaluate their systems.

_____ 3. Advertising, service delivery, and complaint resolution are examples of customer-friendly systems.

_____ 4. To better face daily challenges and opportunities in the workplace, you should strive to increase your knowledge, build your skills, and improve your attitude.

_____ 5. Some of the tools used by organizations to measure service culture include employee focus groups, mystery shoppers, and customer lotteries.

_____ 6. By determining the Added Value And Results For Me (AVARFM), you can develop more personal commitment to service excellence.

_____ 7. Use of "they" language to refer to management when dealing with customers helps demonstrate your commitment to your organization and its culture.

_____ 8. Communicating openly and effectively is one technique for working more closely with customers.

_____ 9. Even though you depend on vendors and suppliers, they are not your customers.

_____ 10. Business etiquette dictates that you should return all telephone calls within four hours.

_____ 11. Your job of serving a customer should end at the conclusion of a transaction so that you can switch your attention to new customers.

_____ 12. Customers want value for their money and effective, efficient service.

Answers to Quick Preview are located at the end of the chapter.

Words to Live By

"You'll never have a product or price advantage again. They can be easily duplicated, but a strong customer service culture can't be copied."

— SOURCE: JERRY FRITZ

LO 2-1 Defining a Service Culture

CONCEPT **Many elements contribute to a service culture.**

What is a **service culture** in an organization? The answer is that it is different for each organization. No two organizations operate in the same manner, have the same focus, or provide management that accomplishes the same results. Among other things, a culture includes the values, beliefs, norms, rituals, and practices of a group or organization. Any policy, procedure, action, or inaction on the part of your organization and its employees contributes to the service culture. Other elements may be specific to your organization or industry. A key point to remember about service culture is that you and every other employee play a key role in communicating the culture of your organization to your customers. You may communicate the culture through your appearance, your interaction with customers, and your knowledge, skill, and **attitude**. The latter element is crucial in your success and that of your organization. As a service provider, if you take a job just to have a paycheck without buying into the service culture and supporting the goals of the organization, both you and the organization will lose. For you to be successful in the service industry (or any other for that matter), you must take ownership of your roles and responsibilities and show commitment to doing the best you can every day that you go to work. Even further, you must project a positive attitude when you are not at work as well. Think about the number of times you have heard friends "bad mouth" their boss, organization, products, and services. Did their attitude toward their job inspire you to want to patronize their workplace or apply for a job there? If you were to take the same approach in sharing information about your organization or the people in it, there can be a negative effect on you and the organization. Such actions can lead to lost customers and revenue that goes to pay salaries and benefits, and to provide the tools and environment necessary to conduct business and deliver effective customer service. What you do or say around others in any environment sends a powerful message about you, your level of professionalism, and your organization. If you cannot support your employer, quit and find a job where you can. To do less is being unfair to yourself, your organization, and your customers.

Culture also encompasses your products and services, and the physical appearance of the organization's facility, equipment, or any other aspect of the organization with which the customer comes into contact. Unfortunately, many companies are top-down–oriented (with upper management at the top of their hierarchy and customers as a final element or afterthought) or product-centered and view customers from the standpoint of what company products or services they use (Figure 2.1). Successful organizations are customer-centered or **customer-centric** and focus on individual needs (Figure 2.2).

An organization's service culture is made up of many facets, each of which affects the customer and helps determine the success or failure of customer service initiatives (Figure 2.3). Too often, organizations overpromise and underdeliver because their cultural and internal systems (*infrastructure*) are not developed in a manner to support customer service initiatives. For example, suppose that management has the marketing department develop a slick piece of literature describing all the benefits of a new product or service provided by a new corporate partner. Then a special

service culture A service environment made up of various factors, including the values, beliefs, norms, rituals, and practices of a group or organization.

attitude Emotional responses to people, ideas, and objects. They are based on values, differ between individuals and cultures, and affect the way people deal with various issues and situations.

customer-centric A term used to describe service providers and organizations that put their customers first and spend time, effort, and money identifying and focusing on the needs of current and potential customers. Efforts are focused on building long-term relationships and customer loyalty rather than simply selling a product or service and moving on to the next customer.

©klenger/Getty Images RF

Organizations that have a solid customer service culture that projects a customer-focused attitude typically generate positive feedback from their customers. *What can you do as a service provider to contribute to your organization's service culture?*

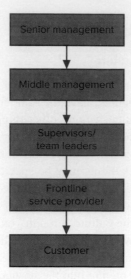

FIGURE 2.1
Typical Hierarchical Organization

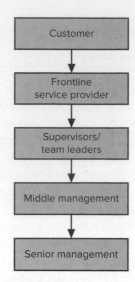

FIGURE 2.2
Customer-Centric Organization

toll-free number or website is set up to handle customer responses, but no additional staff is hired to handle the customer calls or current service providers are not given adequate information or training to do their job. The project is likely doomed to fail because adequate service support has not been planned and implemented.

In the past, organizations were continually making changes to their product and service lines to try to attract and hold customers. They also revert to lowering prices in hopes of drawing in new customers and thwarting the efforts of competitors to do the same. Often this has been their primary approach to customer satisfaction. Now, many major organizations have become more customer-centric and stress relationships with customers. They realize that it is cheaper, and smarter, to focus efforts on better customer service to keep current customers. This is more effective than subscribing to a revolving-door approach of continually trying to attract new customers to replace the ones that they lost to competitors. Advertising campaigns often reflect this new awareness as companies try to communicate that they are focused on their customers.

The following are some familiar customer-focused advertising slogans companies have used in their promotional materials:

Have it your way—Burger King

We try harder—Avis Car Rental

When it absolutely, positively has to be there overnight—Federal Express

You can do it; We can help—Home Depot

Like a good neighbor—State Farm Insurance

When you're here, you're family—Olive Garden Restaurants

You're in good hands—Allstate Insurance Company

We'll leave the light on for you—Motel 6

Think what we can do for you—Bank of America

FIGURE 2.3
Elements of a Successful
Service Culture

Many elements define a successful service organization. Some of the more common for a successful customer-centric organization are shown here.

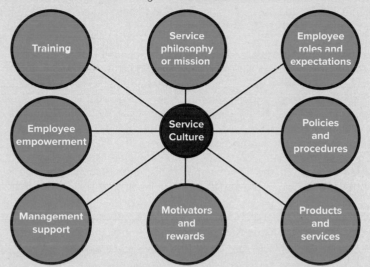

Service philosophy or mission: The succinct direction or vision of an organization that supports day-to-day interactions with the customer.

Employee roles and expectations: The specific communications or measures that indicate what is expected of employees in customer interactions and that define how employee service performance will be evaluated. These elements are outlined in current job descriptions.

Policies and procedures: The guidelines that establish how various situations or transactions will be handled.

Products and services: The materials, products, and services that are state of the art, competitively priced, and meet the needs, wants, and expectations of a diverse customer base.

Motivators and rewards: Monetary rewards, material items, or feedback that prompts employees to continue to deliver service and perform at a high level of effectiveness and efficiency.

Management support: The availability of management to answer questions and assist frontline employees in customer interactions when necessary. Also, the level of management involvement and enthusiasm in coaching and mentoring the professional development of customer service representatives (CSRs).

Employee empowerment: Providing front-line employees with the authority to make on-the-spot decisions that will facilitate efficient and timely customer service based on training they receive and criteria established by supervisors.

Training: Instruction or information provided through a variety of techniques and vehicles that teach knowledge or skills, or attempt to influence employee attitude toward excellent service delivery and achieving customer satisfaction and loyalty.

SERVICE PHILOSOPHY OR MISSION

Generally, an organization's approach to business, its **mission** or its **service philosophy**, is driven from the top of the organization. Upper management, including members of the board of directors, when appropriate, sets the vision or tone and direction of the organization. Without a clearly planned and communicated vision, the service ethic ends at the highest levels. This is often a stumbling block where many organizations falter because of indecision or dissension at the upper echelons (see Figure 2.4).

mission The direction or focus of an organization that supports day-to-day interactions with customers.

service philosophy The approach that an organization takes to providing service and addressing the needs of customers.

FIGURE 2.4

Sample Mission Statements

Coca-Cola: "To refresh the world," "to inspire moments of optimism and happiness," and "to create value and make a difference."

Ford: People working together as a lean, global enterprise to make people's lives better through automotive and mobility leadership.

Leukemia and Lymphoma Society: Cure leukemia, lymphoma, Hodgkin's disease, and myeloma, and improve the quality of life of patients and their families.

Southwest Airlines: Connect people to what's important in their lives through friendly, reliable, low-cost air travel.

Target: We fulfill the needs and fuel the potential of our guests. That means making Target your preferred shopping destination in all channels by delivering outstanding value, continuous innovation and exceptional experiences—consistently fulfilling our Expect More. Pay Less.® brand promise.

Trader Joe's: At Trader Joe's, our mission is to bring our customers the best food and beverage values and the information to make informed buying decisions. There are more than 2000 unique grocery items in our label, all at honest everyday low prices.

Tupperware: We are passionate about changing lives, especially for women by enlightening, educating, empowering.

Walmart: We save people money so they can live better.

Source: Coca-Cola; Ford Mission Statement; Leukemia and Lymphoma Society Mission Statement; Southwest Airlines Mission Statement; Target Mission Statement; Trader Joe's Mission Statement; Tupperware Mission Statement; Walmart Mission Statement

mission statement An organization's mission statement defines its purpose or objectives and *how* it will attain them. It is committed to writing and is publicly shared with employees and customers.

vision statement A vision statement communicates an organization's values and purpose and explains *what* the organization wants to be.

Most successful organizations have written **mission** and **vision statements** that answer the questions of "What does the organization do?" and "Why does the organization exist?" Mission statements should always tie back to the vision statement and be incorporated into the infrastructure (e.g., HR policies and procedures) and service culture of an organization.

Leadership, real and perceived, is crucial to service success. In successful organizations, members of upper management make themselves clearly visible to frontline employees and are in tune with customer needs, wants, and expectations. They also "walk the talk" and continually drive and communicate the mission and vision of the organization through their words, actions, and decisions. Ultimately, these measures set the tone for a more ethical, productive, and customer-conscious organization. If all employees are aware of what their organization stands for, how it accomplishes its mission, and where it is headed in the future, they can play a crucial role in creating a service culture that strives to identify and effectively satisfy customers. Part of ensuring that everyone in the organization is working toward the same goals is to ensure that all policies, infrastructure, and actions support the mission and vision statements. For example, performance appraisals should have language that addresses how supervisors, managers, and employees are doing at addressing established goals and objectives and actions taken to uphold ethical standards. Additionally, all individual and department goals should be tied to the organizational mission and goals.

Although it is wonderful when organizations go to the trouble of developing and hanging a nicely framed formal mission or vision statement on the wall, if they are not a functional way of life for employees, they serve little purpose.

Street Talk **Do not overcommit. Deliver when you promise.**

A boss once criticized me because I told a manager I could not guarantee something that day. She wanted me to say I would do it when I knew I could not. I do not do that. If I cannot do something they request, I tell my manager (my internal customer) when I can get it done and then work 24/7 if I have to in order to meet the deadline. I also tell managers that this process works two ways . . . I remind them if I need something and they remind me if they are waiting on something for me.

COURTESY OF ANNE WILKINSON

©kemalbas/Getty Images RF

Many factors influence service outcome when dealing with customers. *What role do you play in the customer–provider relationship and what might you do to improve your performance in the future?*

EMPLOYEE ROLES AND EXPECTATIONS

Many tasks and responsibilities are assigned to frontline service providers. People who perform direct customer support functions are some of the most crucial in an organization. That is because customers and other people contact customer service representatives (CSRs) for information, to compliment and complaint, and to purchase products and services.

Depending on your job, the size and type of your organization, and the industry involved, the **employee roles** and **employee expectations** may be similar from one organization to another, and yet they may be performed in a variety of different ways. Such roles and expectations are normally included in your job description and in your performance goals. They are updated as necessary during your tenure in the job position. Where goals are concerned, you are typically measured against them during a given performance period. Subsequent decisions on any rewards for which you are eligible are made based on your performance and your organization's policy.

As a service professional, you are the "face" of your organization in interactions that start with a customer contact. Your primary function is to listen actively and gather the information needed in order to make a decision on the best course of action needed to serve the customer in any given situation. This typically requires a polite, professional demeanor and effective and efficient answers to questions or resolutions to problems.

employee roles Task assignments that service providers assume.

employee expectations Perceptions about positive and negative aspects of the workplace.

RUMBA

For you and your organization to be successful in providing superior service to your external and internal customers, your roles and expectations must be defined and communicated clearly in terms of the following characteristics, sometimes referred to as **RUMBA** (**R**ealistic, **U**nderstandable, **M**easurable, **B**elievable, **A**ttainable).

RUMBA An acronym for five criteria (realistic, understandable, measurable, believable, and attainable) used to establish and measure employee performance goals.

Realistic Your behavior and responsibilities must be in line with the reality of your particular workplace and customer base. Although it is possible to transfer a standard of performance from one organization, and even industry, to another, modifications may be necessary to fit your specific situation. For example, is it realistic that all customer calls must be handled within a specified period of time? Many managers set specific goals in terms of "talk time" for their customer service representatives. Can every angry customer be calmed and handled in a two- to three-minute time frame? If not, then a standard such as this sets up employees for failure.

After a performance goal has been set for you, evaluate it fairly and objectively for a period of time (possibly 30 days). This allows time for a variety of opportunities to apply it. At the end of the specified trial period, if you think the goal is unrealistic, go to your supervisor or team leader and discuss modifying it. In preparation for this discussion, think of at least two viable alternatives to the goals. Also, recognize that performance goals are often driven by organizational goals that may be passed down from upper management. Although they might be modified, it may take some time for the change to come about, so be patient. Ultimately, if the goal cannot be modified, do your best to perform within the established standard so that your professional image does not suffer.

 WORK IT OUT 2.1

Organizational Culture

Think about your own organization's service culture or, if you are not actively working as a customer service professional, the culture of an organization with which you are familiar.

1. What do you believe the service philosophy of this organization to be? Why?

2. Are there things that make the organization unique? If so, what are they?

3. What factors (positive or negative) about employee performance in this organization stand out in your mind?

4. Are there factors about the culture that detract from effectiveness? If so, what are they?

5. If you were managing this organization, what service culture aspects would you change? Why?

Understandable You must have a sound understanding of your performance goals before you can act appropriately and effectively, just the way you need to understand how to do your job or how to communicate with others in the workplace. You should first try to participate in the establishment of your performance goals and those of your department or team. To do this, set up a meeting with your supervisor or team leader to discuss goals. Once goals are in place, you and everyone else affected must have a clear understanding of them so that you can effectively reach the assigned goal. If questions or doubts exist about a goal or your role in accomplishing it, make sure to clarify your understanding with a supervisor or team leader since you will ultimately be held accountable if you fail to reach a performance goal. This may impact professional opportunities and personal earning potential.

Measurable Can your performance be measured? The answer is yes. Typically, factors such as time, productivity, quantifiable results, revenue, and manner of performance (how you accomplish your job tasks in terms of following an established step-by-step formula) are used to determine your accomplishment of goals. In a production environment, or in certain sales environments, performance can be measured by reviewing the number of products made or sales completed. In a purely customer-focused environment, **service measurement** can be in terms of factors such as talk time on the telephone, number of customers effectively served, customer feedback surveys and satisfaction cards, and letters or other written correspondence—or, on the negative side, by customer complaints.

service measurement Techniques used by organizations to determine how customers perceive the value of services and products received.

Ethical Dilemma 2.1

Assume that your organizational philosophy states in part that your purpose is "to provide quality products at a competitive price in a low-pressure customer atmosphere." Even so, your supervisor establishes a goal that requires you to have "x" number of sales per shift as an outbound sales representative. Based on your research, this number is two more than the typical industry average for a salesperson during a work shift. You recognize that to achieve this goal, you will have to be more "persuasive" than you usually are when dealing with customers or than you feel comfortable in doing.

1. What ethical issue(s) do you face in this situation?
2. How might these issues impact service delivery?
3. What impact might this situation have on your performance?
4. How might this situation be addressed?

See possible responses at the end of this chapter.

Whatever the measure, it is your responsibility to be sure that you know the acceptable level and do your best to perform to that level. If something inhibits your performance, or if organizational obstacles such as conflicting priorities, overburdening multiple assignments, policies, procedures, equipment, or other employees stand in your way, you should immediately discuss the difficulties with the appropriate authority.

Believable To attain any goal, it must be believable to the people who will strive to reach it and to the supervisors or team leaders who will monitor it. The biggest issues in developing goals are to make them worthy of belief and faithful to the values of the individual and organization, and to ensure that they make sense and tie in directly with the established overall departmental and organizational goals. Too often, assignments given to employees are contrary to the ultimate purpose or mission and overall values or beliefs of the organization. Confusion about what is important and the direction to be taken can occur in such instances. Ultimately, this can affect the level of trust that service providers have with their supervisor and/or organization.

Attainable Given the right training, management support, and organizational environment in which the tools, information, assistance, and rewards are provided, you can attain your goals. The determining factor, however, is you and your attitude toward achieving agreed-upon levels.

Managers should always attempt to set up win/win situations in which you, your organization, and, ultimately, the customer benefit from any service encounter. However, you should be aware that in the "real world," this does not always happen—systems break down. In such cases, it is up to you to ensure that you should continue to deliver service to customers in a seamless fashion. They should not hear about internal problems, and, quite honestly, the customers probably do not care about these problems. They should be able to expect that the products and services they paid for get delivered when promised, in the manner agreed upon, and without inconvenience to them. Anything less is unacceptable and is poor service.

Employee Roles in Larger Retail and Service Organizations

As customers have matured in their knowledge of service standards and what they expect of providers, they look for certain qualifications in those who serve. They gain knowledge from numerous sources that help them be more perceptive in their dealings with businesses (e.g., *Consumer Reports* magazine; Internet research; and television shows such as *20/20*, *Dateline*, and *60 Minutes*). Many times, these customers become sticklers about service and when they do not get the level of service they expect, they take their business elsewhere and/or take legal action. In some cases, they might give the organization a second chance by complaining. This benevolent initiative, allowing organizations to "fix themselves," is often a test. If you or your peers fail, several things can occur. You may not only lose a customer, but you may also "gain" an

Trending NOW

Many companies and small business entrepreneurs are continually looking for new products and services to set them apart from competitors and attract new customers. An article in CNNMoney (http://money.cnn.com/2013/06/24/pf/emergency-savings/index.html) provides insight into one trend. It addressed the move by a small population of North Americans to invest in tiny houses that are typically less than 500 square feet. Following the recession of the first decade of the twenty-first century, a challenge for many people has been not being able to afford traditional living spaces. This is especially true for those consumers who are younger or new to the workplace and those who have seen their income stagnate or shrink. Many have a low level of savings, need or desire to downsize, or preference

for more flexibility in housing options. Some are looking at tiny or small houses as the potential solution to their situation. The trend is picking up speed. In response, a number of companies have stepped in to fill the consumer needs gap by creating customized tiny/small homes that have many deluxe amenities and can be moved anywhere the customer desires. Like many new industries and products, a new idea often takes time to catch on. Zoning laws, financing, and other legal and logistical issues are slowly being worked out across the country. Assuming that the idea does become a craze, new jobs will result for manufacturers and the people who sell and service this new form of housing.

onslaught of negative word-of-mouth publicity that can irreparably damage an organization's image as a whole, and yours specifically. With websites such as www.yelp.com, www.ripoffreport.com, and www.complaintsboard.com, consumers have easy access to forums for voicing their displeasure when something goes wrong.

Typically, customers expect service employees to have at least the following qualifications and competencies in both large and small organizations:

- Broad general knowledge of products and service
- Interpersonal communication skills (e.g., verbal, nonverbal, and listening along with cross-gender and cross-cultural communication)
- Technical expertise related to products sold and serviced
- Positive, customer-focused, "can-do" attitude
- Initiative
- Motivation
- Integrity
- Loyalty (to the organization, to products, and to customers)
- Team spirit
- Creativity
- Sound ethics
- Time management skills
- Problem-solving capability
- Conflict resolution skills

Such skills and capabilities are crucial, whether you are operating a cash register, polishing a car, handling a returned item, repairing a sink, questioning a crime witness or suspect, coaching an executive or technical manager (e.g., a consultant who offers seminars on enhancing interpersonal skills), or dealing with a negative situation (e.g., a shoplifter or disgruntled customer). If you fail to possess and/or exhibit any or all of these factors, the result could be a breakdown in the relationship between you and your customer, with ultimately negative repercussions.

©Spiderstock/Getty Images RF

Employees of both small and large organizations contribute to their service cultures through interactions with customers. *What are some things that they can do to project a positive service image?*

Employee Roles in Smaller Retail and Service Organizations

The growth of small businesses since the early 1990s skyrocketed, especially women- and minority-owned businesses. Many small business entrepreneurs started out of necessity (because of layoffs or downsizing) or out of frustration caused by limitations within a larger structure (e.g. lack of promotion opportunity, low salaries, actual or perceived discrimination, poor management, or continual changes).

The growth of sole proprietorships (one-owner businesses) and small businesses has an upside in that they provide more choices for customers. On the downside, this growth sometimes creates problems for people making the transition from large to small organizations. This is because, in addition to having to possess all the qualifications and characteristics listed earlier, entrepreneurs and employees in small businesses perform greatly varied tasks. Typically, the human resources and technical systems they might call upon for support are limited. If something goes wrong, they cannot "bump the problem upstairs," nor can they obtain immediate, on-site assistance. This often causes customer frustration or anger and can lead to higher customer **churn rate** or desertion to a competitor.

churn rate Refers to the number of customers who leave a supplier during a given time period.

The types of jobs that fall into this struggling category run the gamut of industries. Some examples are the following:

- Administrative assistant (freelance)
- Accountant
- Consultant
- Automotive mechanic
- Computer technician
- Salesperson
- Caterer
- Tailor
- Personal shopper
- Office support staff

- Hair stylist
- Masseuse/masseur
- Office equipment repairperson
- Office cleaning staff
- Child care provider
- Gardener
- Electrician and plumber
- Electronics repairperson
- Visiting nurse or nurse consultant
- Driver
- Temporary worker

Owners and employees in such establishments must continually strive to gain new knowledge and skills in order to stave off failure and help ensure that they identify and satisfy customer needs. They must also work hard to deliver a level of service equal to or superior to that offered by the bigger organizations. This is because many consumers are generally unforgiving and, like an elephant, have long memories—especially when service breaks down.

If you work in this type of environment, look for opportunities to provide stellar customer service and really go out of your way to practice your people skills. Get back to the basics of how to effectively deal with people—listen, ask appropriate questions, provide feedback, communicate well—and do not miss an opportunity to let your customers know that they are special, that you are there to serve their needs, and that you appreciate them.

Employee Roles in Nonprofit Organizations

An option to working for a for-profit company is to seek employment in a nonprofit organization. Even though revenue generation is not the primary goal in such organizations, money is a significant force. Without donations, grants, and other fund-raising efforts, these organizations cannot provide the crucial services, products, and deliverables to their customer/client base (often lower-income and older people or others who have few other alternatives for attainment of needed items and services). In such organizations, administrators, staff, and volunteers provide a wide degree of services and support. Unless these workers maintain a cheerful, positive, and professional attitude, revenue and service levels might plummet. They must never forget that everyone with whom they come into contact is either a potential donor or recipient of products and services.

The following qualifications and competencies are very helpful for anyone working in a nonprofit environment:

- Specific knowledge of the organization and products and services it provides
- Interpersonal communication skills
- Positive, customer-focused "can-do" attitude
- Initiative
- Motivation to succeed
- Integrity
- Commitment to others
- Volunteer spirit
- Team orientation
- Sound ethical attitude
- Time management skills
- Problem-solving ability (ability to think "outside the box")
- Entrepreneur spirit (ability to work in an environment in which freethinking and creativity are encouraged and needed)

POLICIES AND PROCEDURES

Although there are many local, state, and federal regulations with which you and your organization must comply, many policies are flexible. For example, if you go to your bank to deposit a large check that exceeds the maximum amount the bank will accept, the teller may inform you that there will be a seven-day hold put on the check until it clears the sender's bank. In this case, you might petition the branch manager and possibly get this period modified since you are dealing with a "bank" policy.

Many customers negatively meet organizational culture directly when a service provider hides behind "company policy" to handle a problem. The goal should be to respond to customer requests and satisfy needs as quickly, efficiently, and cheerfully as possible. Anything less is an invitation for criticism, dissatisfaction, potential customer loss, and employee frustration.

Return policies in a retail environment are a case in point. Even though customers may not always be "right," you must treat them with respect and as if they are right in order to effectively provide service and generate future relationships. An effective return policy is part of the overall service process. In addition to service received, the return policy of an organization is another gauge customers use to determine where they will spend their time and money. The author of this book received the return statements shown in Figure 2.5 in the past. The language used in each sends specific messages about the organizational culture of both organizations. Notice the tone or service culture that radiates from each example. Think about your "gut" reaction as a customer when you read both policies.

FIGURE 2.5
Sample Return Policies

Policy 1
To err is human; to return is just fine . . .

Already read the book? Pages printed upside down? The package arrived bruised, battered, and otherwise weary from the trip? Actually, the only reason you need to return an item bought from us is this: You're not satisfied . . .

Having the chance to talk with our customer helps us learn and improve our service. It is also an opportunity to demonstrate the [organization's name] customer policy: YOU'RE RIGHT!

Policy 2
Return policy
Returns must meet the following criteria:

1. Books must be received within thirty (30) days of the invoice date. Please allow one week for shipping.

2. Books must be received in salable condition. Damaged books will not be accepted for credit.

3. Refunds will not be made on videotapes and software unless they were defective at the time of purchase. Please notify [organization's name] of any such defects within ten (10) days of the invoice date.

Return shipping information
Returns must be shipped to [organization's name and full address].

Any returns not shipped to the above address will not be credited and FULL PAYMENT for shipping will be the responsibility of the shipper.

All charges incurred in returning materials, including customer's charges, if any, are the responsibility of the shipper.

Ensure that your returns are not lost or damaged.

Comments and feedback
We value your opinion! If you need to return any of the enclosed material, please take a minute to let us know why. Your comments and suggestions will help us better meet your needs in the future.

⚙ **WORK IT OUT 2.2**

Think about the two return policies in Figure 2.5.

What is your reaction to policy example 1? Why?

What is your reaction to policy example 2? Why?

Organizations often hang up fancy posters and banners touting such claims as "The customer is always right," "The customer is No. 1," or "We're here to serve YOU!" But at the moment of truth, when customers come into contact with employees, they frequently hear, "Please take a number so we can better serve you," "I can't do that," or (on the phone) "ABC Company, please hold—CLICK." Clearly, when these things occur, the culture is not customer-focused and service has broken down. The important question for organizations is, "How do we fix our system?" The answer: Make a commitment to the customer and establish an environment that will support that commitment. That is where you come in as a customer service professional. Through conscientious and concerned assistance to customers, the organization can form a solid relationship with the consumer through its employees.

Owners and employees in sole proprietorships must work hard to deliver service equal to that given by larger organizations. *How can an owner make his or her organization special or different?*

Ethical Dilemma 2.2

Your organization's return policy stresses that "Our goal is your total satisfaction," yet your supervisor has told you that returns cost the organization money and negatively impact her quarterly bonus. For that reason, she has instructed you and other employees that you should find a reason not to accept returns and provide refunds whenever possible (e.g., a package was opened, it has been more than seven days since purchase, a receipt is not provided, or the item is being discontinued and the manufacturer will not take it back). She has even suggested that you lie to a customer or make up an excuse rather than accept a return. Further, she instructed you that she must approve all returns and refunds, yet when employees page her over the intercom, she typically does not respond. This leaves you and other service employees to face an escalating negative customer situation.

1. How does such a service atmosphere potentially affect customers? Employees?
2. What message does this approach to service say about the organization?
3. What are potential outcomes of such practices by the supervisor?
4. What can you and other employees do to address the situation?

PRODUCTS AND SERVICES

The type and quality of products and services also contribute to your organizational culture. If customers perceive that you offer reputable products and services in a professional manner and at a competitive price, your organization will likely reap the rewards of loyalty and positive "press." On the other hand, if products and services do not live up to expectations or promises, or if your ability to correct problems in products and services is deficient, you and the organization could suffer adversely.

To get the information you need, you may have to take the initiative. Your customer does not want to hear you say, "Nobody showed me how," "I can't," "I don't know," or "It's not my job." Remember what you read earlier about seamless service. Here are some questions you might ask your supervisor related to job responsibilities:

- What are my exact duties? (Get a copy of your job description in writing, if possible.)
- What are your expectations of me?
- How do I handle (name specific) situations?
- Whom should I see about _____?
- Where are (materials, policies, equipment) located?
- Who is in charge when you are not available?
- What is my level of authority?

MOTIVATORS AND REWARDS

In any employee environment, people work more effectively and productively when their performance is recognized and adequately rewarded. Whether the rewards are in the form of monetary or material items, or a simple verbal pat on the back by the manager, most employees expect and thrive on some form of recognition.

As a way of managing your own motivation level, it is important to remember that there will be many times when your only motivation and reward for accomplishing a goal or providing quality service will come from you. The reality is that every time you do something well or out of the ordinary, you may not receive a financial or any other kind of reward for it. On the other hand, many companies and supervisors go out of their way to recognize good performance. Many use public recognition, contests, games, employee activities (sporting or other events), financial rewards, incentives (gifts or trips), employee-of-the-month or -year awards, and a variety of other techniques to show appreciation for employee efforts (see Figure 2.6). Whatever your organization does, there is always room for improvement and you should take time to make recommendations of your own on ways to reward employees.

FIGURE 2.6

Types of Employee Rewards

Organizations are getting creative in their efforts to recognize and reward positive service practices. By using incentives, they can reward positive behavior and encourage repeat actions by the employee receiving the reward and their peers. The following are some typical forms of recognition that various organizations are using:

Compensation
Commissions paid for service representatives or sales staff members who successfully upsell or encourage customers to buy new or additional products or services are one form of compensation. A tiered system is often used where higher percentages are paid based on the number or level of sales made by the employee during a given performance period. Another form of compensation is a guaranteed annual raise or bonus when an employee meets or exceeds established service standards—for example, number of dissatisfied customers or members "saved" when they contact the organization with an issue and threaten to defect to a competitor (e.g., cable, phone, or lawn care customers). You can find another example of how incentives or awards apply in most call centers. Representatives are often compensated based on meeting standards like "call or contact time" (how long they were on a call or interacted with a customer) or numbers of calls or customers handled during a given time period.

FIGURE 2.6
(*Concluded*)

Flexible Time or Time Off

In a stressful world where many people now value time with their families, many organizations are becoming more lenient in their approach to allowing employees time off to take care of personal activities or just relax.

There are different ways that companies institute flexible work schedules depending on an organization's structure, size, and mission:

- Flexible start and end time for the workday (based on approved scheduling)
- Compressed workweek (e.g., four 10-hour workdays with an additional day of the week off)
- Telecommuting, where employees get to work from remote offices or in their homes, or telework, where employees work part of their week from home and the other portion in their office or other designated worksite
- Project- or results-oriented scheduling, where employees have no set number of hours per week but must reach an established level of productivity or meet required deadlines for project completion
- Two or more part-time employees sharing a job and required to work specific days/hours

Many small businesses use a flextime strategy to attract qualified workers and compete effectively for talent that they might not otherwise be able to afford. Larger organizations use flextime as a way to enhance employee morale.

Of course, like any other policy, there are downsides to flextime. When companies use this work strategy heavily, employees and supervisors may lose a degree of regular contact, and it adds to the burden of scheduling for supervisors. Additionally, some employees do not handle flextime well and disciplinary issues arise that might actually cause an employee to become disgruntled and morale could suffer for them and their peers.

Employee Recognition

One of the easiest and least expensive means of rewarding employees is to acknowledge them as people and applaud their accomplishments. Ways to accomplish this can cost little or no money. There are many inexpensive and effective ways for supervisors to recognize their staff. Some of these include the following:

- Having a buffet breakfast or pizza party once a month to celebrate employees' birthdays that occur during the period
- Giving a round of applause in staff or team meetings for accomplishments
- Giving a handwritten note or card from the CEO or other high-ranking member of management along with a gift card
- Passing around a "floating trophy" of some sort that is retained by the employee who meets an announced performance goal during a specific period and then it moves on to the next person during the following period
- Providing employee-of-the-month parking spaces for the person who excels and meets established criteria for the slot. This often means an indoor parking spot or one closer to the building entrance

The important thing about rewards is that employees perceive that they are being given fairly and in a timely fashion near the completion of an event that precipitated the reward.

Customer Service Success Tip

Work with your customer's interest in mind. Think to yourself, "If I were my customer, what type of service would I expect?" Then, set out to provide that service.

Trending NOW

Many larger organizations (e.g., Best Buy, Walmart, Target, Home Depot, and Staples) are fighting back against the e-commerce challenge, especially during major holiday shopping seasons. They are doing so by promising to match prices offered by online retailers like Amazon. In some instances, they also match local competition pricing and offer 110 percent re-

funds if a customer finds a lower price for the same product than that offered by their store. That means the customer who proves a lower price gets his or her money back, plus 10 percent of the product cost. In most instances, the customer must show a printed or digital receipt for the product to get the match or refund.

MANAGEMENT SUPPORT

Even if you are empowered by managers to resolve a variety of issues that arise, you may not be able to handle every customer-related situation that develops. In some instances, you will have to depend on the knowledge and assistance of a more experienced employee or your supervisor or manager and defer to his or her experience or authority. This could be due to your lack of knowledge or skill or because you are interacting with a customer who only wants to speak to a supervisor or manager. In such instances, it is typically appropriate to escalate a customer issue to someone else.

Another key role for your manager, supervisor, and/or team leader is to provide effective, ongoing coaching, counseling, and training to you and your peers. By doing this, they can pass along valuable information, guide you, and aid in enhancing your knowledge and professional development. In addition, it is their job to monitor your performance and ensure that you receive appropriate rewards based on your ability to interact effectively with customers and fulfill the requirements of your job. Unfortunately, many supervisors have not had adequate training to enable them to provide you with the support you need. In some instances, they were probably good frontline service providers with a high degree of motivation, initiative, and ability. As a result, their management promoted them, often without providing the necessary training, coaching, and guidance to develop their supervisory skills. Another potential limiting factor is that they may be as overwhelmed with job responsibilities as you are. Even though they recognize the importance of coaching you and intend to do so, they may simply not have the time.

If you find that you are not receiving the support you need, there are some things you should consider doing in order to ensure that you have the information, skills, and support to provide quality service to your customers.

Strive for Improvement

Customer service can be frustrating and, in some instances, monotonous. You may need to create self-motivation strategies and continue to seek fulfillment or satisfaction. By remaining optimistic and projecting a can-do image that makes customers enjoy dealing with you, you can influence yourself and others. Smile as an outward gesture of your "I care" philosophy. There are many self-help publications, YouTube videos, and online and in-class courses available that can offer guidance in this area. Many public libraries offer patrons access to instructional videos and classes as part of library membership. If your library system does not have such resources, check surrounding city or county resources. They sometimes will allow non-residents to purchase a library subscription that affords access to services for a nominal fee. If you itemize your federal taxes, such fees may be tax deductible.

WORK IT OUT 2.3

Managing Customer Encounters

Take a few minutes to respond to the following questions. Then your instructor may group you with others to discuss responses.

1. Have you ever witnessed or experienced a customer service situation in which a supervisor or manager became involved in an employee–customer encounter? If so, what occurred?

2. How do you feel the supervisor handled the situation?

3. Could the supervisor's approach have been improved? If so, how?

The reality in many of today's work environments is that organizations have downsized. In some instances, this has negatively influenced productivity, revenue, employee morale, and customer perceptions. The result is that employees and their supervisors are learning to adapt to the changing face of customers related to their needs, wants, and expectations. That means on an individual level you must step back and analyze your job and role in the service culture so that you can better prepare to meet the challenges and opportunities that you will surely encounter.

Look for ways to improve your skills and to raise the level of service you provide to your customer. Whether it is through formal training, mentoring, or simply observing positive service techniques used by others and mimicking them, work to improve your own skills. The more you know, the better you can assist customers and move your own career forward.

Look for a Strong Mentor in Your Organization

With the continuing stream of baby boomers leaving the workforce and taking along decades of knowledge and skills, companies are scampering to cover gaps in expertise. Many organizations have realized that they need to provide succession planning for the future. They must create a system whereby frontline employees, junior supervisors, and managers or future leaders are guided in their personal and professional development by those with more expertise, tenure, and contacts before it is too late to capitalize on that expertise. This is going to become even more crucial in the future since the "brain drain" will accelerate as thousands of older workers continue to retire and exit the workplace in virtually every industry and type of organization. When they go, they will take decades of experience and knowledge and leave behind a huge gap in many organizations, especially those that have not created an effective exit strategy or prepared others to step into key roles and positions.

If your organization does not have a system in place to pair newer employees in the profession with those more knowledgeable and skilled, try to find someone who is a superior customer service professional and get to know him or her. As your relationship grows, become a sponge and soak up as much of his or her knowledge as possible. Additionally, do an Internet search for professional organizations that cater to your profession (e.g., customer service representatives, call center representatives, sales professionals, or whatever your job title). Often, they offer networking opportunities on a regular basis locally where you can attend meetings to hear guest speakers who share their expertise in the field. Through such events, you can likely identify other professionals who are looking to share best practices and information while growing their knowledge and skills.

Mentors are people who are well acquainted with the organization and its policies, politics, and processes. They are well connected (inside and outside the organization), communicate well, have the ability and desire to assist you (the **protégé**), and are capable and experienced. Ask these people to provide support and help you grow personally and professionally. Many good books on the topic of mentoring are available. Figures 2.7 and 2.8 list some characteristics of a mentor and protégé.

Avoid Complacency

Anyone can go to work and just do what he or she is told. Employees who excel, especially in a service environment, are the ones who constantly strive for improvement and look for opportunities to grow professionally. They also take responsibility or ownership for service situations. Take the time to think about the systems, policies, and procedures in place in your organization. Can they be improved? How? Now take that information or awareness and make recommendations for improvements. Even

mentors Individuals who dedicate time and effort to befriend and assist others. In an organization, they are typically people with a lot of knowledge, experience, skills, and initiative, and have a large personal and professional network established.

protégé Typically less experienced recipients of the efforts of mentors.

FIGURE 2.7

Characteristics of an
Effective Mentor

When searching for someone to mentor you, look for these characteristics:

- Willingness to be a mentor
- Experience in the organization or industry and/or job you need help with
- Knowledgeable about the organization and industry
- Good communicator (verbal, nonverbal, and listening skills)
- Awareness of the organizational culture
- Well-connected inside and outside the organization

- Enthusiastic
- Good coaching skills and a good motivator
- Charismatic
- Trustworthy
- Patient
- Creative thinker
- Self-confident
- Good problem solver

FIGURE 2.8

Characteristics of
a Successful Protégé

Since mentoring is a two-way process, you should make sure that you are ready to have a mentor. You should have the following characteristics:

- Willingness to participate, listen, and learn
- Desire to improve and grow
- Commitment to working with a mentor
- Self-confidence

- Effective communication skills
- Enthusiasm
- Openness to feedback
- Adaptability
- Willingness to ask questions

though managers have a key role, the implementation and success of cultural initiatives (practices or actions taken by the organization) rest with you, the frontline employee. You are the one who interacts directly with a customer and often determines the outcome of the contact.

Some people might throw up their hands and say, "It wasn't my fault," "Nobody else cares; why should I," or "I give up." A special person looks for ways around roadblocks in order to provide quality service for customers. The fact that others are not doing their job does not excuse you from doing yours. You are being paid a salary to accomplish specific job tasks. Do them with gusto and pride. Your customers expect no less. You and your customers will reap the rewards of your efforts and initiative.

⚙ **WORK IT OUT 2.4**

Training for Service

Take a few minutes to think about and respond to these questions. Once you have responded, your instructor may form groups and have you share answers.

1. What type of skills training do you believe would be valuable for a customer service professional? Why?

2. What types of training have you had or do you need to qualify for a service position?

EMPLOYEE EMPOWERMENT

Employee **empowerment** is one way for a supervisor to help ensure that service providers can respond quickly to customer needs or requests. The intent of empowerment is a delegation of authority where a frontline service provider can take action without having to call a supervisor or ask permission. Such authority allows on-the-spot responsiveness to the customer while making service representatives feel trusted, respected, and like an important part of the organization. Empowerment is also an intangible way that successful service organizations reward employees. Often someone who has decision-making authority feels better about himself or herself and the organization.

empowerment The word used to describe the giving of decision-making and problem-resolution authority to lower-level employees in an organization. This precludes having to get permission from higher levels in order to take an action or serve a customer.

Customer Service Success Tip

If your supervisor empowers you to make decisions, that means he or she trusts your ability to handle various issues. Do not take this trust lightly. Before taking action, stop, weigh alternatives, and then resolve the situation to the best of your ability in order to send a message of competency and professionalism.

As a service provider, think of customer situations in which you have to get approval from a supervisor or manager before making a decision or taking action to serve your customers. If you feel having to do so is causing a delay in serving your customers, approach your supervisor and suggest having decision-making authority given to you.

Some examples of possible empowerment situations include the following:

- A cashier has to call a supervisor for approval of a customer's personal check.
- A cable television installer has to call the office for approval before adding a hookup for another room.
- A computer technician cannot comply with a customer's request that she make a backup CD-ROM of her hard drive before running a diagnostic test because policy prohibits it.
- A call center representative does not have the authority to reverse late payment charges on the account of a customer who explained that he was in the hospital for three weeks with surgery complications.
- A bank representative cannot waive returned check fees even though she acknowledges the bank created the error that resulted in bounced checks in the first place.
- An assistant cruise purser cannot correct a billing error until the purser returns from lunch.
- A volunteer coordinator must check with the director before allowing a volunteer worker to implement a new process that she recommends to expedite service delivery to a client.

TRAINING

The importance of effective training cannot be overstated. To perform your job successfully and create a positive impression in the minds of customers, you and other frontline employees must be given the necessary tools. Depending on your position and your organization's focus, this training might address interpersonal skills, technical skills, organizational awareness, or job skills, again depending on your position. Most important, your training should help you know what is expected of you and how to fulfill those expectations. Training is a vehicle for accomplishing this and is an essential component of any organizational culture that supports customer service.

KNOWLEDGE CHECK

1. What are the elements included in a successful service organization?
2. What does the acronym RUMBA stand for and how does it relate to your service roles and expectations?
3. What part do rewards and management support play in successful customer service?

Trending NOW

Social media sites are affecting organizational culture as never before. Tech-savvy customers are reaching out to organizations and communicating with those who have adopted technology and created a social presence on sites like Pinterest, Facebook, and Twitter to gather information, communicate complaints, and post compliments. This inexpensive means of connecting with current and potential customers is reducing costs and enhancing product and service awareness, while potentially generating revenue for forward-thinking organizations that have established a social media presence.

Take advantage of training programs offered by your organization. Check with your supervisor and/or training department, if there is one. If you work in a small company or nonprofit organization, have a limited budget for training, or do not have access to training through your organization, look for other resources. Many communities have lists of seminars available through the public library, college business programs, high schools, chambers of commerce, professional organizations, and a variety of other organizations. The Internet also offers a wealth of articles and information in the form of free podcasts or YouTube training videos on a variety of topics. Go to www.youtube.com and search for "customer service training" to get free information. Tap into these resources to gain the knowledge and skills you will need to move ahead. Also, your training and skill level will often determine whether you keep your job if your organization is forced to downsize and reduce staff.

LO 2-2 Establishing a Service Strategy

CONCEPT   **A service provider helps determine approaches for service success.**

The first step a company should take in creating or redefining its service environment is to make sure it knows who its customers really are and how it plans to attract and hold those customers. Many organizations do not even consider this crucial step when creating a business plan or developing their culture.

Next, the organization should periodically conduct an inspection of its systems and practices (e.g., policies, procedures, service and product delivery mechanisms, customer care strategies, and practices for identifying potential customer dissatisfaction in advance and correcting it). This will help determine where the company is now and where it needs to be in order to better serve customers and to be competitive in a global service economy. The manner in which internal (coworkers and supervisors) and external (anyone outside the organization) customer needs are addressed also should be reviewed. For example, are surveys, focus groups, or customer–provider meetings/forums conducted?

It is not just your organization's responsibility to ensure the success of customer service. As a service professional, you have to be familiar with the organization's goals and work toward helping make them successful. A simple way to accomplish this is to give thought to your role in the service process and continually reevaluate what you do on a daily basis when dealing with customers. If you have a positive experience, recognize what made it so and strive to repeat that behavior with other customers. If something went wrong when serving a customer, objectively evaluate the situation and decide what role, if any, you played in a less-than-successful outcome. If you determine that you could have done better, decide on a more positive approach for the future. If you are unsure how to prevent a recurrence of the service breakdown, ask advice from coworkers or your supervisor.

As a service provider, you should do your part in determining needed approaches for service success. From the perspective of a customer service professional, ask yourself the following questions to help clarify your role.

- Who is my customer?
- What am I currently doing, or what can I do, to help achieve organizational excellence?
- Do I focus all my efforts on total customer satisfaction?
- Am I empowered to make the decisions necessary to serve my customer? If not, what levels of authority should I discuss with my supervisor?
- Are there policies and procedures that inhibit my ability to serve the customer? If so, what recommendations about changing policies and procedures can I make?
- When was the last time I told my customers that I sincerely appreciated their business?
- In what areas of organizational skills and product and service knowledge do I need additional information?

LO 2-3 Customer-Friendly Systems

CONCEPT   **System components are advertising, complaint resolution, and delivery systems.**

A service culture starts at the top of an organization and filters down to the frontline employee. By demonstrating their commitment to quality service efforts, managers lead by example. It is not enough to authorize glitzy service promotional campaigns and send out directives informing employees of management's support for customer initiatives; managers must get involved. Further, employees must take initiative to solve problems and better serve the customer. They must be alert for opportunities and make recommendations for improvement whenever appropriate. Only in these situations can changes and improvements in the culture occur.

©Image Source/Getty Images RF

The best way to create a service culture is to get everyone in the organization involved in planning and brainstorming. Everyone should be encouraged to share ideas about how and where internal changes need to be made and to be more responsive to customer needs. *How do you think these ideas can be shared most effectively?*

TYPICAL SYSTEM COMPONENTS

Policies and practices that say, "We care" or "You're important to us" can help ensure effective customer service. Some **customer-friendly systems** that can send positive messages are advertising and complaint or problem resolution.

Advertising

Advertising campaigns should send a message that products and services are competitive in price and that the quality and quantity are at least comparable to those of competitors. Otherwise, customers will likely go elsewhere without even providing an opportunity for employees to display their superior level of service. An advertisement that appears to be deceptive can cost the organization customers and its reputation. Examples of this are as follows:

If an advertisement states that something is "free" (a cup of coffee; a buy-one, get-one-free item; tire rotation; or a consultation), but somewhere in the advertisement (in small print) there are restrictions such as:

"With a purchase of $20 or more"

"While supplies last"

"If you buy two new tires"

"If you sign a one-year contract"

To prevent misunderstandings as a service provider, make sure that you point out restrictions, such as the ones above, to customers when they call or ask questions. If you notice that an advertisement sounds a bit "tricky," inform your supervisor immediately. Possibly the ad was not proofread carefully enough before it was printed and/or aired. Remember, you have a stake in your organization's success. Take ownership.

> ### Customer Service Success Tip
>
> Unhappy people are still your current or potential internal or external customers when they contact you at work. Your goal should be to try to appease them so that they return for future products or services. If you fail at this goal, you and your organization will potentially suffer financial and prestige loss.

Complaint or Problem Resolution

The manner in which complaints or problems are resolved can signal the organization's concern for customer satisfaction. If an employee has to get approvals for the smallest decisions, the customer may have to wait for a supervisor to arrive. In some instances, this is simply a formality and not needed, which can frustrate customers and employees. The CSRs might feel it makes them and the organization look inept (e.g., a supermarket cashier has to call for a manager to approve a check for $10, but when the supervisor arrives, he or she does not even look at the check before signing and walking away).

As a service professional, you should make recommendations for improvement whenever you spot a roadblock or system that impedes provision of service excellence.

SERVICE DELIVERY SYSTEMS

Service delivery systems are a combination of people, technology, and other internal and external elements that make up your organization's method of getting its products and services to customers. Your organization must determine the best way to deliver quality products and service and to provide effective follow-up support to its customers. There should be an ongoing and continuous reevaluation of system success to ensure that it keeps up with the changing needs of your customers. As part of that system, everything that you do is crucial in positioning your organization to be the "go to" source for the types of products and services that are offered to current and potential customers. This includes the way information is made available to customers, initial contacts and handling of customer issues, sales techniques (hard sell versus relationship selling), order collection and processing, price quotations, product and service delivery, processing of paperwork, invoicing, and follow-up. Customers should not have to deal with internal policies, practices, or politics. They should be able to contact you; get the information they need; make a buying decision, where appropriate; and have the products or services they have selected flawlessly delivered in a timely, professional manner. Anything less is poor service and may cost your organization in terms of lost business, customers, or reputation. These concepts also apply to your dealings with your internal customers who request information or services.

Customers also expect value for their money. Part of this is professional, easy-to-access service. For example, if you are in a retail organization and do not have a toll-free number with online customer support, extended hours of operation, top-quality merchandise, and effective resolution of problems, your customers may rebel. They can do this by complaining, spreading negative word-of-mouth publicity, writing letters to consumer advocacy groups (television or radio stations; Better Business Bureaus; local, state, and federal government agencies), and/or going elsewhere for their needs. Additionally, if your company's website is not kept up to date, has page error messages for hyperlinks, is difficult to navigate, or if your company has no web presence, customers may go elsewhere. Customers want to "click" quickly for their information. Websites that are hard to navigate or that take a long time to load will often be abandoned by customers.

There are many ways available for delivering service to customers. Three key factors involved in effective service delivery follow:

1. Transportation modes (how products and services are physically delivered—by truck, train, plane, U.S. Postal Service, courier, or electronically).

2. Location (facilities located centrally and easily accessible by customers). The location can be crucial to nonprofit organizations and medical or dental care providers since many clients or patients do not have access to dependable transportation. They often have to depend on friends, family, and public transportation to access services and products.

3. Technology is the third type of delivery system (type of access that is provided to customers—telephone, chat, e-mail, text, website, or social media). If your organization is in the information business, it likely has a multitiered means of providing access and service delivery to customers. For example, schools, colleges, and training companies that sell knowledge as their product depend heavily on systems that broadcast their information, supports the learning efforts, and handles the related administrative functions. Other entities that depend heavily on technology as a delivery system include help desks, membership organizations, and those companies and organizations that provide information, products, and support to customers (e.g., Veterans Administration, public utilities, and libraries).

Direct or Indirect Delivery

The type of delivery system used (direct or indirect contact) is important because it affects staffing numbers, costs, technology, scheduling, and many other factors. The major difference between the two types of systems is that in a direct contact environment, customers interact directly with people, whereas in an indirect system their needs are met primarily with self-service through technology (possibly integrated with the human factor in customer contact/call centers) integrated with Internet services.

There is a delicate balance in selecting a service delivery system. This is because each customer is unique and has personal preferences. While many prefer a hands-off

> **Customer Service Success Tip**
>
> Successful customer service results from relationships that you forge with others. By taking the time to slow down and let your customers take the lead and discover what they need or want, you increase the opportunity to better meet or exceed their expectations. In doing so, you are contributing to a positive service culture and helping secure your organization's reputation as a customer-focused entity.

self-service approach, others resent it and often view it as a loss of caring. Many banks discovered this fact in recent years. They saw technology as a cost-saving strategy to deliver service. Branches were closed as money was spent to upgrade automated phone systems and add automatic teller machines (ATMs). Many customers rebelled. The result is that companies like Chase Bank are now increasing their branch locations and retrofitting their branches and ATMs. Other banks are looking for ways to send a message that they are customer-oriented. For example, BankUnited, which was in receivership because of failed financial policies during the recession, has since been listed by the Federal Deposit Insurance Corporation (FDIC) as one of the most profitable banks in Florida, where it is headquartered. Some of their turnaround and growth is an emphasis on reaching its customers and providing customer-friendly service. The organization focused on opening new branches across the state and started a process called "bank on wheels" where they sent mobile branches, in the form of large, specially equipped recreational vehicles, into remote areas not served by their brick-and-mortar branches. These mobile branches include ATMs, walk-up tellers, flat-screen video, a small lobby, and two office spaces to meet with employees. Customers are able to get most of the services available in a standard branch. In addition, like many organizations, these companies use automated attendant phone systems that allow callers to speak or manually enter information with their telephone touchpad.

Figure 2.9 shows some ways by which organizations are providing service to customers and prospective customers.

Third-Party Delivery (Outsourcing/Offshoring)

In the past decade, as companies have strived to reduce costs, increase profit, and stay ahead of the competition, an interesting trend has occurred. Many are eliminating internal positions and delegating, assigning, or hiring outside (third-party)

FIGURE 2.9

Direct and Indirect Service Delivery Systems

Many industries are using technology to provide service that has traditionally been obtained by a customer going to a supplier and meeting face-to-face with an organization's representative. The following lists compare the traditional (direct) and technological (indirect) approaches.

Direct Contact	Indirect Contact
Face-to-face	Toll-free telephone number
Bank tellers	Automated teller machines or online banking
Reservationists (airlines, hotels)	Online computer, smartphone, or tablet reservations
Front desk staff (hotels)	On-screen, in-room television checkout and bill viewing
Ticket takers (theme parks)	Ticket scanning kiosks
Customer service representatives	Online viewing or telephone automated attendant to provide balance or billing information (credit card companies)
Lawyers	Telephone tip lines or e-mail
Photo developers	Self-service film kiosk or Internet transmission of digital images
Supermarket clerks	Online ordering and delivery
Towing dispatchers	In-car navigation and notification systems
Cashiers	Self-service checkout cash registers

organizations and individuals to assume eliminated and newly created roles (call center customer support functions, human resource benefits administration, accounting functions, and marketing) for an agreed-upon price (normally without the extra cost of benefits). Typically, outsourced (within your country) and offshored (outside your country) positions are noncore (e.g., call center support, manufacturing, or product design/development). Many third-party providers and the jobs outsourced or offshored are located in India, Mexico, Pakistan, Philippines, and a number of other developing nations where the labor supply is large and the wages and cost of doing business are much lower than they would be in a developed nation. For example, major U.S. companies like American Express, Citigroup, Microsoft, and others have found this strategy of exporting job assignments and processes to other countries to be a lucrative practice. They save millions of dollars in taxes and revenue by distributing call center and service functions outside their own borders.

This practice of outsourcing jobs to a third party provides multiple benefits while also bringing with it some downsides. On the positive side, companies can save money by:

- Eliminating large ongoing salaries
- Reducing health benefits, retirement, and 401(k) payments
- Avoiding the need to purchase and update computers and related equipment and a myriad of other equipment
- Increasing workforce size without necessarily doing likewise to the budget
- Bringing in new, fresh expertise, ideas, and perspectives from outside the organization

Moreover, on the negative side:

- Long-term employee expertise is lost.
- Employee loyalty to the organization suffers.
- Succession planning opportunities and the potential to groom and hire from within an enculturated workforce are reduced.
- The organization's reputation in the eyes of local citizens is potentially tarnished due to sending jobs away.
- The morale of the "survivors" (employees whose jobs were not eliminated) is potentially adversely affected.
- Managing becomes more complex.
- Customers must deal with "strangers" with whom they cannot build a long-term relationship because their provider may be gone the next time they call or stop by.
- Response time in getting a job or task completed may increase because of distance or other factors.
- Quality of work is not always up to expectations internally or for customers (e.g., dealing with service representatives who have hard-to-understand accents or do not fully understand the customer's culture or expectations).

An alternate cost-saving measure that many organizations have adopted is the practice of redesignating job positions as either part time or shared by two employees who are both part time. Because of their status, these employees do not qualify for all benefits because of the number of hours they work. Another common strategy is to fill positions with "temporary" employees contracted through a temporary staffing agency that assumes responsibility for staff benefits like health care. All of this typically occurs to reduce rising employee costs (especially benefits) while providing the necessary customer support.

Customer Service Tip

Be proactive and take ownership for problems you spot. Avoid taking a "not my job" approach in such instances. This can ultimately lead to the issue growing and causing a problem for the organization, customers, and ultimately you if revenue drops due to lost customer patronage. To help prevent this fate, look for ways to resolve issues by being proactive and taking responsibility to fix a problem.

TOOLS FOR SERVICE MEASUREMENT

In a customer-oriented environment, it is important that organizations gauge their service effectiveness continually, as perceived through the eyes of their customers. There are many ways to find out how well you and your peers are doing in serving customers. After obtaining the results of organizational self-assessments, management will likely share them with you and other employees in an effort to determine ways to reduce shortcomings and enhance strengths. If your supervisor fails to share such results, simply ask. Again, you have a stake in improvement and if he or she forgets to include you in the improvement loop—or intentionally omits you—you should take the initiative to demonstrate that you do care and are concerned with customer service delivery. From a selfish standpoint, having this developmental knowledge will allow you to identify resources and work toward improving your knowledge and skills. By doing so, you self-empower and make yourself more marketable inside and outside the organization.

Organizations are continually looking for new ways to gather customer feedback and analyze organizational effectiveness. Often, this is through a combination of strategies. Here are some of the typical techniques or tools available to organizations for service data collection:

- *Employee focus groups.* In such groups, you and others might comment or develop ideas on various topics related to customer service or employee and organizational issues. Although you will be providing interesting and valuable insights from your own perspective, remember that your views may differ significantly from those of your customers. For this reason, if your ideas are not implemented, do not be discouraged. Overriding organizational and customer issues to which you are not privy may be the reason.

- *Employee opinion surveys.* Such surveys are often done yearly to gain employee perspectives on how well policies, procedures, management, technology, and other systems perform.

Among other responsibilities, customer service professionals make a point of communicating their company's commitment to service in face-to-face interactions with customers. *What skills does a customer service representative need to create a positive service culture when talking with customers?*

©Tanya Constantine/AGE Fotostock RF

- *Customer focus groups*. Like the employee groups, these forums provide an opportunity to gather a group of customers (selected geographically; demographically by factors such as age, sex, race, income, or interests; or randomly from lists). Customer focus groups are brought together to answer specific questions related to some aspect of product or service.

- *Mystery shoppers*. These people may be internal employees or external consultants who pose as customers in on-site visits, over the telephone, or online to determine how well customers are being served.

- *Customer satisfaction surveys*. These surveys can be in a written or oral format. They could be a process as simple as an employee or manager chatting with customers at a restaurant and gathering their feedback, or something more formal. Customers sometimes complete a brief questionnaire at the end of their service transaction. Some organizations do follow-up telephone satisfaction surveys; others put their surveys on their website and encourage feedback. Many small businesses use free or inexpensive online survey services like SurveyMonkey. Customers are often enticed to participate in a survey using gifts, prizes, and discounts.

- *Customer comment cards*. Many food service and hospitality businesses use these simple cards to get immediate reactions and comments from customers after a visit. They are also used in the offices of doctors, nonprofit organizations, government offices, and anywhere else where managers really care about what their customers and clients think.

- *Profit and loss statements or management reports*. These reports are invaluable in spotting trends or dramatic changes in profits or losses that might indicate or lead to a service breakdown.

- *Employee exit interviews*. The human resources or personnel department typically administer these interviews or, in smaller organizations, an officer or owner might informally ask questions of a departing employee. Such information can identify trends or concerns. Departing employees often feel that they have nothing to lose and will candidly provide valuable feedback about management practices, policies, and procedures, and a multitude of other organizational issues.

- *Walk-through audits*. Create a checklist of service factors (e.g., responsiveness, friendliness, and so on) for supervisors or managers to use as they walk through a store or service facility to view the operations from a customer's perspective.

- *On-site management visits*. These visits provide firsthand observation of service practice and allow interaction between managers, employees, and customers. They are especially helpful when there are off-site workers (at construction sites or branch offices), operations consulting projects, or in-home services (such as plumbing). A side benefit of these types of visits is that they show the organization is committed to fulfilling the customers' needs.

- *Management inspections*. As a follow-up to employee service delivery, many organizations often have supervisors or managers follow up on service performed by checking the work or asking the customers how they liked the service or product received (e.g., at a carwash after the cleaning of a vehicle). Sometimes, these checks are done over the telephone or via the Internet.

Street Talk **Get permission from customers**

Whenever I call anyone, the first thing I ask is, "Is this a good time to talk?" If they say no, I follow up by asking when would be a better time to talk. I realize that they have other commitments. I think because of this, it increases the chances that they will get back to me. Additionally, when I e-mail people (mainly in my group), I ask about how their evening or weekend went and I strive to remember what they say so it does not seem to be superficial.

COURTESY OF ANNE WILKINSON

1. Why is it important for an organization to conduct inspections of its systems and practices periodically?

2. In what ways can an organization demonstrate that its policies and practices are customer-friendly and show that the organization cares for its customers?

3. How do service delivery systems tie into the culture of an organization?

4. What are some of the measurement tools used by organizations to collect service data?

LO 2-4 Eleven Strategies for Promoting a Positive Service Culture

CONCEPT To perform effectively as a customer service professional, you will need a plan.

Here are 11 strategies for service success:

1. **Partner with customers.** Probably the most important strategy for an organization to adopt in order to create a positive customer-centric service culture is to form a solid relationship with its customers. After all, customers are the reason you have a job and the reason your organization continues to exist. With that in mind, you should do whatever you can to promote a positive, healthy customer–provider relationship. You can accomplish this in a number of ways. Here are some simple techniques:

   • Communicate openly and effectively.

   • Address customers by their preferred name.

   • Smile—project a positive image.

   • Listen intently, and then respond appropriately.

   • Say "Please," "Thank you," and "You are welcome."

   • Facilitate situations in which you meet customer needs and both of you succeed in win/win situations while helping accomplish organizational goals.

   • Focus on developing an ongoing relationship with customers instead of taking a one-time service or sales opportunity approach.

2. **Explore your organization's vision.** In his book, *Employee Engagement for Dummies*, author Bob Kelleher observes that, ". . .vision is 'what could be and what should be, regardless of what is. Vision creates possibilities and inspires people to behave and take action in ways that allow the vision to become a reality'." Successful employees understand their organizational vision, the logic behind it, and work toward making it a reality. They actively engage in activities that help sustain and advance the vision.

   Effective managers strive to get their customer service representatives excited about their organizational vision. They realize that they must win the head and heart of each employee if they are to inspire them to make the vision statement a reality. Ultimately, a lack of employee engagement and support for the vision can lead to poor customer service, lowered morale and motivation, and long-term loss of customers and revenue.

By working to understand the focus of your organization better and asking yourself, "What's the Added Value And Results For Me?" (AVARFM), you can develop your own commitment to helping make the organization successful. An example of AVARFM might occur when a new policy is implemented that requires you to answer a phone by the third ring and a "mystery caller" system is in place as a means of monitoring compliance. As an incentive, you and other employees who meet the three-ring phone standard receive a reward. You now have a reason or benefit associated with meeting the new standard.

For you to succeed, and help your company do the same, you must have a thorough understanding of your role in making the organizational vision a reality. By recognizing how your efforts help internal customers succeed in providing quality customer service to their external customers, you can increase your sense of belonging and pride in your contributions. You can also help inspire other employees to take the same proactive approach in fulfilling their responsibilities toward achieving total customer satisfaction.

3. **Help communicate the culture and organizational vision to customers—daily.** Customers have specific needs, wants, and expectations when they contact a business or other type of organization. Once you are comfortable with the goals and vision on which the organization is focused, you should actively work to communicate them to your customers. It does no good for the organization to have a vision statement with a future objective of customer satisfaction if you do not help demonstrate it to your customers. You can let your customers see what you and your organization are about through your words and actions. When you encounter a customer, you have a unique opportunity to project a positive, customer-centric image. In that initial contact, you can show that you are there to serve the customer and exceed his or her expectations or that you are just doing your job. The first approach projects a positive image, while the second obviously does not.

Many companies place slogans and posters throughout the workplace or service area to communicate their vision. Although these approaches reinforce the message, a more effective means is for you to deliver quality customer service regularly. Through your attitude, language, appearance, knowledge of products and services, body language, and the way you communicate with your customers, they will feel your commitment to serve them.

4. **Demonstrate ethical behavior.** The code of **ethics** of your organization is intertwined with its culture. It is the moral standard that guides actions and defines right from wrong. Positive ethics drive decision making within the organization and in interactions with customers. Ethics also provide the criteria by which customers judge a service provider and his or her organization. By acting in an ethical manner and "doing the right thing," you and your organization can thrive and beat the competition. Figure 2.10 highlights some of the benefits of positive ethical behavior.

ethics The term comes from the Greek word "ethos," meaning character. Ethics is involved with right and wrong or good and evil and is illustrated by the way one responds to situations or acts.

Ethical behavior is an essential element of your career in customer service. It is based on values—those of the society, organization, and employees. These values are a combination of beliefs, ideologies, perceptions, experiences, and a sense of what is right (appropriate) and wrong (inappropriate) and are demonstrated through your words and actions and those of your peers and supervisors. All aspects of organizational and employee conduct come into focus when ethical or moral issues arise. It is how you and others around you handle problems or other situations that arise on a daily basis that paint a picture of the organization's overall ethical values, and, in some cases, your own.

ethical behavior Acting in a manner that sends a message of positive morality and good values when confronted with a customer situation or problem.

FIGURE 2.10

Benefits of Positive Ethical Behavior

Service providers and their organizations often reap the rewards of having a strict code of ethics and doing the right thing. Here are some of the potential benefits:

Enhanced public reputation can be acquired and maintained.

A workplace in which integrity and respect are exhibited daily can be fostered.

Employees take pride in working for the organization and in their own performance, and act more responsibly.

Employees look up to one another when they all take responsibility for their actions and hold one another accountable.

Teamwork and working toward a common goal of customer satisfaction and loyalty are encouraged.

Trust is higher when employees believe that management is truthful and treating them in a fair and professional manner.

Customers prefer doing business with them.

Customer loyalty is often higher.

Negative word-of-mouth publicity is reduced or eliminated.

Legal actions against the organization are less likely.

Many of the unethical instances that surface in organizations can be traced back to personal and societal values. Some of the more common examples of unethical behavior occur when employees fail to follow established laws, policies, and procedures. They often involve interactions between internal customers and the way that employees conduct themselves in the workplace. Examples might include bullying or harassing others, falsifying or stealing time by handling personal activities during work hours or extending breaks, improper use of computers or other organizational equipment, or actual criminal activity, such as, theft of property or embezzlement.

Your customers' values and how they perceive your behavior often determine whether your actions are ethical in their mind. Your customers often hold you and your organization to high standards. Thus, it is crucial for you to be aware of your words and actions so that you do not inadvertently send a negative ethical message to them.

Sometimes, issues are obvious. In other instances, they may fall into more gray areas instead of clearly black and white. How do you know which values your organization holds as important? Many times, they are communicated in an employee manual distributed during new hire orientation. Sometimes, they are emblazoned on a plaque on the wall, possibly as part of the mission or philosophy statement or next to it. However, the reality test or "where the rubber meets the road" related to your organization's values comes in the day-to-day operational actions of you and your organization. Look to your management for guidance on what is acceptable behavior in the workplace.

From an ethical standpoint, it is often up to you and your frontline peers to assess the situation, listen to your customers' requests, scrutinize your organizational policies and procedures, consider all options, and then make the "right" decision. In doing so, ask yourself, "Is this decision fair—to your customer and your organization—and is it morally and legally right?" The 1999 movie *The Insider* (with Al Pacino and Russell Crowe) epitomized the issues of ethical behavior. The movie is based on the true story of a tobacco industry insider who blew the whistle on his company, which publicly denied the harmful side effects of smoking. Even though the man stood to lose everything, possibly even his life, he acted out of conscience in an effort to help others. Another movie, *Erin Brockovich*, demonstrated what can happen if unethical behavior is not immediately caught and corrected by an organization. In that movie, Pacific Gas & Electric (PG&E) dumped chemicals into the soil and water of Hinkley, California, for years. They then covered up the pollution even though many of the local residents developed serious health problems and died. The company even paid medical bills for

⚙ WORK IT OUT 2.5

In the section on ethical behavior, you read about some common unethical behaviors that employees might exhibit in the workplace. List other examples of how actions that you or other employees might take during a workday might be unethical and either be "cheating" an employer or causing you to neglect an internal or external customer. Discuss these behaviors with other students along with ways to avoid them.

some residents to give the appearance of being a good corporate neighbor. Ultimately, Erin was able to piece together the details while working for a small legal firm; the subsequent lawsuit resulted in the largest class-action lawsuit payment in history at the time and severe damage to the reputation of PG&E.

The key to ongoing customer relations is trust. Without it, you have no relationship and cannot win customer loyalty or succeed as a professional.

To get a sense of the types of companies that have been successful in creating and maintaining a positive ethical reputation, visit the Ethical Institute at http://www.ethisphere.com/ to view a listing of ethical companies.

5. **Identify and improve your service skills.** Take an inventory of your interpersonal and customer service skills; use the strengths and improve the weaker areas. By continually upgrading your knowledge and skills related to people, customer service, and products and services offered, you position yourself as a resource to the customer and an asset to the organization. If you wish to pursue learning more about yourself by taking behavioral style surveys, check out some of the Internet resources available to you. Some sites periodically offer a shortened or beta test version of surveys they develop in order to gain feedback and fine-tune the tools before releasing them for commercial purposes.

   For more information on behavioral style surveys, visit www.bing.com and search for behavioral style surveys.

6. **Become an expert on your organization.** As the frontline contact person with customers, you are likely to receive a variety of questions related to the organization. Typical questions involve organizational history, structure, policies and procedures systems, products, or services. By being well versed in the many facets of the organization and its operation, related industry topics, and your competition, you can project a more knowledgeable, helpful, and confident image that contributes to total customer satisfaction.

7. **Demonstrate commitment.** As an employee with customer contact opportunities and responsibilities, you are the organization's representative. One mistake that many frontline employees (and many supervisors) make in communications with customers is to intentionally or unintentionally demonstrate a lack of commitment or support for their company and a sense of powerlessness. A common way in which this occurs is with the use

As a frontline contact with customers, you will be asked a variety of questions about the company and its products. *What skills will you need and what information should you give customers in this situation?*

©gchutka/Getty Images RF

Customer Service Success Tip

Even if your organization does not have a formal policy regarding returning calls, business etiquette dictates that you return all calls and do so within 24 hours or by the next business day. Even better, do so by the close of the business day if possible.

of "they" language when dealing with customers. This can be in reference to management or policies or procedures; for example, "Mrs. Howard, I'd like to help but our policy (they) says . . ." or "Mrs. Howard, I've checked on your request, but my manager (they) said we can't . . ."

An alternative to using "they" language is to take ownership or responsibility for a situation by telling the customer what you can do, not what you cannot do. Customers are not interested in internal strife or procedures; they want to have their needs satisfied. To try to involve customers in situations that are out of their control and that do not concern them is unfair and unwise. Positive language and effort on your part can reduce or eliminate unnecessarily dragging the customer in. Here is one approach: "Mrs. Howard, I'm terribly sorry that you were inconvenienced by our mistake (policy or omission). What I can do to help resolve this situation is . . ."

8. **Treat vendors and suppliers as customers.** Some customer service employees view vendors and suppliers as salespeople whose only purpose is to serve them. In fact, each contact with a vendor or a supplier offers an excellent opportunity to tap into a preestablished network and potentially expand your own customer service base while providing better service to existing customers. People remember how they are treated and often act in kind. By building and nurturing relationships with people outside your organization, you can often learn what is happening with competitors and within the service industry. You can also create opportunities to capitalize on these people's knowledge and expertise to better position yourself as an asset within your own organization.

9. **Share resources.** By building strong interpersonal relationships with coworkers and peers throughout the industry, you can develop a support system of resources. Sometimes customers will request information, products, or services that are not available through your organization. By being able to refer customers to alternative sources, you will have provided a service, and they are likely to remember that you helped them indirectly. After the interaction ends, it is the way your customers perceive they were treated, and how much you cared for their interests, that influences whether they return or recommend you and your organization.

10. **Work with, not against, your customers.** Customers are in the enviable position of being in control. At no time in recent history has the cliché "it's a buyer's market" been truer. Many consumers know this. To capitalize on this situation, many organizations have become very creative and proactive in their efforts to grab and hold customers. Several years ago, one large Colorado-based national supermarket, Albertson's, developed a series of commercials touting "Albertson's—it's your store" and stressing that customer satisfaction was the focus of its corporate efforts. Your efforts should similarly convey the idea that you are working with customers to better serve them.

11. **Provide service follow-up.** Providing follow-up is probably one of the most important service components. Service does not end when the service encounter or sale concludes. There are numerous follow-up opportunities to ensure that customer satisfaction was attained. This can be through a formal customer satisfaction survey or telephone callback system or through an informal process of sending thank-you cards, birthday cards, special sale mailings, and similar initiatives that are inexpensive and take little effort. Think of creative ways to follow up, and then speak to your supervisor about implementing them. These types of efforts reinforce service commitment to customers and let them know that you want to keep them as your customers.

LO 2-5 Separating Average Companies from Excellent Companies

CONCEPT Ask questions to determine the service environment in a company in which you seek employment or are currently employed.

Whether you are currently working in an organization or are seeking employment, the following factors can demonstrate an organization's level of service commitment. You can also use them as a basis for questions you might ask supervisors or interviewers in order to determine what type of service environment exists.

- Executives spend time with the customers.
- Executives spend time talking to frontline service providers.
- Customer feedback is regularly solicited and acted upon.
- Innovation and creativity are encouraged and rewarded.
- Benchmarking (identifying successful practices of others) is done with similar organizations.
- Technology is widespread, frequently updated, and used effectively.
- Employees receive training to keep current on industry trends, organizational issues, skills, and technology.
- Open communication exists between frontline employees and all levels of management.
- Employees are provided with guidelines and empowered (in certain instances, authorized to act without management intervention) to do whatever is necessary to satisfy the customer.
- Partnerships with customers and suppliers are common.
- The status quo is not acceptable.

Trending NOW

Self-service is in vogue in the twenty-first century. In a world driven by instant gratification, customers expect that they can have what they want when, how, and where they want it. Interactive voice response systems, web-based e-commerce, and self-help interactive touch screen kiosks have shown customers that they can receive service without having the annoyance of standing in long lines or sitting on hold waiting for the "next available agent." With the advent of technology that can speak to and understand customers, provide visual images, transact business processes, anticipate what customers want based on choices they make on a touch screen, and much more, people have come to expect that every organization will use the latest technology in its business activities. Organizations that fail to embrace and invest in equipment and software that meet customer wants and expectations will fall by the wayside.

1. How can you determine what type of service environment exists in an organization when speaking to supervisors or interviewers?

LO 2-6 What Customers Want

CONCEPT Customers expect effective, efficient service and value for their money. Customers also expect certain common things that service providers can furnish.

what customers want Things that customers typically desire but do not necessarily need.

Most customers are like you. Moreover, **what customers want** is value for their money and/or effective, efficient service. They also expect certain intangible things during a service encounter. Here are seven common things that customers want and expect if they are to keep doing business with you and your organization:

1. **Personal recognition.** Customers want to be recognized as being important to you and your organization. They want to feel appreciated. This can be demonstrated in a number of ways (sending thank-you cards or notes or birthday cards, returning calls in a timely fashion, or taking the time to look up information that might be helpful even if the customer did not ask for it). A simple way to show recognition to a customer who enters your work area, even if you cannot immediately stop what you are doing to serve him or her, is to smile and acknowledge the person's presence. If possible, you might also offer the customer the option of waiting, having a seat, and so on.

2. **Courtesy.** Basic courtesy involves pleasantries such as "please" and "thank you," as there is no place or excuse for rude behavior in a customer service environment. Even though customers may not always be right, you must treat them with respect. If a situation becomes too intense and you find yourself "losing it," call upon someone else to serve that customer. This is especially important in stressful environments where customers are truly suffering and not likely to be in the mood for poor attitudes or delays (e.g., hospital waiting rooms and doctors' or dentists' offices).

3. **Timely service.** Most people do not mind waiting briefly for service if there is a legitimate reason (as when you are waiting on another customer or obviously serving another customer on the phone), but they do not like to spend what they believe is undue amounts of time waiting to be served.

Your challenge as a customer service professional is to provide prompt yet effective service. It is important to remember that customers value their time as much as you and your managers/bosses do.

Work diligently to stay on schedule and at least explain when delays do occur so that the customer understands the reason for the wait (e.g., in a doctor's office when scheduled appointments are running behind because of a medical emergency or the doctor was delayed while in surgery). If extensive delays are likely to occur, offer the customer an option of possibly rescheduling. Customers probably will not want to, but the gesture of allowing them some decision in the situation is psychologically soothing in many cases.

Customer Service Success Tip

Before you can identify what a customer wants, you have to ask appropriate questions and then actively listen to his or her responses. In some cases, he or she may just want to browse; however, in others, he or she may have specific products or services in mind and likely would appreciate your assistance in locating them and helping him or her complete the transaction in a timely manner. Remember: When the customer talks, you listen. You cannot talk and listen at the same time.

4. **Professionalism.** Customers expect and should receive knowledgeable answers to their questions, service that satisfies their needs and lessens effort on their part, and service personnel who take pride in their work. You can demonstrate these characteristics by exemplifying the ethics talked about earlier, and through effective interpersonal communication.

5. **Enthusiastic service.** Customers come to your organization for one purpose—to satisfy a need. This need may be nothing more than to "look around." Even so, they should find a dedicated team of service professionals standing by to assist them in whatever way possible.

   By delivering service with a smile, offering additional services and information, and taking the time to give extra effort in every service encounter, you can help guarantee a positive service experience for your customer.

6. **Empathy.** Customers also want to be understood. Your job as a service provider is to make every effort to be understanding, and to provide appropriate service.

   To succeed in the service profession, you must be able to put yourself in the customer's position or look at the need from the customer's perspective as much as possible. This is especially true when customers do not speak English well or have some type of disability that reduces their communication effectiveness.

   When a customer has a complaint or believes that he or she did not receive appropriate service, it is your job to calm or appease in a nonthreatening, helpful manner and show understanding.

   A common strategy for showing empathy is the **feel, felt, found technique**. When using it, a service provider is demonstrating a compassionate understanding of the customer's issue or situation. For example, a customer is upset because the product desired is not in stock. A service provider might respond by saying: "Mr. Philips, I know how you feel. I have felt the same way when I had my heart set on a specific item. Many customers have actually found that the alternative product I described to you has the same features and performs several other functions as well. In some instances, it actually outperforms the product you asked about."

   > **feel, felt, found technique** A process for expressing empathy and concern for someone and for helping that person understand that you can relate to the situation.

7. **Patience.** Customers should not have to deal with your frustrations or pressures. Your efficiency and effectiveness should seem effortless. If you are angry because of a policy, procedure, management, or the customer, you must strive to mask that feeling. This may be difficult to do when you believe that the customer is being unfair or unrealistic. By suppressing your desire to speak out or react emotionally, you can remain in control, serve the customer professionally, and end the contact sooner.

> **Street Talk** **Do Not Interrupt Customers**
>
> If the customer is angry and ranting, let the customer complete the ranting before you speak and try to resolve the situation or ask a question. You need to keep wearing your smile and make sure you do not interrupt the customer. Trying to stop an irate customer will be fruitless. Let the customer get it off his or her chest and then you can try to address his or her needs.
>
> **COURTESY OF ANNE HINKLE,** *HR Insurance Benefits Specialist*

  WORK IT OUT 2.6

Your Customer Expectations

Now that you know what goes into making a customer environment "customer-friendly," think about your own expectations when you patronize a company. Share your answers with others in the class.

Drawing on your own experiences, list four or five expectations that you feel are typical of most customers.

KNOWLEDGE CHECK

1. What do you believe is the most important strategy for communicating a positive service culture? Why?
2. What are some strategies for giving personal recognition to your customers?
3. How might you exhibit enthusiastic service to your customers?
4. What is the feel, felt, found technique and what does it potentially communicate to a customer?

Small Business Perspective

No matter what size organization you work for, having great leaders who are visionary and think from a customer perspective will make the organization successful. In small business, such leadership is crucial for success because such organizations do not typically have "deep pockets" with large amounts of expendable resources available. In such companies, every dollar counts. For that reason, it is very important that everyone from the owner or CEO down to frontline employees embrace the concepts that you read about in this chapter. All must go beyond what their job description requires and take personal ownership for the company every day. Employees and management must pull together to share knowledge and skills and create a customer-centric atmosphere.

Typically, employees in successful small companies tend to bond as "family" and really get to know one another. As a result, they are more likely to pitch in when needed without an expectation of reward. This does not mean that if you work for a small company you should not expect to get paid for what you do. It simply means that by getting to know the strengths and areas for improvement of other employees and management, you can help fill gaps if you possess knowledge and skills that they do not have. Such behavior normally results in a higher payout for the organization because customers hear about you and are attracted to do business with the firm. When this occurs, revenue comes in that can fund salary increases, new equipment, and employee functions (e.g., family picnics and celebrations for special occasions or holidays).

In small organizations, effective communication and feedback are powerful and needed. Unlike many large organizations where you might be able to avoid someone or can get assistance and information needed to do your job elsewhere, resources are limited in a small organization. Everyone has to do his or her part and work cohesively together to help guarantee success and deliver customer satisfaction. If a disagreement or misunderstanding occurs, you must work together to resolve and get past it, just as you should with your own family members.

Successful small business employees typically possess many of the following attributes:

- **Self-initiative or ability to recognize what needs to be done.** By identifying potential issues that need to be addressed and accomplishing them without a lot of direction or guidance from others, service providers in small companies aid the overall effectiveness of the organization and address customer expectations.

(continued)

- **Strong powers of persuasion.** There may be no one else around when a customer calls or comes by your office in a small company. For that reason, you must be able to share an opinion, idea, or information in a convincing manner so that your customers believe and trust what you are saying. Strong oral, nonverbal, and written skills will often make the difference in whether you succeed when dealing with customers.

- **Flexibility.** Unlike larger organizations where there may be written policies and procedures and a human resources department to consult for various issues, small business employees often have to be able to "think on their feet" and come up with appropriate solutions when dealing with customers. This comes from having sound knowledge and skills related to products and service procedure.

- **Creativity.** There will be many times when working for a small business where you will have to come up with a solution to a customer question or issue spontaneously. To do this, you must be able to use the products, services, and tools offered by the organization to best satisfy the needs or wants of your customers. You must also have a sound knowledge of the products and services, warranties, policies and procedures, and other operational elements of the organization.

- **Problem-solving ability.** Since you will be working with limited resources in many instances, you must be able to gather data and information about a customer issue through effective questioning, quickly analyze what you learned, and make an appropriate decision.

Before going to work for a small organization, do a self-analysis of your behavioral style (as suggested earlier in this chapter). Based on the results, objectively decide if you have the right temperament or behavioral style preference to succeed in such an environment.

Impact on Service

Based on personal experience and what you just read, answer the following questions:

1. What characteristics or traits do you feel that many employees in small companies lack that causes service problems? Explain.

2. From a service perspective, do you think it is better to work for a small company or large one? Why?

3. To what degree do you feel service providers in small companies differ from their large organization counterparts? Explain.

Use SmartBook to help you read, study, and retain what you have learned. Access SmartBook in your Instructor's Connect course, or go to connect.mheducation.com for help.

SMARTBOOK™

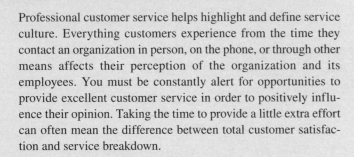

Keyterms

attitudes	ethical behavior	RUMBA
churn rate	ethics	service culture
customer-centric	feel, felt, found technique	service delivery systems
customer-friendly systems	mentors	service measurement
employee expectations	mission	service philosophy
employee roles	mission statement	vision statement
empowerment	protégé	what customers want

Summary

Professional customer service helps highlight and define service culture. Everything customers experience from the time they contact an organization in person, on the phone, or through other means affects their perception of the organization and its employees. You must be constantly alert for opportunities to provide excellent customer service in order to positively influence their opinion. Taking the time to provide a little extra effort can often mean the difference between total customer satisfaction and service breakdown.

Your role in helping create a positive service culture is to continually think like your customers and try to decide how you should best proceed in any situation in which you come into contact with them. Successful service providers have a plan and have strategies in mind for dealing with various issues. Through professional, proactive planning, you can demonstrate that you have your customer's best interest at heart while representing your organization ethically and in a manner that projects a positive attitude.

Review Questions

1. What are some of the key elements that make up a service culture?
2. How does management's service philosophy affect the culture of an organization?
3. How does RUMBA help clearly define employee roles and expectations? Why is each component important?
4. How can policies and procedures affect the customer's impression of customer service?
5. What questions should you ask yourself about your role as a service provider?
6. What are some indicators that a company has customer-friendly systems in place?
7. What are some of the tools used by organizations to measure their service culture?
8. What are some strategies for helping promote a positive customer culture?
9. What separates average organizations from excellent ones?
10. What are some typical things that customers want?

Search It Out

Customer Service and Organizational Culture

1. Log on to the Internet and research the mission statements of the following five organizations: (1) U.S. Department of Education, (2) USAA Educational Foundation, (3) Enterprise Rent-a-Car, (4) Starbucks Coffee, and (5) Florida Hospital. You can locate information by going to available search engines (Yahoo.com, Bing.com, Google.com, AltaVista.com, Excite.com, or Ask.com) and typing in the name of the organization, then searching its site for "mission statement."

As you view each organizational mission statement, answer the following questions:

Are there shared values and beliefs evident in the different mission statements? If so, what are they?

As a customer/client, do you feel that the organization values you? Why or why not?

Does the focus of each mission statement seem to differ between types of organizations (e.g., government, non-profit, not-for-profit, and for-profit)? Why or why not?

If you were writing each mission statement, what would you add or delete?

Be prepared to share your findings at the next scheduled meeting.

2. Conduct an Internet search of models that can be used to determine the cost of obtaining or retaining customers. See if you can find one specific to your industry or desired profession. Once you locate one that you feel is sound, calculate the cost of obtaining one new customer and share your research with classmates and your instructor.

3. For additional articles and information on creating a positive customer service culture, check out the author's Customer Service Skills Blog at http://www.customerserviceskillsbook.com/wordpress and search "Customer Service Culture" and related topics. Also, watch short YouTube videos on customer service culture.

Collaborative Learning Activities

1. Service Culture

Along with assigned group members, go on a field trip to several local organizations before your next class meeting. Use Figure 2.3, Elements of a Service Culture, as a guideline to determine the level and quality of the service culture of each organization visited. Take notes and be prepared to share your observations with other groups when you return to class. As part of your note taking, answer the following questions about each organization:

a. Did you notice any overt signs that indicated the organizations' cultural philosophy (mission or philosophy statements on walls)? If yes, what were they?

b. In what way was service delivered and how did the delivery indicate the organization's philosophy related to customer service?

c. What did the organization's products and services say about its approach to service (quality and quantity, availability, and service support)?

d. What evidence did you see of management support for the service initiatives being used by employees?

e. What indicators of motivators and rewards did you notice (employee-of-the-month or -year plaques; parking space for employee of the month; visible indicators of rewards on employees' clothes or uniforms, for example, items such as pins or buttons)?

f. Were there any indications that training of employees is occurring (employees have a consistent greeting or closing: "Thanks for shopping at _____")?

2. Promoting a Positive Service Culture

a. Form equal-sized groups.

b. Select a group/discussion leader who will take notes and report to the class.

c. Review the 11 strategies discussed in this chapter for promoting a positive service culture.

d. Individually, select the one that you believe you have the most opportunity to focus on as a service provider.

e. Do a tally to count the number of choices for each strategy (1–11).

f. Have each group member discuss why each made the choice he or she did and how he or she might implement that strategy.

Leaders from each group should report their tally and provide a general summary of the discussions to the class.

3. Positive Customer Service Strategies

You have read about customer service and the ways that a service culture can be developed and supported. Think of ways that you, and other service providers whom you have witnessed, can help create positive service culture (e.g., instead of pointing a customer in the direction of a product that he or she seeks, escort the customer to the product as you make small talk. Once there, ask if there is anything else you can do to assist).

a. Form equal-sized groups and brainstorm behaviors or techniques used by professional service providers as they work with customers face-to-face and over the telephone.

b. Generate a list of your ideas.

c. Use your idea list as a basis for your own action plan to help ensure that you are providing the best possible service when you interact with current and potential customers.

Face to Face

You and Your New Job in Customer Service

In the following case study, you are a new employee and are excited and happy to begin your position in customer service with United Booksellers. Read about the company and your role in customer service, and then answer the questions at the end of the case study.

Background

United Booksellers is the fifth-largest retailer of publications on the West Coast in the United States. It started 15 years ago as a family-owned bookstore in Seattle, Washington, and has grown to over 125 stores in seven states. The organization currently employs 3,000 employees, each of whom receives extensive customer service training before being allowed to interact with customers.

Recent issues of *Booksellers Journal* and *Publishers Select* magazine have heralded the quality service and friendly atmosphere of the organization. United Booksellers has been praised for the appearance of the facilities, helpfulness and efficiency of employees, wide selection of publications, and intimate coffee shops where patrons can relax and read their purchases over a hot cup of fresh cappuccino.

Your Role

As a new customer service professional with United Booksellers, you are excited about starting your job, which will require continual customer contact. As a child, you watched your siblings perform customer service functions at the local Burger Mania Restaurant and always thought you would like to follow their lead. Since you like people, enjoy a challenge, do not get stressed out easily, and have hopes of moving into management, you anticipate that this job should be just right for you. In this position, you will be expected to receive new publications from publishers, log in receipts, stock shelves, assist customers, and occasionally work as backup cashier.

Critical Thinking Questions

1. Are there indicators of United Booksellers' service culture? If so, what are they?

2. If you were an employee, in what ways would you feel that you could contribute to the organizational culture?

3. If you were a customer, what kind of service would you expect to receive at United Booksellers? Why?

Planning to Serve

To better understand the role of service providers in helping establish and maintain a positive service culture, think about what you read in this chapter. Also, think about factors related to service cultures in organizations with which you are familiar. Make a list of 5 to 10 key culture elements. Beside these ele-ments, create a list of strategies that you can/could take as a service provider to improve them if you worked in such an organization. Share your list with others in the class.

Quick Preview Answers

| 1. T | 3. T | 5. F | 7. F | 9. F | 11. F |
| 2. T | 4. T | 6. T | 8. T | 10. F | 12. T |

Ethical Dilemma Summary

Ethical Dilemma 2.1 Possible Answers

1. What ethical issue(s) do you face in this situation?

   The supervisor is putting employees in the awkward position of either making their performance goal or facing punitive actions and losing potential rewards. In pressuring customers, you might even alienate and lose them while generating negative word-of-mouth publicity that will hurt the organization in the future. Moreover, this practice can violate some basic principles of ethical behavior because it can damage trust between supervisors and employees and, ultimately, between customers and service providers and the organization. This practice also defeats the part of the organizational philosophy that states, "in a low-pressure customer atmosphere."

2. How might these affect service delivery?

The customer is likely to receive less than stellar service because frontline service providers are going to feel pressured to hurry their service delivery. Additionally, service providers will potentially resent the supervisor, policy, and organization for creating a stressful work environment and/or withholding rewards on the basis of circumstances not always created by the employees. In the long run, employees may act out through tardiness, absenteeism, and high turnover. This can lead to stressed-out supervisors and a revolving-door problem of rotating employees who require ongoing training, increased costs, and loss of expertise to the organization.

3. What impact might this situation have on your performance?

When employees feel that they are in a "no-win" situation or that their supervisor is not listening or being realistic, they often develop poor attitudes and their performance suffers. In a service environment, this often equates to customer complaints and lost business. In any event, if your performance wanes, you will likely receive disciplinary action and could ultimately be terminated or quit out of frustration.

4. How might this situation be addressed?

Supervisors should take a realistic look at the mission statement and philosophy of the organization. They should also benchmark against similar industry organizations to see what types of policies and procedures they use with similar service situations. Ultimately, they should work with employees to develop realistic standards for quality service delivery.

Employees should bring issues related to poor policies and procedures to their supervisor/team leader for discussion. They should take ownership of the issue rather than simply complaining to others about the stress and working conditions. It is possible that your supervisor is receiving pressure from his or her manager and is also frustrated but cannot voice that to you or other employees (since this would be unprofessional). If you perceive this to be the case, and you have a suggestion box or open-door policy, try presenting suggestions for improvement in a manner such that more senior people will hear and can potentially act upon them. Just remain professional in your approach.

Ethical Dilemma 2.2 Possible Answers

1. How does such a service atmosphere potentially impact customers? Employees?

Today's customers are typically better educated and informed and have been bombarded with tips for dealing with poor service by articles, television news stories, and consumer advocates. They often know what their rights are, know whom to contact when those rights are violated, and understand that they have many options for products and services if your organization cannot or will not deliver what they want or expect.

2. What message does this approach to service say about the organization?

When an organization promotes a message of "complete customer satisfaction," and then fails to deliver on that promise, it sends a message of dishonesty, unethical behavior, and lack of concern for customers. It also puts employees in a position of either having to defend the organization or lying to customers. Either option is a losing one for organizations and employees who meet their customers.

3. What are potential outcomes of such practices by the supervisor?

He or she is certain to lose the respect of employees and customers. Depending on whether he or she is acting on his or her own or with the blessing of management, disciplinary action and termination might result for violating organizational policy and for demonstrating poor leadership and bad judgment.

4. What can you and other employees do to address the situation?

In instances when supervisors are blatantly violating policy and putting you and the organization in a negative situation, you should immediately bring it to the attention of management. Of course, if you know that management condones such behavior, you likely are wasting your time and may only have one viable option—find employment in a reputable organization.

PART TWO

SKILLS FOR SUCCESS

3 Verbal Communication Skills

4 Nonverbal Communication Skills

5 Listening Skills

Ginger Marks

Customer Service Interview—Ginger Marks
Name: *Ginger Marks*
Position/job title: *CEO, Publisher/Designer*
Organization: *Calomar, LLC*

Total years of experience providing service to internal and external customers (in all organizations): *38 years*

Website: *http://www.Calomarllc.com*

1 **What are the personal qualities that you believe are essential for anyone working with customers in a service environment?**

Listen with the intent to hear, not with the intent to formulate your answer. If you do not hear the full discourse of what is being said by the person speaking to you, you cannot possibly give a proper response. In listening, you learn what the customer has to say and, at times, he or she will tell you what he or she needs from you to satisfy his or her needs. Also, you should take note of what he or she is saying. Generally speaking, if one person feels strongly enough to bring it to your attention, then chances are there that others do also, but have not voiced their feelings to you.

2 **What do you see as the most rewarding part of working with customers? Why?**

Each customer brings a new set of challenges to the proverbial table. Helping him or her to create unique, professional-looking books and graphics, while conforming to industry standards, results in a job well done. That is extremely rewarding.

3 **What do you believe that the biggest challenge(s) is/are in working with customers?**

Steering the customer or client to make the right choices, without being pushy or overbearing, can be a bit of a challenge for some graphic designers. Ego often comes into play. If you are serious about your business of design, there is no room for ego. This is why listening is so important at the beginning of forming your relationship with your customer/client.

4 What have you done, or could you do, to help overcome the challenges you indicated in question 3 and deliver better customer service?

As I mentioned, listen carefully and fully. Develop a relationship; do not just do the job. Help your customer/client to understand what his or her limitations and options are. If you do not know or cannot do something, do not pretend you do or can.

5 What changes have you seen in the customer service profession since you took your first service provider position—for example, customer demographics, their attitudes, people who work in the service industry and their attitudes, and how technology is applied to provide service?

I come from a precomputer era. Things have changed quite a lot over the course of my career. We used to be limited to face-to-face communication; we then migrated to e-mail, with its missing nuances often being misread or misinterpreted by the recipient. Today, global communication with real-time audio/video is the norm.

6 What future issues do you see evolving in your industry/organization related to dealing with customers in your profession and why do you think these are important?

This global communication brings with it both good and bad. Different cultures have differing norms. Where one culture might see something as totally acceptable and good, it could be just the opposite for another. We must learn to work together in understanding the differences each of us bring to bear as we expand our businesses.

7 What advice related to customer service do you have for anyone seeking or continuing a career in a customer service environment?

What you say is just as important as how you say it. Be careful how and what you say, to whom you say it, and show genuine concern for the other person above yourself. If you do not have excellent communication skills or training, get some!

Application to Customer Service

After reading Ginger's comments, think about how what she said relates to your organization and the customer service profession as a whole and respond to the following:

1. In addition to what Ginger mentioned related to qualities and skills, what other characteristics must a successful customer service professional possess?
2. What additional challenges do you think today's customer service professionals face? How might they effectively handle them?
3. What additional changes have you seen or heard about in the customer service profession? How do these affect the way that you and others in the profession must act when dealing with customers?
4. In addition to Ginger's suggestions, what advice do you have for people in the customer service profession?

Courtesy of Ginger Marks

Verbal Communication Skills

"People don't want to communicate with an organization or a computer. They want to talk to a real, live, responsive, responsible person who will listen and help them get satisfaction."

—Source: Theo Michelson, State Farm Insurance

LEARNING OUTCOMES

After completing this chapter, you will be able to:

3-1 Explain the importance of effective communication in customer service.

3-2 Recognize the elements of effective two-way interpersonal communication.

3-3 Project a professional customer service image through positive communication.

3-4 Provide feedback effectively.

3-5 Avoid language that could send a negative message and harm the customer relationship.

3-6 Use assertive communication techniques to enhance service.

3-7 Identify key differences between assertive and aggressive behavior.

Use SmartBook to help you read, study, and retain what you have learned. Access SmartBook in your Instructor's Connect course, or go to connect.mheducation.com for help. SMARTBOOK™

IN THE REAL WORLD INSURANCE—STATE FARM INSURANCE

State Farm Insurance Company was founded in 1922 and has grown to the largest home, life, and automobile insurer in the United States. It was listed number 35 on the Fortune 500 list of the largest companies in 2016. Over the years, State Farm has grown from a single automobile insurance to over 100 products and services and now handles 37,000 claims a day. The company has over 65,000 employees and over 18,000 agents. In addition to life and health insurance and coverage for homes, automobiles, motorcycles, condominiums, rental property, boats, and other personal property, the company also insures businesses and provides liability insurance. It also operates banks.

Over the years, State Farm has been recognized as one of the top employers in the country and has won employer, community work, and environmental awards from various organizations.

Some of the awards won in 2016 included the following:

- CEO Cancer Gold Accreditation for efforts to reduce the risk of cancer in employees, and their families, through early screening, early detection, and healthy lifestyles.
- Best Companies for Multicultural Women
- Top 100 Most Military-Friendly Companies
- Best Companies for Diversity
- Most Admired Company within the Property and Casualty insurance industry

The organization's founder had a vision of operating fairly and doing the right thing for customers. That vision is alive today as the company pursues a mission of being the first and best in the products and services it provides. Part of doing the right thing for customers extends to communities as well. The organization invests heavily in safety programs and services to help motorists and homeowners. An example of its efforts can be seen as one drives through many states. The company works with various governmental agencies to provide the roadside assistance vehicles that aid stranded motorists at no cost to them. State Farm also provides charitable grants for nonprofit initiatives focused on building stronger, safer, and better-educated communities. Further, it also advocates seat belt legislation and programs addressing teen driver safety. Related to the last issue, State Farm has developed a web-based training program to help raise awareness about different aspects of safe driving for teens (http://teendriving.statefarm.com).

To learn more about the company and its founder, visit https://www.statefarm.com/about-us/company-overview/company-profile/state-farm-story. Also, do an Internet search to learn more about the company.

Think About It

Think about what you read here and online about State Farm Insurance Company, and then answer the following questions. Your instructor may have you work together and share ideas in a group.

1. Have you or anyone from your family ever had an insurance policy through State Farm? If so, what was your experience with service and product quality?
2. Do you believe that State Farm is a good organization to work for? Why or why not?
3. How does the State Farm's service culture reflect on its image and product line?
4. What are the key elements separating State Farm from its competitors in your mind?

Quick Preview

Before reviewing the chapter content, respond to the following questions by placing a "T" for true or an "F" for false on the rules. Use any questions you miss as a checklist of material to which you will pay particular attention as you read the chapter.

For those you get right, give yourself a pat on the back, but review the sections they address in order to learn additional details about the topic.

_____ 1. Feedback is not an important element in the two-way communication model.

_____ 2. Customers appreciate your integrity, and they trust you more when you use language such as "I'm sorry" or "I was wrong" when you make a mistake.

_____ 3. Phrases such as "I'll try" or "I'm not sure" send a reassuring message that you are going to help solve a customer's problem.

_____ 4. When you use agreement or acknowledgment statements, customers can vent without their emotions escalating.

_____ 5. You should attempt to make a positive impression by focusing on the customer and his or her needs during your initial and subsequent contacts.

_____ 6. Having one prepared greeting and closing statement to use with all customers is a good practice.

_____ 7. When you are not certain of an answer, it is a good idea to express an opinion or speculate when something will occur if a customer asks.

_____ 8. An acceptable response to a customer's question about why something cannot be done is "Our policy does not allow . . .."

_____ 9. You should delay feedback whenever possible unless you are communicating in writing.

_____ 10. The appearance of your workplace has little effect on customer satisfaction as long as you are professional and help solve problems.

_____ 11. Assertive communication means expressing your opinions positively and in a manner that helps the customers recognize that you are confident and have the authority to assist them.

_____ 12. Assertiveness is another word for "aggressiveness."

Answers to Quick Preview are located at the end of the chapter.

Words to Live By

"You are serving a customer, not a life sentence. Learn how to enjoy your work."

— SOURCE: LAURIE MCINTOSH

LO 3-1 The Importance of Effective Communication

CONCEPT   **You represent your organization, and customers will respond according to you and your actions.**

For additional information on customer service job opportunities, visit the Bureau of Labor Statistics, Occupational Outlook Handbook—Customer Service Representatives at https://www.bls.gov/ooh/office-and-administrative-support/mobile/customer-service-representatives.htm.

The business of customer service is all about people. With the projected accelerated growth in the number of customer service representative jobs in the United States between 2014 and 2024 (2,581,800 in 2014),[1] organizations must take a proactive approach to ensuring that frontline employees have the requisite communication skills to interact with a diverse customer base. Whether you are the CEO discussing strategic relationships with potential business partners, a salesperson sharing product or service information with a potential customer, a call center representative gathering information from a caller on the phone, or a receptionist greeting a visitor to the organization, they all have one thing in common—effective communication, which is crucial in aiding the exchange of information. Customer satisfaction and successful product and service fulfillment hinge on your ability and that of others in your organization to transmit and receive messages freely and effectively with current and potential customers.

All customer experiences are a combination of people coming together for a common purpose; interacting face-to-face, via technology, or in writing; and merging individual beliefs, values, and expectations. Depending on the skill and finesse of the service provider, this can mean either a positive or negative outcome.

One variable over which you have little control as a service provider is the emotional state of your customers. When you first encounter someone, you have no idea if he or she is happy, sad, optimistic, angry, vindictive, or in some other frame of mind. That is why you must have an arsenal of **interpersonal skills** in your service toolbox upon which you can draw. A key element in this equation is the ability to effectively communicate verbally and to ask appropriate questions, listen, and analyze customer needs, wants, and expectations. You must then take correct and decisive action in order to satisfy the customer.

As a customer service professional, you have the power to make or break the organization. You are the front line in delivering quality service to your customers. Your appearance, actions or inactions, and ability to communicate say volumes about the organization and its focus on customer satisfaction. Additionally, in order to be successful, you need knowledge and skill in communicating verbally, nonverbally, across genders and cultures, and with a variety of personality types. For all these reasons, you should continually work to enhance your knowledge and skills, strive to project a professional image, and go out of your way to make a customer's visit or conversation with you a pleasant and successful one.

Two key elements in making your interactions with customers successful are to recognize how you tend to communicate and understanding how the communication process works. The easiest way to find out how you communicate is to ask those who know you best. Unfortunately, many people are leery about requesting feedback because of what they might hear. Conversely, most people have difficulty giving useful feedback. They have either never learned how to do it effectively or are uncomfortable doing it. In any event, try it. Ask a variety of people for their feedback because each person will likely have a different perspective based on experience with you. In an ideal world, ask people who work with you or who are customers with whom you have developed a sound relationship over a period of time.

As you will read in this chapter, the process of communication involves active participation by both you and your customer. Since you have no control over whether your customer recognizes the importance and steps of the process, the bulk of responsibility for structuring and navigating conversations falls on you as a service professional.

interpersonal skills The skills used by people to relate to and communicate effectively with others. Examples are verbal and nonverbal communication skills and the ability to build trust, empathy, and compassion.

Strengthening Customer Communication

Customers who feel that they have an active role in and control of a service–provider interaction often feel more important and valued. Improved interpersonal communication can lead to higher levels of customer satisfaction and retention and reduced stress for you and your coworkers.

Take advantage of the following strategies to build stronger relationships with your internal and external customers.

Gather Information

Ask for customer input whenever possible. By knowing more about their needs, wants, and expectations, you will be better able to provide services and products that satisfy them. Use strategies you will find in this chapter to gather valuable information from people who you encounter on a daily basis.

Be Consistent

People tend to like what is familiar. If customers come to know that they can depend on you and your organization to provide timely, factual information, they will likely be more loyal. Provide information and updates to customers on a regular basis, not just when it is convenient to you. This is especially true when you are working on a problem or service breakdown. Remember that they do not know what you know. For example, if you are gathering information or need more time than expected, come back to the customer with periodic updates to give a status check.

(continued)

Demonstrate Openness

Customers often want to see that service providers understand them on a personal level. The worst thing that you can do is to hide behind policy or deflect responsibility when dealing with a customer issue or question. Think of how you likely react when a service provider says something like, "I cannot do that because our policy says. . . ." You probably feel the hairs rise on the back of your neck and become agitated. Your customers are no different. When interacting with them, take the time to put yourself in their place before saying something or taking an action that might create an adversarial situation.

Be Personable

Service providers who tend to be "all business" or robotic in their service delivery often fail to get high marks from customers. Even if you are knowledgeable, efficient, and follow all the rules in delivering service, you could end up with a dissatisfied customer if you do not demonstrate some degree of humanness. This means connecting on a personal level and showing compassion and concern for your customers and their emotional needs. For example, if someone tells you during an interaction that he or she is celebrating a special event, take the time to ask about it and explore the topic briefly, or relate a personal example. If it is the birthday of a customer's child, you could wish the child an enthusiastic "Happy Birthday." You might go further to ask the child how old he or she is or what the child hopes to get for his or her birthday. Depending on the type of business you are in, you might even offer a small present (e.g., a free dessert, a piece of candy, a toy, a coupon for a discount on his or her next visit, or whatever is appropriate). At the least, upon concluding the transaction, wish the child well or congratulate him or her one more time.

Customer Service Success Tip

In addition to any communication specifics that you would like to learn for yourself, ask the following questions to those with whom you interact regularly:

- Do I tend to smile when I speak?
- Do I spontaneously smile and greet people who pass me in the workplace?
- What body cues (nonverbal signals) do I use regularly when I speak?
- How would you categorize my overall presence when I speak (confident, uncertain, timid, relaxed)? Why do you perceive that?
- What "pet" words or phrases do I use regularly?
- When I speak, how does my tone sound (assertive, attacking, calming, friendly, persuasive)? What examples of this can you provide?
- When I am frustrated or irritated how do you know it?
- What can I do to improve the way I communicate verbally with people?

KNOWLEDGE CHECK

1. What are two key elements that can make your customer interactions more successful?

LO 3-2 Ensuring Two-Way Communication

CONCEPT **Two-way communication involves a sender and a receiver, each of whom contributes to the communication process. Part of the communication process is deciding the best channel to ensure clear message delivery.**

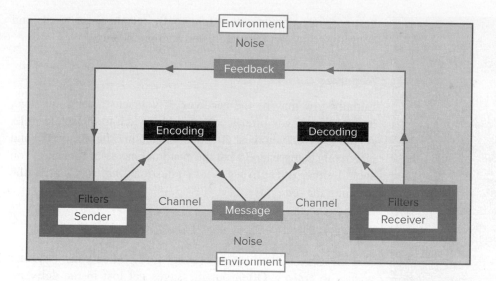

FIGURE 3.1
Interpersonal Communication Model

As a customer service professional, one of your primary roles is to ensure that a meaningful exchange of information takes place each time you interact with a customer. By accepting this responsibility, you can perform your job more efficiently, generate goodwill and customer loyalty for the organization, and provide excellent service. Being aware of the elements of **two-way communication** and the importance of each will help facilitate your communication success. Figure 3.1 shows a communication model that helps the interpersonal communication process.

> **Street Talk** Use Plain Language and Avoid Jargon
>
> Using jargon or unfamiliar vocabulary when explaining a procedure to a student or other customer will leave the listener confused or totally misinformed. Know your audience when explaining any new technique or procedure.
>
> **SOURCE:** SHARON MASSEN, PHD, CAP *MASSEN AND ASSOCIATES*

INTERPERSONAL COMMUNICATION MODEL

Environment

The environment (office, call center, store, and group or individual setting) in which you send or receive messages affects the effectiveness of your message. For example, in a busy business environment, you are likely to be making an effort to meet deadlines, serve all customers, or create a positive experience for each customer. In such an environment, you or others may take shortcuts in communicating and send a perceived curt or abrupt verbal and nonverbal message. This could potentially cause a service breakdown. The key to success in such instances is to take a deep breath when things get hectic, remember to use a calm and professional tone, and think before speaking or responding nonverbally. If things get so stressful that you feel like you are going to "lose it," you might want to take a short break if possible before encountering your next customer. Otherwise, you may inadvertently allow your frustration to carry over from one customer to the next and could come across as being rude or unprofessional to the second person.

Sender

You take on the role of **sender** as you initiate a message with your customer. Conversely, when customers respond, they assume that role. As the sender, you have a responsibility to think of the message that you want the customer to receive, decide the

two-way communication An active process in which two individuals apply all the elements of interpersonal communication (e.g., listening, feedback, positive language) in order to effectively exchange information and ideas.

sender One of the two primary elements of a two-way conversation. He or she selects a communication channel and then creates and encodes the intended message to the receiver. This starts the communication process.

©Cultura RM Exclusive/Nancy Honey/Getty Images

Two-way communication is the foundation of effective customer service. *How can you be sure that you are listening to the customer?*

best way to communicate it (channel), and then use words and nonverbal cues that effectively convey that message.

Receiver

Initially, you may be the **receiver** of your customer's message; however, once you offer feedback, you switch to the sender role. As the receiver, you must effectively listen in order to receive and effectively comprehend what the customer has said. If unsure, you should either **paraphrase** or ask questions that will clarify the meaning for you.

Message

The **message** is the idea or concept that you or your customer wishes to convey. Often our messages get lost in the delivery. Because we choose inappropriate words or nonverbal cues, the customer misinterprets or does not understand our intended point. This can lead to a breakdown in communication and service. In order to prevent this from occurring, it is important to think before speaking. Consider factors such as the customer's gender, age, culture, primary language, experience and knowledge level, ability to hear, and any other factor that might affect the way in which the customer might receive and analyze your message. Then, formulate a message that is clear and concise and communicates your intended meaning.

receiver One of the two primary elements of a two-way conversation. The receiver gathers the sender's message, decodes the message based on his or her interpretation, and then decides how to react to it.

paraphrase The practice of a message receiver giving back in his or her own words what he or she believes a sender said.

message A communication delivered through speech or signals, or in writing.

channel Term used to describe the method through which people communicate messages. Examples are face-to-face, telephone, e-mail, chats, Twitter, written correspondence, and facsimile (FAX).

encoding The stage in the interpersonal communication process in which the sender decides what message to send and how to transmit it along with considerations about the receiver.

Channel

The method you choose to transmit your message is the **channel**. In an ideal world, it is typically best to communicate face-to-face, with a secondary preference being over the telephone. Through these two channels, you and your customer are able to hear words, inflections, tone, and other voice qualities that impact message meaning. In the case of face-to-face, you and your customer both see the nonverbal cues that accompany each other's words. When you revert to written communication through any channel, there is the potential for misunderstanding of meaning, lost opportunity to supplement the words with verbal and nonverbal cues, and the potential feeling of the message being impersonal.

Encoding

Encoding occurs as you evaluate what must be done to effectively put your message into a format that your customer will understand (language, symbols, and gestures are a few options). Failing to correctly determine your customer's ability to decode your message could lead to confusion and misunderstanding. As mentioned under the "message" section above, you must consider many personal factors about your recipient in order to ensure that he or she gets the message that you intend.

Decoding

Decoding occurs as you or your customer converts messages received into familiar ideas by interpreting or assigning meaning. Depending on how well the message was

⚙ **WORK IT OUT 3.1**

Communication Reality Check

To better plan your future service strategy, think about your own past service experiences. Think of your reaction when you walked into a store that used a greeter and the person either did or said nothing other than eyed you up and down or said something like, "Welcome to . . ." in a robotic fashion and without smiling, and then handed you an advertisement flyer, which you likely did not want in the first place. What was your reaction? What message about the organization did his or her words or actions send to you? On a scale of 1–5 (5 being highest), how would you rate his or her level of service? If you were him or her, what could be done differently in the future to change the rating you gave?

encoded or whether personal filters (e.g., gender, background, age, language, or cultural differences) interfere, the received message may not be the one you originally intended. This can lead to a service breakdown and potential conflict.

Feedback

Unless a response is given to messages received, there is no way to determine whether the intended message was received. **Feedback** is one of the most crucial elements of the two-way communication process. Without it, you have a monologue. Feedback typically comes in the form of nonverbal reactions or verbal responses or questions during face-to-face or telephonic communication. When you are using e-mail, texting, or other written formats, you have to wait for a response. In such instances (or when no response is forthcoming), it is a good idea to clarify receipt and proper understanding of your original message based on the type of feedback that you receive. Never assume that someone got and interpreted your message the way you intended. Read the response well before leaping to any potential negative conclusions. There have been too many instances in which people have sent an inappropriate emotional response, which they later regretted, because they initially misinterpreted feedback they received.

Filters

Filters are factors that distort or affect the messages you receive. They include, among other things, your attitude, interests, biases, expectations, experiences, education, beliefs and values, background, culture, and gender. These factors can cloud our perception and judgment and can sometimes result in communication and service breakdowns. Consider your own filters when sending or interpreting messages.

Noise

Noise consists of physiological factors (e.g., health or physical characteristics and abilities) or psychological factors (e.g., level of attention, mood, mental health, or emotional condition) that interfere with the accurate reception of information. It can also include environmental factors (e.g., external sounds or room acoustics) that inhibit communication and listening.

decoding The stage in the interpersonal communication process in which a receiver analyzes the messages received in an effort to determine the sender's intent.

feedback The stage of the interpersonal communication process in which a receiver responds to a sender's message.

filters Psychological barriers in the form of personal experiences, lessons learned, societal beliefs, and values through which people process and compare information received to determine its significance.

noise Refers to physiological or psychological factors (physical characteristics, level of attention, message clarity, loudness of message, or environmental factors) that interfere with the accurate reception of information.

Trending NOW

In recent years, the human attention span in many developed nations has gotten significantly shorter. This can most be attributed to the faster pace of information delivery through technology and the resulting conditioning of the brain to receive and expect material to arrive faster, and on a more regular basis. Think about how fast television commercials are repeated and movie scenes change today. Also, consider the video games to which many people have spent hours playing and have become accustomed.

From an interpersonal communication standpoint, this means that you must structure messages more concisely and deliver information in "sound bites" or short spurts of information for many customers. This is especially true of customers who speak a different primary language. This is opposed to droning on with a long sales pitch or explanation. The key is to watch your customers' nonverbal cues to detect their level of attention and comprehension. If necessary, repeat what you said in a slightly different manner to ensure effectiveness of your message and understanding.

KNOWLEDGE CHECK

1. What are the 10 elements of the interpersonal communication model?

2. Which of the model elements is one of the most crucial in the two-way communication process?

LO 3-3 Communicating Positively

CONCEPT   **A positive approach to addressing customers can be productive.**

You should think out everything from your greeting to your closing statements before you come into contact with a customer. Know what you want and need to say, avoid unnecessary details or discussion, and be prepared to answer questions about the organization, its products and services, and the customer's order. To maximize your potential and create a positive communication outcome with customers, use the PLAN acronym as a guide to effective communication with those with whom you come into contact. The model in Figure 3.2 depicts positive communication.

Just as you can turn customers off with your word choice, you can also win them over. Figure 3.3 contains some tips.

Use action words when trying to persuade your customer to make a purchase or go along with your suggestion or making a decision. For example, when attempting to encourage a customer to choose a specific item or brand, you might say something like, "Your concerns about fitting a new washer into available space are certainly valid. Based on the dimensions that you mentioned, the model I suggested will work fine. If you place your order today, we can also arrange to have it professionally installed to ensure that there are no problems."

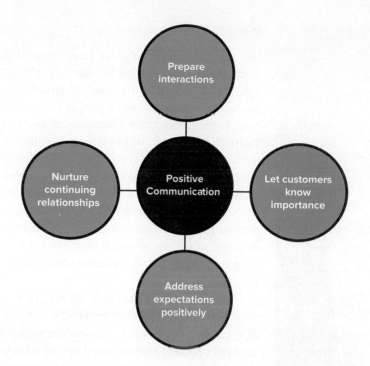

FIGURE 3.2
Positive Communication
Model

FIGURE 3.3

Words and Phrases That
Build Customer Relationships

Some phrases can assist you in strengthening relationships with your customers. Such language reinforces your integrity and encourages customers to trust you. How do you or could you use these words? Which ones do you use the most?

Please.	May I . . .?
Thank you.	Have you considered . . .?
I can or will . . .	I'm sorry (I apologize) for . . .
How may I help?	However, and, or yet (instead of but).
I was wrong.	It is my (our) fault.
I understand (appreciate) how you feel.	Would you mind . . .?
Situation, issue, concern (instead of problem).	What do you think?
Often, many times, some (instead of global terms, such as, all or everybody).	I appreciate . . .
You're right.	Use of customer's name.

PREPARE FOR POSITIVE CUSTOMER INTERACTIONS

The first element of the PLAN acronym is all about getting into a mental state of mind to provide quality service effectively to your customers.

Too often service providers wait for something to happen and then react to the situation. This is a formula for disaster, especially if they do not have the knowledge or skills to address a customer's needs. To prevent this from happening to you, consider the types of potential customer situations you might encounter. Next, get training, discuss possible scenarios and solutions with peers and your supervisor, and role-play handling potential customer issues so that you have in mind possible actions to take should an actual situation arise.

©Wavebreak Media Ltd /123RF RF

Employees should pay close attention to what the customer is saying so that they can anticipate problems. Is *this employee paying attention to what she is hearing?*

pet peeves Refers to factors, people, or situations that personally irritate or frustrate a service provider and that, left unchecked, can create a breakdown in effective service.

Identify Pet Peeves

One way to prepare to serve your customers is to do a quick mental assessment before they arrive or contact you. Part of this analysis revolves around you and your personal preferences. Most people have something that bothers them about how others communicate or behave. These "hot buttons," or **pet peeves**, can lead to customer relationship breakdowns if you are not aware of what your pet peeves are and how you come across to others. By identifying and acknowledging your potential irritants, you can begin to modify your behavior in order to prevent problems with customers. You may also be able to avoid situations in which such behaviors are present or might manifest themselves and cause problems for you.

Your customers also likely have a list of things that they dislike about service providers. If you exhibit one of their pet peeves while serving them, you could find yourself opposite a disgruntled person who is not afraid to voice his or her displeasure. He or she may even escalate his or her complaint to your supervisor or elsewhere.

Some typical behaviors that service providers exhibit, and that might bother customers, include the following:

Disinterest in serving (e.g., talking to coworkers, texting or using smartphone, reading material, or typing on computer)

Standing or walking around the store while texting during work hours

Causing excessive wait times due to inefficiency, lackadaisical attitude, or incompetence

Unprofessional appearance (in the customer's mind)

Lack of cleanliness (environment or service provider)

Abruptly putting someone on telephone hold without his or her permission

---

⚙ WORK IT OUT 3.2

My Pet Peeves

Take a few minutes to think about irritating behaviors that service providers have exhibited when helping you in the past. Make a list of these behaviors and strive not to exhibit similar ones. If you are irritated by them, your customers will likely be too. After you create your list, compare it with others in the class.

As an alternative, your instructor may form groups of four or five learners and do this as a group activity.

Failing to answer telephone within four rings (or within company policy standards)

Eating or chewing while dealing with a customer

Lack of knowledge or authority

Poor quality of service

Condescension (taking an air of superiority to the customer)

Rudeness or overfamiliarity (using first names without permission)

LET YOUR CUSTOMERS KNOW THEY ARE IMPORTANT

The second element of the PLAN acronym deals with making your customers feel as if they are the most important people in the world from the moment they contact you. To do this, you must consider each person who calls, texts, comes into your place of business, or contacts you through a computer or other communication tool to be a guest of your organization. Treat him or her with respect, dignity, and hospitality as you likely would a family member or good friend. Many companies have adopted the term "guests" to describe their customers or visitors as a way to remind employees of this concept.

The following are some proven strategies to help you accomplish the goal of making people feel welcome by you and your peers when they contact the organization.

Extend a welcoming smile and posture whenever interacting with customers. *What are some ways that you can demonstrate that customers are welcome?*

©Tyler Olson/123RF RF

Make Customers Feel Welcome

Personalize your greeting a bit. If appropriate, shake hands, smile often, and offer a sincere welcome, not the canned, "Welcome to . . .." Instead, use whatever your organizational policy dictates, such as, "Good morning/afternoon, welcome to . . . . My name is . . . . How may I assist (or help) you?" Even if you are on the telephone, you should smile and verbally "shake your customer's hand" because your smile can definitely be heard in your voice. Be conscious of the need to sound approachable and receptive.

Most people like to feel as if they belong, be recognized as special, and seen as individuals. To help enhance your service delivery, get to know your customer's name when possible and use it in greeting him or her. Additionally, use it where appropriate throughout the conversation and when closing the encounter. Try to avoid using negative-sounding "you" messages as a primary means of addressing your customer. For example, instead of, "You will need to fill out this form before I can process your refund," try, "Mr. Renaldi, can you please provide some information on this form while I start processing your refund? That way, we will have you out of here quickly." The latter approach makes it sound as if you recognize customers as being important and puts them psychologically in control of the situation as opposed to being told what to do. You are also showing respect for their time. This can often mean the difference between a smile from your customer and a confrontation and demand to speak to a supervisor.

Many companies go out of their way to send the message of "family." For example, the Olive Garden restaurant advertises that "When you're here, you're family." Similarly, CarMax and several other national automobile chains go to great lengths to make the customer feel welcome and special. For example, they drape a huge ribbon over a newly purchased vehicle in a well-lit garage, available sales representatives gather with the customer to congratulate him or her on being part of the "family," and take photographs of this "special moment." While some customers might view the latter as "hokey" or not sincere, others might appreciate the special treatment. Similarly, many less formal restaurants go out of their way to recognize special occasions like birthdays and anniversaries. To recognize patrons who dine with them on their special day, all available staff members clap, sing, and invite other guests to join in. While many new customers to the establishments sometimes find the ceremony to be unnecessary "noise," regular visitors come specifically for the event. The idea is to make customers feel welcome and like they are one of the family.

Customer Service Success Tip

Look for ways to celebrate your customers and make them feel special and valued. For example, congratulate them on special events of which you are aware (e.g., weddings or anniversaries, birthdays, birth of children, graduation from school, and other successes). This will return dividends of increased customer satisfaction, higher levels of customer trust in the organization, and reduced stress for you because you will have fewer instances of unhappy customers with whom you have to deal.

Focus on the Customer as a Person

Strive to let customers know that you recognize them as individuals and appreciate their time, effort, patience, trust, and business. This is important. To deliver quality service effectively, you must deal with the human being before you deal with his or her needs or business concerns. By making contact on an emotional level during interactions, you help ensure a more positive outcome by demonstrating a friendly level of service. After all, friends do not typically confront friends or become irate when something goes wrong.

For example, if someone has waited in a line or on hold for service, as soon as this person steps up or you come back on the line, smile warmly, thank him or her for being patient, apologize for the wait, and ask what you can do to assist him or her. Often in such situations the service provider says something like, "Next" (sounds canned and not customer-focused) or "Can I help the next person?" (better, but it still goes straight to business without an apology or without recognizing the customer's inconvenience or wait). On the phone the service provider goes straight to, "This is Jean; how may I help you?" (this approach gives no acknowledgment of the customer's inconvenience).

Another opportunity to focus on the customer occurs at the end of a transaction or call. If your organization does not have a standard parting comment to use with customers, simply smile and say something like, "Mr. Rinaldi, thank you for coming to (or calling) ABC Corporation. It was my pleasure to serve you. Please come back (or call) again." The key is that you must sound sincere. You may even want to modify your parting statement for subsequent customers so that it sounds more personal—and so the next person in line does not hear you parrot the same words with each customer.

- *Offer assistance.* Even if a problem or question is not in your area of responsibility, offer to help get answers, information, or assistance. Your customer will likely appreciate the fact that you went out of your way to help.

- *Be prepared.* Know as much as possible about the organization, its products and services, your job, and, as appropriate, the customer. Also, make sure that you have all the tools necessary to serve the customer, take notes, and do your job in a professional manner. This allows you to deliver quality information and service while better satisfying customer needs and expectations.

- *Provide factual information.* Do not express opinions or speculate why something did or did not, or will or will not, occur. State only what you are sure of or can substantiate. For example, if you are not sure when a delivery will take place or when a coworker who handles certain functions will return, say so, but offer to find the answer or handle the situation yourself. Do not raise customer expectations by saying, "This should be delivered by 7:30 tomorrow morning" or "Sue should be back from lunch in 10 minutes." If neither event occurs, the customer is likely to be irritated.

- *Be helpful.* If you cannot do something or do not have a product or service, admit it but be prepared to offer an alternative. Do not try to "dance around" an issue in an effort to respond in a manner that you feel the customer expects. Most people will spot this tentative behavior, and your credibility will suffer as a result. Do not insult your customer's intelligence by taking this approach. You and the organization will lose in the end.

- *Accept responsibility.* Take responsibility for what you do or say and, if necessary, for actions taken by someone else that failed to satisfy the customer. Do not blame others or hide behind "they said" or "policy says" excuses. When something goes wrong, take responsibility and work to resolve the problem positively and quickly. If you do not have the authority needed, get someone who does, rather than refer the customer to someone else.

- *Take appropriate action.* You should go to great lengths to satisfy the customer. Sometimes this may mean bending the rules a bit. In such cases, it may be easier to ask forgiveness from your supervisor than to explain why you lost the organization a good customer. If a request really cannot be honored because it is too extreme (a customer demands a free $100 item because he or she had to return one that did not work properly), explain why that specific request cannot be fulfilled and then negotiate and offer alternatives.

ADDRESS YOUR CUSTOMER'S EXPECTATIONS POSITIVELY

The third element of the PLAN acronym focuses on the area of interpersonal communication with your customers.

Communication is a major portion of your job and has a definite impact on the relationships and impressions that you forge with your customers or clients. Each time you interact with a current or potential customer, he or she is assessing you from many standpoints, which plays a large part in how the customer sees and interprets you and your organization.

The following sections provide some guidance on ways that you can project a positive customer service attitude and image.

⚙ WORK IT OUT 3.3

Analyzing Your Verbal Communication Skills

To help you determine how you sound to others, try a bit of objective self-analysis. To do this, place a digital voice recorder nearby, either at home or in the office, and leave it on for about 45 minutes to an hour while you interact with other people. Then play the recording to hear what your voice sounds like when you communicate verbally with others. Be especially alert for verbal cues that send a negative message or seem to be misinterpreted by the other people involved. Also, listen carefully to the manner in which others respond to you. Do their words or voice tone seem different from what you expected? Did they seem to respond to your comments in a way that shows confusion, frustration, or irritation because of what you said or how you said it? If you answer yes to these questions, and this occurs several times on the recording, go back to the people involved in the conversation and ask them to help you interpret what you heard. You may find that your communication style is doing more to hurt than help in gathering information and building relationships with others.

Customer Service Success Tip

When the telephone rings, mentally "shift gears" before answering. Stop doing other tasks, clear your head of other thoughts, focus on the telephone, then cheerfully and professionally answer the call. While on the phone, avoid distractions such as reading information or performing tasks on your computer or electronic devices.

Use Customer-Centric Language

A mistake by many service providers is to communicate as if they are the important element of a transaction. In reality, the customer is the one upon whom a message should be focused. The following examples show the difference in focus:

Provider-Centered Approach

- As soon as I have time, I will . . .
- I will send out a form that we need you to complete and sign.
- Let me explain the benefits of this product.

Customer-Centered Approach

- I will take care of that right away.
- To make sure that we have all the information needed to ensure you the best service, once you get the form, please complete and sign it.
- As a perceptive consumer, you will appreciate the benefits of this product. May I explain?

Another important thing to remember in communicating with customers is to use easily understood words or communication style, especially when interacting with those who speak a primary language other than your own. This does not mean you have to "dummy down" your speech or appear to talk down to someone. Instead, it means that you watch your customer's nonverbal body language for signs of confusion or frustration as you speak, and frequently ask for feedback and questions. This also applies when you are selling or servicing a customer in a technical area where they might not have your level of knowledge or expertise and do not recognize the terminology you might use to describe something.

If you are on the telephone, listen for sounds of confusion or pauses that may indicate that the customer either did not understand something you said or has a question.

Here is an example of how your customer might feel if you use language with which they unfamiliar:

> *Many interpersonal impartation decompositions can be ascribed to one singular customer service professional fallacy—that all customers can discern the significance of the service provider's vernacular.*

How did that statement feel to you? Remember that feeling the next time you are tempted to communicate inappropriately with customers.

Simply stated, what you read means: *Many customer service professionals fail to use language their customers can understand.*

Customer Service Success Tip

Technology has increased the options and speed at which you can communicate with your customers. Even so, there is still a need to stay personally connected with them. There is no substitution for face-to-face or telephone contact. This format allows you to "read" their tone of voice and body language, which you cannot do via other means.

Chances are that you really cannot overcommunicate with your customer, especially when problems exist. It is important that you stay in touch with customers periodically to stay in the forefront of their memory and to demonstrate that you value them. The key is to read their reactions to your efforts and, in those instances when someone might want less contact, act accordingly.

Use "Small Talk"

Look for opportunities to communicate on a personal level or to compliment your customer. If you promptly establish a professional relationship with your customers, they are less likely to attack you verbally or complain. Listen to what they say. Look for specific things that you have in common. For example, suppose your customer mentions that she has just returned from Altoona, Pennsylvania, where she visited relatives. If you grew up in or near Altoona, comment about this and ask questions. By bonding with the customer, you show that you recognize the customer as more than a nameless face or a prospective sale.

One thing to keep in mind about **small talk** is that you must listen to your customer's words and tone. If it is obvious that he or she is impatient or in a hurry, skip the small talk and focus on efficiently providing service.

small talk Dialogue used to enhance relationships, show civility, and build rapport.

Use Positive "I" or "We" Messages

In addition to avoiding the "you" statements that you will read about later in this chapter, focus on what "I" or "we" can do for or with the customer. In addressing the customer, state the specific service approaches you will take; for example, "I'll handle

"I" or "we" messages Communication that is potentially less offensive than the word "you," which is like nonverbal finger-pointing when emotions are high.

this personally," as opposed to "I'll do my best" or "I'll try." Expressions like "I'll handle this personally" sound proactive and positive. **"I" or "we" messages** go a long way in subtly letting the customer know that you have the knowledge, confidence, and authority to help out.

Ask Positively Phrased Questions

Sometimes the simplest things can cause problems, especially if someone is already irritated. To avoid creating a negative situation or escalating customer emotions when things are already amiss, choose the wording of your questions carefully. Consider these two specific techniques.

The first technique is to find a way to rephrase any question that you would normally start with "Why?" The reason is that this word cannot be inflected in a way that does not come across as potentially abrasive, intrusive, or meddlesome. Do not believe it? Get a recording device and attempt to say the word "why" without an inflection that sounds challenging or questioning.

As with many experiences you have, the origin of negative feelings toward the word likely stem from childhood. Do you remember when you wanted to do something as a child and were told no? The word that probably came out of your mouth (in a whiney voice) was "Why?" This was a verbal challenge to the person who was telling you that you could not do something. The response you probably heard was, "Because I said so" or "Because I am the mommy (or daddy); that is why." Most likely, you did not like that type of response then, and neither did your customers when they were children. The result of this early experience is that when we hear the word "*why*" as a question, it can sound like a challenge and can prompt a negative emotional reaction (blame a flashback to memories for this). To prevent this from occurring, try rewording your "Why" question or asking questions that might not be perceived as arrogant, rude, or directive.

Figure 3.4 offers some alternative ways to ask "why" questions.

The second technique to consider regarding question phrasing is to ask ones that do not create or add to a negative impression. This is especially important if you have a

Look for ways to create a positive message exchange between you and your customer. *What are potential outcomes when a service provider communicates a "can-do" attitude with a customer?*

© Terry Vine/Getty Images RF

FIGURE 3.4
Alternatives to "Why"
Questions

Instead of	Try
Why do you feel that way?	What makes you feel that way?
Why do you not like . . .?	What is it that you do not like about . . .?
Why do you need that feature?	How is that feature going to be beneficial to you?
Why do you want that color?	What other colors have you considered?

FIGURE 3.5
Alternative Questioning
Strategies

Instead of	Try
Why?	What prevents . . .? or Could you please provide an alternative suggestion to _____?
Do you not think . . .?	What do you think . . .?
Would this not work as well?	How do you think this would work?
Could we not do . . .instead?	Could we try . . .instead?
Are you not going to make a deposit?	What amount would you like to deposit?
Do you not have two pennies?	Do you have two pennies?
Should you not try this for a week before we replace the part again?	How do you feel about trying it for a week to see how it works before we replace the part again?

customer who is already saying negative things about you, your product, service, or the company. By asking questions that start with a negative word and trying to lead customers to an answer, you can be subtly adding fuel to an emotional fire.

For example, suppose your customer is upset because he ordered window blinds through the mail and did not get the color he wanted. He has called you to complain. You have asked a few questions to determine the color scheme of the room in which he will install the blinds. You say, "Based on what you have told me, do you not think the color you received would work just as well?" Your customer now launches into a tirade. He probably thinks that you were not listening to him, were not concerned about his needs, and presumed you could lead him to another decision.

Figure 3.5 offers some more examples of questions that could cause communication breakdowns, along with some suggested alternatives.

Be Specific

Whenever you have to answer questions, especially details relating to costs, delivery dates, warranties, and other important areas of customer interest, give complete and accurate details. If you believe that something is not important and leave that information out, you can bet that the customer may feel it was important and will be upset.

Examples

If deliveries are free, but only within a 50-mile radius, make sure that you tell the customer about the mileage policy. (The customer may live 51 miles away!)

Trending NOW

Many organizations are offering in-store pickup for items ordered online. Customers are using this service to expedite delivery and save shipping costs. In addition, to fight back against Amazon and other online dealers, brick-and-mortar retailers like Target, Walmart, Toys "R" Us, Home Depot, Staples, and others are offering price-matching guarantees to attract customers back into stores and offline to do their shopping.

If a customer calls to ask for the price of an item and your quote does not include tax, shipping, and handling, say so. Give the total cost so that there are no surprises when the customer drives to the store to make the purchase or orders from your website and ends up paying more.

Listen Carefully and Respond Appropriately

Active listening is a key element of two-way verbal communication. The manner in which you listen and respond often determines the direction of the conversation. When customers feel that they are not being listened to, their attitude and emotions can quickly change from amiable to confrontational.

One technique to ensure that you have received your customer's message correctly is to use a technique called paraphrasing, which you read about earlier in this chapter. To ensure that you got the message that your customer intended to communicate, take time to ask him or her for feedback. Do this by repeating to the customer the message you thought you heard, but in your own words—paraphrase. As an example of this technique, assume that a customer called to complain that a toy that she had purchased for her grandson was defective and missing parts. She went on to describe how she has been a loyal customer of the store since her children were small and that while she normally has no complaints about products and services she receives, she is disappointed by this defective toy. In response, you should thank her for her continued business and personalize by commenting on the length of her patronage. Next, you should paraphrase what you heard by saying something like, "Mrs. Hawthorne, I apologize for the inconvenience that this has caused you. I know that you must be very frustrated. If I understand the issue correctly, you bought this item on June 28 as a present for your grandson and when he tried to assemble it, two parts were missing; is that correct?" Once she confirms, apologize again, assure her that you can help resolve the issue and pursue questions to find out if she would like to exchange the item, just get the missing parts, or return it for a refund.

NURTURE A CONTINUING RELATIONSHIP

The final element of the PLAN model deals with how well you close a transaction, encourage your customers to return, and have them say positive things about their experience.

In order to maintain an ongoing business relationship with customers, each person in the organization has to take responsibility for leaving a positive impression on those with whom they come into contact. As a service provider, it is not enough to just do your job. You also have to cement the transaction and relationship by demonstrating such traits as credibility, trustworthiness, conscientiousness, and other characteristics that many customers expect from a service professional. The following are some easy-to-apply strategies that might help you accomplish this and encourage customers to return and spread positive word-of-mouth publicity about you and your organization.

Ask Permission

Get customer approval before taking action that was not previously approved or discussed, such as putting a telephone caller on hold or interrupting. By doing so, you raise the customers to a position of authority, boost their self-esteem, and empower them (to say yes or no). They will likely appreciate all three.

Agree with Customers

Like most other people, customers like to hear that they are right. This is especially true when a mistake has been made or something goes wrong. When a customer has a complaint or is upset because a product and/or service does not live up to expectations, acknowledge the emotion he or she is feeling and then move on and help resolve the issue. Defusing by acknowledgment is a powerful tool.

However, listen carefully for the level of emotion. If the customer is very angry, you may want to choose your words carefully. For example, suppose you have a customer who has called or returned to your store on four occasions to address a single problem with a product. Because of this, she has been inconvenienced; not gotten satisfaction in the previous encounters; and spent extra time, effort, and money (on gas) in an effort to correct the problem. When she calls or arrives, her voice tone and volume are elevated and she is demanding that you get a supervisor. In this situation, your best approach probably is to let her vent and describe the problem without interrupting, apologize as often as appropriate, and do everything you can to resolve the issue fairly (assuming that she has a legitimate complaint). You would not want to use a statement that could further enflame her.

Although phrases such as "You sound upset Ms. O'Malley" or "I can understand how you feel" can help diffuse some tense situations, they can come across as patronizing and insincere when someone is really angry (such as in the above example). Instead of using such terminology, try looking for something she is saying that you can agree with. Also, remember that when customers get angry, raise their voices, and say certain things, they are not typically angry with you—they are frustrated and angry at the organization and/or system. Try not to become defensive or sound irritated, since this will likely only escalate the customer's emotions.

For example, suppose Ms. O'Malley says something like, "You people are a bunch of idiots. I have been doing business with this company for years and I always have problems. Why do you not hire someone with brains to serve your customers?" A normal human response to such language would be to become defensive or to possibly retaliate. However, think back on what happened when you were a child at the playground and similar situations occurred. When someone pushed you or called you a name and you responded with name-calling or pushed back, emotions escalated until someone either struck out at the other person or ran away crying. No one won. The relationship was damaged, possibly irreparably.

In the case of Ms. O'Malley, if you strike back with language similar to hers, neither of you will win. Moreover, you will likely lose a valued customer who will tell her story to many friends—and you will have to explain to your boss why you acted in that manner. Instead, try a defusing technique in which you seek something upon which you both can agree. For example, you might reply, "I know this is frustrating, especially when it seems we have not done a good job solving your problem. I sincerely apologize for all of your inconvenience." After this, assuming she does not launch back in with another tirade, you might then offer, "Let me help you take care of this right now." If she does verbally attack again, let her vent and then try another calm agreement response, followed by another apology and a second offer to assist or to seek the help of a supervisor, if appropriate. The key is to remain professional and in control of your emotions so that you can find a suitable resolution to the issue.

The value in this approach is that in letting Ms. O'Malley vent, you are discovering her emotions and possibly the history of the problem by listening actively. If you need more information, you can ask questions once you have defused her emotions and she calms down a bit. Typically, if you remain calm and objective and look for minor things with which you can agree, the customer will back off or become more rational. Also, the customer may likely start to see that she is the one out of control and that you are being professional while trying to help her. If the customer truly wants the problem to be resolved, she soon realizes that cooperation with you is necessary.

In many cases, if you resolve the customer's problem professionally, he or she will often apologize for his or her actions and words once the emotion of the moment passes.

Elicit Customer Feedback and Participation

rapport The silent bond built between two people as a result of sharing common interests and issues and demonstrating a win-win, I care attitude.

Make customers feel as if they are a part of the conversation by asking questions. Ask opinions, find out how they feel about what you are doing or saying, and get them involved by building **rapport** through ongoing dialogue. Acknowledge their ideas, suggestions, or information with statements such as, "That's a good idea (or suggestion or decision)." This will foster a feeling that the two of you are working together to solve a problem while putting the customer in psychological control of the situation. The beauty of such an approach is that if the customer comes up with an idea and you follow through on it, he or she often feels a sense of ownership and is less likely to complain later or feel bad if things do not work out as planned.

Close the Transaction Professionally

Instead of some parroted response used for each customer like, "Have a nice day," offer a sincere "Thank you for shopping/calling. . ." and encourage the customer to return in the future. Remember, part of a service culture is building customer loyalty.

Customer Service Success Tip

The techniques and strategies discussed in this chapter are important in nonretail environments as well; for example, a library, dentist's office, nonprofit organization, military, or government agency. Think of similar language that you could use in those environments if you work in one so that you are prepared to effectively deal with customers.

KNOWLEDGE CHECK

1. For what does the PLAN acronym stand?
2. How can you plan for positive customer interactions?
3. What strategies can you use to let customers know they are important?
4. What can be done to positively address customer expectations?
5. How can you continue to nurture customer relationships?

LO 3-4 Providing Feedback Effectively

`CONCEPT`   **Your feedback could affect the relationship you have or are building with your customers. The effect may be positive or negative, depending on the content and delivery.**

Feedback is a response to messages a listener receives. This response may be transmitted verbally (with words) or nonverbally (through actions or inaction). Depending on the content and delivery, your feedback could positively or negatively influence your relationships with your customers. Figure 3.6 offers some tips on providing feedback effectively; the two types of feedback are discussed in the following sections.

FIGURE 3.6
Guidelines for Providing Positive Feedback

Here are 10 tips for effectively providing feedback:

1. When appropriate, give feedback immediately when communicating face-to-face or over the telephone.
2. Communicate in a clear, concise manner.
3. Remain objective and unemotional when providing feedback.
4. Make sure that your feedback is accurate before you provide it.
5. Use verbal and nonverbal messages that are in congruence (agree with each other).
6. Verify your customer's meaning before providing feedback.
7. Make sure that your feedback is appropriate to the customer's original message (active listening helps in getting the original message).
8. Strive to clarify feedback when the customer seems unclear of your intention.
9. Avoid overly critical feedback or negative language (as described in this chapter).
10. Do not provide feedback if it could damage the customer–provider relationship.

WORK IT OUT 3.4

Feeling Special

Think of times when you have been put on hold or stood in a line.

1. How did the service provider address you when it was your turn for service?
2. Did you feel special or did you feel like the next in a long line of bodies being processed? Why?
3. When the service provider simply picked up the phone and offered to assist you or shouted, "Next," while you waited in line, what thoughts went through your mind about the provider and the organization?
4. What could service providers do or say to eliminate negative customer feelings in such situations?

Trending NOW

With the expansion of globalization come millions of people shifting to new geographic locations throughout the world. This means that the likelihood of you encountering someone who is from another country or culture is high. This is a good reason for you to take the time to do some research on various countries and cultural groups related to backgrounds, values, customers, and other facets of daily life and to also consider learning another language. In addition, learn about communication differences and how values and beliefs affect interpersonal communication in different areas of the world.

acronym Words formed by the initial letters of other words and pronounced as a word, such as NASA (National Aeronautics and Space Administration).

verbal feedback Letting both senders and receivers of messages know that a message was correctly received by giving an appropriate response.

nonverbal feedback Messages sent to someone through other than spoken means. Examples are gestures, appearance, and facial expressions.

VERBAL FEEDBACK

The words you choose when providing feedback to your customers are crucial to interpretation and understanding of a message. Before providing feedback, you should take into consideration the knowledge and skill level of your customer(s). This is part of the "encoding" discussed earlier in the interpersonal communication model. Failure to consider the customer could result in comprehension breakdowns. For example, if you choose words that are not likely to be part of your customer's vocabulary because of the customer's education and/or experience, your message may be confusing. In addition, if you use **acronyms** or technical terms (jargon or words unfamiliar to the customer), the meaning of the message could get lost. When providing **verbal feedback**, you should also be conscious of how your customer is receiving your information. If the customer's body language or nonverbal cues (gestures, facial expressions) or words indicate misunderstanding, you should pause and take any corrective action necessary to clear up the confusion.

NONVERBAL FEEDBACK

Nonverbal feedback can be more powerful than the spoken or written word because it is often subject to interpretation based on the customer's background, culture, gender, age, and many other factors. Depending on the way that you sit, stand, move, gesture, make or fail to make eye contact, speak, or even the amount of time you allocate to a customer, you can either send unintended messages or reinforce positive verbal communication. Other factors related to you such as the appearance of your work area, clothing, jewelry, body art, hairstyle, or makeup can send powerful messages.

Manage Body Language

The ways in which you sit, stand, gesture, position your body (face-to-face or at an angle), or use facial expressions can all send positive or negative messages. Think about times when someone has looked at you and you responded with, "What are you looking at?" This is likely because something about his or her glance sent a message that triggered something in your brain that either caused alarm or raised your concern. This is why you should consciously think about your nonverbal cues when interacting with customers.

Use Eye Contact Effectively

In addition to greeting the customer, make regular eye contact (normally no longer than three to five seconds at a time) and assume a positive approachable posture throughout your interaction with a customer. Also, be careful about giving customers the "evil eye" or showing your displeasure with them through your eyes when emotions are high or you are struggling with a difficult situation.

Use Positive Facial Expressions

Over the years, various sources have reported that it takes more muscles to frown than to smile. With that in mind, spend more time (and less facial energy) projecting a pleasant, positive image with your face, rather than one that might send a negative message to your customers. Since customer service is about building relationships with consumers, you must be conscious of the power of your facial expressions. This is because people generally prefer to be around someone who is happy rather than unhappy. Smile often, even if you are having a bad day. The bottom line is that your customers really do not care what kind of day you are having. They do care about how you communicate with and treat them.

Customer Service Success Tip

To check your perception of nonverbal cues received from others so that you can respond appropriately, use the following process:

1. Identify the behavior observed.

Example: "Ms. Shelton, when I said that it would be seven to ten days before we could get your new sofa delivered to your home, your facial expression changed to what appeared to be one of concern."

2. Offer one or two interpretations.

Example: "I wasn't sure whether you were indicating that the time frame doesn't work for you, or whether something else went through your mind."

3. Ask for clarification.

Example: "Which was it?"

By asking for clarification, you reduce the chance of causing customer dissatisfaction. You also send a message that you are paying attention to the customer.

KNOWLEDGE CHECK

1. In what ways can you positively provide verbal feedback?

2. What strategies can you use to communicate with your customers nonverbally?

LO 3-5 Avoiding Negative Communication

CONCEPT **Use positive words or phrases, rather than emphasizing the negative.**

You can squelch customer loyalty and raise customer frustration in a number of ways when communicating. Your choice of words or phrasing can often lead either to satisfaction or to confrontation, or it can destroy a customer–provider relationship. Customers do not want to hear what you cannot do; they want to hear how you are going to help satisfy their needs or expectations. Focus your message on how you can work with the customer to accomplish needs satisfaction. Do not use vague or weak terminology. Instead of "I am not sure . . ." or "I will try . . . ," say, "Let me get that answer for you . . ." or "I can do. . . ."

A good metaphor for avoiding negative communication is the old adage of "see no evil; hear no evil; speak no evil." *What are possible outcomes if you apply this concept with your customers?*

©Stockbroker xtra/AGE Fotostock RF

global terms Potentially inflammatory words or phrases used in conversation. They tend to inappropriately generalize behavior or group people or incidents together (e.g., always, never, everyone, everything, all the time).

Another pitfall to watch out for is the use of **global terms** (all-encompassing or inclusive expressions such as *always*, *never*, *everyone*, *all*). If your customer can give just one example for which your statement is not true, your credibility comes into question and you might go on the defensive. Suppose you say, "We always return calls within four hours," yet the customer has personally experienced a situation when that did not happen. Your statement is now false. Instead, phrase statements to indicate possible variances such as, "We attempt to return all calls within four hours" or "Our objective is to return calls within four hours." Be careful, too, about "verbal finger-pointing," especially if your customer is already upset. This tactic involves the use of the word *you*, as in, "*You* were supposed to call back to remind me" or "*You* didn't follow the directions I gave you." This is like pointing your finger at someone or using a patronizing tone to belittle him or her. People are likely to react powerfully and negatively to this type of treatment. See Figure 3.7 for a list of words and phrases that can damage relationships.

FIGURE 3.7

Words and Phrases That Damage Customer Relationships

Here are some words and phrases that can lead to trouble with your customers. Avoid or limit their use.

You don't understand.	You aren't listening to me.
You'll have to . . .	Listen to me.
You don't see my point.	I never said . . .
Hold on (or hang on) a second.	In my opinion . . .
I (we, you) can't . . .	What's your problem?
Our policy says (or prohibits) . . .	The word *problem*.
That's not my job (or responsibility).	Do you understand?
You're not being reasonable.	Are you aware . . .?
You must (or should) . . .	The word *no*.
The word *but*.	Global terms (always, never, nobody, every time).
What you need to do is . . .	Endearment terms (honey, sweetie, sugar, baby).
Why don't you . . .?	Profanity or vulgarity.
I don't know.	Technical or industry-specific jargon.
You're wrong or mistaken.	

⚙ WORK IT OUT 3.5

Perceptions Are Reality

To emphasize that different people often have different perceptions of what they see, and the importance of appearance, look at the photographs of the people below. Each one of the individuals in these photos will come into your workspace today for service and you will have to interact with them. Number a sheet of paper 1-8 and honestly describe your reactions to and perceptions of the people shown. From a service provider perspective, answer all three questions below about the people in each photo. Once finished, compare your responses to those of fellow students.

1. What are your perceptions about this person?
2. Explain why you have these perceptions.
3. How might your perception affect your ability to effectively serve this person?
4. If you had a child would you want them dating this person or someone who looks like him or her? Explain why or why not.

©wavebreakmedia/Shutterstock.com RF

©wrangler/Shutterstock.com RF

©Rommel Canlas/Shutterstock.com RF

©VGstockstudio/Shutterstock.com RF

©Jelena Aloskina/Shutterstock.com RF

©George Doyle/Getty Images RF

©Don Tremain/Getty Images RF

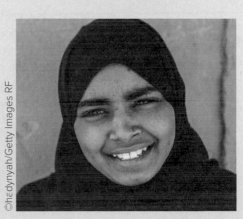
©hadynyah/Getty Images RF

KNOWLEDGE CHECK

1. What are global terms and why should you avoid them?

Customer Service Success Tip

When communicating with customers who speak a primary language other than English, you should avoid using contractions (e.g., can't, won't, or shouldn't) since they may not understand those.

LO 3-6 Dealing Assertively with Customers

CONCEPT Express ideas simply without weakening your position.

assertiveness Involves projecting a presence that is assured, confident, and capable without seeming to be aggressive or arrogant.

Assertiveness is a learned skill. Your **assertiveness** level relates directly to behavioral style preferences and culture. Some people are direct and to the point; others are calm and laid back or come across as being passive or nonassertive. Neither style is better or worse than the other one. The most important thing is your ability to recognize which style to call upon in various situations.

There are going to be times when you and your external customers, coworkers, or supervisors disagree. This is normal when humans interact. In these instances, remember that you need to maintain the relationship and, if necessary, simply agree to disagree and negotiate a solution that both parties can live with. The goal of assertive communication is to disagree, express dissatisfaction, or state your opinion in a manner that does not create a breakdown in the relationship.

Communicating assertively involves elements of self-respect and respect for others. Generally, assertive communication deals with expressing ideas positively and with confidence. An example would be for someone in a Western work environment to stand or sit erect, make direct eye contact, smile, listen empathetically, and then calmly and firmly nod and explain what he or she can do to assist the customer. This approach is sometimes a challenge for people entering a new culture or dealing with a different gender or someone on a higher social, economic, or business level. In such instances because of differing beliefs or because they do not want to potentially offend, some people tend to be less assertive in sharing ideas, giving feedback, or asking questions that may seem to challenge or discredit what someone else has said. The key to being effective, if you are from a different culture and find yourself in such situations, is to listen effectively and to give carefully thought-out candid responses. Planning ahead by researching the cultures, genders, and other diversity factors related to customers with whom you interact can better prepare you for such inevitable contacts. In this diverse world, it is not a question of if, but when, you will meet someone with different values.

Figure 3.8 lists several examples of nonassertive and assertive language and behaviors. Additional resources are listed in the Bibliography.

FIGURE 3.8
Nonassertive and Assertive
Behaviors

The following list contains examples of nonassertive and assertive language and behaviors, along with tips for increasing your assertiveness. Keep in mind that some of the behaviors in both columns are potentially indicative of cultural or gender values and have been learned.

Nonassertive	Assertive
• Poor eye contact while speaking	• Look customer in the eye as you speak (depending on the cultural background of the other person).
• Weak ("limp fish") handshake	• Grasp firmly without crushing (web of your hand against web of the other person's hand).
• Use of verbal paralanguage (ah, um, you know)	• Stop, gather thoughts, speak.
• Apologetic in words and tone	• Apologize if you make a mistake (I am sorry, please forgive me), and then take control and move on with the conversation.
• Soft, subdued tone	• Increase volume; sound firm and convincing.
• Finger-pointing; blaming others	• Take responsibility; resolve the problem.
• Nervous gestures, fidgeting	• Hold something; grasp a table or chair; fold your hands as you talk.
• Indecisive or unsure	• Know your products and services. If possible, prepare a list of points, comments, or questions before calling or meeting with your customer(s).
• Rambling speech, not really stating a specific question or information.	• Think, plan, and then speak a specific question or information.

KNOWLEDGE CHECK

1. What is the goal of assertive communication?

WORK IT OUT 3.6

Standing Up Assertively

To stress the need to speak up assertively when others take advantage of you.
The following are examples of customer situations that you might encounter and a possible means of assertively addressing them.

Scenario 1

An irate customer calls you and starts ranting, yelling, and swearing and will not let you speak. What action would you take?

(continued)

> ⚙ **3.6 (Continued)**
>
> **Scenario 2**
>
> You depend on a coworker to provide data for a report that you must complete by the end of the month. Even though you have asked for and been promised it several times, the report is due tomorrow morning and you still do not have the information. What should you do?
>
> **Scenario 3**
>
> Your coworker just stopped by your desk and asked if you can work late to cover for her because she has to leave early to pick up her son from daycare. You have promised your own son that you would take him shopping after work to get materials he needs for a school project that is due tomorrow. How will you handle this situation?

LO 3-7 Assertive versus Aggressive Service

CONCEPT   Assertive service is good for solving problems; aggressive service may escalate them.

Because of their personal background, some customer service representatives have trouble identifying the difference between assertive and aggressive behavior. The following are some indicators along with some strategies for delivering positive assertive behavior.

Assertive behavior sustains customer relationships while aggressive behavior can destroy them. Your goal should be to achieve an assertive "you win and I win" solution where both you and the customer retain respect for one another and both parties gain something from the compromise.

Do not confuse assertive with aggressive service. Why is the distinction so important in customer service? What is the difference? The answer: Assertiveness can assist in solving problems; aggression can escalate and cause relationship breakdowns. Asserting yourself means that you project an image of confidence, are self-assured, and state what you believe to be true in a self-confident manner. Some ways in which assertiveness might be demonstrated when dealing with customers include the following:

- Interact in a mature manner with customers who may be offensive, defensive, aggressive, hostile, blaming, attacking, or otherwise unreceptive to what you are trying to explain to them. Do not become defensive or confrontational.

- Use appropriate eye contact. Make positive eye contact as you speak. In Western cultures, this behavior typically demonstrates truthfulness, confidence, and friendliness. Maintain intermittent eye contact as you smile. Avoid squinting or glaring.

- Listen openly and use affirmative acknowledgments of what the customer is saying (e.g., "I understand what you are saying" or "Uh huh").

- Use an open body posture if you are face-to-face (e.g., uncross your arms and keep hands off your hips). Stand or sit erectly, but not rigidly. Occasionally lean forward to emphasize key points. Use open gestures with arms and hands. Gesture with open palms, as opposed to pointing.

- Avoid blaming or judging your customer. Simply give your views or explain what you can do to help remedy the situation. Express your feelings when it is appropriate, after you have allowed your customer to vent or state her issue or provide feedback.

- Use "I" statements, where you let customers know how you feel about the situation or something the customer said. Acknowledge that your message comes from your frame of reference and your perceptions ("I feel that this situation is the result of . . ." or "In my opinion, the issue has been caused by . . ." You can also demonstrate ownership of a situation with statements such as, "I not agree with what I just heard you say" (as compared to "You are wrong"). Blaming statements, such as the latter, or "you" statements are like verbal finger-pointing and can irritate and escalate emotions. This will likely foster resentment and resistance rather than understanding and cooperation.

- Ask for feedback and then listen carefully to the other person. For example, "Am I being clear?" "Does that make sense?" or "How do you see this situation?" Asking for feedback can indicate that you are open to dialogue and invite the customer's views or thoughts rather than trying to control the situation or conversation. Through discussion, you can correct any misperceptions either of you have.

- Learn to say no to unreasonable requests in a confident, yet nonthreatening manner. Use the word "no" and offer an explanation if you choose to.

- When appropriate, paraphrase the customer's point of view. This will let him know that you hear and understand his point or request.

©wavebreakmedia/Shutterstock.com RF

Aggressive behavior with customers will almost always end up with negative results. *What can you do as a service provider to ensure that interactions with others do not escalate into confrontational situations?*

- You do not have to say, "I am sorry" every time anything goes wrong. Of course, if something occurred and it was your fault, you should apologize and try to make it right immediately. Many women sometimes tend to put themselves down by saying things like "I am only a doing my job" or "I just work here." There is no need to apologize to customers for what some view as a job that lacks stature. Everything you do has an importance of its own. Without you, customers would not be able to transact their business effectively with your organization.

- Strive for win-win solutions. Work toward mutual understanding and the attainment of resolutions that allow the organization and the customer to succeed. Try to identify a "win-win" solution in handling customer problems or service breakdowns. Some service providers take a "you win and I lose" passive approach where they give up things unnecessarily to appease the customer without first attempting to negotiate an acceptable alternative. The "you lose and I lose" solution is a total passive solution where both you and the customer give up. In this instance, the customer goes away and you lose business for your organization. On the other hand, a "you lose and I win" solution is an aggressive solution where you ignore the customer's needs in order to get your way.

Aggression involves hostile or offensive behavior. Aggressive behavior often manifests itself in the form of either a verbal or physical attack. Aggressive people send messages verbally and nonverbally that imply that they are superior, want to dominate, or are in charge. They often do this through behavior and language that is manipulative, judgmental, or domineering. An assertive person states (verbally and nonverbally), "Here is my position. What is your reaction to that?" An aggressive person sends the message, "Here is my position. Take it or leave it."

Aggressive behavior can lead to relationship failure. When someone verbally attacks another, the chances of emotions escalating and relationships failing increase significantly. Another possibility in a stressed-out world is that violence could result in response to aggressive behavior.

Obviously, the two modes of dealing with customers create very different service experiences. The manner in which you nonverbally or verbally approach, address, and interact with customers may label you as either assertive or aggressive. Consider the following interactions between a customer and a service provider:

Assertive Behavior Example

Customer (returning an item of merchandise): Excuse me; I received this sweater as a present and I would like to return it.

Service Provider (smiling): Is there something wrong with it?

Customer (still smiling): Oh no. I just do not need another sweater.

Service Provider (still smiling): Do you have a receipt?

Customer (not smiling): No. As I said, it was a gift.

Service Provider (handing over a form): That is all right. To help me process your refund a bit faster for you, could you please provide a bit of information and sign this form?

Customer (not smiling): Does this mean I have to get out of line and then wait again? I have already been in line for 10 minutes.

Service Provider (smiling): Well, rather than delay the line, if you could step over to that table to fill out the form, and then bring it back to me, I will take care of you. You will not have to wait in line again.

Customer (smiling): Okay, thanks.

In this example, the service provider is trying to assure the customer through words that he or she is there to assist the customer.

Aggressive Service Example

Customer (returning an item of merchandise): Excuse me, I received this sweater as a present and I would like to return it.

Service Provider (not smiling): What is wrong with it?

Customer (smiling): Oh nothing, I just do not need another sweater.

Service Provider (still not smiling): Do you have a receipt?

Customer (not smiling): No. As I said, it was a gift.

Service Provider (handing over a form): Well, our policy requires that you will have to fill out this form since you don't have a receipt.

Customer (not smiling): Does that mean I have to get out of line and then wait again? I have already been in line for 10 minutes.

Service Provider (not smiling and looking to the next customer in line): The line is getting shorter. It should not take long. Next . . . .

In this example, the service provider is not doing well on service delivery, nor is he or she projecting a positive image. The verbal messages convey an almost hostile attitude. This type of behavior can easily escalate into an unnecessary confrontation.

WORK IT OUT 3.7

Improving Feedback Skills

To strengthen your ability to provide feedback, work with two other people (one partner and one observer) to practice your skill in delivering feedback.

Select a topic for discussion (e.g., a vacation, career goals, or positive or negative customer experiences).

Spend five minutes talking about your selected topic with your partner.

During the conversation, you and your partner should use verbal and nonverbal feedback.

At the end of the five minutes, ask your partner, and then the observer, the following questions.

1. How did I do in providing appropriate verbal feedback? Give examples.
2. How well did I interpret verbal and nonverbal messages? Give examples.
3. What questions did I ask to clarify comments or feedback provided? Give examples.
4. What could I have done to improve my feedback? Rotate roles until all three group participants have shared their vacation experience and practiced their feedback skills.

Ethical Dilemma 3.1

As a child, you were taught that it is always ethically and morally wrong to lie to someone (e.g. a customer), yet your supervisor tells you that it is okay to tell a little white lie (slight exaggeration) to explain a missed delivery.

1. How would you react to or feel about your supervisor's position?
2. Would this cause any change in your relationship with your supervisor? Why or why not?
3. Would you lie to your customer? Why or why not?

See end of chapter for possible answers.

Ethical Dilemma 3.2

Assume that you work in a government office. You observe a coworker taking a defensive stance following a situation in which he promised to send a copy of an official document that the customer requested. The customer never received it and has now come in person to get a copy.

When the customer approached your coworker and explained the situation, the coworker responded, "Well, I specifically remember sending that out after we spoke; according to our records, we sent you a copy two weeks ago. I do not know why you did not get it, but our policy is that we charge 25 cents per page for any additional copies." The coworker offers no additional explanation or assistance to resolve the issue and then excuses herself to go take a phone call.

You are not currently servicing a customer.

1. Would you intervene? Why or why not?
2. If you decide to intervene, what would you say or do? Why?

See end of chapter for possible answers.

Small Business Perspective

The ability to communicate with customers is paramount to any organization's success, but especially to smaller organizations. According to the U.S. Small Business Administration:

- The 28 million small businesses in America account for 54% of all U.S. sales.
- Small businesses provide 55% of all jobs and 66% of all net new jobs since the 1970s.
- The 600,000 plus franchised small businesses in the U.S. account for 40% of all retail sales and provide jobs for some 8 million people.
- The small business sector in America occupies 30–50% of all commercial space, an estimated 20-34 billion square feet.

Furthermore, the small business sector is growing rapidly. While corporate America has been "downsizing," the rate of small business "start-ups" has grown, and the rate for small business failures has declined.

- The number of small businesses in the United States has increased 49% since 1982.
- Since 1990, as big business eliminated 4 million jobs, small businesses added 8 million new jobs.[2]

Often these companies are sole-proprietor operations in which the owner is a consultant or operates a business from home and hires students and/or part-time employees or contracts with other independent businesspeople to provide service to customers. Many of these small businesspeople have multiple ventures going, such as teaching at universities, writing, subcontracting to other organizations, or operating online retail operations, in order to generate income and provide health care to support their families. Their success and ability to generate new clients or make sales are dependent on their communication skills.

Typically, if you should work for such a company, you will have to already possess excellent communication and service skills when you are hired since your employer will provide little or no training. Your employer will depend on you to represent the company in a professional manner and to effectively relate to current and potential customers. Problem solving, negotiation, analytical, and interpersonal knowledge and skills will be your primary tools for success.

Impact on Service

Based on personal experience and what you just read, answer the following questions:

1. Have you or anyone you know ever worked for a small company? If so, what were your experiences from a service standpoint?

2. What situations can you think of that would require excellent communication skills in a small company?

3. What has been your experience with employees of small businesses related to their communication skills? Explain.

Use SmartBook to help you read, study, and retain what you have learned. Access Smart-Book in your Instructor's Connect course, or go to connect.mheducation.com for help.

 SMARTBOOK™

Key Terms

acronym	global terms	pet peeves
assertiveness	"I" or "we" messages	rapport
channel	interpersonal skills	receiver
decoding	message	sender
encoding	noise	small talk
feedback	nonverbal feedback	two-way communication
filters	paraphrase	verbal feedback

Summary

Providing service that makes a customer feel special can lead to customer satisfaction and loyalty to you and your organization. By responding appropriately and in a positive manner verbally, you will increase your likelihood of success. When additional information is required, it is up to you to ask questions that will elicit useful customer feedback. You must then interpret and respond in kind with feedback that lets the customer know you received the intended message. You must also let your customers know that you will take action on their needs or requests. Never overpromise what you cannot deliver. When in doubt, offer to check on something and get back to the customer in a timely manner.

Review Questions

1. As a customer service professional, what are some things you can do to project a positive image to the customer?

2. What element(s) of the interpersonal communication model do you believe are the most important in a customer service environment? Explain.

3. What are some strategies to use to avoid words or phrases that will negatively affect your relationship with your customer?

4. What are some of the tips outlined in this chapter for ensuring effective customer interactions?

5. What is feedback?

6. How can verbal feedback affect customer encounters?

7. Give some examples of nonverbal feedback and explain how they complement the verbal message and how they can affect customer interactions.

8. List at least five tips for providing positive feedback.

Search It Out

Search the Web for Information on Verbal Communication

1. Search the Internet to research topics related to verbal communication, such as those presented in this chapter. Use various search engines (Yahoo, Google, Mozilla, and Excite) as your results will be different with each. Look for one or more of the following, print out pages you feel are helpful, and prepare to share your findings with your peers in class. Some possible topics follow:

   Assertiveness

   Communication with customers

   Conflict resolution

   Customer relationship management

   Customer retention

   Interpersonal communication

   Learning styles

   Nonverbal feedback

   Positive image

   Questioning

   Service recovery strategies

   Two-way communication

   Verbal feedback

2. For additional articles and information on verbal communication skills, visit the author's Customer Service Skills Blog at http://www.customerserviceskillsbook.com/wordpress and search "Verbal Communication Skills" and related communication topics. Also, visit https://www.youtube.com/results?search_query=verbal+communication+skills to search for related videos on verbal communication skills.

Collaborative Learning Activity

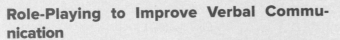

Role-Playing to Improve Verbal Communication

Find a partner (or two) and use the following role-plays to improve your verbal communication skills. After reading the scenarios, pick the two for which you want to practice and receive the most feedback. Next, take a moment to think about how each of you will play your part and then have a two- or three-minute dialogue centering on the situation. If possible, video or audio record the conversation. This will allow each of you to see or hear how you seem when you interact with others. After the role-play, discuss how each of you felt about the way the other person handled the situation. Each of you should ask the other these questions about your own performance:

   What did I do well?

   What did I not do so well?

   What can I do to improve in the future?

Scenario 1

You are a customer service professional in a dry cleaner's shop. A customer who has been coming in for years stops by with a silk shirt that has a stain that, according to him, was not there before the most recent dry cleaning. He is upset because the garment is expensive and he was going to wear it to a class reunion yesterday.

When playing the customer, do not become calmed or satisfied until the service provider offers what you believe is a realistic solution or compensation. As the service provider, try to avoid "giving away the store" by quickly offering to replace the shirt. Try to find other ways to appease and/or compensate the customer.

Scenario 2

You are a member services representative in an automobile club that provides maps, trip information, towing, travel services, and a variety of travel-related products. A member has stopped by to find out whether she can get a replacement membership card and assistance in planning an upcoming vacation.

Scenario 3

You are a counter clerk in a fast-food restaurant. It is lunchtime and the restaurant is full of patrons. As you are taking an order from a customer, a second customer steps to the front of the line, interrupts the first customer, and demands a replacement sandwich because the one she received is not what she ordered. As customer one, you should become indignant at the intrusion. As

customer two, you should be frustrated and express disappointment at having to waste your time to bring the sandwich back for replacement.

Scenario 4

As a clerk in a local electronic game rental store, you see many of the same patrons regularly and have a fairly good relationship with many of them. One of the regular customers has just come in to rent a game but is not sure what he wants. You must determine his needs and properly assist him. Be sure to ask probing, open-end questions, phrased positively, to help you get the information you need to provide service.

Verbal Communication Research on YouTube

Visit https://www.youtube.com/results?search_query=communi cating+verbally+with+customers to view various video segments on the topic of verbal communication skills. Take notes and be prepared to share at least five points that you learned about the topic with your classmates.

Face to Face

Seeking Information from a Client

Background

LKM Graphics has been in business in Norfolk, Virginia, for almost five years. The company employs 17 full-time employees in its graphic design department, a part-time administrative assistant, and three interns from Old Dominion University's graphic arts program. During a typical week, LKM prints 300,000 to 400,000 documents for businesses in the surrounding Tidewater metropolitan area. Most clients have 15 or fewer employees, although there are two active and ongoing government contracts with the Naval Operations Base, which is nearby. The owner of LKM, Linda McLaroy, hired you three years ago when you graduated from the graphic arts program. You are now one of the senior graphics account managers with the company and supervise four other team members.

Your Role

As a quality control measure, each month you are required to visit the clients assigned to your region. During those visits, you are to answer questions, deliver completed orders, verify customer satisfaction, collect feedback data, and look for new

orders. On a recent visit to Brickman's Bakery, you met the new office manager, Sylvia Greco. You had been told by a friend, who works at Brickman's, that Sylvia is considering closing her account with LKM Graphics and moving it to a competitor. Before joining Brickman's last month, she was employed by another organization in the area and had developed a strong relationship with your competitor. Since she is comfortable with the competitor's operation and has friends there, she wants to maintain the relationship. You have also heard through the grapevine that Sylvia prefers to work with your competitor's account representative.

Critical Thinking Questions

1. Since you do not have a relationship with Sylvia, what will you do to get off to a solid start during your visit?

2. How should you approach Sylvia verbally and nonverbally?

3. What strategies among the ones discussed in this chapter can you use to find out where you and LKM stand in Sylvia's mind?

4. What might you propose to Sylvia to try to change her mind if she indicates that she is planning to move the account?

Planning to Serve

Using the content of this chapter as a guide, create a personal action plan focused on improving your verbal communication skills when providing service to your customers. Begin by taking an objective assessment of your current verbal communication

strengths and areas for improvement. Once you have identified areas that need improvement, set goals for improvement.

Start your assessment by listing as many strengths and areas for improvement as you are aware of. Share your list with other people who know you well to see if they agree or can add items. Keep in mind that you will likely be more critical of yourself than will others. Additionally, you may be sending messages that you are not aware of because of the way you currently communicate. For those reasons, keep an open mind when considering their comments.

Once you have a list, choose two or three items that you think need the most work and can add the most value when interacting with others. List these items on a sheet of paper along with specific courses of action you will take for improvement, the name of someone you will enlist to provide feedback on your behavior, and a specific date by which you want to see improvement. When selecting a date, keep in mind that research shows that it takes on average 21 to 30 days to see behavioral change; therefore, set a date that is at least in this range.

Verbal Communication Strength	Areas for Improvement

Top Three Items	Who Will Help	Date for Change
1.		
2.		
3.		

Quick Preview Answers

1. F	3. F	5. T	7. F	9. F	11. T
2. T	4. T	6. F	8. F	10. F	12. F

Ethical Dilemma Summary

Ethical Dilemma 3.1 Possible Answers

1. How would you react to or feel about your supervisor's position?

   Depending on how you were reared and the values that were reinforced to you (e.g., personal from your parents and/or religious), the supervisor's stance might be a real demotivator for you and could lead to loss of respect or other feelings toward him or her. On the other hand, you may share his or her views and reason that you are not harming anything by creating an excuse for failure to deliver to the customer as promised and that he or she will never know the difference. The downside of such logic is that should the customer find out the truth, your credibility and that of the organization are at stake and could result in lost business (from the customer and anyone else he or she tells the story to).

2. Would this cause any change in your relationship with your supervisor? Why or why not?

   This is a personal decision that only you can make. In many cases, such behavior on the part of the supervisor could lead to suspicion (e.g., if he or she lies about this type of thing, what else might he or she lie about in the workplace).

It could also lead to loss of trust in the supervisor's ability to lead and manage effectively. Additionally, if others find out about what the supervisor said, morale and effectiveness within the organization could suffer. There is likely some value in the adage "honesty is the best policy."

Ethical Dilemma 3.2 Possible Answers

1. Would you intervene? Why or why not?

   This is a touchy situation because you do not want to usurp your coworker or make it appear that there are differing standards of service provided within the organization. At the same time, your organization's reputation for effectiveness, efficiency, and customer service are all at stake and all employees represent and influence that reputation.

   Since it seems that neither your organization nor the customer is at fault in this situation, you may want to intervene in order to deliver quality customer service and to prevent an emotional exchange between the customer and coworker.

   A possible solution is to take the coworker aside and quietly suggest that an exception might be in order since it appears that the customer did not receive the copy. Otherwise, why would he have taken time to come to the office personally for a copy? If employees are not empowered to waive the policy, escalate the situation to a supervisor. Another point you can share is that most people are not out to rip off the organization, especially to drive all the way back to the office when they could have just called.

2. If you decide to intervene, what would you say or do? Why?

You might say something like the following to the customer: "I'm sure my coworker is going to handle this, but since she had to step away, let me get your copy rather than keep you waiting and cause further inconvenience." By getting the copy, you have satisfied the customer, who has already waited two weeks and now had to make a trip to the office to get resolution of the issue. You have also potentially salvaged the organization's reputation and prevented any type of confrontation between the customer and your coworker.

Of course, you will likely now have to explain to your coworker why you intervened and gave a "free" copy. In that discussion, it is important to apologize if it seems that you intervened without being asked. Also, put your explanation in terms of how your efforts helped the coworker and sped up service to all customers, since the situation was resolved and the customer left satisfied without becoming emotional. Additionally, stress that it seemed that neither the organization nor the customer was at fault and that you felt it important to deliver a high quality of service to the customer.

Note: To prevent possible future repeats of this type of situation, you may want to bring it up globally (without naming your coworker or pointing fingers) in your next staff meeting. Try to get some guidance on handling similar situations in the future.

Nonverbal Communication Skills

"The most important thing in communication is hearing what isn't said."
— **Source: Peter F. Drucker**

©Roger Bamber/Alamy Stock Photo

LEARNING OUTCOMES

After completing this chapter, you will be able to:

4-1 Define nonverbal communication.

4-2 Recognize various nonverbal cues and their effect on customers.

4-3 Explain the effect that gender has on communication.

4-4 Describe the effect of culture on nonverbal communication.

4-5 Identify unproductive behaviors.

4-6 Use a variety of nonverbal communication strategies.

4-7 Demonstrate specific customer-focused nonverbal behavior.

Use SmartBook to help you read, study, and retain what you have learned. Access SmartBook in your Instructor's Connect course, or go to connect.mheducation.com for help. ☒ SMARTBOOK™

IN THE REAL WORLD (FINANCIAL SERVICES)—AMERICAN EXPRESS

Vision Statement: "We work hard every day to make American Express the World's most respected service brand."

Values:

Customer Commitment

We develop relationships that make a positive difference in our customers' lives.

Quality

We provide outstanding products and unsurpassed service that, together, deliver premium value to our customers.

Integrity

We uphold the highest standards of integrity in all of our actions.

Teamwork

We work together, across boundaries, to meet the needs of our customers and to help the company win.

Respect for People

We value our people, encourage their development, and reward their performance.

Good Citizenship

We are good citizens in the communities in which we live and work.

A Will to Win

We exhibit a strong will to win in the marketplace and in every aspect of our business.

Personal Accountability

We are personally accountable for delivering on our commitments.[1]

A statement in its 2015 Annual Report to investors sums up the company's service philosophy and success, "Our brand and its attributes—trust, security and service—are key assets of the Company. We continue to focus on our brand, and our products and services are evidence of our commitment to its attributes. Our brand has consistently been rated one of the most valuable brands in the world in published studies, and we believe it provides us with a significant competitive advantage."[2]

American Express (also known as AmEx) is a financial services organization that has multinational connections. The company was founded in 1850 as an express mail company and expanded into the money order business to compete with the U.S. Postal Service in 1888. Today, AmEx is headquartered in the financial district of Manhattan, New York.

Primarily known for its credit card, travelers cheques, and charge cards, it also has travel-related services, personal banking, financial advisor, and publishing components. Because of its stature in the world of business, American Express has been ranked 22nd most valuable brands in the world by *Business Week*, 88th on the Fortune 500 listing of companies, one of the Most Admired Companies in the World by *Forbes*, and 62nd Best Company to Work For by *Fortune* magazine.

Financially, the company continues to grow with assets of over 161 billion, over 171 million cards in use, net income of 516 billion, and annual revenue of $32.8 billion. Overall, the company is the world's largest card issuer by purchase volume and seeks to aid merchants' development by offering marketing and information management guidance. It also assists small businesses succeed by offering purchasing power and flexible financial control options.

From a service standpoint, the organization offers a variety of service support options (e.g., telephone support, website assistance, chat capability, and an e-mail response system) 24 hours a day and seven days a week. The employees that staff the customer care centers receive the tools they need to deal with a diverse worldwide customer base. Some of the components of staff development include employee networks, leadership training, personal development programs, and continued education support.

Throughout the years since it opened, American Express has gotten involved in "cause marketing" initiatives in which a portion of income generated from member card usage was earmarked to a variety of causes. Some of these campaigns have been: (1) The Statute of Liberty renovation project, (2) Fight Against Aids, and (3) Charge Against Hunger. In addition to providing funding for these charitable causes, the company reaped significant financial reward as card usage increased. Even so, it cannot be argued that AmEx does not provide benefits to many charitable initiatives. In addition to charitable causes, the organization collaborated with basketball Hall of Famer, Shaquille O'Neill, to promote the Shop Small for 2X Rewards program. The program was designed to encourage shoppers to patronize small businesses in exchange for double their normal reward points when using their American Express cards.

Learn more about American Express by visiting the links in the Notes section at the end of this chapter or by searching "About American Express" on the Internet. For more information about the company, visit http://www.amex.co/2ghHFvK and search through the different page links there.

Think About It

1. How does American Express compare to other credit card companies of which you have personal experience or knowledge?

2. What are some of the organization's strengths related to customer service in your mind and how do you think these might enhance a customer's service experience?

3. What are your thoughts related to American Express' use of technology in the service experience?

4. Would you want to work for this company? Explain why or why not.

Quick Preview

Before reviewing the chapter content, respond to the following questions by placing a "T" for true or an "F" for false on the rules. Use any questions you miss as a checklist of material to which you will pay particular attention as you read the chapter. For those you get right, give yourself a pat on the back, but review the sections they address in order to learn additional details about the topic.

_____ 1. It is possible for you not to send nonverbal messages.

_____ 2. By becoming knowledgeable about body language, you can use the cues you observe to accurately predict the meaning of someone's message.

_____ 3. By leaning toward or away from people as they speak, you can better communicate your level of interest in what they are saying.

_____ 4. Smiling may mean that someone agrees with what you say. Smiling may also mean that the person is listening.

_____ 5. The use of open, flowing gestures could encourage listening and help illustrate key points.

_____ 6. Taking the time to polish your shoes, and clean and press your clothing, can help in presenting a positive personal image.

_____ 7. Vocal qualities have little effect on the way others perceive you.

_____ 8. Pauses in your oral message delivery can nonverbally say, "Think about what I just said" or "It's your turn to speak."

_____ 9. The words you use can distort message meaning.

_____ 10. Spatial preferences are the same throughout the world.

_____ 11. People often draw inferences about you based on the appearance of your office.

_____ 12. The amount of time you allocate for meetings with people could nonverbally communicate your feelings about the importance of those people.

Answers to Quick Preview are located at the end of the chapter.

Words to Live By

"The body never lies."

— Source: Martha Graham

LO 4-1 What Is Nonverbal Communication?

CONCEPT   **Nonverbal messages can contradict or override verbal messages. When in doubt, people tend to place more value on nonverbal messages.**

The study of messages sent via nonverbal means has fascinated people for decades. Many people became aware of this subject with the publication of books like *Body Language*[3] and several others over four decades ago. To date, the book has sold millions of copies and remains in print. In *Body Language*, Julius Fast defined various postures, movements, and gestures by ascribing unspoken messages that people might send as nonverbal cues to someone observing them (e.g., defensiveness or accessibility). Since then, hundreds of articles, books, and research studies have explored the topic and expanded the knowledge on the subject.

To be successful in the service profession, you must be aware that you constantly send **nonverbal messages** to others and that it is impossible for you not to communicate. Through this awareness, you can increase your effectiveness in customer encounters or anytime you meet another person. A significant fact to remember is that in messages between two people, nonverbal signals can contradict or override words. This is especially true when emotions are high. That does not mean that your words are unimportant. They are just overridden by nonverbal cues on many occasions. When in doubt about your message's meaning, people tend to believe the nonverbal (facial, body, and vocal) parts.

Although nonverbal cues carry powerful messages, you should remember that there is considerable room for misinterpretation of the cues used by different people. Based on personality type, gender, cultural and educational background, environment in which people were reared, and many other factors, they may send and receive nonverbal cues differently from the way you would. The skill of recognizing, assigning meaning, and responding appropriately to nonverbal messages is not exact. Human behavior is too unpredictable and the interpretation of nonverbal cues is too subjective for accuracy of interpretation to occur with consistency.

nonverbal messages Consist of such things as movements, gestures, body positions, vocal qualities, and a variety of unspoken signals sent by people, often in conjunction with verbal messages.

KNOWLEDGE CHECK

1. According to Julius Fast, what type of unspoken message might be sent as nonverbal cues?

2. What is a fact related to the power of nonverbal messages that accompany spoken messages?

LO 4-2 The Scope of Nonverbal Behavior

CONCEPT   **Background, culture, physical conditions, communication ability, and many other factors influence whether and how well people use body cues.**

In addition to verbal and written messages, you continually provide nonverbal cues that tell a lot about your personality, attitude, and willingness and ability to assist customers. Customers receive and interpret the messages you send, just as you do theirs.

Customer Service Success Tip

Ask a number of your friends (or customers with whom you have good rapport) if there are nonverbal cues that you use that stand out in their mind or even irritate them in order to get a better understanding of nonverbal cues that you might be using excessively or inappropriately. Based on their response, make necessary modifications in your nonverbal communication behavior.

BODY LANGUAGE

By recognizing, understanding, and reacting appropriately to the body language of your customers, as well as using positive body language yourself, you will communicate with them more effectively. The key to "reading" **body language** is to realize that your interpretations are only an indicator of the customer's true message meaning. This is because background, culture, physical condition, communication ability, and many other factors influence whether and how well people use body cues. Placing too much importance on nonverbal cues could lead to miscommunication and possibly a service breakdown. In the following sections, you will read about some typical forms of body language.

body language Nonverbal communication cues that send powerful messages through gestures, vocal qualities, manner of dress, grooming, and many other cues.

Eye Contact

Some people have said that the eyes are "the windows to the soul." Eye contact is very powerful. This is why criminal investigators are taught to observe eye movement in order to determine whether a suspect is being truthful or not. In most Western cultures, the typical period of time that is comfortable for holding eye contact is 5 to 10 seconds; then an occasional glance away is normal and expected. Looking away in some cultures can often send a message of disinterest, or dishonesty, or lack of confidence (e.g., United States, Canada, and United Kingdom). If either the length or the frequency of eye contact differs from the "norm," many people might think that you are being rude or offensive. They might also interpret your behavior as an attempt to exert power or as flirting. Additionally, looking down before answering questions, glancing away continually as your customer talks, blinking excessively, and other such eye movements can create a negative impression. In any case, your customer might become uncomfortable and may react in an undesirable manner (e.g.,, becoming upset or ending the conversation) if you use eye contact in what they perceive as an inappropriate manner. As with all other aspects of workplace interaction in a multicultural environment, do not forget that cultural values and practices often influence the way in which people communicate and interpret message signals.

Just as you send messages with your eyes, your customer's eye contact can also send meaningful messages to you. A customer's lack of direct eye contact with you could send a variety of messages, such as lack of interest, confidence, or trust, or dishonesty, depending on how you interpret those cues. For example, if you are watching a customer shop and notice a quick loss of eye contact each time you try to engage him or her visually, the customer might be nervous because he or she is shoplifting, or the customer simply might not want your attention and assistance.

Another aspect of nonverbal communication has to do with the size of the pupils. Research on the correlation between a person's interest in an item or object being viewed and the size of the person's pupils has been conducted for decades. Typically, when a customer is interested in an item, his or her pupils will dilate (grow larger). Service providers can potentially parley this fact into increased sales and customer satisfaction. An astute and experienced salesperson can watch for dilation as a customer looks over merchandise. For example, even if a customer displays interest only after asking the price, and then moves on to another, the salesperson who has observed the customer's interest as revealed by dilation of the pupils might be able to influence the customer's buying decision. As with all nonverbal communication, if you are using this technique, remember that there is room for misinterpreting a cue. According to research on **pupilometrics**, other factors such as drugs or a person's physical attraction to someone can also cause dilation. To avoid misinterpreting a

pupilometrics The study of how pupils of the eyes react to stimuli.

©Squaredpixels/E+/Getty Images RF

Nonverbal cues such as eye contact, proximity, smiling, and gesturing send powerful messages. *What cues do you regularly send that impact the way customers perceive you and your organization?*

customer's intent, listen carefully to tone of voice and observe other nonverbal signals so that you do not appear to be pushy or take the wrong action in dealing with a customer.

Facial Expressions

The face is capable of making many expressions. Your face can signal excitement, happiness, sadness, boredom, concern, dismay, and dozens of other emotions. By being aware of the power of your expressions and using positive ones, such as smiling, you can initiate and sustain relationships with others. In fact, smiling seems to be one of the few nonverbal cues that projects a universal meaning of friendship or acceptance. Smiling typically expresses a mood of friendship, cheerfulness, pleasure, relaxation, and comfort with a situation. Even so, like any other nonverbal cue, you have to be cautious of "reading into" the intent of someone's cue because some people smile to mask nervousness, embarrassment, or deceit.

In some situations, smiling (yours and a customer's) may even lead to problems. For example, suppose that you are a male receptionist working at a walk-in care clinic. A male patient from the Middle East and his wife step up to your desk. You smile and greet the husband, and then turn your attention to the wife and do likewise, possibly adding, "That's a very pretty dress you have on." She appears embarrassed, smiles, and giggles as she looks away in an effort to avoid eye contact. At this point, you notice that the husband looks very displeased. A cultural element may be involved. Although your intention was to express friendliness and openness and to compliment the wife, because of his cultural attitudes, the husband may interpret your words and smiling as flirtatious and insulting.

Do not think that this means you should ignore the spouses of your customers. Rather, be conscious of cultural and personal differences that people may have, and take your cue from the customer. As the world grows smaller, it is more crucial than ever that you expand your knowledge of different cultural attitudes and practices, and recognize that your ways are not the same as everyone else.

WORK IT OUT 4.1

Facial Expressions

Take a few minutes to look at each of the faces shown below. Write the emotion that you believe each image portrays and then compare your response to those of others. Did each person have the same reaction to each nonverbal cue?

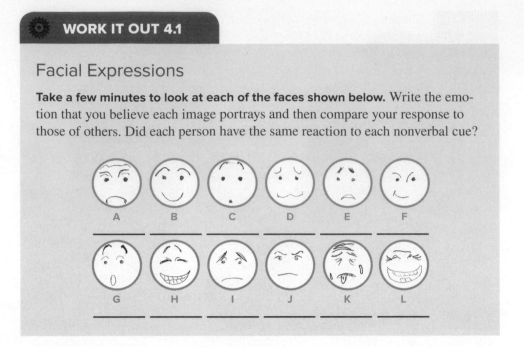

Posture

posture Refers to how one sits or stands in order to project various nonverbal messages.

Your stance or the way that you position your body is known as **posture**. Various terms describe posture based on body positioning, for example, formal, rigid, relaxed, slouched, awkward, sensual, and defensive. In Western-oriented cultures, by sitting or standing in an erect manner, or leaning forward or away as you speak with customers, you can send a variety of messages. By standing or sitting with an erect posture, walking confidently, or assuming a relaxed, open posture, you might appear to be attentive, confident, assertive, and ready to assist your customer. On the other hand, slouching in your seat, standing with slumped shoulders, keeping your arms crossed while speaking to someone, shuffling or not picking up your feet when walking, or averting eye contact can possibly signal that you are unsure of yourself, are being deceitful, or just have a poor or indifferent customer service attitude.

In addition, your nonverbal behavior when listening to a customer speak can affect his or her feedback and reaction to you. For example, if you lean forward and smile as the customer speaks, you can signal that you are interested in what is being said and that you are listening intently. Leaning away could send the opposite message.

Nodding of the Head

Nodding of the head is often used (and overused) by many people to signal agreement or to indicate that they are listening to a speaker during a conversation.

You must be careful when you are using this technique, and when you are watching others who are doing so, to pause occasionally in order to ask a question for clarification. Stop and ask for or provide feedback through a paraphrased message. A question such as "So what do you think of what I just said?" will quickly tell you whether the other person is listening and understands your meaning. The answer will also make it clear if the other person is simply politely smiling and nodding—but not understanding. The latter sometimes happens when there are cultural differences or when someone speaks a native language other than yours.

If you are a woman, be careful not to overuse the nodding technique. Some research has shown that many North American women often nod and smile more than men do during a conversation. Doing so excessively might damage your credibility or effectiveness, especially when you are speaking to a man. The interpretation may be that you agree or that you have no opinion, whether you do or not.

Although nodding your head generally signals agreement, if you nod without a verbal acknowledgment or **paralanguage**, a missed or misinterpreted cue could result. For example, suppose that you want to signal to a customer that you are listening to and understand her request. You may nod slowly, vocalize an occasional "I see" or "uh-huh," and smile as she speaks. She might interpret this to mean that you are following her meaning and are nonverbally signaling acceptance of it. However, if she is stating something contrary to your organization's policy or outside your level of authority, she might misinterpret your signals thinking that you *agree* with her, not that you are merely signaling *understanding*. Later, she might be upset, saying something like, "Well, earlier you nodded agreement when I said I wanted a replacement."

paralanguage Consists of voice qualities (e.g., pitch, rate, tone, or other vocal qualities) or noises and vocalizations (e.g., "hmmm" or "ahhh") made as someone speaks that let a speaker know that his or her message is being listened to and followed.

Customer Service Success Tip

One of the biggest causes of customer dissatisfaction and customer churn is a breakdown in communication between customers and service representatives. By being conscious of the words you choose and the nonverbal messages that you convey through your body language, actions, and inactions, you can potentially reduce the opportunity for disharmony. Educate yourself on effective ways to communicate with all types of customers and then consciously work to improve your skills through practice. Get feedback from coworkers and friends about their perceptions of how well you convey thoughts, ideas, and information.

Gestures

The use of the head, hands, arms, and shoulders to accentuate verbal messages can add color, excitement, and enthusiasm to your communication. Using physical movements naturally during a conversation with a customer may help make a point or result in added credibility.

Typically, such movements are designed to gain and hold attention (e.g., waving a hand to attract someone's attention), clarify or describe further (e.g., holding up one finger to indicate the number 1), or emphasize a point (e.g., pointing a finger while angrily making a point verbally).

Open, flowing gestures (gesturing with arms, palms open and upward, out and away from the body) encourage listening and help explain messages to customers. On the other hand, closed, restrained movements (tightly crossed arms, clinched fists, hands in pockets, hands or fingers intertwined and held below waist level or behind the back) could send a message of coolness, insecurity, or disinterest.

The key is to make gestures seem natural. If you do not normally use gestures when communicating, you may want to practice in front of a mirror until you feel relaxed and the gestures complement your verbal messages without distracting. Figure 4.1 summarizes positive and negative communication behaviors discussed in this chapter.

Ethical Dilemma 4.1

You joined the Federal Emergency Management Agency (FEMA) several months before the catastrophic Hurricane Katrina made landfall along the Gulf Coast from Florida to Texas. At the time, you worked in an agency office in Pearl, Mississippi. Within months after the disaster, you were transferred to Baton Rouge, Louisiana, where you could work with partner emergency management agencies to assist in processing victim claims and help set up low-cost loans and grants to get businesses back into operation in the New Orleans area. After arriving at the office, you set about identifying key resources and communicating with flood victims. There are 25 other specialists performing similar tasks. The work hours are long and stressful, but the job is fulfilling and you really enjoy the opportunity to make a difference in the lives of people whom you are helping get their life back together.

Recently, you were in the corner of the break room, partly hidden by a vending machine as you read a book, when two other employees came in and stood by the coffee machine. From the conversation that you overheard, it was obvious that they were friends and you later found out that they were sisters-in-law. The two were jokingly discussing the amount of money that they dealt with every day and one made a comment to the other that there is really no sound paper trail to track the money. She went on to tell the other woman, "We could very easily 'create' some victims on paper and funnel money to ourselves. Nobody would even notice." The second woman agreed; they laughed and then left the room. As a result of what you heard, you started paying more attention to the two, since one of your jobs was to coordinate claims from the office and track the total amount of money being spent. Within months of their conversation, you noticed that the claims for replacement equipment and rentals from these two increased significantly over the previous quarter compared to those of other representatives in the office.

1. Do you think that these women are doing anything illegal? Explain.

2. Should you take any type of action at this point, based on what you know? If so, what should you do?

3. What are possible consequences if you do take action or fail to do so? Explain.

FIGURE 4.1

Positive and Negative Nonverbal Communication Behaviors

Positive	Negative
Brief eye contact (three to five seconds)	Yawning
Eyes wide open	Frowning or sneering
Smiling	Attending to matters other than the customer
Facing the customer	Manipulating items impatiently
Nodding affirmatively	Leaning away from customer as he or she speaks
Expressive hand gestures	Subdued or minimal hand gestures
Open body stance	Crossed arms
Listening actively	Staring blankly or coolly at customer
Remaining silent as customer speaks	Interrupting
Gesturing with open hand	Pointing finger or object at customer
Maintaining professional appearance	Casual unkempt appearance
Clean, organized work area	Disorganized, cluttered work space

VOCAL CUES

Vocal cues, that is, pitch, volume (loudness), rate, quality, and articulation, and other attributes of verbal communication can send nonverbal messages to customers.

Pitch

Changes in voice tone (either higher or lower) add vocal variety to messages and can dramatically affect interpretation of meaning. These changes are referred to as **inflection** or **pitch** of the voice or tone. For example, a raised inflection occurs at the end of a question and indicates a vocal "question mark." Some people have a bad habit of raising inflection inappropriately at the end of a statement. This practice can confuse listeners for they hear the vocal question mark, but realize that the words were actually a statement. To rectify this communication error, be sure that your inflection normally falls at the end of sentence statements. Another technique is to use a vocal "comma" in the form of a brief pause as you speak.

Volume

The range in which you deliver vocal messages is referred to as the degree of loudness or **volume**. Be aware of the volume of your voice, for changes in volume can indicate emotion and may send a negative message to your customer. For example, if a communication exchange with a customer becomes emotionally charged, your voice may rise in volume, indicating that you are angry or upset. This may escalate emotions and possibly lead to a relationship breakdown.

Depending on surrounding noise or your customers' ability to hear properly, you may have to raise or lower your volume as you speak. Be careful to listen to customer comments, especially on the telephone. If the customer keeps asking you to speak up, check the position of the mouthpiece in relation to your mouth, adjust outgoing volume (if your equipment allows this), and try to eliminate background noise, or simply speak up. On the other hand, if he or she is saying, "You do not have to shout," adjust your voice volume or the positioning of the mouthpiece accordingly or lower your voice.

vocal cues Qualities of the voice that send powerful nonverbal messages. Examples are rate, pitch, volume, and tone.

pitch Refers to the change in tone (highness or lowness) of the voice as one speaks.

inflection Also called pitch, this quality adds vocal variety and punctuation to verbal messages.

volume Refers to loudness or softness of the voice when speaking.

©Thomas Northcut/Photodisc/Getty Images RF

Simple nonverbal cues like smiling at a customer send powerful messages that a service provider is customer-focused. *How do you feel when a service provider smiles at you?*

Rate of Speech

rate of speech Refers to the number of words spoken per minute. Some research studies have found that the average rate of speech for adults in Western cultures is approximately 125–150 words per minute (wpm).

Rate of speech varies for many people. Whether someone was reared in the United States or another country can sometimes affect communication abilities. An average rate of speech for most adults in a workplace setting in Western cultures is 125 to 150 words per minute (wpm). You should recognize that your speed of delivery could affect correct receipt and interpretation of your message. Speech that is either too fast or too slow can be distracting and cause loss of message effectiveness and comprehension.

Voice Quality

voice quality Refers to the sound of one's voice. Terms often attributed to voice quality are raspy, nasal, hoarse, and gravelly.

The sound or quality of your voice can affect message interpretation.

The variations in your **voice quality** can help encourage customers to listen (if your voice sounds pleasant and is accompanied by a smile) or could discourage them (if it is harsh-sounding), depending on their perception of how your voice sounds. Voice quality can be a problem because others are less likely to listen to or interact with you if it is irritating. If others have told you, or you recognize, that your voice exhibits one or more of these characteristics and know that it is not a physiological issue, you may want to meet with a speech coach who specializes in helping improve vocal presentation of messages. Most local colleges and universities that have speech programs can supply the name of an expert, possibly someone on their staff. By taking the initiative to improve your voice quality, you can enhance your customer service image and ultimately your personal relationships.

Articulation

articulation, enunciation, or pronunciation Refers to the manner or clarity in which verbal messages are delivered.

Articulation, enunciation, or pronunciation of words refers to the clarity of your word usage. If you tend to slur words ("Whadju say?", "I hafta go whitja", or "I hadda") or cut off endings (goin', doin', gettin', bein'), you can distort meaning or frustrate listeners. This is especially true when communicating with customers who do not speak your native language well and with customers who view speech ability as indicative of educational achievement or your ability to assist them effectively. If you have a problem articulating well, practice by gripping a pencil horizontally between

---

⚙ **WORK IT OUT 4.2**

Gesture Practice

To see what you look like when you gesture and communicate nonverbally, stand in front of a mirror or video yourself as you practice expressing nonverbal cues that demonstrate the following emotions. Once in class, pair up with another student and each of you select four emotions from the list. Take turns and demonstrate each emotion without telling the other person the intended message. After each attempt, discuss how your partner interpreted the emotion and what message you were actually trying to send. If the two differed, discuss why that might be the case and the potential impact on customer service.

1. Sadness
2. Frustration
3. Disgust
4. Happiness
5. Love
6. Fear
7. Anger
8. Excitement
9. Boredom
10. Frustration

your teeth, reading sentences aloud, and forcing yourself to enunciate each word clearly. Over time, you will find that you slow down and form words more precisely.

Pauses

Pauses in communication can be either positive or negative depending on how you use them. From a positive standpoint, they can be used to allow a customer to reflect on what you just said, to verbally punctuate a point made or a sentence (through intonation and inflection in the voice), or to indicate that you are waiting for a response. On the negative side, you can irritate someone with too many vocal pauses or **interferences**. The latter can be audible sounds ("uh," "er," "um," "uh-huh") and are often used when you have doubts or are unsure of what you are saying, not being truthful, or nervous. Sometimes, these are called **verbal fillers**. Interferences can also be external noises that make hearing difficult (e.g., other people talking, ringing telephones, equipment, or street sounds).

pauses A verbal technique of delaying response in order to allow time to process information received, think of a response, or gain attention.

interferences Noises that can interfere with messages being effectively communicated between two people.

verbal fillers Verbal sounds, words, or utterances that break silence but add little to a conversation. Examples are uh, um, ah, and you know.

Silence

Silence is a form of tacit communication that can be used in a number of ways, some more productive than others. Many people have trouble dealing with silence in a conversation. This is unfortunate because silence is a good way to show respect or show that you are listening to the customer while he or she speaks. It is also a simple way to indicate that the other person should say something or contribute some information after you have asked a question. You can indicate agreement or comprehension by using body language and paralanguage, as discussed earlier. On the negative side, you can indicate defiance or indifference by coupling your silence with some of the nonverbal behaviors listed in Figure 4.1. Obviously, this can damage the customer–provider relationship.

silence Technique used to gain attention when speaking, to allow thought, or to process information received.

Semantics

Semantics has to do with choice of words. Although not nonverbal in nature, semantics is a crucial element of message delivery and interpretation because people interpret your intentions or meanings based on their understanding of word definitions. Think about times when you or someone has inappropriately used the wrong word in a conversation (a **malapropism**). Such incidents are often potentially humorous or confusing to the other person. For example, imagine that you are a server in a restaurant and your male customer says, "Be sure they do not put any of those neutrons on my salad." Obviously, he is referring to bread croutons. Another example might be a customer who says that she does not want any cheese on her burger when you ask her because she is "lack toast intolerant." More likely, she is lactose intolerant and cannot effectively digest milk or dairy products.

semantics The scientific study of relationships between signs, symbols, and words and their meaning.

malapropism The unintentional misuse or distortion of a word or phrase that sounds somewhat like the one intended but with a different context. This often has humorous results.

You can add to or detract from effective communication depending on the words you choose and the manner in which you use them. This can happen if you use a lot of jargon (technical or industry-related terms) or complex words that customers may not understand because of their background, education, culture, or experience. In such instances, you run the risk of irritating, frustrating, or dissatisfying them and thus damaging the customer–provider relationship.

The bottom line related to semantics is that you always want to come across as being intelligent and professional when interacting with your customers. Even so, you must consider your message receiver and talk at a level with which they are comfortable and understand your meaning. Think before you speak and work to hone your communication skills.

Customer Service Success Tip

Sit up straight when speaking, since doing so reduces constriction and opens up your throat (larynx) to reduce muffling and improve voice quality.

appearance and grooming Nonverbal characteristics exhibited by service providers that can send a variety of messages that range from being a professional to having a negative attitude.

APPEARANCE AND GROOMING

The way you look and present yourself physically (hygiene and grooming) and your manner of dress (clothes clean, pressed, and professionally worn with your shoes shined) send a message of either professionalism or indifference. Even though you provide attentive, quality service, the customer will typically form an opinion of you and your organization within 30 seconds based on your appearance and that of your workspace. This opinion may make the difference in whether the customer will continue to patronize your organization or go to a competitor. For example, your clothing, grooming, and choice of jewelry or other accessories could send a negative message to some people. It is crucial to be able to distinguish between what is appropriate or inappropriate for the workplace or business setting. A good starting point in determining this is to ask your supervisor about the organization's dress policy and adhere to it. Also, follow the lead of your supervisor in regards to appropriate appearance, and observe what other employees wear to work.

Through your **appearance and grooming** habits, you project an image of yourself and the organization. Good personal hygiene and attention to your appearance are crucial in a customer environment. Remember, customers do not have to return if they find you or your peers offensive in any manner. Without customers, you do not have a job.

WORK IT OUT 4.3

Adding Emphasis to Words

To practice how changes in your vocal quality affect the meaning of your message, try this activity. Pair up with someone. Take turns verbally delivering the following sentences one at a time. Each time, place the vocal emphasis on the word in boldface type. Following the delivery of each sentence, stop and discuss how you perceived the meaning based on your partner's enunciation and intonation of the key word in the sentence. Also, discuss the impact that you believe such emphasis could have on a customer interaction.

I said I'd do it.

I **said** I'd do it.

I said **I'd** do it.

I said I'd **do** it.

I said I'd do **it**.

Hygiene

Effective **hygiene** (regular washing and combing hair, bathing, brushing teeth, using mouthwash and deodorant, washing hands, and cleaning and trimming fingernails) is basic to successful customer service. This is true even when you work with tools and equipment, or in other skilled trades in which you get dirty easily.

Most customers accept that some jobs are going to result in more dirt and grime. However, they often have a negative feeling about someone who does not take pride in his or her personal appearance and/or hygiene. They often perceive such employees as inconsiderate, lazy, or simply dirty. If you failed to wash your hair, bathe, or shave prior to reporting to work, you could be offensive in appearance to customers and co-workers (you might even have an unpleasant odor) even if you work in a job that requires manual labor. The latter is no excuse for poor hygiene. Think about the times you have encountered such service providers. What was your reaction to them personally? Failing to adhere to these basic commonsense suggestions could result in people avoiding you or complaining about you. Naturally, this would reduce your effectiveness on the job and lower customer satisfaction.

Many Hollywood actors have prompted a number of grooming trends. One of these trends is for men to appear with a one- or two-day beard stubble. While this may look sexy in movies, it has little place in most professional work environments. Depending on the environment, it may cause customers to view the wearer as being too lazy to shave or unprofessional. A second trend that has been around for years, but is growing, is the prevalence of tattoos and piercings. A number of studies show that prominent tattoos and visible piercings are becoming more commonplace in society for all generations. Still, in many instances, these body modifications can raise some customers' eyebrows and cause a negative reaction because of stereotypes that some people have of such things. Often, these reactions are from older customers. Since this group is still one of the largest market forces in many countries, you should consider their views if you want to be a successful service provider. Covering tattoos or not wearing visible body jewelry while at work is a simple "fix" to prevent negative reactions from customers. Obviously, the type of organization for which you work will dictate standards related to this issue. For example, acceptance is more likely when you work in a tattoo parlor, vapor shop, game store, or other location that caters to mostly younger customers, or those places where outward expressions of personal preference are more tolerated.

Although good hygiene and grooming are important, going to an extreme through excessive or bizarre use of makeup, hair coloring, and excessive use of cologne or perfume can create a negative impression and may even cause people to avoid you. This is especially true of people who have allergies or respiratory problems, who think conservatively, or with whom you work in confined spaces. Be conscious of the impact of your grooming preferences on others.

hygiene The healthy maintenance of the body through such practices as regular bathing, washing hair, brushing teeth, cleaning fingernails, and using commercial products to eliminate or mask odors.

Many car owners are capitalizing on a trend to sell advertising space on their vehicles. *How does this trend tie to nonverbal communication for companies?*

©Anton Kovalenko/Alamy Stock Photo

Trending NOW

For years, advertising has been placed on buses, trains, airplanes, trucks, and other vehicles. Companies are now constantly looking for ways to connect and send messages to current and potential customers by paying car owners to allow them to entirely wrap their personal vehicles. In effect, they are turning cars into driving billboards. In exchange for this nonverbal message board, people are able to afford a new car and have someone else pay for it or take a business tax deduction. Search online for more information about this trend.

Being aware of how people may react to violations of their space is necessary for those in customer service. Touching another person is not appropriate in the workplace. This includes hugging a friend or other forms of affection or nontraditional business greeting. Depending on the circumstances, there might be misperceptions (by the person or those who observe your actions) of intentions and sexual harassment claims. *What have been your reactions when someone violated your "personal space" in the workplace?*

©Ryan McVay/Getty Images RF

Clothing and Accessories

For a number of years, casual dress, "dress-down days," and business casual have been buzz words in many organizations in North America as management tries to adapt to the changing values of today's workforce. For example, many hi-tech and graphic work environments often have employees in jeans, T-shirts, and sandals. This trend toward being a bit too lax is now reversing in many companies because some employees have taken the concept of "casual" to an extreme. As a result, there are sometimes negative results in the workplace because customers are voicing their opinion or disapproval. In an economy where every customer counts, organizations are definitely looking for ways to attract and keep this precious commodity. Part of that is rethinking the organizational image and how the public reacts to it.

Work clothing does not have to be expensive, but it should be well maintained and appropriate to your work setting. Certain types of clothing and accessories are acceptable in the work environment, but others are inappropriate. If your organization does not have a policy outlining dress standards, always check with your supervisor before wearing something that might deviate from the standards observed by other employees or might create an unfavorable image to the public. For example, very high heels and miniskirts, or jeans, bare midriffs, pajamas, T-shirts, pants with holes or tattered cuffs, or that hang low on the hips, and tennis shoes or flip flops might be appropriate for a date or social outing, but they may not be appropriate in most workplaces. They could actually be distracting or cause customer disapproval and/or complaints and lost business to your organization.

If you are in doubt about appropriate attire, many publications and videos (e.g., on www.youtube.com) are available on the subject of selecting the right clothing, jewelry, eyeglasses, and accessories. Check with your company's human resources department, your local public library, or the Internet for more information.

SPATIAL CUES

Each culture has its own **proxemics** or **spatial cues** (zones or distances in which interpersonal interactions take place) for various situations (Figure 4.2). When you violate coworkers' spatial preferences based on their culture, their comfort level is likely to decrease, and they may become visibly anxious, move away, and/or become defensive or offended.

Each culture has unwritten rules about contact and interpersonal proximity of which you should be aware and that should be respected when dealing with people from a given culture. In the United States and many Western cultures, studies have resulted in definitions of approximate comfort zones. These may vary, for example, when someone has immigrated to a Western environment but still respects some of his or her own culture practices related to space.

Intimate Distance (0 to 18 inches)

This distance is typically reserved for your family and intimate relationships. Most people will feel uncomfortable when a service provider intrudes into this space uninvited.

Personal Distance (18 inches to 4 feet)

This distance is normally appropriate when close friends or business colleagues, with whom you have established a level of comfort and trust, are together. It might also occur if you have established a long-term customer relationship that has blossomed into a semifriendship. In such a situation, you and the customer may sometimes exchange personal information (about vacation plans, children, and so forth) and feel comfortable standing or sitting closer to one another than would normally be the case in the workplace.

Social and Work Distance (4 to 12 feet)

This is usually the distance range in face-to-face customer service situations. Typically, it is maintained at casual business events and during business transactions.

proxemics Relates to the invisible barrier surrounding people in which they feel comfortable interacting with others. This zone varies depending on the level of relationship a person has with someone else.

spatial cues Nonverbal messages sent based on how close or far someone stands from another person.

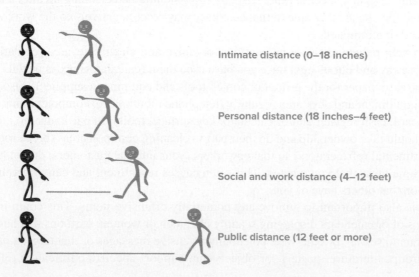

Intimate distance (0–18 inches)

Personal distance (18 inches–4 feet)

Social and work distance (4–12 feet)

Public distance (12 feet or more)

FIGURE 4.2
Typical Spatial Distances in Western Cultures

Public Distance (12 or more feet)

This distance range is likely to be maintained at large gatherings, activities, or presentations where most people do not know one another, or where the interactions are formal in nature.

An important thing to remember about spatial distances in the service environment is how others might perceive your actions. For example, suppose you have an intimate or friendly spatial relationship with a coworker or with someone who regularly comes into your place of business. Outside the workplace, you and this person might engage in interactions from zero to four feet (joking around, touching, kissing, and holding hands). However, if you exhibited similar behavior in the workplace, you could create a feeling of discomfort in others, especially customers or other people who do not know you. Even if they are aware of your relationship with this person, the workplace is not the appropriate place for such behavior. Any touching should be restricted to standard business practices (e.g., a firm business handshake). In fact, touching other than this can lead to claims of a hostile work environment and could lead to a lawsuit according to numerous federal and state laws in the United States. This is especially true if there is a supervisory relationship where one person has the authority to affect another person's career opportunities (e.g., work assignments, training opportunities, pay, or advancement).

ENVIRONMENTAL CUES

environmental cues Any aspect of the workplace with which a customer comes into contact. Such things as the general appearance of an area, clutter, unsightly or offensive items, or general disorganization contribute to the perception of an environment.

The **environmental cues** of the surroundings in which you work and service customers also send nonverbal messages about you and the organization. For example, if your work area looks dirty or disorganized—with tools, pencils, files, and papers scattered about; outdated or inappropriate information or items tacked to a bulletin board; or stacks of boxes, papers stapled or taped to walls, and trash or clutter visible—customers may perceive that you and the organization have a lackadaisical attitude or approach to business. This perception may cause customers to question your ability and commitment to serve. Granted, in some professions keeping a work area clean all the time is difficult (service station, construction site office, manufacturing environment). However, that is no excuse for giving up on cleanliness and organization of your area. If each employee takes responsibility for cleaning his or her area, cleaning becomes a routine event during work hours and no one has to be stuck with the job of doing cleaning tasks at a specific time. Also, by straightening and cleaning up after a task or project, the chance that an external customer may react negatively to the work area is reduced or eliminated.

To help reduce negative perceptions, organize and clean your area regularly, put things away and out of sight once you have used them (calculators, extra pencils, order forms, extra paper for the printer or copier, tools and equipment, supplies). Also, clean your equipment and desk area regularly (telephone mouthpiece, computer monitor and keyboard, cash register and/or calculator key surface, tools). In particular, all employees should take ownership and do their part in cleaning common areas (break rooms or departmental refrigerators) so that coworkers (your internal customers) do not have to pick up a mess that you created. This often causes resentment and can affect the perception that others have of you.

It is also important to remove any potentially offensive items. This could include photos of or calendars displaying scantily clad men or women; cartoons that have ethnic, racial, sexual, or otherwise potentially offensive messages or that target a particular group; literature, posters, or objects that support specific political or religious views; or any item that could be unpleasant or offensive to view. These items have no place in a professional setting. In addition to sending a negative message to external customers who might see them, failure to remove such material might result in legal liability for you and your organization and create a hostile work environment.

MISCELLANEOUS CUES

Other factors, such as the **miscellaneous cues** discussed in the following sections, can affect customer perception or feelings about you or your organization.

miscellaneous cues Refer to factors used to send messages that influence a customer's perception or feelings about a service provider or organization. Examples are personal habits, etiquette, and manners.

Personal Habits

If you have annoying or distracting habits, you could send negative messages to your customer. For example, eating, smoking, drinking, or chewing food or gum while servicing customers can lead to negative impressions about you and your organization. Any of the following habits can lead to relationship breakdowns:

- Touching the customer (other than a professional handshake upon greeting and at the conclusion of a transaction, if appropriate)
- Scratching or touching certain parts of your body typically viewed as personal
- Using pet phrases or speech patterns excessively ("Cool," "You know," "Groovy," "Am I right?" "Awesome," "Solid," "Whatever")
- Talking endlessly without letting the customer speak
- Talking about personal problems
- Complaining about your job, employer, coworkers, or other customers

---

WORK IT OUT 4.4

Spatial Perceptions

Pair up with someone and stand facing him or her from across the room. Start a conversation about any topic (e.g., how you feel about the concepts addressed in this chapter or how you feel about the activity in which you are participating) and slowly begin to move toward one another. As you do so, think about your feelings related to the distance at which you are communicating. Keep moving until you are approximately one inch from your partner. At that point, start slowly backing away—again thinking about your feelings. When you get back to your side of the room, have a seat and answer these questions:

1. How did you feel when you were communicating from the opposite side of the room (what were your thoughts)?
2. At what distance (moving forward or back) did you feel most comfortable? Why?
3. Did you feel uncomfortable at any point? Why or why not?
4. How can you use the information learned from this activity in the customer service environment?

Customer Service Success Tip

To determine if you have any annoying or potentially distracting personal habits that could cause relationship issues, ask someone who knows you well to be alert to gestures, movements, habits, or phrases that you repeat or use often. Once identified, make a conscious effort to reduce or eliminate the habits

Ethical Dilemma 4.2

Assume that you are a receptionist in a hospital emergency room waiting area and an older homeless male who is dirty, with cutoff jeans, sandals, and a T-shirt with holes in it, comes up to your desk. He has a dirty bloody rag wrapped around his hand and complains that he has cut himself with a rusty can lid. You greet him without a smile, hand him a clipboard with paperwork, and tell him to have a seat and complete the forms. At the same time that the indigent patient arrived, a well-dressed older woman wearing a suit arrives with a small crying girl and states that the child fell out of a tree and hurt her shoulder. There are no visible wounds, but the woman said that she just wanted to check it out to make sure she was not hurt. You greet her warmly with a smile and proceed to engage her in conversation and assist attentively. Meanwhile, the injured homeless patient waits to have a question answered about his paperwork.

1. How do you think you would feel if you were the homeless patient? Why?
2. Why do you think you might have used different standards of service for the two patients?
3. Do you think this approach to service is appropriate? Why or why not?
4. What could you have done differently/better to improve the service delivery in this situation?
5. How do you think other waiting patients might react to the difference in service that you provided?
6. What is the likely impact of the service delivery outlined in this situation?

Time Allocation and Attention

time allocation Amount of attention given to a person or project.

Some organizations have standards for servicing customers within a specific time frame (e.g., returning phone calls within four hours), but these **time allocations** should be targets, not absolute deadlines, since all customer transactions cannot be resolved in a specified period of time. The key is to be efficient and effective in your efforts. Continually reevaluate your work habits and patterns to see whether you can accomplish tasks in a more timely fashion. The amount of time you spend with customers often sends subliminal messages of how you perceive their importance. If your organization has service standards that dictate how much time to spend with customers and it is adversely affecting your ability to provide quality service, consider discussing your concerns in a positive manner with your supervisor or manager. Make realistic suggestions for change. If nothing else, taking the opportunity to do this can open up communication between the two of you. You might also learn the logic behind such a policy in the event that you do not already know.

Street Talk Perceptions Trump Reality

It is how a problem is perceived by the parties that is reality.

SOURCE: SHARON MASSEN, Ph.D., CAP MASSEN AND ASSOCIATES

Follow-Through

Trust is the basis for any sound relationship. Without it, you really have no relationship.

When you deal with your customers, it is crucial that they can depend on you. Follow-through, or lack of it, sends a very powerful nonverbal message to customers. If you tell a customer you will do something, it is critical to your relationship that you do so. If you cannot meet agreed-upon terms or time frames, get back to the customer and renegotiate. Otherwise, you may lose the customer's trust. For example, suppose you assure a customer that an item that is out of stock will arrive by Wednesday. On Tuesday, you find out that the shipment is delayed. If you fail to inform the customer, you may lose the sale and the customer's trust, along with potential future business. The result could be that the customer may view you and your organization negatively and then share that perception with others.

Proper Etiquette and Manners

People appreciate receiving appropriate respect and prefer dealing with others who have good **etiquette and manners**.

    Tied to nonverbal messages, the polite things you do (saying "please" and "thank you," asking permission, or acknowledging contributions) go far in establishing and building relationships. Such language sends an unspoken message that says, "I care" or "I respect you." In addition, behavior that affects your customer's perception of you can also affect your interaction and ability to provide service. For example, if you interrupt others as they speak; talk with food in your mouth at a client luncheon; chew food with your mouth open; point with your finger, fork, or other items; or rest your elbows on the table while eating lunch with a customer, he or she might form a negative opinion about you. There are many good books available on business manners and dining etiquette if you are unsure of yourself or want to grow professionally. Visit www.amazon.com to start your search for information. Additionally, there are dozens of blogs and other Internet resources that address the dos and do nots of providing service to and working with customers. Visit www.customerserviceskillsbook.com to explore one such blog written by the author of this book.

Color

Although color is not as important as some other factors related to nonverbal communication in the customer service environment, the way in which you use various colors in decorating a workspace and in your clothing could have an emotional impact on

etiquette and manners Include the acceptable rules, manners, and ceremonies for an organization, profession, or society.

Etiquette and manners can send powerful nonverbal signals about your professionalism and background. By fine-tuning your basic dining and business etiquette skills, you can positively influence your customers. *In what ways have you seen poor etiquette or manners in various situations influence your opinions of others?*

©Ron Chapple Photography, Inc./Alamy Stock Photo RF

FIGURE 4.3

The Emotional Messages of
Color: Emotion or Message
in Western Cultures

	Color	Message
	Red	Stimulates and evokes excitement, passion, power, energy, anger, intensity. Can also indicate "stop," negativity, financial trouble, or shortage.
	Yellow	Indicates caution, warmth, mellowness, positive meaning, optimism, and cheerfulness. Yellow can also stimulate thinking and visualizing.
	Dark blue	Depending on shade, can relax, soothe, indicate maturity, and evoke trust and tranquility or peace.
	Light blue	Projects a cool, youthful, or masculine image.
	Purple	Projects assertiveness or boldness and youthfulness. Has a contemporary "feel." Often used as a sign of royalty, richness, spirituality, or power.
	Orange	Can indicate high energy or enthusiasm. Is an emotional color and sometimes stimulates positive thinking.
	Brown	An earth tone that creates a feeling of security, wholesomeness, strength, support, and lack of pretentiousness.
	Green	Can bring to mind nature, productivity, positive image, moving forward or "go," comforting, growth, or financial success or prosperity. Also, can give a feeling of balance.
	Gold and silver	Prestige, status, wealth, elegance, or conservatism.
	Pink	Projects a youthful, feminine, or warm image.
	White	Contains all the colors of the color spectrum. Typically used to indicate purity, cleanliness, honesty, and wholesomeness. Is visually relaxing.
	Black	Lack of color. Creates sense of independence, completeness, and solidarity. Often used to indicate financial success, death, or seriousness of situation.

KNOWLEDGE CHECK

1. What are the four forms of body language discussed in the text and why are they important in customer service?

2. What are the five vocal cues that can send unintentional nonverbal messages to your customers?

3. How do appearance and grooming affect the level of customer service that you provide?

4. What are the four spatial distances and how might they impact your ability to effectively serve your customers?

5. How do environmental cues send messages to others?

6. What are some of the miscellaneous cues discussed in the text and what role do they have in customer service?

customers. You should at least consider the colors you choose when dressing for work. This is especially true when dressing for a meeting with some international customers or business associates, since colors have different meanings around the world. For example, the color red in some African countries symbolizes death. The same is true of the color white in China, Korea, and other Asian nations where it symbolizes death, mourning, and bad luck. A lot of research has been done by marketing and communication experts to determine which colors evoke the most positive reactions from customers. In various studies involving the reaction people had to colors, some clear patterns evolved. Figure 4.3 lists various colors and the possible **emotional messages of color** they can send.

> **emotional messages of color** Research-based use of color to send nonverbal messages through advertisements and other elements of the organization.

LO 4-3 The Role of Gender in Nonverbal Communication

CONCEPT Research indicates that boys and girls, and men and women behave differently. Young children are sometimes treated differently by their parents because of their gender preference (either male or female may be the preferred gender, no matter the gender of the parent).

There has been a lot of research on the topic of gender communication in the past couple of decades. As a result, crucial information concerning differences in the way males and females interact and communicate has been discovered and written.

Gender communication is an important factor for you to consider before dealing with customers. By better understanding the nuances often exhibited when people of the opposite gender come into contact with you increases your chances of providing customer satisfaction. For example, some researchers have found that females are more comfortable being in close physical proximity with other females than males are being close to other males. Although similarities exist between the ways in which males and females relate to one another, there are distinct differences in behavior, beginning in childhood and carrying through into adulthood.

> **gender communication** Term used to refer to communication between genders.

Numerous books have been written that hypothesize that boys and girls are different in many ways, are acculturated to act and behave differently, and have some real biological differences that account for their actions (and inactions). These are often examined from a number of perspectives. These books often reference various studies that

 WORK IT OUT 4.5

Gender Communication

To get a better idea of how males and females communicate and interact differently, go to a library or to the Internet and gather information on the topic. Look specifically for information on the following topics:

Brain differences between men (males) and women (females) and the impact of these differences on communication and relationships

Differences in nonverbal cues used by men (males) and women (females)

Base for the communication differences in the workplace or business world between men (males) and women (females)

FIGURE 4.4

General Behavioral
Differences between Men
and Women in North
America

	Females	Males
Body	Claim small areas of personal space (e.g., cross legs at knees or ankles). Cross arms and legs frequently. Sit or stand close to same sex. Use subdued gestures. Touch more (both sexes). Nod frequently to indicate receptiveness. Glance casually at watch. Hug and possibly kiss both sexes upon greeting. Use high inflection at end of statements (sounds like a question).	Claim large areas of personal space (e.g., use figure-four leg cross). Use relaxed arm and leg posture (e.g., over arm of a chair). Sit or stand away from same sex but closer to females. Use dramatic gestures. Touch males less, females more. Nod occasionally to indicate agreement. Glance dramatically at watch (e.g., with arm fully extended and retracted to raise sleeve). Hug and possibly kiss females upon greeting. Use subdued vocal inflection.
Vocal	Speak at faster rate. Express more emotion. Use more polite "requesting" language (e.g., "Would you please?") Focus on relationship messages. Use vocal variety. Interrupt less; more tolerant of interruptions. Maintain eye contact. Smile frequently.	Speak at slower rate. Express less emotion. Use more "command" language (e.g., "Get me the …). Focus on business messages. Often use monotone. Interrupt more, but tolerate interruptions less. Glance away frequently. Smile infrequently (with strangers).
Facial	Use expressive facial movements. Focus more on details. Are more emotional in problem solving.	Show little variation in facial expression. Focus less on details. Are analytical in problem solving (e.g., try to find cause and fix problem).
Behavior	View verbal rejection as personal. Apologize after disagreements. Hold grudges longer. Commonly display personal objects in the workplace. Use bright colors in clothing and decorations.	Do not dwell on verbal rejection. Apologize less after disagreements. Do not hold grudges. Commonly display items symbolizing achievement. Use more subdued colors in clothing and decorations.
Environmental	Use patterns in clothing and decoration.	Use few patterns in clothing.

have found that boys and girls typically learn to interact with each other, and with members of their own gender, in different ways. Females generally tend to learn more nurturing and relationship skills early, whereas males approach life from a more aggressive, competitive stance. Females often search for more "relationship" messages during an interaction and strive to develop a collaborative approach; males typically focus on competitiveness or "bottom-line" responses in which there is a distinct winner. Obviously, these differences in approaches to relationship building can have an impact in the customer service environment, where people of all types come together.

The lessons learned early in life usually carry over into the workplace and affect customer interactions. Communication and customer–provider relationships can break down if you fail to recognize the differences between the sexes and the gender roles assigned to them in any given culture. You must develop the skills necessary to interact with both men and women if you want to succeed in the customer service profession.

The basis for gender differences is the fact that the brains of males and females develop at different rates and focus on different priorities throughout life. Some research studies indicate that women often tend to be bilateral in the use of their brain. They can switch readily between the left (analytical, logical, factual, facts-and-figures-oriented) and right (emotional, creative, artistic, romantic, and expressive of feelings) brain hemispheres in various situations. Men, on the other hand, tend to be more lateral in their thinking. This means that they typically favor either the left hemisphere or the right hemisphere. These differences can result in the way each gender communicates, relates to others, perceives, and deals with various situations.

Another factor that influences the manner in which a man or woman interacts with the opposite gender is behavioral preferences. Again, some research focuses on why some individuals prefer working with people while others prefer to work alone or focus on tasks. This research stretches back thousands of years to biblical times and continues today as researchers try to understand the human psyche.

Figure 4.4 lists some basic behavioral differences between females and males.

KNOWLEDGE CHECK

1. In what ways might gender affect customer service?

LO 4-4 The Impact of Culture on Nonverbal Communication

CONCEPT   To be successful in a global economy, you need to be familiar with the many cultures, habits, values, and beliefs of a wide variety of people.

Cultural diversity is having a significant impact on the world and the customer service environment. The number of service providers and customers with varied backgrounds is growing at a rapid pace. This trend provides a tremendous opportunity for expanding your personal knowledge and interaction with people from cultures you might not otherwise encounter. However, with this opportunity comes challenge. If you are to understand and serve people who might be different from you, you must first become aware that they are also very similar to you. In addition, if you are to be successful in interacting with a wide variety of people, you will need to understand the **impact of culture** by learning about many behaviors, habits, values, and beliefs from around the

impact of culture Refers to the outcome of people from various countries or backgrounds coming into contact with one another and potentially experiencing misunderstandings or relationship breakdowns.

world. The Internet is a fertile source for such information. Take advantage of it, or visit your local library to check out books on different countries and their people. Join the National Geographic Society, and you will receive its monthly magazine, which highlights different cultures and people from around the globe.[4]

To become more skilled at dealing with people from other cultures, develop an action plan of things to learn and explore. At a minimum, familiarize yourself with common nonverbal cues that differ dramatically from one culture to another. Specifically, look for cues perceived as negative in some cultures so that you can avoid them. Learn to recognize the different views and approaches to matters such as time, distance, touching, eye contact, and use of colors so that you will not inadvertently violate someone's personal space or cause offense.

KNOWLEDGE CHECK

1. How can an awareness of the varying cultures in a service environment help or hinder your service delivery?

Traditional palm-to-palm handshakes are used and expected in most Western business environments and in Westernized business environments around the world. *Have you ever been caught off guard when someone tried a different handshake version (other than traditional palm-to-palm) when you first met? How did that feel?*

©Somos/SuperStock RF

LO 4-5 Negative Nonverbal Behaviors

CONCEPT You should be aware of habits or mannerisms that can send annoying or negative messages to customers.

People develop unproductive nonverbal behaviors without even realizing it. These may be nervous habits or mannerisms carried to excess (scratching, pulling an ear, or playing with hair). In a customer service environment, you should try to minimize such actions because they might send a negative or annoying message to your customers. An easy way to discover whether you have such behaviors is to ask people who know you well to observe you and share potential problem behaviors that they observe. The following are some more common behaviors that can annoy people and cause relationship breakdowns or comments about you and your organization.

UNPROFESSIONAL HANDSHAKE

Hundreds of years ago, people in many cultures began to use a handshake as a way to determine whether a person was holding a weapon. Later, a firm handshake became a show of commitment, of one's word, or of "manhood."

Today, in Western cultures and many others that have adopted the "Western" approach of doing business, both men and women in the workplace are expected to convey greeting and/or commitment with a firm handshake. Failure to shake hands appropriately (palm-to-palm), with a couple of firm pumps up and down, can lead to an impression that you are weak or lack confidence or that you do not respect the other person. The grip should not be overly loose or overly firm. In regard to an overly firm handshake, it can cause problems. An overly powerful handshake may inadvertently injure a person who has specific medical issues (arthritis). That type of handshake can be just as much a turn-off as a limp or clammy handshake.

One key point to remember related to handshakes is that some people are averse to participating for a number of reasons. Some people do not like to touch strangers, others are germaphobic, and in other instances it is not a culturally preferred form of greeting. A good practice is to exhibit positive relationship cues (e.g., smiling and greeting the customer professionally) and then follow the customer's lead. If he or she extends a hand to shake, you should do so as described above.

In addition, when doing business in other countries or with people from other cultures, learn about their traditional forms of greeting so that you can greet people appropriately, depending on where you are serving them (e.g., in another country). If you typically exchange handshakes with customers, and that practice is not a greeting with which they might be accustomed in their culture, remember that everyone does not traditionally adhere to your form of greeting. In many instances, a customer may just be shaking hands as a show of respect for your culture, so you should appreciate his or her effort rather than critique or criticize it.

One mistake that some people make in a business setting is to carry their informal forms of greetings outside the office over to the workplace. For example, while it may be appropriate for you to greet friends and peers with a "high five," slap of the palm of the hand, knuckle bump, or grip their hand with fingers curled and a brief hug or chest press, this is not appropriate in a professional environment with a customer. In order to project a positive professional protocol, use the traditional handshake when in the workplace if you are in a Westernized business environment.

FIDGETING

Using some mannerisms can indicate to a customer that you are anxious, annoyed, or distracted. You should avoid these when possible. Such signals can also indicate that you are nervous or lack confidence. Cues such as playing with or putting hair in your mouth, tugging at clothing, hand-wringing, throat-clearing, playing with items as you speak (pencil, pen, or other object), biting or licking your lips, or drumming your fingers or tapping a surface with a pencil or other object can all send a potentially annoying and/or negative message.

POINTING A FINGER OR OTHER OBJECT

Many people view this gesture as a very accusatory mannerism; it can lead to anger or violence on the part of your customer. If you must gesture toward a customer or toward an area or item, do so with an open flat hand (palm up) in a casual manner. The result is a less threatening gesture that almost invites comment or feedback because it looks as if you are offering the customer an opportunity to speak. Additionally, this is the appropriate means for pointing toward something in many cultures.

©Eyecandy Images/AGE Fotostock RF

Our nonverbal cues tell others a great deal about us, particularly when we display unproductive behaviors. *What are some possible reasons for the behaviors displayed in this photo?*

RAISING AN EYEBROW

This mannerism is sometimes called the *editorial eyebrow* because some television broadcasters raise their eyebrow. With the editorial eyebrow, only one eyebrow is arched upward at the corner, usually in response to something that the person has heard. This mannerism often signals skepticism or doubt about what you have heard and that you are questioning the customer's honesty.

PEERING OVER TOP OF EYEGLASSES

Many people who need glasses to read but not to see for distances may forget that they have on glasses when interrupted while they are reading or using them. As a result, they may speak to others while wearing their glasses sitting low on the end of their nose. This gesture might be associated with a professor, teacher, or someone who is in a position of authority looking down on a student or subordinate. For that reason, customers may not react positively if you peer over your eyeglasses at them. Typical nonverbal messages that this cue might send include displeasure, condescension, scrutiny, or disbelief.

CROSSING ARMS OR PUTTING HANDS ON HIPS

Typically viewed as a closed or defiant posture, crossing your arms or putting your hands on your hips may send a negative message to your customer and cause a confrontation. People often view this gesture as demonstrating a closed mind, resistance, or opposition.

HOLDING HANDS NEAR MOUTH

By holding your hands near your mouth, you will muffle your voice or distort your message. If someone is hearing impaired or uses a language other than your native tongue, and relies partly on reading your lips, he or she may be unable to understand your message. By placing your hands over or in front of your mouth, you can also send messages of doubt or uncertainty, or suggest that you are hiding something.

KNOWLEDGE CHECK

1. What are examples of negative nonverbal behaviors and how might they affect service delivery?

LO 4-6 Strategies for Improving Nonverbal Communication

CONCEPT Nonverbal cues are all around us. Vocal and visual cues related to customers' feelings or needs are important and may mean the difference between a successful or unsuccessful customer service experience.

Nonverbal communication is not a science. That is because each person is a unique combination of factors such as personal backgrounds, educational experiences, cultures, and life experiences. There is no one answer related to what a given nonverbal cue means since each signal is interpreted differently by the person observing it. This is why learning as much as you can about people and what makes them function, and then mimicking what they do, is so crucial in the customer service profession.

The four strategies discussed in this section will help provide some basic tools that can help you improve your nonverbal communication skills if you practice them and try to understand the behavior of others.

SEEK OUT NONVERBAL CUES

Too often, service providers miss important vocal and visual clues related to customer feelings or needs because they are distracted doing other things or not being attentive. These missed opportunities can often mean the difference between successful and unsuccessful customer experiences. Train yourself to look for nonverbal cues by becoming a "student of human nature."

Nonverbal cues are all around you, if you simply open your eyes and mind to them. Start spending time watching people in public places, such as supermarkets, malls, airports, bus stops, school, or wherever you have the chance. From your observations, objectively evaluate what works and what does not, and then modify your behavior accordingly to reflect the positive things you learn.

Try the following strategies to aid you in focusing on the nonverbal cues sent by others:

- Watch the behavior of others you see and the behavior of the people with whom they are interacting. Try to interpret the results of each behavior. However, keep in mind that human nature is not exact and that many factors affect the nonverbal cues used by yourself and others (culture, gender, environment, and many more).

- Be aware that you may be viewing through your own filters or biases, so evaluate carefully.

- Look at **clusters** of nonverbal behavior and the language accompanying them instead of interpreting individual signals. These clusters might be a combination of positive (smiling, open body posture, friendly touching) or negative (crossed arms, looking away as someone talks, or angry facial expressions or gestures) mannerisms. Evaluating clusters can help you gain a more accurate view of what is going on in a communication exchange.

clusters Groupings of nonverbal behaviors that indicate a possible negative intent (e.g., crossed arms, closed body posturing, frowning, or turning away) while other behaviors (smiling, open gestures with arms and hands, and friendly touching) indicate positive message intent.

CONFIRM YOUR PERCEPTIONS

Let others know that you have received and interpreted their nonverbal cues. Ask for clarification by **perception checking** if necessary. This involves stating the behavior observed, giving one or two possible interpretations, and then asking for clarification of message meaning.

perception checking The process of clarifying a nonverbal cue that was received by stating what behavior was observed, giving one or two possible interpretations, and then asking the message sender for clarification.

Perception Checking Example

Suppose that you are explaining the features of a piece of office equipment to a customer and she reacts with a quizzical look. You might respond with a statement such as, "You seem astonished by what I just said. I am not sure whether you were surprised by something I said or whether I was unclear in my explanation. What questions do you have?"

Notice in the example above that the focus of the error is on the service provider (I) rather than the customer (you). It also does not include a potentially accusatory question of "What did you not understand?" that many people use in similar situations. This latter type of question potentially implies that the customer may not be smart enough to grasp what you were saying. It may seem especially pointed if the person speaks another primary language.

By taking the approach in the example, you focus on the customer's behavior and provide an opportunity for her to gain additional necessary information.

SEEK CLARIFYING FEEDBACK

In many instances, you need feedback in order to adjust your behavior. You may be sending cues you do not mean to send or to which others may react negatively.

Clarifying Feedback Examples

1. Assume that you are on a cross-functional work team with members of various departments in your organization and have been in a meeting to discuss ideas for creating a new work process.

   During a heated discussion of ideas, you excuse yourself briefly to get a drink of water in order to take a prescribed pill.

   Later, a teammate mentions that others commented about your frustration level and the fact that you bolted out of the room.

   To determine what behaviors led to the team's reaction, you might ask yourself something like, "What did I do that made people perceive that I was upset?"

   If you later find out why people viewed your behavior the way they did, you can offer an explanation in your next team meeting and avoid exhibiting similar behaviors in the future.

2. Another example might be to ask a coworker whether the clothing you have on seems too formal for a presentation you will give later in the day.

   Keep in mind, though, that some people will not give you honest, open feedback. Instead, they tell you what they think you want to hear or what they think will not hurt your feelings. For this reason, it is usually best to elicit information from a variety of sources before making any personal behavior changes, or deciding not to make them.

> **Street Talk** Customers have expectations of service providers
>
> Customer service representatives are expected to be dedicated, proactive, self-managed, and brand ambassadors.
>
> **Source: Jennifer Harper**

ANALYZE YOUR INTERPRETATIONS OF NONVERBAL CUES

One way to ensure that you are accurately evaluating nonverbal cues given by a variety of people is to analyze your own perceptions, stereotypes, and biases. This is important because the manner in which you view certain situations or groups of people might negatively affect your ability to provide professional and effective service to all your customers. This is especially true of customers in the groups toward which you feel a bias. Without realizing it, you may send negative nonverbal cues that could cause a relationship breakdown and lead to either customer dissatisfaction or even a confrontation.

KNOWLEDGE CHECK

1. What are four strategies for improving your nonverbal behavior with customers?

LO 4-7 Customer-Focused Behavior

CONCEPT **Being customer-focused in your behavior may help you solve a customer's problem or eliminate the opportunity for a problem to develop. The nonverbal cues discussed in this section can help you stay customer-focused.**

The nonverbal behavior you exhibit in the presence of a customer can send powerful messages. You should constantly remind yourself of advice you may have heard often: "Be nice to people." One way in which you can indicate that you intend to be nice is to send customer-focused messages regularly and enthusiastically through your nonverbal cues. Figure 4.5 lists some important benefits of customer-focused behavior. It gives some simple ways to accomplish this when you are dealing with internal and external customers.

FIGURE 4.5
Courtesy Pays

Because of the competitive nature of business, organizations and customer service professionals should strive to pull ahead of the competition in any positive way possible. Simple courteous nonverbal behavior can be one way to beat the service quality levels of other companies. Why should you be courteous?

- *Image is enhanced.* First impressions are often lasting impressions. You can create a more professional impression when you and the organizational culture are customer-focused. When your customers feel comfortable about you and the image projected, they are more likely to develop a higher level of trust and willingness to be more tolerant when things do go wrong occasionally.
- *Employee–customer communication improves.* By treating customers in a professional, courteous manner, you encourage them to freely approach and talk to you. Needs, expectations, and satisfaction levels can then be more easily determined. Additionally, when communication works well, you are less likely to have to deal with a customer who is dissatisfied or have to implement service recovery strategies.
- *Word-of-mouth advertising increases.* Sending regular positive nonverbal messages can help create a feeling of satisfaction and rapport. When customers are satisfied and feel comfortable with you and your organization, they typically tell three to five other people. This increases your customer base while holding down formal advertising costs, such as newspapers and other publications, television, and radio.
- *Employee morale and esteem increase.* If employees feel that they are doing a good job and get positive customer and management feedback, they will probably feel better about themselves. This increased level of self-esteem affects the quality of service delivered. Keep in mind that your role in helping peers feel appreciated. They are often your internal customers and expect the same consideration and treatment as your external customers.
- *Complaints are reduced.* When you treat people fairly and courteously, they are less likely to complain. If they do complain, their complaints are generally directed to a lower level (below supervisory level) and expressed with low levels of anger. Simple things like smiling or attentive actions can help customers relax and feel appreciated.
- *Financial losses decrease.* When customers are satisfied, they are less likely to desert to competitors, file lawsuits, steal, be abusive toward employees (who might ultimately resign), and spread negative stories about employees and the organization. Building good rapport through communication can help in this area.
- *Customer loyalty increases.* People often return to organizations where they feel welcome, serviced properly, and respected. Your role as a service provider is to create an atmosphere where people feel comfortable and trust that you and the organization are working in their best interest to provide quality products and services that meet their needs, wants, and expectations.

Stand Up, If Appropriate

Depending on the layout of your work area, if a customer arrives or approaches you and you are seated behind a desk, stand up and greet him or her. Use the customer's name if you know it and extend a handshake. These actions show that you respect the person as an equal and are eager to assist her or him. Obviously, if you are a cashier behind a glass enclosure or have some other physical constraints, this would not apply. Just use common sense based on your environment in such instances.

Act Promptly

The speed with which you recognize and assist customers, gather information, or respond tells them what you think of their importance. If your service to the customer will take longer than planned or will be delayed, notify the customer, tell him or her the reason, and offer service alternatives if they are appropriate and available. If on the telephone and they are on hold, come back on the line every 30 seconds or so to let them know that you are working on their issue or question. An alternative to the latter is to tell them how long it will take to get their information or answer. Offer them the options that either they can hold for that period or you can take their phone number and call them back within a specified time frame. This psychologically puts the customer back in control and he or she feels empowered.

Guide Rather Than Direct

If customers must go to another person or area in the organization, or if they ask directions, personally guide them or have someone else do so, if possible. Do not simply point or direct. If you are on the telephone and you need to transfer a customer, give the extension of the person you are connecting to (in case of disconnection), transfer the call, and stay on the line to introduce the customer to the other service provider. Once the customer and one of your peers are connected, thank the customer for calling; then disconnect quietly.

Courteous behaviors foster positive interactions. *What does this photo depict?*

©Robert Kneschke/Shutterstock.com RF

Be Patient with Customers

Provide whatever assistance is necessary without appearing to push customers away. Patiently take the time to determine whether a customer has additional needs. It is fine to ask questions such as, "Will there be anything else I can do to assist you?" to signal the end of your interaction with a customer. Just be sure that you do it with a smile and pleasant tone so that the customer does not feel "dumped," rushed, or abandoned.

Offer Assistance

Offer to assist with doors, packages, directions, or in other ways, especially if a customer is elderly, has a disability, has numerous packages, or appears to need help. Similarly, if someone needs assistance with a door or in getting from one place to another, offer to help. If the person says, "No, thank you," smile and go on your way but monitor the person periodically in case he or she changes his or her mind or wants to signal to you. Do not assume that someone needs help, grab an arm to guide him or her, or push open a door. Such actions could surprise a person and throw him or her off balance. This is especially true of someone with a mobility or sight impairment who has learned to navigate using canes or other assistance devices or animals. Upsetting a person's momentum or "system" could cause a fall or injury, which in turn could result in embarrassment and/or a liability situation for you or your organization.

Reduce Customer Wait Times

Nobody likes waiting, so keep waits to a minimum. If you anticipate a long delay, inform the customer, offer alternatives, and work to reduce the wait time. If you notice that customers routinely have to wait for service, approach your supervisor about the situation and offer any suggestions for preventing this in the future. Remember that, as a responsible service professional, you have a role in ensuring that customers are welcomed and getting the appropriate levels of service that they deserve.

Allow Customers to Go First

Typically, you should encourage and allow customers to precede you through cafeteria lines or doors, onto escalators or elevators, into vehicles, and so on as a show of respect. This is especially important if you are dealing with people from cultures in which the senior or eldest person in the group routinely goes ahead of others (e.g., South Korea and other Asian countries) so that others will be able to identify him or her based on his or her status. This projects an air of respect and courtesy. If he or she declines, do not make a scene and insist; simply go first yourself.

Offer Refreshments, If Appropriate

Take care of your "guests" the same way you would at home. Offer to get them something to drink if they come to your office or if they are attending lengthy meetings. You may also want to offer reading materials if they are in a waiting area. Be sure that reading materials in waiting areas are current, are professional-looking, and do not have any offensive material in them, such as scantily clad men or women, offensive jokes, or cartoons that target specific groups. Discard old, worn, and inappropriate materials. Also, if you are in an office, ensure that it is tidy, trash cans are emptied, and it projects a professional image before visitors arrive.

Be Professional

Avoid smirking, making faces, or commenting to other customers or coworkers after a customer leaves or turns his or her back. Such activity is unprofessional and will probably make the second customer wonder what you will do when he or she leaves.

KNOWLEDGE CHECK

1. What are the actions that you can use to exhibit customer-focused behavior?

Small Business Perspective

Small business owners and employees should uphold the same quality standards and commonsense rules related to nonverbal communication as you just read in this chapter. Because of their size and the fact that they typically have limited resources, it is crucial that each employee in a small company strives to project a strong professional image. Each customer contact is crucial in gaining and maintaining customers who will help add to the organization's revenue base.

Customer service training is an important component in making smaller organizations more competitive in a global marketplace. Since funding and resources for training are often limited, owners must get creative in helping prepare workers to provide quality service. To accomplish this, if some employees have the benefit of knowledge about effective nonverbal customer service skills because they have attended training or educational classes on the topic while they worked for larger companies in the past, they might be powerful coaches or mentors to other employees. Additionally, supervisors or owners might attend professional development workshops to gain knowledge and skills that they can come back and share with all employees. Another option is for employees to be allowed and encouraged to sign up for online courses or attend local colleges or schools that teach courses on effective nonverbal communication. These courses are often less expensive than professional development seminars or workshops and in many instances held on-site. If small businesses are hiring new workers, they can often receive grants for training from local and state government entities because they are adding to the economy by employing someone and increasing the local tax base.

By sharing the knowledge learned in training with other company employees, owners and employees can help gain a more competitive edge over larger, better trained or equipped organizations.

Impact on Service

Based on personal experience and what you just read, answer the following questions:

1. Why do employees from small businesses need to be aware of the impact of their nonverbal messages? Explain.

2. What personal example can you think of where an employee of a small organization sent you, or someone you observed, an inappropriate nonverbal message? What was the result?

3. If you worked for a small business, what type of situations might require a sound knowledge of nonverbal cues when dealing with customers? Explain.

Use SmartBook to help you read, study, and retain what you have learned. Access SmartBook in your Instructor's Connect course, or go to connect.mheducation. com for help.

Key Terms

appearance and grooming

articulation, enunciation, or pronunciation

body language

clusters

emotional messages of color

environmental cues

etiquette and manners

gender communication

hygiene

impact of culture

inflection

interferences

malapropism

miscellaneous cues

nonverbal messages

paralanguage

pauses

perception checking

pitch

posture

proxemics

pupilometrics

rate of speech

semantics

silence

spatial cues

time allocation

verbal fillers

vocal cues

voice quality

volume

Summary

Once you become aware of the potential and scope of nonverbal communication, it can be one of the most important ways you have of sharing information and messages with customers. You can covey numerous messages through a look, a gesture, a posture, or a vocal intonation. To ensure that the messages received by your customers are the ones you intended to send, be vigilant about what you say and do, and how you communicate. Also, watch carefully the responses of your customers. Keep in mind that gender, culture, and a host of other factors affect the way you and your customers interpret received nonverbal cues.

To avoid distorting customer messages, or sending inappropriate messages yourself, keep these two points in mind: (1) Use a nonverbal cue you receive from others as an indicator and not as an absolute message. Analyze the cue in conjunction with the verbal message in order to assess the meaning of the message more accurately. (2) Continually seek to improve your understanding of nonverbal signals.

One final point: Remember that you are constantly sending nonverbal messages. Be certain that they complement your verbal communication and say to the customer, "I'm here to serve you."

Review Questions

1. What are six categories of nonverbal cues?

2. What are some of the voice qualities that can affect message meaning?

3. What are some examples of inappropriate workplace attire?

4. How can grooming affect your relationship with customers?

5. What four spatial distances are observed in Western cultures, and for which people or situations is each typically reserved?

6. What are some of the miscellaneous nonverbal cues that can affect your effectiveness in a customer environment?

7. What are some ways in which men and women differ in their nonverbal communication?

8. What are some examples of unproductive communication?

9. List four strategies for improving nonverbal communication.

10. What are five examples of customer-focused behavior?

Search It Out

Search the Internet to Further Your Knowledge of Nonverbal Communication

Now that you have learned some of the basics of nonverbal communication and the impact it can have on your customer relationships, search the Internet to explore the topic further.

1. Select two topics from the following list, check out as many reputable sites as you can find, and prepare a report of at least two pages in length to present to your peers.

   Body language

   Nonverbal cues

   Gender communication

   Spatial distances

   The impact of color on people

   The role of vocal cues in nonverbal communication

   Professional appearance and grooming for the workplace

   The impact of culture on nonverbal cues

2. Go online and research communication differences between men and women. Use your new knowledge of how males and females differ to improve your service by structuring your communication and approach to their preferences; however, remember that each person is unique, so service customers individually.

3. For additional articles and information on nonverbal communication, check out the author's Customer Service Skills Blog by visiting http://www.customerserviceskillsbook .com/wordpress and search "Nonverbal Communication" and related topics. Also, visit YouTube through https:// www.youtube.com/watch?v=9_IzvsRuu84 to watch short videos on nonverbal communication.

Collaborative Learning Activity

1. Focus on Your Speech Patterns

Set up a recording device. Then pair up with someone to discuss what you believe are the benefits of understanding and using nonverbal cues for building customer relations (spend at least five minutes presenting your ideas). Your partner should then present his or her views to you. Once both of you have presented your ideas, listen to the recording with your partner and focus on your speech patterns.

a. Are you using appropriate verbal cues in your relationships with others? In what ways?

b. Do you use silence effectively? If so, how?

c. How did you sound in regard to the following four speech components?

   Rate

   Pitch

   Volume

   Articulation

d. Once you have identified positive and negative areas in your communication, set up an action plan for improvement by targeting the following:

   Area(s) for improvement

   Target improvement date

   Resources needed to improve (assistance of others, training, training materials)

   Support person(s)—who will coach or encourage you toward improvement

2. Gesture Meaning Around the World

As you read in this chapter, common gestures take on different meanings around the world. As a service provider, you have to be cautious not to send unplanned messages with a gesture when you are dealing with a customer from another country or region of the world.

Form a group of two to three students and explore the Internet or locate books on the topic of nonverbal communication and identify meanings of the hand gestures in these photos in the following countries. Be prepared to share your findings with your classmates.

China

Russia

Japan

Mexico

United Kingdom

Kuwait

Greece

Turkey

India

South America

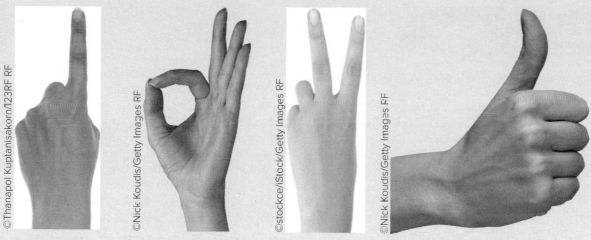

©Thanapol Kuptanisakorn/123RF RF ©Nick Koudis/Getty Images RF ©stockce/iStock/Getty Images RF ©Nick Koudis/Getty Images FF

Common gestures can take on different meanings in different cultures. *What do these gestures signify to you?*

3. Greetings Around the World

Depending on where you are in the world and the environment in which you find yourself, you may experience different greetings.

Do an Internet search and identify forms of business greetings (eye contact, gestures, or otherwise) for the following countries. Note specifically if these customs differ between men and women or between people from different socioeconomic classes. Share findings with your classmates.

China

Indonesia

Mexico

Thailand

Philippines

England

India

Turkey

Japan

South Korea

Italy

Face-to-Face

Handling Customer Complaints at Central Petroleum National Bank

Background

Central Petroleum National Bank is one of the largest financial institutions in the Dallas–Fort Worth, Texas, area. With revenues of more than $200 million and investment holdings all over the world, the bank does business with many individuals and organizations in the region and other parts of Texas. The bank has 17 branch offices in addition to the home office in downtown Dallas.

Your Role

As one of the 125 employees of Central Petroleum's Western Branch Office, you provide customer service and establish new checking and savings accounts.

On Tuesday, a new customer, Mr. Gomez, came in to open an account. He stated that he was moving his money, over $200,000, from an account at a competing bank because of poor service. As you spoke with Mr. Gomez, one of your established patrons, Mrs. Wyatt, came into the office. As she signed in, you looked over, smiled, nodded, and held up one finger to indicate that you would be with her momentarily. She smiled in return as she went

to sit in the waiting area. As you were finishing the paperwork with Mr. Gomez, his teenage son came in and joined him. The son had been working at a summer job and had saved several hundred dollars. He also wished to establish a checking account. He placed his money on your desk and asked what he needed to do. He stated that he was on his lunch break and had only 20 more minutes to fill out the necessary forms. By then, you noticed that Mrs. Wyatt was looking at her watch and glancing frequently in your direction. Shortly thereafter, she left abruptly.

When you arrived at work the next day, the branch vice president called you into her office to tell you that she had received a complaint letter from Mrs. Wyatt concerning your lack of customer service and uncaring attitude.

Critical Thinking Questions

1. What did you do right in this situation?

2. What could you have done differently?

3. Do you believe that Mrs. Wyatt was justified in her perception of the situation? Explain.

4. Could Mrs. Wyatt have misinterpreted your nonverbal messages? Explain.

Planning to Serve

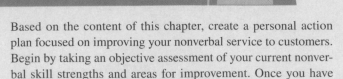

Based on the content of this chapter, create a personal action plan focused on improving your nonverbal service to customers. Begin by taking an objective assessment of your current nonverbal skill strengths and areas for improvement. Once you have identified deficit areas, set goals for improvement.

Start your assessment by listing as many strengths and areas for improvement as you are aware of. Share your list with other people who know you well to see if they agree or can add additional items. Keep in mind that you will likely be more critical of yourself than other people will. Additionally, you may be

sending nonverbal signals of which you are not aware. For those reasons, keep an open mind when considering their comments.

Once you have a list, choose two or three items that you think need the most work and can add the most value when interacting with others. List these items on a sheet of paper along with specific courses of action you will take for improvement, the name of someone you will enlist to provide feedback on your behavior, and a specific date by which you want to see improvement. Related to the last, keep in mind that it takes on average 21 to 30 days to see behavioral change; therefore, set a date that is at least in this range.

Nonverbal Communication Strengths	Areas for Improvement

Top Three Items	Who Will Help	Date for Change
1.		
2.		
3.		

Quick Preview Answers

1. F	3. T	5. T	7. F	9. T	11. T
2. F	4. T	6. T	8. T	10. F	12. T

Ethical Dilemma Summary

Ethical Dilemma 4.1 Possible Answers

1. Do you think that these women are doing anything illegal? Explain.

   While you have no concrete proof at this point that the women are doing anything illegal, the circumstantial evidence of their conversation and the increased volume of their claims should be a red flag or indication that something might be wrong. Since pointing a finger at them and identifying them as criminals can result in damage to their reputation, firing, arrest, or result in a lawsuit for slander or libel if you are wrong. You should gather more information before alerting your supervisor to the situation. Certainly, you should not discuss it with anyone else who does not need to know in order to provide you with additional documentation or validation. This is how rumors get started. Remember that at this point, all you have are suspicions.

2. Should you take any action at this point, based on what you know? If so, what?

It is not illegal for people to joke about criminal activity. Many people have done so in the past without ever intending to act upon their comments. If you do anything to implicate them and nothing is wrong, you could end up with a defamation-of-character lawsuit or worse.

Your first step is to determine if all the claims being submitted are factual and that actual hurricane victims are receiving the money. If you have a system for cross-referencing and verifying that each claim is for a real victim, do whatever you can to determine validity of claims. This might mean checking computer files, background information gathered on claimants, and other sources or checking with claimants to see if they received checks. Just be careful about taking the last action unless your normal job requires that, since the victims are working with their assigned representative (one of the women) and are likely to mention your contact to them at some point. This could cause your coworkers to wonder why you are calling their claimant and they are likely to ask that question of you. Should you determine that all the claims are valid, you might continue to monitor the situation, but do nothing further.

If it becomes evident that there is something wrong, immediately approach your supervisor to explain what you heard and share the data that you have gathered. He or she should then take action to bring it to the attention of proper authorities.

3. What are the possible consequences if you take action? Explain.

Should criminal activity be occurring, the two women will likely be questioned, arrested, and potentially fired from their jobs, if a court finds them guilty. However, you should also be aware that in the real world, even if they are arrested, they will likely get bail and get out of jail before their trial. That means that they might potentially retaliate against you, your supervisor, and the agency. Unfortunately, workplace violence is a serious threat in today's world. Even so, you have a responsibility to your employer, claimants, and the federal government to report any illegal activity. Failure to do so means that criminals are free to steal your tax dollars while they take needed funds away from needy victims of the hurricane.

Ethical Dilemma 4.2 Possible Answers

1. How do you think you would feel if you were the homeless patient? Why?

He likely feels that there is a double standard—that the receptionist views him as less important because he has no assets or resources—and that the quality and degree of service that he will receive, if any, will be inferior to that of other patients. This is likely due to his financial standing and social status level and the perception that the receptionist might have of such people.

2. Why do you think you might have used different standards of service for the two patients?

You possibly have preconceived ideas about homeless people and negative stereotypes (e.g., they are lazy, drug/alcohol abusers, etc.) and also that the hospital will not recoup its costs for treatment from the homeless man.

3. Do you think this approach to service is appropriate? Why or why not?

Assuming that the older woman was talking about information related to the little girl's injury rather than some unrelated topic, you should not ignore the man who is likely in pain and needing assistance. Based on the situation at hand, you could either indicate to the man that you will be right with him as soon as you get the little girl checked in or, if the woman is discussing information not pertinent to the little girl's condition, politely interrupt her and ask if she would mind letting you answer the man's question. Point out to the woman that the man had already started to check in and has a bleeding injury. Be careful not to imply that either person is more important than the other.

4. What could you have done differently or better to improve the service delivery in this situation?

Attempt to avoid stereotypes about homeless people, treat the homeless man with more respect and as a customer who was not homeless, and use more positive nonverbal signals when dealing with all customers.

5. How do you think other waiting patients might react to the difference in service that you provided?

Unfortunately, some patients might not care about potentially different treatment levels being provided to those less fortunate. On the other hand, some might perceive that you are providing preferential treatment to someone who appears to be better off economically or socially, and that you relegated the homeless man to a lower status because he might not have funding to pay for the service he will receive. Such perceptions can tarnish your reputation and that of the hospital as a "place of caring" and might even lead to complaints or negative word-of-mouth publicity by others who view the incident.

6. What is the likely impact of the service delivery outlined in this situation?

The homeless person will likely have a negative impression about you and the medical facility; he may possibly have lowered self-esteem as a result of his treatment. Stereotypes might be reinforced with other patients, and possible legal action might result, especially if the homeless man has medical complications due to lack of timely or proper treatment.

Listening to the Customer

"The most basic of all human needs is the need to understand and be understood. The best way to understand people is to listen to them."
—SOURCE: RALPH NICHOLS

©Goran Bogicevic/123RF RF

LEARNING OUTCOMES

After completing this chapter, you will be able to:

5-1 Describe why listening is important to customer service.

5-2 Define the four steps in the listening process.

5-3 List the characteristics of a good listener.

5-4 Recognize the causes of listening breakdown.

5-5 Develop strategies to improve your listening ability.

5-6 Use information-gathering techniques learned to better serve customers.

5-7 Apply concepts discussed to generate meaningful responses to your questions from customers.

Use SmartBook to help you read, study, and retain what you have learned. Access SmartBook in your Instructor's Connect course, or go to connect.mheducation.com for help. ▉SMARTBOOK™

IN THE REAL WORLD RETAIL—NORDSTROM

According to the company website, "Nordstrom, Inc. is a leading fashion specialty retailer offering compelling clothing, shoes and accessories for men, women and children. Since 1901, we've been committed to providing our customers with the best possible service—and to improving it every day."

Source: Nordstrom—About Us

The company was started by a 16-year-old (John W. Nordstrom) Swedish immigrant who could not speak English and arrived in New York with only $5 in his pocket. After spending time in mining and logging camps in Washington and California, he moved to Alaska and made enough money in a gold mine stake to return to Seattle, Washington. There, he partnered with a friend from Alaska and opened a shoe store, which would grow to be the largest independent shoe chain in the country.

Nordstrom retired in 1928 and turned the company over to his sons. By the 1960s, they had expanded throughout several Western states and added clothing apparel to their stores and in 1968 turned the company over to their children and other relatives.

In 1971, the company went public, changed its name to Nordstrom, Inc., was recognized as the largest volume West Coast fashion specialty store, and surpassed the $100 million sales mark.

In the late 1980s, Nordstrom opened its first Nordstrom Rack (clearance center) expanded to the East coast and focused on catering to customers' needs, individually. As stated on its website, "Instead of categorizing departments by merchandise, Nordstrom created fashion departments that fit individuals' lifestyles."

In recent years, Nordstrom has analyzed customer needs and has added online shopping capabilities to allow customers more options for accessing products. The result has been the continued growth. In 2015, Nordstrom reported an all-time record high for sales of $14.1 billion.

Throughout the Nordstrom history, the founder's guiding principle "offering the customer the best possible service, selection, quality, and value" (Source: Nordstrom—Company History) has led to national reputation as a truly service-focused organization that caters to the wants and needs of its customers. The result of its efforts has paid off. The organization regularly receives awards from a variety of organizations. Nordstrom has been named as one of the "100 Best Places to Work" numerous times by *Fortune* magazine, "Most Admired Company," and "100 Best Corporate Citizens" by *Business Ethics*. Additional awards include, "Top Employers for Minorities" and "Retailer of the Year" by the American Apparel and Footwear Association.

With over 347 stores in the United States and Canada and more being added each year, the company has the infrastructure to provide quality service. The goal is to live up to John W. Nordstrom's founding philosophy of "offering the customer the best possible service, selection, quality, and value." To help accomplish that, Nordstrom has offered customers 24-hour shopping access to its website since 1988 and now offers free shipping and returns. It has also embraced mobile technology to better serve customers with shopping apps and register-free transactions. The latter is possible because store employees carry tablets to allow them to complete sales transactions from anywhere on the sales floor.

In addition to its efforts to provide quality service through innovative retail strategies, the company actively participates in community, charitable, and other programs to give back to the people it serves. Nordstrom also has active environmental protection programs in place to reduce its impact on the earth.

For more information about this organization, search the Internet and visit the company website at www.nordstrom.com/.

Think About It

1. Based on what you read here and found on the Internet, what are the company's strengths related to customer service?

2. Why do you think Nordstrom has such a solid reputation for quality service?

3. How does Nordstrom compare in its customer service initiatives to other major retail store chains of which you are familiar.

4. How does the company's approach to giving back to people and organizations make it a better organization?

5. Would you like to work for Nordstrom? Why or why not?

Quick Preview

Before reviewing the chapter content, respond to the following questions by placing a "T" for true or an "F" for false on the rules. Use any questions you miss as a checklist of material to which you will pay particular attention as you read the chapter. For those you get right, give yourself a pat on the back, but review the sections they address in order to learn additional details about the topic.

_____ 1. Listening is a passive process similar to hearing.

_____ 2. Listening is a learned process.

_____ 3. During the comprehending stage of the listening process, messages received are compared and matched to memorized data in order to attach meaning to the messages.

_____ 4. The two categories of obstacles that contribute to listening breakdowns are personal and professional.

_____ 5. Biases sometimes get in the way of effective customer service.

_____ 6. A customer's inability to communicate ideas effectively can be an obstacle to effective listening.

_____ 7. A faulty assumption arises when you react to or make a decision about a customer's message based on your experiences or encounters.

_____ 8. A customer's refusal to deal with you, coupled with a request to be served by someone else, could indicate that you are viewed as a poor listener.

_____ 9. Many people can listen effectively to several people at one time.

_____ 10. By showing a willingness to listen and eliminate distractions, you can encourage meaningful customer dialogue.

_____ 11. Two types of questions that are effective for gathering information are reflective and direct.

_____ 12. Open-end questions elicit more information than closed-end questions do because they allow customers to provide what they feel is necessary to answer your question.

Answers to Quick Preview are located at the end of the chapter.

Words to Live By

"Spend a lot of time talking to customers face-to-face. You'd be amazed how many companies don't listen to their customers."

—SOURCE: ROSS PEROT

LO 5-1 Why Is Listening So Important?

listening An active, learned process consisting of four phases: receiving/hearing the message, attending, comprehending/assigning meaning, and responding.

CONCEPT **To be a better customer service professional, it is necessary to improve your listening skills.**

Listening effectively is the primary means that many customer service professionals use to determine the needs of their customers. Many times, these needs are communicated through inferences, indirect comments, or nonverbal signals rather than directly to you. A skilled listener will notice a customer's words and these cues or nuances and conduct follow-up questioning or probe deeper to determine the real need.

Most people take the listening skill for granted. They incorrectly assume that anyone can listen effectively. Unfortunately, this is untrue. Many service providers are complacent about listening and only go through the motions of focusing on what a customer is saying.

In a classic study on listening conducted by Dr. Ralph G. Nichols, who is sometimes called the *Father of the Field of Listening*, data revealed that the average white-collar worker in the United States typically has only about a 25 percent efficiency rate when listening. This means that 75 percent of the message is lost. Think about what such a loss

Customer Service Success Tip

Stop doing other tasks and focus on what your customers are saying in order to increase your listening efficiency. Ask clarifying questions where appropriate.

©Clerkenwell/Getty Images RF

To effectively deal with customers, you must listen to their needs, wants, and issues. *What do you do to show others that you are listening as they speak?*

Opportunities	Action Taken	Impact
100 customers a day, each with a $10 order	25 orders were filled successfully	Loss of $750 per day ($273,750 per year)
1,000 customers went to a store in one day	250 were serviced properly	750 were dissatisfied
1,000,000 members were eligible for membership renewal in an association	250,000 returned their applications after receiving a reminder call	750,000 members were lost

FIGURE 5.1
Missed Opportunities (Based on a 25 Percent Efficiency Rate)

in message reception could mean in an organization if the poor listening skills of customer service professionals led to a loss of 75 percent of customer opportunities. Figure 5.1 gives you some idea of the potential impact of a 25 percent efficiency rate on an organization. The implications of such loss include higher customer churn rates, potential negative word-of-mouth publicity, and reduced revenue for your organization. The latter could mean inability to purchase or update of new equipment and software, lowered benefits and employee salaries, and organizational solvency is endangered.

KNOWLEDGE CHECK

1. Why is effective listening so important for service providers?

LO 5-2 What Is Listening?

CONCEPT Listening is a learned process, not a physical one.

True listening is an active learned process, as opposed to hearing, which is the physical process of gathering sound waves through the ear canal. When you listen actively, you go through a number of phases: hearing or receiving the message,

WORK IT OUT 5.1

Implied Messages

To help reinforce the concept that many customer messages are implied rather than actually spoken to service providers, form a group with two other students and role-play the following scenarios. Choose one in which you play the customer, one in which you play the service provider, and one in which you are the observer. Each group member assumes one of the roles during scenarios.

When you are the customer, simply state your issue or need in a way that does not ask the service provider to do something. Also, do not suggest a solution to the problem or issue. Let the person playing the provider role figure out your need and offer one or more solutions.

At the end of each scenario, you and your teammates should take time to answer the following questions:

1. What unspoken need was the customer sending to the service provider?

2. How well did the service provider do in listening and identifying the customer's issue or need?

3. Specifically, what did the service provider do or say to address the customer's need or issue?

4. What could the service provider have done differently to improve service or satisfy the customer?

Possible answers to these scenarios can be found at www.mhhe.com/customerservice.

Scenario 1

A customer has a mortgage payment due on the first day of each month. In the past, his paydays were on the 10th and 25th; however, he started a new job and now paid on the 15th and 30th of each month. He recently bought a new car and that payment is due on the 27th of each month. This does not leave him much extra cash for living expenses at the end of the month. He is asking to change his mortgage due date.

Scenario 2

You work in a customer care center as a call center representative. A customer contacts you because she just placed an order on your company website but forgot to enter an e-coupon code for free shipping that she received last week. Her credit card had already been charged for the shipping when the order was sent.

Scenario 3

A customer moved into his newly built house in February and subsequently requested the cable company (your organization) to install cable service to the home. The installers came out with a backhoe, dug a trench, and installed the cable. It is now June and service has been fine until the customer turned on his lawn sprinkler system for the first time this season. The water pressure dropped immediately and, upon investigation, soggy ground was found where the cable company dug to install the cable months ago. He just called to complain and wants the problem resolved.

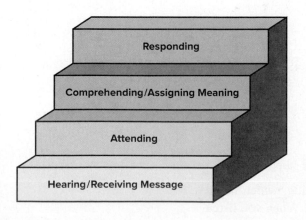

attending, comprehending or assigning meaning, and responding. Figure 5.2 illustrates the process.

HEARING AND RECEIVING THE MESSAGE

Hearing is a passive physiological process of receiving sound waves and transmitting them to the brain for analysis and action. This is usually a simple process. However, because of external noises and internal distracters (psychological and physical), a customer's message(s) may be lost or distorted.

Personal Listening Experiences

Think about experiences you have had in which a customer or someone else did a good job listening to you. Write these down on a piece of paper and be prepared to share these in class.

Describe some of these experiences.

How did the behavior of the person make you feel?

How did you react to the behavior of the person?

Did you enjoy your interaction with the person? Why or why not?

What did you tell others about your experience?

Use your reactions as a reminder that if you practice good listening skills with customers, they might also feel as you did in the situations above. That can enhance the customer–provider relationship, which can mean success for you and your organization.

ATTENDING

Once your ears pick up sound waves, your brain goes to work focusing on, or **attending** to, what you heard. In the process, it sorts out every sound being received. The effort involves deciding what is important so that you can focus attention on the proper sound. This becomes extremely difficult when you are receiving multiple messages or sounds. That is why it is important to eliminate as many distractions as possible. For example, during a meeting you could forward phone calls, turn off your computer, or shut your door. Another option is to find a quiet place to meet.

COMPREHENDING OR ASSIGNING MEANING

Once you have decided to which message or customer you will listen, your brain begins a process of **comprehending or assigning meaning** to what you heard. It "decodes" the message. Just like a computer, your brain has files of information—sounds, sights, shapes, images, experiences, and knowledge on various topics in memory—through which it sorts. As it compares what you heard to what is stored, it tries to match the pieces. For example, when you hear a voice on the phone that sounds familiar, the brain goes to work trying to match the voice to a name or person you have dealt with before. This is called **memory** and **recognition**.

RESPONDING

The last phase of the listening process is **responding**. Selecting an appropriate response is crucial to the success of your customer interactions. The words you select, the way you deliver them, the timing and location, and the nonverbal signals you send all have meaning, and all affect the way others perceive and interpret your message. This is why you should carefully select the appropriate response and method of delivery when dealing with customers. In other words, you should properly "encode" the message considering such things as who your receiver is, his or her background, the location, possible message delivery systems available, and any other factor that might aid reception and comprehension by your listener. A wrong choice of words or message delivery method could mean lost business or worse (the customer could get angry or violent).

hearing A passive physiological means of gathering sound waves and transmitting them to the brain for analysis. It is the first phase of the listening process.

attending The phase of the listening process in which a listener focuses attention on a specific sound or message being received from a person or the environment.

comprehending or assigning meaning The phase of the listening process in which the brain attempts to match a received sound or message with other information stored in the brain as a memory in order to recognize or extract meaning from it.

memory The ability to gain, store, retain, and recall information in the brain for later application. Short-term memory stores small bits of information (seven items, plus or minus two) for approximately 20 seconds while long-term memory can store much larger quantities of information for potentially unlimited duration.

recognition A process that occurs in thinking when a previously experienced pattern, event, process, image, or object that is stored in memory is encountered again.

responding Refers to sending back verbal and nonverbal messages to a message originator.

Figure 5.3 gives some suggested questions you might ask yourself to verify your listening effectiveness. Figure 5.4 provides questions for a self-assessment of your listening skills.

FIGURE 5.3

Questions for the Listener

In analyzing your customer's message(s), ask yourself the following questions:

- Am I practicing active listening skills?
- What message is the customer trying to get across?
- What does the customer want or need me to do in response to his or her message?
- Should I take notes or remember key points being made?
- Am I forming premature conclusions, or do I need to listen further?
- Are there personal biases or distractions I need to avoid?
- Is the customer failing to provide information needed for me to make a sound decision?
- In addition to words, what other feedback clues are being provided? Are they important to message meaning?
- What questions do I need to ask as a follow-up to the customer's message?

FIGURE 5.4

Listening Self-Assessment

To prepare yourself for effective customer interactions and to quickly assess effectiveness of you listening skills, take a few moments to take the following assessment. Depending on your responses, you may need to develop a listening improvement plan using some of the strategies in this chapter and available from other sources.

Place a check mark in the appropriate column.

	Always	Sometimes	Never
1. When a customer speaks to me, I stop what I am doing to focus on what he or she is saying.			
2. I listen to customers, even if I disagree with what they are saying.			
3. When I am unsure of a customer's meaning, I ask for clarification.			
4. I avoid daydreaming when listening to others.			
5. I focus on main ideas, not details, when a customer speaks to me.			
6. While listening, I am also conscious of nonverbal cues sent by the customer.			
7. I consciously block out noise when a customer speaks to me.			
8. I paraphrase the messages I receive in order to ensure I understood the customer's meaning.			
9. I wait until I have received a customer's entire message before forming my response.			
10. When receiving negative feedback (e.g., a customer complaint), I listen with an open mind.			

Rating key: Always = 5   Sometimes = 3   Never = 0
Add your total score. If you rated:

40–50	Your listening is excellent.
26–39	Your listening is above average.
15–25	Your listening likely falls into the range identified by Dr. Nichols' study mentioned earlier in this chapter.
Below 15	You have a serious listening problem and should seek additional training or resources to improve.

KNOWLEDGE CHECK

1. What are the four phases of the active listening process?

2. How would you describe the process of hearing?

3. What occurs during the attending phase of the listening process?

4. What happens in your brain during the comprehending/assigning meaning phase of listening?

5. Why should you be sure to select the appropriate response during the responding phase of listening?

> **Customer Service Success Tip**
>
> Take time to slow down and actively listen to customers in order to make them feel important and allow you to better identify and meet their needs. This is important because many people spend time thinking about what they will say next rather than listening to what the message sender is saying. If you do this, your customer–provider relationship could suffer.

LO 5-3 Characteristics of a Good Listener

CONCEPT Listening will improve as you "learn" in the customer's shoes.

Successful listening is essential to service excellence. Like any other skill, listening is a learned behavior that some people learn better than others do. The following sections contain some common characteristics possessed by most effective listeners. Figure 5.5 summarizes the characteristics of effective and ineffective listeners.

Empathy. By putting yourself in the customer's place and trying to relate to the customer's needs, wants, and concerns, you can often reduce the risk of poor service. Some customer service professionals neglect the customer's need for compassion, especially when the customer is dissatisfied. Such negligence tends to magnify or compound the effect of the initial poor service the customer received.

Understanding. The ability to listen as customers verbalize their needs, and to ensure that you understand them, is essential in properly servicing the customer. Too often, you hear people say, "I understand what you mean," when it is obvious that they have no clue as to the level of emotion being felt. When this happens while a

FIGURE 5.5

Characteristics of Effective and Ineffective Listeners

Many factors can indicate an effective or ineffective listener. Over the years, researchers have assigned the following characteristics to effective and ineffective listeners:

Effective Listeners	Ineffective Listeners
Focused	Inattentive
Responsive	Uncaring
Alert	Distracted
Understanding	Unconcerned
Caring	Insensitive
Empathetic	Smug/conceited
Unemotional	Emotionally involved
Interested	Self-centered
Patient	Judgmental
Cautious	Disorganized
Open	Defensive

customer is upset or angry, flared tempers, loss of business, bad publicity, and, at the far end of the continuum, acts of violence might result. You will read about some techniques for demonstrating understanding later in this chapter.

Trending NOW

Customers need to know companies are truly listening to them. One solution now available to organizations is the use of personalized customer interactions through automated chats. Companies are either creating their own communication software or contracting with third-party companies like Zendesk to provide them (visit www.zendesk.com for information on additional software sources). This is often an economical means for smaller organizations to provide service support without having to increase staff and technology resources internally. It is a win-win situation because the organizations provide necessary support and customers feel heard or attended to right away.

Patience. Keep in mind that it is your job to serve the customer. Not everyone communicates in the same manner. Each customer has different needs and expectations based on age, gender, behavioral style, preference, background, cultural background, and other factors. That is why you must never try to use a cookie-cutter approach to delivering service where you assume all people are the same and respond to the same approach in service delivery. Take the time to ask questions and actively listen to their responses before choosing a course of action.

©Spencer Grant/PhotoEdit

Active listening involves complete attention, a readiness and willingness to take action, and an open mind to evaluate customers and determine their needs. *What should customer service professionals do to achieve these goals of active listening?*

Do your best to listen well so that you can get at the customer's meaning or need. Do not rush a customer who seems to be processing information and forming opinions or making a decision. This is especially important after you have presented product information and have asked for a buying decision. Answer questions and provide additional information requested, but do not appear impatient. Doing so could frustrate, anger, and ultimately alienate the customer. You could end up with a complaint or lost customer.

Patience is especially important when a language barrier or speech disability is part of a customer's situation. Your job is to take extra care to determine customer needs and then respond appropriately. In some cases, you may have to resort to the use of an interpreter or written or other visual communication techniques in order to determine the customer's needs.

Attentiveness. By focusing your attention on the customer, you can better interpret his or her message and satisfy his or her needs. Attentiveness can be displayed through nonverbal cues (nodding or cocking of the head to one side or the other, smiling, or using paralanguage). When you are reading, talking on the phone to someone while servicing your customer, or doing some other task while "listening" to your customer, you are not really focusing. In fact, your absorption rate will fall into the 25 percent of listening efficiency category about which you read earlier. The ability to competently multitask or juggle multiple tasks is a myth. Research studies support the fact that the human brain cannot efficiently conduct two activities simultaneously.

Objectivity. In dealings with customers, try to avoid subjective opinions or judgments. If you have a preconceived idea about customers, their concerns or questions, the environment, or anything related to the customers, you could mishandle the situation. Listen openly and avoid making assumptions. Allow customers to describe their needs, wants, or concerns in their own words, and then analyze them fairly before taking appropriate action. If necessary or appropriate, have a colleague join in the discussion to get an objective second opinion.

KNOWLEDGE CHECK

1. Name the five characteristics possessed by most effective listeners and describe their relationship to customer service.

LO 5-4 Causes of Listening Breakdown

CONCEPT **Poor customer service may result from a breakdown of the listening process.**

Many factors contribute to ineffective listening. Some are internal or in your brain, but others are external and you cannot control them. The key is to recognize actual and potential factors that can cause ineffective listening and strive to eliminate them. The factors discussed in the following sections are some of the most common.

PERSONAL OBSTACLES

As a listener, you may have individual characteristics or qualities that get in the way of listening effectively to the customer. Some of these **personal obstacles** follow.

Biases

Your opinions or beliefs about a specific person, group, situation, or issue can sometimes cloud your ability to listen objectively to a message. These **biases** may result in preconceived and sometimes incorrect assumptions. They can also lead to service breakdowns, complaints, angry or lost customers, or even violence.

Often personal biases are a result of things learned earlier in life and not even recognized on a conscious level. Everyone has such biases to some degree because children often repeat what they hear from caregivers, in the media, through music, and via other sources in juvenile jokes or taunts. Unfortunately, some of the things they hear are inappropriate negative stereotypes about individuals or groups of people. Repeating such comments helps to lock them into long-term memory. As adults, we have these retained images or "tapes" continually playing in the back of our subconscious mind. This is why many people who do not consider themselves as racist or biased against other people whom they perceive to be different will sometimes shout or use slurs or derogatory comments based on race or some other aspect of a person (e.g., weight, color, dialect, or physical condition) in emotional situations. For example, someone cuts them off in traffic, bumps into them in a crowded store, or acts in a way that the person believes is "typical" of "those" people. In such instances, they might react with a derogatory remark or nonverbalized thought because of the mental "tape" or memories in their head from an earlier point in their life.

personal obstacles Individual factors that can limit performance or success in life. Examples are disabilities, lack of education, attitude, and biases.

biases Beliefs or opinions that a person has about an individual or group. Often based on unreasonable distortions or prejudice.

As a service provider, you must never allow such biases to impact the way you listen to or deal with others. Often we see this occur when a service provider has an emotional exchange with a customer. After the customer leaves or hangs up the phone, the provider makes a derogatory comment to him- or herself or to a coworker that is overheard by others. This portrays the provider in a negative light and potentially degrades the reputation of the organization, especially if another customer or coworker hears the comment.

Psychological Distracters

psychological distracters Refers to mental factors that can cause a shift in focus in interacting with others. Examples are state of health and personal issues.

Your psychological state can impede effective listening. **Psychological distracters**, such as being angry or upset, or simply not wanting to deal with a particular person or situation, may negatively affect your listening. Think about a time when you had a negative call or encounter with a customer or someone else and you became frustrated or angry. Did your mood and possibly your voice tone change as a result? Did that emotion then carry over and affect another person later?

Often when people become upset, they need time to cool off before they deal with someone else. If you do not calm down emotionally, the chance that you will raise your voice or become frustrated with the next person you encounter increases greatly. If this second encounter escalates because of the person's reaction to your perceived negative tone or attitude, you might respond inappropriately. Thus, a vicious cycle starts. You get angry at a person; your tone carries over to a second, who in turn gets upset with your tone; your emotions escalate, and you carry that mood to a third person; and so on. All of this lessens your ability to listen and serve customers effectively.

> ### Street Talk
>
> Empower each customer service representative to make a decision that will bring closure for the customer. This will leave the customer feeling good about the organization and how he or she was treated by the service provider.
>
> **SOURCE: SHARON MASSEN, Ph.D., CAP *Massen and Associates***

Physical Condition

Another internal factor that can contribute to or detract from effective listening is your state of wellness and fitness. When you are ill, fatigued, in poor physical condition, or just not feeling well, listening can suffer. Because of the hectic pace of today's world, the prevalence and easy access of television, and the belief by many people that they "need" to check their e-mail, text, or voice messages immediately when communication arrives, we are a world of tired people. All of this can cause problems when trying to effectively listen to others or function effectively each day. According to the National Sleep Foundation, the depth and quality of sleep are impacted by a number of environmental factors. Ultimately, a loss of sound sleep can impact your effectiveness on the job.[1] Further, "A study from the National Health Interview Survey which examined the sleep duration of individuals across several occupations ranging from manufacturing to public administration found that the percent of workers who reported a sleep duration of 6 hours or less per night increased from 24 to 30% in the last 20 years."[2]

We often hear that a good diet and exercise are essential to good health. They are also crucial for effective listening. Try not to skip meals when you are working, stay away from foods high in sugar content, and get some form of regular exercise. These all affect physical condition. Try something as simple as using the stairs rather than the elevator or escalator. Another option is a brisk walk at lunchtime. All of these can help you maintain your "edge" so that you are better prepared for a variety of customer encounters. Also, avoiding meals that are heavy in carbohydrates can aid you in staying more alert.

©MONKEY BUSINESS - LBR/AGE Fotostock RF

When a customer service professional gets angry, his or her tone and mood may likely carry over to a customer. *How do you feel when a customer service professional is angry and raises his or her voice?*

Circadian Rhythm

All people have a natural 24-hour biological pattern (**circadian rhythm**) by which they function. The physiological cycle is associated with the earth's rotation. It affects metabolic and sleep patterns in humans as day replaces night. This "clock" often establishes the body's peak performance periods.

"Most people feel the strongest desire to sleep between 1:00pm and 3:00pm (a.k.a. the post-lunch, afternoon crash) and then again between 2:00am and 4:00am, but this can vary from person to person. That's why some people are 'morning people,' while others function best in the evening. Your circadian rhythm can also change as you age. When you were a teenager, for example, your body was programmed (so to speak) to sleep for more total hours, as well as go to bed and wake up later."[3]

Morning people typically wake early, "hit the ground running," and continue until after lunch, when the natural rhythm or energy level in their body begins to slow down. For such people, afternoons are often a struggle. They may not do their best thinking or perform physically at peak during that point in the day. Contrarily, the pattern of

circadian rhythm The physiological 24-hour cycle associated with the earth's rotation that affects metabolic and sleep patterns in humans as day displaces night.

⚙ WORK IT OUT 5.3

Personal Habits

Take a few minutes to think about your personal nutritional (e.g., how many meals a day you eat, snacks, quantities, and when you eat) and exercise (e.g., how often, duration, and type of exercise) habits since these can affect attention span and your ability to listen effectively; then create a list of the ones that are positive and negative. Next, make an action plan for any adjustments that might be appropriate to enhance your workplace or personal performance.

Leaders in many organizations realize the importance of employee work–life balance. To address the issue, they are now instituting benefits that provide services like child care, elder care, and in some instances even pet care in order to attract and retain qualified employees. Often, these services are provided on-site where employees work. Such options often relieve personal pressure and allow customer service representatives to better listen and focus on customer needs.

energy for evening people is often opposite to that of their morning counterparts. They struggle to get up or perform in the morning; however, during the afternoon and in the evening, they are just hitting their stride. They often stay awake and work or engage in other activities until the early hours of the next day, when the morning people have been sound asleep for hours. From a listening standpoint, you should recognize your own natural body pattern so that you can deal with the most important listening and other activities during your peak period if possible. For example, if you are a morning person, you may want to ask your boss to assign you to customer contact or to handling problem situations early in the day. At that time, you are likely to be most alert and productive, less stressed, and less apt to become frustrated or irritated by abusive or offensive behavior by others.

Preoccupation

In recent years, many people have become distracted from work and listening activities by personal factors (e.g., financial issues, relationship or family problems, schooling, or stress because of issues at home) that override their efforts to do a good job each day. When you have personal or other matters on your mind, it sometimes becomes difficult to focus on the needs and expectations of the customer and your job tasks. This can frustrate both you and your customers. It is difficult to turn off personal problems, but you should try to resolve them before going to work, even if you must take time off to deal with them. Many companies offer programs to assist employees in dealing with their personal and performance issues. Through **employee assistance programs (EAPs)**, organizations are providing counseling in such areas as finance, mental hygiene (health), substance abuse, marital and family issues, smoking cessation, weight loss, and workplace performance problems. Check with your supervisor or human resources department to identify whether such resources are available in your organization. Also, if you are applying for a new job, ask during the interview process if the company offers EAPs.

employee assistance program (EAP) Benefit package offered by many organizations that provides services to help employees deal with personal issues that might adversely affect their work performance (e.g., legal, financial, behavioral, family, and mental health counseling services).

Hearing Loss

Many people suffer from hearing loss caused by physiological (physical) problems or extended exposure to loud noises (personal and workplace). Sometimes they are not aware that their hearing is impaired. Often, out of vanity or embarrassment, people take no action to remedy the loss and prolong taking remedial action. If you find yourself regularly straining to hear someone, having to turn an ear toward the speaker, or asking people to repeat what they said because you did not get the entire message, you may have a hearing loss. If you suspect that you have hearing loss, go to your physician or an audiologist (hearing specialist) quickly to avoid complications or further loss of hearing. Failure to do so could lead to issues where your supervisor perceives that your workplace listening issues are caused by poor attitude or some other issue. That could result in negative performance ratings for you.

LISTENING SKILL LEVEL

People communicate on different levels, depending on their knowledge and experiences in the area of communication. Childhood experiences influence adult behavior. That is, they are likely to repeat behavior they learned as children. For example, if you grew up in an environment where the people around you practiced positive listening skills, providing feedback and using nonverbal communication and effective interpersonal skills for dealing with others, you will likely use similar techniques as an adult (Figure 5.6 shows some indicators of poor listening skills). On the other hand, if your childhood experiences were negative, where active conversation with multiple people talking simultaneously was normal, or you did not have good communication role models, the chances are that you struggle in listening to others effectively. This may not be true if, as an adult, you have taken steps (e.g., attended courses on active listening and practiced listening more effectively) to improve your listening skills.

As you read earlier, listening is the primary skill most people have for gathering information. Unfortunately, in the United States (and other countries), the skill of listening is not routinely taught in many public school systems. People learn the proper listening techniques only if they take the personal initiative to read, listen to professional development recordings, watch videos, and attend seminars or college courses on active listening skills. Too often, even though a parent's intentions might be well meant, techniques used to teach listening to children are often ineffective.

Two other factors can also create barriers and inhibit effective listening when dealing with your customers. These are thought speed and faulty assumptions (biases) that you have about others or a situation.

FIGURE 5.6

Indicators of Poor Listening

You cannot afford the luxury of failing to listen to your customer. Periodically, you should do a self-check on your listening style to see whether you need to improve. If any of the following events occur, you may need to refocus.

- Customers specifically ask to speak to or be served by someone else.
- You find yourself missing key details of conversations.
- You regularly have to ask people to repeat information.
- You end phone calls or personal encounters not knowing for sure what action is required of you.
- Customers often ask questions or make statements such as, "Did you hear what I said?" "Are you listening to me?" or "You are not listening."
- You find yourself daydreaming or distracted as a customer is speaking.
- You miss nonverbal cues sent by the customer or others as the two of you communicate.
- You answer a question incorrectly because you did not actually "listen" to it.

Thought Speed

thought speed The rate at which the human brain processes information.

Your brain is capable of comprehending messages delivered at rates of as much as four to six times faster (**thought speed**) than the speed at which the average adult speaks. In the United States, this rate is approximately 125 to 150 words per minute (wpm), while in other countries or cultures this rate might vary. The difference between the two rates can be referred to as a **lag time** or **listening gap** during which the mind is momentarily idle or focused on another activity. The result is that your brain does other things to occupy itself (e.g., daydreaming or formulating a response before gathering all relevant information). To prevent or reduce such distraction, you must consciously focus on your customer's message, look for key points he or she makes, ask pertinent questions, and respond appropriately. One way to help yourself focus is to take notes about an issue, suggestion, or complaint as your customer speaks. You then have something to which you can refer or provide feedback from once the customer stops talking. Another benefit of this technique is that you can demonstrate to customers that you are truly interested in their ideas or subject of the conversation.

lag time The term applied to the difference in the rate at which the human brain can receive and process information and at which most adults speak.

listening gap The difference in the speed at which the brain can comprehend communication and the speed at which the average adult speaks in the United States.

Ethical Dilemma 5.1

A customer comes into your office at the Department of Water and Sewer on a Tuesday following a three-day holiday weekend. She has a toddler and a five-year-old daughter with her and is very upset. She is cursing and screaming that on the previous Thursday another employee promised that her water, which was turned off due to two-month bill payment delinquency, would be turned back on Friday afternoon. It was not. She states that she and her two infant children had no water or bathroom to use all weekend.

You know that no turn-offs/turn-ons are routinely scheduled on Fridays since maintenance staff members have mandatory in-service training every Friday afternoon.

In checking your database, you find that she had promised to come in last Wednesday to give a money order for the delinquent bills, but never showed up. You also see that she has a history of nonpayment.

1. How would you handle this situation? Explain.
2. Exactly what would you say to this customer? Explain why you would use the wording you intend to use.
3. What actions would you take to remedy the situation and get her water back on so that she and her children would have access to services?

Faulty Assumptions

faulty assumptions Service provider projections made about underlying customer message meanings based on past experiences.

Because of experiences or encounters with others, you may be tempted to make **faulty assumptions** about your customer's message(s). Do not do so. Each customer and each situation is different and you should regard them as such. Because you had a certain experience with one customer does not mean that you will have a similar experience with another. For example, because one customer lies about an issue with your organization's products or services does not mean that everyone who complains is lying. Take the time to effectively gather information in each customer encounter so that you can make an informed decision on the correct course of action. Once you have done so, make a judgment on what needs to be accomplished in order to remedy the situation.

For additional articles and tips on effective listening, visit the author's Customer Service Skills Blog at http://www.customerserviceskillsbook.com/wordpress.

EXTERNAL OBSTACLES

You cannot remove all barriers to effective listening, but you should still try to reduce them when dealing with customers. Some typical examples of **external obstacles** that often create problems include the following.

external obstacles Factors outside an organization or the sphere of one's influence that can cause challenges in delivering service.

Information Overload

Each day, information from many sources piles up. You get information in meetings, e-mail and text messages, from the radio and television, from customers, and in a variety of public places. In many instances, you spend as much as five to six hours a day listening to customers, coworkers, family members, friends, and strangers. Such **information overload** can result in stress, inadequate time to deal with individual situations, and reduced levels of customer service.

information overload Refers to having too many messages coming together and causing confusion, frustration, or an inability to act.

Other People Talking

It is not possible for you to give your full attention to two speakers simultaneously. In order to serve customers effectively, deal with only one person at a time. If someone else approaches, smile, acknowledge him or her, and say, "I will be with you in just a moment" or at least signal that message by holding up your index finger to indicate "one minute" while you smile. If after a minute, it appears that you will need more time with your current customer, either call for assistance or ask the waiting person if he or she just has a simple question that you might answer. If he or she indicates this to be the case, ask the current customer if he or she would mind your answering a question. Should you determine that the second customer's question is going to take some time to address, either ask him or her to continue waiting or call for assistance.

Employees rarely have control over external distractions in the workplace. *What are some strategies to help cope with a noisy work environment?*

©Digital Vision/Getty Images RF

Ringing Phones

Ringing telephones can be annoying, but you should not stop helping one customer to get into a discussion with or try to serve another customer over the phone. This creates a dilemma, for you cannot ignore customers or others who depend on you to serve their needs over the telephone. Still, you cannot effectively do two things at once.

Several options are available in such instances. You might arrange with your supervisor or coworkers to have someone else answer ringing phones. Those people can either provide service or take messages, depending on the business your organization conducts and the knowledge and experience of employees. Another option is the use of a voice mail system or answering service for message collection. Still another possibility would be to ask the person to whom you are speaking face-to-face to excuse you, professionally answer the phone, and either ask the caller to remain on hold or take a number for a callback. Just be aware that this approach could irritate the current customer, so try to read their personality style, evaluate the situation, and watch their non-verbal cues.

No one solution is best. You can only try to provide the best service possible, depending on your situation. In a world of downsized organizations where employees are required to multitask and perform more than their normal job tasks, delivering quality service can sometimes be a challenge. Before such situations develop, it is a good idea to speak with your supervisor or team leader and peers to determine the policy and procedures for handling customers in these instances. During the conversation(s), make any suggestions that you have for improving the system. This will improve the quality of service delivery that customers receive and help your supervisor recognize that you take initiative to solve problems. Thus, promotion and incentive opportunities might follow for you.

⚙ WORK IT OUT 5.4

Dealing with Interruptions

Think about a situation in which you were a customer and talking to a service representative when another customer approached or the phone started ringing. The service representative stated, "Please excuse me and started talking to the new customer or answered the telephone"

How did that make you feel?

If in person, what was your reaction to the other customer or how did you handle the situation with him or her?

What was your reaction to the service provider or how did you handle the situation with him or her?

Next, think of a situation in which you were a service provider talking to a customer and another person arrived, interrupted, and started asking questions or talking to you.

What was the reaction of the first person to whom you were talking?

What was your reaction?

How did you handle the situation?

Discuss these scenarios in class to identify effective ways to handle them should you encounter them in the future.

Office and Maintenance Equipment

Noisy printers, computers, photocopying machines, electric staplers, vacuum cleaners, humming overhead lights, and other devices can also be distractions. When servicing customers, eliminate or minimize the use of these types of items. If others are using noisy equipment, try to position yourself or them as far away from the customer service area as possible.

Speakerphones

These devices allow for hands-free telephone conversations. They are great because you can continue your conversation while searching for something the customer has requested. If you want to use one, inform the customer and ask if he or she minds. Also, make sure that you can be heard and that there are no distracting background noises that might interfere with reception on either end. The negative part of using speakerphones is that many people put callers on the loudspeaker while continuing to do work not related to the caller. This not only is rude, but it results in ineffective communication and poor customer service.

Because the speakerphone picks up background noise, it is often difficult to hear the caller, especially if you are moving around the room and are not next to the phone. This is one reason that many people dislike speakerphones. Improper use of them could cause customers to stop calling or to complain.

An additional issue with the speakerphone is confidentiality. Since others can hear the conversation, the caller may be reluctant to provide certain information (credit card and Social Security numbers, medical information, or personal data). Whenever you use a speakerphone, inform the caller if someone else is in the room with you and/or close your office door, if possible. If you are in a cubicle environment, it is best to avoid using these devices because of loss of confidentiality.

Physical Barriers

Desks, counters, furniture, or other items separating you from your customer can stifle communication. Depending on your job function, you might be able to eliminate barriers. If possible, do so. These obstacles can distance you physically from your customer or depersonalize your service. If you have an option, be conscious of how you arrange your office or workspace. Side-by-side (facing the customer at an angle)

 WORK IT OUT 5.5

Inattentive Listening Behavior

To help you improve your listening skills and offer better service to your customers, complete the following activity. Think of a time when someone was verbally communicating ideas to you and he or she realized (from your verbal and nonverbal responses) that you were distracted and not really listening.

1. What was going on that prevented you from listening effectively?
2. What reaction did your listener have to your distraction or lack of focus?

Compare your answers with those of others. Use the collective responses to these questions to improve your listening skills.

The rise of social media and mobile technology has opened an entirely new opportunity for companies regarding "listening" to their customers and potential customers. Through technology such as smartphones, organizations are now able to solicit feedback as close to the end of a customer experience as possible. Once a customer has visited a store, contacted a service representative, made a purchase, or otherwise contacted an organizational representative, his or her feedback should be requested. This enables the organization to obtain almost immediate emotional and empirical responses and record them for future analysis and integration into service improvement strategies. For example, if a company has obtained contact information from a customer during a store visit or phone call, it might send a tweet or e-mail message conveying an offer of a gift certificate or discount in exchange for the customer completing a survey on the company website or through websites such as Survey Monkey (www.surveymonkey.com).

From a customer standpoint, technology allows organizations to capture customer feedback as they go about their daily business or life functions without the intrusion of calling them at home during dinner or family time.

seating next to a table is preferable to sitting across from a customer in most situations. That is because having a table between you nonverbally creates an obstacle to effective interaction. It can potentially project a perception of authority, dominance, and inequality. An exception to this approach would be appropriate if you provide service to customers who might become agitated or violent. Some examples of situations when you might want a physical barrier include the following:

- City or state clerks who deal with people charged with traffic or other violations of the law
- Public utility employees who deal with people who are complaining about service problems
- Employees in tax or motor vehicle offices where problems with drivers' licenses or vehicle registrations are common.

ADDITIONAL OBSTACLES TO EFFECTIVE LISTENING

In addition to the issues you just read, customers themselves can negatively affect communication—through their inability to convey a message to you.

Although it is not specifically a listening issue, if customers are unable to deliver their message effectively, you may be unable to receive and properly analyze their meaning. No amount of dedication and effort on your part will make up for a language barrier, a disability (speech, physical) that limits speech and nonverbal body language, or a customer's poor communication skills. In these situations, it is often necessary to seek out others to help (translators, signers) or to use alternative means of communication (gestures, written, symbols, or a text telephone [TTY/TDD]) to discover the customers' meaning and satisfy their needs.

By recognizing these limiting factors, you can improve your chances of communicating more effectively.

KNOWLEDGE CHECK

1. What are six personal obstacles that might cause a listening breakdown?
2. How do thought speed and faulty assumptions affect your listening skill level?
3. What can you do to reduce the external obstacles you just read about?

LO 5-5 Strategies for Improved Listening

CONCEPT You can improve your listening skills in several different ways. One important way is to listen more than you talk.

There are numerous techniques for becoming a more effective listener. You can use the following as a basis for self-improvement.

STOP TALKING!

You cannot talk and actively listen at the same time. When the customer starts talking, the first thing you should do is stop talking and listen carefully. One common mistake that many people make is to ask a question, hesitate, and immediately ask a second question or "clarify" their meaning by providing additional information if no answer was immediately received. A habit like this is confusing to the listener. It is also rude. Some people (e.g., people who speak a different language, have certain **behavioral styles**, are elderly, or have certain disabilities) take a bit more time to analyze and respond to messages they receive. Others may be simply trying to formulate just the right answer before responding. If you interrupt with additional information or questions, you may interfere with their thought patterns and cause them to become frustrated or forget what they were going to say. The result is that the listener may not speak or respond at all because he or she believes that you are not really listening or interested in the response anyhow, or because he or she is embarrassed or confused.

Listening behavior such as that which you just read about could lead to a complaint to your supervisor because of what a customer believes to be rude, uncaring, or an

behavioral styles Descriptive term that identifies categories of human behavior identified by behavioral researchers. Many of the models used to group behaviors date back to those identified by Carl Jung.

WORK IT OUT 5.6

Correcting Common Listening Problems

Here are some common listening problems. Work in a small group with other students to try to think of one or two means for reducing or eliminating these problems in your customer service.

Listening to words, not concepts, ideas, or emotions

Pretending interest in a customer's problem, question, suggestion, or concern

Planning your next remarks while the customer is talking

Being distracted by external factors

Listening only for what you perceive is the real issue or point

Reacting emotionally to what the customer is saying

WORK IT OUT 5.7

Active Listening Strategies

Think about someone whom you believe to be a good listener. List some of the behaviors and listening techniques that he or she demonstrates and use this list as a guide to set personal listening improvement goals.

unprofessional service attitude. To avoid such a scenario, plan what you want to say, ask the question, and then stop speaking. You might ask, "Mr. Swanson, how do you think we might resolve this issue?" Once you have asked the question, stop talking and wait for a response. If a response does not come in a moment or so, or the customer states that he or she is unsure or seems confused by what you said, try asking the question another way (paraphrase). Possibly offer some guidance to a response and conclude with an open-end question (one that encourages the listener to give opinions or longer responses). You might say, "Mr. Swanson, I would really like to help resolve this issue. Perhaps we could try _____ or _____. How do you think that would work?"

PREPARE YOURSELF

Before you can listen effectively to someone, you must be ready to receive what this person has to say. Focus on your customer by not reading, writing, talking to others, thinking about other things, working on your computer, answering phones, dealing with other business matters, or doing anything else that might distract you. For example, if a customer approaches while you are using a calculator to add up a row of figures, smile and say, "I will be with you in just a moment" or smile and hold up your index finger to indicate "One minute." As quickly as possible, complete your task, apologize for the delay, and then ask, "How may I assist you?"

Other things to do in order to be ready to listen include having within easy access all the administrative supplies, forms, reference materials, and other information needed to answer a question or serve your customer. This will preclude your having to stop serving or listening to a customer to retrieve such items.

By demonstrating that you are actively listening to customers, you can strengthen the service–provider relationship while gaining information you need to serve them. *How do you show customers that you are listening to them?*

LISTEN ACTIVELY

Use the basics of sound communication when a customer is speaking. The following strategies are typically helpful in sending an "I care" message when done naturally and with sincerity:

- SMILE!
- Do not interrupt to interject your ideas or make comments unless they help to clarify a point made by the customer.
- Sit or stand up straight and make eye contact with the customer.
- Lean forward or turn an ear toward the customer, if appropriate and necessary.
- Paraphrase the customer's statements occasionally.

- Nod and offer affirmative statements or utterances (e.g. "I see," "Uh-huh," "Really," "Yes") to show that you are following the conversation.
- Do not finish a customer's sentence. Let the customer talk.

In addition, focus on complete messages. A complete message consists of the words, nonverbal messages, and emotions of the customer. If a customer says that she is satisfied with a product but is sending nonverbal signals that contradict her statement, you should investigate further. Suppose that the supply of blue bowls given away as gifts to people who stop by your trade show exhibit is gone. The customer might say, "Oh, that is okay. I guess a green one will do." However, her tone and facial expression may indicate disappointment. You could counter with, "I am sorry we are out of the blue bowls, Mrs. Zagowski. If you would like one, I can give you a certificate that will allow you to pick one up when you visit our store, or I can take your address and ship one to you when I get back to the store. Would you prefer one of those options?" By being "tuned in" to your customer and taking this extra initiative, you have gone beyond ordinary service and moved into the realm of exceptional customer service. Mrs. Zagowski will probably appreciate your gesture and tell others about the wonderful, customer-focused person she met at the trade show exhibit. In such instances, you have to be prepared for the result of your offering. For example, what if Mrs. Zagowski tells others and they stop by wanting you to ship them a bowl. You time and cost investment for shipping will go up. The point is to think through what you offer before saying it to a customer.

Ethical Dilemma 5.2

Assume that you work in a college registrar office. You see many students and hear lots of stories when they try to change from one class to another or drop a course. One day a student comes into your office and asks to cancel her registration in one class in order to register for another even though the designated time period for such a class change has passed. Your immediate inclination might be to quote policy since you have "heard this one before." Your response might sound like, "I am sorry, Ms. Molina, the period for adds or drops has passed." However, do not respond so quickly; instead, hear the student (customer) out. She may provide information (verbally or nonverbally) that will change your view. For example, Ms. Molina (crying) might emotionally say, "I have got to get out of that class. I need one more course to graduate, but I cannot stay in this class."

If you are proactive in this situation and practicing active listening, you will identify the emotions and ask some questions in order to find out her real need or issue. For example, you might say, "Ms. Molina, you seem very upset, is anything wrong?" She might respond, "Yes. I need to graduate this semester and return to my country to help support my family. But I cannot stay in Mr. Broward's class. He is ... he is always leering at me and making lewd remarks. And, in a previous class, he would regularly massage my shoulders and that of other girls during class."

1. Were you practicing good service skills in this situation? Explain.
2. Is the student's request to transfer reasonable even though the add/drop period has passed? Explain.
3. Would you allow the student (customer) to transfer to another class? Why or why not?
4. As an employee of the college, do you have any further responsibilities? Explain.

SHOW A WILLINGNESS TO LISTEN

By eliminating distractions, sending positive verbal and nonverbal responses, and actively focusing on delivered messages, you can help a customer relax and have a more meaningful dialogue. For example, when dealing with customers, you should make sure that you take some of the positive approaches to listening outlined earlier (turning off noisy equipment, facing the person, making eye contact, and smiling while responding in a positive manner). These small efforts can pay big customer dividends in the form of higher satisfaction, lower frustration, and experiencing a sense of caring.

SHOW EMPATHY

Put yourself in the customer's place by empathizing, especially when the customer is complaining about what he or she perceives to be poor service or inferior products. This is sometimes referred to as "walking a mile in your customer's shoes." For example, if a customer complains that she was expecting a specific service by a certain date but did not get it, you might respond as follows: "Mrs. Ellis, I apologize that we were unable to complete _____ on the tenth as promised. We dispatched a truck, but the driver was involved in an accident. Can we make it up to you by _____? (Offer a gift, suggest an alternative such as hand delivery, and so on.) This technique, known as **service recovery**, is a crucial step in delivering quality service and remaining competitive into the twenty-first century.

service recovery The process of correcting a wrong or something that has not gone as promised involving provision of a product or service to a customer. The concept involves not only replacing defective products, but also going the extra step of providing compensation for the customer's inconvenience.

LISTEN FOR CONCEPTS

Instead of focusing on one or two details, listen to the entire message before analyzing it and responding. Instead of trying to respond to one portion of a message, wait for the customer to provide all the details. Then ask any questions necessary to get the information you need to respond appropriately. For example, assume that a customer (Mr. Chi), who works for a manufacturing company, has requested a special fabricated part to replace one his company currently has for a new machine assembly that it is working on. The part is a special order and not one currently in your company's inventory. He indicates that his company's development budget for the part is $10,000.

After he explains his need, you might respond with something like, "Mr. Chi, if I understand you correctly, you would like us to build a new prototype part to replace the one currently being used in the assembly. You are looking for a total cost for development and manufacture not to exceed $10,000. Is that correct?"

LISTEN OPENLY

Avoid the biases discussed earlier. Remember that you do not have to like everyone you encounter, but you do have to respect and treat customers fairly and impartially if you want to maintain a positive business relationship. For example, whenever you encounter a person

©Jupiterimages/Getty Images RF

Note taking can help focus listening and later aid recall of discussion on topics. *What system do you use to take notes while talking on the phone or to follow up on customer issues?*

who is rude or is the type of person for whom you have a personal dislike, try to maintain your professionalism. Remember that you represent your organization and that you are being paid by your employer to serve the customer (whoever he or she is). If a situation arises that you feel you cannot or prefer not to handle, call in a coworker or supervisor. However, be careful in taking this action because you may potentially reveal a personal preference or bias. That might hurt you when you apply for other positions in your organization or positions in other companies. Try to work through your differences or biases rather than let them hinder your ability to deal with others or your career potential. Your ability to serve each customer fairly and competently is important to your job success.

SEND POSITIVE NONVERBAL CUES

Be conscious of the nonverbal messages you are sending. Even when you are verbally agreeing or saying yes, you may be unconsciously sending negative nonverbal messages. When sending a message, you should make sure that your verbal cues (words) and nonverbal cues (gestures, facial expressions) are in **congruence**. For example, if you say, "Good morning. How may I help you?" in a gruff tone, with no smile, and while looking away from the customer, that customer is not going to feel welcome or believe that you are sincere in your offer to assist.

congruence In communication, this relates to ensuring that verbal messages sent match or are in agreement with the nonverbal cues used.

DO NOT ARGUE

Do you remember the "did not/did too" quarrels you might have witnessed when you were a child and one person accused the other of doing something? Such verbal exchanges often resulted in heated discussions in which voices were raised, tempers escalated, and someone might have started hitting or pushing. Who won? The answer is—no one. You should avoid similar childish behaviors in dealing with others—especially your current or potential customers. Do not let these memories, or "tapes" in your head, get in the way of good service.

When you argue, you become part of the problem and cannot be part of the solution. Learn to phrase responses or questions positively. Keep in mind that even when you go out of your way to serve customers, some of them will respond negatively. Some people seem to enjoy conflict or have a need to dominate or win in such situations. Always remember to maintain your composure (count to ten silently before responding), listen, and attempt to satisfy their needs. If necessary, refer such customers to your supervisor or a peer for service rather than let the encounter turn confrontational or emotional.

Street Talk

Do what you say you are going to do. Always show up as promised and always answer phone calls.

SOURCE: GARY GOLDBERG *Owner, Weeding by Hand*

TAKE NOTES, IF NECESSARY

Most people do not have a photographic memory and cannot remember all details about a discussion or situation. If information is complicated, or if names, dates, numbers, or numerous details are involved in a customer encounter, you may want to take notes for future reference and to ensure accuracy. Notes can help prevent your forgetting or confusing information. Once you have made your notes, verify your understanding of the facts with your customer before proceeding. For example, in a client or customer meeting, you may want to jot down key issues, points, follow-up actions, or questions. Doing so demonstrates that you are indeed listening and committed to getting things right or taking appropriate action.

KNOWLEDGE CHECK

1. In order to actively listen, what is the first thing you must do?

2. What are seven active listening strategies that can send a message of "I care"?

3. What can you do to ensure that your verbal and nonverbal messages are in congruence?

LO 5-6 Information-Gathering Techniques

CONCEPT   Use appropriate questions to sort out facts from fiction.

Your purpose in listening to your customers is to gather information about their needs or wants on which you can base decisions on how to best satisfy them. Sometimes, you will need to prompt your customers to provide additional or different types of information.

Use questions to determine customer needs and to verify and clarify information received. This will ensure that you thoroughly understand the customer's message prior to taking action or responding. For example, when you first encounter a customer, you must discover his or her needs or wants. Through a series of open-end questions and closed-end questions, you can gain useful information.

OPEN-END QUESTIONS

This type of questioning follows the time-tested approach of the five Ws and one H used by journalists, who ask questions that help determine who, what, when, where, why, and how about a given situation. **Open-end questions** establish a number of facts and are used to seek substantial amounts of information and encourage dialogue. They:

Identify Customer Needs

By asking questions, you can help determine **customer needs** and what he or she wants or expects. This is a crucial task because some customers are either unsure of what they need or want or do not adequately express their needs or wants.

Examples

"Ms. Deloach, for what type of car are you looking?"

"Mr. Petell, why is an extended warranty important to you?"

Gather a Lot of Information

Open-end questions are helpful when you are just beginning a customer relationship and are not sure what the customer has in mind or what is important. By uncovering more details, you can better serve your customer.

open-end questions Typically start with words like who, when, what, how, and why and are used to engage others in conversation or to gain input and ideas. They invite participation in a conversation.

customer needs Motivators or drivers that cause customers to seek out specific types of products or services. These may be marketing-driven by advertising that customers have seen or may tie directly to Dr. Abraham Maslow's hierarchy of needs theory.

Example

"Mr. and Mrs. Milton, to help me better serve you, could you please describe what your ideal house would look like if you could build it?"

Uncover Background Data

When a customer calls to complain about a problem, often he or she has already taken unsuccessful steps to solve it. In such cases, it is important to find out the background information about the customer or situation. By asking open-end questions, you allow customers to share as much information as they feel is necessary to answer your question. This is why open-end questions are generally more effective for gathering data than are closed-end questions. If you feel you need more information after your customer responds to an open-end question, you can always ask further questions.

Example

"Mrs. Chan, will you please tell me the history behind this problem, including all of your previous contacts with this office?"

Uncover Objections during a Sale

If you are in sales or cross-selling or upselling products or services (getting a customer to buy additional, higher quality, or different brand of product, or extend or enhance existing service agreements) to current customers as a service representative, you will likely encounter **objections**. The reasons for a customer not wanting or needing your product and/or service can be identified through open-end questions.

Such questions help you determine whether your customer has questions or objections. Many times, people are not rejecting what you are offering outright; they simply do not see an immediate need for the product or cannot think of appropriate questions to ask. In these cases, you can help them focus their thinking or guide their decision through open-end questions. Be careful to listen to your customer's words and tone when he or she offers objections. If the customer seems adamant, such as, "I really do not want it," do not go any further with your questions. The customer will probably become angry because he or she will feel that you are not listening. A fine line exists between helping and pushing, and if you cross it, you could end up with a confrontation on your hands. Often active listening and experience will help you determine what course of action to take.

> **objections** Reasons given by customers for not wanting to purchase a product or service during an interaction with a salesperson or service provider (e.g., "I don't need one," "I cannot afford it," or "I already have one").

Example

"Ms. Williams, from what you told me, all the features of the new RD10 model that we talked about will definitely ease some of your workload, so let me get the paperwork started so you can take it home with you. What do you think?"

After asking the question in this example; stop talking and listen actively. Watch nonverbal cues and, depending on how the customer responds, either provide additional information or thank her for her time and offer additional assistance, as appropriate.

Give the Customer an Opportunity to Speak

Although it is important to control the conversation in order to save time and thus allow you to serve more customers, sometimes you may want to give the customer an opportunity to talk. This is crucial if the customer is upset or dissatisfied about something. By allowing a customer to "vent" as you listen actively, you can sometimes reduce the level of tension and help solve the problem. You might also discover other details that will more appropriately allow you to address the situation.

It is important for service providers in any environment to ask appropriate questions in order to determine what the customer wants, needs, and expects. *What types of questions do you typically ask your customers to get the information you need to ensure their satisfaction?*

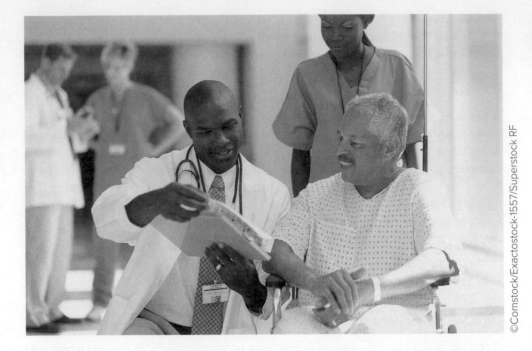

©Comstock/Exactostock-1557/Superstock RF

Examples of Open-End Questions

"What suggestions for improving our complaint-handling process should I present to my supervisor?"

"Why is this feature so important to you?"

"Jim, how has the printer been malfunctioning?"

"What is the main use of this product?"

"What are some of the common symptoms that you have been experiencing?"

"When would you most likely need us come out each month?"

"Where have you seen our product or similar ones being used?"

"Why do you feel that this product is better than others you have tried?"

"How do you normally use the product?"

"How has the new hearing aid been performing for you?"

"Mr. O'Connell, I can see you are unhappy. What can I do to help solve this problem?"

CLOSED-END QUESTIONS

closed-end questions Inquiries that typically start with a verb; solicit short, one-syllable answers (e.g., yes, no, one word, or a number); and can be used for such purposes as clarifying, verifying information already given, controlling conversation, or affirming something.

Open-end questions help to draw out a lot of information. Traditionally, **closed-end questions** start with verbs such as *do*, *did*, *are*, and *will*; elicit short, one-syllable responses; and gain little new information. Many closed-end questions can be answered yes or no or with a specific answer, such as a number or a date. Use closed-end questions for:

Verifying Information

Closed-end questions are a quick way to check information already shared or agreements made. Using them reinforces that you are listening and also helps prevent you from making mistakes because you misinterpreted or misunderstood information.

Example of a Verifying Question

"Mr. Christopherson, earlier I believe you said that you saw Doctor Naglapadi about this problem in the past. Is that correct?"

Closing an Order

Once you have discovered needs and presented the benefits and features of your product and service, you need to ask for a buying decision. This brings closure to your discussion. Asking for a decision also signals the customer that it is his or her turn to speak. If the customer offers an objection or declines to make a purchase, you can try to use the open-end questioning format discussed earlier in order to determine the reason for his or her hesitancy. Just remember in such situations to LISTEN to his or her words and tone when he or she responds. The word No often means just that. If you fail to recognize the difference between uncertainty and a decision not to purchase, you might irritate or offend the customer and the situation could escalate negatively.

Example of an Attempt to Close a Sale

"Mr. Jones, this tie will go nicely with the new suit you are purchasing. May I wrap it for you as well?"

Gaining Agreement

When there has been ongoing dialogue and closure or commitment is needed, closed-end questions can often bring about that result.

Example of a Question to Gain Agreement

"Veronica, with everything we have accomplished today, I would really like to be able to conclude this project before we leave. Can we work for one more hour?"

Clarifying Information

Closed-end questions can also help ensure that you have the details correct and thus help prevent future misunderstandings or mistakes. Closed-end questions also help save time and reduce the number of complaints and/or product returns you or someone else will have to deal with.

Example of a Clarifying Question

"Ms. Jovanovich, if I heard you correctly, you said that the problem occurs when you increase power to the engine. Is that as soon as you turn the ignition key or after you have been driving the car for a while?"

Examples of Closed-End Questions

"Do you agree that we should begin right away?" (obtaining agreement)

"Mrs. Leonard, did you say this was your first visit to our restaurant?" (verifying understanding)

"Mr. Morris, did you say you normally travel three or four times a month and have been doing so for the past 10 years?" (verifying facts)

"Is the pain in your tooth constant or just periodic?" (gathering information)

"So, shall I wrap these items for you so that you can make that appointment you mentioned, Mr. Carroll?" (closing an order)

KNOWLEDGE CHECK

1. What two types of questions can you use to determine a customer's needs or wants?

2. With what words do open-end questions typically begin?

3. Why are closed-end questions typically used?

LO 5-7 Additional Question Guidelines

CONCEPT   Use questions to further your feedback.

In order to generate meaningful responses from customers, keep the following points in mind.

AVOID CRITICISM

Be careful not to seem to be critical in the way you ask questions. For example, a question such as, "You really are not going to need two of the same item, are you?" sounds as if you are challenging the customer's decision making. What customers choose should not be your concern. Your job is to help them by providing excellent service. Remember that nonverbal messages delivered via tone or body language can suggest criticism, even if your spoken words do not.

ASK ONLY POSITIVELY PHRASED QUESTIONS

You can ask for the same information in different ways, some more positive than others do. As you interact with your customers, it is crucial to send messages in an open, pleasant manner. You can accomplish this by tone of voice and proper word selection. In the following examples, you can see how a negative or positive word choice affects meaning.

Examples
"You really do not want that color do you, Mrs. Handly?" (potentially negative or directive)

"We offer a wide selection of colors. Would you consider another color as an alternative, Mrs. Handly?" (positive or suggestive)

ASK DIRECT QUESTIONS

You generally get what you ask for. Therefore, being very specific with your questions can often result in your receiving useful information and can save time and effort. This does not mean that you should be abrupt or curt in your communication with customers or anyone else.

Example
If you want to know what style of furniture the customer prefers, but you know that only three styles are available, do not ask a general open-end question, such as "Mrs. Harris, what style of furniture were you looking for?" Instead, try a more structured, closed-end question, such as "Mrs. Harris, we stock Colonial, French provincial, and Victorian styles. Do any of those meet your needs?"

This approach prevents you from having to respond, "I am sorry, we do not stock that style," when Mrs. Harris answers your open-end question by telling you that she is looking for Art Deco or Contemporary style furniture.

ASK CUSTOMERS HOW YOU CAN BETTER SERVE

You will find no better or easier way to determine what customers want and expect than to ask them. They will appreciate it, and you will do a better job serving them. *Note*: If appropriate, a good follow-up approach to gain additional information after a customer has responded to a question is "That is interesting; will you please explain to me what makes you feel that way (or believe that's true)?"

Small Business Perspective

Listening to the customer makes all the difference in the world when you are the owner or employee of a small business. Because many small business people typically work with established customers for long periods once they establish a good service relationship, they often have the chance to get to know customers on a more personal basis. This affords them the opportunity to learn about immediate product and service needs. Additionally, business goals, likes and dislikes about competitors, and why they choose to do business with the organization can be identified through conversations with customers.

If an organization has a physical presence (bricks-and-mortar store or shop) as opposed to a primarily technology-based (Internet/e-commerce) one, owners can often gain customer feedback on a regular basis. This is true because many of their customers are from the same local geographic location. This provides the opportunity for the owners and employees to encounter customers in more relaxed settings (e.g., golf course, supermarket, restaurant, or repair shop) and talk about things other than business while building a strong customer–provider relationship. There is also the potential for inviting customers in for social functions such as holiday parties. You can also ask them to participate in focus groups where they answer questions about needs, products, and services available or that might be offered in the future.

In a globally competitive marketplace, smart small business owners and employees take advantage of some of the strategies mentioned above. Every employee plays a pivotal role in gaining and keeping customers. While they may not have a large staff or budget, small businesses can capitalize on these strategies to better position themselves competitively. Additionally, they can show customers that they truly do listen to and care about their wants, needs, comments, and suggestions. In effect, they put a personal face on service by doing this.

Another vehicle for enhanced customer communication is the proliferation of social media sites. These allow small business owners and employees to inexpensively reach out and connect on a different level with their customers.

Impact on Service

Based on personal experience and what you just read, answer the following questions:

1. Have you ever experienced a situation as a customer where you felt an employee of a small business was not listening to you? What did you do as a result?

2. What is the impact on a small business if its employees fail to listen to their customers? Explain.

(continued)

3. Why might small business employees not listen to their customers?

4. If you were a small business employee, what would you do to enhance your own listening skills?

5. If you owned or worked for a small business, what strategies would you use to more effectively develop communication with and retain customers?

 **SMARTBOOK** **Use SmartBook to help you read, study, and retain what you have learned. Access SmartBook in your Instructor's Connect course, or go to connect. mheducation.com for help.**

Key Terms

attending

behavioral styles

biases

circadian rhythm

closed-end questions

comprehending or assigning meaning

congruence

customer needs

employee assistance programs (EAPs)

external obstacles

faulty assumptions

hearing

information overload

lag time

listening

listening gap

memory

objections

open-end questions

personal obstacles

psychological distracters

recognition

responding

service recovery

thought speed

Summary

No matter what your current level of listening skill is, there is usually room for improvement. Customers expect and should receive your undivided attention in any contact they have with you. You should continually reevaluate your own listening style, decide which areas need development, and strive for improvement. In addition, you should keep in mind that active listening involves more than just focusing on spoken words. Remember that many obstacles can impede listening. To overcome them, you need to develop the characteristics of an effective listener and strive to minimize negative habits. By using the active listening process and positive questioning strategies you read about in this chapter, you can better determine and satisfy customer needs.

Review Questions

1. What phases make up the active listening process?

2. What is the difference between hearing and listening?

3. According to studies, what is the average rate of listening efficiency for most adults in the United States? Why is this significant in a customer service environment?

4. List 14 characteristics of effective listeners.

5. Of the characteristics common to good listeners, which do you consider the most important in a customer service organization? Explain.

6. What is an important reason for practicing good listening skills in a customer service environment?

7. What obstacles to effective listening have you experienced, either as a customer service professional or as a customer?

8. How can you determine when someone is not listening to what you say?

9. What techniques or strategies you use to improve your listening skills?

10. How is the outcome of customer service encounters improved by using a variety of questions?

Search It Out

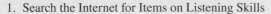

1. Search the Internet for Items on Listening Skills

   To find out more about the listening process and how you can improve your listening skills, search the Internet for "Listening" or any of the other topic headings or subheadings in this chapter. For example, you might search for the following items:

   Listening activities

   Quotations about listening

   Books and articles on listening (create a bibliographic list) or interpersonal communication

   Research data on listening

   Any other topic covered in this chapter (open-end or closed-end questions, handling sales objections)

   Listening in customer service

   Bring your findings to class and be prepared to discuss them with your group.

2. For additional articles and information on listening, visit the author's Customer Service Skills blog at http://www.customerserviceskillsbook.com/wordpress and search "Listening" and related topics.

3. Visit YouTube through https://binged.it/2sD2QSM to watch short videos on listening.

Collaborative Learning Activity

Developing Team Listening Skills

To give you some practical experience in using the techniques described in this chapter, you will now have an opportunity to interact with others in your group. Do this activity in groups of three or four members. One person will be the listener, one will be the speaker, and one or two will be observers. Each person will have an opportunity to play the different roles. For example, if there are four people in the group, there will be four rounds of activity. In the first round, one member of the group will be the listener, one will be the speaker, and the other two will be observers. The roles will change in each of the next three rounds so that everyone will have had a turn at each role.

The speaker will spend about five to seven minutes sharing a customer service experience he or she has had in the past few weeks (it can be positive or negative). The experience should have been one that lasted for several minutes so that there will be enough detail to share with the other members of the group. The speaker should describe:

The type of organization

Why he or she was there

How he or she was greeted by the service provider

Behavior exhibited by the customer service provider

How the provider dealt with concerns and questions

Any other important point the speaker can recall

As the speaker talks, the listener should pay attention and use as many of the positive listening skills discussed in this chapter as possible. The observers should watch and take notes on what they see. Specifically, they should look for use of the positive listening skills and any other behaviors exhibited (positive or negative).

After each speaker has finished his or her story, the listener, then the speaker, and finally the observers (in that order) should answer the following questions about the listener's behavior:

What did the listener do well?

What needed improvement?

What comments or suggestions for the listener came to your mind as you participated or observed?

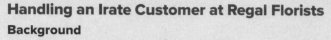

Face-to-Face

Handling an Irate Customer at Regal Florists

Background

Regal Florists is a small, third-generation, family-owned flower shop in Willow Grove, Pennsylvania. Most customers are local residents, but Regal has a website and an FTD delivery arrangement so that it serves customers throughout the United States. Mr. and Mrs. Raymond Boyle have been doing business with Regal for more than 20 years and know the owners well. They often order centerpiece arrangements for holidays and dinner parties, which they host frequently because of Mr. Boyle's position with a public relations firm. They also occasionally send flowers to their six children and four grandchildren living in various parts of the United States and overseas. Regal's owners and employees are usually especially cheerful, helpful, and efficient. That is one of the reasons the Boyles are loyal customers even though Regal's prices have risen above the industry average in recent years.

Your Role

During the past years, you have worked part-time at Regal's, at first delivering arrangements and for the past year creating arrangements and managing the shop. Mr. Boyle stopped by first thing this morning, just as you were opening the store. He was irate, demanding to know what happened with the arrangement delivered yesterday to his assistant for Secretary's Day, and swearing he would never patronize Regal's again. Apparently, he

had phoned in the order last week. The order was taken by a former 16-year-old part-time employee, who resigned. According to Mr. Boyle, he had ordered a small arrangement with carnations and various other bright spring flowers for his assistant. Instead, his assistant received a dozen red roses along with a card, on the outside of which was a border of little hearts and the statement "Thinking of you." Inside the card was a message intended for his wife: "I do not know what I would do without you." Unfortunately, Mrs. Boyle had dropped by Mr. Boyle's office and was near the assistant's desk when the flowers arrived, saw the card and flowers, and was quite upset. Rumor has it that Mr. and Mrs. Boyle are having marital problems. You were the only person in the shop when Mr. Boyle came in. Answer these questions.

Critical Thinking Questions

1. Do you think that Mr. Boyle should take Regal's past performance record into consideration? Why or why not?

2. What listening skills addressed in this chapter should you use in this situation? Why?

3. What can you possibly do or say that might resolve this situation positively?

4. Based on information provided, how would you have reacted in this situation if you were Mr. Boyle? Why?

5. If you were Mr. Boyle, what could Regal say to convince you to continue to do business with the company?

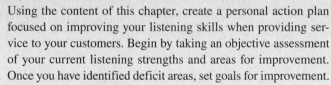

Planning to Serve

Using the content of this chapter, create a personal action plan focused on improving your listening skills when providing service to your customers. Begin by taking an objective assessment of your current listening strengths and areas for improvement. Once you have identified deficit areas, set goals for improvement.

Start your assessment by listing as many strengths and areas for improvement as you are aware of. Share your list with other people who know you well to see if they agree or can add additional items. Keep in mind that you will likely be more critical of yourself than other people will. Additionally, you may be sending nonverbal signals related to listening of which you are

not aware. For those reasons, keep an open mind when considering their comments.

Once you have a list, choose two or three items that you think need the most work and can add the most value when you are interacting with others. List these items on a sheet of paper along with specific courses of action you will take for improvement, the name of someone you will enlist to provide feedback on your behavior, and a specific date by which you want to see improvement. Related to the latter, keep in mind that research shows that it takes on average 21 to 30 days to see behavioral change; therefore, set a date that is at least in this range.

Listening	Areas for Improvement

Top Three Items	Who Will Help	Date for Change
1.		
2.		
3.		

Quick Preview Answers

1. F	3. T	5. T	7. T	9. F	11. F
2. T	4 F	6. T	8. T	10. T	12. T

Ethical Dilemma Summary

Ethical Dilemma 5.1 Possible Answers

1. What would you say to this customer? Explain.

   There are a couple of issues in this scenario. First, there is the fact that she is cursing and screaming, which is not conducive to effective conflict resolution. She also has her children with her. They are being exposed to not only their mother's attitude and demeanor but also whatever you decide to do. This could leave a negative impression on them related to public utility workers in the future. Finally, there is the fact that she is providing potentially untrue information.

   Before you can even begin to deal with the water issue, you should address her use of profanity and her emotion. Try using the emotion-reducing model that you will read about in Chapter 7 (Figure 7.4). Explain in an assertive manner that her tone and language are interfering with your ability to help her and that if she wants to get this issue resolved, she needs to calm down and treat you in a civil manner. Should she be unwilling to do so, say "Please excuse me for a second" and go to get a supervisor to intervene.

2. What actions would you take to remedy the situation and get her water back on so that she and her children would have access to services?

   To deal with this situation, you should keep in mind some of the strategies for effective listening and apply some of the information-gathering techniques described in this chapter. Specifically, be careful of faulty assumptions (e.g., that everything she is telling you is untrue). Spend a bit of time asking open-end questions, such as "Who did you speak with that promised to turn on your water on Friday" and "I see that you were to come in last Wednesday with a money order. When did you make payment on the account?" (This affords her the benefit of the doubt that she did make payment and no one updated your system). If she states a time/date, ask for documentation of payment.

   Once you have determined whether payment was or was not made and that your department either did not fail to deliver service as promised, or failed to follow through as promised, proceed as you normally would to collect payment and/or schedule to have services reinstated immediately. Certainly, if there was an error, apologize sincerely and make necessary adjustments to her account.

   As an added service touch to reinforce your concern for the customer as a person, if you have lollipops or candy available, ask the customer if she would mind if the children have a piece.

Ethical Dilemma 5.2 Possible Answers

1. Were you practicing good service skills in this situation? Explain.

   Yes. By making the effort to listen to Ms. Molina's spoken and unspoken messages, you were able to pick up emotion that was driving her feelings or needs. Had you not been watching for nonverbal cues or practicing active listening skills, you might have simply told her that she could not transfer because she had missed established cut-off dates.

2. Is the student's request to transfer reasonable even though the add/drop period has passed?

   Yes. If you are authorized in these extenuating circumstances, you should certainly permit a change of classes. If not, you should check with your supervisor to get permission to make the change immediately.

3. Would you allow the student (customer) to transfer to another class? Why or why not?

   Obviously, the rules do not apply in this case. If you did not listen, you would never know, and there would be a dissatisfied and distraught customer as a result. If you fail to do so, you might be setting up the institution for a harassment lawsuit by forcing Ms. Molina to stay in the class or could create other situations in which Ms. Molina feels compelled to take other actions to remedy the situation (e.g., lawsuit, violence, or going to the media to expose the teacher and the institution).

   In a positive customer service environment, there are few instances (except where exceptions would violate regulatory or legal guidelines) in which exceptions to organizationally established policies cannot be made.

4. As an employee of the college, do you have any further responsibilities? Explain.

   Absolutely, you have moral and legal obligations to bring this situation to the attention of your supervisor immediately. He or she should then take prompt action to document and report the behavior to the human resources department or other appropriate authorities at the college. The institution and employees are required by state and federal laws to act in order to prevent discrimination of any type and to protect students, customers, employees, and vendors from exposure to inappropriate behavior.

©Robert W. Lucas

PART THREE

BUILDING AND MAINTAINING RELATIONSHIPS

6 **Customer Service and Behavior**

7 **Service Breakdowns and Service Recovery**

8 **Customer Service in a Diverse World**

9 **Customer Service via Technology**

Venkatesh P. Nagalapadi

Position/job title: *President*

Organization: *CFP Physicians Group, CFP Care Team, Central Florida Medical Directors*

Website: *http://www.cfpphysiciansgroup.com/*

Total years of experience providing service to internal (people within your organization) and external customers/patients (in all organizations): 15

---

1 **What are the personal qualities that you believe are essential for anyone working with customers (patients) in a service environment?**

A calm welcoming demeanor, confidence in what you do, satisfaction in your line of work, belief in the fact that you do make a difference in people's lives, and knowing that a kind word or gesture can alleviate turmoil, anger, and suffering.

2 **What do you see as the most rewarding part of working with customers (patients)? Why?**

My personal mantra has always been making a difference in patients' lives. That is the reason why I chose geriatrics as a specialty. I do believe that as long as I am happy and content and am personally satisfied in what I do, I will have a favorable effect on people's lives. Patients come to you in times of need and when they are weak and vulnerable. They do expect their doctor to treat them as an individual and pay personal attention in making them feel better. I think it is important to establish a mutually trustful and open relationship with your patients.

3 **What do you believe the biggest challenge(s) is/are in working with customers (patients)?**

The biggest challenges are busy schedules and time constraints. It is a balancing act every time. As much as I would like to spend an hour or two with my patients, it does become impossible to comply with insurance paperwork. Bureaucracy is a big burden on the time factor too.

4 **What have you done, or could you do, to help overcome the challenges you indicated in and deliver better customer service?**

Being honest and candid with my patients as to why my time with them was limited and explaining why they have had to wait 30 minutes for their appointment. It is not because I do not value their time and respect their schedules, but because of the time I have had to spend with other patients while also fulfilling other paperwork requirements.

5 **What changes have you seen in the customer service (medical) profession since you first started working with customers (patients)—for example, customer (patient) demographics, their attitudes, people who work in the medical profession and their attitudes, how technology is applied to provide better customer (patient) service, etc.?**

I think the medical profession is finally coming to terms with the importance of customer service and satisfaction. I have seen more training with regards to improving the patient experience as a whole. We are adapting to a rapidly changing and ever-evolving patient demographics with regards to race, economic background, educational background, and age distribution as well. We have since adopted electronic health records and the practice management software, but we have resisted converting the front office and back office to a computer-based system. This is because I believe patients have come to expect a certain personal touch to their customer experience.

6 **What future issues do you see evolving in your industry/organization related to dealing with customers and why do you think these are important?**

I think the future of medicine is going to be driven by physician extenders and telemedicine. There are fewer physicians going to school and fewer wanting to deal with the challenges of medicine.

7 **What advice related to customer service do you have for anyone seeking or continuing a career in the medical profession?**

Go into the medical profession not for financially driven motives. Go into medicine because you want to help patients while fully understanding that there are challenges and obstacles, and that it is a mentally and physically taxing profession.

Application To Customer Service

After reading Dr. Nagalapadi's comments, think about how what he said relates to your experiences and the customer service profession as a whole and then respond to the following questions.

1. How do the doctor's comments relate to your own customer (patient) experience with people in the medical profession? Explain.

2. Do his comments give a better appreciation for the customer challenges that he and others in the medical field face daily? Explain.

3. In what ways would you enhance a patient's (customer's) experience if you worked in a doctor's office?

4. In what ways do the challenges he discussed relate to customer service in other organizations and industries?

5. Would you want to work in a doctor's office in a support role? Explain why or why not?

Courtesy of Dr. Vankatesh Nagalapadi

Customer Service and Behavior

"To be successful, you have to be able to relate to people; they have to be satisfied with your personality to be able to do business with you and to build a relationship with mutual trust."
—Source: George Ross

LEARNING OUTCOMES

After completing this chapter, you will be able to:

6-1 Explain what behavioral styles are and why you should be concerned with them.

6-2 Identify four key behavioral styles and the roles they play in customer service.

6-3 Develop strategies for communicating effectively with each behavioral style.

6-4 Respond to customer problems effectively while building relationships.

6-5 Use knowledge of behavioral styles to help manage perceptions of others.

Use SmartBook to help you read, study, and retain what you have learned. Access SmartBook in your Instructor's Connect course, or go to connect.mheducation.com for help. ▉ SMARTBOOK™

IN THE REAL WORLD SUPERMARKET—TRADER JOE'S

The beginnings for Trader Joe's started in 1958 with a small chain of convenience stores called Pronto Markets. The company operated that way, as a privately held company, until 1967 when the owner changed the name to Trader Joe's and opened his first store in Pasadena, California. The business model evolved over the next few years and included developing larger stores in which employees dressed in Hawaiian shirts. Ahead of its time, it started using recyclable canvas bags for shoppers.

Eighty percent of the products it stocks are its own goods. Early on in its life cycle, the company started offering innovative, hard-to-find foods that contain no colors or preservatives before many of its competitors joined this trend. It markets these products under the trademarked "Trader Joe's" brand along with an expanded selection of its own wines. Its wines include Trader Joe's own "Three Buck Chuck" merlot, named after the company's founder Charles Shaw. In addition to Trader Joe's, it has also created other trademarked product names (e.g., Trader Ming's and Trader Jose's).

As the organization grew, new and fun ways to communicate and connect with customers and employees evolved, starting with a newsletter that, to this day, is its primary form of advertising. It also began using brass nautical bells to communicate (island style) with employees instead of the annoying public address systems that some stores use. One bell lets crew members (employees) know when to open another register. Two bells mean there are additional questions that need to be answered at the checkout. Three bells call over a manager-type person.

By the 1990s, the company's efforts to grow and gain market share paid off as it expanded throughout the Pacific Northwest. In 1993, it opened its 70th store and by 2013, it had 400 locations. In 1996, www.traderjoes.com went online and the following year, the organization moved to the East Coast with a store in Boston. Stores in the Midwest and Southeast followed in coming years. Since its beginning, the organization has developed almost a "cult" following of loyal customers who love its products and believe in its business ethic and philosophy. Part of this loyalty stems from Trader Joe's approach to doing business:

The mission of Trader Joe's is to give our customers the best food and beverage values that they can find anywhere and to provide them with the information required to make informed buying decisions. We provide these with a dedication to the highest quality of customer satisfaction delivered with a sense of warmth, friendliness, fun, individual pride, and company spirit.

Source: Mission of Trader Joe

According to its website, its philosophy is to provide value to customers. Simply stated, it touts: "We just focus on what matters—Great food + Great prices = Value."

Source: Trader Joe's

The ways it accomplishes this is to strive to continually cut costs in the way it procures products and manages its stores. Trader Joe's tries to buy directly from local suppliers whenever possible and it does not tack additional supplier and customer fees onto its products. The result of its efforts is that customers do not have to shop with coupons or membership cards or search out discounts or sales in order to save money and get fair value for their money. They always get the best prices available every day. If a customer is ever dissatisfied, part of Trader Joe's promise to customers is "If you don't, bring it back for a refund or exchange—no hassles."

Source: Trader Joe's

For more information about Trader Joe's, do an Internet search and visit its website (www.traderjoes.com).

Think About It

1. Why do you think Trader Joe's might have such a loyal customer base?

2. Based on what you read above, on its website, and on an Internet search for the company, what do think about its approach to satisfying customer needs?

3. Is this a company that you would patronize as a customer? Why or why not?

4. Would you want to work for this company? Why or why not?

Quick Preview

Before reviewing the chapter content, respond to the following questions by placing a "T" for true or an "F" for false on the rules. If you do not know an answer, put a question mark. Use any questions you miss as a checklist of material to which you will pay particular attention as you read the chapter. For those you get right, give yourself a pat on the back, but review the sections they address in order to learn additional details about the topic.

_____ **1.** Understanding behavioral styles can aid in establishing and maintaining positive customer relationships.

_____ **2.** You should treat others as individuals, not as members of a category.

_____ **3.** People whose primary behavioral style category is "E" focus their energy on working with people.

_____ **4.** People whose primary behavioral style category is "D" focus their energy on tasks or getting the job done.

_____ **5.** Some behavioral styles are better than others.

_____ **6.** People who exhibit the "D" style often tend to move slowly and speak in a low-key manner.

_____ **7.** People who exhibit the "E" style often tend to be highly animated in using gestures and speaking.

_____ **8.** People who exhibit the "R" style often tend to be very impatient.

_____ **9.** People who exhibit the "I" style often tend to express their emotions easily.

_____ **10.** You should attempt to determine a customer's behavioral style and then tailor your communication accordingly.

_____ **11.** To deliver total customer satisfaction, you need to make your customers feel special.

_____ **12.** When you say no to a customer, it is important to let him or her know what you cannot do and why.

_____ **13.** Service to your customers should be seamless; customers should not have to see or deal with problems or process breakdowns.

_____ **14.** Perceptions are based on education, experiences, events, and interpersonal contacts, as well as a person's intelligence level.

_____ **15.** Once you have made a perception, you should evaluate its accuracy.

Answers to Quick Preview are located at the end of the chapter.

Words to Live By

"Here is a simple but powerful rule: Always give people more than they expect to get."

—SOURCE: NELSON BOSWELL

LO 6-1 What Are Behavioral Styles

CONCEPT Behavioral styles are actions or reactions exhibited when you and others deal with tasks or people. As a customer service professional, you need to be aware that not everyone is the same.

A couple of things to remember about behavioral styles are that there is no "one best type" of behavior and that behavior can change from one situation to another. Humans have a variety of style behaviors within them. Much of the way that people react in a given situation is driven by personal knowledge, experience, culture, and other background features. Various studies indicate that while most people have primary style preferences, they also have secondary styles from which they pull, depending on situations and the people with whom they are interacting. This is especially true in customer service environments. Another key point to remember as you read through this chapter, and any material you read on the topic of behavioral styles, is that you should NEVER try to put people into a box. Avoid thinking "I should deal with this person in a specific manner because he or she seems to be demonstrating 'x' style behavior." The key to effectively managing your behavior and addressing that of others is to listen what the customer is saying, watch nonverbal cues, and consider the information you are about to read in this chapter. The skills addressed in this chapter provide general guidance and are designed to raise awareness about behavioral styles, and not give a pat answer for dealing with any specific situation. Human behavior is adaptable and often unpredictable. By learning more about your own behavioral styles, and how others might behave in various situations, you can increase the chance of service success.

For thousands of years, people have devised systems in an attempt to better understand why they do what they do and how they accomplish what they do—and to categorize behavioral styles. Many of these systems are still in use today.

Behavioral styles are observable tendencies (actions that you can see or experience) that you and other people exhibit when dealing with tasks or people. As you grow from infancy, your personality forms based on your experiences and your environment. These form the basis of your behavioral style preference(s).

Have you ever met someone with whom you either did not feel comfortable or with whom you felt an immediate bond? If so, you were possibly experiencing and reacting to the effect of behavioral style. As a customer service professional, you need to be aware that everyone is different. Not everyone behaves as you do, yet many still demonstrate behaviors that are similar to yours. For this reason, you should strive to provide service in a manner that addresses not only the behaviors that you prefer, but also those that fulfill the needs and desires of others as well.

Part of being a customer service professional is that you need to understand human behavioral style characteristics. The more proficient you become at identifying your own behavioral characteristics and those of others, the better you will be at establishing and maintaining positive relationships with customers. Self-knowledge is the starting point. To help in this effort, we will examine some common behaviors that you exhibit and that you may observe in customers.

When dealing with your customers, you should recognize that someone else doing something or acting differently from the way you do does not mean that the person is wrong. It simply means that he or she approaches situations differently. Relationships are made when participants learn to accept the characteristics of others.

In customer service, adaptability is crucial, for many people do not always act the way you want them to. As you will read later in this chapter, there are many strategies that can be used to help modify and adapt your behavior so that it does not clash with

behavioral styles Descriptive term that identifies categories of human behavior identified by behavioral researchers. Many of the models used to group behaviors date back to those identified by Carl Jung.

Customer Service Success Tip

Take the time to obtain one or more of the commercial self-assessment surveys available on the Internet (e.g., DiSC [https://www.discprofile.com/what-is-disc/overview/], DISC [https://discpersonalitytesting.com/blog/what-are-the-four-disc-types/], or Myers-Briggs Type Indicator [http://www.myersbriggs.org/my-mbti-personality-type/mbti-basics/]) in order to learn more about yourself and be better equipped to interact with others in the workplace.

that of your customers. This does not mean that you must make all the concessions when behaviors do not mesh. It simply means that, although you do not have control over the behavior of others, you do have control over your own behavior. Use this control to deal more effectively with your customers.

KNOWLEDGE CHECK

1. What are behavioral styles?

LO 6-2 Identifying Behavioral Styles

CONCEPT Each contact in a customer service environment has the potential for contributing to your success. Each person should be valued for his or her strengths and not belittled for what you perceive as shortcomings.

Through an assessment questionnaire, you can discover your own behavioral tendencies in a variety of situations. An awareness of your own style preferences can then lead you to a better understanding of customers, since many also possess similar style preferences. By understanding these characteristics, you can improve communication, build stronger relationships, reduce conflict and misunderstandings, and offer better service to the customer.

Many self-assessment questionnaires in use today are based on the work begun by pioneers in the field, such as, psychiatrist Carl Jung, William Moulton Marston, PhD, and others in the earlier part of the twentieth century. Jung explored human personality and behavior. He divided behavior into two "attitudes" (introvert and extrovert) and four dominant impulses that drive behavior or "functions" (thinking, feeling, sensation, and intuition). These attitudes and functions can intermingle to form eight psychological types; knowledge of these types is useful in defining and describing human behavioral characteristics. Marston focused on a simpler model that addresses four dominant personality traits that influence behavior (dominance, influence, steadiness and compliance). Based on Marston's research, Walter Clark developed the first DiSC behavioral survey in 1940.

From Jung's complex research (and that of others) have come many variations, additional studies, and a variety of behavioral style self-assessment questionnaires (surveys) and models for explaining personal behavior. An example of such an assessment is the Myers-Briggs Type Indicator (MBTI) developed by Katherine Cook Briggs and her daughter Isabel Briggs Myers in 1962.

While various assessments are sold and administered by trained consultants, several organizations allow you to complete similar free surveys online. You can find information on these surveys by searching the Internet for "behavioral styles" surveys or related topics. You can also explore websites listed in the Search It Out section at the end of this chapter.

To help give you a sense of what behavioral styles involve and understand the concepts without incurring additional cost to the reader, this chapter provides a hybrid model that the author has created. It is based on nearly three decades of researching and teaching behavioral characteristics to thousands of people. During that period, he has been certified to use and distribute several commercial behavioral surveys that use a variety of characteristic categories and are based on the research mentioned earlier. While the RIDE model is not designed to provide in-depth knowledge on the topic, you will learn the basics of how to identify behaviors of customers and how to better interact with them.

For more in-depth information on the topic, check out some of the resources referenced above and consider purchasing a commercial product. To better understand your own styles and those of others, consider purchasing an online computerized survey that will provide you with a multipage printout of your style preferences and descriptive information. You will learn about these during your Internet research at the end of the chapter.

Although everyone typically has a **primary behavior pattern** (the way a person typically acts or reacts under certain circumstances) to which he or she reverts in stressful situations, people are a combination of various behavioral styles that they pull from as situations change. Because of this, your customers have characteristics in common and regularly demonstrate similar behavioral patterns. Identifying your own style preferences helps you understand and relate to behaviors in others.

primary behavior pattern Refers to a person's preferred style or approach for dealing with others.

To informally identify some of your own behavioral style preferences, complete Work It Out 6.1. This is not a validated behavioral survey. However, it will give a strong indication of your behavioral preferences in dealing with others. Keep in mind that your behavior is adaptable based on a given situation in which you find yourself.

Note: The questionnaire in Work It Out 6.1 is only a quick indicator. A more thorough assessment, using a formal instrument (questionnaire), will help you better predict your style preferences.

 WORK IT OUT 6.1

Describing Your Behavior

As a quick way to determine your behavioral style preference, make a copy of this page and then complete the following survey.

Step 1

Focus on how you interact with customers or others in a typical workplace situation. Before proceeding to Step 2, read the following list of words and phrases and rate (score) yourself by placing a number (from 1 to 5) next to each item. A "5" means that the word is an accurate description of how you most often behave in a workplace situation, a "3" indicates a balanced agreement about the word's application (often you behave this way), and a "1" means that you do not feel that the word describes your behavior in dealing with others in the workplace well.

Your Numerical Rating Value	Behavior Trait	Your Letter Value
	Relaxed	
	Logical	

(continued)

6.1 (Continued)

Your Numerical Rating Value	Behavior Trait	Your Letter Value
	Decisive	
	Talkative	
	Consistent	
	Nonaggressive (avoids conflict)	
	Calculating	
	Fun-loving	
	Loyal	
	Quality-focused	
	Competitive	
	Enthusiastic	
	Sincere	
	Accurate	
	Pragmatic (practical)	
	Popular	
	Patient	
	Detail-oriented	
	Objective	
	Optimistic	
TOTAL	R = I = D =	E =

Step 2

Once you have scored each word or phrase, start with the first word, "Relaxed," and put the letter "R" to the right of it. Place an "I" to the right of the second word, "Logical," a "D" to the right of the third word, and an "E" to the right of the fourth word. Then start over with the fifth word and repeat the "RIDE" pattern until all words have a letter at their right.

Step 3

Next, go through the list and count point values for all words that have an "R" beside them. Put the total at the bottom of the grid next to the letter "R =." Do the same for the other letters "IDE." For example, if the words *relaxed*, *consistent*, *loyal*, *sincere*, and *patient* all had a number "4" by them, the total would be 20 and that number would go in the total area next to R =.

Once you have finished, one letter will probably have the highest total score. This is your natural style tendency. For example, if "R" has the highest

6.1 (Continued)

score, your primary style preference is *rational*. If "I" has the highest score, you exhibit more *inquisitive* behavior. "D" indicates *decisive*, and "E" is an *expressive* style preference. See Figure 6.1 as an example of a completed survey page.

If two or more of your scores have the same high totals, you probably generally put forth similar amounts of effort in both these style areas. As a result, you likely exhibit numerous characteristics listed under both style categories depending on the situation. Most people have primary and secondary styles. Some even have a tertiary preference.

Because of the complexities of human behavior, you should not try to use behavioral characteristics and cues as absolute indicators of the type of person with whom you are dealing. You and others have some of the characteristics listed for all four of the style categories shown in this chapter; you simply have learned through years of experience which behavior you are most comfortable with and when adaptation is helpful or necessary. Generally, most people are adaptable and can shift style categories or exhibit different characteristics depending on the situation or environment in which they are in. For example, a person who is normally very personable and amiable can revert to more directive behavior, if necessary, in order to manage an activity or process for which he or she is accountable. Similarly, a person who normally exhibits controlling or task-oriented behavior can socialize and react positively in social or "people" situations.

An important point to remember about this short questionnaire, and any other behavioral survey that you use, is that there is no "best" or "worst" style. Each person should be valued for his or her strengths and not belittled because of what you perceive as shortcomings. In a customer environment, each contact has the potential for contributing to your success and that of your organization. By appreciating the behavioral characteristics of people with whom you interact, you can avoid bias or prejudice and better serve your customers.

How can a person who demonstrates one of the four styles be described? How might this person act, react, or interact? In this section, you will read some generalizations about behavior. Remember that even though people have a primary style, they have all four behavioral style characteristics within them and demonstrate other style behaviors as needed depending on the situation in which they find themselves.

By becoming familiar with the style characteristics in Figure 6.1, recognizing them in yourself, and observing how others display them, you can begin to learn how to better adapt to various behaviors. When interacting with others, make sure that you monitor their overall actions and behavior in order to get a better perception of their style preferences rather than react to one or two actions. Also, recognize that *these characteristics are generalities* and not absolutes when dealing with others. People can and do adapt or change behavior depending on a variety of circumstances. There is also the possibility that, based on your perceptions, you might misinterpret their actions or behaviors.

While there is no definitive research related to preferences based on gender or cultural background, these factors obviously play a role in how someone dresses, acts, and communicates. When dealing with customers, consider all possible factors and

FIGURE 6.1

Sample Completed Self-Assessment

Your Numerical Rating Value	Behavior Trait	Your Letter Value
5	Relaxed	R
3	Logical	I
1	Decisive	D
4	Talkative	E
5	Consistent	R
3	Nonaggressive (avoids conflict)	I
5	Calculating	D
3	Fun-loving	E
5	Loyal	R
1	Quality-focused	I
3	Competitive	D
2	Enthusiastic	E
5	Sincere	R
1	Accurate	I
3	Pragmatic (practical)	D
1	Popular	E
5	Patient	R
2	Detail-oriented	I
1	Objective	D
2	Optimistic	E
TOTAL	**R = 25 I = 10 D = 13**	**E = 12**

analyze the situation objectively. When all else fails, use your positive verbal communication skills to ask if your perception is correct.

The following descriptions of the four behavioral style categories are general. Since people are a combination of all four styles, they may exhibit some, but not all, of these characteristics at any given time. They may also exhibit characteristics from other style categories based on a given situation or their emotional state.

R: RATIONAL

rational style One of four behavioral groups characterized by being quiet, reflective, task-focused, and systematic.

People who have a preference for the **rational style** may tend to:

- Listen and observe more than they talk (especially in groups).
- Be very patient.
- Wait or stand in one place for periods of time without complaining, although they may be internally irritated about a breakdown in the system or lack of organization.

- Exhibit congenial eye contact and facial expressions.
- Prefer one-on-one or small-group interactions instead of large-group ones.
- Seek specific or complete explanations to questions (e.g., "That's our policy" does not work well with an "R" customer).
- Dislike calling attention to themselves or a situation.
- Avoid conflict and anger.
- Often wear subdued colors and informal, conservative, or conventional clothing styles and accessories.
- Ask questions rather than state their opinion.
- Communicate more in writing and like the use of notes, birthday cards, or thank-you cards just to stay in touch.
- Like to be on a first-name basis with others.
- Have intermittent eye contact, with a brief, businesslike handshake.
- Have informal, comfortable office spaces, possibly with pictures of family in view.
- Like leisure activities that involve people (often family).

People who exhibit the *rational* behavioral style preference are congenial and often prefer to seek explanations for actions you take, rather than accepting that "policy says." *How might you serve such a person effectively?*

inquisitive style One of four behavioral groups, characterized by being introverted, task-focused, and detail-oriented.

I: INQUISITIVE

People who have a preference for the **inquisitive style** may tend to:

- Rarely volunteer feelings freely.
- Ask specific, pertinent questions rather than make statements of their feelings.
- Rely heavily on facts, times, dates, and practical information to make their point.
- Prefer to interact in writing rather than in person or on the phone.
- Prefer formality and distance in interactions. They often lean back when talking, even when emphasizing key points.
- Use formal titles and last names as opposed to first names. They may also stress the use of full names, not nicknames (e.g., Cynthia instead of Cindy or Charles instead of Chuck).
- Use cool, brief handshakes, often without a smile. If they do smile, it may appear forced.
- Wear conservative clothing although their accessories are matched well.
- Be impeccable in their grooming but may differ in their choice of styles from those around them (e.g., hair and makeup).
- Be very punctual and time-conscious.
- Carry on lengthy conversations, especially when trying to get answers to questions.
- Be diplomatic with others.

People with a primary behavioral preference of *inquisitive* are often more intrapersonal and focus on details, facts, and practicality. *How would you address a customer who exhibits these characteristics?*

- Prefer solitary leisure activities (e.g., reading or listening to relaxing music).
- Keep their personal life separate from business.

Ethical Dilemma 6.1

A supervisor at your company who typically demonstrates high decisive-type behavior criticizes you and other employees publicly, does not seem to respect people of other races, and very rarely asks for your opinion. You perceive that when she does take the time to get your input, and that of other employees, it seems that she really does not listen to what you have to say and usually does not take your advice or suggestions. In the past, you have heard employees and external customers comment about the supervisor's behavior. You know of at least one customer who said she was defecting to a competing company because of it. Should you address your perceptions with her? Why or why not?

People with a primary behavioral preference of *decisive* tend to appear more formal and use direct statements and questions. *How would you address a customer who exhibits these characteristics?*

©Thinkstock Images/Getty Images RF

D: DECISIVE

decisive style One of four behavior styles, characterized by a direct, no-nonsense approach to people and situations.

People who have a preference for the **decisive style** may tend to:

- Move quickly.
- Seek immediate gratification of needs or results.
- Work proactively toward a solution to a problem.
- Be forceful and assertive in their approach (sometimes overly so).
- Project a competitive nature.
- Display a confident, possibly arrogant demeanor.
- Ask specific, direct questions and give short, straight answers.
- Discuss rather than write about something (e.g., call or come in rather than write about a complaint).
- Talk and interrupt more than listen.

- Display symbols of power to demonstrate their own importance (e.g., expensive jewelry, clothes, cars, and power colors in business attire, such as, navy blue or charcoal gray).
- Be solemn and use closed, nonverbal body cues.
- Have firm handshakes and strong, direct eye contact.
- Have functionally decorated offices (all items have a purpose and are not there to make the environment more attractive).
- Prefer active, competitive leisure activities.

E: EXPRESSIVE

People who have a preference for the **expressive style** may tend to:

- Look for opportunities to socialize or talk with others (e.g., checkout lines at stores, bus stops, waiting areas).
- Project a friendly, positive attitude.
- Be enthusiastic, even animated when talking, using wide, free-flowing gestures.
- Use direct eye contact and enthusiastic, warm (often two-handed) handshake.
- Smile and use open body language.
- Get close or touch when speaking to someone.
- Talk rather than write about something (e.g., call or come in with a complaint rather than writing to complain).
- Initiate projects.
- May wear bright, modern, or unusual clothes and jewelry because it gets them noticed or fits their mood.
- Dislike routine.
- Share feelings and express opinions or ideas easily and readily.
- Get distracted in conversations and start discussing other issues.
- Prefer informal use of names and like first-name communication.
- Not be time-conscious and may often be late for appointments.
- Speak loudly and expressively with a wide range of inflection.
- Like action-oriented, people-centered leisure activities.

©Ingram Publishing RF

People with a primary behavioral preference of *expressive* tend to be very people oriented, more relaxed, and often "go with the flow." *How would you address a customer who exhibits these characteristics?*

Street Talk Responsiveness

Every time your client/customer has a need, your responsiveness is being evaluated anew. The speed, accuracy, degree of helpfulness, and courtesy shown are key ingredients that matter each time you pick up the phone, respond to an e-mail or text, or resolve a challenge on behalf of your client. Responsiveness matters and your score is constantly being updated with each service interaction.

SOURCE: LEILANI POLAND, *Owner, The Resource Connection*

expressive style One of four behavior groups characterized as being people-oriented, fun-loving, upbeat, and extroverted.

KNOWLEDGE CHECK

1. What is meant by primary behavior pattern?
2. What are the four behavioral style categories?
3. What are five characteristics that a customer with a primary style of rational might demonstrate?
4. What are five characteristics that a customer with a primary style of inquisitive might demonstrate?
5. What are five characteristics that a customer with a primary style of decisive might demonstrate?
6. What are five characteristics that a customer with a primary style of expressive might demonstrate?

LO 6-3 Communicating with Each Style

CONCEPT Each behavior style features various indicators of this style in practice. Remember, these cues are indicators, not absolutes, as you begin to use them to interact appropriately with others.

Once you recognize people's style tendencies, you can improve your relationships and chances of success by tailoring your communication strategies. As you examine Figure 6.2, think about how you can use these strategies with people you know in each style category. Keep in mind that these and other characteristics outlined in this chapter are only general in nature. Everyone is a mixture of all four styles and can change to a different style to address a variety of situations. Use these examples as indicators of style and not as absolutes. Also, be careful *not* to label a person as being one style (e.g., Toni is a high "R") since people use all four styles—and most people do not appreciate stereotypes and labeling.

FIGURE 6.2

Communicating with Different Personality Styles

Style	Behaviors Exhibited	Provider Response	Customer Relationship Strategies
RATIONAL	**Nonverbal Cues** Gentle handshake; flowing, nondramatic gestures. Fleeting eye contact.	Return firm, brief handshake; avoid aggressive gestures. Make intermittent (three to five seconds) eye contact.	• Work to maintain peace and group stability. • Focus on his or her need for security and amiable relationships. • Show a sincere interest in the customer and his or her views.
	Verbal Cues Steady, even delivery. Subdued volume. Slower rate of speech.	Mirror their style somewhat. Relax your message delivery. Slow your rate if necessary; be patient.	• Organize your information in a logical sequence and provide background data, if necessary. • Take a slow, low-key approach in recommending products or services.
	Keeps communication brief. Communication follows a logical pattern (e.g., step 1, step 2).	Ask open-end questions to draw out information. Use structured approach in communications.	• Use open-end questions to obtain information. • Explain how your product or service can help simplify and support the customer's relationships and systems.
	Additional Cues Avoids confrontation.	Attempt to solve problems without creating a situation in which they feel challenged or obliged to defend themselves.	• Stress low risk and benefits to him or her. • Encourage the customer to verify facts, and so on, with others whose opinions he or she values. • When change occurs, explain the need for the change and allow time for the customer to adjust. • Provide information on available warranties, guarantees, and support systems.

FIGURE 6.2 *(Continued)*

Style	Behaviors Exhibited	Provider Response	Customer Relationship Strategies
INQUISITIVE	**Nonverbal Cues** Deliberate body movements. Uses little physical contact. Correspondence is formal and includes many details.	Use careful, restrained body cues. Avoid touching. Respond similarly.	• Often desire quality, efficiency, and precision. • Focus on the customer's need for accuracy and efficiency by methodically outlining steps, processes, or details related to a product or service.
	Verbal Cues Quiet, slow-paced speech (especially in groups). Minimal vocal variety.	Mirror rate and pattern. Use subdued tone and volume.	
	Additional Cues Values concise communication. Uses details to make points. Prefers confirmation and backup in writing. Uses formal names instead of nicknames.	Use brief, accurate statements. Provide background information and data. Respond in writing and provide adequate background information. Address them by title and last name unless told otherwise.	• Tie communication into facts, not feelings. • Prepare information in advance and be thoroughly familiar with it. • Approach encounters in a direct, businesslike, low-key manner. • Avoid small talk and speaking about yourself.
	Additional Cues Sharing of personal information is minimal. Focus on task at hand.	Communicate on business level unless they initiate personal conversation. Organize thoughts before responding.	• Have documentation available to substantiate your claims. • Do not pressure his or her decisions. • Follow through on promises.
DECISIVE	**Nonverbal Cues** Steady, direct eye contact. Writing tends to be short and specific. Gestures tend to be autocratic (e.g., pointing fingers or hands on hips).	Return eye contact (three to five seconds) and smile. Respond in similar fashion; minimize small talk and details. Stand your ground without antagonizing. Maintain a professional demeanor.	• Often want to save time and money. • Focus on the customer's need for control by finding out what he or she wishes to do, what he or she wants or needs, or what motivates him or her. • Provide direct, concise, and factual answers to the customer's questions. • Keep explanations brief and provide solutions, not excuses.
	Verbal Cues Forceful tone. Speaks in statements. Direct and challenging (short, abrupt). Fast rate of speech.	Do not react defensively or in a retaliatory manner. Use facts and logic and avoid unnecessary details. Listen rather than defend. Match rate somewhat.	• Avoid trying to "get to know him or her." The customer often perceives this as a waste of time and may distrust your motives. • Be conscious of time, by making your point and then concluding the interaction appropriately. • Provide opportunities for the customer to talk by alternately providing small bits of information and asking specific questions aimed at solving the problem and serving the customer.

(continued)

FIGURE 6.2   (*Concluded*)

Style	Behaviors Exhibited	Provider Response	Customer Relationship Strategies
	Additional Cues Short attention span when listening. Very direct and decisive.	Keep sentences and communication brief. Support opinions, ideas, and vision.	• Be prepared with information, necessary forms, details, warranties, and so on, before the customer arrives. • When appropriate, provide options supported by evidence and focus on how the solution will affect the customer's time, effort, and money. • Focus on new, innovative products or services, emphasizing especially those that are environmentally sensitive or responsive.
EXPRESSIVE	**Nonverbal Cues** Enthusiasm and inflection in voice. Active body language. Very intense, dramatic. Writing tends to be flowery and includes many details.	Listen and respond enthusiastically. Use open, positive body language and smile easily. Return firm, professional one-hand shake. Acknowledge but use caution in returning touch (this action could be misinterpreted by them or others).	• Typically people-oriented and want to be around people. • Focus on the customer's need to be liked and accepted by appealing to his or her emotions. • Give positive feedback, acknowledging the customer's ideas. • Listen to his or her stories and share humorous ones about yourself.
		Show interest and ask pertinent questions. When writing, use a friendly reader-focused style.	• Use an open-ended, friendly approach. • Ask questions such as "What attracted you to this product or service?" • Keep product details to a minimum unless the customer asks for them. • Describe how your product or service can help the customer get closer to his or her goals or to fulfilling his or her needs.
	Verbal Cues Excessive details when describing something. Fast rate of speech. Emphasizes storytelling and fun.	Ask specific open-end questions to help them refocus. Mirror or match their rate and excitement where appropriate. Relax, listen, laugh, and respond as appropriate.	• Explain solutions or suggestions in terms of the impact on the customer and his or her relationships with others. • If appropriate, provide incentives to encourage a decision.
	Additional Cues Inattentive to details in tasks. Shares personal information and virtually anything else freely.	Ask questions to involve them. Reciprocate if you are comfortable doing so; however, stay focused on the task at hand.	• Provide information verbally and in writing to ensure details are not missed. • Provide solid examples and success stories to emphasize the value and importance of products or services.

KNOWLEDGE CHECK

1. What nonverbal cues might someone with a primary style of rational exhibit?

2. What nonverbal cues might someone with a primary style of inquisitive exhibit?

3. What nonverbal cues might someone with a primary style of decisive exhibit?

4. What nonverbal cues might someone with a primary style of expressive exhibit?

5. What verbal cues might someone with a primary style of rational exhibit?

6. What verbal cues might someone with a primary style of inquisitive exhibit?

7. What verbal cues might someone with a primary style of decisive exhibit?

8. What verbal cues might someone with a primary style of expressive exhibit?

LO 6-4 Building Stronger Relationships

CONCEPT **Sometimes, building stronger customer relationships means that you discover customer needs, seek opportunities for service, and respond appropriately to customers' behavioral styles. Occasionally you will need to deemphasize a no and say it as positively as you can.**

Recognizing and relating to customers' behavioral styles is just the first step in providing better service. To deliver total customer satisfaction, you will need to make the customer feel special, which often requires skills such as relationship building through effective communication and **problem solving**.

Whether a situation involves simply answering a question, guiding someone to a desired product or location, or performing a service, customers should leave the interaction feeling good about what they experienced. Providing this feeling not only is good business sense on your part but also helps guarantee the customers return or spread favorable word-of-mouth advertising.

There are many ways of partnering with either internal or external customers to solve problems and produce a **win-win situation** (one in which both the customer and you and your organization succeed and feel good about the outcome). Whatever you do to achieve this result, your customers should realize that you are their advocate and are acting in their best interests to solve their problems. Some suggestions for building stronger customer relationships follow.

problem solving The system of identifying issues, determining alternatives for dealing with them, and then selecting and monitoring a strategy for resolution.

win-win situation An outcome to a disagreement in which both parties walk away feeling that they got what they wanted or needed.

People send verbal and nonverbal clues to their behavioral style preference. Observe your customers' eye contact, their level of directness or evasiveness, how quickly or slowly they speak, and their level of warmth versus formality. Once you can read these clues, you will be better able to individualize the customer service you can provide. *Can you think of a person in your life who exhibits clues to his or her other behavioral style?*

©Cathy Yeulet/123RF RF

Trending NOW

For decades, advertisers have done research on what appeals to customers and encourages them to buy a product or service. Such research applies to the behavioral style preferences in this chapter, since customers with varying primary styles will react differently to each of the five identified appeals.

In today's changing global marketplace in which customers have a variety of backgrounds and personal preferences, service representatives need to understand the impact of these appeals. This can allow them to address individual needs, wants, expectations, and preferences. The five traditional appeals used in advertising include the following:

Fear or the customer's belief that his or her action or inaction will cause a loss of something (e.g., products, knowledge, personal appeal to others, health, or life)

Rational or logical approach that focuses on perceptions of functionality or practicality of a product or service (e.g., increased vehicle mileage, increased income or savings, lowered energy use).

Belonging or camaraderie that pushes the perception that by using a specific product or service a customer can be part of a group (e.g., social network bonding while using a product such as cigarette or soft drink, having the latest trendy item, or using something that everyone else does)

Humor that helps create an emotional memory to a product or service advertisement (e.g., Aflac Duck, GEICO Gecko, and Farmers Insurance advertisements that show humorous situation then the spokesperson stresses "We know a thing or two because we've seen a thing or two")

Sex designed to attract a specific target audience (e.g., beer advertisements that focus on men capturing the attention of attractive women by drinking a particular brand, or fragrance commercials focused on creating a romantic or glamorous image to attract women)

DISCOVER CUSTOMER NEEDS

Using sound listening and verbal and nonverbal communication skills, engage customers in a dialogue that allows them to identify what they really want or need. If you can determine a customer's behavioral style, you can tailor your communication strategy to that style. Keep in mind that some customers may not be express their needs aloud. In these instances, you should attempt to validate your impressions or suspicions by asking questions or requesting feedback. Gather information about a customer by observing vocal qualities, phrasing, nonverbal expressions and movements, and emotional state. Also, look for signs that help identify his or her primary behavioral style preference. For example, while providing service to Mr. Delgado, you told him that the product he was ordering would not arrive for three weeks. You noticed that he grimaced and made a concerned sound of "Um." At this point, a perception check would have been appropriate. You could have said, "Mr. Delgado, you looked concerned or disappointed when I mentioned the delivery date. Is that a problem for you?" You might have discovered that he needed the item sooner but resigned himself to the delay and did not ask about other options. In effect, he was exhibiting "I" or possibly "R" behavior (silence and low-key reaction). Rather than have a confrontation, he accepted the situation without voicing disappointment or concern. A potential outcome in such instances might be that your customer decides to check a competitor to see if it has what is wanted or needed. By reacting positively to the customer's nonverbal signals in this scenario, you could identify and address a concern, seek an alternative solution, and thus prevent a dissatisfied and/or lost customer.

⚙ WORK IT OUT 6.2

Monitoring Behavior

To practice matching behavior with styles, try this activity. Select four or five friends or coworkers whom you see and interact with regularly. Write one of their names at the top of a sheet. Covertly (without their knowledge) observe these people for a week or so in various settings and make notes about their behavior under the categories listed below:

Writing pattern or style

Body movements and other nonverbal gestures

Interpersonal communication style (e.g., direct, indirect, specific or nonspecific questions, good or poor listener)

Dress style (e.g., flashy, conservative, formal, informal)

Surroundings (e.g., office decorations or organization, car, home)

Personality (e.g., activities and interactions preferred—solitary, group, active, passive)

Behavioral style(s) (e.g., primary, secondary, tertiary)

At the end of the week, decide which primary and/or secondary style(s) of behavior each person exhibits most often. Then ask these people to assist you in an experiment that will involve them completing the quick style assessment that you did earlier (Figure 6.1).

After they have rated themselves, explain that you have been observing them for the past week.

Compare their ratings to the characteristics described in this chapter, and to your own assessment. Were you able to predict their primary or, at least, their secondary style?

SAY "YES"

If you must decline a request or cannot provide a product or service, do so in a positive manner. Deemphasizing what you cannot do and providing an alternative position the customer in a power position. That is, even though she may not get her first request, she is once again in control because she can say yes or no to the alternative you have offered, or she can decide on the next step. For example, when a customer requests a brand or product not stocked by your organization, you could offer alternatives. You might counter with, "Mrs. Hanslik, although we do not stock that brand, we do have a comparable product that has been rated higher by *Consumer Reports* than the one you requested. May I show you?" This approach not only serves the customer but also (sometimes) results in a sale and is important if the person is a primarily high "D" behavioral type and prefers to take the lead in situations.

Figure 6.3 provides some strategies to use when responding to customer complaints and solving problems involving people who demonstrate the four behavioral styles that you have learned. By tailoring customer service strategies to individual style

FIGURE 6.3

Strategies for Responding to Customer Problems

Style	Customer Behaviors	Service Strategies
RATIONAL	Seeks systematic resolution to the situation.	Stress resolution and security of the issue.
	Avoids conflict or disagreement.	Smile, when appropriate.
	Strives for acceptance of ideas.	Provide references or resources.
	Intermittent eye contact.	Listen actively; make eye contact.
	Uses hand and subdued body movements and speech to emphasize key points.	Focus on personal movements to convey your feelings about the incident (e.g., "How do you feel we can best resolve this problem?").
INQUISITIVE	Listens to explanations.	Focus on the problem, not the person.
	Demands specifics.	Have details and facts available.
	Mild demeanor.	Approach in nonthreatening manner.
	Intermittent eye contact.	Listen actively, make eye contact, and focus on the situation.
	Gives list of issues, in chronological order.	Be specific in outlining actions to be taken by everyone.
	Exhibits patience.	Follow through on commitments.
	Seeks reassurance.	Offer guarantees of resolution if possible.
	Focuses on facts.	Give facts and pros and cons of suggestions.
DECISIVE	Seeks to avoid conflict; just wants resolution.	Use low-pitched, unemotional speech; be patient; listen.
	Loud voice.	Be patient; listen empathetically.
	Finger-pointing or aggressive body gestures.	Do not internalize; he or she is angry with the product or service, not necessarily you.
	Firm, active handshake.	Return a firm businesslike handshake.
	Directly places blame on service provider.	Be brief; tell him or her what you can do; offer solutions.

Style	Customer Behaviors	Service Strategies
	Direct eye contact.	Be formal, businesslike.
	Sarcasm.	Do not take a happy-go-lucky or flippant approach.
	Impatient.	Be time conscious; time is money to a "D."
	Demanding verblage (e.g., "You'd better fix this"; "I want to see the manager *now!*").	Project competence; find the best person to solve the problem.
	Irrational assertions (e.g., "You people *never* or *always* ...").	Ask questions that focus on what he or she needs or wants (e.g., "What do you think is a reasonable solution?").
EXPRESSIVE	Threats (e.g., "If you can't help, I'll go to a company that can.").	Reassure; say what you can do.
	Intermittent smiling along with verbalizing dissatisfaction.	Be supportive; tell the customer what you can do for him or her.
	Uses nonaggressive language (e.g., "I'd like to talk with someone about . . .").	Allow him or her to vent frustrations or verbalize thoughts.
	Steady eye contact.	Smile, if appropriate; return eye contact while conversing.
	Elicits your assistance and follow-up (e.g., "I really don't want to run all over town searching. Will you please call ...").	Take the time to offer assistance and comply with his or her requests, if possible.
	Shows sincere interest.	Focus on feelings through empathy (e.g., "I feel that . . .").
	Enthusiastic active handshake.	Return a firm businesslike handshake.
	Enthusiastically explains a situation.	Patiently provide active listening; offer ideas and suggestions for resolution.

preferences, you address the customer's specific needs. Active listening is a key skill in any service situation. As you review these strategies, think of other things you might do to serve each behavioral type.

SEEK OPPORTUNITIES FOR SERVICE

View complaints as a chance to create a favorable impression by solving a problem. Watch the behavioral characteristics that your customer is exhibiting. Using what you see and hear, take appropriate action to adapt to the customer's personality needs and solve the problem professionally. For example, Mrs. Minga complained loudly to you that the servicewoman who installed her new washing machine tracked oil onto the dining room carpet. As she is speaking, Mrs. Minga is pointing her finger at you, raising her voice, and threatening to go to the manager if you do not handle this situation immediately. You can take the opportunity to solve the problem and strengthen the relationship at the same time. You might try the following. Make direct eye contact (no staring), smile, and empathize by saying, "Mrs. Minga, I am terribly sorry about your carpet. I know that it must be very upsetting. If you will allow me to, I will arrange to have your dining room carpet cleaned, and for your inconvenience, while they are at it we will have them clean the carpets in adjoining rooms at no cost to you. How does that sound?" In reacting this way, you professionally and assertively took control of the situation. This is important because Mrs. Minga is exhibiting high "D" behavior.

Customers should not be kept waiting because your systems or processes break down. By striving for seamless service delivery, customers of all behavioral styles are more likely to be satisfied. *What can you do on a daily basis to enhance the service that your customers receive?*

©Claudiad/Getty Images RF

Responding in a less decisive manner might result in an escalation of her emotions and a demand to see an authority figure that she feels can resolve the issue.

FOCUS ON PROCESS IMPROVEMENT

Customers generally do not like having to wait when your system is not functioning properly. They rightfully view their time as valuable. In today's "I want it and I want it now" society, inconveniencing your customers will likely lead to emotional reactions, complaints, and customer defection to a competitor. To expect them to patiently wait while a new cashier tries to figure out the register codes, someone gets a price check because the product was coded incorrectly, you have to call the office for information or approvals, and so on, is unfair and unreasonable.

Handle defects in your system or processes or delays when the customer is not present. You should strive to provide **seamless service** to customers. This means that they should get great service and never have to worry about your problems or breakdowns. When breakdowns do occur, remedy them quickly, and then soothe over the customer relationship. In addition, recognize that customers with varying behavioral styles will react differently to such breakdowns. Here are some examples of how each style might react to service glitches:

- "R" style customers may smile but are likely to complain in an inoffensive manner, and also may seek out a supervisor.
- "I" style individuals may seem to be patient and not say anything or cause a confrontation. Even so, they may request directions to the supervisor's office, send a detailed letter or e-mail message of complaint, or go online to blast you and the organization on websites like yelp.com, ripoff.com, or complaintsboard.com.
- "D" style people may get loud, aggressive, and vocal and demand a supervisor after only a brief delay.
- "E" behavioral types may get upset but will often make the best of their time complaining to other customers and comparing notes on similar past experiences.

seamless service Service that is done in a manner that seems effortless and natural to the customer. Processes and systems are fully functional, effective, and efficient. Service representatives are well trained and proficient in delivering service, and there is no inconvenience to the customer.

No matter what style the customer exhibits, you should strive to reduce or eliminate customer inconvenience and distress.

In all cases, after an extensive delay you may want to compensate the customer for the inconvenience. At the least, such a situation warrants a sincere apology. Such an occurrence might be handled in the following manner: "Mr. Westgate, I am sorry for the delay. We have been experiencing computer problems all day. I would like to make up for your inconvenience by giving you a 10 percent discount off your meal check. Would that be acceptable?" Although this is not a significant offering, your intention is to show remorse and to placate the customer so that he or she will continue to use your products and/or services.

After you have dealt with a problem, your next concern should be to personally address the process that caused the breakdown or make a recommendation to your supervisor or other appropriate person. All employees are responsible for quality service and **process improvement**.

MAKE CUSTOMERS FEEL SPECIAL

Most people like to feel special and appreciated. Creating that feeling in others is what stellar customer service is all about. Through simple things like a warm smile, pleasant tone, and welcoming words, you can make your customers feel like the most important people in the world to you … because at that moment they should be.

By creating a bond with your customers through positive words and actions, you can easily help them feel as if there is no other place they would rather be or with whom they would rather do business. With a few simple gestures or phrases, you can be on the way to developing a sound customer–provider relationship that not only results in a loyal customer, but is also likely to generate positive word-of-mouth advertising from the customer to other people that he or he knows.

Keep in mind that when customers feel good about themselves because of something you did or said, they are likely to better appreciate what you and your organization can offer them. Small tokens of appreciation can be worth their weight in customer gold. For example, to demonstrate appreciation for long-term patronage, you may want to recognize a customer as follows: "Mr. and Mrs. Hoffmeister, we really appreciate your loyalty. Our records indicate that you have been a patient in our office for over 20 years. In recognition, on behalf of Dr. Seiffert, here is a complimentary dinner certificate for $25. Please accept it with our compliments." Consider how unusual it is to have a customer's loyalty for 20 years and how much revenue such a relationship brings—not just from the customer, but also referrals. Such a reward would likely surprise and amaze most patients since many doctors have a reputation of not valuing a patient's time or business. This type of strategy goes a long way in guaranteeing customer loyalty.

BE CULTURALLY AWARE

The reality of a multicultural customer service environment further challenges your ability to deal with behaviors. This is because, in today's multicultural business environment, it is likely that you will interact with someone of a different background, belief system, or culture on any given day. Many challenges that develop in these encounters are a result of diversity ignorance.

Even after you master the concepts of behavioral styles, you must remember that because values and beliefs vary from one culture to another, behavior is also likely to vary. For example, in many countries or cultures, the nonverbal gestures that North

process improvement Refers to the process of continually evaluating products and services to ensure that maximum effectiveness, efficiency, and potential are being obtained from them.

> **Customer Service Success Tip**
>
> Go out of your way to make your customers feel appreciated by recognizing the value of those with whom you come into contact. Do this by communicating with customers effectively, asking questions essential to discovering their needs and expectations, listening to their needs, and providing valid feedback designed to show that you value them and their issues and are willing to help them. All of this can help raise their self-esteem and result in a better customer–provider relationship.

Americans use have completely different meanings. Likewise, the reactions to such gestures will differ based on the recipient's personality style and background. For example, variations of symbols such as joining the thumb and index finger to form an O, signaling "Okay," have sexual connotations in parts of several countries (e.g., Germany, Sardinia, Malta, Greece, Turkey, Russia, the Middle East, and parts of South America). Likewise, variations of the V symbolizing "victory" or "peace" to many people in Western cultures have negative connotations in some parts of the world (e.g., British Isles and parts of Malta).[1] Symbols and gestures, therefore, might anger or offend some customers. Additionally, seemingly innocent behaviors such as crossing your legs so that the sole of your shoe points toward someone or patting a small child on the top of his or her head may cause offense. That is because the sole of the foot is the lowest part of the body and touches the ground. In some parts of the world, pointing the sole of the foot toward a person implies that the person is lowly. Males from a Western culture, and specifically males who have "D," "I," and "R" styles and tend to adopt a formal posture when seated, should be aware of the effect crossing their legs might have on certain customers. ("E" style people tend to be more relaxed and sprawling in their posture.) As for the head, many countries (e.g., in the Far East, especially Thailand)[2] view it as a sacred part of the body. Patting a child on the head in some cultures is sometimes considered to invite evil spirits or bad omens. This action might easily be taken by people who have high "E" behavioral tendencies, for they tend to be touchy-feely.

To help send a positive message to customers from other cultures, you can do simple things that might have major effects. For example, if you work in a restaurant and want to show appreciation for the large numbers of customers from another country that patronize the restaurant, you might recommend to your boss that a special dish from that area of the world be added to the menu. This offering could be promoted through flyers or advertisements. Such a strategy shows appreciation of the customers and their culture while encouraging them to eat at your establishment. However, be sure that the special dish is correctly prepared and uses the correct ingredients. Otherwise, you might offend and displease rather than satisfy the customer.

All these strategies, combined with a heightened knowledge of behavioral styles, can better prepare you to serve a wide variety of customers.

⚙ WORK IT OUT 6.3

Determining Styles

Read the following descriptions and then determine with which behavioral style you are dealing. Keep in mind that each person can switch behavioral styles, depending on the situation. To help you determine style characteristics, refer to the style tendencies described in previous sections of this chapter.

Situation 1

You are a salesperson at a jewelry counter and observe a professionally dressed female customer waiting in line for several minutes. She is checking her watch frequently, anxiously looking around, and sighing often. When she arrives at the counter, she makes direct eye contact with you and without smiling states, "I want to buy a 16-inch 14-karat gold twisted-link necklace like the one advertised in today's paper. I also want a small gold heart pendant and would like

(continued)

6.3 (Continued)

these to cost no more than $125. Can you help me? Oh yes, I almost forgot. Wrap that in birthday paper. This gift is for my daughter's birthday."

Situation 2

You stop by the office of a director of a department that provides data you use to prepare your end-of-month reports. As you look around, you see a photograph of his family. Your coworker smiles weakly and asks you to have a seat. As you begin to state your purpose by saying, "Thanks for taking the time to see me, Mr. Cohen," he interrupts and says, "Call me Lenny, please."

Situation 3

As a customer service representative for an automobile dealer, you return a phone message from Cynthia McGregor. When the phone is answered, you say, "Good morning, may I speak with Cindy McGregor?" The curt response is, "This is Cynthia McGregor. How may I help you?" During the conversation, Ms. McGregor asks a variety of very specific questions about an automotive recall. Even though it seems obvious that the recall does not apply to her car, she asks very detailed follow-up questions such as why the recall was necessary, who was affected, and what was being done. Throughout the conversation, she is very focused on facts, times, dates, and technical aspects of the recall.

Situation 4

You are a teller in a bank. Mrs. Vittelli, one of the customers, comes into your branch several times a week. You know that she has just become a grandmother because she has brought along photos of her grandson. She has shared them, and all the details of her daughter's pregnancy, in a loud, exuberant manner with several of your coworkers. As she speaks, you have noticed that she has a beautiful smile, and that throughout conversations she is very animated, using gestures and often reaching over to lightly touch others as they speak.

KNOW YOUR PRODUCTS AND SERVICES

Customers expect that you will be able to identify and describe the products and services offered by your company. Depending on the behavioral style of the customer, the type of questions will vary. The following are some examples of questioning approaches that may be used by the four style types. Just remember that like other suggestions throughout this chapter, these are possibilities. Since people have all four styles within them, they might react differently based on a given situation.

- An "R" personality type may want to know who uses your services and products and ask to see the instructions and warranty.
- An "I" behavioral style customer may ask many questions related to options, testing, rebates, and similar detailed technical information.
- A person with a strong "D" behavioral tendency may want to know the "bottom line" of using your service or product benefits.

- A person with an "E" style preference may want to talk about uses, colors, and sizes.

If you cannot answer their questions, frustration, complaints, and/or loss of a customer may result.

Service providers need to have a sound knowledge of the products and services they are offering so that they can provide the best customer service possible. For example, when a new service or product line is introduced, orientation classes for employees can be arranged. In the classes, the features, benefits, and operation of the new items can be explained and demonstrated. Taking this approach increases knowledge of products and helps ensure better customer service. If your organization does not offer such product and service training, take the time and responsibility to read manuals, do research, and ask questions of vendors, suppliers, and your supervisor so that you become proficient in demonstrating and explaining what you are providing.

KNOWLEDGE CHECK

1. What are some strategies for handling a situation in which you cannot say "yes" or provide a product or service to a customer with a primary style of rational?

2. What are some strategies for handling a situation in which you cannot say "yes" or provide a product or service to a customer with a primary style of inquisitive?

3. What are some strategies for handling a situation in which you cannot say "yes" or provide a product or service to a customer with a primary style of decisive?

4. What are some strategies for handling a situation in which you cannot say "yes" or provide a product or service to a customer with a primary style of expressive?

5. How might you make your customers feel special?

LO 6-5 Dealing with Perceptions

CONCEPT   **Often there are many different perceptions of an event. Our perceptions are often influenced by many factors such as physical qualities, social roles and behaviors, psychological qualities, and group affiliations.**

perceptions How someone views an item, situation, or others.

Everyone has **perceptions** about the people and events he or she encounters (see Figure 6.4). A person's behavioral style as well as background, based on education, experiences, events, and interpersonal contacts, can influence how he or she views the world. In effect, there are sometimes as many different perceptions of an event as there are people involved.

FIGURE 6.4

Factors Affecting Perceptions

How are our perceptions shaped within a customer service framework? In essence, there are six categories that form the basis of many perceptions. We tend to base our perceptions of others and categorize people by thinking about the following:

- *Personal appearance.* How does the customer generally look related to factors such as dress, jewelry, grooming, and hygiene?
- *Physical qualities.* What does a person look like? What gender? What body shape? Color of skin? Physical characteristics (hair color or type, facial features, height, or weight)?
- *Social roles.* What is a person's position in society? Job title? Honors received? Involvement in social or volunteer organizations?
- *Social behaviors.* How does this person act in terms of the behavioral style characteristics? What social skills does he or she exhibit in social and business settings? How well does he or she interact with people (peers, customers, seniors, subordinates, and people of other races, gender, or backgrounds)?
- *Psychological qualities.* How does he or she process information mentally? Is this person confident? Stressed out? Insecure? Curious? Paranoid?
- *Group affiliations.* Does this person belong to a recognizable religious, ethnic, or political group? What kinds of qualities are associated with each group? Does he or she assume leadership roles and demonstrate competence in such roles?

PERCEPTIONS AND STEREOTYPES

People's perceptions of events vary greatly, as do their perceptions of each other. As a customer service provider, you should be aware of how you perceive your customers and, in turn, how they perceive you.

Ethical Dilemma 6.2

You often hear one of your coworkers making improper and derogatory comments about customers from other cultures (e.g., the way they dress, their accent, their values and beliefs, and so on). Often this occurs when other people from outside the organization (e.g., vendors, suppliers, or customers) can hear. Assume that another employee tries to engage you in a conversation in which he or she is making derogatory comments about people from another culture while there are people from a variety of countries within the hearing range.

What would you do about the situation, if anything?

In some cases, you may **stereotype** people and, in doing so, adversely affect delivery of services. In some instances, the factors that you might be tempted to project onto an individual (e.g., age, gender, race, or ethnic background) might actually stem from the person's behavioral style preference. For example, your perception of older customers may be that they are all slow, hard of hearing, argumentative, disagreeable, and politically conservative. Other than the physiological issues, you may be witnessing behavioral characteristics that they have likely displayed most of their life. In some instances, your perceptions may be based on your experiences with one person (or more) from the same demographic or from what you have heard or seen on television or in movies. In any event, such views of a group of people might cause you to treat

stereotype Generalization made about an individual or group and not based on reality. Similar people are often lumped together for ease in categorizing them.

most older people in the same way, rather than treating each person as unique. In these instances, you would be basing your behavior on a stereotype, not on reality. Think about it—are there many older people who do not have these characteristics? Thus, you need to be very careful that your perceptions about any group of people are not influenced by stereotypes because this clearly works against treating each customer as an individual.

⚙ WORK IT OUT 6.4

Discovering Common Characteristics

Refer to Work It Out 6.1 (Describing Your Behavior). Select four to eight friends or coworkers and ask them to rate themselves using Work It Out 6.1. Next, ask each person to answer the following questions:

What do I look for when I shop?

What is my main reason for shopping?

What do I do when I need to buy or replace something?

What is the most important thing to me when I am looking to replace something?

Once everyone has finished, gather in a group to compare and discuss answers. Focus on the fact that each person and each style is unique but that we all have common characteristics and needs. Discuss how this knowledge of common needs or drives can be used to provide customer service more effectively.

---

disparate treatment Term meaning discrimination against a person or group of people based on factors, such as, age, race, sex, ethnicity, or ability level.

Stereotyping people affects your relationships with customers. The practice could even lead to legal charges of **disparate treatment** and liability for you and your organization. This is one reason why you should consciously guard against stereotyping when you interact with customers. If you pigeonhole people right away because of preconceptions, you may negatively affect future interactions. For example, suppose you use your new knowledge about behavioral styles to walk up to a coworker and say something like, "I figured out what your problem is when dealing with people. You are a "D."" Could this create a confrontational situation? Might this person react negatively? What impact might your behavior have on your relationship with your coworker (and possibly others who witness your behavior)? There are several things wrong with such an approach. First, no one always exhibits only "D" behavior. Although a person might exhibit this behavior a lot, he or she draws from all four styles, just as you do. Second, exhibiting any particular style is not a "problem." As you have seen in this chapter, "D" behavior can provide some valuable input to any situation. Finally, although a behavioral style may contribute to a person's actions, many other factors come into play (e.g., communication ability, timing, age, gender, location, and situation).

To avoid categorizing or stereotyping people, spend time observing them, listen to them objectively, and respond according to each unique situation and person. Doing this can lead to better relationships and improved customer service. It can also add to your appearing more professional.

Many preconceived ideas about an individual or group can lead to different or disparate treatment and poor service. *What preconceived ideas might affect how a server treats each of the groups of diners shown in these photographs?*

KNOWLEDGE CHECK

1. What is the difference between a perception and a stereotype?
2. What are six factors that influence perceptions?
3. What is disparate treatment and why should it be avoided?

Small Business Perspective

Since many small business employees often deliver service face-to-face with customers and have an opportunity to get to know their customers on a more personal basis, knowledge of behavioral styles can come in handy. As noted in the chapter, by recognizing specific traits or behaviors related to the various style preferences, you can adjust your service delivery to meet the likes of customers if you work for a small company. You might even keep an informal file on each customer that you can reference when a planned meeting is coming. In it, you can note what you believe to be the customer's primary, and any secondary, style preferences. When possible, before actually meeting with the customer, refer to the file and mentally think of ways to deal with the customer. Just remember to focus on a given situation and the dynamics occurring since people can switch to other behavioral styles depending on what is happening and with whom they are dealing.

If service interactions are typically over the telephone, you can still use the strategies you read about in this chapter. Simply by listening to customer tone, timing, delivery of messages, and their reactions to what you say, you can adjust your tone, selection of words, and the approach you take to handling the interaction.

Impact on Service

Based on personal experience and what you just read, answer the following questions:

1. How might behavioral styles play an important role in dealing with fellow employees in a small company? Explain.

2. If you worked for a small business, what strategies for using what you read in this chapter might help strengthen your service to customers? Explain.

3. What specific challenges could you have in dealing with a customer who has a different style preference than your own? Explain.

 SMARTBOOK™   Use SmartBook to help you read, study, and retain what you have learned. Access SmartBook in your Instructor's Connect course, or go to connect.mheducation.com for help.

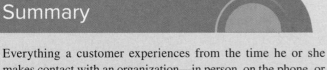

Key Terms

behavioral styles

decisive style

disparate treatment

expressive style

inquisitive style

perceptions

primary behavior pattern

problem solving

process improvement

rational style

seamless service

stereotype

win-win situation

Summary

Everything a customer experiences from the time he or she makes contact with an organization—in person, on the phone, or through other means—affects that customer's perception of the organization and its employees. In order to positively influence the customer's opinion, service professionals must constantly be alert for opportunities to provide excellent service. Making a little extra effort can often mean the difference between total customer satisfaction and service breakdown.

As you have seen in this chapter, people are varied and have different behavioral styles. Recognizing the differences and dealing with customers on a case-by-case basis form the foundation of solid customer service. By examining individual behavioral tendencies, actions, communication styles, and needs, you can better determine a course of action for each customer. The test of your effectiveness is whether your customers return and what they tell their friends about you and your organization.

Review Questions

1. What are behavioral styles?

2. What are the four behavioral style categories discussed in this chapter?

3. What are some of the characteristics that can help you identify a person who has the following style preferences: R, I, D, E?

4. When communicating with someone who has an "R" preference, what can you do to improve your effectiveness?

5. When communicating with someone who has an "I" preference, what can you do to improve your effectiveness?

6. When communicating with someone who has a "D" preference, what can you do to improve your effectiveness?

7. When communicating with someone who has an "E" preference, what can you do to improve your effectiveness?

8. What are some strategies for eliminating service barriers by using your knowledge of behavioral styles?

9. What are perceptions?

10. How can perceptions affect customer relations?

Search It Out

1. Search for Behavioral Styles on the Internet

   Search the Internet and look for information and research data on behavioral styles and other types of personal surveys. Specifically look for the various theories and surveys that describe and categorize behavior. Also, try to find information about some of the people who have done research on behavior. The following list will get you started:

   Sigmund Freud

   Carl Jung

   Alfred Adler

   Abraham Maslow

   William Moulton Marston

   Ivan Pavlov

   B. F. Skinner

   Behavioral style surveys

   Personality surveys

   www.myersbriggs.org

   www.inscapepublishing.com

   www.tracomcorp.com

   www.personalitypathways.com

   Be prepared to present some of your findings at the next scheduled class.

2. For additional articles and information on dealing with a variety of customer service behaviors and behavioral styles, visit the author's Customer Service Skills Blog at http://www.customerserviceskillsbook.com/wordpress and search "Customer Service Behavior," "Behavioral Styles," and related topics. Also, visit YouTube through http://bit.ly/2tNEd5A to search and watch short videos on the customer service behavior, behavioral styles, and related topics.

Collaborative Learning Activity

Observing and Analyzing Behavioral Styles

With a partner or team, go to a public place (park, mall, airport, train or bus station, or restaurant) to observe three different people. Note the specific behaviors each person exhibits. After you have finished this part of the activity, take a guess at each person's behavioral style preference based on behaviors you saw. Compare notes with your teammates and discuss similarities and differences among findings. Also, discuss how this information can be helpful in your workplace to deliver better customer service.

Face-to-Face

Working through Technology and People Problems at Child's Play Toy Company

Background

Since the opening of its newest store in Princeton, New Jersey, Child's Play Toy Company of Minneapolis, Minnesota, has been getting mixed customer reviews. Designed to be state of the art, open, and customer friendly, the store includes an attended activity area where small children can play while parents shop. In addition, an innovative system makes it possible for local customers to order products from catalogs or from the company's website and then go to a drive-up window to pick up their purchases without leaving their cars. Another creative feature involves interactive television monitors in the store—where customers can see a customer service representative at the same time the representative sees them. To reduce staffing costs, the customer service representatives are actually at a Philadelphia, Pennsylvania, location and are remotely connected via satellite and computer to all new stores. This system is used for special ordering, billing questions, and complaint resolution. Customers can also use a computer keyboard to enter data or search for product information online through the company's website while in the store.

In recent months, the number of customer complaints has been rising. Many people complain about not getting the product that they ordered over the system. Some are uncomfortable using the computer keyboard, while others dislike the impersonal touch and that they have to answer a series of standard questions asked by a "talking head" on the screen. Further, some customers have encountered system or computer breakdowns and say that they cannot get timely service or resolution of problems.

Your Role

As a customer service representative and cashier at the store, you are responsible for operating a cash register in the store at Child's Play when all lines are operational and more than two customers are waiting in each line. You are also responsible for supervising other cashiers on your shift and dealing with customer questions, complaints, or problems. You report directly to the assistant store manager, Meg Giarnelli. Prior to coming to this store, you worked in two other New Jersey store branches during the five preceding years.

This afternoon, Mrs. Sakuro, a regular customer, came to you. She was obviously frustrated and pointed her finger at you as she shouted, "You people are stupid!" She also demanded to speak with the manager and threatened that "if you people do not want my business, I will go to another store!" Apparently, a doll that Mrs. Sakuro had ordered two weeks ago over the in-store system had not arrived. The doll was to be for her daughter's birthday, which is in two days. Although Mrs. Sakuro has a heavy accent, you understood that she had been directed by a cashier to check with a customer service representative via the monitor to determine the status of the order. When she did this, she was informed that there was a problem with the order. The representative who took the original order apparently wrote down the credit card number incorrectly and the order was not processed. When Mrs. Sakuro asked the customer service representative why someone had not called her, the representative said that the customer service department was in another state and that long-distance calls were not allowed by frontline employees. She was told that the local store where she was picking up is responsible for verifying order status, contacting the customer via telephone, and handling problems. There was no valid explanation given when Mrs. Sakuro asked why someone in New Jersey had not just e-mailed her since they had her e-mail address. Mrs. Sakuro's behavior and attitude are upsetting to you.

Critical Thinking Questions

1. From the behavioral style information in this chapter and other subjects discussed in this book, what do you think is causing the complaints being made?

2. What system changes would you suggest for Child's Play? Why?

3. What can you do at this point to solve the problem?

4. What primary behavioral style is Mrs. Sakuro exhibiting? What specific strategies should you use to address her behavior?

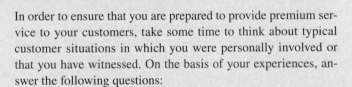

Planning to Serve

In order to ensure that you are prepared to provide premium service to your customers, take some time to think about typical customer situations in which you were personally involved or that you have witnessed. On the basis of your experiences, answer the following questions:

1. What types of behaviors does the average customer exhibit?

2. Based on what you learned about behavioral styles in general, and your preferred style, what service strategies could you use if you were involved with the behaviors identified in question 1?

3. In difficult or emotional service situations, what behaviors are often manifested?

4. What strategies might help you in dealing with such customer behaviors?

Quick Preview Answers

1. T	4. T	7. T	10. T	13. T
2. T	5. F	8. F	11. T	14. F
3. T	6. F	9. F	12. F	15. T

Ethical Dilemma Summary

Ethical Dilemma 6.1 Possible Answers

High "D" behavior, such as your supervisor is displaying, can be frustrating and create challenges in the workplace. If you have observed your supervisor exhibiting the behavior in question on numerous occasions to arrive at your conclusions, and have validated them by talking to some of your coworkers, you may be doing the supervisor and employees a good deed by bringing your perceptions to her attention. This is because most people exhibit behavior of which they are often unaware. If the person is not made aware or does not change them, such unintentional displays can create communication and relationship breakdowns. In a service environment, this can be a real issue.

The key to providing such feedback is to do so at a nonemotional time (e.g., not immediately following an event in which the supervisor does not get input or listen and you are upset about it). Try the following approach:

Pick a time when both of you can calmly and rationally sit down to discuss the issue, perhaps over a cup of coffee in the break room when no one else is present. Doing this might prevent a situation in which the supervisor feels that she has to "stand her ground" because of having to maintain an image of being in control (remember she does have a high "D" type of personality preference). Also, remember the old adage of "the boss may not always be right, but he or she is always the boss."

When sharing your observations, focus on specific examples of her behavior and not on the person. For example, you might say something like, "Susan, I wanted to share my perceptions about how we are allowed to provide suggestions or feedback in the department. I have discussed my feelings with a couple of other people and they mentioned that they have had similar reactions or experiences. A specific example of what I am referring to happened when Matt, Shirley, and I offered a suggestion about . . . and then the process changed to something totally different without any explanation about why our idea could not be used. It made us feel that our opinion and experience are really irrelevant." Notice in this example, the word "you" (referring to the supervisor) is avoided. Instead, the focus is on what you and others did, the end action or behavior, and how it made you feel. This potentially reduces the chance that your supervisor will feel attacked or threatened and therefore may seriously consider your feedback, or at least offer an explanation about why she took the action that she did.

An important point to consider in this situation is that you have already witnessed one customer defection. There are likely others of which you are not aware. Such business loss is costing the company, and ultimately you and all other employees, due to lost revenue. Avoiding the issue is not an option. If all else fails and your supervisor is not receptive or responsive to feedback, you might even have to go to your supervisor's manager.

Ethical Dilemma 6.2 Possible Answers

Comments about factors that someone cannot change (e.g., culture or physical characteristics) are often a sign of more underlying prejudices against a group or type of people. They can lead to bias and discrimination as well as to provoking emotional confrontations with others.

In the workplace, you sometimes have to walk a fine line between doing what is right and potentially offending your coworkers. In this case, if you have a good rapport with the coworker, you might consider approaching the person in a nonthreatening, rational manner and using unemotional language. If you do not know the person well, perhaps you can get one of his or her friends to take action to correct the situation.

If you do decide to speak to your coworker, point out that such language is offensive and can actually get him or her into trouble with the customer and the organization. In a nonthreatening tone, point out that such behavior can also be viewed as discriminatory and might lead to possible legal action against the employee and the organization. This approach is often best done through a question format (e.g., "When you say things like that about people from other countries, do you really dislike them or are you just trying to be funny?"). Depending on the answer, you may want to try to get the coworker to see that others might perceive him or her as being prejudiced because of such comments. In some cases, depending on the remarks, the attitude of the coworker, and the situation, it may even be appropriate to advise a supervisor of the incident. The bottom line is to try to share your views in a manner that helps the other person see that such actions may not be appropriate and to help that person curtail future such language without damaging your work relationship or creating more serious situations.

Service Breakdowns and Recovery

"Never underestimate the power of the irate customer."
—SOURCE: JOEL ROSS

©Kevin Brine/123RF RF

LEARNING OUTCOMES

After completing this chapter, you will be able to:

7-1 Define what a service breakdown is.

7-2 Apply knowledge of behavioral styles in difficult customer situations.

7-3 Recognize different types of difficult customers and effectively deal with them.

7-4 Use the emotion-reducing model to help keep difficult situations from escalating.

7-5 Explain why customers defect.

7-6 Develop effective strategies for working with internal customers.

7-7 Identify strategies for preventing customer dissatisfaction and problem solving.

7-8 Explain the six steps of the problem-solving model.

7-9 Implement a frontline service recovery strategy, and spot roadblocks to service recovery.

7-10 Discuss the importance of disaster planning initiatives in the service recovery process.

Use SmartBook to help you read, study, and retain what you have learned. Access SmartBook in your Instructor's Connect course, or go to connect.mheducation.com for help. ▪ SMARTBOOK™

IN THE REAL WORLD   RETAIL/MANUFACTURING—COCA-COLA

Mission Statement: "Our Roadmap starts with our mission, which is enduring. It declares our purpose as a company and serves as the standard against which we weigh our actions and decisions."

Source: Mission of The Coca-Cola Company

- To refresh the world.
- To inspire moments of optimism and happiness.
- To create value and make a difference.

Vision

The six "Ps" of the company vision statement highlight Coca-Cola's purpose and desired future objectives.

- **People.** Be a great place to work where people are inspired to be the best they can be.
- **Portfolio.** Bring to the world a portfolio of quality beverage brands that anticipate and satisfy people's desires and needs.
- **Partners.** Nurture a winning network of customers and suppliers; together we create mutual, enduring value.
- **Planet.** Be a responsible citizen that makes a difference by helping build and support sustainable communities.
- **Profit.** Maximize long-term return to shareholders while being mindful of our overall responsibilities.
- **Productivity.** Be a highly effective, lean and fast-moving organization.[1]

Coca-Cola is a soft drink brand that is recognized worldwide. In fact, the drink is one of the most recognized corporate logos and the brand is sold in over 200 countries through 250 bottlers throughout the world. According to the company website, Coca-Cola has the world's largest beverage distribution system and is the no. 1 provider of sparkling and still beverages. It has over $20 billion sales brands, and over 1.9 billion servings of Coke are consumed a day.

The Coca-Cola story began in Atlanta, Georgia, in 1886 when pharmacist John Pemberton was experimenting with a recipe that he later mixed with carbonated water and began to sell at his drugstore. Two years after its invention, Pemberton sold his secret formula to a businessman by the name of Asa Candler, who formed a corporation to bottle and distribute the trendy drink. He later sold the rights to two other businessmen who wanted to bottle the drink and enhance distribution. Candler sold syrup that his company produced to these distributors, but not his secret formula. They simply mixed the syrup with carbonated water and bottled it. From there, the product became a household name as more people began to take Coca-Cola home to enjoy.

As with many successful products, competitors soon emerged. To ensure that people could tell the original from these wannabes, the distributors created the trademarked contour bottle in 1916 so that customers would recognize the original product.

Candler ultimately sold his company in 1919 to a group of investors with Robert Woodruff as the president. The new group wanted to make Coca-Cola available anytime and anyplace. To accomplish this, the new company started adding bottling plants all over the world. Today, Coca-Cola owns nearly 500 trademarked brands including popular products like Dannon, Campbells, Evian, Nestea, Bacardi Mixers, Powerade, Dr. Pepper, Minute Maid, and many others. Interbrand ranked the company as the world's third most valuable brand in 2015.

Coca-Cola has a long history of promoting its products while giving back to the world. Some examples of this follow:

The company is the sponsor of the Olympic Games since 1928.

In 1943, the company operated an ammunition loading plant in Alabama to supply ammunition to U.S. troops in World War II.

To assist in accomplishing its vision, the company established the Coca-Cola Foundation in 1984. This entity focuses on helping and giving back to communities worldwide. Some of the issues supported in various countries include water stewardship (providing safe, clean drinking water), lifestyle/behavioral change programs (e.g., nutrition, exercise, and behavior modification), recycling, and education.

In 2001, the company contributed $12 million in disaster relief following the 9/11 terrorist attacks.

Between 2008 and 2010, the Coca-Cola foundation and company donated almost $700 million to numerous causes.

In 2010, following a devastating earthquake, the company launched the Haiti Hope Project to help develop a sustainable mango industry in that country.

For more information about Coca-Cola, do an Internet search and visit the website (www.coca-colacompany.com/).

Think About It

1. What is your opinion of the Coca-Cola company? Explain.

2. Based on what you know or read on the Internet or through other sources, do you believe that the company is customer focused? Why or why not?

3. How does the company's community involvement potentially affect its image in the eyes of customers or potential customers?

4. Would you want to work for this company? Why or why not?

Quick Preview

Before reviewing the chapter content, respond to the following questions by placing a "T" for true or an "F" for false on the rules. Use any questions you miss as a checklist of material to which you will pay particular attention as you read the chapter. For those you get right, give yourself a pat on the back, but review the sections they address in order to learn additional details about the topic.

_____ 1. Service breakdowns often occur because service providers fail to meet customer needs and wants.

_____ 2. Customer expectations do not affect service delivery.

_____ 3. Behavioral style preferences do not affect customer needs or satisfaction levels.

_____ 4. An upset customer is usually annoyed with a specific person rather than the organization or system.

_____ 5. When you cannot comply with the demands of an angry customer, you should try to negotiate an alternative solution.

_____ 6. Competency in communicating can eliminate the need for service recovery.

_____ 7. Demanding customers often act in a domineering manner because they are very self-confident. This is a function of behavioral style.

_____ 8. Service recovery occurs when a provider is able to make restitution, solve a problem, or regain customer trust after service breakdown.

_____ 9. One key strategy for preventing dissatisfaction is to learn to think like a customer.

_____ 10. Adopting a "good neighbor policy" can help in dealings with internal customers.

_____ 11. As part of trying to help solve a customer problem, you should assess its seriousness.

_____ 12. When something does not go as the customer needs or expects, service recovery becomes a vital step in maintaining the relationship.

Answers to Quick Preview are located at the end of the chapter.

Words to Live By

"The goal as a company is to have customer service that is not just the best but legendary."

— SOURCE: SAM WALTON (1918–1992)

LO 7-1 What Is a Service Breakdown?

CONCEPT Service breakdowns occur whenever any product or service fails to meet the customer's expectations.

Service breakdowns occur daily in all types of organizations. They occur whenever the product or service delivered fails to meet customer expectations (see Figure 7.1). In some cases, the product or service delivered may function exactly as designed, but if the customer perceived that it should work another way, a breakdown occurs. Additionally, when a product or service fails to meet what the customer **wants** or **needs** or

service breakdown Situations when customers have expectations of a certain type or level of product or service that are not met by a service provider.

wants Things that customers typically desire but do not necessarily need.

needs Motivators or drivers that cause customers to seek out specific types of products or services. These may be marketing-driven, based on advertising they have seen, or may tie directly to Abraham Maslow's hierarchy of needs theory.

FIGURE 7.1

Examples of Service Breakdowns

Here are some examples of service breakdowns:

- A food service professional brings a meal containing an ingredient not expected or wanted by the customer, or one that the customer specified she did not want. For example, a customer orders a hamburger with only lettuce, tomato, and mayonnaise, and specifically tells the server she wants no onion or pickle on the plate due to an allergy. The burger arrives with both onion and pickle. The server states, "I told them not to put that on there, but they preset the condiments for sandwiches before lunch to save time. Can you just pick it off?"

  A note of caution: If you are in food service, be vigilant in monitoring orders when customers ask you not to include certain ingredients. Check food and drinks before you deliver them to your customer to be sure that the cook staff or bartender did not forget the special request. Also, do not simply remove a food item when the kitchen staff inadvertently places it on a customer's plate. Some people have severe allergies to certain foods that could cause serious illness and even death—and a huge liability for you and your organization.

- On Friday morning, you realize that the pain medication you are taking following surgery is about to run out and that there are no refills left on the prescription. You call your doctor's office at 9:00 A.M. and are transferred to an automated nurse's hotline, which tells you the office will return calls by the end of the day or the next business day. At 4:00 p.m., you check with the pharmacy and find the prescription has not been called in from the doctor, so you call back to the doctor's office only to find that the office closes at 3:30 p.m. on Fridays. You now have no pain medication for the weekend.

- A hotel room is not available when the customer arrives. (In some cases, a stated check-in time may exist and the customer may be early. Make every effort to accommodate the customer if this happens.)

- According to the customer, room service food was cold when delivered (e.g., not at the degree of warmth desired or expected).

- An optometrist provides glasses or contact lenses that do not adequately correct a patient's vision because a technician misread the prescription.

- A volunteer at a silent auction for charity misplaces an item won by a donor.

- A coworker expects your assistance in providing information needed for a monthly report, but you failed to get it to her on time or as agreed.

- A manufacturer does not receive a parts delivery as you promised and has to shut down an assembly line.

- A garment you needed for a meeting the following morning returns from the laundry with broken buttons and cannot be worn.

In any of the situations described, customers may have not received what they were promised or expected, or at least they perceived that they did not. When such incidents occur, there is a breakdown and they often lead to emotional or difficult situations. In many instances, service providers are uncomfortable and unprepared to deal with such events because of lack of either confidence, training, or empowerment. Issues, such as those listed above, should be addressed and rectified before coming into contact with customers.

customer expectations The perceptions that customers have when they contact an organization or service provider about the kind, level, and quality of products and services they should receive.

does not live up to advertised promises or standards, dissatisfaction and frustration could result.

In addition to wants and needs, **customer expectations** can affect how service is delivered to and perceived by your customers. Today's customers are more discerning and better educated, have access to more up-to-date and accurate information, and are often more demanding than in the past. They have certain expectations about your products and services, and the way that you will provide them. Figure 7.2 shows some common expectations customers might have of a service organization. Failure to fulfill some or all of these expectations can lead to dissatisfaction and in some cases confrontation and/or loss of business. Keep in mind that they also have many more options offered by your competitors.

 WORK IT OUT 7.1

Handling Service Breakdowns

Pair up with one or two other students and discuss possible ways to prevent the service breakdowns listed in Figure 7.1 and solutions if they do occur.

FIGURE 7.2

Typical Customer Expectations

Customers come to you expecting that certain things will occur concerning the products and services they obtain. Customers typically expect the following:

Expectations Related to People

Friendly, knowledgeable service providers

Respect (they want to be treated as if they are intelligent)

Empathy (they want their feelings and emotions to be recognized)

Courtesy (they want recognition as "the customer" and as someone who is important to you and your organization)

Equitable treatment (they do not want to feel that one individual or group gets preferential benefits or treatment over another)

Expectations Related to Products and Services

Easily accessible and available products and services (no lengthy delays)

Reasonable and competitive pricing

Products and services that adequately address needs

Quality (appropriate value for money and time invested)

Ease of use

Safe (warranty available and product free of defects that might cause physical injury)

State-of-the-art products and service delivery

Easy-to-understand instructions (and follow-up assistance availability)

Ease of return or exchange (flexible policies that provide alternatives depending on the situation)

Appropriate and expedient problem resolution

Ethical Dilemma 7.1

You are an employee of a local retail organization that typically closes at 6:00 p.m. At 5:52 p.m., your supervisor tosses you the keys to the front door and tells you to lock up for the evening because he wants to get out early so that he can pick up his wife. They have tickets for a play and are going out to dinner to celebrate their anniversary.

As you lock the door and start to return to your cash register to begin your end-of-day activities, you hear a frantic knock on the front door. An obviously distraught customer is yelling that she needs to buy a gift for her son's birthday and is pointing to the clock on the wall next to your register that indicates 5:56 p.m. There is a sign on the door that lists the closing time as 6:00 p.m.

1. What would you do in this situation?
2. How do you think the customer will view this matter?
3. Are there possible repercussions from a service standpoint? If so, what are they?

Customer Service Success Tip

Be prepared and conscientious and think like a customer in order to identify and satisfy customer needs and expectations.

KNOWLEDGE CHECK

1. What is a service breakdown?
2. What is the difference between a customer need and a want?
3. How can customer expectations impact the perceived level of product or service quality that they receive?

LO 7-2 The Role of Behavioral Style

CONCEPT **Behavioral preferences have a major effect on the interactions of people. The more you know about style tendencies, the better you will understand your customers.**

Behavioral style preferences play a major part in how people interact. Styles also affect the types of things people want and value. Depending on how a customer approaches a given situation, he or she may have a perception that you will or will not take certain actions while serving him or her. He or she might also expect that products will perform in a specific manner based on his or her knowledge, background, research, or experience. If you or your products and services fail to meet those expectations, you can find yourself in the midst of a service breakdown and have to deal with an emotional situation that you might not be prepared to handle. For example, those customers with high expressive behavioral tendencies (e.g., outgoing, flexible, and people-oriented) will probably buy more colorful and people-oriented items and may be more willing to accept alternative suggestions from you than someone who has high decisive (e.g., formal, direct, status-, and task–oriented people) behavioral tendencies.

The more you know about behavioral style preferences, the easier it becomes to deal with people in a variety of situations and to help match their needs with the products and services you and your organization can provide. Keep in mind that everyone possesses one or a combination of the following four different behavioral styles:

- *Rational.* Prefer one-on-one or small-group interaction, are congenial and patient, avoid conflict, and dislike calling attention to themselves.

- *Inquisitive.* Rarely volunteer feelings, ask "why" questions, desire facts and figures, and are formal, task-oriented, conservative, and punctual.
- *Decisive.* Are decisive, directive, task- and goal-focused, confident, and competitive; seek immediate gratification or results; and talk more than listen.
- *Expressive.* Are open, laid back, flexible, positive, enthusiastic, and informal; prefer dealing with people; and easily share feelings and emotions.

Because customers can display various types of behavior from time to time, you should carefully observe their behavior and learn about each style as an indicator of the type of person with whom you are dealing. Just remember that human beings are complex and react to stimuli in various ways—so adapt your approach as necessary. For that reason, do not use information you learn about behavioral styles as the definitive answer for resolving the situation. In addition, learn to deal with your emotions so that you can prevent or resolve heated emotional situations that might arise when dealing with a personality different from your own.

KNOWLEDGE CHECK

1. How might the four behavioral styles play a role in the perceived level of service received by a customer?

⚙ WORK IT OUT 7.2

Service Breakdown Examples

What examples of service breakdown have you experienced or can you recall from someone else's story? List and then discuss them with classmates. After discussing your lists, brainstorm ways that the organization did or could have recovered.

LO 7-3 Difficult Customers

CONCEPT **Ultimately, successful service is delivered through effective communication skills, positive attitude, patience, and a willingness to help the customer.**

difficult customers People who challenge a service provider's ability to deliver service and who require special skills and patience.

You may think of **difficult customer** contacts as those in which you have to deal with negative, angry, demanding, or aggressive people. These are just a few of the types of potentially difficult interactions that you may encounter as a service representative. From time to time, you will provide assistance to customers who can be described in one or more of the following ways:

- Dissatisfied with your service or products
- Indecisive or lack knowledge about your product, service, or policies

- Rude or inconsiderate of others
- Talkative
- Internal customers with special requests
- Speak a primary language other than yours
- Elderly and need extra assistance
- Young and inexperienced who might need to be guided in making a good choice
- Have some type of a disability or special needs

Each of the above categories can be difficult to handle, depending on your knowledge, experience, and abilities. A key to successfully serving all types of customers is to treat each person as an individual. If you stereotype people, you will likely damage the customer–provider relationship and might even generate complaints to your supervisor or legal action against you and your organization based on perceived discrimination. Avoid labeling people according to their behavior. Do not mentally categorize people (put them into groups) according to the way they speak, act, or look—and then treat everyone in a "group" the same way.

Ultimately, you will deliver successful service through your effective communication skills, positive attitude, patience, knowledge, service experience, and willingness to help the customer. Your ability to focus on the situation or problem and not on the person will be a very important factor in your success. Making the distinction between the person and the problem is especially important when faced with difficult situations in the service environment. Although you may not understand or approve of a person's behavior, he or she is still your customer. Try to make the interaction a positive one, and if necessary ask for assistance from a coworker or refer the problem to an appropriate level in your operational chain of command.

Many difficult situations you will deal with as a service provider will be caused by a perceived failure to meet your customer's needs, wants, and expectations. You will read about service challenges in this chapter, along with their causes and some strategies for effectively dealing with them.

©Montgomery Martin/Alamy Stock Photo RF

Handling difficult customers will be one of your biggest challenges, so be prepared. *How would you deal with an unhappy customer?*

DEMANDING OR DOMINEERING CUSTOMERS

demanding or domineering customers Customers who have definite ideas about what they want and are unwilling to compromise or accept alternatives.

Customers might be **demanding or domineering** for a number of reasons. Many times, domineering behavior is part of a personality style or simply behavior that they have learned. In other instances, their behavior could be a reaction to past customer service encounters and an expectation that they now have about what should or should not occur. A demanding customer may feel a need to be or stay in control, especially if he or she has felt out of control in the past. Often, such people are insecure or have a behavioral style that lends itself to wanting to be in control or to "win." The following sections provide strategies for effectively handling demanding customers:

- *Be professional.* Do not raise your voice or retaliate verbally. Try to work with your customer to negotiate an acceptable alternative when problems arise. Also, keep in mind that children engage in name-calling, which often escalates into shoving matches. Unfortunately, some adults "regress" to childish behavior and may revert to negative actions learned in the past. Both you and the customer lose when this happens.

- *Respect the customer.* You do not necessarily have to like your customer, but you should show respect. This does not mean that you must accommodate your customer's every wish. It means that you should make positive eye contact (but not glare), remain calm, use the customer's name, apologize when appropriate and/or necessary, and let the customer know that he or she is important to you and your organization. Also, let the customer know that you are there to assist him or her or make the situation right and work positively toward an acceptable resolution of the problem. If accommodations are appropriate and possible, consider making them. If they are not, explain the reason in an assertive, but not aggressive manner. You can reason with most adults if you take the time to talk to them on a professional and equal level.

- *Be firm and fair and focus on the customer's needs.* Assertive behavior is an appropriate response to a domineering or demanding person; aggression is not. Also, remember the importance of treating each customer as an individual. If you are dealing with a customer who is being unreasonable, contact your supervisor. Try to get the customer to accompany you to a more private location where the three of you can discuss the issue in an unemotional manner out of sight of other customers.

- *Tell the customer what you can do.* Do not focus on negatives or what cannot be done when dealing with your customers. Stick with what is possible and what you are willing and able to do. Be flexible and willing to listen to requests. If something suggested is possible and will help solve the problem, compliment the person on his or her idea (e.g., "Mr. Hollister, that is a great suggestion, and one that I think will work"), and then try to make it happen. Doing this will show that you are receptive to new ideas, are truly working to meet the customer's needs and expectations, and value the customer's opinion. Also, remember that if you can partner with a customer psychologically, he or she is less likely to attack. You do need to make sure that you do not appear to be giving in or backing down through your willingness to assist and comply. If it is, the customer may make additional demands or return in the future with similar attempts to get his or her way. Many scam artists look for weaknesses in an organization's system so that they can exploit them for their own gain. To avoid this, you could add to the earlier statement by saying something like, "Mr. Hollister, that's a good suggestion, and although we cannot do this in every instance, I think that your suggestion is one that will work out this time." This puts the customer on alert that although he or she may get his or her way this time, it will not necessarily happen in the future. Another strategy is to make a counter offer in an effort to find a win-win solution in which both the customer and your organization get partial satisfaction and needs fulfillment.

By being thoroughly familiar with your organization's policies and procedures and your limits of authority, you will be prepared to negotiate with demanding customers. If they want something you cannot provide, you might offer an alternative that will satisfy them. Remember that your goal is complete customer satisfaction but not at the expense of excessive loss to your organization.

Customer Service Success Tip

Put yourself in a customer's situation when he or she is demanding and trying to control you. Ask yourself, "Is there something that I have said or done that might have escalated or added to this situation?" If the answer is "yes," apologize, listen, and move toward resolution. If you do not believe that you are at fault, engage the customer with nonthreatening but firm language and explain that your goal is to help the customer. Stress that you need him or her to calmly explain the issue so that you can figure out what needs to be done. If all else fails, you may eventually have to call in a supervisor or other employee to handle the customer's issue.

WORK IT OUT 7.3

Handling the Demanding Customer

Survey customer service professionals in various professions to see how they handle demanding or domineering customers. Make a list for future reference and role-play a variety of scenarios involving demanding customers with a peer.

INDECISIVE CUSTOMERS

You will encounter people who cannot or will not make a decision. In some instances, this may be a result of their behavioral style or it might be due to something in their background from which they learned such behavior. Such customers sometimes spend long periods vacillating between several options as they seemingly struggle to choose one over the other. They might even leave and come back later to continue their decision-making effort. Sometimes, they will even bring along a friend or family member on the second visit to help facilitate a decision. In some cases, **indecisive customers** truly do not know what they want or need, as when they are looking for a gift for a special occasion. In other instances, such customers are afraid that they will choose incorrectly or need reassurance that the product has the features they really need or will use later. In the latter situation, use all your product or service knowledge and communication skills to provide them with the information they need to make a buying decision. Otherwise, indecisive customers will occupy large amounts of your time and detract from your ability to do your job effectively or to assist other customers. In addition, they will likely return the item in the future. This will take up additional

indecisive customers People who have difficulty making a decision or making a selection when given choices of products or services.

Indecisive people can be frustrating as you try to serve their needs. *What steps would you take to help a customer make a decision?*

©Thomas Barwick/Getty Images RF

service provider time and could cost the organization money (e.g., they used a credit card to which you will have to refund money. In that instance, the company pays a card processing fee on both ends of the transaction. Those fee amounts add up over time).

An important point to keep in mind is that some people really are just looking or researching a product or service as they check out sales, kill time between appointments, or relax, or they may simply be lonely and want to be around others. Strategies for dealing with an indecisive person are:

- *Be patient.* Do not forget that although indecisive people can be frustrating, especially if you have a high decisive or "D" behavioral style preference and get impatient easily, they are still customers.

- *Ask open-end questions.* Just as you would do with a dissatisfied customer, try to get as much background information about the customer's likes, needs, wants, and expectations as possible. The more data you can gather, the easier it is for you to evaluate the situation, determine needs, and assist in the solution of any problems.

- *Listen actively.* Focus on customer verbal and nonverbal messages for clues to determine emotions, concerns, and interests. Watch for reaction when you show them a new item or make a suggestion.

- *Suggest other options.* Offer alternatives that will help in decision-making and reduce the customer's anxiety. Pointing out a warranty or exchange option available on a product or service may make the customer more secure in the decision-making process.

- *Guide decision-making.* By assertively, not aggressively, offering suggestions or ideas and providing product and/or service information, you can help guide customers to a decision. Try giving examples of how you or others have purchased or used products or services being considered, and the satisfaction received. Remember that you are helping them, not making the decision for them. If you push your preferences on them, they may be dissatisfied later or have buyer's remorse, where they regret their decision and return the item or even complain that you pressured their decision. Then you or someone else will have to potentially deal with an unhappy customer.

DISSATISFIED AND ANGRY CUSTOMERS

Occasionally, you will encounter **dissatisfied customers** or angry ones. They may feel that the treatment being received is unfair, that you or someone else is lying to or taking advantage of them, or that they are not getting the service they want or expect. Possibly, you or one of your peers, or a competitor, improperly served them in the past, and they now have a preconceived idea about anyone who is in the sales or service profession. For example, think of the stereotypes that many people have about telephone solicitors or used car salespeople.

The challenge is that in instances where you encounter a dissatisfied or angry customer, you represent the organization or you may be considered "just like that last service employee." This can happen even if you were not personally involved in his or her previous experience. Unfair as this may be, you have to try to calm these customers and make them happy. To do so, try the following strategies:

- *Listen* with an open mind to discover the basis for their anger or dissatisfaction.
- *Remain positive and flexible* while showing a willingness to work with the customer or negotiate.
- *Smile, give your name, and offer assistance* by projecting a "can do" attitude and lowering defenses. By doing so, you can potentially get the customer to do likewise and salvage the situation and customer–provider relationship.
- *Be compassionate and empathize without making excuses.* Angry or dissatisfied customers typically want and expect that you will try to see their side of the situation and will make concessions in order to appease them. This does not mean that you should bow down to them if the situation was truly not your fault or that of your organization. It does mean that you should try to understand their position and work to bring them back around to a point where you can negotiate and resolve the issue.
- *Ask open-end questions and verify information.* That allows your customers to talk and vent while providing the degree of information needed to identify what went wrong and offer potential solutions. The only way to start to resolve the issue is to find out what caused it in the first place.
- *Take appropriate action.* Once you have gotten the customer to lower his or her emotions to the point where the two of you can intelligently discuss the situation, you will be on your way to a solution. If you know your organization's policies and procedures and are knowledgeable about products and services, you have the tools to potentially get the relationship back on track and resolve the issue.

dissatisfied customer Someone who does not (or perceives that he or she does not) receive promised or quality products or services.

 WORK IT OUT 7.4

Dealing with Angry Customers

Work with a partner. Discuss situations in which you had to deal with an angry person. Think about what made the person angry and what seemed to reduce tension. Make a list of these factors and be prepared to share your list with the class. Use the results of this discussion to develop strategies to help calm angry people in the future.

FIGURE 7.3
Positive Wording

When faced with a customer encounter that is not going well, remain positive in language. This will help you avoid escalating the situation.

Negative Words or Phrases	Positive Alternatives
Problem	Situation, issue, concern, challenge
No	What I (or we) can do is...
Cannot	What I (or we) can do is...
It is not my job (or my fault)	Although I do not normally handle that, I am happy to assist you.
You will have to (or you must...)	Would you mind...? Would you please...?
Our policy says...	While I am unable to..., what I can do is...

angry customer Consumers who become emotional because either you do not meet their needs they are dissatisfied with the services or products purchased from an organization.

Remember that if you get defensive, you become part of the problem and not part of the solution. By maintaining a positive approach and using positive language, you are more likely to bring about a successful outcome when dealing with an angry or dissatisfied person. Figure 7.3 shows some examples of negative wording and some possible alternatives.

Dealing with angry people requires a certain amount of caution. To effectively serve an **angry customer**, you must move beyond the emotions to discover the reason for his or her anger. *Note*: Before dealing with customers, check with your supervisor to find out what your policies are and what level of authority you have in making decisions. This relates to employee empowerment. By having this information before interacting with a customer, you will have the tools and knowledge necessary to handle your customers effectively and professionally. Here are some possible resolution strategies:

- *Be positive.* Tell the customer what you can do rather than what you cannot do.
- *Acknowledge the customer's feelings or anger.* By taking this approach, you have addressed the customer's emotional state, demonstrated a willingness to assist, and encouraged the customer to participate in solving the problem. For example, "Mr. Philips, I can see that you are obviously upset by _____ and I want to help find a solution to this issue; however, I need your assistance to do that. Please explain what caused the issue from your perspective.
- *Reassure.* Indicate that you understand why he or she is angry and that you will work to solve the problems. For example, "Ms. O'Hara, based on what you have explained, I can see why you are not satisfied with this product. I am going to immediately see what we can do to repair or replace the unit."
- *Remain objective.* In most instances, angry customers are usually upset with the organization, product, or service that you represent, not at you.
- *Listen actively; determine the cause.* Whether the customer is "right" or "wrong" makes no difference in situations like these. Actively listening and trying to discover the problem without attempting to place blame will assure the customer that you are trying to take care of it for him or her.
- *Reduce frustrations.* Do not say or do anything that will create further tension. Do your best to handle the situation with this customer before serving another.
- *Negotiate a solution.* Elicit ideas or negotiate an alternative with the customer. Be willing to compromise, if appropriate, needed, and possible.

- *Conduct a follow-up.* Contact your customer as soon as possible after your attempted resolution contact in order to show the customer that you are truly concerned that the issue was correctly resolved and that you value the relationship with him or her. Do not assume that the organization's system will work as designed or intended and that all is well. If the customer was not satisfied completely, or other issues remain, you may lose a customer and generate negative word-of-mouth publicity as the customer shares the experience with others.

Customer Service Success Tip

Strive to do the unexpected and provide quality service to create a memorable customer experience—**under promise and over deliver**. Do whatever you can (within your authority) to rectify a situation in which a customer is dissatisfied with your product or service in order to ensure customer satisfaction.

under promise and over deliver
A service strategy in which service providers strive for excellent customer service and satisfaction by doing more than they say they will do for the customer and exceed customer expectations.

⚙ WORK IT OUT 7.5

Responding to Rudeness

Working with a partner, develop a list of rude comments that a customer might make to you. For example, the comment might be, "If you are not too busy, I would like some assistance." Also, list the responses you might give; for example, "If you could please wait, I will be happy to assist you as soon as I finish, sir (or madam). I want to be able to give you my full attention and do not want to be distracted."

RUDE OR INCONSIDERATE CUSTOMERS

Some people seem to go out of their way to be offensive or to get attention. Although they seem confident and self-assured outwardly, they are often insecure and defensive. Some behaviors that they might exhibit include:

Raising their voice

Demanding to speak to a supervisor

Using profanity

Cutting in front of someone else in a line

Being verbally abrupt (snapping back at you) even though you are trying to assist; calling you by your last name, which they see on your name tag (e.g., "Listen, Smith"); and ignoring what you say

Otherwise going out of the way to be offensive or in control

Try the following strategies for dealing with **rude or inconsiderate customers**:

- *Remain professional.* Just because the customer exhibits inappropriate behavior does not justify your reacting in kind. Remain calm, assertive, and in control of the situation. For example, if you are waiting on a customer and a rude person barges in or cuts off your conversation, pause, make direct eye contact, smile, and firmly say, "Good morning/afternoon, I will be with you as soon as I finish with this customer,

rude or inconsiderate customers
People who seem to take pleasure in being obstinate and contrary when dealing with service providers and who seem to have their own agenda without concern for the feelings of others.

Before you can deal with a customer's business needs, you must first address the customer's emotional issues and try to calm him or her. *What would you do to calm such a customer?*

©Image Source/Getty Images RF

sir (or madam)." If he or she insists, repeat your comment and let the person know that the faster you serve the current customer, the faster you can get to the person waiting. Additionally, by maintaining decorum you may win over the person or at least keep him or her in check.

● *Do not resort to retaliation.* Retaliation will only infuriate this type of customer, especially if you have embarrassed him or her in the presence of others. Remember that such people are still customers, and if they or someone else perceives your actions as inappropriate, you could lose more than just the situation at hand.

TALKATIVE CUSTOMERS

Some people phone or approach you and then spend excessive amounts of time discussing irrelevant matters such as personal experiences, family, friends, schooling, accomplishments, other customer service situations, and the weather. The following tips might help when dealing with **talkative customers**:

talkative customers People exhibiting extroverted behavior who are very people-oriented.

● *Remain warm and cordial, but focused.* Recognize that this person's personality style is probably mainly expressive and that his or her natural inclination is to connect with others. You can smile, acknowledge comments, and carry on a brief conversation as you are serving this customer. For example, if the person comments that you spell your last name exactly as his or her great aunt's does and then asks the origin of your family, you could respond with, "That's interesting. My family is from . . . but I do not believe we have any relatives outside that area." You have responded but possibly cut off the next question. The customer may perceive anything less than a personal response to be rude. Anything more could invite additional discussion. Your next statement should then be business-related and designed to get the conversation back on service (e.g., "Is there anything else I can assist you with today?").

● *Ask specific open-end questions.* These types of questions can assist in determining needs and addressing customer concerns. For example, "Ms. Pruitt, what type of ring did you have in mind for your husband's Father's Day gift?"

● *Use closed-end questions to control.* Once you have determined the customer's needs, switch to closed-end questions to better control the situation and limit the opportunity for the customer to continue talking. For example, "If I understand you correctly, Mr. Hawkins, the two features most important in a new television are that it is Wi-Fi capable and features the latest HD technology; is that correct?"

- *Manage the conversation.* Keep in mind that if you spend a lot of time with one customer, other customers may feel neglected. You can manage a customer encounter through questioning and through statements that let the customer know your objective is to serve customers. You might say, "If you have no further questions, I know you said you have a lot of shopping to do, so I will not keep you any longer. Thanks for coming in. Please let me know if I can assist in the future." This approach implies that you are ending the interaction to benefit the customer.

KNOWLEDGE CHECK

1. What constitutes a "difficult customer"?
2. How might you handle a demanding or domineering customer?
3. Why might a customer be indecisive?
4. What strategies might help diffuse an angry or dissatisfied customer situation?
5. What can you do to address rude or inconsiderate customers?
6. In what ways could you manage a talkative customer situation?

WORK IT OUT 7.6

Building Your Skills

Go on a field trip to a variety of businesses or stores (possibly a mall). As you visit these establishments, play the role of a customer and engage customer service professionals in lengthy conversation. Take note of the techniques they use to regain control of the conversation. Chances are, most, especially the more experienced, will allow you to talk and will respond to you rather than risk being rude. Remember the effective techniques described and jot them down.

LO 7-4 Handling Emotions with the Emotion-Reducing Model

CONCEPT Using the emotion-reducing model helps to calm the customer so that you can then solve the problem.

It is important to remember when dealing with people who are behaving emotionally (e.g., irritated, angry, upset, crying, or raising their voice) that they are typically upset with the structure, process, organization, or other factors over which you and/or they have no control. They are usually not upset with you (unless you have provoked them by exhibiting poor customer service skills or attitude). Remain rational and do not react to them emotionally.

Before you can get your customer to calm down, listen, and address the situation, you must first deal with her or his emotional state. Once you do this, you can proceed to use problem-solving strategies discussed later in this chapter to assist in solving the problem. A customer will likely not be receptive to what you are saying or your attempts to assist until you reduce his or her emotional level. In some cases, she or he may even become irritated because you seem uncaring.

To help calm the customer down, you must send customer-focused verbal and nonverbal messages. You need to demonstrate patience and use positive communication skills such as properly phrased verbal messages and questions, effective nonverbal cues, and active listening skills. Most important among those skills are the ability and the willingness to listen calmly to what the customer has to say without interrupting or interjecting your views. Because of the importance of the latter approach, this strategy is taught to many law enforcement officers to help them deal with crisis intervention situations, such as, domestic disturbances. This approach often helps prevent situations from emotionally escalating. If your customer perceives that you disregard his or her emotional needs, or thinks that you are not working in his or her best interest, you will likely be unsuccessful.

Keep in mind that a customer generally wants to be respected and acknowledged as an individual and as being important. As you interact with a customer, you can soften the situation and reduce emotion by providing customer-focused responses. Simple messages can put you on a friendly (human) level while at the same time helping to calm the emotion. For example, "Ms. Hernandez, I can appreciate why you are so frustrated about the service you have received thus far. It seems as if we truly did make an error on your order and I sincerely apologize for that. You are important to us and I am going to do my best to resolve this issue as quickly as possible."

emotion-reducing model Process for reducing customer emotion in situations when frustration or anger exists.

The key to helping resolve any service breakdowns is to frame your problem resolution with customer-focused messages through use of the emotion-reducing model (Figure 7.4). Here is how the five steps of the **emotion-reducing model** are implemented: Assume a customer has a problem. As the customer approaches (or when you answer the telephone), greet him or her with "Good morning (or afternoon)," a smile, and open body language and gesturing (1. customer-focused message). Then, as the customer explains the issue (2. emotional issue), you can offer statements such as, "I see," "I can appreciate your concern (or frustration, or anger)," or "I understand how that can feel" (3. customer-focused message). Such statements can help you connect psychologically with the customer. Continue to use positive reinforcement and communication throughout your interaction. Once you define the problem and resolve it (4. problem solving), take one more opportunity at the end of your interaction to send a customer-focused message by smiling and thanking the customer for allowing you to assist. In addition, one last apology may be appropriate for inconvenience, frustration, mistreatment, and so on (5. customer-focused message).

FIGURE 7.4

Emotion-Reducing Model

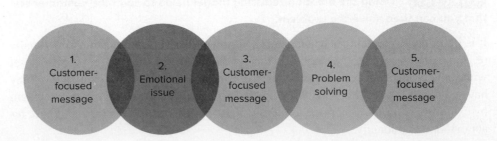

KNOWLEDGE CHECK

1. What are the five phases of the emotion-reducing model?

Customer Service Success Tip

Customers are not always right, but they are human, make mistakes, and have emotions. For these reasons, you should always interact with them professionally and do whatever possible and appropriate to rectify a situation when problems arise. This is important because other customers may see or hear of a situation in which you failed to do so. That could cast you and your organization in a negative light and might result in lost revenue or additional problems in the future.

LO 7-5 Reasons for Customer Defection

CONCEPT **Failing to meet the customer's needs, handling problems inefficiently, treating the customer unfairly, and using inadequate systems are reasons for the customer to leave you and go elsewhere.**

Following a service breakdown, there is often a possibility that you may never see the customer again. This is potentially disastrous to your organization because it costs five to six times as much to win a new customer as it costs to retain a current one. Moreover, as we saw earlier in this chapter, a dissatisfied customer is likely to tell other people about the bad experience. Thus, you and others in your organization must be especially careful to identify reasons for **customer defection** (Figure 7.5) and remedy potential and actual problems before they negatively affect customers.

So often, service providers make the mistake of trying to project their personal needs onto others. The feeling might be "I like it, so everybody should like it." However, today's diverse world requires you to be more knowledgeable and accepting of the ideas, values, beliefs, and needs of others. Failure to be sensitive to diversity may set you, your organization, and your customers on a collision course. Never lose sight of the fact that establishing and maintaining trust is crucial in sustaining customer–provider relationships.

customer defection Customers often take their business to competitors when they feel that their needs or wants are not met or if they encounter breakdown in customer service or poor quality products.

- *Price.* Customers are often willing to switch product and service providers because of pricing. If prices increase or they perceive that they are not getting value for what they pay, then a move to another provider often occurs. You may not be able to do much about prices set by your organization, but you can prepare to counter customer comments regarding costs. By being aware of what competitors charge for the same or similar products and services, you can help educate customers on value. A convincing argument relates to the quality of service that your organization provides. This is especially true if you work in a small business environment where price competition is sometimes difficult.

- *Poor service and complacency.* Never forget that if a concern is important enough for the customer to verbalize (formally or informally) or to write down, it is important enough for you to take seriously. If customers perceive that you and/or

FIGURE 7.5

Reasons for Customer Defection

(continued)

your organization do not sincerely care about them or about solving their problems, they may go elsewhere. You should immediately address any identified problem by listening, gathering information, and taking appropriate action. Customer comments might be casual, for example, "You know, I sure wish you folks stocked a wider variety of rose bush colors. I love shopping here, but your selection is so limited." In this instance, you might write down the customer's name, phone number, and address and then follow up with your manager or buyers about it. Also, practice your questioning skills by asking, "What color did you have in mind?" or "What is your favorite color?" If the customer has a specific request, you could pass that along. You or someone else should try to obtain the item and then contact the customer to discuss your efforts and findings. Sometimes the obvious solutions are the ones that are overlooked, so be perceptive when dealing with customers and look for little clues such as these. It could mean the difference in continued business and word-of-mouth advertising by your customer.

- *Inappropriate complaint resolution.* The key thing to remember about complaint resolution is that it is the customer's perception of the situation, not yours, that counts. If customers believe that they are not treated fairly, honestly, in a timely manner, and in an appropriate fashion, or if they are still dissatisfied, your efforts failed. Remember that only a small percentage of your customers complain. Second attempts at resolution by customers are almost unheard of.

- *Unmet needs.* Customers have very specific needs to which you must attend. Failure to address or satisfy customer needs will likely cause customers to seek an alternative source of fulfillment. By using effective communication strategies, you can work with customers to identify their expectations and begin to meet them.

KNOWLEDGE CHECK

1. What are four reasons that customers defect to competitors?

LO 7-6 Working with Internal Customers (Coworkers)

CONCEPT **Relationships with your internal customers are important. You should meet your commitments and build a professional reputation.**

If you are a service provider, you have external customers who purchase or use your products or services. In addition to these external customers or organizations, if you are a service provider and work in any type of organization that has more than one employee, you also have to deal with internal customers. The bottom line is that, if you give information, products, or services to another person or entity (e.g., team, department, division, or subsidiary), you are a service provider and have customers. If you receive information, products, or services from another person or entity, you are a customer to them.

Although your interactions with internal customers may not be difficult, they can often be more sensitive than your dealings with outsiders. This is because if someone within your organization becomes irritated or dissatisfied with you, he or she does not necessarily go away. Instead, he or she might tell coworkers or your supervisor about the encounter, which can damage your reputation and even put your standing in the

Effective relationships with internal customers allow you to gain access to information and services that you need to better serve your external customers. *What are some things that you can do better to serve your internal customers and build stronger relationships with them?*

organization in jeopardy. The customer might also withdraw, which means that you might lose access to knowledge, information, or support that you need from him or her in the future.

After all, you see peers and coworkers regularly, and because of your job, office politics, and protocol, your interactions with them are ongoing. Therefore, extend all the same courtesies to internal customers that you do to external ones—in some cases, more so.

The importance of effective internal customer service cannot be underestimated. That is because your relationships with individuals and departments within your organization have far-reaching effects on the organization. Sound internal customer service practices can help to boost employee communication and morale while helping to enhance processes and procedures, reduce costs, increase productivity, and replace interdepartmental competition with interdepartmental cooperation. Through such internal collaboration, external customer service improves because employees have access to information and services they need to better serve external customers. Below are some suggestions that might help you enhance your interactions with internal customers.

STAY CONNECTED

Since relationships within the organization are so important, go out of your way to contact internal customers regularly. You can do this by dropping by their work area to say hello, sending an e-mail, texting, or leaving a voice mail message. You might also friend one another on Facebook, connect on LinkedIn, or otherwise tap into social media channels to get to know one another better outside the workplace and build a more solid relationship. By following coworkers on various websites, you learn more about one another outside the work setting.

If you know of a special occasion for a coworker (e.g., birthday, anniversary, or the birth or adoption of a child), consider sending a card or an e-card to congratulate him or her. This helps strengthen the relationship and can keep the door to communication open so that if service does break down someday, you will have a better chance of hearing about it and solving the problem amiably.

> **Street Talk Service Recovery**
>
> When a customer is unhappy with the result of an interaction, performed by either you or a colleague, sincerely ask the customer, "What can I do to make this right for you?" Many times, the answer will be a surprisingly simple request that you can execute to keep the customer–organization relationship intact.
>
> **SOURCE: STACEY OLIVER-KNAPPE,** *Owner, The Customer Service Gurus LLC*

You might describe your departmental or team coworkers as your "normal" internal customers. However, do not forget the importance of your relationships with other organizational employees, such as the cleaning crew (they service your office and work area), security force (they protect you, your organization, and your vehicle), support staff (who provide services like purchasing, payroll, travel, mail, and print services and logistical assistance), and the information technology staff (they maintain computer equipment). All these groups or individuals and many others within the organization add value and might be a big help to you at some point. If nothing else, they have connections with other people who might aid in your service delivery efforts. Go out of your way to build and maintain strong interpersonal relationships with others in the workplace, especially if you have a behavioral style to which personal interactions are not second nature or as comfortable. A little extra effort to say good morning or do something nice for others can pay big dividends in the future. For example, if you have good rapport with coworkers and are someday downsized, you still have a support network of people who may know other people in the industry where you might find another job.

MEET ALL COMMITMENTS

Too often, service providers forget the importance of internal customers. Because of familiarity, they sometimes become lax and fail to give the same degree of attention to internal customers that they give to external customers. This can be a big mistake. For example, if you depend on someone else to obtain or send products or services to external customers, that relationship is as crucial as the ones you have with external customers. Do not forget that if you depend on internal suppliers for materials, products, or information, these people can negatively affect your ability to serve external customers by delaying or withholding the items you need. Such actions might be unintentional or intentional, depending on your relationship. Your external customers suffer either way and your reputation and that of the organization are on the line.

To prevent, or at least reduce, the possibility of such breakdowns, honor all commitments you make to internal customers. If you promise to do something, do your best to deliver, and in the agreed-upon time. If you cannot do something, say so when your internal customer asks. If something comes up that prevents you from fulfilling your commitment, let the customer know of the change in a timely manner.

Remember, it is better to exceed customer expectations than not meet them. If you beat a deadline, they will probably be pleasantly surprised and appreciative.

Ethical Dilemma 7.2

A coworker promised to help you complete a project where you were to compile information and mail it to customers on Tuesday even though it was not her job. You have helped her in similar situations in the past. It is now Thursday, the coworker still has not come to your aid, and you are now behind schedule.

1. How would you handle this situation? Why?
2. Would you report the situation to your supervisor? Why or why not?
3. What effect might her behavior have on your relationship? Why?

DO NOT SIT ON YOUR EMOTIONS

Some people hold on to anger, frustration, and other negative emotions rather than getting their feelings out into the open and dealing with them. Not only is this potentially damaging to health, for it might cause stress-related illnesses, but it can also destroy working relationships. Whenever something goes wrong or someone troubles you, go to the person and use feedback skills to talk about the situation. Failure to do so can result in disgruntled internal customers, damage to the customer–supplier relationship, and damage to your reputation. Do not forget that you will likely have to continue to rely on your customers in the future, so you cannot afford a relationship problem.

Customer Service Success Tip

Be proactive in dealings with individuals and departments within your organization. This can go a long way to building and strengthening relationships and support. Instead of waiting for someone to ask for information, anticipate needs and provide it before he or she needs it. As you read articles or attend training programs, think of information, data, statistics, or pertinent information that would benefit others in the organization and share it with them. Most people will appreciate your interest and initiative and will likely reciprocate.

BUILD A PROFESSIONAL REPUTATION

Through your words and actions, go out of your way to let your customer and your supervisor know that you have a positive, can-do, customer-focused attitude. Let them know that you will do whatever it takes to create an environment in which internal and external customers are important.

   Part of projecting a professional image is to demonstrate your commitment to proactive service regularly. This means gathering information, products, and other tools before engaging with a customer so that you are prepared to deal with a variety of situations and people. It also means doing the unexpected for customers and providing service that makes them excited about doing business with you and your organization.

ADOPT A GOOD-NEIGHBOR POLICY

Take a proactive approach to building internal relationships so that you can head off negative situations. If your internal customers are in your department, act in a manner that preserves sound working relationships. You can accomplish this in part by adopting the following work habits:

- *Avoid gatherings of friends and loud conversation in your workspace.* This can be especially annoying if the office setup consists of cubicles, as sound travels easily. Respect your coworkers' right to work in a professional environment. If you must hold meetings or gatherings, go to the cafeteria, conference room, break room, or some other place away from the work area.
- *Maintain good grooming and hygiene habits.* Demonstrate professionalism in your dress and grooming. Avoid excessive amounts of colognes and perfumes. This is important because some people have severe allergies to such products and if you are creating an environment where they cannot work, their performance and health suffer.

- ***Do not overdo call forwarding.*** Sometimes you must be away from your workspace. Company policy may require that you forward your calls. Do not overdo forwarding your calls, especially if you are actually in your office and only use that practice as a way to avoid interruptions and focus on a work task. Your coworkers may be inconvenienced and resentful if you do.

- ***Avoid unloading personal problems.*** Everyone has personal problems now and then. Do not bring personal problems to the workplace and burden coworkers with them. If you have personal issues and need assistance, go to your supervisor, team leader, or human resources department and ask for some suggestions. Many organizations have professionally trained counselors available through their employee assistance programs (EAPs). If you get a reputation for often having personal problems that interfere with your effectiveness and efficiency—and bringing them to the workplace—your career could suffer.

- ***Avoid office politics and gossip.*** Your purpose in the workplace is to serve the customer and do your job. If you have extra time to spread gossip and network often with others, you should approach your supervisor or team leader about job opportunities in which you can learn new skills or take on additional responsibilities. This can increase your effectiveness and marketability in the workplace and enhance your value to the organization. The latter can be important in a bad economy where downsizing staff to save costs is an option used by many organizations.

- ***Pitch in to help.*** If you have spare time and your coworkers need assistance with a project, volunteer to help. They may do the same at some point in the future when you are feeling overwhelmed with a project or assignment.

- ***Maintain a clean, organized work area.*** How you maintain your work area sends nonverbal messages about your professionalism, personal values, and level of initiative to many people. Additionally, pick up after yourself (e.g., leave the breakroom clean and regularly clean out any of your items from the refrigerator, if there is one).

homesourcing The practice of bringing jobs formerly outsourced to organizations in other countries back to a company's home country.

- ***Be truthful.*** One of the fastest ways for you to suffer a damaged relationship, or lose the trust and confidence of your coworkers and customers, is to be caught lying. Regard your word as your bond.

Trending NOW

Due in part to the last economic recession, and to some degree with overall dissatisfaction with a lower level of service effectiveness, a number of companies have reversed the trend of offshoring service jobs to countries such as India, the Philippines, and other nations. Instead they are **homesourcing** jobs back to their own country in an effort to make customers feel more comfortable with the service they are receiving and to reduce communication breakdowns.

While sending jobs to countries where salaries are lower and labor issues are reduced makes sense financially, many organizations have found that there is often a disconnect with customers. This is due in part to language differences, but more so to a breakdown with service contractors not effectively understanding the values, expectations, and needs of their customers. Having technical proficiency and knowledge of products and services is not sufficient to satisfy customer needs and expectations. To serve customers effectively, customer service representatives must be able to connect on an emotional and intellectual level with their clients.

KNOWLEDGE CHECK

1. What is the definition of a customer?

2. What is the definition of a service provider?

3. List some strategies for staying connected with internal customers.

4. Why is it important to meet commitments with internal customers?

5. What are possible results of "sitting on emotions"?

6. What are ways to build a professional reputation?

7. What are some work behaviors to adopt that can build internal relationships?

LO 7-7 Strategies for Preventing Dissatisfaction and Problem Solving

CONCEPT Focusing on the customers' needs and seeking ways to satisfy them quickly while exceeding customer expectations are ways to prevent dissatisfaction.

The best way to deal with a service breakdown is to prevent it from occurring. Here are some specific **strategies for preventing dissatisfaction**.

MAKE POSITIVE INITIAL CONTACT

First impressions are crucial and often lasting. To ensure that you put your best effort forward, remember the basics of positive verbal and nonverbal communication—giving a professional salutation, projecting a positive attitude, and sincerely offering to assist. This is crucial because the average customer will come into an initial contact with certain expectations. If the expectations are not met, you and your organization can lose **relationship-rating points** that can ultimately cost the organization a customer. Such points are like the ones on performance appraisals used in many organizations to evaluate and rate employee performance (see Figure 7.6). Use this **relationship-rating point scale** frequently to evaluate your rating as you deal with various customers. Ratings range from exemplary to unsatisfactory, with average being assigned when service occurs as expected.

THINK LIKE THE CUSTOMER

In order to be successful in serving customers, research and learn to use interactive communication techniques. Once you have mastered them, set out to discover what customers want by observing nonverbal behavior, asking specific questions, and listening to their comments and responses. Learn to listen for their unspoken as well as verbalized needs, concerns, and questions. Think about the manner in which you want to be served under the conditions you are dealing with and act accordingly. Why not ask your customers what they want in order to ensure your assumptions about service are correct?

strategies for preventing dissatisfaction Techniques used to prevent a breakdown in needs fulfillment when you are dealing with customers.

relationship-rating points Values mentally assigned by customers to a service provider and his or her organization. They are based on a number of factors starting with initial impressions and subsequently by the quality and level of service provided.

relationship-rating point scale The mental rating system that customers apply to service and service providers.

FIGURE 7.6
Relationship-Rating Point
Scale

Exemplary (4) Service that is out of the ordinary and unexpected falls into this category. *Examples*: An auto repair shop details a customer's car after replacing a transmission. A beauty salon owner provides a free Swedish massage to a regular patron on her birthday. A restaurant server provides a complimentary meal and a coupon for a discount on a future visit or asks the manager to write off the cost of the meal to a customer who had to send her steak back twice to be cooked properly. A nurse visits one of his patients in the intensive care unit after his 12-hour shift ends to ensure that everything is okay and to ask the spouse if she needs anything.

Above Average (3) Service in this category goes beyond the normal and may pleasantly surprise the customer, but it does not dazzle the customer. *Examples*: A regular customer at a bar gets a free second drink from the bartender. A clerk at a bank gives a customer a free wall calendar at the end of the transaction. A customer's son, who just received his first haircut, is given a lollipop by the barber.

Average (2) Service at this level is what is expected by a customer. *Examples*: A customer drops off laundry and when it is picked up, his shirts are starched as requested, on hangers, and in a plastic garment bag. A grocery store bagger asks, "Paper or plastic?" and then proceeds to comply with the customer's request. An accountant finishes a client's tax return on time, as promised. A receptionist properly processes a new dental patient and gathers pertinent health and insurance information in a pleasant manner.

Below Average (1) Service provided at this level is not as expected and disappoints customers. *Examples*: A newspaper deliverer brings a replacement paper after a customer calls to complain, leaves it on the doorstep, rings the bell, and departs without apologizing. A patient waits in a doctor's waiting room 15 minutes or longer beyond her scheduled appointment, and when she is finally seen, no one apologizes. A call center representative gives a customer a $15 credit on service because the customer had to call back three times to have a problem resolved.

Unsatisfactory (0) Service at this level is unacceptable and typically leads to a breakdown in the customer–provider relationship. *Examples*: A customer's cat is neutered by a veterinarian when taken in for a flea dip. A plumbing company that advertises "immediate emergency service" takes over four hours to send a repairperson to fix a leaking pipe in a wall; meanwhile, all carpeting in the living room is being saturated and one wall is crumbling. A contracted tree-trimming worker cuts a large section from a tree that crashes through the garage roof and onto a brand-new car. A doctor operates on the wrong leg of a patient.

PAMPER THE CUSTOMER

You do not have to give into a customer's every whim and request, but you should certainly attempt to provide the products and services promised in a timely manner. Additionally, provide the best quality of service that you can deliver, and address the customer's concerns quickly and professionally.

Make customers feel special and important. Treat them as if they are the center of your attention and that you are there for no other purpose than to serve them. To help accomplish this, do the unexpected, and take any extra effort necessary to meet and exceed their needs and expectations. Even if you cannot satisfy all their wishes, if you are positive and enthusiastic and show initiative, customers might walk away feeling good about the encounter.

RESPECT THE CUSTOMER

Respect is a basic value that most people expect and in some cases demand. To show customer respect, you have to demonstrate that you care about, listen to, and are

©NuStock/Getty Images RF

Go out of your way to build strong relationships with your customers and exceed their expectations. *What are some strategies for exceeding customer expectations?*

concerned for your customers and their well-being. Additionally, you must show that they are important to you and the organization and that you appreciate them and value their business.

When problems arise, you can show your respect by actively listening to your customers and empathizing with them. This means that before you can begin focusing on your customers' problems, you have to take the time to try to understand their concerns and demonstrate that you support the customer and his or her viewpoint. By using a people-centered approach to problem analysis and problem solving, you can win the customer over. With both of you working together, you can define the problem and jointly reach an acceptable solution. See Figure 7.7 for some strategies that you might use to focus on the customer's concerns.

Street Talk

Everything speaks in your physical appearance and demeanor, many times before you even say a word. Think of yourself going onto a stage every day. What is the impression you want people to have of you? It becomes your brand.

SOURCE: TERI YANOVICH, *President, T.A. Yanovich, Inc.*

FIGURE 7.7
Customer-Focused Strategies

Look at complaints as a favor from your customer. Most dissatisfied customers simply leave without telling you why. They then express their displeasure to others and online. When a customer takes the time to share a concern, complaint, or question, thank him or her for giving you an opportunity to correct a problem area and then take the following five actions:

- **React to remarks or actions.** Let the customer know that you heard what she said or received her written message. If a customer delivers information in person, remember to use the verbal, nonverbal, and listening skills discussed earlier in this book. Smile and acknowledge the customer's presence and comments. If you cannot deal with her at that moment because you are serving another customer, let her know when you will be available to assist. If a customer's comments are in writing, respond quickly. If a phone number is available, try calling to speed up the response and add a more personal customer-oriented approach and then follow up in writing.

- **Empathize.** Let customers know that you are concerned; that you do appreciate their views, feelings, or concerns; and that you will do your best to serve them. Really try to "feel their pain" and act as if you were resolving a personal issue of your own. Chances are you will then put more effort into it and appear sincerer.

(continued)

- *Take action.* Once you have gathered enough information to determine an appropriate response, get agreement from your customer on a proposed course of action and then act. The faster you act, the more important the customer will feel.

- *Reassure or reaffirm.* Take measures to let customers know that you and the organization have their best interests at heart. Stress their value to you and your commitment to resolving their complaints. Part of this is providing your name and phone number, and telling them what actions you will take; for example, "Mrs. Lupe, I appreciate your concern about not receiving the package on time. My name is Bob Lucas, my phone number is 407-555-0000, and I will research the problem. Once I have discovered what happened, I will call you back this afternoon, unless I discover that it will take more than a day. In that case, I will call you by 4 p.m. tomorrow to update you. Is that acceptable?"

- *Follow up.* Once a customer transaction is completed, make sure that you begin any necessary follow-up actions. For example, if appropriate, make an additional phone call to customers to be sure that they received their orders and are satisfied with your actions. While speaking with them, reassure them and provide an opportunity for questions. If you promised to take some action, do so and coordinate with others who need to be involved. In the latter instance, if someone else in your organization commits to handle the issue, follow up with that employee and the customer to ensure that everything went as agreed. Remember that your name is often the last that a customer has when issues are transferred to another department or individual. If satisfaction is received, you will likely be the one answering questions from your supervisor.

 WORK IT OUT 7.7

Focusing on the Customer

Think about the techniques described in this chapter for focusing on the customer. Make a list of additional strategies that you can think of and then work with others to see what suggestions they have. Discuss how to implement the strategies in the workplace.

EXCEED EXPECTATIONS

Go the extra mile by giving your customers exemplary service. Strive to get the highest rating possible on the relationship-rating point scale that you read about earlier. To do so, work hard to understand what the customer wants and expects. Observe customers, monitor trends, and talk to customers. Constantly look for opportunities to exceed customer expectations and beat your competitors. Provide service faster, better, and more efficiently than others. Do things for your customer that set your service attitude apart from that of other providers. Some things cost little or nothing and return your "investment" many times over through goodwill and positive word-of-mouth publicity. Depending on your occupation, you can raise your rating and please customers, with strategies such as these:

Auto repair technician: "After I rotated and balanced your tires, I checked and filled all your fluids, and also inspected all your hoses free of charge."

Clothing salesperson: "While you try on that outfit, I will go pick out a couple of other blouses that I think you might like."

Bank customer service representative: "While you are waiting for a loan officer, can I get you a cup of coffee or a bottle of water?"

Hotel operator: "Along with your wake-up call, I will have some complimentary coffee or tea brought up. Which would you prefer?"

Restaurant host: "I apologize, but the wait for a table is approximately 30 minutes. Can I get you a complimentary glass of wine or soft drink from the bar?"

Travel agent: "Since this is your honeymoon cruise, I have arranged for a complimentary bottle of champagne to be delivered to your room along with a book of discount coupons for onboard services."

Call center representative: "Because you were on hold so long to place your order, I am taking 10 percent off your order."

Dentist: "For referring your friend to us, I have told my receptionist to take $25 off your next cleaning fee."

Plumber: "While I was fixing your toilet stopper, I noticed that the lift arm was almost rusted through, so I changed it too, at no charge."

Dry Cleaning Clerk: "When we pressed your blouse, we noticed several buttons were cracked, so we replaced them. We also replaced the remaining buttons so they would all match."

KNOWLEDGE CHECK

1. List some strategies for preventing customer dissatisfaction.

2. What are customer-rating points and how do they impact an organization?

3. What are five customer-focused behaviors you can take to demonstrate respect for your customers?

4. What are some ways to exceed customer expectations?

RESPONDING TO CONFLICT

Conflict should be viewed as neither positive nor negative. Instead, it is an opportunity to identify differences that may need to be addressed when dealing with your internal and external customers. It is not unusual for you to experience conflict when dealing with someone else. In fact, it is normal and beneficial as long as you stay focused on the issue rather than personalizing and internalizing the conflict. When you focus on the individual, or vice versa, conflict can escalate and ultimately do irreparable damage to the relationship. Figure 7.8 describes various forms of conflict.

conflict Involves incompatible or opposing views and can result when a customer's needs, desires, or demands do not match service provider or organizational policies, procedures, and abilities.

CAUSES OF CONFLICT

There are many causes of conflict. The following are some common ones.

- *Conflicting values and beliefs.* These sometime create situations in which the perceptions of an issue or its impact vary. Since values and beliefs have been learned over long periods of time and are often taken personally at face value, individuals get very defensive when their foundations are challenged. For example, you have

FIGURE 7.8

Forms of Conflict

Conflict typically results when you and someone else disagree about something. The following are examples of five forms of conflict that might occur in your organization:

- *Between individuals.* You and your supervisor (or another employee) disagree on the way a customer situation should be handled.
- *Between an individual and a group.* You disagree about a new customer procedure created by your work team.
- *Between an individual and an organization.* A dissatisfied customer feels that your organization is not providing quality products or services.
- *Between organizational groups.* Your department has goals (e.g., the way customer orders or call-handling procedures are processed) that create additional requirements or responsibilities for members of another department.
- *Between organizations.* Your organization is targeting the same customers to sell a new product similar to one that an affiliate organization markets to that group.

been taught that stealing is not only illegal, but also morally wrong. One of your coworkers, who is a friend, regularly takes pens, paper, and other administrative supplies home for her child to use at school. Her logic is that "it (the organization) is a big company and can afford it." You disagree because this creates an ethical dilemma for you—do you confront her, simply avoid her, report the issue to your supervisor, or say nothing?

- *Personal style differences.* Each person is different and requires special consideration and a unique approach in interactions. For example, your supervisor has a high behavioral D style (decisive, direct, and to-the-point), is very focused, and typically wants to know only the bottom line in any conversation. You have a high E (expressive) behavioral style and find it difficult to share information without providing a lot of details in a highly emotional fashion. When the two of you speak, this can lead to conflict unless one or both of you are aware of the other's style and willing to adapt your communication style.

- *Differing perceptions.* People often witness or view an incident or issue differently. This can cause disagreement, frustration, and a multitude of other emotional feelings. For example, an employee (Sue) tells you that she is upset because a deadline was missed because another employee (Fred) did not effectively manage his time. Fred later commented to you that your supervisor pulled him off the project in question in order to work on another assignment. This resulted in his missing the original assignment deadline and a perception by Sue that he could not manage time.

- *Inadequate or poor communication.* Any time there is inadequate communication, the chance for conflict escalates. For example, a coworker (Leonard) confides to you that he may have forgotten to tell a customer about limitations on your organization's return policy. As a result, when the customer brought a product back to return it, another coworker had to deal with a frustrated and angry customer.

- *Contrary expectations.* When one party expects something not provided by another, conflict will likely result. For example, your company offers a 90-day parts-only warranty on equipment that you sell; however, when it breaks down within that period, the customer expects free service also. If you fail to meet the customer's expectation, you have to deal with conflict and the customer potentially becomes dissatisfied.

- *Inadequate communication.* Employees generally like to know what to expect and do not want negative surprises from their supervisor. When they receive mixed signals because of inconsistency, frustration and conflict could result. For example, your supervisor told the entire service staff that in the future, each employee would have an opportunity to earn bonuses based on how many customers he or she could convince to upgrade their membership in the organization. You believe that you have sold the most for the month, yet when you point this out to your supervisor, he tells you that the bonus applies only if you have high sales for two months in a row.

- *Goals out of sync with reality.* Frustration and resentment can result from mis-aligned efforts. For example, you have been working as a service technician for over a year and have learned that, on average, it takes about one and half hours to install a new telephone line. Your supervisor regularly counsels you because you do not accomplish the feat within the goal of one hour.

- *Competition for shared resources.* When two people or groups vie for the same re-sources, conflict usually results. For example, all monies for employee training are lumped into a central training budget in your organization. You have been request-ing to attend a customer service training skills program for the past six months; however, you are told that there is only enough money to train people from the technical staff to learn the new computer software.

- *Outcomes dependent on others.* Whenever you have two or more people, depart-ments, teams, or organizations working jointly toward goal attainment, the potential for conflict exists. For example, your department receives customer orders over the telephone and then forwards them to the fulfillment department for processing and order shipment. If the fulfillment process breaks down, a customer has your name and number, and he or she typically contacts you. If the customer is unhappy, you are the person who has to placate him or her and spend time resolving the conflict.

- *Misuse of power.* Resentment, frustration, and retaliation often result when employ-ees believe that their supervisor is abusing his or her authority or power. For ex-ample, you overhear your supervisor telling an attractive new employee that unless certain sexual favors are granted, she will not receive a desired promotion. This creates an ethical dilemma for you about whether to report the problem or stay out of the situation. Ultimately, it can lead to conflict with your supervisor who is in a power position that can affect your job.

There are various ways you can deal effectively with conflict. Figure 7.9 gives some guidelines.

SALVAGING RELATIONSHIPS AFTER CONFLICT

Managing conflict involves more than just resolving the disagreement. If you fail to address the emotional and psychological needs of those involved, you may find the conflict returning and/or severe damage to the customer–provider relationship may occur. Often poorly handled service recovery efforts result in such things as com-plaints to a service provider's supervisor or consumer agencies, bad word-of-mouth publicity, and lost customers.

Depending on the severity of the conflict and how you handle it at each step of the resolution process, it may be impossible to go back to the relationship as it was before the disagreement. The key to reducing this possibility is to identify and address con-flicting issues as early as possible. The longer an issue remains unresolved, the more damage it can cause. Make the effort to help protect and salvage the relationship be-tween you and your customers.

Often, customers are rational once they can get past their need for emotional own-ership of the situation. If you can apply some basic communication strategies that

FIGURE 7.9

Guidelines for Effective
Conflict Management

Even though each situation and person you deal with will differ, there are some basic approaches that may help in resolution of disagreement(s). Try the following strategies.

- *Remain calm.* You cannot be part of the solution if you become part of the problem. If you are one of the factors contributing to the conflict, consider getting an objective third party to arbitrate, possibly a coworker or your supervisor.

- *Be proactive in avoiding conflict.* As a customer service representative for your organization, you must try to recognize the personalities of those with whom you come into contact daily. If you are dealing with coworkers or peers, try to identify their capabilities and the environments most conducive to their effectiveness. When interacting with a customer, use verbal and nonverbal techniques discussed to help determine the customer's needs. Approach each person in a fashion that can lead to win-win situations; do not set yourself or others up for conflict or failure.

- *Keep an open mind.* Be cautious in order to avoid letting your own values or beliefs influence your objectivity when working toward conflict identification and resolution. This can cause damage to your long-term relationship(s).

- *Identify and confront underlying issues immediately.* Because of the emotional issues often involved in dealing with problem situations, few people enjoy dealing with conflict. However, if you fail to acknowledge and confront issues as soon as you become aware of them, tensions may escalate.

- *Clarify communication.* Ensure that you elicit information on the causes of the conflict from everyone involved and provide the clear, detailed feedback necessary to resolve the issue. This effort can sometimes test your patience and communication skills, but it is a necessary step in the resolution process.

- *Stress cooperation rather than competition.* One of your roles as a service provider is to ensure that you work toward common goals with your coworkers, supervisor, and customers. When one person succeeds at the expense of another's failure, you have not done your job. Encourage and develop teamwork and cooperation when dealing with others.

- *Focus resolution efforts on the issues.* Do not be caught up in or allow finger-pointing, name-calling, or accusations. Keep all efforts and discussions directed toward identifying and resolving the real issue(s). Avoid criticizing or blaming others.

- *Follow established procedures for handling conflict.* It is easier to implement a process already in place than to have to come up with one quickly. That is why most customer service organizations have set customer complaint handling procedures.

can reduce emotions (e.g., empathize, agree with the customer, lower your volume, and monitor your voice tone), the situation may become more manageable. Just remember that your customers are human just like you and human behavior is sometimes volatile. Allow them to vent and calm down and then focus on recovering and rebuilding the relationship. The following strategies can assist in your service recovery efforts:

- *Reaffirm the value of the relationship.* You cannot assume that others feel the same as you or understand your intent unless you communicate it. Apologize sincerely and tell them how much you value the relationship between them and the organization. Also, stress that your goal is to assist them in whatever manner possible.

  Customers typically tell others about the bad experiences they have. The result is that damage can occur to your organization's reputation. This is a strong reason for you to do whatever possible to resolve the issue and appease your customer.

- *Demonstrate commitment.* You must verbalize and demonstrate your desire to continue or strengthen your relationship. The way to do this with customers is through sound interpersonal communication efforts (e.g., active listening, empathy, and positive verbal and nonverbal messages). Once you have smoothed things over a bit emotionally with the customer, take definitive action to address the service or product breakdown positively. If that means involving a coworker or supervisor, do so.

- *Be realistic.* Because of cultural, gender, generational, and behavioral style differences, it is difficult for some people to "forgive and forget." You have to help restore their trust systematically. It can take a while to accomplish this, but the effort is well worth it. Take the time to follow up with your customer after a recovery initiative. Send a card, discount, or gift certificate or take some other proactive measure to show the customer that you are truly sorry for the breakdown in communication and that you are willing to work to regain his or her trust.

- *Remain flexible.* A solid customer–provider relationship involves the ability to give and take. It is especially crucial that you and the other people involved make concessions following conflict. Avoid any references to policy or organizational standard procedure. If you cannot satisfy a customer's complete desires or demands, work toward a compromise and offer possible alternatives.

- *Keep communication open.* One of the biggest causes of conflict and destroyed relationships is poor communication. Service breakdowns usually result in escalated emotions on both sides. Step back mentally and take a deep breath before saying anything that you might regret or that could further frustrate or even anger your customer. Be willing to compromise and let the customer take the lead in the discussion if that appears to help calm him or her and allows you time to work toward an agreeable solution.

- *Gain commitment.* You cannot do it all by yourself. Get a commitment to work toward reconciliation from any other person(s) involved in the conflict. Also, once he or she has relaxed a bit and seems to be more receptive to listening to your suggestions, reaffirm that you have acted in a manner to resolve the issue to his or her satisfaction. Let him or her know that your goal is to help him or her as best you can. Additionally, ask him or her to let you know in the future if any service or product that you and your organization provide does not meet his or her needs or expectations. That will allow you to try to rectify the situation immediately.

- *Monitor progress.* Do not assume that, because the conflict or problem was resolved, it will remain that way. Deep-seated issues often resurface, especially when you do not obtain commitment from the other party. Be sure to do follow-up shortly afterward to ensure that a spark does not rekindle into a blazing fire in their mind. Statistically, a large percentage of customers who desert to a competitor because of dissatisfaction do so without letting you know why. They simply go away and then tell others about their negative experience.

KNOWLEDGE CHECK

1. Describe the difference between assertive and aggressive service.
2. What are some causes of conflict?
3. What are some strategies for salvaging a customer relationship following conflict?

Customer Service Success Tip

Be a problem solver by first being a good listener. When customers have a complaint or a problem, they want solutions, not excuses. To ensure that you address customer needs effectively in these situations, you need to be proficient at problem solving by listening to customers' needs and then providing information, products, or services that remedy their issue(s). Learn the process of problem solving and practice its use before a customer situation actually surfaces.

LO 7-8 The Problem-Solving Process

CONCEPT   Helping customers find a solution to a problem through use of the six-step problem-solving model strengthens customer–provider relationships.

problem-solving model The process used by a service provider to assist customers in determining and selecting appropriate solutions to their issues, concerns, or needs.

To solve a problem, you need to first identify the cause and result of the issue and determine if it needs to be solved. For instance, some customers will complain about things that are legitimately not your responsibility (e.g., a customer bought a drill and used it for over 30 days, and then wanted to return it for a replacement because he left it outside on a construction site during a rain shower and now it will not work). Once you decide to solve the problem, follow the six proven steps to problem solving. Figure 7.10 shows a concise six-step **problem-solving model**.

Before you begin to solve a customer's problem, consider the fact that he or she may not really want you to "solve the problem." In some cases, a person simply wants to vent frustration or be heard. This is where empathetic listening—where you actively listen for messages being sent by the customer and then respond with statements such as "I can appreciate your frustration," "I hear the irritation in your voice and can understand why you feel that way," or "I know that it is disappointing not to get exactly what you are hoping for"—will come in handy.

In many cases, your customer will often have a solution in mind when he or she calls or contacts you. Your role may be to simply listen and offer to facilitate the implementation of the suggested solution. In some situations, you may have to "plant a seed" of a possible solution by asking an open-end question that suggests your recommended approach. If the customer takes your "seed" and nourishes it, you end up with an outcome for which he or she feels ownership, yet is actually one that you thought would be best. For example, assume that a customer wants a product that you do not have in stock. Instead of simply saying, "I am sorry, that item is out of stock," you could ask an additional question such as, "How do you think _____ would work as an alternative?" You have now subtly made a suggestion without saying, "You could use _____ instead. It does the same thing." By taking such an approach, you demonstrate that you listened and are taking a proactive approach to help resolve the issue with his or her best interests in mind.

If you jointly solve a problem, the customer often feels ownership for the solution—that he or she has made the decision. In such instances, the customer is likely to be a satisfied customer. The following six steps describe some key actions involved in this process.

1. IDENTIFY THE PROBLEM

Before you can decide on a course of action, you must first know the nature and scope of the issue you are facing. Often, the customer may not know how to explain his or her problem well, especially if he or she primarily speaks another language or has a

FIGURE 7.10

The Problem-Solving Model

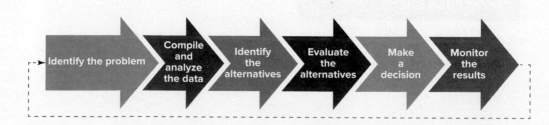

©Robert W. Lucas

Just as each customer is unique, problems are unique and you should approach them in a manner that allows you to gather information and take the appropriate course of action to solve it. *How can a more systematic approach to solving a problem improve customer service?*

communication-related disability. In such cases, it is up to you to do a little detective work and ask questions or review available information. In some cases, you might have to seek the assistance of someone else (a coworker or nearby customer) to act as a translator. In the case of persons with a disability, perhaps they can write down their message.

Begin your journey into problem solving by apologizing for any inconvenience caused by you or your organization. The customer likely wants someone to be responsible. A simple, "I am sorry you were inconvenienced; how may I assist you?" coupled with some of the other techniques listed in this book can go a long way to mending the relationship. Take responsibility for the problem or concern, even if you did not actually cause it. Remember that you represent the organization to the customer. In that role, you are "chosen" to be responsible. Do not point fingers at other employees, policies, procedures, or other factors. It is important to let the customer know that you are sincerely remorseful (on behalf of the organization) and that you will do whatever possible to resolve the issue quickly and effectively.

To learn as much about the issue as you can, start by speaking directly to the customer, when possible. Collect any documentation or other background information available.

For example, if the problem were a malfunctioning television, ask questions to your customers similar to the following (assuming they apply). In some instances, you might ask a "why" question, but be careful about how you phrase the question because someone might take offense or become irritated. This is because the word "why" has a harsh sound to it.

Where and when did you buy the unit?

How long has the problem existed?

What model is it?

What, exactly, is wrong?

Thus far, how have you tried to rectify the situation?

Does it have an antenna attached?

Is there a remote control? If so, is it functioning properly?

Have you checked to see that the power cord is attached firmly?

Have you tried using a different electrical outlet?

Have you checked to make sure that the power strip is turned on?

2. COMPILE AND ANALYZE THE DATA

To effectively determine a course of action, you need as much information as possible and a thorough understanding of what you are dealing with. Getting that data requires the active listening and a little investigative work. You may need to collect information from a variety of sources, such as sales receipts, correspondence, the customer, public records, the manufacturer, coworkers, organizational files, and the manufacturer.

In gathering data, you should also do a quick assessment of the seriousness of the problem. You may be hearing about one incident of a defective product or inefficient service. In fact, there may be many unspoken complaints. Also, look for patterns or trends in complaints received.

Spend some time looking over what you have found after collecting information through questioning and other sources. If time permits and you think it necessary or helpful (e.g., the customer is not standing in front of you or on the telephone), ask for opinions from others (e.g., coworkers, team leader/supervisor, technical experts). Ultimately, what you are trying to do is determine alternatives available that will help satisfy the customer and resolve the issue.

3. IDENTIFY THE ALTERNATIVES

Let customers know that you are willing to work with them to find an acceptable issue resolution. Tell them what you can do, gain agreement, and then set about taking action.

You have an advantage when a customer notifies you of a problem or his or her dissatisfaction. You can offer an objective, outside perspective. In effect, you are performing as an outside consultant. Use this outside vantage point to offer suggestions or viewpoints that the customer may not see or has overlooked. Additionally, make sure you consider various possibilities and alternatives when thinking about potential resolutions.

Look out for the best interests of your customer and your organization throughout the problem-solving process. Be willing to listen to customer suggestions and think "outside of the box" for ideas other than the ones that you and your organization typically use. Do not opt for convenience at the risk of customer satisfaction. If necessary, seek any necessary approval from higher authority to access other options (e.g., to make a special purchase of an alternative item from a manufacturer for the customer, or to give a refund even though the time frame for refunds has expired according to the organizational policy).

4. EVALUATE THE ALTERNATIVES

Once you have collected all the facts, look at your alternatives or possible options. While you should certainly strive to hold down costs to your organization, be careful not to let cost be the deciding factor. A little extra time and money spent to resolve an issue could save a customer and prevent recurring problems later. It can also help bolster your organization's reputation as a customer-centric company. Consider the following factors in this evaluation process:

What is the most efficient way to solve this problem?

Which are the most effective options for solving this problem?

Which options are the most cost-effective?

Will the options solve the problem and satisfy the customer?

Will the selected alternative create new issues?

5. MAKE A DECISION

Based on the questions in step 4, and any others you wish to use in evaluation, make a decision on what your course of action will be. To do this, ask the customer, "Which option would you prefer?"

This simple question now puts the customer into the decision-making position and he or she feels empowered. It now becomes his or her choice, and you can potentially avoid recurring problems. Proceed and resolve the issue if the customer's request is reasonable and possible. If not, negotiate a different alternative.

6. MONITOR THE RESULTS

Once you have made a decision, monitor the effect or results. Do not assume that your customer is satisfied, especially if any negotiation occurred between the two of you.

You can monitor the situation with a follow-up call, by asking if the customer needs anything else when you next see or speak to him or her, or by sending a written follow-up (e.g., a thank-you letter with a query concerning satisfaction, a service survey, or an e-mail). Many companies now use inexpensive online surveys through websites like SurveyMonkey.

If you determine that your customer is not satisfied or additional needs are present, go back to step 1 and start over.

KNOWLEDGE CHECK

1. What are the six steps of the problem-solving model?

LO 7-9 Implementing a Service Recovery Strategy

CONCEPT **The job of a service provider is to return the customer to a satisfied state. Not listening, poor communication, and lack of respect are roadblocks to service recovery.**

Humans make mistakes. Mistakes often appear glaring to customers, who can be very demanding and unforgiving at times. The best you can hope for when something goes wrong is that you can identify the cause and remedy it quickly to the satisfaction of your customer.

The primary purpose of any good service recovery program should be to return the customer–provider relationship to its normal state. If done well, a disgruntled customer can often become one who is very loyal and who acts as a publicist for the organization. Some typical reasons that necessitate service recovery action are:

- Product or service did not deliver as expected.
- There was a failure to keep a promise (e.g., failure to follow up).
- A deadline was missed.
- Customer service was not adequately provided (the customer had to wait excessively or was ignored).
- A service provider lacked adequate knowledge or skills to handle a situation.
- Actions taken by you or the organization inconvenienced the customer (e.g., a lab technician took blood during a patient's visit and the sample was mishandled, requiring the patient to return for a retest).
- A customer request or order was not handled properly (e.g., wrong product or service delivered).
- Attempts to return or exchange an item were hampered by policy or an uncooperative employee.
- A Customer was given the "runaround," by being transferred to various employees or departments and being required to explain the situation to each individual.
- A Customer was treated (or perceived he or she was treated) unprofessionally or in a rude manner.
- Corrective action was taken for any of the above reasons and the customer is still not satisfied.

Actually, there are numerous factors in the service process that can lead to a failure to meet customer expectations. Ultimately, they can all influence service recovery.

According to a consumer survey by the internationally known training company AchieveGlobal of Tampa, Florida, customers—regardless of industry, geography, or product/service—want the service they receive to be:

- ***Seamless.*** The company is able to manage behind-the-scenes service factors so that they remain invisible to the customer.
- ***Trustworthy.*** The company provides what is promised, dependably and with quality.
- ***Attentive.*** The company provides caring, personalized attention to customers, recognizing both their human and business needs.
- ***Resourceful.*** The company efficiently provides flexible and creative solutions.

Typically, there are five phases to the service recovery process (see Figure 7.11).

1. APOLOGIZE, APOLOGIZE, AND APOLOGIZE AGAIN

Showing sincere remorse throughout the recovery cycle is crucial. Listen carefully. Empathize with the customer as he or she explains and do not make excuses, interrupt, or otherwise indicate (verbally or nonverbally) that you do not have time for the customer.

Street Talk

Constantly seek out feedback from your customers and thank them in return. Customers now want to be appreciated and valued more than ever. In the age of social media, just a few words tweeted or a quick picture shared via an online platform can make or break your organization. If you simply show that you care, your customers will more likely be your most zealous agents.

SOURCE: WENDY RICHARD, *HRD Specialist*

FIGURE 7.11
Service Recovery Process

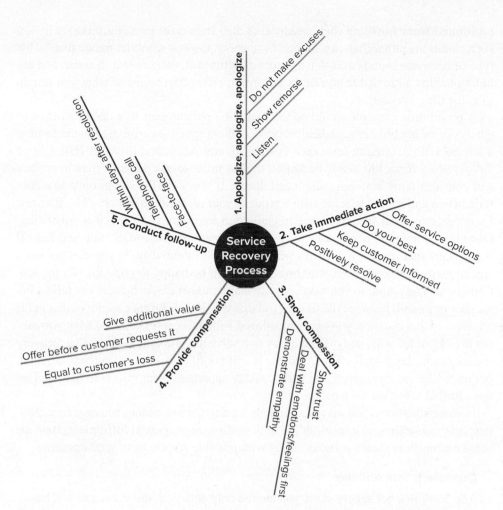

You want to retain the customer and have an opportunity for recovery. You must demonstrate that you care for the customer and that he or she is very important to you and your organization. Interestingly, many service providers do not accept responsibility and/or apologize when customers become dissatisfied. Such an apology should come immediately after the discovery of the customer's dissatisfaction and be delivered in person, if possible. The phone is a second option. Written apologies are the last choice.

2. TAKE IMMEDIATE ACTION

As soon as your customer has identified a problem, you must set about positively resolving it. As you proceed, it is crucial that you keep the customer informed of actions, barriers encountered, or successful efforts. Even if you are unable to make a quick resolution, the customer may be satisfied if he or she perceives your efforts as sincere and ongoing. You must convince customers through your actions and words that you are doing your best to solve the problem in a timely manner. Also, do not forget what you read earlier in the book about avoiding having to say no without offering **service options**. Remember that your customers want to hear what you can do for them, not what you cannot.

Even though you may want to, there may be times when you will not be able to give customers what they want because of regulations or **prohibitions** (e.g., local, state, or federal laws or regulations). In such cases, it is important to use all the interpersonal skills discussed throughout this book to let customers know that you are

service options Alternatives offered by service providers when an original customer request cannot be honored because of such restrictions as governmental statutory regulations, nonavailability of products, or inability to perform as requested.

prohibitions Local, state, or federal regulations that prevent a service provider from satisfying a customer's request even though the provider would normally do so.

prohibited from fulfilling their needs. It is also important to explain the "why" in such situations rather than just saying, "I'm sorry; the law won't let me do that." This type of response sounds as if you are not being truthful, do not want to assist, and are hiding behind an invisible barrier. In any event, offer alternatives of what you can do to assist the customer.

A prohibition example would be the sister of a patient goes to a doctor's office to get a copy of her brother's medical records. Without specific permission in the form of a signed HIPPA (Health Insurance Portability and Accountability Act [HIPAA] of 1996) release form, this would be against the law because of a patient's right to privacy and confidentiality between patient and doctor. If you were the receptionist in a doctor's office and someone made such a request, your response might be: "Ms. Ramsey, I apologize for your inconvenience in coming in for nothing. I know it is frustrating. However, although I would love to assist you, I cannot because of state and federal regulations that protect a patient's privacy and confidentiality. If you can get me a signed medical release from your brother, I would be happy to copy his file for you. Can you do that? And, so you won't have to make another trip in here, if you have a fax number or e-mail, I can get the files to you that way if your brother approves that in his release." In this instance, you have empathized with the customer, stated what you cannot do, explained why, and offered a way to resolve the problem along with a recovery strategy (e.g., fax/e-mail). The customer is still not likely to be 100 percent satisfied, but under the circumstances, she will probably appreciate your efforts to help and reduce further effort on her part.

In some situations, you may want to help a customer but cannot because your abilities, time constraints, resources, or the timing of a request prevent fulfillment. Here are some examples of such situations, along with possible responses to your customer:

Example 1: Your Abilities

You work in a pet supply store, you are the only person in the store, and you have a severe back injury that prevents you from lifting anything over 25 pounds. A customer comes in and buys 50 bags of chicken feed, each weighing 100 pounds. She asks that you help her load the bags onto her truck.

Your Response

"Ms. Saunders, we appreciate your business. I know your time is valuable and I would love to help you. However, I have a back injury and the doctor told me not to lift anything over 25 pounds. I am the only person working here during the lunch hour. If you can come back in half an hour, I will have two guys who will load bags for you in no time. Would that be possible? For your inconvenience, I will even take $10 off your order total."

Example 2: Time Constraints

You work in a bakery and a distraught customer comes in at 3 p.m. Apparently, he had forgotten that he was supposed to stop by on the way to work this morning to order a chocolate cake for his daughter's first birthday party, which is at 5 p.m. He wants you to make him a two-layer chocolate cake with her name and butterflies on it.

Your Response

"Mr. Simon, that first birthday party sounds exciting, and I want to help you make it a success. However, we sold our last chocolate cake half an hour ago, and if I bake a new one, it will still have to cool before I can decorate it. You will never make it by five o'clock. I know it is frustrating not to get exactly what you want. However, since your daughter is only one year old and will not know the difference in the type of cake, can I suggest an alternative? We have a chocolate swirl and virtually any other kind of cake you could want, and I can put on chocolate icing and decorate it for you in less than 15 minutes. Would that work?"

Example 3: Available Resources

You are in North Carolina, near the coastline. A customer comes into your lumberyard in search of plywood to board up his house a day before a major hurricane is due to hit the area. Since the announcement of the impending hurricane on the morning news, you have been overwhelmed with purchases of plywood and sold out two hours ago.

Your Response

"Mr. Rasheed, I can appreciate the urgency of your need. Unfortunately, as you know, everyone in town is buying plywood and we sold out two hours ago. However, I do have a couple of options for you. I can call our store in Jacksonville to find out whether any plywood is left. If there is some, I can have it held if you want to drive over there. The other option is that we have a shipment on the way that should arrive sometime around midnight. I will be here and can hold some for you if you want to pay now and come back at that time. Would either of those options work for you?"

Example 4: Timing

It is April 13 and you are an accountant. With the federal tax filing deadline two days away, you and the entire staff of your firm have been working 12- to 14-hour days for weeks. A regular customer calls and wants to come in the next couple of days to discuss incorporating her business and to get some information on the tax advantages for doing so.

Your Response

"Ruth, it is great that you are ready to move forward with the incorporation. I think you will find that it will be very beneficial for you. However, with tax deadlines two days away, we are swamped and there is just no way I can take on any nonrefund-related work. Since your incorporation is not under a deadline, can we set up our meeting sometime around the first of next week? That will give me time to wrap up taxes, take a breather, and then give you the full attention you deserve."

In all of these instances, you show a willingness to assist and meet customer needs even though there are obstacles to meeting original requests. You also work with them and offer alternatives for consideration. This is important, since you do not want to close the door on customer opportunities. Doing so will surely send customers to a competitor.

There might be other occasions when you or your organization cannot meet a customer's need even though it is possible to do so. In such cases, company restrictions keep you from fulfilling the customers' request. In this type of situation, you sometimes hear service providers hide behind a phrase such as "Policy says. . . ." The reality is that someone in the organization has decided for business reasons that certain actions cannot, or should not, be taken. If you encounter such "policies" that prohibit you from delivering service to customers, bring them to the attention of your team leader or management for discussion. These restrictions will most likely cost your organization some customers and result in bad word-of-mouth publicity. The following is an example of such a situation, along with a possible response:

Example

You work in a gas station in a major tourist area that has a policy that prohibits accepting out-of-town checks. There is a sign on the gas pumps stating payment policy. It includes a statement that out-of-town checks are not accepted. A tourist from another state has her family with her and fills her car with gas. She then comes to you to pay for her purchase. She tells you that she has only personal checks and $2 in cash with her. She is leaving town to return home at this time.

Your Response

"I know that this is an inconvenience, and I apologize. However, because of problems we have experienced in the past, we do not accept checks from banks out of this area. We will gladly accept major credit cards, travelers' checks, or cash. Does anyone else in your car have a credit card or cash? We also have an ATM machine where you can use a bank debit card to get cash."

In this example, the customer either failed to read the policy sign on the pump or intentionally chose to ignore it. Either way, you had to initiate a problem-solving intervention and have provided several viable alternatives for payment.

 WORK IT OUT 7.8

Recovering from Policy Restrictions

Work in small groups to discuss ways that you might handle the situation in the gas station example provided. What would you do if none of your suggested alternative solutions was acceptable or possible (e.g., no one else had cash, or credit or debit cards)?

3. SHOW COMPASSION

To help the customer see that your remorse and desire to solve a problem are genuine, you must demonstrate empathy. Expressions such as "I can appreciate your frustration," "I understand how we have inconvenienced you," or "I can imagine how you must feel" can go a long way in soothing and winning the customer over. Before you can truly address the customers' problem, however, you must deal with their emotions or feelings. If you disregard their feelings, customers may not give you a chance to help resolve the breakdown. Also, keep in mind what you read about trust in an earlier chapter: You must give it to receive it.

4. PROVIDE COMPENSATION

Prove to customers that they are valuable and that you are trying to make up for their inconvenience or loss. This penance or symbolic self-punishment should be significant enough that the customer feels that you and your organization have suffered an equal loss. The value or degree of your atonement should equal the customer's loss in time, money, energy, or frustration. For example, if your chef cooked a customer's meal improperly and the customer and others in the party had to wait, you might give her a free meal and free coffee or tea to everyone in the group. If she ordered a vegetable that came much later because you forgot to include it on the order you sent to the kitchen, a free dessert might suffice. The key is to make the offer without the customer having to suggest or demand it.

Not only must the recovery compensate original loss, it should give additional value. This is known as "making the customer whole." In other words, it means providing the product or service for which the customer originally paid and compensating for the inconvenience experienced. For example, if a customer had an oil change done on his or her car and oil his carpet was soiled by oil on a mechanic's shoes, an appropriate gesture might be to give the oil change free and have the carpet cleaned at your company's expense. This solution compensates for inconvenience and lost time while providing added value (saving the cost of the oil change).

5. CONDUCT FOLLOW-UP

Following up after service is the only way to find out whether you were successful in your recovery efforts or whether the customer is truly satisfied. The preferable methods are face-to-face questioning or a phone call. This contact should come within a few days after the complaint was resolved. It could take the form of a few simple statements or questions (e.g., "I am following up in case you had any additional questions" or "I am calling to make sure that it is now working as it should be. Is there anything else we can do to assist you?").

This last step in the recovery process can be the deciding factor in whether the customer returns to you or your organization. This phase that reemphasizes the message "We truly care."

KNOWLEDGE CHECK

1. According to AchieveGlobal, what four things do customers want service they receive to be?

2. What are the five phases of the service recovery process?

LO 7-10 Disaster Planning Initiatives in the Service Recovery Process

Hurricanes Katrina and Sandy, the Oklahoma tornadoes of 1999 and 2013, the 2013 earthquake and typhoon in the Philippines, the 2004 earthquake and tsunami in the Indian Ocean, the earthquake in Nepal in 2015, and other similar natural catastrophes all have one thing in common—they devastated homes and businesses on a massive scale.

For organizations in those areas that did not have an active **disaster preparedness** or contingency plan, the results were dramatic and paralyzing financially and from an operational standpoint. Physical structures were lost in the devastation, organizational records and assets were lost, and customer service was virtually stopped. Customers had limited access to cell and landline phone service and Internet service was severed or radically disrupted. There was also little or no way to contact companies and businesses for needed services. Call centers were offline or destroyed totally and employees stayed

disaster preparedness A process through which an organization creates an active plan to contain the effects of a disastrous event in order to minimize injury and loss of life and property.

home to deal with their own personal calamity and loss. All of this had a crippling effect on the ability of affected organizations to communicate with and deliver any degree of service.

In the chaos that followed, companies struggled for weeks and months to regain any semblance of their previous operational effectiveness. Many businesses were closed permanently; employees were out of work with no income. Many people struggled with the loss of precious items and with the loss of a loved one. Insurance companies scrambled to appraise the damage and pay insured claims, and utter confusion was the word of the day.

The U.S. Small Business Administration suggests that organizations take at least the following actions to prepare for potential disaster situations. This will allow them to remain functional or to more effectively recover should a similar catastrophe strike:

- Create a preparedness program for the business.
- Identify critical business functions and systems.
- Create an emergency communications plan.
- Test preparedness systems regularly.
- Build a disaster preparedness kit.

Because of the potential destructive loss caused by unexpected catastrophes, many organizations have taken proactive measures to create and rehearse disaster preparedness and contingency plans. They store vital information and data at reinforced offsite facilities in various geographic regions and via cloud technology. They also train their employees about the need to think proactively and decide what information is crucial for storage and how they might better prepare in the event of emergencies from a service and personal perspective.

Customer service professionals also play individual roles in the preparedness process. On a basic level, if you work with data, ensure that you save files every five to ten minutes and make backup copies of all your work regularly. This is especially important if related to customer orders and information. If you work face-to-face with customers, take time to survey your work area. Know the nearest evacuation routes from every area, be alert for potential safety hazards and report them, and speak to your supervisor about the company's disaster preparedness plan. If your organization includes disaster preparedness in its employee handbook or on its website, take time to read it and make sure you understand your role(s) in implementation. As an additional step, volunteer for training in first aid and cardiopulmonary resuscitation (CPR) so that you are prepared to render medical assistance, if necessary. Finally, make sure that you update your emergency contact information with human resources whenever there is a change so that your family members receive notifications in the event of a disaster or emergency.

KNOWLEDGE CHECK

1. What are some of the things that businesses can do to prepare for disasters that interrupt operations?

2. What roles do service providers play in the service recovery process?

3. How can service providers better prepare to play an active role in the preparedness process?

Small Business Perspective

Customers do not expect any less degree of quality service from a small business. They are still spending their money and putting forth the same amount of effort when they patronize a small organization as they would with a larger one.

The challenge for small businesses in service recovery is that they typically do not have training available for employees on the process. Because of the limited number of employees, they typically do not have the luxury of a customer service department to handle follow-ups. Additionally, small businesses do not have large budgets and in some cases have limited liquid assets or money that they can apply to service recovery efforts. Even so, recovery efforts are equally as important to small businesses because they really count on every customer and sale to survive.

To compensate for limited resources, every employee must take responsibility for providing quality service in order to reduce the need for service recovery. When something does go wrong, the service representative making contact with the customer must assume responsibility and do his or her best to follow the steps of the problem-solving model. If situations escalate, the service representative should immediately contact a supervisor or the owner, as appropriate, to bring the issue to management's attention and ask for guidance.

If you work for a small company, you should still strive to be the most competent, conscientious, and professional service provider that you can be.

Impact on Service
Based on personal experience and what you just read, answer the following questions:

1. Why do you think that service recovery efforts are often limited in small companies? Explain.

2. What could better prepare employees of small businesses to handle service breakdowns? Explain.

3. If you were an employee of a small business and a customer received the wrong product, what would you do to appease the customer? Explain.

Use SmartBook to help you read, study, and retain what you have learned. Access SmartBook in your Instructor's Connect course, or go to connect.mheducation.com for help.

Key Terms

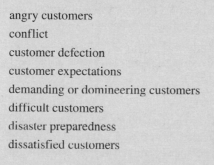

angry customers

conflict

customer defection

customer expectations

demanding or domineering customers

difficult customers

disaster preparedness

dissatisfied customers

emotion-reducing model

homesourcing

indecisive customers

needs

problem-solving model

prohibitions

relationship-rating points

relationship-rating point scale

rude or inconsiderate customers

service breakdowns

service options

strategies for preventing dissatisfaction

talkative customers

under promise and over deliver

wants

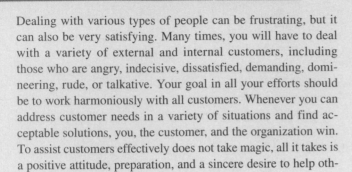

Summary

Dealing with various types of people can be frustrating, but it can also be very satisfying. Many times, you will have to deal with a variety of external and internal customers, including those who are angry, indecisive, dissatisfied, demanding, domineering, rude, or talkative. Your goal in all your efforts should be to work harmoniously with all customers. Whenever you can address customer needs in a variety of situations and find acceptable solutions, you, the customer, and the organization win. To assist customers effectively does not take magic, all it takes is a positive attitude, preparation, and a sincere desire to help others. If you use the techniques outlined in this chapter, and others in this book, you are on your way to providing stellar customer service and satisfying customer needs. Whenever a customer experiences an actual or perceived breakdown in service, prompt, appropriate recovery efforts may be your only hope of retaining the customer. In a profession that has seen major strides in quality and technology as well as increased domestic and global competition, service is often the deciding factor. Customers often expect and demand their rights. When they are disappointed, they simply go elsewhere. Your role in the process is to remain vigilant, recognize customer needs, and provide service levels that will keep them coming back.

Review Questions

1. What does the term *service breakdown mean*? Define.

2. What causes customers to become dissatisfied?

3. What tactics can you use to deal with angry customers?

4. What can you do to assist indecisive people in coming to a decision?

5. Why might some customers feel they have to demand things from others?

6. How can you effectively deal with rude or inconsiderate customers?

7. What are some strategies for refocusing a talkative customer?

8. What are some strategies for preventing customer dissatisfaction? List them.

9. How does the emotion-reducing model work?

10. Why do customers defect?

11. What strategies can you use to build strong relationships with coworkers?

12. List the strategies for effective problem solving.

13. What is service recovery and when do you need to implement it?

Search It Out

1. **Search the Internet for Information on Problem Solving**

   Search the Internet and locate information on providing customer service to irate customers. Also, look for information on the following topics:

   Conflict resolution

   Problem solving

   Handling stressful situations

   Service breakdown

   Service recovery

   Be prepared to share what you find with your classmates at the next scheduled class.

2. **Search the Internet for Factors That Have Influenced Societal Groups**

   Each generation has societal and cultural issues that have influenced its members. These factors (e.g., values, beliefs, economy, world situation, and others) help people form opinions and affect the manner in which they deal with life situations.

   Spend some time searching the Internet for information on the factors that have influenced each of the major societal groups—Traditionalist (1900–1945), Baby Boomers (1946–1964), Generation X (1965–1980), and Millennials (1981–2000). Make a listing of what you find for each group.

   Be prepared to share your list with classmates at the next session.

3. **Contingency Planning**

   Give some thought to what it would mean to your organization if a natural disaster struck your area and what that would mean to you personally and to your customers. With this in mind, spend some time on the Internet searching information about what organizations are doing to prepare for catastrophic events or disasters.

Once you gather the information, prepare a checklist of things that you could do as a service provider to prepare for such a catastrophe. Also, think of what recommendations you could offer your supervisor for developing contingencies to keep service flowing to your customers.

Be prepared to share your thoughts with your classmates.

4. **Additional Resources**

For additional articles and information on service breakdowns and service recovery, check the author's Customer Service Skills Blog at http://www.customerserviceskillsbook.com/wordpress and search "Customer Service Representatives" and related topics. Also, visit YouTube at https://www.youtube.com/results?search_query=customer+service+breakdowns to watch short videos on customer service breakdowns.

Collaborative Learning Activity

1. Role-Playing Difficult Customer Situations

Work with a partner and role-play one or more of the following scenarios. Each of you should choose at least one scenario in which you will play the service provider role. The other person will play the customer. In each instance, discuss what type of difficult customer you are dealing with and how such an encounter might go. At the end of each role-play, both persons should answer the following questions and discuss ideas for improvement:

Scenario 1

Terry Welch entered your shoe store over 30 minutes ago and seems to be having trouble deciding the style and color of shoes she wants.

Scenario 2

Chris Dulaney is back in your lawn mower repair shop. This is the third time in less than two weeks that he has been in for repairs on a riding mower. Chris is getting upset because the problem stems from a defective carburetor that he was told you repaired on each previous visit. He is beginning to raise his voice, and his frustration is becoming evident.

Scenario 3

You are a telephone service representative for a large retail distribution center. You have been at work for about an hour when you receive a call from Pat Mason, who immediately starts making demands (e.g., "I have only got a few minutes for you to tell me how to order." "Look, I have read all the articles about the scams telemarketers pull. I will tell you what I want, and you tell me how much it will cost." or "Listen, what I want you to do is take my order and get me the products within the next two days. I need them for a conference.").

Scenario 4

You are a cashier in the express lane at a supermarket. As you are ringing up a customer's order, a second customer approaches, squeezes past several people in line, and says, "I am in a hurry. All I have is a quart of milk. Can you just tell me how much it costs, and I will leave the money right here on the register."

Scenario 5

You are a very busy switchboard operator for ComTech, a large corporation. A vendor whom you recognize from previous calls has just called to speak with your purchasing manager. As in previous calls, the vendor starts a friendly conversation about the weather, how things are going, and other topics not related to business.

Questions

1. How well was service provided?
2. Were any negative or unclear verbal or nonverbal messages communicated? If so, discuss.
3. How can you incorporate the improvements you have identified into a real customer service encounter?
4. What open-end questions did the service provider use to discover customer needs? What other questions could have been used?

2. Generation Breakdowns and Recovery

Each generation has societal and cultural issues that have influenced its members. These factors (e.g., values, beliefs, economy, world situation, and others) help people form opinions and affect the manner in which they deal with life situations. Using the information you discovered in your Search It Out activity on factors that impact each of the major generational groups:

a. Form equal-sized groups.
b. Use the generational value lists to discuss possible conflicts that might occur between customers and service providers who come from the different generational groups. Also, discuss why such breakdowns might occur.
c. What role do someone's perceptions play in breakdowns between generations? From where might those perceptions originate and how might those be avoided?
d. Once you have identified potential breakdowns, discuss what might be done by service providers to prevent them and how they should handle any breakdowns that do occur.

3. Maximizing Generational Interactions

The way people from different generations interact with one another sometimes causes communication and relationship breakdowns. In a customer service environment, these glitches can mean lost revenue and business and negative word-of-mouth publicity about service providers or their organization.

a. Brainstorm examples of ways that younger (under 21 years of age) and older (over 21 years of age) service providers and customers can sometimes create challenges when interacting with one another. These examples might include variations in language/terminology used, clothing styles, personal appearance preferences, personal mannerisms, or behavioral habits.

b. Put your challenges identified above into lists using the following categories:
Younger service providers dealing with older customers
Older service providers dealing with younger customers
Younger customers interacting with older service providers
Older customers interacting with younger service providers

c. After creating your lists of challenges, discuss strategies to help avoid breakdowns in each category as either a service provider or a customer.

d. Use your strategy lists as guidelines to avoid problems in your own service interactions with people from different age groups.

Face-to-Face

Handling Service Breakdowns at AAA Landscaping

Background

You are the owner of AAA Landscaping, a small company in Orlando, Florida, that specializes in resodding and maintenance of lawns. Much of your business is through word-of-mouth advertising. Once a contract is negotiated, portions of it are subcontracted out to other companies (e.g., sprinkler system repair and pesticide services). Recently, you went to the home of Stu Murphy to bid on resodding his lawn. He obtained several other bids, but yours was the lowest. You arranged for work to begin to remove old grass and replace it with the St. Augustine grass sod that he requested.

As part of the contract, Stu also asked that some basic maintenance be done (e.g., hedge and tree trimming, hauling away of old decorative wooden logs from around flower beds, and general sprucing up of the front area of the house). In addition, fertilizer and pesticide were to be applied within two weeks. Stu signed the contract on Wednesday and the work was to be completed by Saturday, when he had planned a party.

Your Role

You were pleased to get the contract, worth over $1,200. This is actually the third or fourth contract in the same subdivision because of word-of-mouth advertising. Your employees completed the initial sod removal and replacement, weeding, and pruning on Friday, and you received full payment on Monday.

You received a call from Stu on Tuesday afternoon stating that several trees were not trimmed to his satisfaction, debris covering decorative rocks along hedges was not removed as agreed, and bags of clippings had been left behind. Because of other commitments, it was only on Friday that you sent someone out to finish the job. On Saturday, Stu left another message on your answering machine stating that there was still an untrimmed tree, the debris remained, and the clippings were still in the side yard. You did not get around to returning his call. Stu called again Monday, repeating the message he had left before and reminding you that the contract called for pesticide and fertilizer to be applied to the lawn. You called back and said that someone would be out the next day. Again, other commitments kept you from following through. Stu called on Wednesday and left a fourth message on your answering machine. He said that he was getting irritated at not getting callbacks and action on his needs. Without returning Stu's call, you responded by sending someone out on Thursday to take care of the outstanding work.

It has been several days since the work was completed, and you assume that Stu is now satisfied since you have heard nothing else from him.

Critical Thinking Questions

1. Based on information in this chapter, how have you done on providing service to Stu? Explain.

2. What were Stu's needs in this case?

3. Could you have done anything differently?

4. Are you sure that Stu will give a good recommendation to neighbors or friends in the future? Why or why not?

Planning to Serve

To help better prepare yourself to deal with difficult customer service situations and to help you to prevent service breakdown or to aid in service recovery, respond to the following statements. Based on your responses below, seek out resources (e.g., materials, training programs, and people) that can help broaden your knowledge on these topics. Try to discuss these questions—and your answers—with your coworkers or classmates. This can ultimately help improve your own skills, employee morale, and service to customers.

1. I approach what I believe to be a difficult customer with a positive attitude and believe that I can reverse the situation.　　**Yes**　　**No**

2. In dealing with customers, I seek to determine their true needs before offering a service solution.　　**Yes**　　**No**

3. What actions or circumstances have you noticed lead to service breakdowns in organizations where you were either a customer or service provider?

4. When you were a customer and service broke down, what recovery strategies were used effectively to help "make you whole"?

5. I consciously monitor my language, and elicit feedback from peers on it to ensure that I typically use positive words and phrases when communicating.　　**Yes**　　**No**

6. When dealing with the types of difficult customers described in this chapter, I maintain my professionalism and actively listen in order to better serve their needs.　　**Yes**　　**No**

7. When working with coworkers, I afford the same courtesies and professionalism that is required for external customers.　　**Yes**　　**No**

8. When you were a customer and service broke down, what ineffective recovery strategies did you experience?

Quick Preview Answers

1. T　　　3. F　　　5. T　　　7. T　　　9. T　　　11. T
2. F　　　4. F　　　6. T　　　8. T　　　10. T　　　12. T

Ethical Dilemma Summary

Ethical Dilemma 7.1 Possible Answers

1. What would you do in this situation?

   You are in an awkward situation. Your boss wants to leave and has made that clear; however, your customer is in need of service. An appropriate strategy would be to call your supervisor, make him aware of the situation, and ask him how you should handle it.

2. How do you think the customer will view this matter?

   In effect, you are violating your own store policy regarding closing times. Customers have a legitimate expectation that if you have a written policy displayed (the time on the door), you will follow it. By failing to adhere to posted times, you are not only potentially violating your customer's trust, but also creating a situation where you lose merit in their eyes and the organization will likely sustain negative word-of-mouth publicity as they recount the story to many others and likely on social media.

3. Are there possible repercussions from a service standpoint? If so, what are they?

   If you allow the customer to come in to get the item(s) needed, she will likely be thankful and less stressed, although the fact that you locked up earlier than announced may play a role in future end-of-day visits. In the future, she might opt to go elsewhere in similar circumstances. If you do not allow her to shop, you will likely lose her future business and she will spread word of the incident to anyone who will listen to her. She might even call or send a letter or e-mail to the store manager to complain.

Ethical Dilemma 7.2 Possible Answers

1. How would you handle this situation? Why?

   This is a touchy situation in which you asked the coworker to do you a favor and she agreed to do so. Rather than jump to conclusions, it is probably best to approach the coworker in a friendly and nonthreatening manner, using some strategies you read about in Chapters 3 and 4. Ask why she failed to assist as she agreed and listen to her response rationally. Depending on what she tells you, let her know that you are disappointed that she failed to either help or come to you before now to explain that she could not do so. Also, let her know how you feel about her failure to come forward. The last is important because people often do not realize the effect their behavior has on others and how it might affect relationships.

2. Would you report the situation to your supervisor? Why or why not?

   Since this was not a task assigned to both of you, it is probably best not to go to your supervisor or to point fingers and blame your coworker for your missing the deadline. After all, it is your job and not hers.

3. What effect might her behavior have on your relationship? Why?

   Because relationships depend on trust, your coworker's behavior could certainly negatively affect your relationship in the future, depending on her reason for failing to assist you. Even if she has a good reason, the fact that she did not at least let you know of the obstacle could influence how you feel toward her and your ability to trust and work with her effectively in the future.

Customer Service in a Diverse World

CHAPTER

8

LEARNING OUTCOMES

After completing this chapter, you will be able to:

8-1 Recognize that diversity is not a bad thing.

8-2 Describe some of the characteristics that make people unique.

8-3 Embrace the need to treat customers as individuals.

8-4 Determine actions for dealing with various types of people.

8-5 Identify a variety of factors that make people diverse and that help to better serve them.

8-6 Communicate effectively with a diverse customer population.

Use SmartBook to help you read, study, and retain what you have learned. Access SmartBook in your Instructor's Connect course, or go to connect.mheducation.com for help. ▧ SMARTBOOK™

IN THE REAL WORLD RESTAURANT FRANCHISE—SUBWAY

Vision: "To make our restaurants and operations as environmentally and socially responsible as possible."

Organizational Commitment:

Continue to evolve our menu of great tasting, nutritious options, as well as provide access to nutrition and healthier lifestyle information;

Ensure our food meets the highest quality and safety standards;

Find sustainable and cost-effective solutions that serve the business needs of our franchisees

Focus on sustainability initiatives on energy efficiency, water and resource conservation, waste reeducation, sustainable sourcing, and supply chain management;

Encourage our franchises to contribute to their communities, promote diversity, and choose "environmentally friendly" options and business practices.

Source: In The Real World Restaurant Franchise — Subway

What does a 17-year-old graduate who wants to become a medical doctor do in order to pay his college tuition? He starts a sandwich business that morphs into a multimillion global dollar franchise operation. This is how Peter DeLuca started Pete's Super Submarine shop in Bridgeport, Connecticut in 1965. On opening day, the store sold 312 sandwiches and its owner knew he was onto something.

To get his venture started, DeLuca borrowed $1,000 from a family friend, Dr. Peter Buck. The two partners set a goal of opening 32 restaurants within 10 years. By 1974, they owned 16 submarine shops around Connecticut and realized that they needed to change their plan in order to reach their original goal, so they began to franchise the operation. Subway is the world's largest submarine chain with over 44,000 restaurants owned by over 21,000 franchisees in over 100 countries worldwide. There are no corporate-owned sites and the company is privately held and not traded on any stock exchange.

Part of the appeal of Subway products is that it sources them locally whenever possible, thus supporting the economies in which franchises are located. It is also environmentally conscious. Ninety-five percent of its salad bowls, trays, and lids are made from recycled content and its napkins are made from 100 percent recycled fiber. Further, in many stores, recycling and composting bins are available to reduce landfill contributions. Product distribution centers are located geographically to support restaurants and reduce the number of miles driven for deliveries. This reduces vehicle carbon emissions. In addition, all new and remodeled franchise locations use energy-efficient lighting and low-flush toilet systems to reduce their impact on the planet.

All of these initiatives help protect the environment.

The Subway corporate website stresses that from an organizational standpoint the franchise headquarters "is committed to increased representation of women and minorities in our workforce and does not tolerate discrimination of any kind on the basis of race, sex, sexual orientation, gender identity, creed, religion, color, or national origin."[1]

For additional information about the Subway organization, search the Internet or visit its website at http://www.subway.com/en-us/aboutus/.

Think About It

1. Based on what you know personally about the organization and what have read and researched about the company, on a scale of 1–10 (1 being lowest) how would you rate it from a service perspective? Explain your rating.

2. What do you think it does well as an organization?

3. If you were looking to buy a franchise, would you consider Subway? Why or why not?

Quick Preview

Before reviewing the chapter content, respond to the following questions by placing a "T" for true or an "F" for false on the rules. Use any questions you miss as a checklist of material to which you will pay particular attention as you read the chapter. For those you get right, give yourself a pat on the back, but review the sections they address in order to learn additional details about the topic.

_____ 1. Diversity is an important aspect of everyone's life that can present many positive opportunities or negative challenges depending on your knowledge of other people and groups.

_____ 2. Many people only associate the term diversity with the word cultural, which describes the differences between groups of people from various countries and with differing beliefs.

_____ 3. The diverse nature of your customer population requires you to be aware of the various ways people from different cultures interact in the business setting.

_____ 4. Values are the "rules" that people use to evaluate situations, make decisions, interact with others, and deal with conflict.

_____ 5. In some cultures, direct eye contact is often discouraged, for it suggests disrespect or overfamiliarity.

_____ 6. Today, all cultures use less formality in the business environment and do not stress the importance of using titles and family names as often as they did in the past.

_____ 7. When encountering someone who speaks a language other than yours, you should avoid jokes, words, or acronyms that are tied to sports, historical events, or specific aspects of your own culture.

_____ 8. In serving customers from some cultures, it is important to avoid the use of the word "no" because this word may cause the customer to become embarrassed or experience a "loss of face."

_____ 9. According to the U.S. Census Bureau, under 54 million Americans have some level of disability.

_____ 10. When a customer has a disability, deemphasize the disability by thinking of the person first and the disability second.

_____ 11. When dealing with an elderly customer, you should always be respectful.

_____ 12. Younger customers are as valuable as those in any other age group and should be served professionally.

Answers to Quick Preview are located at the end of the chapter.

Words to Live By

"It starts with respect. If you respect the customer as a human being, and truly honor their right to be treated fairly and honestly, everything else is much easier."

—**Source: Doug Smith**

LO 8-1 The Impact of Diversity

CONCEPT   **Diversity is an important aspect of everyone's life. Encounters with others give us an opportunity to expand our knowledge of others.**

diversity The characteristics, values, beliefs, and factors that make people different, yet similar.

As the world grows smaller economically and otherwise (e.g., in world trade, ease of international travel, outsourcing and offshoring of jobs, worldwide Internet access, international partnerships between organizations, and technologically transmitted information exchange), the likelihood that you will have contact on the job with people from other cultures, or who are different from you in other ways, increases significantly. This likelihood also carries over into your personal life. **Diversity** is encountered everywhere (e.g., over the telephone, on the Internet, in supermarkets, in religious organizations, and on public transportation) and is an important aspect of everyone's life. Although it presents challenges in making us think of differences and similarities, it also enriches our lives—each encounter we have with another person gives us an opportunity to expand our knowledge of others and build relationships, while growing personally.

One significant impact that diversity has on customer service is that people from varied backgrounds and cultures bring with them expectations based on the "norm" of their country or group. Whether this diversity pertains to cultural or ethnic differences, beliefs, values, religion, age, gender, ability levels, or other factors, a potential breakdown in customer satisfaction can occur if people get other than what they want or expect.

Part of creating a positive diverse customer business environment is to train each service provider on the nuances of dealing with people who have backgrounds that are different from their own. Additionally, this effort involves each employee taking ownership for enhancing his or her knowledge and skills related to working with a diverse customer base. By taking such initiative and expanding their understanding of others, employees become a valued asset for their organization. They also enhance their career and professional opportunities.

As you begin your journey through the concept of dealing with diverse customers in this chapter, stop and think about the following questions.

- How do you define *diversity*?
- What do you already know about diverse cultures around the world?
- In what ways do your cultural beliefs and values differ from those of cultures with which you have contact as a service provider?
- In what ways are your cultural beliefs and values similar to those of cultures with which you have contact as a service provider?
- How do the beliefs and expectations of people from a gender other than your own affect your ability to serve them effectively?
- What is your personal interest in learning about other cultures or diverse groups?
- What training or research have you done on diversity and how has that influenced your views or perspectives toward others who may be different from you?

©Digital Vision./Getty Images RF

The people of the world are becoming more increasingly integrated each day as ease of travel and the Internet close the distance gap between them. *What are you doing to educate yourself about differences in gender, generations, and other factors that influence the way the diverse customers that you will encounter think and act?*

KNOWLEDGE CHECK

1. What does the term *diversity* mean to you?

LO 8-2 Defining Diversity

CONCEPT Diversity is not a simple matter; it is not difficult to deal with if you are fair to people and keep an open mind.

WORK IT OUT 8.1

Encountering Diversity

Take a few minutes to ask yourself what diversity is and what it means to you. Write your own definition of diversity.

During the past week, in what situations have you encountered someone from a different culture, group, or background in the workplace or at school (someone whose values or beliefs differed from yours or who looked or dressed differently from you or your group)? Make a list of the diverse people that you met (e.g., where they were from, why they were different from you, and how they were similar to you) and the situations encountered.

Once you have created your responses, form a group with two to three other students, share your responses, and discuss the implications of providing quality service to customers who are different from you.

cultural diversity The different racial, ethnic, and socioeconomic varieties, based on factors such as values, beliefs, and experiences, that are present in people grouped together in a given situation, group, or organization.

The word *diversity* encompasses a broad range of differences. Many people only associate the term *diversity* with race or color of skin. However, it also encompasses a variety of other individual and group characteristics such as **cultural diversity**. This term has to do with the differences between groups of people, depending on their country of origin, backgrounds, and beliefs. An important point for service providers to remember is that diversity occurs within each cultural group; however, many other characteristics are involved. For example, within a group of Japanese people are subgroups such as males, females, children, the elderly, athletes, thin people, gay or lesbian people, Buddhists, Christians, grandparents, and married and single people, to mention just a few of the possible diverse characteristics, beliefs, and values.

Customer Service Success Tip

A key point to remember is that the concept of treating others as you would like to be treated (a value common in many religions—e.g., the Golden Rule) can lead to service breakdowns. This is because your customers are unique and may not value what you do or want to be treated as you do.

To better ensure service success, find out what customers want and treat them as they want to be treated. This concept has been termed the **Platinum Rule**.[2]

Platinum Rule Term coined by speaker and author Tony Alessandra related to going beyond the step of treating customers the way you want to be treated, to the next level of treating them the way they would like to be treated.

Diversity is not a simple matter, yet it is not difficult to deal with. Start your journey to better understanding of diversity by being fair to people and keeping an open mind when interacting with them. In fact, when you look more closely at, and think about, diversity, it provides wonderful opportunities because people from varying groups and geographic locations bring with them special knowledge, experience, and value. This is because even though people may have differences or potentially look different, they also have many traits in common. Their similarities form a solid basis for successful interpersonal relationships if you are knowledgeable and think of people as individuals; you can then capitalize on their uniqueness. Contrarily, if you cannot think of the person instead of the group, you may stereotype people—lump them together and treat them all the same. This is a recipe for interpersonal disaster, service breakdown, and organizational failure.

You can apply the basic customer service techniques related to communication found in this book to many situations in which you encounter customers from various groups. Coupled with specific strategies for adapting to special customer needs, these techniques provide the tools you need to provide excellent customer service.

Some factors that make people different are innate, that is, they are born with them, such as height, weight, hair color, gender, skin color, physical and mental condition, and sibling birth order. All these factors contribute to our uniqueness and help or inhibit us throughout our lives, depending on the perceptions we have. We gain or learn other factors that make us unique through our environment and our life experiences. Examples of these factors include religion, **values**, **beliefs**, economic level, lifestyle choices, profession, marital status, education, and political affiliation. Often, we use these factors to assign people to categories. Use caution when considering any of these characteristics, since grouping people can lead to stereotyping and possible discrimination.

The bottom line is that all of these factors affect each customer encounter. Your awareness of differences and of your own preferences is crucial in determining the success you will have in each instance.

values Long-term appraisals of the worth of an idea, person, place, thing, or practice held by individuals, groups, or cultures. They affect attitudes and behavior.

beliefs Perceptions or assumptions that individuals or cultures maintain. These perceptions are based on experiences, memories, and interpretations and influence how people act and interact with certain individuals or groups.

KNOWLEDGE CHECK

1. How does cultural diversity differ from diversity?
2. In what ways might a customer's values and beliefs influence your ability to deliver effective service to him or her?

LO 8-3 Customer Awareness

CONCEPT Applying your own cultural practices and beliefs to a situation involving someone from another culture can result in frustration, anger, poor service, and lost business.

Are all customers alike? Emphatically, no! No two people are alike, no two generations are alike, and no two cultures are alike. In addition, each customer has needs based on his or her own perceptions and situation.

In our highly mobile, technologically connected world, you are likely to encounter a wide variety of people with differing backgrounds, experiences, religions, modes of dress, values, and beliefs within the course of a single day. Many of these factors can affect customer needs, wants, and expectations and potentially create situations in which you must be alert to the verbal and nonverbal messages that indicate those needs. Moreover, the diverse nature of your customer population requires you to be aware of the various ways people from different cultures or groups interact in the business setting. Applying your own cultural practices and beliefs to a situation involving someone from another culture can result in frustration, anger, poor service, and lost business.

A changing customer world brings potential differences in the way some people perceive factors such as time, communication style, gender roles, religion, dress, and members of other countries and cultures. By better understanding other cultures and contexts, you have a prime opportunity for building a solid customer–provider relationship. You also significantly reduce the chance for communication and service breakdowns due to differing perspectives and expectations.

Because people from various cultures approach situations in different ways, you run the risk of misunderstanding that can occur due to the way people deal with communication, conflict, problem solving, task completion, and decision making. This is why cultural awareness training and research are so crucial to your job success and effective customer service.

KNOWLEDGE CHECK

1. How can better understanding the cultural differences of your customers potentially assist in enhancing the customer service you provide?

LO 8-4 The Impact of Cultural Values

CONCEPT Values often dictate which behaviors and practices are acceptable or unacceptable. These values may or may not have a direct bearing on serving the customer.

Although many cultures have similar values and beliefs, specific cultural values are typically taught to members of particular groups starting at a very young age. This does not mean that a particular group's values and beliefs are better or worse than those of any other group; they are simply important to that particular group. These values often dictate which behaviors and practices are acceptable or unacceptable. They may or may not have a direct bearing on serving the customer, but they can have a very powerful influence on what the customer wants, needs, thinks is important, and seeks or accepts. Values can also influence your perceptions and actions toward others. Being conscious of differences can lead to a better understanding of customers and potentially reduce conflict or misunderstandings in dealing with them.

Many service providers take values for granted. This is a mistake. Values are the "rules" that people use to evaluate issues or situations, make decisions, interact with others, and deal with conflict. As a whole, a person's value system often guides thinking and helps him or her determine right from wrong or good from bad. From a customer service perspective, values often strongly drive customer needs and influence the buying decision. Values also differ from one culture to another,

Education, cultural nuances, family backgrounds, and other factors cause people to behave based on their own experiences. The more informed you are about similarities and differences possessed by people from various cultures, the greater the likelihood that you will provide quality service. *How should you provide customer service to someone of another culture?*

depending on its views on ethics, morals, religion, and many other factors. For example, if customers perceive clothing as either too sexy or too conservative, they may not purchase the items, depending on what need they are trying to meet. Likewise, they may not buy a house because it is in the perceived "wrong" neighborhood.

Values come from deeply held beliefs of a culture or subculture. Often, they are founded in religion, politics, or group mores. They drive thinking and actions and are so powerful that they have served as the basis for arguments, conflicts, and wars for hundreds of years.

To be effective in dealing with others, service providers should not ignore the power of values and beliefs, nor should they think that their value system is better than that of someone else. The key to service success is to be open-minded and accept that someone else has a different belief system that determines his or her needs. With this in mind, you, as a service provider, should strive to use all the positive communication and needs identification you have read about thus far in order to satisfy the customer.

You might demonstrate cultural values through open expression or subtle behavior. Your values can affect your interactions with your customers in a variety of ways. In the next few pages, consider the connection of values with behavior. Also consider how you might adjust your customer service to ensure a satisfactory experience for diverse customers. Keep in mind that the degree to which customers are **acculturated** to prominent cultural standards will determine how they act. Assimilation often occurs when someone is exposed to the values and beliefs of a new group or country for a long period of time.

Your goal is to provide excellent service to the customer. In order to achieve success in accomplishing this goal, you must be sensitive to, tolerant of, and empathetic toward customers. You do not need to adopt the beliefs of others, but you should adapt to them to the extent that you provide the best service possible to all of your customers. As mentioned earlier, apply the Platinum Rule of service when dealing with customers.

acculturated The cultural and psychological changes in one's beliefs and behavior that often occur as a person or group of people are integrated into another culture or country and adopt the habits and beliefs of their new environment.

©Cathy Yeulet/123RF RF

MODESTY

modesty Refers to the way that cultures view propriety of dress and conduct.

Modesty can be exhibited in many ways. In some cultures (e.g., Muslim and Quaker), conservative dress by women is one manifestation of modesty. For example, in some cultures, women demonstrate modesty and a dedication to traditional beliefs by wearing a veil or headdress. Such practices tie to religious and cultural beliefs that originated hundreds of years ago. In other cultures, nonverbal communication cues send messages. For example, direct eye contact is viewed as an effective communication approach in many Westernized cultures. Lack of eye contact could suggest dishonesty or lack of confidence to a Westerner. In some cultures (India, Iran, Iraq, and Japan), direct eye contact is often discouraged, in particular between men and women not married to one another or between people who are of different social or business status. Such behavior is considered disrespectful or rude. Modesty is encouraged between sexes. At an early age (more so in females), people in some cultures are taught a sense of modesty. They might demonstrate this value by covering the mouth or part of the face with an open hand when laughing or speaking, or through avoiding direct eye contact in certain situations.

Another way that you might offend someone's modesty is through your environment. For example, if you have a waiting room that has magazines that show advertisements with scantily clad models or a television or radio station broadcasting that contains sexual situations (e.g., soap operas) or racy talk show hosts, you may want to rethink the situation. That can help avoid offense to some customers.

Street Talk Customer Loyalty

You can help customers stay loyal to your company by being attentive to every question and concern posed by the customer. During your career, you will hear the same issue many times, but it is always the first time for that customer. By letting the customer know that every concern he or she has is important to you and your organization, you demonstrate compassion in short-term interactions that will eventually develop into a loyal long-term relationship.

SOURCE: STACEY OLIVER-KNAPPE, *Owner, The Customer Service Gurus LLC*

Impact on Service

When encountering examples of potentially modest behavior, evaluate the situation for the true message or meaning. The person may really be exhibiting suspicious behavior. However, instead of assuming that the customer is being evasive or dishonest, consider the possible impact of culture as part of your assessment of the situation. If you suspect illegal intentions, certainly call your risk management staff or a supervisor; however, do not quickly jump to conclusions or draw undue attention to a customer's nonverbal behavior, cultural dress, or beliefs being demonstrated. Instead, continue to verbally probe for customer needs and address them. In addition, provide the same quality of friendly service as you would to others who display behavior or cultural characteristics that do not differ from your own.

EXPECTATIONS OF PRIVACY

Based on your personality and prior life experiences, you may be more or less likely to disclose personal information, especially to people you do not know well. You should be aware that disclosing personal information about oneself is often a cultural factor and that **expectations of privacy** vary. For example, many people who are British, German, Australian, Korean, or Japanese may display a tendency to disclose less about themselves than many North Americans do.

expectations of privacy The belief that personal information provided to an organization will be safeguarded against inappropriate or unauthorized use or dissemination.

Impact on Service

Being congenial and welcoming is a good thing during a customer interaction; however, if you tend to be gregarious and speak freely about virtually any topic, you should

Ethical Dilemma 8.1

Assume that you are an employee in a lingerie store at a local shopping mall, and you and a fellow employee have been discussing world events because of a news story about a terrorist bombing you saw on the television this afternoon. You were talking about how, in a post-9/11 world, there is ongoing scrutiny and reevaluation of handling different situations because of security concerns worldwide. Airports limit what can be carried onto planes, people are checked by security personnel and devices (e.g., metal detectors and scanners), and organizational policies and procedures related to service and various situations have been modified (e.g., entrance into buildings, background checks for current and new employees, and access to certain types of data and equipment).

Shortly after your conversation with the other employee, a male customer or client comes in carrying a paper bag. Based on the man's mode of dress, you and another employee debate on what country he is from before you approach him to offer assistance. When you do, he states that he is "just killing time while his wife has her hair done." You observe him leave your store, wander into several others, and then return a second time about an hour later. Your fellow employee jokes that, "He is probably a terrorist casing the place to blow it up."

1. Does the man's dress or the other employee's comments make a difference in this situation? Explain why or why not.

2. What action should you take, if any? Why or why not?

3. Does the conversation that you had with your coworker have any bearing on the course of action you choose in this situation? Explain.

4. What are possible repercussions if you either act or decide not to act?

5. If the person were dressed differently, would you take a different course of action? Explain.

curtail this tendency in the customer service environment. Be cordial but do not talk excessively. Failure to do so could slow service to waiting customers and might make some customers feel uneasy and uncomfortable. Their discomfort may result from the fact that if you are conducting business in a Western culture, when someone asks a question or shares information, there is often an expectation that the other party will reciprocate. When you are reluctant to do so, customer might perceive you as being unfriendly or even rude. A good rule of thumb is to stay focused on the business of serving your customer in an expeditious and professional manner. Keeping your conversations centered on satisfying the customer's needs can accomplish this. This does not mean that you should totally avoid "small talk"; just keep it under control and watch customer reactions closely. Talking about the weather, traffic, or some other impersonal topic might be fine. Avoid controversial topics that might be emotional hot buttons or sensitive to other people (e.g., politics, religion, other customers, or perspectives on birth control).

FORMS OF ADDRESS

Although many North Americans often pride themselves on their informality, people from other countries may see informality as rudeness, arrogance, or overfamiliarity. For example, if you were from the United States, doing business in another country and failed to greet the customer appropriately (e.g., with a slight bow, sign of the **wai**,

wai (pronounced "why") Traditional gesture in Thailand used in conjunction with a slight bow as a greeting to say "thank you" or "sorry." You execute this posture by placing the palms and fingers of both hands together as in a prayer position in the center of the chest. Holding the hands higher in relation to the face is an indication of more respect or reverence to the other person in certain countries.

Forms of address and greetings differ around the world. When meeting someone from another culture, it may be appropriate to use their cultural greeting format rather than a handshake, depending on the situation. *What do you know about greetings used by other cultures and how might a lack of knowledge or cultural insensitivity hinder perceptions of your level of service to some customers?*

namaste Traditional greeting gesture in India (pronounced "NAH-mes-tay") that is performed with a slight bow and by placing the palms and fingers of both hands together as in a prayer position in the center of the chest.

namaste, or other traditional greeting) or called customers from a more formal culture by their first name without their permission (e.g., in a doctor's office or a waiting area), you might possibly irritate or anger them.

When meeting someone from another culture who has not been acculturated into your own, you might greet the customer according to his or her cultural background. This demonstrates sensitivity and respect to the customer and his or her culture and can create an instant bond. For example, many cultures (e.g., Argentina, many European countries, China, and other parts of Asia) stress formality in greeting someone in the business environment and place importance on the use of titles and family names when addressing others.

To further confuse the issue of how to address a customer, some cultures have differing rules on how family names are listed and used. For example, in parts of China and Taiwan, many people are given a family name, a generational name (for the period during which they are born), and a personal name at birth. The generational and personal names might be separated by a hyphen or space (e.g., a female might be named Li [family name] Teng [generational name] Jiang [personal name], or Li Teng-Jiang]. Women typically do not take their husband's surnames. When addressing someone from the Chinese culture, use an appropriate title such as *Mr.* or *Mrs.* followed by the family name (Mrs. Li) unless you are asked to use a different **form of address**.

form of address Title used to address people. Examples are Mister, Miss, and Doctor.

Many service providers from other cultures who move to a Westernized culture often adopt a Western first name (e.g., Amanda or Richard) when they immigrate to, or work with, people from that culture. This makes it easier for their customers and co-workers to pronounce their names.

Hispanic culture Refers to people who were born in Mexico, Puerto Rico, Cuba, or Central or South America.

Chicano culture Refers primarily to people with a heritage based in Mexico.

Latino culture Refers to people of Hispanic descent.

In Argentina (and most **Hispanic**, **Chicano**, and **Latino cultures**), people have two surnames: one from their father (listed first) and one from their mother (e.g., Jose Ricardo Gutierrez (father's surname) Martinez (mother's surname). Usually, when addressing the person, use a title only with the father's surname (e.g., Mr. or Mrs. Gutierrez).

Impact on Service

A customer's preference for a particular name or form of address can have an impact upon your ability to effectively deal with him or her. If you start a conversation with someone and immediately alienate the person by incorrectly using his or her name, you may not be able to recover. Moreover, informality or improper use of family names could send a message of lack of knowledge or concern for the customer as an individual or as being important to you. Take the time to learn some of the global rules of doing business. No matter what job you get in the future, this information will likely come in handy when dealing with internal and external customers and other acquaintances.

RESPECT FOR ELDERS

In most cultures, some level of respect is paid to older people. Often this **respect for elders** is focused more on males (when older men are viewed as revered, as among Chinese). This stems from a belief that with age come knowledge, experience, wisdom, authority, and, often, higher status. Thus, respect for or deference to elders is normal. In numerous cultures, age brings with it unique privileges and rights (such as the right to rule or to be the leader). For example, this is true in many Native American cultures.[3]

Impact on Service

You must be careful to pay appropriate respect when speaking to older customers (of both sexes). Further, you should be sensitive to the fact that if the customer demands to speak to a senior person or to the manager or owner, he or she may simply be exhibiting a customary expectation for his or her culture or generation. If you can assist without creating conflict in such situations, do so; if not, honor the request when possible.

> **Customer Service Success Tip**
>
> Rather than assume familiarity and make the choice yourself, ask your customer his or her preference for being addressed. The latter can lead to a service relationship breakdown.

respect for elders A value held by people from many cultures.

Trending NOW

Many organizations and employees have realized the importance of creating a fair and equal environment in which everyone feels respected and valued. This is especially important in a service environment where employees encounter customers who have different characteristics daily.

To ensure that you are ready for potential situations in which you will be serving people of different ages, genders, abilities, cultural and religious backgrounds, and numerous other diversity factors, consider participating in the following initiatives:

1. Objectively evaluate your own biases toward people from a given group and develop some strategies for overcoming them.

2. Visit a restaurant that serves ethnic foods other than that of your native culture.

3. Share your own story with someone from a different group (e.g., age, gender, ethnic background, or religion) and see how their life experiences compare or differ from yours.

4. Identify at least one resource for diversity information and visit it each month.

5. Take a language course to learn a new language.

6. Visit a religious institution, museum, or historical monument of a culture different from your own.

7. Volunteer to work with people whose race, gender, or cultural backgrounds are different from your own.

IMPORTANCE OF RELATIONSHIPS

Before business is conducted in many Asian, Latin American, and Middle Eastern cultures, building of a strong **interpersonal relationship** is extremely important. For example, in China, Egypt, El Salvador, Indonesia, Korea, Japan, and Myanmar

interpersonal relationship Focuses on the need for service providers to build strong bonds with customers.

FIGURE 8.1

Relationship-Focused Countries (Partial Listing)

Bangladesh	Indonesia	Myanmar	Saudi Arabia
Brazil	Iran	Pakistan	Singapore
China	Iraq	Philippines	South Korea
Colombia	Japan	Poland	Thailand
Egypt	Kuwait	Qatar	Turkey
Greece	Malaysia	Romania	Vietnam
India	Mexico	Russia	

face Refers to the important concept of honor, dignity, or self-esteem in many Asian cultures. In such cultures, one tries not to cause embarrassment or otherwise create a situation in which someone looks bad in the eyes of others.

(formerly Burma), having a number of informal meetings with people in an organization to build a relationship is often expected before coming to an agreement. Lunch, dinner, and office meetings often occur for weeks before discussing any serious business or reaching an agreement. Additionally, unless you reach the right level of management in the organization for these meetings, all your efforts may be wasted. Figure 8.1 shows a partial listing of some of the world's more relationship-focused countries where building relationships before conducting business is often crucial.

Related to relationships is the concept of "**face**" (sense of dignity or self-esteem) that is important in some Asian cultures (e.g., Chinese and Japanese). Using the equivalent to the word "no" in some cultures could lead to embarrassment or bad impressions from peers or friends. This is a violation of social and business etiquette and is not taken lightly or quickly forgotten. For these reasons, when a person is invited to a meeting or social event, but cannot or does not want to attend, he or she may say something like, "That is possible" rather than declining. This approach allows the person inviting to save face and avoid embarrassment by a declined invitation. In such instances, the invited individual often has no intention of attending. Westerners who are not acculturated into societies in which this practice is common are often confused or angered when they invite someone who does not show up under such circumstances. Conflict can result when the cultures collide because in Western countries, being "brutally honest" is often appreciated and expected. The opposite is true in Asia.

Impact on Service

Failure to establish support or an environment of trust could lead to a breakdown in service and/or lost customers. This does not mean that you should hesitate to assume a quicker familiarity with customers from such cultures. This could also alienate them. Instead, when you will be having ongoing contact or doing repeat business, follow the customers's lead. Get to know them and share information about your organization and yourself that can lead to mutual respect and trust. You may find that you also have to take time at the beginning of each encounter with your established customers to reestablish the relationship. This may involve spending time in conversations related to nonbusiness topics (e.g., their health, sports, hobbies, pets, or other topics in which the customer is interested). Just remember to familiarize yourself with cultural manners and etiquette for the customer's country before meeting in order to avoid cultural taboos. For example, it is often inappropriate for a male to ask a male counterpart from many Middle Eastern countries about his wife or daughter. Unless you know your client well and have established a degree of friendship and he has brought up the topic of family, avoid such topics. In many instances, some of these strict interpersonal rules may be relaxed depending on the degree to which your customer has dealt with Westerners, understands their culture and practices, and has traveled to the United States and other Westernized countries.

Relationship building may also involve presenting gifts to persuade various people in the organization that you are a friend and have their interests at heart. Only then can you proceed to determine needs and provide service. People from many countries view this as an appropriate form of etiquette, while others may label such gratuities as bribes. Whatever your belief, if the practice is a cultural norm, you may do well to follow it when dealing with customers from other regions of the world.

GENDER ROLES

Culturally and individually, people view the role of men and women differently. Although **gender roles** are continually evolving throughout the world, decision-making and authority are often clearly established as male prerogatives within many cultures, subcultures, or families. For example, in many Middle Eastern, Asian, South American, and European countries, women have often not gained the respect or credibility in the business environment that they have achieved in many parts of North America.

gender roles Behaviors attributed to or assigned by societal norms.

In some countries, women are often expected to take a "seen and not heard" role or to remain out of business transactions. In parts of Korea and other Pacific Rim countries, it is rare for women to participate in many business operations. Men often still have higher social status than females. You do not have to agree with these practices, but you will need to consider them when facing them in some customer encounters.

When serving customers from different countries, you would do well to remember that people may leave a country, but they take their cultural norms and values with them. Failure to consider alternative ways of dealing with people in certain instances might cause you to react negatively to a situation and nonverbally communicate your bias.

Impact on Service

If you are a female dealing with a male whose cultural background is like one of those just described, he may reject your assistance and ask for a male service provider. If you are a male dealing with a male and female from such a culture, do not be surprised if your conversation involves only the male. Attempts to draw a woman into such a transaction or make direct eye contact and smile may embarrass, offend, or even anger customers and/or their family male members who are present. Generally, people who have lived or worked in Western cultures for longer periods will acculturate and not take offense to more direct behaviors that are meant to convey friendliness and to engage customers (e.g., smiling, engaging in small talk about families, or complimenting on dress).

ATTITUDE TOWARD CONFLICT

Conflict is possible when two people come together in a customer environment, but it does not have to happen. By recognizing your biases and preferences, and being familiar with other cultures, you can reduce the potential for disagreement. Certainly, there will be times when a customer initiates conflict. In such instances, all you can do is to use the positive communication techniques described throughout this book. If necessary, you may need to involve a coworker or supervisor to resolve a conflict situation.

attitudes Emotional responses to people, ideas, and objects. They are based on values, differ between individuals and cultures, and affect the way people deal with various issues and situations.

individualistic cultures Groups in which members value themselves as individuals who are separate from their group and responsible for their own destiny.

collective cultures Members of a group sharing common interests and values. They see themselves as an interdependent unit and conform and cooperate for the good of the group.

conflict resolution style The manner in which a person handles conflict. People typically use one of the five approaches to resolving conflict: avoidance, compromise, competition, accommodation, or collaboration.

monochronic Refers to the perception of time as being a central focus with deadlines being a crucial element of societal norms.

polychronic Refers to the perception of time as a fluid commodity that does not interfere with relationships and elements of happiness.

©Stockbyte/Getty Images RF

The perception of time and how it is viewed and used vary between cultures. *What do you know about the ways that various cultures view time, and how might that affect your ability to interact with and serve customers from those groups?*

concept of time Term used to describe how certain societies view time as either polychromic of monochronic.

Many times, **attitudes** toward conflict are either rooted in the individual's culture or subculture or based on personal behavioral style preference. Some cultures are **individualistic cultures** (emphasis is placed on individuals' goals, as in Western countries), and some are **collective cultures** (individuals are viewed as part of a group, as in Japan or in Native American cultures). Members of individualistic cultures are likely to take a direct approach to conflict, whereas people whose culture is collective may address conflict indirectly, using an informal mediator in an effort to prevent loss of face or embarrassment for those involved. Even within subcultures of a society, there are often differing styles of communication and dealing with conflict. Of course, regardless of culture or group, people choose different **conflict resolution styles** based on personality style preferences.

Impact on Service

Depending on the individuals you encounter and their cultural background, you and your customers may deal differently with conflict. If you use the wrong strategy, emotions could escalate and customer dissatisfaction could follow. The key is to listen and remain calm, especially if the customer becomes agitated.

THE CONCEPT OF TIME

In relation to time, people and societies are often referred to as being either **monochronic** or **polychronic**. People from monochronic societies tend to do one thing at a time, take time commitments seriously, are often focused on short-term projects or relationships, and adhere closely to plans or timelines. On the other hand, polychronic people are used to distractions and juggle multiple things (e.g., conversations with two or more people) simultaneously without feeling stressed. They consider time as a guide and flexible commodity, work toward long-term deadlines, and view relationships more important than deadlines.

People from the United States are typically very time-conscious (monochronic). You often hear such phrases as "time is money," "faster than a New York minute," and "time is of the essence," which stress their impatience and need to maximize time usage. Similarly, in Germany, punctuality is almost a religion, and being late is viewed as very unprofessional and rude. In most business settings in the United States, anyone over five minutes late for a meeting is often chastised. In many colleges and universities, etiquette dictates that students wait no longer than 15 to 20 minutes before leaving when an instructor (depending on whether he or she is a full or associate professor) is late for a class.

Many North Americans tend to expect people from other cultures to be as time-conscious as they are; however, this is not always the case. For example, it is not unusual for people from Arab countries (polychronic) to be a half hour or more late for an appointment or for a person from Hispanic and some Asian cultures to be up to an hour late for social engagements. It is also not unusual for people from such cultures to fail to show up for an appointment at all without notifying other attendees. A phrase used by some Asian Indians sums up the concept and justifies the lateness: "Indian standard time." Such tardiness is not viewed as disrespect for the time of others or rudeness; it is simply indicative of a cultural value or way of life. Figure 8.2 lists countries according to their **concept of time**.

Impact on Service

In Western and other monochronic cultures, you are expected to be punctual. This is a crucial factor in delivering effective service. Although others may not have the

FIGURE 8.2
Monochronic and
Polychronic Countries

Most cultures can be described as either monochronic or polychronic. Some are both in that people exhibit one focus in the workplace and another with relationships. In some countries, a monochronic approach is prevalent in major urban areas, whereas a polychronic view is taken elsewhere. The following is a sampling of countries and their perspective on time.

Monochronic	Polychronic		Both
Australia	Africa	Latvia	Brazil
Canada	Bahrain	Lebanon	France
Czech Republic	Bangladesh	Mexico	Japan
England	Cambodia	Myanmar (Burma)	Spain
Germany	China	Native American tribes	
Hungary	Croatia	Pakistan	
The Netherlands	Estonia	Philippines	
New Zealand	Ethiopia	Portugal	
Norway	Greece	Romania	
Poland	India	Russia	
Slovakia	Indonesia	Saudi Arabia	
Sweden	Ireland	Serbia	
Switzerland	Italy	South Korea	
United States	Java	Thailand	
	Jordan	Turkey	
	Kuwait	Ukraine	
	Laos	Vietnam	

same beliefs and may be late for meetings, you must observe time rules in order to project an appropriate image and to satisfy the needs of your customers and organization.

OWNERSHIP OF PROPERTY

In many cultures or groups (e.g., Buddhist, certain African tribes, and the Chickasaw Indian Nation), **ownership of property**, or accumulation of worldly goods or wealth, is frowned upon. In the case of the Chickasaw Indians and other native tribes in North America, such things as the earth, nature, natural resources, possessions, and individual skills are shared among the tribal group. They are not to be owned or kept from others, for the Creator gave these things.[4] Many devout Buddhists believe that giving away personal belongings to others can help them reach a higher spiritual state. Thus, the amassing of material things is not at all important to them and is often frowned upon.

Impact on Service

People have differing levels of needs. Ask customers what their needs are and listen to their responses. Do not persist in upgrading a customer's request to a higher level or more expensive product if he or she declines your suggestion. You may offend and lose a customer. Of course, if you are in sales, you must make a judgment on whether an objection is one that you should attempt to overcome or whether it is emphatic or culturally based and means no.

> **Customer Service Success Tip**
>
> By being aware of the time values that you and your customers have and proceeding accordingly, you can reduce your own stress level when dealing with customers or clients from other cultures.

Ethical Dilemma 8.2

Assume that you work for an organization that has a zero-tolerance policy related to discrimination based on characteristics such as race, color, national origin, and other protected categories. While working one day, you overhear one coworker talking to another about a customer from a Middle Eastern country who just walked out of the store. The customer had been dressed in his native garb (e.g., a flowing floor-length garment called a jellabiya with a turban). Apparently, the customer did not speak English well and had difficulty getting his point across to your coworker. You heard the coworker make disparaging remarks about the customer. He finishes by saying, "That guy might have gotten what he wanted, but I will have the last laugh. I told him that I would make sure his credit card gets credited for an overcharge as soon as the system comes back online, but that is never going to happen." The workers both laughed as they walked away.

You are well aware of the organization's nondiscrimination policy and have respect for anyone who comes to this country and makes an effort to assimilate into the culture. This is because your parents and grandparents all immigrated from Eastern Europe and you are a first-generation North American.

1. Have you ever witnessed similar situations in the workplace? Explain.
2. From a service perspective, is this situation a problem? Explain.
3. What would you do or say about the incident that you just witnessed? Explain.
4. If you fail to act in this situation, what are possible repercussions? What about if you do act?

KNOWLEDGE CHECK

1. How can a customer's personal values and beliefs impact a service situation?
2. On what are values based and how do they potentially impact a customer's decisions?
3. How might the value of modesty be misinterpreted in a service situation?
4. How can someone's differing expectation of privacy create challenges for a service provider who is very outgoing?
5. What is a good rule of thumb when addressing customers?
6. In what ways are elderly people viewed in various cultures?
7. In what ways might the value of building strong interpersonal relationships potentially affect your service delivery?
8. How do gender roles differ in various cultures and what impact might that have on service delivery?
9. How do individualistic and collective cultures differ in their handling of conflict?
10. What potentially happens when monochronic and polychronic people find themselves engaged in business settings?
11. How would someone's perception of property ownership potentially impact customer service?

LO 8-5 Providing Quality Service to Diverse Customer Groups

CONCEPT As a service provider, you should become proficient in working with customers with language differences and disabilities; you also need to work with young and elderly customers.

Given the potential diversity of your customer base, it may be impossible to establish a service strategy for each group. However, you should think of what you might do to address the needs of some of the larger categories of customers with whom you will probably come into contact. The next few sections provide some strategies for dealing effectively with people from four diverse groups: customers with language differences, those with varying abilities, elderly customers, and young customers.

CUSTOMERS WITH LANGUAGE DIFFERENCES

One major obstacle for service providers in the United States is that many adults believe that most of the world's population speaks English. In actuality, English is the third most spoken language behind Mandarin Chinese and Spanish. However, if you combine the number of native English speakers and nonnative people who speak English as a second language, English moves up to first or possibly second behind Chinese.[5]

The Bureau of Labor Statistics figures estimate that over 25 million (16.1 percent) of the U.S. workforce are **foreign-born people**.[6] These figures are representative of the number of people who live in the United States but were not born in the country. The key to effectively serving all customers, and particularly people from different cultures, is flexibility. Since you are likely to encounter customers from virtually any country in the world when you work in today's business environment, you need to be prepared. You need to have a way to use alternative methods or strategies for providing service. For example, you might identify people in your organization who speak languages other than English so that you can call upon them, if necessary. Some larger organizations provide an on-call list of translators who can assist at point-of-sale locations. There is a posted listing in different languages next to the cash register that says something like, "Point to the text that you can read." This allows a service provider to see what language the person speaks and dial a phone code that connects to an appropriate translator.

foreign-born people Refers to people not born in a given country.

Another strategy for dealing with people from other countries is to do research on the Internet and at the library to learn about different cultures or countries. To help accomplish this, you might subscribe to publications that focus on cultural issues and a variety of countries, such as *National Geographic*.[7] If a customer speaks a little English, or has a heavy accent, try the strategies described in the following sections.

Customer Service Success **Tip**

Keep in mind when dealing with people from another cultural background that their reaction to your language and actions depends on how acculturated (familiar with your culture and language) they are. If you are aware of how their culture acts or communicates nonverbally or verbally, it sometimes helps to address people from that perspective in order to show that you respect them and their cultural values and traditions.

When communicating with customers from other cultures, you must monitor your speech pattern and choice of words in order to ensure understanding of what you say. *What are some things you can do to ensure that the message you send is the message received by customers who speak a primary language other than yours?*

Let Your Customer Guide the Conversation

When possible, let your customer take the lead in guiding the service interaction. Some customers may want to spend time getting to know you, others may take a rigid or formal approach and get right down to business by taking the lead, and still others may choose to have someone else act as a mediator or an intermediary. Learn to recognize the cues and follow along when you can.

Be Flexible

Communicating with people from other cultures who do not speak your language fluently can be frustrating and complicated. Even if you do not understand their culture or language, using positive listening, nonverbal, and verbal techniques can help. If you are having difficulties, try some of the specific ideas included in this section of the book.

Part of being flexible is recognizing that your views are not the way of the world. Making the mistake of believing that everyone has the same experiences and sees things the way you do can lead to communication and relationship breakdown. It is probably wise to assume that people from other cultures with whom you come into contact do not have the same knowledge and experience that you have. You can then proceed to share information with each other openly and freely. Listen for points of agreement or commonality.

Listen Patiently

You may be frustrated, but so is the other person. Focus on what he or she is saying and try to understand the meaning of the message and the needs being communicated by your customer.

Speak Clearly and Slowly

Depending on what survey results you view, most adults in the United States speak at a rate of about 125 to 150 words a minute. Other cultures have different rates of speech. The key to successful customer service is to speak at a rate slow enough to allow your customers to understand you without being insulting.

Speak at a Normal Volume and Tone

Yelling or changing tone does nothing to enhance understanding. A customer who is unable to speak your language is not necessarily deaf. You may naturally raise your voice if a customer cannot speak your language, but if you do, the customer may become offended or think that you are hard of hearing and raise his or her voice also. This is not an effective way to communicate or provide effective customer service.

Use Open-End Questions

Open-end questions that typically start with "what," "when," "how," "where," or "why" encourage customers to share information. On the other hand, closed-end questions that start with verbs (e.g., do, did, has, is, are, or will) do not allow you to accurately gauge a customer's viewpoint or understanding. Either because of embarrassment or to avoid saying no, some customers from other cultures may not admit that they do not agree, have an answer, or want to do something if you used a closed-end question. This reluctance can lead to misunderstandings and possibly resentment if you do not recognize a customer's nonverbal signals.

Pause Frequently

Pausing allows your customer to translate what you have said into her or his language, comprehend, and then respond in your language or ask questions.

Use Standard English (or whatever the primary language is for the country in which you are doing business)

Avoid technical terms specific to a product, organization, process, or industry; contractions (e.g., *don't, can't*); slangs (e.g., *like, you know, whoopee, rubberneck*); or broken language (e.g., sentences that fail to follow standard rules of grammar or syntax). Some people, when encountering nonnative-language-speaking customers, revert to an insulting singsong, almost childish, form of communication (e.g., in English, this might sound like, "You wantee me to takee this back?"). This does nothing to aid communication, for it is offensive and any English language that the customer does understands gets lost in translation.

It is helpful to recognize that some people understand your language though they may not be able to speak it well. Also, some people do not speak your language because they are self-conscious about their ability or choose not to out of fear of being embarrassed or losing self-esteem from you or others who hear them. In addition, many cultures (e.g., Asian) value and use silence as an important aspect to communication, something that some people of Western cultures find difficult to understand. Many Westerners often believe that silence means that a person either does not understand or has nothing to add.

A scene in the classic first *Rush Hour* movie, with Chris Tucker and Jackie Chan, is a perfect example of how some people make assumptions about people from other cultures and end up communicating ineffectively. Tucker (playing a Los Angeles police officer) is sent to the airport to pick up a Chinese police officer (Chan). Tucker immediately makes assumptions about Chan's ability to communicate in English:

Tucker [upon meeting Chan]: "Please tell me you speak English."

Chan [gives no response; just looks at a Chinese airline pilot standing next to him]

Tucker [raises his voice]: "I'm Detective Carter. You speaka any English?"

Chan [again looks at others and says nothing]

Tucker [in a loud, exaggerated voice and gesturing toward his mouth]: "Do you understand the words coming out of my mouth?"

Chan [smiles and says nothing]

Later in the movie, as the two are riding in Tucker's car, Chan finally speaks in English.

Tucker: "All of a sudden, you're speaking English now."

Chan: "A little."

Tucker: "You lied to me."

Chan: "I didn't say I didn't speak English. You assumed I didn't. Not being able to speak is not the same as not speaking."

Use Globally Understood References

To reduce the risk of misunderstandings by people who speak your language as a second language, stick with basic verbiage. Avoid jokes, words, or acronyms that are uniquely tied to sports, historical events, or your culture. For example, people from the United States should avoid these types of statements:

- "I will need your John Hancock on this form" (referring to John Hancock signing the Declaration of Independence).
- "If plan A fails, we will drop back and punt" (referring to North American football).
- "We scored a base hit with that proposal yesterday" (referring to baseball).

These phrases might be understood by someone acculturated to the North American society but will likely make no sense to many others.

Be Conscious of Nonverbal Cues

Continually monitor nonverbal reactions as you converse with a customer. If you sense confusion or lack of comprehension, stop and try to reestablish a bond. Also, be aware of the cues you send and make sure that they are in line with your verbal message.

Paraphrase the Customer's Message

After focusing on what you think is the customer's message, you may convey your understanding to the customer in your own words. When you think that you do not understand, either paraphrase the part of the customer's message up to the point at which you did understand or ask clarifying questions. For example, "Mr. Rasheed, I understand your complaint, but I am not sure I understand what you expect us to do. How can I help make this better for you?"

Try Writing Your Message

Some people who speak another primary language understand written English words better than they speak them. If a customer seems to be having trouble understanding what you are saying, try printing your message (legibly) to see if he or she can understand your meaning. You might even try using recognizable symbols, if appropriate (e.g., a stop sign when you are giving directions or a picture of an object if you are describing something).

Try a Different Language

If you speak a second language, try using it. Your nonnative-language-speaking customers may understand, since many countries require students to learn multiple languages in school. At the very least, your customer may appreciate your efforts to communicate with him or her.

Avoid Humor and Sarcasm

Humor and sarcasm are common to many Westerners but do not work well with customers whose first language is not English. They could lead to customer confusion and embarrassment. Differing cultural values and beliefs result in alternative points of view about what is socially acceptable. Also, jokes and other types of humor are typically based on incidents or people connected to a specific culture. They do not "travel well" and may not be understood by someone not of that culture.

Look for Positive Options

Many North Americans are often very direct. Many tend to use an abrupt *no* in response to a request they cannot fulfill. This behavior is viewed as rude, arrogant, and closed-minded in many cultures. Some countries do not even have a literal word in their language for *no* (e.g., Burmese). In many cases (e.g., parts of Asia), the response *no* in a conversation may cause a person embarrassment or loss of personal sense of honor, worth, or self-esteem. Many people try to avoid such embarrassment at all costs. In some instances, people from certain parts of Asia may even say yes to your proposal and then not follow through on your suggestion rather than tell you no. Such behavior is acceptable in some cultures.

If you are dealing with customers who might react to your saying no in these ways—and you must decline—smile, apologize, and then try something like, "I am not sure we can do this" or "That will be difficult to do." Then, offer an alternative.

Customer Service Success Tip

Do not point out the mistake if a customer makes an error or is wrong about something (e.g., improperly fills out a form or uses an incorrect word when speaking). Instead, take responsibility for correcting the error or clearing up the misunderstanding (e.g., "I am sorry that these forms are so confusing. I have trouble with them too." or "I apologize that I did not clearly explain what you needed to do to get a refund."). This strategy allows you to assume responsibility and helps him or her avoid embarrassment (save face). It also sends a nonjudgmental message that you are there to assist the customer.

Use Questions Carefully

As mentioned earlier, phrase questions simply and avoid the use of closed-end questions that require a yes or no. Watch your customer's nonverbal responses so that you will be able to gauge his or her reactions to your questions.

In some cultures, people believe that questioning someone is intrusive, and they therefore avoid it. This is especially true if the questions are personal (e.g., "How is your family?").

Use a Step-by-Step Approach

When explaining something, outline exactly what you will do or what will be expected of the customer. Write this information down for the customer's future reference in order to prevent misunderstandings. If the customer cannot read it, and does not want to admit this out of embarrassment, he or she now has something to take to someone else for translation.

Keep Your Message Brief

Avoid lengthy explanations or details that might frustrate or confuse your customer. Use simple one-syllable words and short sentences. But also avoid being too brisk. Make sure you allow time for interpretation of, translation of, and response to your message.

Check Frequently for Understanding

In addition to using short words and sentences, pause often to verify the customer's understanding of your message before continuing. Avoid questions such as "Do you understand?" Not only can this be answered with a "yes" or "no" as you read in an earlier chapter, but it can also offend someone who speaks and understands English reasonably well. The nonverbal message is that the person may not be smart enough to get your meaning. Instead, try tie-in questions such as "How do you think you will use this?" or others that will give you an indication of whether the customer understands the information you have provided. These types of questions help you and the customer visualize how the information will be put to use. They also give you a chance to find out if the person has misunderstood what you explained.

Keep Smiling

Smiling is a universal language; speak it fluently (when appropriate).

CUSTOMERS WITH DISABILITIES

According to *Disabled World*, approximately 10 percent of the world's population has some type of disability.[8] This is not just an issue in the United States. Around the world, populations are aging. The future impact on societies is going to be huge because these numbers are projected to continue to grow as populations age.

Many People Experience Disabilities at Some Point in Their Lifetime

Some people are born with a disability, others become disabled as a result of an illness or injury, and some people develop them as they age. At some point in our lives almost all of us will have some type of disability.

About 1 in 5 people in America currently has a disability.

33% of 20-year-old workers will become disabled before reaching retirement age.

Over a billion people, around 15% of the world's population, have some form of disability.

Between 110 million and 190 million adults worldwide have significant difficulties in functioning.

Rates of disability are increasing due to population aging and increases in chronic health conditions.

Source: Disabled World, https://www.disabled-world.com/

From a customer service perspective, you will certainly encounter someone in the workplace who has a disability and that may require your assistance in serving him or her.

Some service professionals are uncomfortable working with **customers with disabilities**. This is often because they have had little prior exposure to people who have special needs, they are uninformed about various disabilities, or they have an unfounded fear or anxiety in relating to them.

customers with disabilities
Descriptive phrase that refers to anyone with a physical or mental disability.

Even though you may be unfamiliar with how people with disabilities adapt to life experiences, you should strive to provide excellent service to them. In most cases, customers who have disabilities have learned to accommodate their own personal needs and do not want to be treated differently; they want to be treated equally. Related to this, a point to remember is that many people with disabilities will not disclose the fact out of concern that they might be treated differently or discriminated against. In reality, their disability is the norm for them and they do not see it as big of an issue as someone who does not share their disability or have knowledge about it.

In addition to all the factors you have read about previously, to be effective in dealing with customers in the United States, you must be aware of the **Americans with Disabilities Act of 1990** (ADA), the ADA Amendments Act of 2008, and other legislation passed by Congress to protect individuals and groups.

Americans with Disabilities Act of 1990 A U.S. federal act signed into law in July 1990 guaranteeing people with disabilities equal access to workplace and public opportunities.

Customer Service Success Tip

Do not assume that just because someone has an obvious disability that he or she requires or wants your assistance. Offer assistance, if appropriate, and follow your customer's lead in offering assistance. Unsolicited assistance can be offensive and might even be dangerous if it is unexpected and causes the person to lose his or her balance or distracts him or her.

Legislation similar to the ADA now exists in many other countries as well, so if you work in such an area, you should familiarize yourself with and comply with those laws. You should also understand the court interpretations of these laws that require businesses to provide certain services to customers with disabilities and to make certain premises accessible to them. The laws also often prohibit any form of discrimination or harassment related to a disability.

Since the passage of the ADA, much has been published about the rights of and accommodations for people with disabilities. Figure 8.3 provides general strategies for working with customers and others with disabilities and complying with the ADA. In addition, the following sections discuss specific approaches you can take to work well with people with certain disabilities.

FIGURE 8.3

General Strategies for Servicing Customers with Disabilities

In addition to the suggestions offered in this chapter for serving customers with specific disabilities, here are some general guidelines for success:

- *Be prepared and informed.* You can find a lot of literature and information about disabilities. Do some reading to learn about the capabilities and needs of customers with various disabilities.
- *Be careful not to patronize.* Refrain from talking "down" to customers with disabilities. Just because they have a physical or mental disability does not mean that they cannot help themselves or understand what you are saying. Customers with disabilities should be valued no less as a customer or person than someone who does not exhibit a disability.
- *Treat them equally, not differently.* Just as you would other customers, work to discover their needs and then set about satisfying them.
- *Refer to the person, not the disability.* Instead of referring to *the blind man,* refer to *the man wearing the red shirt* or *the man who is standing by the...,* or, better yet, *the man who needs....*
- *Offer assistance, but do not rush to help without asking.* Just as you would ask someone without a disability whether you might assist him or her, hold a door, or carry a package, do the same for a person with a disability. If he or she declines, drop the issue and move ahead in your service efforts.
- *Be respectful.* The amount of respect you show to all customers should be at a consistently high level. This includes tone of voice (showing patience), gestures, eye contact, and all the other communication techniques you have learned about.

Customers with Hearing Disabilities

hearing disabilities Conditions in which the ability to hear is diminished below established auditory standards.

Hearing loss is common as people age or because of a medical condition and can be a real challenge in service environments. According to the Centers for Disease Control and Prevention (CDC), 40.3 million noninstitutionalized Americans over the age of 18 (16.8 percent of population) have hearing trouble.[9] As people age, this issue will become more prevalent. Remember that customers who have **hearing disabilities** may have special needs, but they also have certain abilities. Do not assume that people who are hearing impaired are helpless. In interactions with such customers, you can do a variety of things to provide effective service:

- Face your customer directly when speaking.
- Speak louder (assuming they only have partial hearing loss).
- Provide written information and instructions where appropriate and possible.
- Use pictures, objects, diagrams, or other such items to communicate more clearly, if appropriate.
- To get the person's attention, use nonverbal cues such as gesturing.
- Use facial expressions and gestures to emphasize key words or express thoughts.
- Enunciate your words and speak slowly so that the customer can see your mouth form words (but do not overexaggerate your mouth's movements).
- Use short sentences and words.
- Check for understanding frequently by using open-end questions to which the customer must provide descriptive answers.
- Communicate in a well-lighted room when possible.
- Watch backlighting (light coming from behind you that can cast a shadow on your face), which may reduce the ability to see your mouth.
- Reduce background noise, if possible.

As the population ages, hearing deficits become more prominent in customers. *How can you ensure that your message is heard and understood when serving someone with a hearing loss?*

Street Talk

I encountered a deaf customer who could not speak and I was totally unprepared to serve him. Due to an inability to speak, he simply pointed at products that he wanted. When I did not comprehend or hesitated, he became obviously aggravated. Luckily, a crew member recognized what was happening and stepped in to serve him. By pointing to products to confirm the customer's preference, and then watching his response, the crew member was able to correctly fulfill the man's order by showing that the two were attuned and "communicating."

This demonstrated the need to do research on people with various disabilities and have a plan developed to serve people before actually encountering a situation where such knowledge and skills are necessary.

SOURCE: TONY PETROVICH, *Restaurant Manager, Dunkin Donuts/Baskin Robbins*

Telecommunications Relay Service (TRS) Through such services, specially trained operators act as intermediaries between people who are deaf, hard-of-hearing, speech disabled, or deaf and blind and standard telephone users.

If you serve customers over the telephone or Internet, you may find yourself interacting with a **Telecommunications Relay Service (TRS)**, also called relay service, relay operator, and IP-relay. Through such services, specially trained operators act as intermediaries between people who are deaf, hard-of-hearing, speech disabled, or deaf and blind and standard telephone users. This is accomplished when a customer with a disability uses a keyboard or assistive device to contact the operator service. Those people then add the intended service provider onto the call and translate messages verbally back and forth between the customer and provider. The customer types comments and the operator then relays them to the service provider. When the provider responds, the operator responds back to the customer in writing. As you can imagine, this is a time-consuming process. If you are contacted by such an operator, be patient and speak slowly so that your message gets translated properly.

Real-Time IM Relay for Customers with Hearing and Speech Loss services are now available to assist people with hearing loss. The relatively new technology has virtually replaced the previous relay services (telecommunications device for the deaf [TDD] or telephone typewriter [TTY]). The new system is currently offered exclusively by AT&T and at no cost to people who sign up for AT&T's Relay Services. Users log in to a specialized AOL AIM interface through an Internet connection on a PC and on a wireless device. Specially trained relay operators read the instant messages to hearing callers and then type IMs, which are displayed—in real time—to the hearing-impaired end user.

Unlike with the previous TTY system, instead of having to wait until a relay operator types a full phrase or sentence and sends it to the recipient, IM users can see the text messages word-by-word as they are typed. In effect, this makes conversations being transmitted seem more like a call that a hearing customer might experience.

Like many other aspects of life involving technology these days, there are people who try to abuse "the system." There are many scam artists (e.g., Nigerian-based con artists) who attempt to use the TRS systems to steal from unsuspecting organizations, especially small businesses. This can create a potential trust issue between you and legitimate customers with disabilities who contact you via an assistance system. Provide quality service whenever you are contacted by a relay operator; however, always beware. To protect your organization, make sure that you receive payment in advance via a credit card or a money order or check (ensure the check clears your bank) before shipping products.

> **Real-Time IM Relay for Customers with Hearing and Speech Loss** Instant messaging system that allows people with hearing loss who have signed up for AT&T's free Relay Service to receive real-time instant messages from callers.

Customers with Vision Disabilities

As with hearing loss, many people experience vision loss because of medical conditions or as a result of the aging process. According to the National Federation of the Blind, almost 7.4 million people (2.3 percent of the population) in the United States between the ages of 16 and 75+ have a visual disability.[10] This means that you are likely to encounter someone with a vision impairment or sight loss on any given day.

Like people who have hearing impairments, customers with **vision disabilities** may need special assistance, but they are not helpless. Depending on your organization's product and service focus, you can do things to assist visually impaired customers. Be aware that, depending on the type of impairment, a person may have limited vision that can be used to advantage when serving him or her.

Here are some strategies to use that can potentially help improve the quality and level of service you provide:

> **vision disabilities** Conditions resulting from lost visual acuity or disability.

- Talk to a person with a visual impairment the same way you would talk to anyone else.

- You do not have to raise your voice; the person is visually impaired, not hard of hearing.

- Do not feel embarrassed or change your vocabulary. It is okay to say things like "Do you see my point?" or "Do you get the picture?"

- Speak directly to the customer.

- Speak to the person as he or she enters the room or approach the person so that he or she knows where you are. Also, introduce others who are present, or at least inform the customer of their presence.

- If appropriate, ask how much sight he or she has and how you can best assist.

- Give very specific information and directions (e.g., "A chair is approximately 10 feet ahead on your left").

- If you are seating the person, face him or her away from bright lights that might interfere with any limited vision he or she may have.

- When walking with someone who is blind, offer your arm. Do not take the person's arm without permission; this could startle him or her. Let the person take your elbow and walk slightly behind you.

- When helping a person who is blind, to a chair, guide his or her hand to the back of the chair. Also, inform the person if a chair has arms to prevent him or her from overturning the chair by leaning or sitting on an arm.

- Leave doors either completely closed or open. Partially open doors pose a danger to visually impaired people.

Customers with Mobility or Motion Impairments

In the United States and Canada, more than 18 million people have limited mobility caused by such things as disease, accidents, and aging. Six million of those people are veterans. Additionally, one in five elderly people struggle with mobility.[11] The term "mobility impairment" typically refers to disabilities that impact someone's ability to move without assistance, manipulate objects, and interact with the physical world. Impairments may affect the person's movement of head, hands, body, legs, and/or feet and could impact his or her coordination or balance and sensation or ability to feel. Mobility-impaired users include those who are confined to bed, use a wheelchair or other assistive device to navigate, or have permanently incapacitated or reduced hand movements. Causes range for mobility impairments. Someone might have had an accident or may have a disabling disease such as spina bifida, muscular dystrophy, or cerebral palsy.

mobility or motion impairments Physical limitations that some people have, requiring accommodation or special consideration to allow access to products or services.

Customers who have **mobility or motion impairments** often use specially designed equipment and have had extensive training in how to best use assistive devices to compensate for the loss of the use of some part of their body. You can best assist them by offering to help and then following their lead or instructions. Do not make the

The number of people with mobility impairments is on the rise. What are some strategies that you can use to better serve customers with a mobility impairment?

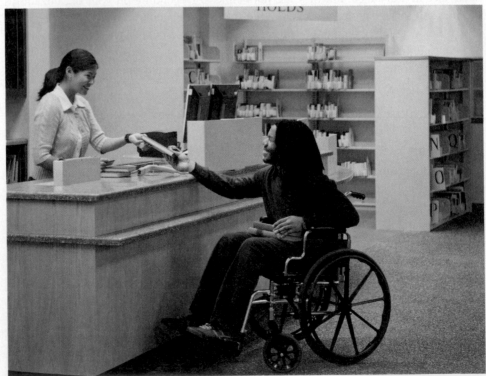

©Andersen Ross/Blend Images RF

assumption that they need your assistance and then set about giving it. You can cause injury if you upset their balance or routine. Here are some strategies for better serving these customers:

- Prior to a situation in which you may have to accommodate someone who uses a walker, wheelchair, crutches, or other device, do an environmental survey of your workplace. Note areas where space is inadequate to permit mobility (a minimum of 36 inches is needed for a standard wheelchair) or where hazards exist. If you can correct the situation, do so. For example, move or bring in a different table or chair or rearrange furniture for better access. Otherwise, make suggestions for improvements to the proper people in your organization. Remind them that the ADA and state regulations require an organization to accommodate customers with such disabilities.

- Do not assume that someone who has such an impairment cannot perform certain tasks. As mentioned earlier, people who have disabilities are often given extensive training. They have learned how to overcome obstacles and perform various tasks in different ways.

- Make sure that you place information or materials at a level that makes it possible for the person to see without undue strain (e.g., eye level for someone in a wheelchair so that he or she does not have to look up).

- Do not push or lean on someone's wheelchair without his or her permission.

> **Customer Service Success Tip**
>
> Stand or sit so that you can make direct eye contact with a person in a wheelchair without forcing the person to look up at an uncomfortable angle for extended periods. This reduces discomfort and neck strain on his or her part.

ELDERLY CUSTOMERS

Being older does not make a person or a customer less valuable. In fact, many older customers are in excellent physical and mental shape, are still employed, and have more time to be active now than when they were younger. Studies show that aging citizens have more disposable income now than at any other time in history. And, as the **baby boomer** population (people born between 1946 and 1964) ages, there are more older Americans than ever. U.S. Census reports indicate that "the population is projected to age over the coming decades, with a higher proportion of the nation's total population in the older ages (65 and over). Overall, the percentage of the total population that is under the age of 18 is projected to decrease from 23 percent to 20 percent between 2014 and 2060. Similarly, the working-age population is projected to decrease from 62 percent to 57 percent of the total population over the same interval. In contrast, the percentage of the population that is aged 65 and over is expected to grow from 15 percent to 24 percent, an increase of 9 percentage points."[12] Moreover, as the population ages, there will be a greater need for services—and service providers—to care for people and allow them to enjoy a good quality of life.

> **baby boomer** A term applied to anyone born between 1946 and 1964. People in this age group are called "boomers."

Be Respectful

As you would with any customer, be respectful. Even if the customer seems a bit arrogant, disoriented, or disrespectful, do not lose your professionalism. Recognize that sometimes these behaviors are a response to perceptions based on your cues. When this happens, quickly evaluate your behavior and make adjustments, if necessary. If an older customer seems abrupt in his or her response, think about whether you might have nonverbally signaled impatience because of your perception that he or she was slow in acting or responding.

WORK IT OUT 8.2

Identifying Resources

Check with local advocacy groups or on the Internet for information on the types of accommodations you might make for people with various disabilities and how best to interact with people who have specific disabilities (e.g., sight, mobility, hearing impairment). Collect and read literature on the subject. Share the information with other students and/or coworkers (if you currently work in a customer service environment).

What to look for:

Definitions of various disabilities

Strategies for better communication

Accommodations necessary to allow customer access to products and services

Resources available (e.g., tools, equipment, training, or organizations)

Bibliographic information on disabilities (e.g., books or articles)

Customer Service Success Tip

Use the following strategies to help enhance communication with all customers:

- Face the person.
- Talk slowly and enunciate words clearly (but do not overexaggerate your mouth's movements).
- Keep your hands away from your mouth.
- Talk without food or chewing gum in your mouth.
- Observe the customer's nonverbal cues.
- Reword statements or ask questions again, if necessary.
- Be positive, be patient, and practice the good listening skills covered in Chapter 5.
- Stand near good lighting, and keep background noise to a minimum, when possible.

If an interpreter is with the customer, talk to the customer and not the interpreter. The interpreter will know what to do.

Be Patient

Allow older customers the time to look around, respond, react, or ask questions. Value their decisions. Also, keep in mind that as some people age, their ability to process information lessens and their attention span becomes shorter. Do not assume that this is true of all older customers, but be patient when it does occur.

Answer Questions

Providing information to customers is crucial in order to help them make reasonable decisions. Even though you may have just explained something, listen to the customer's questions, respond, and restate. If it appears that the customer has misunderstood, try repeating the information, possibly using slightly different words.

Try Not to Sound Patronizing

If you appear to talk down to older customers, problems could arise and you could lose a customer. Customers who are elderly should not be treated as if they are senile! A condescending attitude will often cause any customer, elderly or otherwise, to take his or her business elsewhere.

Remain Professional

Common courtesy and professionalism should always be extended to customers without regard for their age. Words such as please, thank you, yes sir/ma'am, and other such pleasantries can go a long way in building customer–provider relationships and show that you respect and appreciate your customers.

Unfortunately, some service representatives get caught up in being overfamiliar with customers, especially if they seem easy-going and kind. This is a common error for many people in more informal cultures such as in the United States. Do not let yourself fall into the trap of addressing older customers accompanied by their children or grandchildren with "Good morning, Grandma" or some similar comment just because one of their family members used that language. Such an approach is unprofessional, inappropriate, disrespectful, and rude. It is also likely to offend either the person whom you are addressing or his or her companion. Additionally, avoid overly familiar terms of address, such as "Here is your change partner" or "I hear you brother" that you might use with friends or in peer groups.

Guard against Biases

Be careful not to let biases about older people interfere with good service. Do not ignore or offend older customers by making statements such as "Hang on, old timer. I'll be with you in a minute." Such a statement might be in jest, but nonetheless it is potentially offensive to the person, and to others who might hear it. Similarly, do not use such age-based comments when referring to an older coworker or external customer since these might be overheard by others and may cause people to form opinions about your level of professionalism or your beliefs regarding older people as a result. Either could cause problems in the workplace and ultimately impact service potential.

YOUNGER CUSTOMERS

You have heard the various terms describing the "younger generation"—Generation Y, Nexters, MTV generation, Millennial Generation (1981–2000), or cyber kids. Whatever the term, this group follows Generation X (born 1964–1980) and is now in the workplace in great numbers as employees and consumers. The youngest members of this group were born in 2000 and are now teenagers while the oldest members of the generation are over 30 years of age. Many of these older Gen Yers now have children of their own, who you may also end up serving.

Financially, the group accounts for billions of dollars in business revenue for products such as clothes, music, videos, electronic entertainment equipment, and entertainment consumption. Generation Y is a spending force to be reckoned with, and marketers are going after them with a vengeance. If you do not believe this, pick up a magazine and look at the faces of the models, look at the products being sold, and watch the shows being added to television lineups each year. All of this affects the way you will provide service to this generation of customers. Depending on your own age, your attitude toward them will vary. If you are of Gen Y, you may make the mistake of being overly familiar with your age group in delivering service.

> **Street Talk**
>
> Different cultures and different ways of doing things in a business today mean that you need to be a wealth of information about how to work positively with your colleagues, your customers, and the management team in your company. If you work with a diverse population, study the cultures in the resources you can locate in the library or on the Internet.
>
> **SOURCE: SHARON MASSEN, Ph.D., CAP** *Massen and Associates*

Younger customers can often have a completely different set of needs. *What are some effective strategies for handling customers of a younger generation?*

©Dan Dalton/Getty Images RF

younger customers Subjective term referring to anyone younger than the service provider. Sometimes used to describe members of Generation X (born to baby boomers) or later.

If you are a Gen Xer, you may potentially treat members of this generation as you would your own children. Be careful not to do this or to come across as domineering or controlling since this will likely irritate your customer(s).

If you are a baby boomer or older, you may feel paternalistic or maternalistic or might believe some of the stereotypical rhetoric about this group (e.g., low moral values, fragmented in focus, lack motivation, and overprotected by legislation and programs). Although some of these descriptions may be accurate for some members of the group, it is dangerous to pigeonhole any group or individual, as you have read. This is especially true when addressing customer expectations, since quality service is based on satisfying personal needs and wants.

Remember when you were young and felt that adults did not understand or care about your wants or needs? Well, your **younger customers** probably feel the same way and will remember how you treat them. Their memories could prompt them to take their business elsewhere if their experience with you is negative.

If you are older, you may be tempted to talk down to them or be flippant. Do not give in to the temptation. Keep in mind that they are customers. If they feel unwelcome, they will take their business and money elsewhere, and they will tell their friends about the poor treatment they received. Just as with older customers, avoid demeaning language and condescending forms of address (*kid, sonny, sweetie, sugar,* or *young woman/man*).

An additional point to remember when dealing with younger customers is that they may not have the product knowledge and sophistication in communicating that older customers might have. You can decrease confusion and increase communication effectiveness by using words that are appropriate for their age group and by taking the time to explain and/or demonstrate technical points. Keep it simple without being patronizing if you are older than your customers and make sure not to allow any frustration to show in your tone of voice.

WORK IT OUT 8.3

Serving a Variety of Customers

Pair up with a peer and use the following scenarios as the basis of role-plays to give you practice and feedback in dealing with various categories of customers. Before beginning, discuss how you might deal with each customer in a real-life situation. After the role-plays, both persons should answer the following questions and discuss any ideas for improvement.

Questions

1. How well do you feel that service was provided?
2. Were any negative or unclear messages, verbal or nonverbal, communicated? If yes, discuss.
3. What open-end questions were used to discover customer needs? What others could have been used?
4. How can identified areas for improvement be incorporated into a real customer service encounter?

Scenario 1

You are an airport shuttle driver and just received a call from your dispatcher to proceed to 8172 Dealy Lane to pick up Cassandra Fenton. You were told that Ms. Fenton is blind and will need assistance getting her bags from the house to the bus. Upon arrival, you find Ms. Fenton waiting on her front porch with her bags.

Scenario 2

Mrs. Zagowski is 62 years old and is in the library where you are working at the circulation desk. As you observe her, you notice that she seems a bit frustrated and confused. You saw her browse through several aisles of books, then talk briefly with the reference librarian, and finally go to the computer containing the publication listings and their locations. You are going to try to assist her. Upon meeting her, you realize that she has a hearing deficit and has difficulty hearing what you are saying.

Scenario 3

You are the owner of a small hobby shop that specializes in coins, stamps, comics, and sports memorabilia. Tommy Chin, whom you recognize as a regular "browser," has come in while you are particularly busy. After looking through numerous racks of comic books and trading cards, he is now focused on autographed baseballs in a display case. You believe that he cannot afford them, although he is asking about prices and requesting other information about the cards.

KNOWLEDGE CHECK

- What are some strategies that you might use to ensure effective communication with your customers who speak a primary language other than your own?
- How can you better assist customers who have a hearing disability?
- What are some ways that you can better serve customers with vision impairments?
- What should you remember to do when serving older customers?
- How should you approach and interact with customers who are younger than you?

LO 8-6 Communicating with Diverse Customers

CONCEPT Many considerations need to be taken into account when you are delivering service to a diverse customer base. Appropriate language usage is a meaningful tool that you should master for good customer service.

Given all this diversity that you have read about, you must be wondering how to provide service that is acceptable to all of these customer groups. As you have seen, there are many considerations in delivering service to a diverse customer base. Therefore, consider the following basic guidelines for communicating; these tips are appropriate for dealing with all types of customers.

> ### Customer Service Success Tip
>
> Learn as much technology as you can if you plan to effectively provide service to members of Generations X and Y, since they are very technically savvy. Technology examples include smartphones, iPads, computer hardware and software, Internet options and services, social media, and service delivery technology such as **wikis**, **blogs** (web logs), and **podcasts**.

wiki A website that allows nontechnical personnel to create and edit website pages using any web browser and without complex programming knowledge. These An interactive websites allow where users are freedom to in adding, modifying, or deleteing information. Because of the casual and flexible nature of such sites, many people, especially educators, do not consider them a valid resource.

blogs Online journals (web logs) or diaries that allow people to add content. Many organizational websites use them to post "what's new" sections and to receive feedback (good and bad) from customers and website visitors.

podcasts A word that is a derivative of Apple® Computer's iPod® media player and the term *broadcasting*. Through podcasts, websites can offer direct download or streaming of their content (i.e., music or video files) to customers or website users.

inclusive The concept of ensuring that people of all races, genders, and religious and ethnic backgrounds, as well as a multitude of other diverse factors, are included in communications and activities in the workplace.

Be Careful with Your Remarks and Jokes

Comments that focus on any aspect of diversity (religion, sexual preference, weight, hair color, age) can be offensive and should not be made. Also, humor does not cross cultural boundaries well. Each culture has a different interpretation of what is humorous and socially acceptable.

Make Sure That Your Language Is "Inclusive"

When speaking, address or refer to the people from various groups that are present. If you are addressing a group of two men and one woman, using the term *guys* or *fellows* excludes the woman and thus is not **inclusive**.

Respect Personal Preferences When Addressing People

As you read earlier, do not assume familiarity when addressing others. (Do not call someone by her or his first name unless she or he gives permission.) Do not use *Ms.* if a female customer prefers another form of address. Also, avoid derogatory or demeaning terms such as *honey*, *sugar*, and *sweetheart* or other overly familiar language with either gender.

Use General Terms

Instead of singling a customer out or focusing on exceptions in a group, describe people in general terms. That is, instead of referring to someone as a *female supervisor*, *black salesperson*, or *disabled administrative assistant*, say *supervisor*, *salesperson*, or *administrative assistant*.

Recognize the Impact of Words

Keep in mind that certain words have a negative connotation and could insult or offend. Even if you do not intend to offend, the customer's perception is the deciding factor of your actions. For example, using the derogatory or demeaning terms, such as *handicapped* or *crippled*, *boy*, *girl*, *homo*, *retard*, or *idiot* may conjure up a negative image to some groups or individuals and label you as unprofessional, biased, and inconsiderate. Using such terminology can also reflect negatively upon you and your organization and should never be used.

Use Care with Nonverbal Cues

The nonverbal cues that you are familiar with may carry different meanings in other cultures. Be careful when you use symbols or gestures if you are not certain how your customer will receive them. Figure 8.4 lists some cues that are common in Western cultures but have negative meanings in other cultures.

FIGURE 8.4

Nonverbal Cue Meanings

The following are symbols and gestures that are commonly used in the United States but have different—and negative or offensive—meanings in other parts of the world.

American Gesture or Symbol	Meaning in Other Cultures	Country
Beckoning by curling and uncurling index finger*†	Used for calling animals or ladies of the evening	Australia, Hong Kong, Indonesia, Malaysia, Yugoslavia
V for victory sign (with palm facing you)*‡	Rude gesture	England
Sole of foot pointed toward a person*‡	You are lowly (the sole is the lowest part of the body and contacts the ground)	Egypt, Saudi Arabia, Singapore, Thailand
"Halt" gesture with palm and extended fingers thrust toward someone*†‡	Rude epithet	Greece
Thumb up (fingers curled) indicating *okay, good going, or everything is fine**‡	The number 5; rude gesture	Australia, Nigeria, Japan
Thumb and forefinger forming an O, meaning okay*‡	Zero or worthless; money; rude gesture	Brazil, France, Greece, Italy, Japan, Malta, Paraguay, Russia, Tunisia, Turkey
Waving good-bye with fingers extended, palm down, and moving the fingers up and down toward yourself*‡	Come here	Parts of Europe, Colombia, Myanmar, Peru
Patting the head of a child	Insult; inviting evil spirits	Parts of the Far East
Using red ink for documents	Death; offensive	Parts of China, Korea, and Mexico
Passing things with left hand (especially food)	Socially unacceptable	India, Pakistan

*R. Axtell, *Gestures: The Do's and Taboos of Body Language around the World* (New York: John Wiley and Sons, 1991).
†A. Wolfgang, *Everybody's Guide to People Watching* (Yarmouth, MA: International Press, Yarmouth, 1995).
‡D. Morris, *Bodytalk: The Meaning of Human Gestures* (New York: Crown Trade Paperback, 1994).

KNOWLEDGE CHECK

1. What are some strategies that you might use to ensure effective communication with all types of customers?

Small Business Perspective

In order for small businesses to compete effectively with larger ones, they must utilize all resources available to them. That means that they must openly embrace a diverse workforce and learn more about people from various cultures, races, generations, genders, religions, and other diverse factors. In addition, employees have to be aware of the laws regarding fair and equitable treatment of others. By recognizing the needs and preferences of different groups and individuals, employers can better prepare their employees, products, and services to address what customers want and expect.

Part of the initiative to prepare to better deal with diversity involves providing training and job aids that can support employees as they serve customers. Programs such as effective multicultural communication, cultural sensitivity, diversity awareness, behavioral styles, and others that provide insights into how people behave, what they value and believe, their special needs, and any cultural background information are valuable in educating employees about others.

By doing research on the products and services desired and typically used by various groups of customers, small business employees can become a valuable resource for those seeking specific products and services. This can lead to them being recognized as a prime source or organization that specializes in particular products or in the delivery of culturally and group-specific products and can help them stand out from the competitive crowd.

Impact on Service

Based on personal experience and what you just read, answer the following questions:

1. What specific customer needs might employees of a small business have to meet? Explain.

2. How does the changing demographic environment impact the ability of small businesses to compete for customers? Explain.

3. If you worked for a small business, what do you think you would need to know in order to deliver appropriate service to a diverse customer base? Explain.

ISMARTBOOK™　**Use SmartBook to help you read, study, and retain what you have learned. Access Smart-Book in your Instructor's Connect course, or go to connect.mheducation.com for help.**

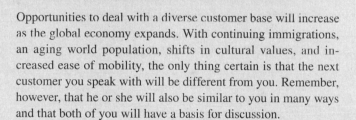

Key Terms

acculturated

Americans with Disabilities Act of 1990

attitudes

baby boomer

beliefs

blogs

Chicano culture

collective cultures

concept of time

conflict resolution style

cultural diversity

customers with disabilities

diversity

expectations of privacy

face

foreign-born people

form of address

gender roles

hearing disabilities

Hispanic culture

inclusive

individualistic cultures

interpersonal relationship

Latino culture

mobility or motion impairments

modesty

monochronic

namaste

ownership of property

Platinum Rule

podcasts

polychronic

Real-Time IM Relay for Customers with Hearing and Speech Loss

respect for elders

Telecommunications Relay Service (TRS)

values

vision disabilities

wai

wiki

younger customers

Summary

Opportunities to deal with a diverse customer base will increase as the global economy expands. With continuing immigrations, an aging world population, shifts in cultural values, and increased ease of mobility, the only thing certain is that the next customer you speak with will be different from you. Remember, however, that he or she will also be similar to you in many ways and that both of you will have a basis for discussion.

The success you have in the area of dealing with others is totally dependent on your preparation and attitude toward providing quality service. Learn as much as you can about various groups of people in order to effectively evaluate situations, determine needs, and serve all customers on an equal basis.

Review Questions

1. What are some innate qualities or characteristics that make people unique?

2. What external or societal factors affect the way members of a group are seen or perceived?

3. What are values?

4. Do beliefs differ from values? Explain.

5. Why would some people be reluctant to make eye contact with you?

6. When dealing with customers with a disability, how can you best help them?

7. How can recognition of the cultural value of "importance of family" be helpful in customer service?

8. What are some considerations for improving communication in a diverse environment?

9. How can you effectively communicate with someone who has difficulty with the English language?

10. What are some techniques for effectively providing service to older customers?

Search It Out

1. **Search the Internet for Diversity Information**

   Search the Internet to locate information and articles related to topics covered in this chapter. Be prepared to share what you found at your next scheduled class or session. The following are some key words you might use in your search:

   Any country name (e.g., Australia, Canada, Sri Lanka)

   Any religion (e.g., Muslim, Hindu, Buddhist, Christian)

   Baby boomers

   Beliefs

   Cultural diversity

   Cultural values

   Disabilities

   Disability advocacy

   Diversity

   Elderly

   Generation X

   Generation Y

   Intercultural communication

   Intercultural dynamics

   IP-Relay

   Jellabiya

   Population projections

   Relay operator

   Relay Service

   Telecommunications Device for the Deaf (TDD)

   Telecommunications Relay Service (TRS)

   Telephone typewriter (TTY)

   Turban

2. **YouTube Search**

   Visit YouTube and conduct a search for video segments related to diversity and customer service. Search terms such as:

   Communicating with people from different cultures

   Gender roles in different cultures

   Dealing with diverse customers

   Dealing with customers with disabilities

   Dealing with customers from (insert various country names)

   Multicultural customer service

   Improving relationships with (fill in a category such as people with disabilities, customers from _____)

   Search https://www.youtube.com/watch?v=-RF0lavUcvk as a starting point. Take notes as you view numerous videos and be prepared to share what you learn with your classmates.

3. **Additional Resources**

   For additional articles and information on dealing with a diverse customer base, visit the author's Customer Service Skills Blog at http://www.customerserviceskillsbook.com/wordpress and search "Diverse Customer Service" and related topics.

Collaborative Learning Activity

Awareness of Diversity

To help raise your awareness of diversity in the customer service environment, try the following activities:

1. Pair up with someone to role-play scenarios in which you are a service provider and have customers from the following groups:

   An elderly person who has a hearing loss and wants directions on how to use some equipment (you choose the equipment and provide instruction)

   Someone who speaks English as a second language (with a heavy accent) and needs to fill out a credit card application or some other form

   Someone with a sight impairment who wants to "see" several blouses or shirts or needs directions to another part of your store

   A 10-year-old who wants a new computer and has questions about various types, components, and how they work

2. Interview a variety of people: from different cultures, from various age groups, with disabilities, male or female (opposite of your sex), or gay or lesbian. Find out whether they have preferences in the type of customer service they receive or in the kind of language used to refer to their group. Also, ask about ways you can better communicate with and understand them and people from their group.

3. Suggest to your supervisor, team leader, or workgroup peers that employees meet as a group to discuss situations in which all of you have encountered people from different cultures or groups. Exchange ideas on how to better serve such people in the future. Report the results of your efforts to your class members at the next scheduled meeting.

4. Working in teams assigned by your instructor, set up an appointment to visit a local advocacy group for people with disabilities or aging, or contact a national group (e.g., the National Society to Prevent Blindness, assisted-living facilities, World Federation of the Deaf, National Information Center on

Deafness, National Eye Institute, National Institute on Aging). Focus on gathering information that will help you understand various disabilities and develop strategies for effectively communicating with and serving people who have disabilities. Write a brief summary of your experience and report back to your peers.

Face to Face

Dealing with Difficult People on the Phone at MedMobile

Background

MedMobile is a medical supply business located in Los Angeles employing 62 full-time and 11 part-time workers. The company specializes in equipment designed to improve patient mobility (walkers, motorized carts, wheelchairs, mechanized beds, and chairs). Average yearly sales are in the area of $1.5 million.

The primary client base for the company is insurance companies that pay for rehabilitation after worker accidents or injuries. Medical professionals who conduct the patient's medical case file reviews and recommend treatment programs are in regular contact with the account representatives for MedMobile.

Your Role

As an account representative with MedMobile, you have been with the company for about 18 months. Your main job is to help clients determine and obtain the correct equipment needed to assist their patients. To do this, you spend hours on the phone daily and often know clients by voice. You have become extremely frustrated in the past month, almost to the point of anger. A new claims adjuster works for one of your primary account companies, TrueCare Insurance Company. His name is Abeyola Pepukayi, and he has been with TrueCare for 8 weeks. He has been an adjuster for a little over a year.

You just got off the phone after a lengthy conversation with Abeyola and you are agitated. For over half an hour, you tried unsuccessfully to explain why you felt the equipment being ordered by Abeyola was not the best for the patient's injury, as he described it to you.

Because this is not the first time such an encounter has taken place, you are now in your supervisor's office venting. While discussing the situation with your boss, you note the following about Abeyola:

- He does not listen. No matter what you say, he asks totally irrelevant questions about other equipment.

- He usually has no idea what you are talking about.

- He is rude and interrupts, often making statements such as "One moment, please. That makes no sense."

- You have spent hours discussing equipment design and function because he does not know anything about it.

- He spends endless amounts of time getting off track and trying to discuss other issues or topics.

After your conversation, your boss called a friend at TrueCare to see what he knew of the situation. The friend, David Helmstedter, supervises Abeyola. Apparently, Abeyola has been venting to David about you. From what David has been told:

- You are rude and abrupt and are not very friendly. Abeyola has tried to establish a relationship, but you have ignored his efforts.

- Abeyola is trying hard to learn the terminology and equipment, but you are unwilling to help.

- You speak rapidly, using a lot of technical language that you do not explain.

Critical Thinking Questions

1. What seems to be happening here? Does Abeyola have any legitimate complaints? If so, what are they?

2. What steps or process can you use to clarify understanding?

3. What cultural differences might be involved in this scenario?

Planning to Serve

Identifying Your Biases

We sometimes have biases that interfere with our interactions with others. Typically, these biases are learned behavior (something we have personally experienced or have been taught by others). By thinking of your biases and bringing them to a conscious level, you can better control or eliminate them in dealing with your customers and others.

Think about the qualities of other people or groups that you do not like or prefer to avoid. List them, along with the basis (why you believe them to be true) for each.

Share your list with other students and discuss their potential impact on service.

Quick Preview Answers

1. T	3. T	5. T	7. T	9. F	11. T
2. T	4. T	6. F	8. T	10. T	12. T

Ethical Dilemma Summary

Ethical Dilemma 8.1 Possible Answers

1. Does the man's dress or the other employee's comments make a difference in this situation? Explain why or why not.

   Even though we live in a global society where someone can get on a plane and be on the other side of the world within 24 hours, a majority of people in any country have never traveled outside their own borders. They also have little or no contact with people from different ethnic groups or cultures, and have not taken the time to do research on the dress, values, religion, beliefs, and other aspects of other groups. The result is quite honestly ignorance that is often supplanted by negative stereotypes seen in the media, on television, in movies, and from their like-minded, uneducated peers.

   In this instance, the people involved might be reacting to post-9/11 stereotypes that "all of those people" are terrorists simply because they look similar, have the same religion, or come from the same country or geographic region. In reality, nothing is further from the truth. Like any other service situation, this customer should be evaluated based on one-on-one contact and information provided, and not on potentially irrational and unprofessional decisions.

2. What action should you take, if any? Why or why not?

   As a service professional, you should be polite, attentive, and responsive to all customers. Additionally, as an employee of any type of organization (retail or otherwise) you should take ownership of your environment. After all, your employer pays you to be professional and alert on the job. In this situation, the customer seems to be acting in an unusual and possibly suspicious manner. Certainly, security is a concern for anyone these days. You would be correct and prudent to monitor the man's actions and to notify your supervisor, a coworker, and/or security of the situation just in case the person is up to some unlawful or otherwise inappropriate activity. Because of potential risk, you should not confront such a person yourself, and certainly not alone without others watching the situation.

   Any action you take would likely be precautionary to prevent loss (financial or physical) to your organization, yourself, and others. Also, in the event that the person is really up to illegal activity, you would likely be doing it out of concern for safety (yours and others).

3. Does the conversation that you had with your coworker have any bearing on the course of action you choose in this situation? Explain.

   Obviously, such conversations raise awareness and possibilities in your mind; however, since the customer has displayed friendly actions (smiling) and has not done anything other customers might do, you should continue to be professional and courteous.

4. What are possible repercussions if you either act or decide not to act?

   If you fail to act and the person is engaged in some unlawful or mischievous activity, you, others, and the organization could sustain loss, damage, and possible injury. If you do act and the man is not doing anything more than "killing time," the person's perception could be that you are targeting him and potentially could become upset or even claim some sort of discrimination. You could also lose his business and that of anyone to whom he relates his experience.

5. If the person was dressed differently, would you take a different course of action? Explain.

   Truthfully, no matter how a customer is dressed, you should always maintain a positive, attentive, and professional manner. Should other factors (e.g., actions or comments) by the customer indicate that you should treat him or her otherwise, then you should act accordingly (e.g., ask him or her to leave or request assistance from a supervisor, peer, or security).

Ethical Dilemma 8.2 Possible Answers

1. Have you ever witnessed similar situations in the workplace? Explain.

   Spend some time discussing your experience(s) with other students along with the results of such behavior.

2. From a service perspective, is this situation a problem? Explain.

   Even though the customer may not have heard the remarks in this situation, this is unacceptable behavior. You (and possibly others, including customers) may have overheard the remarks. As a service provider, employees represent not only themselves, but also the organization. People form opinions based on what they see workers do and say. This type of incident can lead to lost business, negative word-of-mouth publicity, and claims of defamation and discrimination. Not only is there potential for financial loss, but also damage to the reputation of the service providers involved, other workers, and the organization.

3. What would you do or say about the incident that you just witnessed? Explain.

   At the very least, you should intervene to point out that the language is disrespectful, derogatory, and discriminatory and can cause problems for the two employees, others at the organization, and the organization itself. Depending on the reaction you get when approaching the others, you may need to escalate this matter to your supervisor for appropriate action.

4. If you fail to act in this situation, what are possible repercussions? What about if you do act?

   Failure to act to correct this situation can create a number of issues. First, you recognize that what happened is ethically and morally wrong. Failing to act is likely to have a personal impact on your conscious and impact your perceptions as a professional as guilt possibly seeps into your thinking. What you witnessed is unprofessional and as a representative of the organization, you have a responsibility to protect the assets and reputation of the company. Failure to do so might cause damage to the company and lead to negative publicity, especially if the incident is shared with others or on social media and other people become aware of what happened. If it becomes apparent that you knew of the incident and did nothing to intervene, you become complicit in the act and may even experience repercussions should your boss or others find out. On the other hand, if you do take action by either speaking up to your coworkers or reporting the incident to a supervisor, you could experience other fallout. You might become alienated from the two employees your witnessed and other employees who share their views or consider you a "snitch." Thus, the level of trust between you and others could suffer. That can have an impact on your ability to interact with other employees and get your job done effectively. In some extreme cases, your coworkers might even retaliate in some way (e.g. physically, emotionally, in a harassing manner, or they might try to undermine you as an employee to make you look bad). On the positive side, if you report the incident or speak to your coworkers, you might enhance your level of self-esteem while gaining merit in the eyes of others. By pointing out a wrong in dealing with others and helping them see your perspective you might even help sway your coworkers attitude toward those who might seem different from them. You might even be rewarded by your supervisor for your professionalism and attention to doing the right thing when dealing with customers.

Customer Service via Technology

"In the world of Internet customer service, it's important to remember that your competitor is only one mouse click away."
—Source: Doug Warner

©Chuck Pefley/Alamy Stock Photo

LEARNING OUTCOMES

After completing this chapter, you will be able to:

9-1 Recognize the role of technology-effective service delivery.

9-2 Describe ways in which technology enhances an organization's service delivery capabilities.

9-3 Discuss ways in which companies are integrating the evolving web-based and mobile technologies into their service strategies.

9-4 Communicate effectively via e-mail, the Internet, and fax.

9-5 Deliver quality service through effective telephone techniques.

Use SmartBook to help you read, study, and retain what you have learned. Access SmartBook in your Instructor's Connect course, or go to connect.mheducation.com for help. ■ SMARTBOOK™

IN THE REAL WORLD TECHNOLOGY—MICROSOFT

Mission Statement: At Microsoft, "Our mission is to empower every person and every organization on the planet to achieve more."

Source: Mission of Microsoft

According to the Microsoft website, the organization was founded by Bill Gates in 1975 in Albuquerque, New Mexico and is now "the worldwide leader in software services, devices, and solutions to help people and businesses reach their full potential." (Source: Microsoft) Headquartered in Redmond, Washington, the company incorporated in 1981 and went public in 1986. It continues to be a technology megaforce, rolling out a continual stream of new and updated products every year. As most people recognize, the company's name and products are synonymous with computing. For example, there are now more than 1.2 billion people in 140 countries and 107 languages using Microsoft Office. Additionally, there are more than 400 million devices running Windows 10 in 192 countries across the world. Some of the company's more familiar products and services include Office suite, Bing search engine, Office 365Xbox, Kinect, Windows Phone, Skype, Surface Pro, and Microsoft Cloud.

A unique factor related to Microsoft is that its developer Bill Gates is a recognized philanthropist who strives to give back to the world. The Bill and Melinda Gates Foundation was established in 2000. It is potentially the largest transparently operated private foundation in the world. The foundation's purpose is to provide enhanced health care worldwide, help reduce extreme poverty, and increase educational opportunities and access to information technology. As of 2016, Bill Gates had donated over $28 billion to the organization.

In addition to personal contributions, Microsoft also provides millions of dollars in company resources. This funding is dedicated to creating and expanding tools for people with special needs to make sure that technology and information is available to everyone. The company donates more than $2.6 million in software each day to more than 86,000 nonprofit groups around the world. In addition, there are teams of computer scientists, programmers, engineers, and other experts working with scientists and researchers around the world to develop algorithms and computers that can help identify new ways to enhance cancer research and process information that can help doctors develop more targeted treatments for the disease. Employees are also into the giving mode and have donated more than $1 billion to over 31,000 charities.

On an organizational level, Microsoft has been a leader in workplace diversity. In addition to programs and support efforts for women, Latino/Hispanics, Asians, blacks, and other diverse groups, the organization was one of the first companies in the world to provide same-sex domestic partner benefits. Today, there are over 2,000 members in its GLEAM employee resource group working for its lesbian, gay, bisexual, and transgender workers. In 2009, the company formed its disability employee resource group to help represent the interests of employees, family, and friends with disabilities. It also holds an annual Ability Summit and continues to work on initiatives that improve products and services to support the needs of customers with disabilities.

For additional information about Microsoft, visit http://www.microsoft.com and do an Internet search for the company name and products and for Bill Gates.

Think About It

Based on this organization's profile, answer the following questions and be prepared to discuss your responses.

1. From your personal experiences as a customer, information that you just read, and what you found on the Internet, what do you feel are the strengths of the company? Explain.

2. What societal factors do you feel have influenced Microsoft and contributed to its popularity and growth? Explain the relationship of these factors to Microsoft's growth.

3. What do you think are some future opportunities for growth related to customer service at Microsoft? Explain.

4. As a consumer, are you a fan of Microsoft and what it has accomplished? Why or why not?

5. As a current customer or potential customer, what do you think about Microsoft's approach to business? Explain your views.

6. Would you want to work for Microsoft? Why or why not?

Quick Preview

Before reviewing the chapter content, respond to the following questions by placing a "T" for true or an "F" for false on the rules. Use any questions you miss as a checklist of material to which you will pay particular attention as you read the chapter. For those you get right, give yourself a pat on the back, but review the sections they address in order to learn additional details about the topic.

_____ 1. According to the Cellular Telecommunications Industry Association, over 276 million people in the United States subscribe to a wireless telephone service.

_____ 2. E-commerce is a term that means that the commerce of the United States is in excellent condition.

_____ 3. A customer service representative might also have one of the following job titles: associate, sales representative, consumer affairs counselor, consultant, technical service representative, operator, account executive, attendant, or engineer.

_____ 4. The acronym TTY is used by call center staff members to indicate that something is to be done today.

_____ 5. Businesses have not yet learned to harness the power of web-based and mobile technologies to serve their customers.

_____ 6. Many organizations think of technology as a way to reduce staff and save money.

_____ 7. One way to improve your image over the telephone is to evaluate your speech regularly.

_____ 8. Jargon, slang, and colloquialisms can distort message meaning.

_____ 9. Adjusting your rate of speech to mirror a customer's rate can aid comprehension.

_____ 10. Quoting policy is one way to ensure that customers understand why you cannot give them what they want.

_____ 11. To ensure that accurate communication has taken place, you should summarize key points at the end of a telephone conversation.

_____ 12. Chewing food and gum, drinking, or talking to others while on the telephone can be distracting and you should avoid these practices.

_____ 13. Using voice mail to answer calls is an effective way to avoid interruptions while you are speaking to a customer.

_____ 14. Planning calls and the information you will leave on a voice mail is an effective way to avoid service breakdown.

_____ 15. Because of the cost of technology, small businesses cannot effectively benefit from its use as a customer service tool.

Answers to Quick Preview are located at the end of the chapter.

Words to Live By

"Your website isn't the center of your universe. Your Facebook page isn't the center of your universe. Your mobile app isn't the center of your universe. The customer is the center of your universe."
—BRUCE ERNST

LO 9-1 The Role of Technology in Customer Service

CONCEPT **Customer service is a 24/7 responsibility, and technology can assist in making it effective.**

To say that technology has permeated almost every aspect of life in most developed countries would be an understatement. With the number of Internet users continuing to climb throughout the world, it is no wonder that online sales of products and services continue to rise.

Research conducted by McKinsey Global indicates that "the Internet is changing the way we work, socialize, create and share information, and organize the flow of people, ideas, and things around the globe . . . The Internet accounted for 21 percent of the GDP growth in mature economies over the past 5 years."[1] Figure 9.1 illustrates the impact of the Internet around the world.

Computers and other forms of technology are continually becoming smaller, more complex, and more powerful; we have only started to see the impact that technology will have on shaping the future. Most businesses in the United States are technologically dependent in some form. Calculators, cash registers, maintenance equipment, telephones, radios, cellular phones, pagers, and computer systems are typical examples of technology that we rely upon. We have become a 24/7/365 society (we access technology 24 hours a day, seven days a week, 365 days a year) and can communicate at any time and in many places throughout the world. Examples of the way that people use technology to give and receive service include students who communicate with their instructors or register and take courses online, arranging to order or return merchandise, and tracking package shipments. According to reports from the United Nations International Telecommunication Union, by the end of 2016, 47.1 percent of the world's population was using the Internet with 80.1 percent of developed nations doing so. Almost two-thirds of households in the Americas and half of those globally were connected to the Internet. Almost 1 billion households worldwide had Internet access and 90.3 percent of people in developed nations had mobile broadband subscriptions.[2]

FIGURE 9.1

Internet Usage Worldwide

Various sources track Internet usage throughout the world and report data related to demographics, penetration rates, and other factors. The following are some attention-getting figures:

- There are over almost 3.7 billion worldwide Internet users. Asia has the largest percentage of users with 50.2 percent, while North America has 8.7 percent of users, www.internetworldstats.com/stats.htm

- 50.1 percent of world population has Internet access, www.internetrworldstats.com/stats3.htm

- 88.6 percent of the U.S. population uses the Internet, www.internetworldstats.com/america.htm#us

- The top five Internet usage countries in Europe with millions of users are Russia (103.1), Germany (71.7), United Kingdom (59.3), France (55.4), and Turkey (46.3), www.internetworldstats.com/stats4.htm

QR Codes

A **QR code (Quick Response code)** is similar in concept to the standard barcode that appears on retail products. Those products contain embedded product and price information accessed by handheld readers. Originally, QR codes were used in the automotive industry in Japan. They have moved beyond to other industries due to faster readability and capacity to store more information. The codes allow access to virtually any type of stored information about products, services, or organizations.

Businesses have realized the potential of the code and started to use it other than for product information. By scanning a code with a smartphone or other specially equipped camera device, consumers can be directed to a website where additional information about a product or supplemental resources can be accessed.

In 2011, the Royal Dutch Mint issued a special coin with a three-dimensional image on one side and a QR code on the back that, when scanned, takes users to a special website where interested people can read historical information about the coin. This is just one of the creative uses for this useful technology.

Courtesy of the Royal Dutch Mint

Courtesy of the Royal Dutch Mint

First coin minted in the world with a QR code on one side and a three-dimensional image on the other. Minted by the Royal Dutch Mint in 2011.

QR Code (Quick Response Code) Similar in concept to the standard barcode that appears on retail products, this code can allow access to virtually any type of stored information about products, services, or organizations.

As a result, more people are accessing telephone-related customer service. This is significantly influencing the economies of many countries via technology-based customer services. More than ever, people are using their smartphones and other electronic mobile applications, devices, and computers to surf the Internet and place orders. This is especially true of younger consumers, in particular members of the millennial generation, who make up one-fourth of the U.S. population and spend over $200 billion a year. This group rivals the baby boomer generation in size and potential

The technology of today progresses more rapidly than most people can keep up with. *What are you doing to stay abreast of industry technology changes?*

©Vladyslav Starozhylov/Alamy Stock Photo RF

spending clout. Many of them view e-mail and personal computers as old technology. "As a generation defined by their use of technology, the majority of Millennials aren't willing to delay upgrading their PCs and mobile devices to save money . . . About 92% of Millennials own a smartphone, compared to 76% of Baby Boomers. Because technology is an integral part of their lives, it's a key component of their shopping experience. Roughly 19% of the total generation and 31% of upscale Millennials spent over $1,000 online in the past year."[3]

Younger consumers are not the only ones tapping into technology. A Pew Research Center report indicates that "more than half of older adults (defined as those ages 65 and older) were internet users. Today, 59% of seniors report they go online . . . and 47% say they have a high-speed broadband connection at home. In addition, 77% of older adults have a cell phone."[4]

There has been some shrinkage in the number and size of call centers in the United States due to the following: offshoring call center functions to other countries (e.g., India, Mexico, or the Philippines), outsourcing to third-party companies that specialize in call center operations, and the rise in self-service web or speech recognition technologies that allow customers to place their own orders and access information without contacting a customer care representative. Since the recession ended in 2009, the number of call centers has increased in part due to an increased demand by customers for technology-based ordering and service systems. With a decline in the economy in the first decade of the twenty-first century, and associated factors such as reduced family incomes and fluctuating gasoline prices, more people have opted to do their shopping and business from the comfort of their own home. According to the U.S. Census Bureau, retail e-commerce sales were $101.3 billion in the third quarter of 2016.[5] Black Friday online sales were $3.34 billion, up 21.6 percent from the previous year. Over one-third or $1.2 billion of that number were from mobile sales.[6] Because of the convenience of online shopping, the trend is likely to continue to grow in the future. For example, instead of driving to the bank to check their account or deal with an issue, customers now simply log online or call. They also simply scan checks with their smartphones to make deposits. This saves time and vehicle operating costs.

All of this means that companies that are not prepared to meet the future using technology will lose business as customers migrate to providers that are better prepared. With access to products and services at almost any time through telephones, smartphones, mobile devices, and the Internet, customers are in a power position as never before. Many organizations are looking for new service applications for available technology. Figure 9.2 illustrates how some organizations are embracing technology to serve their customers.

> **Street Talk Never Discount Customer Value**
>
> Your customers are vital to your success—make them feel important. Be available—listen—respond. You can use technology to enhance your availability, but never let it replace the personal interaction.
>
> **SOURCE: BARBARA TANZER,** *Owner, The TBS Group LLC*

KNOWLEDGE CHECK

1. In what ways are the Internet and technology affecting people and businesses around the world?

2. What is causing the number and size of call centers in the United States to shrink?

FIGURE 9.2

Using Technology to Better Serve

Many organizations are striving to find new ways to apply technology to enhance service and connect with customers and others.

Organization	Application
American Automobile Association www.aaa.com	AAA mobile services are being provided via GPS-enabled wireless telephones. Members can access directions and restaurant and hotel information, and in case of a need for roadside assistance, their vehicle's location can be determined in order to dispatch help.
Travelocity, Expedia, and Priceline www.travelocity.com www.expedia.com www.priceline.com	All three services and others like them act as online discount brokers for hotels, car rental companies, airlines, and other travel-related services. These organizations have pulled together a huge system of discounted travel services that consumers can access and through which they can make reservations for a fee.
Meriwether Lewis Elementary School www.lewiselementary.org/	This school uses blogs as an organization as well as providing a location for educators to create their own blogs related to their classes and extracurricular activities. Parents, staff, students, and other interested parties can access important information 24/7 via the Internet, even when the school is closed.
Political Candidates	Since the value of using technology to raise funds for political campaigns was demonstrated during Barack Obama's bid for president of the United States in 2008, other candidates have capitalized on the use of smartphones, Twitter, social media, websites, and other technology to raise millions of dollars in campaign funds and communicate with supporters in a short period of time. Obama's campaign set a new precedent for future political campaigns by showing the power and value of technology in reaching out to potential contributors.

Trending NOW

Virtual Reality in Business

Virtual reality has long been the stuff of science fiction and space odyssey movies. Today, a number of companies are starting to capitalize on the technology to serve internal and external customers. The uses are expanding as more companies recognize the potential value. One application already in place includes employee training (e.g., law enforcement, military, or safety workers) that requires familiarization and practice in various life-threatening functions and environments.

Other applications allow realtors and others who need to provide a 360-degree property tour or an organization providing tours of company properties in remote sites for employees so that they can better describe them to customers. Medical schools are also starting to tap the technology to provide students with an internal look into the body so that they can examine and discuss organs and systems without the use of cadavers.

LO 9-2 The Customer Contact/Call Center or Help Desk

CONCEPT **Electronic commerce is an expanding and powerful way to employ technology to conduct business.**

The growing trend of customer care center or call center expansion that provide technology-based service has resulted in reduced staff and costs, while maintaining or increasing service effectiveness. Most organizations now have free 800 or 888 numbers that customers can use to call the organization to get information, place orders, receive service, and for a variety of other functions. Organizations are also employing **fee-based 900 numbers** through which customers and others can call for information and service (e.g., computer technical support). Such numbers are pay-as-you-go with the caller incurring a per-minute charge for service from the telephone company and/or a flat fee from the organization for services rendered.

> **fee-based 900 number** A premium telephone number provided by organizations and individuals that, when called, can provide information and services that are billed back to the caller's local telephone bill.

In the past, operations that used technology were seen as labor-intensive (because of the need to maintain and operate equipment) and behind-the-scenes or "back-office" functions. They were not viewed as a strategic initiative related to the overall operation of the organization. Instead, they typically supplemented the frontline service providers. Savvy customers who are comfortable with technology, along with qualified computer-trained employees, have made customer contact centers an integral part of many organizations. Corporate and organizational officers and stakeholders in all types of organizations now recognize the potential of such operations and are pumping billions of dollars into the development, maintenance, and improvement of customer contact center operations. Customer contact centers, or **help desks**, are more powerful and complicated than ever before. They also provide more functions than their rather ineffectual predecessors did. Additionally, because of changing expectations from customers and new regulatory guidelines related to how technology can be applied (e.g., restrictions on telesolicitations and use of automated messages), traditional business metrics and approaches to interacting with customers and potential customers need to be reexamined by organizations. Any technology application considered today must incorporate a real-time solution for all customer interactions, while effectively monitoring employee performance and productivity results and tying directly to workflow processes that will best satisfy customer needs. Additionally, such systems should provide opportunities for creating future business opportunities (e.g., gathering customer needs data that can potentially lead to additional sales or leads). All of this maximizes profit potential by positioning the organization to generate new revenue while reducing staffing costs through technology usage.

> **help desk** Term used to describe a support center in which service providers are trained and assigned to assist customers with information, questions, problems, or suggestions.

The influence of technology-based applications is so significant in terms of dollars that organizations doing business with them have been labeled electronic commerce (e-commerce) businesses or websites.

Even with all the technological advances, one thing remains clear: Many customers still appreciate old-fashioned personalized customer service. Notice the qualifier "many" in that last statement. Factors such as a customer's age, socioeconomic and educational background, comfort level with technology, access to technology, and behavioral style preference can influence whether or not he or she would rather deal with a person or technology. Successful service organizations realize that each customer is unique and provide multichannel customer support that offers a variety of means for customer access (e.g., telephone, e-mail, live chat, or face-to-face). Some

Technology has drastically changed and, along with it, customer service expectations have also shifted in regard to response time and accessibility of information. *What are some innovations that have contributed to this trend?*

people are *high touch* (preferring assistance) while others are *low touch* (preferring to serve themselves); therefore, offering a variety of service delivery systems is smart business. Whether you deliver service face-to-face or via technology, there is often no substitute for a dedicated, knowledgeable, and well-trained employee to assist when needed. You and your customer service peers are the lifeline of your organization.

CALL CENTER TECHNOLOGY

Call center technology is advancing at such a rapid rate that typical organizations and their employees struggle to keep up with the changes, especially smaller businesses. Previously, when a customer had a question or needed assistance, he or she would call a toll-free number. When the call arrived at the call center, a customer service representative would answer and, after obtaining information, might be able to handle the customer's situation.

Today, customer service representatives have a vast amount of technology at their disposal and the industry and regulations governing it are continuing to evolve. For example, the U.S. Congress passed a law banning virtually all organizations from "robocalling" (automated machines that trigger when someone answers and start delivering a message). Organizations that violate the regulations face fines of up to $1,600 per call. Government agencies, nonprofits, and some others may still use the technology, but because of the disdain that most consumers have for the system, tighter restrictions are sure to follow. Some of the typical systems found in customer care centers follow.

TRADITIONAL CALL CENTER TECHNOLOGY

Call centers have been around for years. During that time, representatives or agents have used traditional technology to access data and communicate with customers in order to provide a standardized level of service. As you will read later in this chapter, technology shifts are changing the roles of call centers and the people who staff them.

The following are some of the traditional equipment used to provide call center-based customer service.

Automated Attendant

Automated attendant systems can be used to provide prerecorded responses to frequently asked questions (FAQs) and to route callers to specific representatives or other employees and departments. These are the machines that customers encounter, which welcome them and provide automated selections to reach various departments or automated functions by pressing numeric keys on the telephone.

automated attendant systems
Provide callers with a menu of options from which they can select by pressing a key on their telephone pad.

Automatic Call Distribution (ACD) System

Automatic call distribution (ACD) systems route incoming calls to the next available agent based on number called, time of day, caller ID, or caller-selected codes. When agents are busy or lines are full, an ACD automatically places callers on hold and plays a prerecorded announcement. Many companies use the announcement device to make callers aware of other products and services offered by the organization.

automatic call distribution (ACD) systems Telecommunications system used by many companies in their call centers and customer care facilities to capture incoming calls and route them to available service providers.

Automated Computer Telephone Interviews

Automated computer telephone interviews allow organizations to conduct automated phone surveys of customers. Typically, programs are built around advanced interactive voice response (IVR) technology along with voice broadcasting technology. By using an auto-dialer phone system that calls customers programmed into the computer, and CATI software, organizations call potential interviewees and play a custom greeting. Callers are often offered the option of responding to automated interview questions or being transferred to a representative. The caller can also leave a voice message, hear additional information, or simply decline to be interviewed. Organizations often use this type of system to collect customer satisfaction data. For example, when you buy fast food at Burger King, Wendy's, Chick-fil-A, and other fast food restaurants, there is often a satisfaction survey through their website or toll-free number offered on the back of your receipt. You can visit the website or call and go through the automated survey in exchange for a free food item on a future visit.

The call survey applications are usually programmed to accept touch phone responses or can record each question's response for later analysis.

automated computer telephone interviews A voice recognition computer mechanism that queries survey respondents with questions and stores their responses. Depending upon answers received, the system can branch and follow scripted prompts.

Automatic Number Identification (ANI)

Automatic number identification (ANI) systems allow customers to be identified by their country/area code and have their calls directed appropriately before an agent talks to them. For example, the system can route a customer to a special agent who is multilingual or who has specialized product or service knowledge. This saves time, since the agent does not have to key in the customer's telephone number and the geographic location is identified before speaking with him or her. The agent might also be able to access information on a computer screen about the customer's history with the organization (e.g., memberships, prior orders, or past issues addressed). In addition, calls can be routed to the same agent who most recently handled a specific caller. Finally, with ANI, calls are routed to the service center closest to the customer's home.

automatic number identification (ANI) systems (pronounced "Annie") A form of caller identification technology similar to home telephone caller ID systems. ANI allows incoming customers to be identified on a computer screen with background information so that they can be routed to an appropriate service representative for assistance.

Global access to technology and communications equipment has propelled customer service headlong into a world not even imagined several decades ago. *What changes in service technology have you witnessed in your lifetime?*

©LOVELUCK/Shutterstock.com RF

Computer Telephony Integration (CTI)

computer telephony integration (CTI) A system that integrates a representative's computer and phone to facilitate the automatic retrieval of customer records and other information needed to satisfy a customer's needs and requests.

Computer telephony integration (CTI), or computer–telephone integration, systems help integrate a customer service representative's computer, phone, fax, web, and e-mail systems to facilitate the automatic retrieval of customer records and other information needed to satisfy a customer's needs and requests. Other functions controlled by CTI include the following:

- Screen population of customer data when the customer answers the phone
- Phone control (e.g., answer, hold, conference, and hang up)
- Coordinated transfer, where a caller is transferred to another representative along with the data populated on a service representative's computer screen
- Call quality monitoring and recording
- Representative/agent state control (e.g., a set period for after-call work then automatically switching to a ready status)

Customer Relationship Management (CRM) software

customer relationship management (CRM) software Systems designed for use by organizations to assist their marketing, sales, and service professionals to better manage their relationship with current and potential customers by providing a database function for storage and retrieval of information about customers, products, and services.

Customer relationship management (CRM) software systems are designed to automate and integrate service and other functions within an organization. They help manage interactions between service representatives and current or prospective customers. CRM uses software that helps to organize, automate, and synchronize marketing, sales, technical support, and customer service initiatives. Among other things, CRM systems can perform the following functions:

- Capture contact information.
- Track suppliers and vendors.
- Monitor sales, returns, deadlines, and other important dates.
- Develop e-mail/direct-mail lists.
- Log correspondence, set follow-ups and alerts, and record comments.

- Automatically maintain a detailed audit history on customer accounts, transactions, and individual events.
- Attach files (documents, images, etc.) to event or customer records.
- Generate event-related invoices and track payments.

Some CRM systems can also integrate with social media sites like Facebook, Google Plus, and LinkedIn to track opinions and feedback on experiences about the organization, products, and services and then communicate with those consumers.

Electronic Mail (E-mail)

Electronic mail (e-mail) provides an inexpensive, rapid way of communicating with customers in writing worldwide. It allows customers to access information via telephone and then, through prompting (and using the telephone keypad), have the information delivered to them via e-mail. A big advantage of e-mail is that you can write a single message and have it delivered to hundreds of people worldwide in a matter of minutes at little or no cost. The downside of using this vehicle from a customer standpoint is that **spamming** or sending **spam** by unscrupulous people and organizations has given e-mail advertisers in general a bad reputation.

Facsimile (Fax) Machine

A **facsimile (fax) machine** allows users to transport graphics and text messages as electronic signals via telephone lines or from a personal computer equipped with a modem. Information can be sent anywhere in the world in minutes, or a customer can make a call, key in a code number, and have information delivered to his or her fax machine or computer without ever speaking to a person (**fax-on-demand** system).

In most instances, fax machines have given way to computer technology that allows senders to use the scan function on higher-end printers to convert images into electronic format and then use their computer and send the images as attachments to e-mail messages. The images can also be stored on computer hard drives for later.

Instant Messaging

Instant messaging is a type of technology that allows online chats in real-time text transmission over the Internet between customers and service representatives. Short messages are typically transmitted between the two parties. Once someone types in his or her message and hits send, the other person sees it immediately and can respond. Some more advanced systems use technology that provides real-time texting in which a message receiver can view each character simultaneously as the message is being written by the sender.

Intelligent Callback Technology

Customer expectations continue to grow and change with the introduction of new technology into the workplace. One result is that they have become far less tolerant of long wait times to receive service. To address this concern, many organizations have introduced **intelligent callback technology** into their call centers. With this equipment, customers decide whether they prefer to wait on hold to speak to a representative or would rather receive a scheduled callback. Such technology gathers information from the customer (e.g., return telephone number) and tells the customer when he or she can expect a callback. Thus, the customer manages a call center experience that is more convenient and potentially provides a greater degree of customer satisfaction.

---

electronic mail (e-mail) System used to transmit messages around the Internet. Instant messaging (IM) is replacing this technology in some call centers as many younger consumers embrace it as a primary form of communication.

spamming or spam An abusive use of various electronic messaging systems and technology to send unsolicited and indiscriminate bulk messages to people (also used with instant messaging, web search engines, blogs, and other formats).

facsimile (fax) machine Older form of technology that converts printed words and graphics into electronic signals and allows them to be transmitted across telephone lines and then reassembled into a facsimile of the words and graphics on the receiving end.

fax-on-demand Technology that allows information, such as a form, stored in a computer to be requested electronically via a telephone and transmitted to a customer.

intelligent callback technology Technology that gathers information from the customer and tells the customer when he or she can expect a callback.

Interactive Kiosks or Digital Displays

Interactive kiosks or digital displays are an evolving technology that allows customers and customer contact centers equipped with video camera computer hookups to interact via the computer. Similar to interactive kiosks by companies like INTOUCH Interactive and Four Winds Interactive where customers can view product videos or other product information, this technology allows customers and agents to see one another during their interactions. Many organizations are now using these in lobbies to allow self-service to customers. You may have seen these at airline check-ins, banks (ATMs), or in theme parks or other entertainment venues. Walt Disney World has been using this technology at its theme parks for years to allow guests to use kiosks to make their restaurant reservations upon arrival in the park. Because of privacy concerns or preference, some software allows customers to block their image, yet they still see the agent to whom they are speaking.

Interactive Voice Response (IVR) System or Voice Response Unit (VRU)

An interactive voice response (IVR) system or **voice response unit (VRU)** allows customers to call in 24 hours a day, seven days a week, even when customer service representatives are not available. By keying in a series of numbers on the phone, customers can get information or answers to questions. Such systems perform a text-to-speech conversion to present database information audibly to a caller. They also ensure consistency of information. Banks and credit card companies use such systems to allow customers to access account information. Once they are connected, customers are prompted to enter membership/account numbers, passwords, and security codes or pins to verify their identity before proceeding to access account information. They may also have to respond to security questions.

Internet Callback Technology

Internet callback technology allows someone browsing the Internet to click on words or phrases (e.g., *Call me*), enter his or her phone number, and continue browsing. This triggers a predictive dialing system (discussed later in this chapter) and assigns an agent to handle the call when it rings at the customer's end.

Internet Telephony

Internet telephony allows users to have voice communications over the Internet. Although widely discussed in the industry, call center Internet telephony is in its infancy, lacks standards, and is not currently embraced by consumers. Power outages, quality issues with transmissions, and other technical glitches have prevented this medium from becoming widely used by most organizations.

Media Blending

Media blending allows agents to communicate with a customer over a telephone line while simultaneously displaying information over the Internet to the customer. As with Internet telephony, this technology has not reached its full potential.

Online Information Fulfillment System

Online information fulfillment systems allow customers to go to the World Wide Web, access an organization's website, and click on desired information. This is one of the fastest-growing customer service technologies. Every competitive

---

interactive kiosks or digital displays Computer terminals that have customized software and hardware and set up in a public area where users can touch a screen display to access application for information, commerce, education, or entertainment.

interactive voice response (IVR) system Technology that allows customers to call an organization to get information from recorded messages or a computer by keying a series of numbers on the telephone keypad in response to questions or prompts.

voice response unit (VRU) System that allows customers to call 24 hours a day, seven days a week by keying a series of numbers on the telephone keypad in order to get information or answers to questions.

internet callback technology Technology that allows someone browsing the Internet to key a prompt on a website and have a service representative call a phone number provided.

internet telephony Technology that allows people to talk to one another via the Internet as if they were on a regular telephone.

media blending Technology that allows a service provider to communicate with a customer via telephone while at the same time displaying information to the customer over the computer.

online information fulfillment system Technology that allows a customer to access an organization's website and click on desired information without having to interact with a service provider.

business will eventually use this system so that customers can get information and place orders.

Predictive Dialing System

Predictive dialing systems automatically place outgoing calls and deliver incoming calls to the next available agent. This type of system is often used in outbound (tele-marketing/call center) operations. Because of numerous abuses, the government is continually restricting its use.

Screen Pop-Ups

Screen pop-ups are used in conjunction with ANI and IVR systems to identify callers. As a call is received and dispatched to an agent, the system provides information about the caller that "pops" onto the agent's screen before he or she answers the telephone (e.g., order information, membership data, service history, contact history).

Speech or Voice Recognition

Speech- or voice-recognition programs allow a system to recognize keywords or phrases from a caller. These systems can be used for routing callers to a representative and for retrieving information from a database. This technology is incorporated into a customer contact center's voice response system. Such systems allow individuals to dictate data directly into a computer, which then converts the spoken words into text. There are various applications of voice-recognition systems for all contact centers. Some organizations are recording customers' voices (passwords and phrases) as a means of identification so that customers can gain access to their accounts without allowing unauthorized persons to break into them and steal personal information. With other applications, agents speak into a computer, instead of typing data, and people who have disabilities can obtain data from their accounts by speaking into the computer.

Call centers and many of the world's largest companies are using voice-recognition software to facilitate customer service and provide services through their products. Examples of this technology are the Siri attendant in Apple products, Alexa in Amazon's Echo, automotive manufacturers that have telephone and media integration built into many of their cars, and banks (e.g., Wells Fargo and Bank of America) that use it for their automated attendant systems.

predictive dialing system Technology that uses programmed data to automatically place outgoing calls and also deliver incoming calls to the next available service representative in a call center.

screen pop-ups Small screen images that are programmed to appear on someone's computer monitor when a website is accessed.

speech or voice recognition The ability of a machine or software program to identify words and phrases in spoken language and convert them to a machine-readable format that can respond to vocal prompts and branch to optional responses.

artificial intelligence (AI) Computer systems that perform tasks normally requiring human intelligence.

Trending NOW

Companies are finding new ways to make the customer experience more fun and useful for consumers. Numerous organizations are now using **artificial intelligence (AI)** Facebook Messenger chatbots to engage and assist customers looking for information or products and services on their Facebook pages. The chatbot technology expedites information delivery, eliminates the need to talk to a customer service representative, and reduces employee labor costs for companies.

For example, Whole Foods applies the technology to allow customers browsing through the store to find products. With a couple of taps, they can select emoji images, like an apple or cucumber, which directs them to recipes containing those ingredients that they might like to try. American Express also uses the technology to allow customers to make requests, such as getting a copy of a receipt and redeeming reward points.

Telephone Typewriter System (TTY)

Partly because of the passage of the 1990 Americans with Disabilities Act in the United States, and similar laws in other countries, which required that telecommunication services be available to people with disabilities, organizations now have the technology to assist customers who have hearing and speech impairments. By using a **telephone typewriter system (TTY)**—a typewriter-like device for sending messages back and forth over telephone lines—a person who has a hearing or speech impairment can contact someone who is using a standard telephone. The sender and the receiver type their messages using the TTY. To do this, the sender or receiver can go through an operator-assisted relay service provided by local and long-distance telephone companies to reach companies and individuals who do not have TTY receiving technology, or the user can get in touch directly with companies that have TTYs. The service is free of charge. Operators can help first-time hearing-disabled users understand the rules in using TTY. In addition, local speech and hearing centers can often provide training on the use of TTY in a call center environment.

The federal government has a similar service (Federal Information Relay Service, or FIRS) for individuals who wish to conduct business with any branch of the federal government nationwide.

Voice over Internet Protocol (VoIP)

Another video-based service option for businesses, used by individuals for a number of years, is known as **Voice over Internet Protocol (VoIP)**. It allows voice communications combined with multimedia, such as video images, to be transported over the Internet. This free or low-cost means of communication has been popular with users as an alternative to long-distance calling that does not allow speakers to see one another.

telephone typewriter system (TTY) A typewriter-like device used by people with hearing disabilities for typing and sending messages back and forth via telephone lines. The system is also referred to as telecommunications device for the deaf (TDD). Newer text based communication methods, such as short message service (SMS), Internet relay chat (IRC), and instant messaging have been developed as an alternative to TDD.

Voice over Internet Protocol (VoIP) Technologies, methodologies, and transmission techniques involved in the delivery of voice and image communication via the Internet.

With the advent of technology in phones, cars, and other electronic devices that can accept, translate, and respond to spoken words, new tools are being developed daily that can enhance the customer experience. *In what ways have you experienced speech recognition technology and how do you think it will impact customer service?*

©nihatdursun/Getty Images RF

Various software and service providers, such as Microsoft's Skype, Linphone, and Google Voice, offer this means for organizations to connect via voice and images with their customers. In addition to video capability, companies can transfer files and conduct videoconferences.

KNOWLEDGE CHECK

1. How have changes in technology changed the look and operation of call centers?

2. What are some traditional call center technologies and how have they improved customer service?

3. How is CRM software being used in call centers?

LO 9-3 Tapping into Web-Based and Mobile Technologies

CONCEPT **Evolving technology is changing the way the businesses and other organizations of all sizes around the world do business.**

Web-based and mobile technologies continue to multiply and expand on a daily basis, and so do ways in which businesses are rapidly learning to harness their power. Everything from organizational branding, sharing information, introducing new products, and communicating and helping satisfy customer needs is possible on technology that is evolving rapidly. While service representatives do not typically use all of the technology approaches discussed in this chapter, and are typically trained by their organization on the ones they will need to perform their job, a familiarity with terminology and technological capabilities is important to professional success.

The following are some ways that organizations are tapping into today's evolving web-based and mobile technology to better serve potential, new, and existing customers.

WEBSITES

Websites provide organizations with a valuable tool for presenting a "face" to the entire world. They are a component of an organization's professional brand. Few successful businesses can survive today without having a professional-looking and functional website. These standards of technology are able to share information about a person or a company's organization, products and services, contacts, service options, and much more. As part of their overall marketing strategy, they can offer informative blogs, advertising links, and important connections to their social media accounts. All of these can better promote the organizational brand, generate leads, identify potential customers, provide service to current customers, and create residual income streams. Small, one-person businesses and bloggers often capitalize on affiliate, banner, and other types of web advertising to generate income.

One key to effective website effectiveness is recognition and connections. People must know about the organization and be able to find its website in order to access information on it. Search engine optimization is crucial in positioning a company's website link at the top of a search engine results page when people use Google, Yahoo, or other search engines to scour the Internet looking for information. By going to

websites A series of electronic "pages" that are hosted on a web server and provide vital organizational, product, and service information, and multiple ways for consumers to get in touch with key company representatives.

statistical tracking sites and using tools like Alexa and Google Analytics, owners and others can track valuable statistics related to the number of visitors to their sites, how long they stayed on a website, site ranking on the Internet, demographic data, referring websites, and more. With such valuable information, businesses are able to determine where they are getting leads and sales and how to better spend marketing dollars and target their marketing initiatives.

The thing to remember about websites is that they are basically a "pull" mechanism. That means that site owners post information, provide service **chat support**, and encourage people to come to the site to retrieve information, use services and support, and make purchases. This is opposed to "push" technology, which proactively sends out information to customers and potential customers. Examples of push technology or initiatives are e-mail and Twitter messages, blog articles, eNewsletters sent to subscribers, and mailings through the post office. These methods put information into the hands of customers. By getting website domain links into the hands of potential site visitors through social media or one of the other methods mentioned, organizations can encourage them to come to the website and potentially access products, services, or information provided. This strategy often helps take some workload off call center representatives and other service providers because companies can post frequently asked questions (FAQs) on the site and potentially provide assistance to people who would normally pick up a phone and call or come by the organization's physical site.

Having live chat capability is an easy way for organizations to provide an instant and convenient support vehicle for their unseen customers. Both agents and customers can actually multitask during the chat experience since one types, while the other waits and then responds. This type of service technology continues to gain popularity according to the research by Forrester on customer service channel (types of service technology) rate trends. The organization found that "channel rates are also quickly changing: we've seen a 12% rise in web self-service usage, a 24% rise in chat usage, and a 25% increase in community usage for customer service in the past three years."[7]

chat support An online chat support system provides customers with access to a "real person" to get answers and help resolve issues. By going to an organization's website that has chat capability, a customer can avoid having to navigate a cumbersome toll-free phone system that often requires him or her to sit on hold for endless amounts of time waiting for a service representative to become available.

According to Digital Shift Media:

1. 75 percent of total search traffic is directed to positions one through five in Google search results.

2. Positions six through ten in Google search results receive approximately 16 percent of all traffic.

3. Search results that appear on the second page of Google (results 11 through 20) are still important as they receive the remaining 10 percent spread across those 10 results.

Source: https://digitalshiftmedia.com/blog/.

Cloud Computing

Cloud computing technology involves using hardware and software delivered over a network, such as the Internet. In effect, this form of computing allows end users (e.g., customers) to use mobile phones, tablets, computers, or laptops to access data through a mobile application on the device through a web browser such as Internet Explorer, Firefox, Opera, Safari, or Google Chrome. From a cost perspective,

cloud computing Technology that allows for remote storage of a user's data, which can then be accessed through a web browser using a mobile application on the user's tablet, mobile device (e.g., smartphone), laptop, or computer. The term relates to storing information "off in the electronic clouds" rather than on a user's storage device.

©Tetra Images/Getty Images RF

With the ability for companies to now store massive amounts of data and connect various electrical components via the Internet, customers and companies now have more options for communicating, downloading, and saving data. *In what ways has cloud technology affected you as a customer?*

it provides a means for individuals and organizations to access service and products without having to pay for additional equipment and infrastructure for the storage and operation of data and applications.

An example of how cloud technology works occurs whenever customers of Amazon or Apple order music, videos, or books. Customers can either download the purchased product to their device or they can store it on the organization's server (storage unit) and access it when they want to read, listen to, or view it. The use of this cloud storage negates customers from using up internal storage space, which at some point may push them to their maximum capacity and require the purchase of additional memory or a new device. In effect, this saves customers additional money while allowing them to access their product when they want it. The only caveat is that they must have Internet access via a connection or Wi-Fi (wireless access) capability in order to access their application and data.

SOCIAL MEDIA

The Internet has exploded with social networking websites (e.g., LinkedIn, MySpace, Twitter, Pinterest, and Facebook) that allow people and organizations a vehicle to post information about themselves, products, and services. Most of these sites were originally envisioned as a way to connect with old and new friends and relatives and to share personal messages or information.

Social media has become so popular and available to consumers that businesses and other organizations are tapping into it to help establish their brand, share information, identify and connect with customers, and target specific demographic groups while keeping their name in front of millions of people. Research from Nielsen indicates that Americans are spending a good portion of their time on social media: "44 percent of American tablet owners and 38 percent of smartphone users have their devices in hand while watching TV. About a third of 18–34-year-olds are on social media sites while using the bathroom."[8] These numbers indicate the power of social media and the opportunity awaiting companies that are tapping into the phenomenon.

Users connect on various social and media sharing sites for a variety of reasons. This potentially provides a wealth of opportunity for companies that want to share their message about products and services with the world since there are hundreds of millions of visitors to these websites each year. Sites such as Ignite Social Media (http://www.ignitesocialmedia.com) can provide a wealth of demographic information about social media website usage to organizations.

Obviously, organizations hoping to tap this revenue-generating gold mine should develop a strategic marketing plan to target specific audience demographics and to determine what site users are looking for on each media site that is part of the plan. There are many factors to consider before moving forward into the social media arena. Part of the initiative should be to identify what is in it for site users and the organization. For example, e-commerce blog article for the e-commerce support company, Volusion,[9] outlines five reasons that people are likely to follow your company brand on social media: (1) to receive coupons and discounts, (2) to show their friends that they like your brand, (3) to receive entertaining or educational content, (4) to receive customer support, and (5) to receive exclusive information and content.

One of the biggest advantages to using social media to get information out to current and potential customers is that the sites are almost exclusively free. As long as the organizations follow site guidelines, they are free to share information and benefit from the mass exposure. Since many of these sites focus on target demographics (e.g., www.BlackPlanet.com [African Americans], www.CafeMom.com [mothers], and www.TravBuddy.com [travelers]), they offer opportunities for organizations specializing or diversifying into a specific market to tap that resource. If you had to pay to

Social media has influenced many aspects of life for millions of people and taken hold of much of society. Successful organizations are striving to harness its power and are now embracing it as a tool for connecting to current and potential customers. *In what ways have you seen companies tap this lucrative free network of websites to enhance business operations?*

©Pankaj Kumar/AGE Fotostock RF

- Lead generation by identifying and targeting key decision makers in world-class companies who have the authority to make buying decisions.
- Identifying and solidifying their position in niche markets by separating themselves from competitors and emphasizing why their products and services are superior.
- Increase search engine ranking and website traffic by posting interesting content that drives people to the company website.
- Provide customer service support to people who go to social media to complain or search for advice on products and services.
- Product and service brand management (e.g., rolling out new products and services or sharing information to educate customers and influence buying decisions).
- Gaining customer insights to gather relevant information about preferences, ideas, feedback, or suggestions related to the organization, competition, and current and potential products and services.
- Share information and content faster and less expensively than creating mailing lists or posting information on a company website.
- Run inexpensive targeted advertisements based on age, gender, job title, geographic area, interests, and other factors before rolling out an ad campaign to the general public.
- Identify competitors and find out what they are doing to capture and serve customers.
- Crisis management or damage control when something goes wrong (e.g., products or services are not delivered or do not perform as advertised or intended).

FIGURE 9.3

Organizational Uses of Social Media

get the exposure that you and your organization might want, it would cost millions of dollars. Imagine the simplicity of creating a short video that discusses your organization's mission, vision, and value statements or provides an overview of products and services and then uploading it to a site like YouTube. This simple free tool could direct job candidates, vendors, consumers, and anyone else with an interest in the organization to your website link to view the content. Such vehicles could save companies time and money in their marketing effort or in orienting new employees to what the organization is all about.

Companies are using social media in many ways as an inexpensive means of getting information out at low costs. They are now hiring specialists to oversee their social media efforts. Figure 9.3 shows some of the ways that social media sites are being used by organizations.

An important thing for companies to realize is that their employees are networking with other employees and possibly their customers directly or indirectly through social media. This impact can be either positive or negative on the company image depending on what is being shared. As employees discuss their job, talk about issues, or, in some cases, vent their frustrations, they may inadvertently or intentionally share private or proprietary information with others who do not have a need to know. This is why many organizations now have designated people in the information technology (IT) department monitoring social media. It is up to each employee to be vigilant and professional in his or her communications online and with others so that no unintentional breakdowns in policy and ethical standards occur.

The following are some of the more popular social media websites and technology that individuals and organizations are using to share information or for promotion.

Trending NOW

Another innovative way that organizations are tapping social media is through **data mining**. This is a relatively new concept through which companies develop part of their marketing strategy through social media involvement. Marketing and other designated personnel actively participate on a social media platform like Twitter, Facebook, Pinterest, or others. These are websites where participants freely disclose likes, dislikes, comments, personal information, and other pertinent information. By capturing and analyzing data, companies can create profiles of potential customer audiences. The process can be slow and tedious because it is difficult to match up current customers with participants on a social media site. For example, if Sally Hanson is a customer of Company A and there is a Sally Hanson profile on several platforms, someone has to correlate or match the two to ensure they are the same person. However, once that happens, the company can identify a wealth of potential information that might help target a product or service to Sally. For example, if the company has an outdoor clothing product line and Sally identifies on Twitter or Facebook that she loves summer or winter sports, the company can now offer specific special offers to her to help generate sales. As with all technology, it is progressing rapidly, so the pace of social media data mining is accelerating quickly. There are software companies already offering AI technology products that can electronically collect and correlate data and then create algorithms. Law enforcement agencies are already using the same type of technology to locate and match criminals.

data mining The process of searching through social media data to identify trends and potential customer bases by extracting information offered by social media participants.

YouTube The largest video-sharing website on the Internet, where users can upload, share, and view videos.

YouTube

YouTube was established in 2005 by three former PayPal (a subsidiary of eBay) employees. The company is a subsidiary of Google and provides a forum for users to upload and view videos containing movie and TV clips or music, educational content, and personal or organizational messages and content. Primarily used by individuals at inception, entrepreneurs, small and large organizations, businesses, and other organizations have realized the potential for free advertising and reaching large demographic audiences, particularly younger users. While the primary goal and slogan of the site are to "Broadcast Yourself" and have people share personal, funny, and entertaining video content, organizations use the format to train, educate, inform, and brand themselves. With a billion visitors per year, this is a viable resource for potentially sharing information in an upbeat and entertaining format. More YouTube views come via mobile devices, which is why websites must be set up to be viewed in that format. YouTube mobile reaches more 18–49-year-olds than any cable network in the United States. It can be navigated in 76 different languages (covering 95 percent of the Internet population).

Twitter

Twitter An online social networking and microblogging service that enables its users to send and read text-based messages.

tweets Messages limited to 140 characters sent via Twitter to other mobile equipment and computer users. Direct messages to connected individuals can be longer.

Twitter is a real-time, short messaging service that works with a variety of communication networks and electronic devices. It is primarily used by many people as a social networking tool to stay in touch through text messaging. Users can quickly ask questions and receive responses from others. Because of its rapid delivery potential, many organizations are using **tweets** to interact with customers in order to share information about products and services, respond to complaints, and answer questions. The technology is being used to supplement call center phone lines and take some of the workload off those representatives. This is because anyone in an organization (e.g., marketers, salespeople, human resources professional, or others) can provide information about his or her area of responsibility to callers and customers as needed. They do not need to go through a call center to get information or resolve issues related to a specific department.

According to StatisticBrain.com:

- Twitter has over 695 million users. Of that number, 342 million are active "tweeters."
- 135,000 new users sign up daily.
- Average number of tweets sent per day is 58 million.
- 9,100 tweets are sent every second.
- 43 percent of Twitter users use their phone to tweet.

Source: "Twitter Statistics," Statistic Brain Research Center. http://www.statisticbrain.com/twitter-statistics

Twitter is a great vehicle for checking customer reactions to a commercial or product rollout, asking for ideas, or gathering information regarding other organization-sponsored events or activities. For example, when PepsiCo was considering a new Mountain Dew product, they conducted a Twitter campaign to have customers visit its DEWmocracy website and vote on one of the three choices for a new Mountain Dew flavor. They got more than 350,000 tweets in response.

Facebook

Facebook was founded in 2004 by Mark Zuckerburg and his college roommates as a social networking tool for students at Harvard University. It quickly expanded to other major educational institutions and then to the world. It allows users to register free, set up a personal and professional account, create a profile about themselves, and then share photos and other information and send messages. They can also join community groups with like-minded people or organizations. All these activities have resulted in 1.79 billion active monthly users (people who have logged in during the last 30 days). In recent years, large and small organizations have realized the potential of tapping into the Facebook network. They are setting up professional profiles to which people and organizations can link and share information. Using Facebook provides another creative option for communicating with current and potential customers. For example, Entergy Arkansas has used its Facebook page as a communication tool and a service channel supplement by providing customers with updates on power outages during severe weather situations in their area.

Pinterest

Pinterest was founded in 2009 and initially run from a New York apartment by its founders, and had around 5,000 users in the first year. Statistically, 71 percent of Pinterest's 72.5 million users are women but that is changing as 33.33 percent of new sign-ups are men. Around 2.75 percent of usage occurs on mobile devices and 93 percent of Pinners shopped online in the past six months.[10]

Since the site started allowing people to establish business accounts, in addition to their personal accounts, there has been an influx of organizations using it to act as a storefront or inexpensive means of promoting its brand, products, and services. The site has proven to be very helpful for small business owners with limited marketing dollars who are trying to compete with larger companies. For example, a nationwide U.S. plumbing firm by the name of Mr. Rooter launched a fun campaign called "Where in the world is Mr. Rooter?" They impose images of their plastic Mr. Rooter figurine

Street Talk **Get Permission from Customers**

Whenever I call anyone, the first thing I ask is "Is this a good time to talk?" If they say no, I follow up to ask when would be a better time to talk. I realize that they have other commitments. I think because of this, it increases the chances that they will get back to me. Additionally, when I e-mail people (mainly in my group), I ask about how their evening or weekend went and I strive to remember what they say so it doesn't seem to be superficial.

SOURCE: COURTESY OF ANNE WILKINSON

Facebook This social networking site is open for use by anyone over the age of 13 to share information, send messages, and network socially.

Pinterest A pin- or cork-board type of forum where users can share photos and images on various themes or interests.

into world-famous travel location photos and pin them on their account boards in Pinterest along with thank you messages and other images from customers in order to maintain brand recognition. The result is that other users capture the images and repin them to their own boards or share them with others on various social media channels. You can view their campaign by visiting http://pinterest.com/Mrrooterllc.

Podcasts (Portable On-Demand Broadcasts)

With podcasts, service providers can share information (e.g., advertisements, product information, training program content, entertainment, or information updates) with potential and current customers or the community. People subscribe to and download the content through their mobile device or computer. Organizations can transmit scheduled material to customers as a free service or as a subscription or per-event/item purchase. Consultants often use this vehicle to conduct client meetings or train employees. Other organizations tap into the technology to save money on travel by providing information or training to remote clients or employees.

If you have visited a museum or taken a college campus tour where you listened to prerecorded information, then you have experienced one use of podcasts. Some educators use podcasts to provide a review of session content or supplemental information regarding topics covered in class or their text. Even the White House uses podcasts to share the president's weekly addresses, White House speeches, and White House press briefings.

Trending NOW

A negative side to wireless technology is that it can easily be used by criminals. For example, there have been many instances of credit card fraud by unscrupulous food servers who scanned their customer's card with an illegal device called a skimmer and later used or sold the stolen credit card information for their own benefit. An innovative tablet E la Carte (http://www.elacarte.com) called the Presto Smart Dining System, now being used in restaurants such as HMSHosts at many airports, might help stem that practice, increase efficiency, and save time for servers and customers. It is a tablet device, similar in appearance to an iPad, that shows menus and food photos, provides recommendations on specials of the day, and allows customers to place their order. They can also pay to play electronic games while waiting for their food to arrive. The latter is a popular function for parents with small kids who accompany them. All of these functions can be performed at the convenience of the customer's table. They can even split their check with others and pay by swiping their credits card(s) at their table, thus eliminating the possibility of card fraud. The system eliminates having to let their credit or debit card leave their sight and provides more individualized service. Customers can also print a copy of their transaction so that they have a record for future reference.

Smartphones and Tablets

smartphones Mobile telephones that are built with a mobile operating system similar to a computer that allows them to perform a myriad of functions using what are called applications or apps.

tablets A personal computer (PC) that is a hybrid between a notebook or laptop computer and a personal digital assistant (PDA) and has a flat-screen viewing panel.

Smartphones and **tablets** (e.g., the iPad) are becoming more sophisticated every day. While the phones have traditionally functioned as a way to share voice and text information with customers, technological developments by major industry companies like Apple, Samsung, Microsoft, and others have expanded competition to develop faster, stronger, and more robust pieces of equipment that can perform multiple functions. In addition to simply making calls and sending text messages, modern-day phones and tablets can take photographs and make movies comparable to many modern-day cameras. Users can navigate the functions on a tablet by using a plastic-tipped stylus, tapping icons, or swiping and tapping on the screen with their fingers.

People can also use **applications (apps)** on their smartphones, tablets, and other devices to perform hundreds of tasks previously available only through a computer. The devices can connect to the Internet through wireless (**Wi-Fi**) connections; provide information; play music; allow users to read books; act as navigational devices, cameras, and calculators; and perform myriad other processes and functions. These amazing devices have provided new opportunities to organizations wishing to get information and services to mobile phone customers. Couple these innovative smartphones and tablets with broadband Internet access and high-speed wireless delivery and the potential for helping customers is huge. Customers have instant access to service providers to find information, search for the best pricing, order products and services, and perform all sorts of consumer-related functions from virtually anywhere there is wireless phone access. They can contact their bank, membership organizations, and other companies with which they do business from anywhere in the world if they have access to adequate wireless networks.

applications (apps) Software that can process information and perform various tasks on smartphones, tablets, electronic devices, and computers using Internet wireless (Wi-Fi) and wired connections.

Wi-Fi Technology that enables electronic devices such as smartphones, computers, and tablets to send and receive data wirelessly (using radio waves) over a computer network.

Trending NOW

Instagram, a popular application for iPhone and Android phones, is one way in which individuals and organizations are passing images around in the world of technology. This website is a favorite of the 18–29-year-old population and had over 600 million users at the end of 2016. Since it integrates with other social media sites like Facebook, organizations are realizing the potential for targeting these sites' demographics. For example, during the 2008 presidential elections in the United States, the Obama campaign group wisely tapped into this technology to get its message out and connect with younger voters. Recognizing the power of Instagram, many companies are using it to help capture the interest of potential customers by running product photo contests and soliciting feedback on new and existing brands. Some examples are Burberry (https://www.instagram.com/burberry and Nike (https://www.instagram.com/nike).

Text Messaging

Text messaging or **texting**, an electronic form of messaging between mobile, portable, or fixed devices over a telephone network, has been popular, especially among younger users. For over a decade, businesses have adopted the practice as a readily available and inexpensive way to interact with customers. The following are some ways that organizations are applying the technology.

text messaging or texting The process of someone typing and sending a brief electronic message to another person over a phone network using a mobile phone or fixed or portable device.

- Travel agencies, entertainment companies, and others that deal with scheduling, events, and changing information for customers use this format to send short updates or information related to products and events to customers' cellular phones.
- Notifications are being sent to on-call personnel such as maintenance, engineering, and medical staff when an issue or emergency needing their attention arises.
- Service organizations, such as auto repair, hair salon, and dentists' and doctors' offices remind customers and patients of upcoming appointments or changes.
- Retail and other organizations send confirmations of bill payments.
- Schools notify students and/or parents of upcoming events, tasks that need to be handled, school closings, class cancellations, or in emergency situations.

Wikis

Many employers and organizations are using websites called wikis to allow a form of social networking among their internal customers (employees). These sites provide a means of collecting and exchanging information and brainstorming ideas related to a project. This exchange of knowledge and ideas can facilitate harmony as well as enhance productivity if used effectively. They are the "water coolers" of today's technically savvy employees, who might prefer to fire off thoughts via their keypad rather than gather at a bar after work. Wikis allow users to add and edit content at any time by simply logging on.

Wikis are also being used by some employers to provide information that would normally be delivered in a training session, thus saving time and money. For example, if an organization uses a lot of acronyms or jargon, it could use a wiki as a place to define terms so that employees can determine the meaning of a term they come across in the workplace without having to go to the supervisor or someone else. To see what a wiki looks like, visit wikipedia.org on the Internet.

Blogs

bloggers Individuals who write content that is posted on blogs on the World Wide Web.

posts Articles or other content published on blogs for site visitors to read, comment on, share, or download.

A relatively new tool being used by individuals and organizations is the web log (blog). These chronological "diaries" are a creative way for individual **bloggers**, and those within organizations, to provide updates, product or service commentary, and information and graphics or video to internal and external customers (e.g., product recalls, updates, procedures, processes, policy changes) in the form of **posts**. Many blogs contain only text; however, they can have images and other media in them as well as links to helpful websites. Typically, readers are able to ask questions or leave comments in the blog. A key component of a successful blog is to have a web master or editor who monitors comments to prevent someone from posting obscenities or other competing, embarrassing, or damaging information.

According to Hubspot, companies that use blogs get 55 percent more web traffic and 70 percent more leads than those that do not. Further, 57 percent of companies have acquired at least one customer through their blog. Part of this success comes from the fact that people believe a company that publishes articles and useful information in their blogs is more trustworthy.

The key to successfully using a blog as a marketing tool is consistency and frequency.

Ethical Dilemma 9.1

During a break during your work shift you are sitting with friends when you overhear another employee at another table sharing with his friend that he is very discontent with his supervisor and the organization due to a new policy that has been implemented. Apparently, it has affected the number of work hours he will get and puts him into a part-time position where he will lose some of his benefits in addition to having less income. You hear him say that he has been posting negative comments on his Facebook and LinkedIn accounts so that others will know what a bad company he works for. He also admitted to sharing proprietary information about his job to "get back" at the company.

1. Is there anything wrong with how the employee is handling this situation? Explain.
2. What is the potential consequences of his actions for the company and other employees?
3. What action, if any, should you take?

Trending NOW

Biometric Entry Systems

In addition to telephonic and call center-based technology used to serve customers better, there are other types being explored by various organizations. One example is a biometric entry system. Many larger organizations are using fingerprint or thumbprint and retinal eye verification to prohibit unauthorized entry into restricted areas and from preventing access to a customer's personal data or property without permission. For example, Walt Disney World in Orlando requires guests who purchase an annual pass to their parks in Florida to provide a fingerprint at the time of purchase. Subsequently, when using their pass at the security/entrance gate at one of the parks, they must place their finger onto the security pad three times to verify they are the authorized users. This prevents fraudulent users from getting into the park and costing the company money, since Disney often provides specials at different times of the year (e.g., discounted passes to military family members or Florida resident discounts). It also protects a guest who loses a pass from having an unauthorized person use it. In the latter instance, customers can rest assured that if they buy a pass in January and subsequently misplace or lose it, they will be able to replace it and prevent some unauthorized person from using their visits.

Financial institutions and retail organizations are using evolving biometric technology to reduce customer wait times by speeding up the customer authentication process for sensitive transactions (e.g., check cashing) and to help deter identity thieves and fraudsters. Additionally, security agencies in over 100 countries are using biometric passports (called e-passports) to decrease the likelihood of counterfeit documentation and strengthen border security.

ADVANTAGES AND DISADVANTAGES OF TECHNOLOGY

Like anything else related to customer service, technology offers advantages and disadvantages. The following sections briefly review some of the issues resulting from the use of technology.

Organizational Issues

Distinct advantages accrue to organizations that use technology. By using computers, software, and various telecommunication devices, a company can extend its presence without physically establishing a business site and without adding staff. Simply by setting up a website, organizations can become known and develop a worldwide customer base while helping to equalize the playing field with multinational and distant competitors. This is because, on the Internet, visitors do not know how many employees or buildings and how much money an organization has when they view a website. The company can provide information and services on demand to customers. Often, simultaneous service is provided to many customers through the telephone, fax, and so on.

The challenge for organizations is to have well-maintained, state-of-the-art equipment with trained, qualified, competent, and customer-oriented people to operate it. In a low-unemployment period, this can be a challenge and can possibly result in disgruntled customers who have to wait on hold for service until an agent is available to help them. However, in recent years with the availability of large numbers of qualified candidates in the workplace, many forward-thinking organizations have been able to overcome this challenge by staffing up with the right employees to handle their jobs. As the organizational "brain drain" continues with many baby boomers retiring, expertise and qualified staffing will likely become a challenge for managers. If they fail to attract and train enough qualified, competent replacement workers, customers are likely to receive lowered levels of service.

Staying on top of competition with technology is an expensive venture. New and upgraded software and hardware appear almost every day. If a company is using systems that are six months old, these systems are on their way to becoming obsolete. In addition, new technology typically brings with it a need to train or retrain staff. The result is that employees have to be taken away from their jobs for training. This often leads to fewer people available to serve customers.

Employee Issues

Technology brings many benefits to employees. The greatest one is that it frees them from mundane tasks such as taking information and mailing out forms, information, or other materials. These tasks can be done by using fax-on-demand, IVR, or online fulfillment systems and self-service mechanisms where customers can access information and get answers on websites or interactive store kiosks. Additionally, potential and existing customers can receive information through automated surveys sent to them to find out preferences, satisfaction levels, and other valuable information that can be used to market products and services and provide better service. Technology also allows employees to serve more people in a shorter period of time—and to do it better.

The downside for employees is that many organizations see technology as a way to reduce staff costs and overhead related to employees. They often eliminate positions following procurement of new hardware and software. Moreover, new technology requires new training and skills. Some people have difficulty using technology and are not able to master it quickly. This in turn can lead to reassignment or dismissal. To avoid such negative outcomes, you and your peers should continually work to stay abreast of technology trends. Do this by checking the Internet or taking refresher courses through your organization's training department or local community resources. Often these resources are inexpensive or free on sites through YouTube and various Internet audio, video, and text-based podcast sites. For example, iTunes store advertises hundreds of thousands of free podcasts on various topics.

Another problem created by technology is an increase in stress levels of both employees and customers. This arises from factors such as the increased pace of business and daily life, the need for employees to keep up to date with technology, and equipment and technology breakdowns. Stress accounts for some of the high turnover rate in call center and retail staff and for customer defections. It also is one of the

Sometimes, the stress of dealing with a variety of customers can take its toll. *What can you do to prevent your frustration from coming through to your customers?*

© YAY Media AS/Alamy Stock Photo RF

highest medical expenses with which companies have to deal. But it does not necessarily have to be that way. For more information on dealing with stress and time more effectively in a service environment, visit http://www.mhhe.com/customerservice to read the additional chapters on time and stress management that supplement this text.

Customer Issues

In the age of technology, people contacting your organization typically expect immediate responses or assistance. They do not care about problems with your system or that you are experiencing. They likely expect that issues related to services, phone systems, and other equipment are anticipated and an alternative is available—and that you have a backup plan in place to handle them when something fails. If that is not the case and you make excuses for why you cannot deliver service (e.g., "I am sorry, my system just went down. Can you call back later?"), chances are that you may never again hear from the person in a positive manner. If you do hear, it is often in a form of complaint to your supervisor or in this day of social media from comments about you and your organization on consumer opinion sites like:

http://www.yelp.com

http://www.ripoffreport.com

http://www.complaintsboard.com

http://usa.gov/consumer-complaints

http://ftccomplaintassistant.gov

It is not the fault of your customer, nor is it his or her responsibility to call you back. There should be a process for circumventing technical problems and you should take the initiative to get the information he or she needs and get back to him or her as soon as possible (e.g., "My apologies, Mr. Hernandez; my computer system just went offline. Rather than keep you waiting, please tell me exactly what information you need. As soon as the system comes back online, I will research the issue and get back to you with an answer. Is that acceptable?" If the customer agrees, say something like, "Please give me a phone number and an e-mail address where I can reach you."). If customers tell you they need an answer right away, ask them to hold while you check with someone else to try and get an answer. Certainly, these steps will not work in every situation or satisfy every customer; however, you should make a positive, good-faith effort to assist them right away.

From a customer standpoint, if service providers and organizations use it correctly and professionally, technology can be a blessing. From the comfort and convenience of a home, office, car, or anywhere a customer may have a telephone or laptop computer, he or she can access products and services. More people than ever have access to the Internet and computers. Technologies allow a customer to get information, order products, have questions about billing or other matters answered, and access virtually anything she or he wants on the World Wide Web.

However, this convenience comes with a cost to customers, just as it does for organizations. To have the latest gadgets is costly in terms of time and money. For example, when a customer calls a toll-free support number, or must pay for a call to a support center, it is not unusual for the customer to wait on hold for the next available agent. In addition, technology does not always work as designed. This might occur on a website when the instructions about how to enter an account number or how to get a password are not clear. Even if a customer follows the instructions exactly, he or she might repeatedly get a frustrating error message instructing him or her to reenter the data. At

> **Customer Service Success Tip**
>
> Make sure that you have a "backup plan" to use in case technology fails (e.g., the electricity fails and the cash register will not work or the computer system goes down). Discuss how to handle this type of situation with your supervisor before something goes wrong and customer service fails or a situation escalates.

some point, the customer will simply give up and go to another website. Another example would be for a customer to be caught in "voice mail jail." In this situation, the customer follows the instructions, pressing the appropriate phone keys to get to a representative, only to find that the representative has forwarded his or her calls to another voice mailbox. Eventually, either the instructions lead the customer back to the first message or the customer is automatically disconnected.

Customer Service Success Tip

These days, most customers with whom you will interact are more savvy and have access to the Internet. They often know what effective customer service should "feel" like and are likely to be less tolerant if the service they perceive they receive is substandard. Unlike past CSRs, you will be less likely to get away with passing a customer off to another representative or lying to him or her (e.g., "I am sorry, my supervisor is in a meeting at the moment and not available. Can I get you name and I will have him call you back when he is available?"). If you fail to follow through, many customers will now bypass your level (and that of you supervisor) to go directly to the top of the organization. Websites like http://www.connect.data.com make it a simple search to get the name and address of a company CEO to which customers can send a letter. And, do not forget that the last name in your organization that the customer heard was likely yours. It is always better to professionally handle a customer situation than try to avoid or ignore it.

---

robocall A term used to describe a type of automated phone auto-dialer that delivers a personalized, prerecorded message to recipients.

Another major consumer issue related to telephone usage is that many organizations conduct direct marketing (telemarketing) and/or collections activities via the telephone. Unfortunately, many unscrupulous telemarketers pressure-call recipients or use **robocall** machines, illegally take advantage of them, and/or violate personal privacy. Often these callers are scammers who offer fraudulent offers to unsuspecting recipients in an effort to get them to send money or to extract personal information from them. The calls are robotic in nature, thus the name. One scam that surfaced in recent years is an automated message purporting to be from the IRS telling the recipients that they owe back taxes and instructing them to call a number. When the recipients call that number, they may fall victim to a scammer on the other end who tries to get them to send money. To stem the use of robocalls, they have been made illegal unless the caller falls into certain categories (e.g., political organizations, charities, telephone surveyors, or companies with which a consumer has an existing business relationship). As a result, many states and the federal government have passed laws dictating how companies must conduct business via the telephone. If you are involved in this type of outbound calling, it is crucial that you and your organization adhere to laws prohibiting when you may call someone and how to conduct business. To help reduce the number of annoyance calls consumers receive, they can now apply to be on a national do-not-call registry. Many states have similar lists.

Additional Issues

Just as with any system, there are people who will take advantage of it. Technology, especially the Internet, has spawned a new era of fraud and manipulation. This is a major concern for consumers and can create many challenges for you and your peers when you work in a call center. Some of the biggest problems you must deal with are customers' fears of fraud, violation of privacy, and concerns that their personal and financial information might be compromised, leading to future issues with their credit.

Many news stories warn of criminal activity associated with technology. The result is that customers, especially those who are technically naive, have a level of distrust and paranoia related to giving information via the Internet and over the phone to unsolicited callers. This is why many websites involved in e-commerce offer the option of calling a toll-free number to talk to a customer service representative instead of entering credit card and other personal information into an Internet order form. If you, as a customer service provider, encounter a lot of this type of reluctance, notify your supervisor. Some systemic issues may be adding to your customers' fears. You have a personal responsibility and a vested interest to improve processes and procedures in the organization. Working to identify these issues and dealing with them professionally can make life easier for you and your customers. It can also help the organization improve the quality of service delivered and potentially increase revenue streams. The latter can lead to more available cash for new equipment, facilities, salaries, and benefits.

One thing to remember is that a customer's reluctance to provide you with information is not necessarily a reflection on you or your peers; it is based more on a distrust in the system. Figure 9.4 lists some strategies you can use to help reduce customer fears related to communicating via technology.

> **Street Talk**
>
> When talking on the telephone, be sure that the phone is inactive before commenting on the conversation to a colleague nearby. If the phone call is still active, the customer will hear any comments you may make before the line is inactive.
>
> **SOURCE: SHARON MASSEN, Ph.D., CAP** *Massen and Associates*

Customer Service Success Tip

Informed customers go to great lengths to protect their credit card, merchant account, social security numbers, addresses, and other personal data (e.g., arrest records, medical history, and family information). You should educate yourself about potential fraud issues and discuss security measures that your organization has in place with your supervisor and peers so that you are prepared to address customer concerns. For example, if your processes require collection of a customer's social security number, be prepared to explain why that information is needed and how it will be protected. So many scams are perpetrated by people stealing social security numbers that many consumers are reluctant to provide their numbers to strangers, especially over the telephone.

Trending NOW

Wait Time Reduction Technology

According to *The Wall Street Journal*, retail organizations are taking steps toward better customer satisfaction by using technology to reduce service wait times.[11] Some examples of this are the following:

- Kroger Supermarkets have installed infrared body heat-sensing cameras and sensors (like those used by the military and law enforcement) developed by Irisys, known as QueVision, at entrances and cash registers of 95 percent of its stores.

These devices sense the number of people waiting and signal a need to open additional service lanes. The result is that average wait times have been lowered from four minutes to 26 seconds. Of course, like any system, there are downsides and potential impacts on staff. Managers must be proactive to ensure that there are enough employees on-site to respond from other departments when new registers need to be opened to handle customers.

- Chili's, Applebee's, Smokey Bones, UNO's, and other casual dining restaurants now allow diners to pay at their table with a small flat-screen device. This provides a level of convenience, customers' credit card never leaves their sight, and they do not have to wait for a server's assistance to check out.

- Walmart is testing a "Scan & Go" iPhone application that allows customers to scan bar code items they are buying

as they shop and place them in bags. When they get to the register, they hold their phone to the self-checkout screen and the information is wirelessly transferred.

- Nordstrom department stores are using handheld devices that allow customers to pay an associate anywhere in their store, rather than proceeding to a single checkout line.

FIGURE 9.4

Reducing Customer Fears about Technology

Avoiding customer concerns is often as simple as communicating effectively. Try some of the following approaches to help reassure your customers about the security of technology:

- Emphasize the organization's policy on security and service. If customers voice concerns about providing a credit card number over the phone or on the Internet, you might respond with "This is not a problem. You can either fax or mail the information to us."
- If your organization is a member, stress participation in consumer watchdog or community organizations (e.g., Better Business Bureau or Chamber of Commerce).
- Direct customers to areas on your website that show your digital certificate or security level (e.g., a Secure Socket Layer [SSL] logo from a third-party certifying source like VeriSign or Thawte) and that indicate the encryption of information entered into the order system and transferred electronically. Also, point to the "https" component of your domain name at the top of their screen. This indicates that they are on a secure website.
- Point out any website page that shows the organization's history and shows how long you have been in business (assuming the company has been in business for a while). The longevity of a company can subconsciously allay fears and convince people that you have been around for a while and are not likely to go out of business tomorrow.
- Ask for only pertinent information.
- Answer questions quickly and openly (e.g., if a customer asks why you need certain information, respond in terms of benefits to the customer—for example, "We need that information to ensure that we credit the right account.").
- Avoid asking for personal and financial account information when possible.
- Offer other options for data submission, if they are available.
- When using the telephone, smile and sound approachable in order to establish rapport (customers can "hear" a smile over the telephone).
- Listen carefully for voice tones that indicate hesitancy or uncertainty and respond appropriately (e.g., "You sound a bit hesitant about giving your credit card information, Mr. Hopkins. Let me assure you that we will not process your charge until we have actually shipped your order. And, you will receive an e-mail to the address you provided so that you know when the order was charged and the amount.").
- Communicate in short, clear, and concise terms and sentences. Also, avoid technical or "legal" language that might confuse or frustrate the customer.
- If calls are recorded, remind the customer of that and point to it as an added layer of security in case there is a question about a charge later.
- Explain how your organization uses and stores personal information.

1. What are some reasons why technology has assumed a more dominant role in customer service?

2. What are some trends leading to the expansion of the use of technology to serve customers?

3. How many common call center technologies can you list?

4. In what ways are organizations tapping technology to better serve potential and existing customers?

5. What are some advantages of technology related to customer service?

6. List some of the disadvantages of technology related to customer service.

LO 9-4 Technology Etiquette and Strategies

CONCEPT **Using technology ethically and with correct etiquette is important.**

As with any other interaction with people, you should be aware of some basic dos and do nots related to using technology to interact with and serve your customers. Failure to observe some commonsense rules can cause loss of a customer.

E-MAIL

E-mail provides an inexpensive, quick way of communicating via the World Wide Web. It was never intended to replace formal written correspondence. Even so, many organizations now use it to send things like attached correspondence and receipts. They also use it to notify customers of order status, gather additional information needed to serve a customer, and for other business-related issues. No matter what the function, e-mail has its own set of guidelines for effective usage. These guidelines help ensure that you do not offend or otherwise create problems when dealing with customers. The following 13 tips offer some e-mail etiquette guidelines for effective usage:

1. *Use abbreviations and initials.* Since e-mail is an informal means of communicating, using acronyms and other short forms or abbreviations (e.g., USA versus United States of America) works fine in some cases. Just be sure that your receiver knows what the letters represent; otherwise, miscommunication could occur. Figure 9.5 lists some common abbreviations employed by e-mail users who typically know and e-mail one another frequently (e.g., internal customers,

LOL	Laughing out loud or lots of luck	ROTFL	Rolling on the floor laughing
BCNU	Be seeing you	TTFN	Ta-ta for now
FYI	For your information	TTYL	Talk to you later
IMHO	In my humble opinion	BTW	By the way
FWIW	For what it's worth	ASAP	As soon as possible

FIGURE 9.5

Common Abbreviations

friends, and family members). When communicating with external customers, you may want to use abbreviations sparingly or avoid them altogether in order to prevent confusion, communication breakdown, and the perception that you are unprofessional.

2. *Proofread and spell-check before sending a message.* Checking your message before sending an e-mail may help prevent damage to your professional image. This is especially true when writing customers because you are representing your organization. Poor grammar, syntax, spelling, and usage can paint a poor picture of your abilities and professionalism and can leave a bad impression about your organization and its employees. If you are using Microsoft e-mail products (e.g., LIVE or Outlook), there is a spell-check function available. Even so, remember that correctly spelled variations of a word (e.g., their and there) will not be caught if used incorrectly in a sentence. Also, spell-check searches the message text and not the title line. You will have to ensure those words are spelled correctly on your own.

3. *Think before writing.* This is especially important if you are answering an e-mail when you are upset or emotional. Take time to cool off before responding to a negative message ("flame" is the name given to an insulting or provocative e-mail message) or when you are angry. Remember that once you send an e-mail, you cannot take back your words. Your relationship with your receiver is at stake and the recipient can easily share your message with others (think about all the e-mailed messages you get regularly that have been forwarded to many other people and whose names appear in the text section of the e-mail). The latter is why you should never forward potentially discriminatory or racist jokes, articles, or other materials that could cast a negative light on you and your organization. For this reason, most companies prohibit personal use of their e-mail systems.

4. *Use short, concise sentences.* The average person will not read lengthy, multiparagraph messages sent by e-mail. Scrolling up and down pages of text is time-consuming and frustrating. Therefore, put your question or key idea in the first sentence or paragraph. Keep your sentences short and use new paragraphs often, for easier reading. A good rule of thumb is that if the entire message does not fit on a single viewing screen, consider whether another means of communication is more appropriate. An option would be to use the attachment feature in order to allow lengthy documents to be printed by the recipient.

5. *Use both upper and lowercase letters.* With e-mail, writing a sentence or message in all-capital letters is like shouting at a person and could offend or cause relationship problems. In addition, reading a message written in all-capital letters is difficult and is likely to annoy your customer.

6. *Be careful with punctuation.* As with all-capital letters, you should use caution with punctuation marks, especially exclamation points. Like all-capital letter messages, those can potentially cause offense because they indicate strong emotion.

7. *Use e-mail only for informal correspondence.* Although it is becoming more acceptable to send business correspondence (e.g., contracts, resumes, and other information) via e-mail, it is probably better to use a more formal format in most instances (see the additional information on the Business Writers' Workshop available in your Connect course). For example, it would be inappropriate to send a membership cancellation notice via e-mail. The receiver might think that the matter is not significant enough to warrant your organization buying a stamp to mail a letter. However, this caution does not mean that you should not attach letters or other documents to an e-mail. Just consider the effect on the recipient.

Another important thing to remember about e-mail is that it is sometimes unreliable. Many people do not check their e-mail regularly, especially if they use free e-mail accounts offered by yahoo.com, gmail.com, google.com, and other companies. Computer systems also fail and individuals often change service providers or e-mail addresses and forget to inform everyone with whom they correspond. If your message is critical and delivery is time-sensitive, choose another method (e.g., a telephone call or express mail). If nothing else, call as a follow-up to ensure that the customer received the e-mail. Do not assume the addressee got your message.

In some cases, e-mail that is not delivered does not get returned to the sender, so you may not know why the recipient did not respond. If your computer system allows, you can also request a return receipt notification showing the time and date that a message was opened. The downside of that is that your receivers can cancel the return notification on their end or it could get directed to their spam folder, and you will not know if the message ever arrived.

8. *Use organization e-mail for business only.* Many companies have policies prohibiting sending personal e-mail via their system. Some companies have started to monitor outgoing messages for system abuses. Many organizations now can use unauthorized use of the e-mail as grounds for employee dismissal. Avoid violating your company's policy on this. Remember, too, that while you are sending personal messages, you are wasting productive time and your customers may be waiting. A good rule of thumb is: Never send anything by e-mail that you would not want to see in tomorrow's newspaper.

9. *Use blind courtesy copies sparingly.* Most e-mail systems allow you to send a copy to someone without the original addressee knowing it (a blind courtesy copy or bcc). If the recipient becomes aware of the bcc, he or she might view your actions as suspicious and your motives brought into question. A customer might wonder if your actions are an attempt to hide something from him or her. Thus, a relationship breakdown could occur if the original recipient discovers the existence of the bcc or if the recipient of the bcc misuses the information.

10. *Copy only necessary people.* Nowadays, most people are overloaded with work and do not have the time to read every e-mail. If someone does not need to see a message, do not send that person a copy with the "reply to all" function available in e-mail programs. When you do the latter, anyone listed as a recipient or copied will get the return e-mail.

11. *Get permission to send advertisements or promotional materials.* As mentioned earlier, people have little time or patience to read lengthy e-mail messages, especially from someone trying to promote or sell them something. Unsolicited information is viewed the same way you probably think of unsolicited junk mail or telemarketing calls at home. Companies should routinely have an "opt-out" check box available when they are soliciting e-mail information from their customers. If your company does not have this option, you should recommend adding one to your management as a service to your customers and potential customers.

12. *Be cautious in using emoticons.* **Emoticons (emotional icons)** are the faces created by using computer keyboard characters. Many people believe that their use in business correspondence is inappropriate and too informal. In addition, since humor is a matter of personal point of view, these symbols might be misinterpreted and confusing. This is especially true when you are corresponding with someone from a different culture. Figure 9.6 shows examples of emoticons.

emoticons (emotional icons)
Humorous characters that send visual messages such as smiling or frowning. They can be created with various strokes of the computer keyboard characters and symbols.

FIGURE 9.6

Sample Emoticons

:-)	Happy	:-}	Embarrassment or sarcasm
:-(	Sad	:-D	Big grin or laugh
;-)	Flirting or wink	<:-)	Stupid question (dunce cap)
O /\	Defiant or determined	O:-)	Angel or saint
:-O	Yelling or surprised	>:-)	Devil
:-x	Lips are sealed	:-/	Really confused

It is so easy to send a potentially offensive message via the computer, especially if you are in a hurry. *What do you do to ensure that you follow accepted e-mail protocol and etiquette when sending messages?*

13. *Fill in your address line last.* This is a safety mechanism to ensure that you take the time to read and think about your message before you send the e-mail. A message cannot be transmitted until you address it. You will have one last chance to consider the effect of the content of the message on the recipient (e.g. tone, word selection, and emotion expressed).

FACSIMILE

Facsimile (FAX) machines have been around for decades. Many companies now use computers with scanners to replace them. Even so, they are still used by some organizations, especially small businesses. As with any other form of communication, there are certain dos and do nots to abide by when you use a fax machine to transmit messages. Failing to adhere to these simple guidelines can cause frustration, anger, and a breakdown in the relationships between you and your customers or others to whom you send messages.

- *Be considerate of your receiver.* If you plan to send a multipage document to your customer, telephone in advance to make sure that it is OK and a good time to send it. This is especially true if you will be using a business number during the workday or if there is only one line for the telephone and fax machine. It is frustrating and irritating to customers when their fax is occupied for long periods because large documents are being transmitted, especially if they are not expecting or did not solicit them. If you must send a large document, try to do so before or after working hours (e.g., before 9 a.m. or after 5 p.m.). Also, keep in mind geographic time differences. Following these tips can also help maintain good relationships with coworkers who may also depend on the fax machine to conduct business with their customers.

- *Limit graphics.* If graphic images are unnecessary to clarify written text, eliminate them. They waste the receiver's printer cartridge ink, tie up the machine unduly, and can irritate your receiver. Therefore, delete any unnecessary graphics (or solid colored areas) including your large corporate logo on a cover sheet. If appropriate, create a special outline image of your logo for your fax cover sheets.

- *Limit correspondence recipients.* As with e-mail and memorandums, limit the recipients of your messages. If someone does not have a need to know, do not send message copies to that person. Check your broadcast mailing list (a list of people who will receive all messages, often programmed into a computer) to ensure that it is limited to people who "have a need to know." This is important from the standpoint of confidentiality. If the information you are sending is proprietary or sensitive in any way, think about who will receive it. Do not forget that unless the document is going directly to someone's computer fax modem, it may be lying in a stack of other incoming messages and accessible by people other than your intended recipient. If a message that you are transmitting has sensitive information or data (e.g., credit card or social security numbers), call recipients to alert them to check their fax machine when you are about to send it.

Customer Service Success Tip

When a customer calls or contacts your organization, you should personally accept responsibility and do whatever you can to help ensure that he or she gets the finest level of service available. Remember that, to provide quality customer service, everyone in the organization has to take ownership for customer satisfaction. The first person interacting with a current or potential customer sends a powerful message about the organization and may be the only person with whom that customer ever deals. The way that person is treated will often determine the memory of the organization and whether the customer becomes a supporter or spreads the word about the poor service received.

KNOWLEDGE CHECK

1. List many strategies that organizations are using to maintain a high-touch relationship with current and potential customers.

2. What are some commonsense etiquette rules related to using e-mail to deliver customer service?

3. When sending facsimile messages, what should you consider?

LO 9-5 The Telephone in Customer Service

CONCEPT   **The telephone is the second most important link in customer service.**

Not all service via technology is delivered from a customer contact center. Although many small- and medium-sized organizations may have dedicated customer service professionals to staff their telephones, others do not. In the latter cases, the responsibility for answering the telephone and providing service falls on anyone who is available and hears the telephone ring (e.g., administrative assistant, salesperson, driver, nurse, partner, owner, or CEO).

Employees no longer have to take time to physically travel to another location to interact with customers and vendors. To counter that, modern businesses rely heavily on the use of telephones to conduct day-to-day operations and communicate with internal and external customers. Effective use of the telephone saves employee time and effort. By simply dialing a telephone number or typing in a text message on a cell phone, you are almost instantaneously transported anywhere in the world. And with the use of the fax and computer modem, documents and information can be sent in minutes to someone thousands of miles away—even during nonbusiness hours. Figure 9.7 lists some advantages of telephone customer service.

With telephones (and supporting equipment), more businesses are setting up inbound (e.g., order taking, customer service, information sources) and outbound (e.g., telemarketing sales, customer service, customer surveys) telephone staff. Through these groups of trained specialists, companies are expanding and enhancing their customer contact efforts. They are also more likely to accomplish total customer satisfaction.

FIGURE 9.7

Advantages of Telephone Customer Service

Even though there are some disadvantages to telephone communication (e.g., lack of face-to-face contact with the customer), there are many advantages. Some of the advantages follow:

- *Convenience*. Sales, information exchange, money collection, customer satisfaction surveys, and complaint handling are only a few of the many tasks effectively handled by using the telephone and related equipment. If someone needs a quick answer, the telephone can provide a vehicle to receive it without the need to travel and meet someone face-to-face or to endure the delays caused by the mail.
- *Ease of communication*. Some countries have more advanced telephone systems and capabilities than others. Still, you can call someone in nearly any country in the world. With advances in cellular phone technology, even mobile phones have international communication capability.
- *Economy*. Face-to-face visits or sales calls are expensive and can be reduced or eliminated. Phone contacts eliminate the need to travel to a customer's location. Since the deregulation of the telephone industry in the United States, competitive rates offered by many telephone companies provide companies and customers with many options for calling plans. For example, customers can purchase a calling card and use it from any telephone. All of this makes accessing customer services a simple and relatively inexpensive task, especially when combined with the other technology discussed in this chapter.
- *Efficiency*. You and your customer can interact without the delay of writing and responding by mail or e-mail. Telephones are so simple to operate that kindergarten and grade school children are taught to use them.

COMMUNICATION SKILLS FOR SUCCESS

Just as when you are delivering service face-to-face with a customer, the same skills apply to providing effective customer service over the telephone, especially the use of vocal quality and listening skills. Your customer cannot communicate with or understand you if she or he does not accurately receive your message. To reduce the chances of message failure, think about the following 11 communication techniques:

1. *Speak clearly.* By pronouncing words clearly and correctly, you increase the chances that your customer will accurately receive your intended message. Failure to use good diction could decrease a customer's comprehension of your message. It might also be interpreted to mean that you are lazy, unprofessional, or lack intelligence and/or education. If you are unsure how to improve your diction, do an Internet search to find helpful tips. Clear diction is especially important when speaking to someone with a hearing deficit or who speaks a different native language.

2. *Limit jargon, slang, and colloquialisms.* Technical jargon (terms related to technology, an industry, a specific organization, or a job), slang (informal words used to make a message more colorful; c.g., *whoopee*, *blooper*, *bummer*), and colloquialisms (regional phrases or words such as "fair to middling," "as slow as molasses," "if the good Lord's willing and the creek don't rise," or "faster than a New York minute") can distort your message and detract from your ability to communicate effectively. This is especially true when your recipient speaks a language other than your native language. By using words or phrases unfamiliar to the customer, you draw the customer's attention away from listening to your message. This is because, when people encounter a word or phrase that is unfamiliar, they tend to stop and reflect on that word or phrase. When this occurs, they miss the next part of the message while their mind tries to focus on and decipher the unfamiliar element they encountered. You must then either repeat the missed portion or risk miscommunication.

3. *Adjust your volume.* As your conversation progresses, it may become apparent that you need to speak more loudly or more softly to your customer. Obvious cues are statements from the customer, such as "You do not have to yell" or "Could you speak up?" If your customer is speaking really loudly, he or she may have a hearing impairment. To find out if this is the case, you could say, "I am sorry, Mrs. Reynolds, are you able to hear me clearly? I am having trouble with loud volume on my end." Taking this approach can potentially help alleviate the issue and avoids potential embarrassment to the customer.

4. *Speak at a rate that allows comprehension.* Depending on the person to whom you are speaking, you may need to adjust your rate of speech by either speeding up or slowing down. A good rule of thumb is to mirror or match the other person's rate of speech to some extent, since he or she is probably comfortable with it. Otherwise, you risk boring the customer by speaking too slowly, or confusing the customer by speaking too rapidly. Be careful not to be too obvious or unnatural when doing this; otherwise, some customers may think that you are making fun of them.

5. *Use voice inflection.* By raising or lowering the pitch or tone of your voice and avoiding a tendency to speak in a monotone (flat or unchanging pitch), you can help communicate your message in an interesting manner that will hold your customer's attention. The result might be saved time, since your message may be received correctly the first time and you will not have to repeat it.

Customer Service Success Tip

Avoid distractions while you are on the phone in order to help prevent breakdowns in communication. It is difficult to listen effectively when you are reading something not related to serving your customer, writing notes to yourself, using a cash register or mobile device, typing, polishing your fingernails, and so on.

6. *Use correct grammar.* Just as important as enunciation, good grammar helps project a positive, competent image. When you fail to use good grammar in your communication, the perception might be that you are lazy or uneducated. Keep in mind that your customer forms an image of you and the company you represent simply by listening to you and the way you speak.

7. *Pause occasionally.* This simple yet dramatic technique can sometimes affect the course of a conversation. By pausing after you make a statement or ask a question, you give yourself time to breathe and think. You also give your customer an opportunity to reflect on what you have said or to ask questions. This practice can greatly aid in reducing tension when you are speaking with an upset customer or one who does not speak your language fluently.

8. *Smile as you speak.* By smiling, you project an upbeat, warm, and sincere attitude through the phone. This can often cheer the customer, diffuse irritation, and help build rapport. A technique some telephone professionals use to remind themselves to smile when placing or answering a call is to put a small mirror or a picture of a "smiling face" in front of them or next to their telephone. This reminds them to smile as they talk.

9. *Project a positive image and attitude.* All the tips related to using your voice that were presented in earlier chapters contribute to how people envision you. Customers generally do not want to hear what you cannot do for them or about the bad day you are having. They want a timely, affirmative answer to their questions or solution of their problems. Giving anything less is likely to discourage or annoy them and result in a service breakdown.

10. *Wait to speak.* Many people tend to interrupt a customer to add information or ask a question. This is not only rude but can cause a breakdown in communication and possibly anger the customer. If you ask a question, or if the customer is speaking, allow him or her to respond or to finish speaking before interjecting your thoughts or comments.

11. *Listen actively.* Just as with face-to-face communication, effective listening is a crucial telephone skill for the customer service provider. The need to focus is even more important when you are speaking on the phone, since you do not have nonverbal cues or visual contact to help in message delivery or interpretation.

The sound of your voice projects your true attitude and mood. Make sure that you remember to put a smile in your tone when talking to customers. *How do you ensure that you project a positive message when talking to people on the phone?*

©Fuse/Getty Images RF

TIPS FOR CREATING A POSITIVE TELEPHONE IMAGE

People quickly form an opinion of you and your organization in any interaction. The message they receive often determines how they interact with you during the conversation and in your future relationship. Keep in mind that when you answer your organization's telephone, or call someone else as part of your job, you represent yourself and the organization. Since many telephone calls are short, you have a limited opportunity to make a positive impression.

Ethical Dilemma 9.2

Before discussing the following dilemma with other students, research the National Do-Not-Call Registry on the Internet.

You have heard that there are federal laws that prohibit call centers from contacting people with whom they have no prior business relationship or who are on the National Do-Not-Call Registry. Your organization has recently started a phone campaign to identify potential customers and is using a number of phone lists obtained from various other companies. When you remind your supervisor about the nonsolicitation law, she tells you not to worry about it. She instructs you that if someone complains about the interruption or states they are on a do-not-call registry list when you call, that you should just hang up.

1. Are there any potential legal problems with this policy? If so, what might they be?

2. Are there any ethical issues here? Explain.

3. What would you do in this situation?

When you feel good about yourself, you normally project a naturally confident and pleasant image. On days when things are not going so well for you, your self-image may tend to suffer. Here are eight suggestions to help serve your customers effectively and leave them thinking well of you and your organization.

1. *Continually evaluate yourself.* You are your own best critic. From time to time, think about your conversation—what went well and what could you have improved? If possible, occasionally record your daily conversations with family and friends with their permission; evaluate your voice qualities and message delivery. Have someone else listen to the tape and provide objective feedback. To help in your self-assessment, you may want to make copies of Worksheet 9.1 (available in your Connect course) and evaluate all your calls for a specific period (e.g., a couple of hours or a day).

2. *Use proper body posture.* The following behaviors can negatively affect the sound and quality of your voice:

   - Slouching in your chair
   - Sitting with your feet on a desk, with your arms behind your head, as you rock back and forth in your chair
   - Looking down, with your chin on your chest, to read something or search through drawers
   - Resting the telephone handset between your cheek and shoulder as you do other work (e.g., type data into a computer, look for something, write, doodle, or file your nails)

Strive to sit or stand upright and speak clearly into the mouthpiece whether you are using a headset or handheld receiver. If you are using a handheld receiver, make sure that you place the earpiece firmly against your ear and the mouthpiece is directly in front of your mouth.

3. *Be prepared.* Answer a ringing phone promptly and use a standard greeting as outlined later in this chapter.

4. *Speak naturally.* Whether you are calling someone or providing information to a caller, speak in a conversational voice. Do not use a "canned" or mechanical presentation, and do not read from a prepared script, unless you are required to do so by your company. If you must read from a script, *practice, practice, practice.* Before you connect with a customer, become very comfortable with your presentation so that you can deliver it in a fluid, warm, and sincere manner. Nothing sends a negative message more than a service provider who mispronounces a customer's name, stumbles through opening comments, and seems disorganized.

5. *Be time-conscious.* Customers appreciate prompt, courteous service. Be aware that time is money—yours, the organization's, and the customer's. Have your thoughts organized when you call a customer. It is a good idea to have a list of questions or key points ready before calling (see Worksheet 9.2 available in your Connect course as an example). If a customer phones you and you do not have an answer or information readily available, offer to do some research and call back instead of putting the customer on hold. Respect your customer's time. Chances are that customers will prefer to hold if they will be waiting only a short time, but give them the option. In addition to helping better organize your calls, a written call planning sheet will provide a good record of the call.

6. *Be proactive with service.* If you must say no to a customer, do so in a positive manner without quoting policy. Tell the customer what you can do. For example, if your policy prohibits refunds on one-of-a-kind or closeout items, you might make an offer such as this (depending on your level of authority or empowerment): "Mr. Targowski, I see that the computer you ordered from our website was a closeout item. That information is shown on your receipt. I understand that you have decided that you need more RAM. Although I cannot give refunds on a closeout item, I can give you a voucher good at any of our retail locations for a $50 discount on a memory upgrade or free installation, whichever you prefer."

7. *Doing more than the customer expects after a breakdown is important*, especially if you or your company made an error. There will be times when you or your company is not responsible for a service or product error, but you want to maintain a positive customer–provider relationship—going out of your way to help make it better is just good business practice.

8. *Conclude calls professionally.* Ending a call on an upbeat note, using the caller's name, and summarizing key actions that both parties will take are all recommended practices. For example, you might say, "All right, Ms. Herrick, let me confirm what we've discussed. I will get _____ by the 23rd, and call you to confirm _____. You will take care of _____. Is that also your understanding?" Once you reach agreement, thank the customer for calling, ask what other questions he or she has or with what else you can assist, and then let the customer disconnect first. By following this type of format, you can reduce misunderstandings and elicit any last-minute questions or comments the customer might have. If you fail to bring the conversation to a formal close and hang up abruptly, the customer may feel you are in a hurry to finish servicing him or her (regardless of the fact that you have just spent 15 minutes talking with him or her!). Think of

this final step as wrapping a gift: It looks fine, but adding a nice ribbon and bow in the form of a professional close makes it look even better. The thank you and polite sign-off are your ribbon and bow.

EFFECTIVE TELEPHONE USAGE

One basic strategy for successfully providing effective customer service over the telephone is to thoroughly understand all phone features and use them effectively. This may seem to be a logical and simple concept, but think about times when you called a company and someone attempted to transfer you, put you on hold, or did not communicate clearly. If the transfer was successful, you were lucky. If not, you probably could not understand what happened, got disconnected, were connected to the wrong party, or heard the original person come back on the telephone to apologize and say something like, "The call did not go through. Let me try again." Sound familiar? If so, use the strategies in Figure 9.8 to ensure that you do not deliver similar poor service.

FIGURE 9.8
Transfer Calls and Use the Hold Function Properly

Be sure you understand how the telephone call transfer (sometimes called the link) and hold functions work. Nothing is more frustrating or irritating than callers being shuffled from one person to the next or to be placed on what seems to be an endless hold. Here are some suggestions that can help to increase your effectiveness in these areas:

- **Always request permission before transferring a caller.** This shows respect for the caller and psychologically gives the caller a feeling of control over the conversation. You can also offer options: You can ask the caller to allow a transfer or let you take a message. This is especially helpful when the customer is already irritated or has a problem. Before transferring the call, explain why you need to do so. You might say, "The person who handles billing questions is Shashandra Philips at extension 4739. May I transfer you, or would you prefer I take a message and pass it along to her?" This saves you and the caller time and effort, and you have provided professional, courteous service. If the caller says, "Yes, please transfer me," follow by saying something like, "I will be happy to connect you. Again, if you are accidentally disconnected, I'll be calling Shashandra Philips at extension 4739." You might also ask for the caller's number in case a disconnection occurs and you need to call him or her back.

- **Once you have successfully reached the intended person,** announce the call by saying, "Shashandra, this is (your name), from (your department). I have (customer's name) on the phone. She has a (question, problem). Are you the right person to handle that?" If Shashandra answers yes, connect the caller and announce, "(Customer's name), I have Shashandra Philips on the line. She will be happy to assist you. Thanks for calling (or some similar positive disconnect phrase)." You can then hang up, knowing that you did your part in delivering quality customer service.

- **If the call taker is not available or is not the appropriate person,** reconnect with the customer and explain the situation. Then offer to take a message rather than trying to transfer to different people while keeping the customer on hold. You would make an exception if the call taker informed you of the appropriate person to whom you should transfer, or if the customer insisted on staying on the line while you tried to transfer to the right person.

- **You should avoid making a blind transfer.** This practice is ineffective, rude, and not customer-focused. A **blind transfer** happens when a service provider asks a caller, "May I transfer you to Cathy in Billing?" or may even say, without permission, "Let me transfer you to Tom in Shipping." Once the intended transfer party answers, the person transferring the call hangs up. Always "announce your caller" by waiting for the phone to be picked up and saying, "This is (your name) in (your department). I have (customer's name) on the line with a question/issue about _____. Can you take the

blind transfer The practice of transferring an incoming caller to another telephone number without an introduction to the second service provider, and then hanging up.

(continued)

call?" Failure to do this could result in a confrontation between the customer and the second service provider. If the calling customer is already upset, you have just set up a situation that could lead to a lost customer and/or angry coworker, especially if the second provider is not the one who can handle the customer's issue.

- **If you place someone on hold,** it is a good idea to go back on the line every 20 to 30 seconds to let the person know that you have not forgotten the call. This action becomes more important if the phone system you are using does not offer information or music that the customer hears during the holding time. Once you return to the phone to take the call, thank the caller for waiting.

- *Eliminate distractions.* Do not eat food, chew gum, drink, talk to others, read (unless for the purpose of providing the customer with information), or handle other office tasks (e.g., filing, stapling, stamping, sealing envelopes, or using the computer) while on the phone unless you are checking information for the customer on the line and with his or her permission. Your voice quality will alert the customer to the fact that you are otherwise preoccupied.

- *Answer promptly.* You communicate a lot by the way you handle a phone call. One tip for success is to always answer by the third or fourth ring. This sends a nonverbal message to your customers of your availability to serve them. It also reduces the irritating ringing that you, coworkers, or other customers who are present have to hear. Check with your supervisor, employee handbook, or intranet website to learn your organization's standard for answering.

Customer Service Success Tip

Use equipment properly. Ensure that the earpiece and mouthpiece rest squarely against your ear and in front of your mouth, respectively, when speaking to customers. This allows you to accurately hear what a customer says and accurately and clearly transmit your words to the customer. Your success or failure in receiving and delivering messages often hinges on simply holding the receiver or wearing a headset properly.

- *Use titles with names.* Dale Carnegie once said, "There is no sweeter sound to one's ears than the sound of his name." However, until you are told otherwise, use a person's title (e.g., Mr., Mrs., Ms., or Dr.) and last name. Do not assume that you can use first names. Some people regard the use of their first name as insolent or rude. This may especially be true of older customers and people from other cultures where respect and use of titles are valued. When you are speaking with customers, it is also a good idea to use their name frequently (do not overdo it, though, or you will sound mechanical). Repeat the name directly after the greeting (e.g., "Yes, Dr. Carmine, how may I help you?"), during the conversation (e.g., "One idea I have, Mr. Perrier, is to . . . "), and at the end of the call (e.g., "Thanks for calling, Mrs. Needham. I will get that information right out to you. Is there anything else I can do to assist you today?").

- *Ask questions.* You read about the use of questions earlier in the book. Use them on the telephone to get information or clarify points made by the customer. Ask open-end questions; then, listen to the response carefully. To clarify or verify information, use closed-end questions.

- *Use speakerphones with caution.* Speakerphones make sense for people who have certain disabilities and in some environments (where you need free hands or are doing something else while you are on hold or are waiting for someone to answer a phone). From a customer service standpoint, they can send a cold or impersonal message, and their use should be minimal. Many callers do not like them and even think that speakerphone users are rude. In addition, depending on the equipment used and how far you are from the telephone, the message received by your customer could be distorted, or it might seem as though you are in an echo chamber. Before using a speakerphone, ask yourself whether there is a valid reason for not using a headset or handheld phone.

  When you are using a speakerphone, make sure that others will not overhear your conversation, especially if you are discussing personal, proprietary, or confidential information. Also, if someone is listening in on the customer's conversation, make sure that you inform the customer of that fact and introduce the two people. Also, explain why he or she is listening. As you read earlier, some people are very protective of their privacy and you should respect their feelings.

- *Use call waiting.* A useful feature offered by many phone systems is call waiting. While you are on the phone, a signal (usually a beep) indicates that there is an incoming call. When you hear the signal, you have a couple of options: Excuse yourself from your current call by getting permission to place the person on hold, or ignore the second caller. If you have a voice mail system, the system makes the choice for you by transferring incoming calls to your message system. Both options have advantages and disadvantages.

  By taking the second call, you may irritate your current caller, who might hang up. This results in potential lost business. On the other hand, by not taking the second call, you might miss an important message and/or irritate that caller.

  By ignoring the signal, you might offend the second caller. Research indicates that many customers forget to or decide against placing later calls to busy numbers, especially if they have already made several attempts. Customers may feel that you are too busy to properly serve them.

  So, how do you handle the dilemma? Make a judgment about how the customer to whom you are speaking might react and then act accordingly. In some instances, company policies tell you what to do, so you do not have to decide.

VOICE MAIL AND ANSWERING MACHINES OR SERVICES

Although voice mail is hailed by many people as a time-saver and vehicle for delivering messages, when an intended recipient is unavailable, many other people have difficulty dealing with this technology (including answering machines). Some people simply refuse to interact with a machine. Let us take a look at some ways to use voice mail.

- *Managing incoming calls.* In order to effectively use voice mail, you must first understand how your system works.

It is important to project a professional image whether talking to customers face-to-face or by telephone. *In what ways do you project a professional image to your customers over the telephone?*

©nyul/123RF RF

Check the manuals delivered with your system or speak with your supervisor and/or the technical expert responsible for its maintenance.

A key to using voice mail effectively is to keep your outgoing message current, indicating your availability, the type of information the caller should leave, and when the caller can expect a return call. If your system allows the caller the option of accessing an operator or another person, you should indicate this early in your outgoing message to save the caller from having to listen to unnecessary information. Figure 9.9 provides a sample outgoing message. Also, Work It Out 9.1 can be used to evaluate the voice mail messages of others when you call them. Another key to effective voice mail usage is to retrieve your calls and return them as soon as possible. Usually within 24 hours, or by the next working day, is a good guideline for returning calls. If you return a call immediately, your callers will likely appreciate and respect you more. Doing so sends a positive customer service message.

FIGURE 9.9

Sample Outgoing Message

- "Hello. This is (your name) of (company and department).
- I am unavailable to take your call at the moment, but if you leave your name, number, and a brief message, I will call you as soon as possible.
- (Optional) If you need immediate assistance, press #_____/call _____ at #_____.
- Thanks for calling."

If you know when you will be returning calls (e.g., at the end of the workday), tell the caller so. If your voice mail system offers callers the option to press a number to speak with someone else, let the caller know this right after you mention that they can leave a message. This avoids requiring the caller to listen to a lengthy message before he or she can select an option.

WORK IT OUT 9.1

Evaluating Voice Mail

To help increase your awareness of the effect of voice mail messages, make note of the following questions during the coming week. As you call people or organizations, consider the outgoing messages that they leave on their voice mail or answering machines and evaluate them, using the following questions. Incorporate practices that you like into your own voice message process if your organization does not provide a standard format.

1. Was the call answered by the fourth ring?

2. Did the announcement contain the following:

Greeting (hello, good morning, or good afternoon)?

Organization's name?

Departmental name?

A statement of when the person will return?

An early announcement of an option to press a number for assistance?

Instructions for leaving a message?

When calls will be returned?

- *Placing calls to voice mail.* Many normally articulate people cannot speak coherently when they encounter an answering machine or voice mail. One technique for success is to plan your call before picking up the phone. Have a 30-second or less "sales" presentation in mind that you can deliver whether you get a person or machine. For example, if you get a person, try, "This is (your first and last name) from (company) calling (or returning a call) for Wilhelm Tackes. Is he available?" Also, have available a list of the key points you want to discuss so that you do not forget them as you talk.

  If you get a machine, try, "This is (first and last name) from (company) calling (returning a call) for Inez Montoya. My number is _____. I will be available from _____ to _____." If you are calling to get or give information, you may want to add, "The reason I am calling is to _____." This allows the return caller to leave information on your voice mail or with someone else and thus avoid the game of telephone tag if you are not available when he or she returns your call.

- *Avoiding telephone tag.* You have probably played telephone tag. The game starts when the intended call receiver is not available and a message is left. The game continues when the call is returned, the original caller is not available, a return message is left, and so on.

  Telephone tag is frustrating and a waste of valuable time. It results in a loss of efficiency, money, and, in some cases, customers. To avoid telephone tag, plan your calls and make your messages effective by giving your name, company name, phone number, time and date of your call, and a succinct message, and by indicating when you can be reached. If appropriate, emphasize that it is all right to leave the information you have requested on your voice mail or with someone else. In addition, you may suggest that your message recipient tell you a time when you can call or meet with him or her face-to-face. By doing this, you end the game and get what you need. Use Worksheet 9.3 (available in your Connect course) to help plan your calls effectively.

TAKING MESSAGES PROFESSIONALLY

If you have ever received an incomplete or undecipherable telephone message, you can appreciate the need for practice in this area. At a minimum, when you take a message you should get the following information from the caller:

  Name (correctly spelled—ask caller for spelling)

  Company name

  Phone number (with area code and country code, if appropriate)

  Brief message

  When call should be returned

  Time and date of the call and your name (in case a question about the message arises)

If you are answering someone's phone while he or she is away, let the caller know right away. This can be done by using a statement such as, "Hello, (person's name)'s line. This is (your name). How may I assist you?" In addition, be cautious of statements you make regarding the intended recipient's availability. Sometimes, well-meant comments can send a negative message to customers. See Figure 9.10 for typical problem messages and better alternatives.

FIGURE 9.10

Communicating Messages

Message	Possible Interpretation	Alternative
"I am not sure where he is" or "He is out roaming around the building somewhere."	"Do they not have any control or structure at this company?"	"He is not available. May I take a message?"
"I am sorry. She is *still* at lunch."	(Depending on the time of the call.) "Must be nice to have two-hour lunch breaks!"	Same as above or "I am sorry; she is at lunch or is unavailable. May I assist you or take a message?"
"We *should* have that problem taken care of soon."	"Do you not know for sure?"	"I apologize for the inconvenience. We will attempt to resolve this by."
"He is not available right now. He is taking care of a crisis."	"Is there a problem there?"	"He is not available right now. May I assist you or take a message?"
"She is not in today. I am not sure when she will be back."	Same as above.	"She is not in today. May I assist you or take a message?"
"He left early today."	"Obviously, you people are not very customer-focused or he would be there during normal business hours to assist me."	"He is out of the office. May I assist you or take a message?"
"I do not know where she is. I was just walking by and heard the phone ringing."	"Nice that you are so conscientious. Too bad others are not."	"She is not available right now, but I will be happy to take a message."
"I will give him the message and try to get him to call you back."	"So there is a 50-50 chance I will be served."	"I will give him the message when he returns and ask him to call you back."
"Hang on a second while I find something to take a message with."	"Does not sound as if people at this company are very prepared to serve customers."	"Would you mind holding while I get a pen and paper?"

GENERAL ADVICE FOR COMMUNICATING BY TELEPHONE

Do not communicate personal information (someone is at the doctor's, on sick leave, etc.), belittle yourself (e.g., "I do not know," "I am only . . . ") or the company (e.g., "Nobody knows"), or use weak or negative language (e.g., "I think," "I cannot"). Instead, simply state, "Malik is unavailable. May I take a message?" or, if appropriate,

KNOWLEDGE CHECK

1. What are some of the advantages of conducting service via the telephone?
2. List some effective communication techniques when talking to customers over the telephone.
3. How can you create a positive image over the telephone?
4. What are some strategies for delivering effective telephone service?
5. When transferring a call, what should you remember to do?
6. List several ways to use voice mail effectively.
7. What elements should an effectively taken message over the telephone contain?

"I will be happy to assist you." After you have taken the message, thank the caller before hanging up and then deliver the message to the intended receiver in a timely manner. If you discover that the receiver will not be available within a 24-hour period, you may want to call the customer and convey this information. If you do so, again offer to assist or suggest some other alternative, if one is available.

Small Business Perspective

Small businesses can benefit from technology in ways similar to larger organizations. Even though many may not have the human resources and finances to have their own call centers and internal support staff members, they have options for applying technology to their day-to-day operations. The Internet has provided a tremendous resource that allows even single-person or small family-run, home-based businesses to look like much larger organizations. By setting up a professional-looking website and arranging to accept credit cards and/or PayPal as cash transaction systems, they can now participate in e-commerce activities.

In addition, through contracting arrangements with third-party organizations, small businesses can look like major players in the business world. For example, the author's former online company, Creative Presentation Resources, Inc., offered many large and electronic items that would have required a lot of warehouse space and tie up large amounts of revenue if it had stocked them internally. Instead, special orders were handled through established business accounts with major manufacturers and distributors who drop-shipped the items when they were ordered via the website, telephone, or fax by customers around the world. When those orders were received, they were processed, and a purchase order was faxed to suppliers, who in turn shipped the item(s) and invoiced the author's company. In turn, the author's company invoiced or collected payment from the customer. There are many small businesses using this process all over the world.

The key to successful e-commerce for a small business is to plan before getting involved. There are many elements that must be considered (e.g., website design, maintenance, and support; merchandise types and sources; marketing; distribution; payment processing; and staffing). To be successful, small businesses need a high-quality computer system with a quality printer, fax machine, telephone, answering machine, and copier. A toll-free number is also valuable and sends a subliminal message that the company is larger and more professional.

Impact on Service

Based on personal experience and what you just read, list three to five small businesses with which you had business dealings within the past month, and then answer the following questions about them:

1. What are some of the types of technology that you have witnessed these businesses using to serve their customers?

2. How successful were their employees in using the technology provided to them to service customers? Explain and give examples.

3. In what ways has technology hindered one or more of these companies from delivering effective customer service? Explain.

4. How could these companies improve service with new, different, or upgraded technology?

Key Terms

applications or apps

artificial intelligence

automated attendant systems

automated computer telephone interviews

automatic call distribution (ACD) system

automatic number identification (ANI) systems

blind transfer

bloggers

chat support

cloud computing

computer telephony integration (CTI)

customer relationship management (CRM) software

data mining

electronic mail (e-mail)

emoticons (emotional icons)

Facebook

facsimile (fax) machine

fax-on-demand

fee-based 900 numbers

help desk

intelligent callback technology

interactive kiosks or digital displays

interactive voice response (IVR) system

Internet callback technology

Internet telephony

media blending

online information fulfillment system

Pinterest

posts

predictive dialing system

QR code (Quick Response Code)

robocall

screen pop-ups

smartphones

spamming or spam

speech or voice recognition

tablets

telephone typewriter system (TTY)

text messaging or texting

tweet

Twitter

Voice over Internet Protocol (VoIP)

voice response unit (VRU)

websites

Wi-Fi

YouTube

Summary

Delivering customer service via technology can be an effective and efficient approach to use in order to achieve total customer satisfaction. However, you must continually upgrade your personal technology knowledge and skills, practice with the applications and equipment, and consciously evaluate the approach and techniques you use to provide service.

In the quality-oriented organizational cultures now developing in the United States and in many other countries, service will make the difference between survival and failure for individuals and organizations. You are the front line, and you are often the first and only contact a customer will have with your company.

Learn as much as you can about the technology that your organization has available to it for service delivery. Strive to use that technology to its fullest potential, but do not forget that you and your peers ultimately determine whether customer expectations are met.

Whether a company is large or small, technology can help make it successful when used properly. Smart and successful managers and frontline service providers stay current on societal trends and act quickly to implement strategies that incorporate technology to address evolving customer needs.

Review Questions

1. In what ways can technology play a role in the delivery of effective customer service? Explain.

2. What are some advantages of using technology for service delivery?

3. What are some disadvantages of using technology for service delivery?

4. What are some of the communication skills for success?

5. How can you project a more positive image over the telephone?

6. What information should you always get when taking telephone messages?

7. When transferring calls, what should you avoid and why?

8. When you leave a message on voice mail, what information should you give?

9. What is telephone tag, and how can you avoid or reduce it?

10. How are small businesses benefitting from today's technology?

Search It Out

1. **Search the Internet for Customer Service Technology Resources**

   a. Visit http://www.youtube.com and search the phrase "customer service technology." Identify and download one video that addresses customer service technology and/or its use that you can share with the class.

   b. Search the Internet for sites that deal with customer service and the technology used to deliver quality customer service. Also, look for the websites and organizations that focus on the technology and people involved in the delivery of customer service. Be prepared to share what you find with the class.

   c. Search the Internet for additional information about one of the technologies addressed in sections LO 9-2 and LO 9-3 of this chapter. Report your findings to your classmates.

   d. Search the Internet for books and other publications that focus on customer service and technology. Develop a bibliographic listing of at least 7 to 10 publications, make copies of the list, and share it with your classmates.

2. **Additional Resources**

   For additional articles and information on customer service via technology and related topics, visit the author's Customer Service Skills Blog www.customerserviceskillsbook.com in your Connect course and search "Customer Service Technology" and related topics discussed in this chapter.

3. **Search Ted Talks**

   Here is a starting point for videos on customer service: https://binged.it/2gs2Z10.

Collaborative Learning Activity

Practice Customer Service with Your Team Members

Get together in teams of three members each. One person will take the role of a customer service provider, one will be a customer, and one will be the observer. Use the following scenarios to practice the skills you have learned in this chapter. Incorporate other communication skills covered in previous chapters as you deal with your "customer." Use three of the four scenarios so that each person in a group has a chance to play each of the three roles. Depending on the scenario, you might use copies of Worksheet 9.2 (available in your Connect course) to plan your call.

Scenario 1

You are a customer service representative in a customer contact center that provides service to customers who have purchased small appliances from your company. A customer is calling to complain that she purchased a waffle iron from one of your outlet stores two weeks ago and it no longer works. She is upset because her in-laws and family are arriving in two days for an extended visit and they love her "special" waffles.

Scenario 2

You are a customer care specialist for a company that provides answers to travel-related questions for a national membership warehouse retail store. A customer calls to find out about the types of travel-related discounts for which he qualifies through his membership.

Scenario 3

You are a telemarketing sales representative for a company that sells water filtration systems. You are calling current customers who purchased a filtration system 7 to 10 years ago to inform them of your new Oasis line of filters, which is better than any other system on the market. You can offer them:

- A 30-day money-back guarantee
- Billing by all major credit cards or invoice
- A one-year limited warranty on the system that replaces all defective parts but does not cover labor
- If they find a less expensive offer for the same product, your company matches the prices plus pays 10 percent of the price difference.

Scenario 4

This scenario has two parts. In Part 1, you are a mechanic in an automotive repair shop. You answer a phone call from an irate customer calling to complain about what he perceives is an inflated billing charge for a recent air-conditioner repair. He is asking for your manager, who is at lunch and will not be back for 45 minutes. You take the incoming call, using the message-taking format covered in this chapter. In Part 2, you are the manager. You have just returned from lunch and find a message from the irate customer described in Part 1 and must call the customer. Use Worksheet 9.3 (available in your Connect course) to plan your return call based on the message you received.

Face to Face

Telephone Techniques at Staff-Temps

Background

Staff-Temps International is a temporary employment agency based in Chicago, Illinois. It has six full-time and three part-time employment counselors. The office is part of a national chain owned by Yamaguchi Enterprises Ltd., headquartered in Tokyo. The chain places over 100,000 temporary employees annually in a variety of businesses and offices.

Most of Staff-Temps' contacts are made by telephone; therefore, greater emphasis is placed on selecting and training employees who have a good phone presence. Each employee is required to meet certain standards of quality in dealing with customers on the telephone. To ensure that employees apply these standards uniformly, an outside quality control company (Morrison and Lewis) is used to occasionally make "phantom calls" to staff members. In these calls, Morrison and Lewis staff members pretend to be potential clients seeking information. The "employee–customer" calls are randomly recorded. Through the calls and recordings, customer service levels are measured.

Your Role

Your name is Chris Walker. As an employment counselor with Staff-Temps, you are aware of the customer service standards, which include the following:

- Answer a ringing telephone within four rings.
- Smile as you speak.
- Use a standard salutation (good morning, afternoon, or evening).
- Give your name and the name of your department and company.
- Offer to assist the customer ("How may I assist you?").

On the way back to the office after lunch, you were involved in a minor automobile accident. Even though it was not your fault, you are concerned that your insurance may be canceled, since you had another accident and got a speeding ticket earlier this year. Because of the accident, you were an hour late in returning from lunch. Upon your arrival, the receptionist handed you six messages from vendors and customers. Two of the messages were from Aretha Washington, human resources director for an electronics manufacturing firm that has been a good client for over two years. The two of you had spoken earlier in the day.

As you walked into your office, the telephone started to ring. By the time you took your coat off and got to your desk, the phone had rung five or six times.

When you answered, you heard Aretha's voice on the line. Her tone told you that she was upset. This was the conversation:

You: Staff-Temps. Chris speaking.

Aretha: Chris, what's going on? You told me when I called first thing this morning that you would find out why my temp did not show up today and would call me back. I have left messages all day and have not heard a thing! We have got a major deadline to meet for a very important client, and I cannot get the work done. My boss has been in here every half hour checking on this. What is going on?

You: Aretha, I am truly sorry. I just got in from lunch and have not been able to get back to you.

Aretha: Just got back from lunch! It's after 2:30! It must be nice to have the luxury of a long lunch break. I did not even get to eat lunch today!

You: Listen, Aretha, I could not help . . . (obviously anxious and raising your voice).

Aretha: You do not "listen" me! I am the customer, and if you cannot handle my needs, I know someone else who can. If I do not hear from you within the next half hour, I do not ever want to hear from you again! Goodbye!
[Slamming receiver down.]

Critical Thinking Questions

1. How well was this customer call handled? Explain.

2. What should you have done differently?

3. Do you believe that Aretha was justified in how she treated you? Explain.

4. How do personal problems or priorities sometimes affect customer service?

Planning to Serve

To get a better idea of how well your own organization uses technology to serve customers, use the following checklist to ensure that you and the organization are delivering the best possible service to customers, using technology effectively, and sending a positive image to others.

Call your own organizational (office) telephone number, or choose any large company or government agency from the phone book, to determine:

- How many times the telephone rings before being routed to another person or voice mail. (Four rings should be the maximum unless an organization has another standard.)

- If the "O" (operator) option is chosen, does the call go to a live person at another number? In other words, do you have service coverage when you are away from your telephone?

If you choose the voice mail option, is your outgoing message:

- Upbeat and friendly?
- Concise?
- In compliance with organizational guidelines for voice messages? If no standards exist, does your message comply with the suggested message format in this chapter?

E-mail yourself to determine:

- If the message is delivered properly to your mailbox.
- If your "out of office" message is sent automatically (assuming that you have this option on your system and have activated it). For example, a response might be generated that tells correspondents, "I'll be out of the office from (date) until (date), but I will be checking my e-mail during that period and will respond as soon as possible."

Examine your fax cover sheets (if used) to ensure that excessive information and graphics (e.g., bulky logos or icons) have been removed and that your name and phone number are provided.

Quick Preview Answers

1. T	4. F	7. T	10. F	13. T
2. F	5. F	8. T	11. T	14. T
3. T	6. T	9. T	12. T	15. F

Ethical Dilemma Summary

Ethical Dilemma 9.1 Possible Answers

1. Is there anything wrong with how the employee is handling this situation? Explain.

   Your coworker is obviously frustrated and "blowing off steam," which is a human reaction when we feel wronged. However, the manner in which he is doing it is unprofessional and disloyal and potentially could cause harm to the organization in terms of financial and reputation losses (and indirectly to you and other employees).

2. What action, if any, should you take?

   If you know the employee well, you might meet with him and share that you and others overheard his remarks. Empathize, but also share your concerns that his discussing the situation in front of you and other employees is making you uneasy. Additionally, you might mention that while the situation may seem unfair, the reality is that organizations (and employees) make decisions all the time that potentially have a negative impact on the other. Often there are overriding business issues driving management's decisions to which employees are not privy in such cases. Caution your coworker that what he is doing is also seemingly unprofessional and could even have serious consequences for him professionally and legally.

Based on the reaction you get from your coworker, you may want to consider escalating the situation to your supervisor and sharing what happened.

Ethical Dilemma 9.2 Possible Answers

1. Are there any potential legal problems with this policy? If so, what might they be?

   The National Do-Not-Call Registry is overseen by the Federal Trade Commission (the consumer protection agency in the United States) and applies to any plan, program, or campaign selling goods or services through interstate phone calls. This includes telemarketers who solicit consumers, often on behalf of third-party sellers. It also includes sellers who provide, offer to provide, or arrange to provide goods or services to consumers in exchange for payment.

   The National Do-Not-Call Registry does not limit calls by political organizations, charities, or telephone surveyors.

   Under the law, a telemarketer or seller may call a consumer with whom it has an established business relationship for up to 18 months after the consumer's last purchase, delivery, or payment—even if the consumer's number is on the National Do-Not-Call Registry. In addition, a company may call a consumer for up to three months after the consumer makes an inquiry or submits an application to the company.

Additionally, if a consumer has given a company written permission, the company may call even if the consumer's number is on the National Do-Not-Call Registry.

If a consumer asks a company not to call, the company may not call, even if there is an established business relationship. Indeed, a company may not call a consumer—regardless of whether the consumer's number is on the registry—if the consumer has asked to be put on the company's own do-not-call list.

Since 2005, telemarketers and sellers have been required to search the registry at least once every 31 days and drop from their call lists the phone numbers of consumers who have registered. A consumer who receives a telemarketing call despite being on the registry will be able to file a complaint with the FTC, either online or by calling a toll-free number. Violators could be fined up to $16,000 per incident.

2. Are there any ethical issues here? Explain.

Yes, if you know that the supervisor is asking you to violate a federal law, you have to decide whether to participate in the illegal activity or to take some type of action.

3. What should you do in this situation?

Ethically, you have to decide whether you want to escalate your concerns about calling people illegally to your supervisor's boss, report the company to the FTC, and/or resign from the company.

©Robert W. Lucas

PART FOUR

RETAINING CUSTOMERS

10 Encouraging Customer Loyalty

Richard Ulrych

Position/job title: *Partner (owner/operator)*
Organization: *Waterways Car Spa*

Total years' experience providing service to internal and external customers: 38

Website: *http://www.waterwayscarspa.com*

1 **What are the personal qualities that you believe are essential for anyone working with customers in a service environment?**

Customers purchase a service comprising of the "product" itself as well as the experience. This is either positively enhanced or negatively impacted by every one of the service providers. On that basis, some of the most essential qualities required to work in the service industry are the following:

a. Having an upbeat persona in order to transmit enthusiasm and promote the sense of enjoyment and satisfaction

b. Demonstrating a positive attitude in order to maintain focus and overcome issues

c. Understanding and dealing with customer concerns and expressing empathy in order to ensure that they feel as if service providers are treating them as people

Many customers go to an establishment to have a service that they are either unwilling or unable to perform themselves. They view that service as an unwanted chore. At Waterways, we want to turn that chore into an enjoyable experience. In other circumstances: hospitality—customers purchase services to enjoy, relax, and/or separate themselves from their "daily grind."

In any event, the objective is to expansively package services or products provided in such a way that they exceed customer expectations. In addition, if an issue exists, deal with it quickly and properly and do not let it linger or take half-measures. You have an opportunity to show exactly who you are and what you stand for as you deal with the complaint/issue.

2 **What do you see as the most rewarding part of working with customers? Why?**

I believe in people having pride in their accomplishments and a job well done. Although you can see when a customer is pleased and satisfied, there are times when it can be difficult to perceive these results tangibly and immediately in the service industry. You need to believe that you have done all that you could for the customer (e.g., knowing that you have done a good job—*from the customer's point of view*). At that point, you then have the satisfaction of having done a good job or deed and of providing a plus in a customer's day. That is what you are there to do.

The most rewarding aspect of customer service for me is those instances in which I have tried my utmost to assist a customer but he or she still leaves unsatisfied. Later, he or she returns or calls to express gratitude for the manner in which I treated her or him, and the attempts I made to accommodate. This is confirmation that I have actually achieved something positive.

3 **What do you believe the biggest challenge(s) is/are in working with customers?**

Although there are a few circumstances when it is genuinely not possible to help or satisfy a customer, the biggest challenge comes when a customer does not want help or to have an issue resolved. Whether the issue is real or concocted, this situation often occurs when a customer has other issues going on that are affecting responses and receptiveness to your attempts to resolve an issue. In such instances, you must always maintain your bearing, your level of service and attention, as well as that of the business you represent.

An example that I experienced: A customer's vehicle came out of the automated car wash tunnel. After the customer circled the vehicle, he started shouting that his car had been scratched. I went to investigate and saw it had scratches all over it. The scratches were incompatible with any damage that the car wash equipment could have caused. While trying to ascertain more details of the issue from the customer, he stated, "When I came in, my car had 26 scratches. It now has 27 scratches. You scratched my car. What are you going to do about it?" As I did in this instance, I typically try to address a problem by talking through the issue with the customer. However, the customer was adamant that we had damaged his vehicle and would not accept any settlement less than restoring the condition of his vehicle. In this instance, we reached an unfortunate and unsatisfactory impasse. I stated, "Tell me which scratch we caused and we will deal with it."

4 **What have you done, or could you do, to help overcome the challenges you indicated in question 3 and deliver better customer service?**

Being involved in a small business operation, there have been moments that a lack of personnel to cover other aspects of the business has meant that I have not been able to dedicate the time I would like for dealing with issues such as those I described.

Although the outcome may not have changed in the instance above, the fact that I had covered all possible aspects of the issue with the customer is often sufficient to placate any irate customer.

Generally, by taking time to address a customer's concerns or complaints, you give importance to the issues raised and how you have treated them respectfully. This is often the greatest tool in resolving an issue. From that point, the customer is more likely to be more responsive in your attempts to resolve the issue.

5 **What changes have you seen in the customer service profession since you took your first service provider position?**

I first started in the service industry nearly 40 years ago, working at an airport dealing with both scheduled and charter flights. I then spent many years employed in the hospitality industry catering to different clientele (mass and exclusive).

Although the question is not quite so relevant in my present industry, I have seen how the levels of service as a whole have filtered down to far smaller business operations. Smaller businesses that previously provided customized services have adopted the economic structure of larger operations and now provide a "mini-mass production" level of service. Because of economics, businesses that promoted an image of refined service in the past have trimmed back to little more than the essentials. Economics means ensuring market share and enabling the organization to progress and succeed.

Around 40-plus years ago, there were distinct levels of service providers. Largely, these rigid service segment divisions have blurred. Social mobility and the economy have led many customers to bridge service level segmentation. As such, businesses have opened up to tourist class, tourist menus, short break specials, and similar shortcuts. In addition, they have consolidated operations via association or acquisition.

For example, the era of the travel agent who would individually create a specific custom-made itinerary for his or her clientele has all but disappeared. The proportion of travel agencies that are still able to cater to clientele requiring such services is minute.

6 **What advice related to customer service do you have for anyone seeking or continuing a career in a customer service environment?**

If you are not prepared to bend over backward for a customer, and do it willingly, think very carefully before choosing a move into the service industry. Of course, that does not mean you have to accept being insulted or abused but realize that there will be many instances when you will be severely tried, especially in the early part of your career.

Ultimately, in the service industry, you are there to help a customer. You should understand that this is the reason why you occupy your position and what this entails. The satisfaction you receive can be significant on a personal level and can bring career success. However, all that is solely dependent on you.

Application to Customer Service

After reading Richard's comments, think about how what he said relates to your organization and the customer service profession as a whole and respond to the following:

1. Do you think the qualities and skills that Richard highlighted are important in any service position? Explain.
2. Do you agree with the rewards of customer service that Richard mentioned? What other rewards do you believe can be derived from working with customers?
3. How do the challenges suggested by Richard apply to other organizations? What challenges have you experienced as a service provider or from a customer perspective?
4. If you had experienced the customer situation that Richard described in question 3, how would you have handled it?
5. What changes have you experienced or heard about in the customer service profession?
6. What advice do you have for those working in the customer service profession to increase their effectiveness and success?

Courtesy of Richard Ulrych

Encouraging Customer Loyalty

You don't earn loyalty in a day. You earn loyalty day-by-day.

—SOURCE: JEFFREY GITOMER

©Cassiohabib/Shutterstock.com RF

LEARNING OUTCOMES

After completing this chapter, you will be able to:

10-1 Relate the role of customer and brand loyalty to organizational success.

10-2 Establish and maintain trust with customers.

10-3 Explain customer relationship management and its importance to quality service.

10-4 Develop the service provider characteristics that will enhance customer loyalty.

10-5 Describe the provider's responsibility for establishing and maintaining positive customer relationships.

10-6 Identify strategies that can be used to make customers feel like they are number one.

10-7 Discuss strategies that can enhance customer satisfaction.

10-8 Define quality service.

Use SmartBook to help you read, study, and retain what you have learned. Access SmartBook in your Instructor's Connect course, or go to connect.mheducation.com for help. SMARTBOOK™

IN THE REAL WORLD   WHOLESALE—COSTCO

Mission: "To continually provide our members with quality goods and services at the lowest possible prices."

Source: Costco Code of Ethics

Code of Ethics:

Obey the law.
Take care of our members.
Take care of our employees.
Respect our suppliers.
Reward our shareholders.

Sustainability Responsibilities:

Take care of our employees.

Support the communities where our employees and members live and work.

Operate efficiently and in an environmentally responsible manner.

Strategically source our merchandise in a sustainable manner.

According to its website, "Costco started the wholesale warehouse phenomenon in 1976 under the name Price Club in a converted airplane hangar in San Diego, California. The company found it could achieve greater buying power by serving small businesses and a select audience of non-business customers." (Source: The History of Costco) Costco was started by James Sinegal (an employee at Price Club) and Jeffrey Brotman (a lawyer from an old Seattle retailing family). The two began a wholesale distribution center and quickly became a success. They opened the first Costco warehouse in Seattle, Washington in 1983 and in 1993 merged with Price Club (owned by Sol Price and his son Robert) after Price declined a bid to merge by Sam Walton and Walmart. The combined PriceCostco company became the first to grow from zero to $3 billion in sales in less

than six years. After Price left the company in 1994, the organization formally changed its name to Costco in 1997.

As of July 2016, Costco had 705 warehouses in nine countries staffed by 117,000 employees. The formula for success obviously worked because the company has flourished into a worldwide brand with a total of over $116 billion in sales in 2016. With a large membership base and a philosophy of keeping prices down and passing savings along to members, the company continues to flourish and outsells its nearest competitor Sam's Club.

In 2014, Costco was listed in the National Retail Federation's "Top 100 Retailers" as the third largest retailer in the United States. Part of Costco's success can be attributed to its membership base. Many of its stores are located in geographic locations where salaries are higher and people have better job stability. This helps explain why the Costco annual membership fee is higher than that of Sam's Club. Contrarily, according to a 2014 article in *The Huffington Post*, "Sam's Club CEO Rosalind Brewer noted in an earnings call that the chain suffered in the past quarter from a decline in public assistance to poor customers." The article also pointed out that as less affluent customers cut back on purchases, Sam's laid off 2,300 workers.[1] Since a major portion of operating profits in warehouse stores comes from membership fees, Costco has an advantage over competitors. Some reports show that Costco's members renew at around a 90 percent rate, so they are obviously happy about the way the company does business.

Since its inception, Costco has expanded its product and service offerings. Today, in addition to food and household items, Costco facilities provide a variety of services including auto, electronics, jewelry, travel, insurance, appliances, gas, pharmaceuticals, hearing aids, photo processing, and much more. The company also created its own trademarked private brand called "Kirkland Signature." This name was derived from the location of Costco's former corporate headquarters location in Kirkland, Washington. To ensure that customers are completely happy with their purchases and the company, Costco has a return policy that guarantees almost all of their products with a full refund. Exceptions include electronics and telephones that have a 90-day return window. After 90 days, items fall under the manufacturer's return policy. Additionally, members who are unsatisfied with their membership can cancel at any time before their membership expires for a full refund of their membership fees.

Think About It

1. What do you personally know about Costco and how does this impact your perspective of the company as a current or potential customer?

2. From a customer perspective, why do you think some companies like Costco have flourished when other retailers have not?

3. What role do you think management decisions to improve services since its inception have played in impacting customer service from Costco? Explain.

4. What positive aspects about the company do you think help contribute to its worldwide success and reputation? Explain.

5. Would you like to work for a company like Costco? Why or why not?

For more information about Costco, search the Internet and visit the company website at http://www.costco.com.

Quick Preview

Before reviewing the chapter content, respond to the following questions by placing a "T" for true or an "F" for false on the rules. Use any questions you miss as a checklist of material to which you will pay particular attention as you read through the chapter. For those you get right, pat yourself on the back, but review the sections they address in order to learn additional details about the topic.

_____ 1. Customer satisfaction and loyalty are the result of effective product and service delivery, resolution of problems, and elimination of dissatisfaction.

_____ 2. The number of customers with major problems who continue to do business with an organization if their complaint is resolved is about 9 percent.

_____ 3. One way to take responsibility for customer relationships is to personalize your approach when dealing with customers.

_____ 4. Customers usually decide to purchase or repurchase from a supplier on the basis of the quality and performance of the products and services.

_____ 5. Many customers return to organizations because of relationships established with employees even though comparable products and services are available elsewhere.

_____ 6. As customers develop long-term relationships with an organization, they tend to become more tolerant of poor service.

_____ 7. Projecting an enthusiastic "I'm happy to serve you" attitude is one way to have a positive effect on customer relationships.

_____ 8. Customers usually exhibit six common needs that must be addressed by service providers in order to ensure customer loyalty.

_____ 9. Using a customer's name is a good way to personalize your relationship with a customer.

_____ 10. Trust is not a major concern for most customers.

_____ 11. Handling complaints quickly and effectively is a good strategy for aiding customer retention.

_____ 12. An important step often overlooked in dealing with customers is follow-up.

Answers to Quick Preview are located at the end of the chapter.

Words to Live By

"Merely satisfying customers will not be enough to earn their loyalty. Instead, they must experience exceptional service worthy of their repeat business and referral. Understand the factors that drive this customer revolution."

—Source: Rick Tate

LO 10-1 Customer Loyalty

CONCEPT **Customer and brand loyalty are a crucial element of any organization's success.**

Customer loyalty is an *emotional* rather than a *rational* thing. Each time there is contact at a **touch point** where the customer and provider come together, there is opportunity for further cementing the customer relationship and loyalty or driving a wedge between the customer and organization due to failure to meet expectations or needs. With every contact, service providers should strive to demonstrate commitment to exceed customer expectations and provide an experience that is beyond anything for which they might have hoped. Tied to commitment, loyalty is typically based on customer interest in maintaining a relationship with your organization. Often, customer interest is created and maintained through one or more positive experiences that lead to a relationship.

An important point to keep in mind about customer loyalty is that it does not happen as a result of a single customer–provider encounter. Nor does it happen just because of periodic special promotions, sales, or passive loyalty programs that provide only minimal rewards. Rather, true customer loyalty stems from an organization's concerted, ongoing efforts that are part of its strategic goals to meet and exceed the expectations and needs of its customers.

Trust builds lasting customer relationships! The most important thing to remember about trust is that, without it, you have no relationship. This applies to all human situations, not just the customer service environment. In the business world, trust typically results in positive word-of-mouth advertising. This mode of endorsement can be powerful and contribute to organization or product success. In a time when mom and pop shops have shuttered their doors and been replaced by nationwide chains, consumers still have the most powerful tool for ensuring that they receive the best possible customer service: their mouths.

customer loyalty Term used to describe the tendency of customers to return to a product or organization regularly because of the service and satisfaction they receive.

touch point Any instance in which a service provider or organization (e.g., face-to-face, in writing, through technology) comes in contact with a customer; it is an opportunity to influence customer loyalty and enhance the customer relationship.`

Impact of Customer Service on Business Results

Dimensional Research did a survey on the long-term impact of customer service on business results with 1,046 people who had customer service experiences with mid-sized companies. The survey results showed that good customer service drove personal and business purchases while bad service led people to seek alternative sources for products and services.

Some of the findings included the following:

- Customer service was the top factor in trusting a vendor.
- Sixty-two percent of business-to-business and 42 percent of business-to-consumer customers continued to purchase following good customer service.
- Sixty-six percent of business-to-business and 52 percent of business-to-consumer customers stopped doing business following a negative service experience.
- Seventy-two percent of customers blamed having to explain their problem to multiple people for their bad service experience.
- Thirty-nine percent continue to avoid a vendor more than two years following a negative experience.
- Ninety-five percent share bad experiences and 87 percent share good service experiences.
- Fifty-four percent shared their bad experience and 33 percent shared their good experience with five or more people.
- Forty-five percent shared bad experiences and 30 percent shared good customer service experiences via social media.[2]

The advent of mobile and other types of electronic communication devices that allow consumers to easily find a way to provide feedback on products and services to others and to reach out for information that helps them make a buying decision has impacted customer loyalty to some degree. With competing products being only a mouse click away, a customer can research numerous sources and make a buying decision within a matter of minutes without ever leaving the comfort of his or her desk chair or chaise lounge. This is one reason why many business owners and marketing professionals espouse the belief that customer loyalty is dead. That may be true to some degree based on applying old standards of what loyalty looked like. However, in an era where society and the mechanisms of business have morphed dramatically toward technology integration and a melding of world economies, it is still possible for successful and innovative companies to carve out a niche and have a degree of customer loyalty toward their brands.

Examples of Brand Loyalty

- Cadillac and Lincoln automobiles are still very popular with the parents of baby boomers (born between 1964 and 1980) who grew up with that icon of quality and prosperity.
- Trader Joe's, Whole Foods, Fresh Foods, and other natural food markets have almost a cult following of people who believe that fresh, natural products are a must to ensure longevity and health.
- The Four Seasons and Ritz Carlton hotel chains have a following of more affluent customers who appreciate luxury when they travel.
- Nordstrom's department stores have die-hard customers who love being catered to as they shop.
- Harley Davidson motorcycle riders would rather be found dead than on another type of cycle. They wear shirts and other products that promote the company brand.
- Apple has created a customer following that anticipates its next edition of just about every one of its products. They are often willing to camp outside its stores the day of a scheduled product release.

All of these organizations have identified and targeted a specific category and have successfully delivered their message about products and services to them through advertising and ultimately word-of-mouth consumer promotions.

While the use of technology to shop and research information varies between generational and other customer groups, it plays a more significant role than ever might have been imagined in the past and certainly has an impact on overall customer satisfaction and loyalty. By using technology, customers can access product and service experts from around the world in a matter of seconds to find out about a company's reputation, products, and services. They can check forums that focus on and organizations that gather consumer feedback to see if an organization or person is credible and worthy of their trust and business.

For many consumers, the concept of what are acceptable product quality and service level has changed dramatically over the years, along with whom they believe. For example, in the case of millennials (people born between 1981 and 2000—depending on what source you reference) "… the definition of 'expert'—a person with the credibility to recommend brands, products, and services—has shifted from someone with professional or academic credentials to potentially anyone with firsthand experience, ideally a peer or close friend. U.S. Millennials also tend to seek multiple sources of information, especially from noncorporate channels, and they're likely to consult their friends before making purchase decisions…."[3]

The key to establishing and maintaining customer loyalty is to put forth an honest and ongoing series of initiatives and efforts that demonstrate to customers that they are important to the organization. Through words and actions, service providers can show that they are truly there to assist customers meet their needs, wants, and expectations.

One way that organizations try to cement relationships and encourage customer loyalty and retention is through loyalty or rewards programs. Such programs have been around since the nineteenth century when soap manufacturers offered certificates redeemable for color lithographs. Later, merchants created various incentive programs that were designed to give additional value and create brand loyalty for products and companies. One of the most recognized incentive initiatives in the late 1800s and up to today in the United States and overseas has been the Sperry and Hutchinson (S&H) Green Stamps program. For decades, millions of customers dutifully collected small green stamps with S&H emblazoned on them from stores and businesses and pasted the stamps into books. Customers traded their books for housewares and other items. Stores bought the stamps from S&H and then distributed them with purchases based on criteria that each company set. Customers often chose who to trade with based on the value of the stamps given. S&H went through various iterations due to the economy and a Supreme Court ruling that restricting the distribution of stamps was illegal. The stamps were in use up until the 1990s when the Internet made them obsolete. The company morphed into a system of S&H "greenpoints" that are still in use today to get gift certificates and rewards from Home Depot, Papa John's, L.L. Bean, Barnes & Noble, and other recognizable companies. People who still have green stamps can redeem them through the company's website (https://www.greenpoints.com/).

Trending NOW

Walt Disney was a visionary and innovator and his company often leads the way with service-related processes and procedures often mimicked by its competitors and other companies. With recent expansions to its theme parks, the company has introduced a new radio frequency wristband device called MagicBands that will eliminate the need for guests at its Walt Disney World Resort to carry room keys, park tickets, passes, or even money and credit cards. These high-tech bracelets will be worn by guests, who can scan them at special kiosks or points of sale to make purchases in their gift shops and food venues, to enter the parks, to access "fast passes" that allow them a designated reservation time for various rides and venues in the parks, to enter their hotel room, and much more.

The devices have a code that securely links to guest information stored in an encrypted database to prevent loss of personal and financial information. The bands then allow access to various Disney locations and to make purchases, if a credit card has been associated with the band at guest services. In the latter case, a personal identification number (PIN) is required to make a purchase in order to prevent unauthorized use should the band get lost. Parents can set dollar limits on types of items and the amount that children may purchase to avoid overspending.

The implications for use of such devices span many industries where customers stay in a facility or location owned by a company and make purchases or access services. For example, in a hotel, resort, or on cruise ships, guests are able to easily access various services without having to sign for each transaction and end up with a stack of receipts that they have to track.

The convenience of high-tech devices such as the MagicBand is one way that Disney is showing that it is always thinking of new ways to make the guest experience seamless, better fortify the customer–provider relationship, and lead to higher levels of satisfaction and brand loyalty.

LO 10-2 The Role of Trust

CONCEPT Trust is the most important criterion for a relationship. Trust depends on many factors. Communicating effectively, keeping your word, caring, and trusting your customers are some of these factors.

trust Key element in cementing interpersonal relationships.

Trust is at the heart of any relationship, especially when there is an exchange of money for products or services. For a customer to hand over his or her hard-earned cash to you and your organization typically takes a bit of persuasion through advertising or word-of-mouth endorsements from previous customers. All of this is developed by an ongoing investment of time, effort, and money from your organization and commitment and initiative from each service provider.

For trust to start and grow, your customers must believe several things about you and your organization:

1. You and the organization have the customer's best interests in mind before, during, and after the transaction.

2. You and the organization are honest and forthcoming with customers and your goal is to deliver the best products and services possible in a timely manner and at a fair price.

3. You have quality products and services that are backed by a guarantee that should something go wrong, it will be quickly and earnestly taken care of.

Customer Service Satisfaction Tip

The process of potentially satisfying a customer begins from the moment you make contact with someone. To prepare for this encounter, you must prepare your knowledge, attitude, appearance, and many other factors in order to project the most positive image possible. By becoming thoroughly familiar with your organization, its mission, products and services, and putting together a solid toolbox of service skills, you can increase your opportunity for achieving customer satisfaction. Ultimately, customers will evaluate the entire service experience from the time of contact until they receive the product or service that they purchased. This includes any follow-up service or warranty work that may be required.

For customers to continue doing business with you, they must trust you and your organization. The thing about trust is that you must earn it. That does not happen overnight. Only through continued positive efforts on the part of everyone in your organization can you demonstrate to customers that you are worthy of their trust and thereby positively affect customer retention. Through actions and deeds, you must deliver quality products and services that are competitively priced and information that satisfies the needs of your customers. Every touch point with a customer is an opportunity for you and your organization to influence customer loyalty.

Even when you win trust and achieve **customer satisfaction**, the customer relationship is very fragile. It is easy to destroy trust quickly; an inappropriate tone, a missed appointment, failure to follow through on a promise, a lie, and a misleading statement or information to a customer are just some of the ways you can sabotage this relationship.

customer satisfaction A marketing term that is used to describe how well an organization is doing in providing products and services that meet or exceed a customer's needs and expectations.

The good news for North American businesses is that as the economic recession of the past decade is past and the economy has begun to show continued signs of growth. Customer satisfaction levels for a number of industries have begun a slow movement toward improvement on the University of Michigan American Customer Satisfaction Index (ACSI) scale of 100 possible points (visit http://bit.ly/19lrvqq for more information). Even so, there is still a long way to full recovery in the United States and around the world as consumers begin struggle to trust the government and economic systems that let so many down and resulted in grave financial consequences around the world. Compounding this are factors related to the contentious and unorthodox U.S. 2016 presidential election.

While organizations are starting to gain access to more capital due to loosening of restrictions on lending and other economic factors, many low- to middle-class consumers struggle to achieve higher income flows or levels of disposable income. Many are still unemployed or underemployed. Still, recent reports are that stocks have rebounded and the housing industry has moved to a point where houses are in higher demand and people are actually getting into cash bidding wars. There are reports that in some housing markets, buyers are paying as much as $100,000 over the asking price. This is putting money into people's pockets, and, as a result, other areas of the economy (e.g., automotive, home goods, and clothing) have returned to normal.

To gain and maintain trust, you and the organization must actively work toward incorporating the values and beliefs into daily actions. Failure to do so can send a message that you are not trustworthy or that you act according to a double standard of saying one thing but doing another.

You must exhibit trustworthiness in words and actions, for although it takes a long time to gain trust, it can be lost in seconds. Once trust is gone, if you do not act quickly to correct the situation through a sound service recovery initiative, you may never regain total customer confidence.

One way that consumers are turned off from a trust standpoint is through a loss of confidence that follows a breakdown in an organization's manufacturing and distribution processes. Often glitches occur that result in recalls of products, which can immediately take away most or all of the consumer confidence in the safety and/or reliability of products they have used regularly for years. See Figure 10.1 for examples.

These continued recalls, and those of many consumer products in the past (e.g., toy, tire, car, and dishwasher manufacturers that produce products that cause death, injury, and product loss to users), are causing a lot of uneasiness and distrust of many manufacturers. Some companies (e.g., Johnson & Johnson) immediately took steps to recall affected products, even if they did not know whether they were at fault, while others (Toyota) delayed recalls and denied liability until forced to take action by safety organizations and consumers. Obviously, the manner in which a company handles such situations has a potentially lasting positive or negative impact on consumer confidence and trust in the future.

FIGURE 10.1 Examples of Product and Service Breakdowns

Examples of product and service breakdowns can be found in virtually any industry. Here are some of the more prominent ones that have caused severe financial and trust issues for companies in the past:

Company	Product	Year	Issue(s)
Johnson & Johnson	Tylenol	1982	Poison in product/death/ illness of consumers
Bi Mar Foods	Hot dogs	1998	Consumer deaths
Sam's Clubs	Beef	2007	*E. coli* illnesses
Mattel Toys	Various Chinese-made toys	2007	Small magnets/lead paint
Toyota	Multiple brands	2009	Sticking accelerator
Kellogg's	Mini-Wheats cereal	2012	Metal shavings in product
Trader Joe's	Peanut butter	2012	Salmonella outbreak
Boeing	B787 Dreamliner	2013	Battery fires

In addition to loss of consumer confidence and trust, there is also the potential for huge financial loss as a result of a recall. As an example of the cost of just one recall, in 2010 when the egg industry issued a recall of eggs due to a salmonella outbreak, "The US recall involved almost half a billion eggs through 11 states. It is estimated that the $0.40 per dozen decrease, between the projected benchmark price and actual realization, cost the generic shell-egg industry over $100 million in September 2010 alone."[4]

There are numerous things that you can do to personally help build trust with your customers in recall situations and when minor service breakdowns occur. Some potential trust-building success strategies are discussed below.

Displaying caring and respect for customers is essential. *What are some ways you can go "above and beyond" when providing customer service?*

©DON EMMERT/Getty Images

COMMUNICATE EFFECTIVELY AND CONVINCINGLY

If you cannot articulate or clearly explain (verbally and in writing) information in a manner that customers can comprehend and act upon, they will not believe in you. You must provide more than facts and figures; you must send a message of sincerity, knowledge, and honesty. Never forget that customer–provider relationships are based on personal interactions, not on policy and procedures.

As you communicate, project your feelings and emotions by being positive and enthusiastic. Let customers know that you are human and approachable. Also, communicate frequently and keep customers informed. This is especially important when a problem has occurred or they are awaiting a product or service that has been delayed. If you fail to update them regularly, they may become frustrated and believe that you are lying or trying to hide something from them. The result of such perceptions is that they might cancel their order, complain, take their business elsewhere, and tell others about their disappointing experience.

> **Customer Service Success Tip**
>
> Always act in the best interest of your customers. Listen to them, ask questions, anticipate their needs, deliver what you promise, and exhibit high levels of professionalism in everything that you do whether your customers are present or not.

WORK IT OUT 10.1

Preventing Customer Defection

Working in groups of three to five members, create a list of industries or companies that you know of that offer incentives to new customers, seemingly at the expense of existing ones. Discuss the impact that such policies have on existing customer loyalty. Also, talk about actions that customers might take as a result of such initiatives and how you as a frontline service provider might help stem such behavior.

Present your conclusions to the rest of the group.

DISPLAY CARING AND CONCERN

Emphasize to your customers that you have their best interests at heart. Work to demonstrate that you are willing to assist in satisfying their needs. Asking questions that uncover their needs and then taking positive action to satisfy them can do this. It can also be accomplished through passionate efforts to solve problems. Remember that their problem is your problem.

Too often, service providers send a message that customers are not really that important. This can happen when service providers adopt a "next" mentality and treat customers as if they were numbers, not people. For example, think about the difference wording can make. Which of the following sends a more caring message to a group of customers standing in line as they wait for service?

1. A provider calls out "Next."
2. A provider looks over to the next person in line, smiles, and motions the person over with a waving hand gesture while saying, "May I help the next person in line?"

If you chose number 2, you are on your way to providing caring service.

BE FAIR

Make sure that you treat all customers (internal and external) with respect and consistency. For example, if you give special discounts to established or return customers while other customers are present, do so discreetly. Failure to exercise discretion in these cases could cause other customers to be offended because they perceive "preferential treatment" and they might take their business elsewhere. Similarly, if your organization offers special incentives to attract new customers that are not offered to current customers, the latter may resent this practice and feel that even though they have demonstrated brand loyalty, they are not valued. As a result, they may search out competitors who provide them incentives to come aboard as a customer.

People like to feel that they are special. If a customer believes that another customer is getting something that he or she is not, you could have problems. Such perceptions might even lead to legal action if customers perceive that your actions are discriminatory.

> ### Street Talk
>
> Customers remain loyal to companies that make them feel they made a smart decision to engage with that particular organization. You can help reinforce this idea about your organization with your customers by using complimentary words, thanking them for their business, and pointing out how your company values them as important and special.
>
> **SOURCE: STACEY OLIVER-KNAPPE, *OWNER, THE CUSTOMER SERVICE GURUS LLC***

ADMIT ERRORS OR LACK OF KNOWLEDGE

You are human and are expected to make mistakes. The key is to recover from errors by apologizing, accepting responsibility, and then quickly and appropriately solving the problem or getting the necessary information. One of the biggest mistakes any service provider can make is to deny accountability in dealing with a customer. When you or your organization, or the products or services it sells, cause customer inconvenience, loss, or dissatisfaction, take responsibility immediately, apologize, and work toward an acceptable resolution with the customer. To do otherwise is courting disaster. In some cases, even if a customer incorrectly perceives that you contributed to his or her dissatisfaction or loss, it may be wise to take responsibility and implement a service recovery initiative.

> ### Ethical Dilemma 10.1
>
> You work as a pharmacy technician at a major drugstore chain and you have hopes of one day being selected for the company's management training program after graduating from college.
>
> A patient calls to complain that the medication she was given causes headaches when she takes it and the symptoms for which it was prescribed are not going away. You instruct her to stop by the pharmacy at her convenience and to bring the prescription with her. Once the pharmacist sees the pills and compares it to her doctor's prescription, he realizes that the patient was given the wrong medication. The pharmacist instructs you to tell the patient that he will call the doctor to get a new prescription, but he actually just refills the original prescription and gives it to her.
>
> 1. What would you say or do to the pharmacist? Explain.
> 2. Should you notify anyone else about the incident? Explain.
> 3. What do you do or say to the patient? Explain.
> 4. What are the ethical issues here and how would you deal with them?
> 5. How do such instances potentially affect customer loyalty?

An urban legend about the power of such action has been circulated for years. It involves the highly successful department store Nordstrom. As the story goes, a disgruntled customer brought a used car tire into a Nordstrom's store and complained that it was defective. After some discussion, the manager looked at the customer's receipt and cheerfully accepted the tire and refunded the customer's money. This may not seem too unusual, except that Nordstrom does not sell automobile tires! So, why would the manager take such an extreme action? Think about the word-of-mouth publicity (how many people in your class now know this story from just reading it?) and the customer loyalty that likely resulted from it. Whether the event actually took place or someone made it up is irrelevant. The point is that taking unusual actions to solve ordinary customer problems can pay dividends long into the future. Of course, in any organization where you work, you should discuss your level of authority and what is acceptable in similar situations. Not many companies would approve of a solution like the one you just read.

In another classic example of taking responsibility for a problem, in 1982 an unknown person or group contaminated bottles of Extra-Strength Tylenol with cyanide. Seven people used the product and died. Upon finding out about the situation, the parent company (Johnson & Johnson) immediately called a press conference to announce the total recall of the product from store shelves (approximately 264,000 bottles). Johnson & Johnson started a major media campaign to reassure the public that its other products were safe. The company also helped lead the way in developing tamper-resistant packaging. The cost—millions. The result—walk into any store that sells over-the-counter drug products and look for Extra-Strength Tylenol. Tylenol is right there with all its competitors and is a strong seller. How did Johnson & Johnson pull this off? The actions of the company in taking responsibility for a situation that was not of its making communicated strong values and concern for public safety, and the public remained loyal as a result.

Other companies have not fared so well in the face of adversity. For example, think about the Exxon oil tanker *Valdez*, which spilled more than 200,000 gallons of crude oil along the Alaska coastline in 1989. The fishing and associated industries in the region were devastated and many people and animals suffered in various ways as a result. This disaster caused major environmental as well as financial losses in the millions of dollars. This does not include the almost $3 billion Exxon has spent cleaning up the environmental damage and paying legal settlements. Similarly, when the British Petroleum (BP)–owned oil platform in the Gulf of Mexico exploded in 2010, killing several workers and pumping 4.9 million gallons of oil and gas into the water, outrage was swift and people were unforgiving of BP. That spill resulted in the following action: "The United States Department of Justice settled federal criminal charges with BP pleading guilty to 11 counts of manslaughter, two misdemeanors, and a felony count of lying to Congress. BP also agreed to four years of government monitoring of its safety practices and ethics, and the Environmental Protection Agency announced that BP would be temporarily banned from new contracts with the US government. BP and the Department of Justice agreed to a record-setting $4.525 billion in fines and other payments. As of February 2013, criminal and civil settlements and payments to a trust fund had cost the company $42.2 billion."[5]

In both oil spills, the companies were slow to react and did not initially take responsibility. As a result, both organizations are still the object of litigation and jokes today. From a trust standpoint, people harbor resentment over the incidents and, in protest, many will still not patronize Exxon and BP gas stations.

Why companies make such bad decisions related to quickly taking responsibility for and dealing with problem situations is a mystery. It likely comes down to a culture of apathy and poor judgment that starts at the highest level of the organization. When employees are not empowered to make decisions that help customers or are not held accountable for their actions, they often make bad choices when dealing with customers. In some instances, this is out of lack of concern or training, or possibly fear.

In light of the costs associated with procuring new customers and keeping current ones, Forrester Research found that when service providers exceed customer expectations in solving problems, loyalty levels rise. However, when customer expectations are not met, loyalty is eroded. To expand on this, Forrester's study of North American consumers found the following:

- Eighty-one percent of respondents who said a company's problem resolution experience far exceeded their expectations also said that they're very likely to do business with that company again. Only 5% of those who said problem resolution experiences fell far below expectations said that they're very likely to do business with the same company again.

- Sixty-five percent of respondents who said that problem resolution experiences far exceeded their expectations also said that they're very likely to tell someone about the experience. Even more—71%—of those who said that their experiences fell far below expectations said that they're very likely to tell someone.[6]

In an era of strong competition and product and service availability worldwide, failure to work proactively to resolve issues quickly and efficiently makes little fiscal sense and does nothing to stimulate and maintain customer loyalty. This is why every service provider should be trained and take responsibility for identifying and handling customer problems effectively.

TRUST YOUR CUSTOMERS

Most customers are not out to cheat or "rip you (or your organization) off." They do want the best value and service for their money and expect you to provide it. Make a good-faith effort to accomplish this and deal effectively with customers by communicating openly, listening objectively to their questions and concerns, providing service to the best of your ability, showing compassion for their needs, and demonstrating that you are their advocate when things go wrong (if appropriate).

One of the most common mistakes service providers make in dealing with customers who have a complaint or problem is to verbally acknowledge and agree, but nonverbally send a message of skepticism. For example, suppose a customer comes in to complain about a defective product she purchased. As she is describing the symptoms of the problem, you use some of the paralanguage discussed in earlier chapters (e.g., "Uh huh," "I see," "Hmmm"); however, the inflection you use or your tone of voice communicates questioning or doubt (e.g., "I seeee?" or "Hmmm?"). How do you think the customer might feel or perceive you at that point?

KEEP YOUR WORD

Customers have many choices in selecting a service or product provider. If they feel you cannot be depended upon to take action, they simply leave, often without complaint or comment. When you tell customers you will do something, do it. Do not promise what you cannot deliver; many people take your word as your bond. Your goal should be to provide customers with competitively priced, reliable products or services that you deliver with little or no inconvenience or difficulty. Break the bond and you risk destroying the relationship.

If feasible after delivering a product or providing service, contact your customer to make sure that he or she was satisfied and that your service met expectations. This follow-up can be an informal call, a more formal questionnaire, or a friendly e-mail or text message (assuming he or she authorized you to send such correspondence). Always strive to underpromise and overdeliver. An example of this concept in action would be for you to suppose that a customer drops off film to be processed at your store on Tuesday. The store guarantees that the photos will be ready on Saturday. If possible, develop the film before Saturday and call to tell the customer it is ready. When he or she comes to pick it up, give a coupon for a discount on the next roll of film. Such proactive actions help secure customer loyalty.

PROVIDE PEACE OF MIND

Be positive and assertive. Assure customers through your words and actions that you are confident, have their best interests at heart, and are in control of the situation. Let them know that their calls or messages, questions, and needs will be addressed professionally and in a timely manner. Reassure them that what they purchase is the best quality, has a solid warranty, will be backed by the organization, and will address their needs while providing many benefits. Also, assure them that their requests and information will be processed rapidly and promises will be met. All of these things can lead them to the belief that they made the right decision in selecting you and your organization and that you will take care of their needs.

Being technically proficient at your job is not enough. You also have to build and maintain strong customer relationships in order to be successful. *What can you do to create a lasting relationship with your customers?*

©Eric Audras/Getty Images RF

BE RESPONSIBLE FOR YOUR CUSTOMER RELATIONSHIPS

Taking a concerned, one-on-one approach to working with customers helps satisfy immediate needs while building a basis for long-lasting relationships. Customers tend to enjoy dealing more with people whom they believe are caring and have their best interests at heart. Interacting with someone they like is a pleasant experience and is likely to encourage trust and an enhanced relationship.

PERSONALIZE YOUR APPROACH

If you have ever seen the syndicated television show *Cheers,* you may recall the catchy show theme song. The idea of the theme song was that *Cheers* was a great place to go because "everyone knows your name." Mostly, people are a social species and need to be around others to grow and flourish. Helping your customers feel accepted can create a bond that will keep them coming back.

To create a social bond with customers, you will need to take time to get to know your regular customers and serve them individually. Recognizing them and using their names while interacting goes a long way toward creating that bond. For new customers, immediately start using the positive interpersonal communication skills you have learned. Treating customers as individuals and not as a number or one in a series is a very important step in building rapport and loyalty.

> **Customer Service Success Tip**
>
> Take the time to personalize your customer interactions and to make each customer feel special. Use a customer's name often during an interaction, listen, smile, ask questions to show interest, and strive to project a positive image. This can all lead to enhanced trust and helps ensure that the customer returns.

⚙ WORK IT OUT 10.2

Problem Solving

Working in teams of three or four members, decide on a course of action to resolve the problem posed in the following scenario. You have been a cashier at Gifts Galore for a little over one month. A customer comes into your gift shop and wants to return a lamp that she says she purchased from your store as a gift for a wedding. Apparently, she discovered later that the intended recipient already had a lamp exactly like the one she bought. She tells you that she remembers the salesperson, Brittney, because her daughter's name is spelled the same way. You know that Brittney used to work at the gift shop but quit about the time you started. The customer has no receipt, and you do not recognize the product as one that your store sells. You are empowered to make exchanges and give refunds up to a product value of $50. The customer says the lamp was $49.95 before tax. Store policy says that the customer must have a receipt if a refund is to be made, otherwise, a store credit is issued. The customer is not happy about this policy. What questions would you ask to clarify the situation? How would you handle the problem?

KEEP AN OPEN MIND

To develop and maintain an open mind, make it a habit to assess your attitude about your job, customers, products, and services periodically before making contact with your customers. Make sure that you are positive, objective, prepared, and focused. Do not let negative attitudes block good service. Many service providers, even the more seasoned ones, go through slumps during which they feel down about themselves, their job, supervisors, organizations, customers, and so on. This is normal. Customer service is a stressful job, and external and internal factors (e.g., circadian rhythm, workload, and personal problems) influence one's perceptions of people and the world in general; however, guard against pessimism.

If you are facing personal problems that seem overwhelming, contact your supervisor, human resources, or personnel department, or any other appropriate resource (e.g., employee assistance program [EAP] representative) to help you sort out your problems. Failure to do so could lead to poor customer service or a less-than-professional image.

INDIVIDUALIZE SERVICE

Each customer is unique and has his or her own desires and needs. For that reason, every situation you handle will be slightly different. You should view each person as an individual and not deal with customers on the basis of preconceived ideas or the demographic group of which they are part. By addressing a customer as an individual, listening so that you can discover his or her personal needs and problems, and then working to satisfy the needs or solve the problems, you potentially create a loyal customer. A simple way of accomplishing individualized service is to ask what else the customer would like. For example, in the case of a restaurant server who uses such a question, a customer might respond, "Do you have any (item)?" If the item is available, the server could cheerfully reply, "We certainly do. I will get it for you right away." If the item is not available, the server might reply, "I am sorry we do not have (item). However, we do have (alternative item) or we could special order the item for you and have it within a week. Would one of those options be acceptable?"

> ⚙ **WORK IT OUT 10.3**
>
> ## Showing Respect
>
> **Take a few minutes to think of other ways that you can show respect for a variety of customers (e.g., older, younger, people with disabilities, or people of various cultural backgrounds).** Make a list of the different categories of customers discussed in this chapter and write down your service ideas for each group. Discuss how these can positively influence service.

SHOW RESPECT

Even if you do not agree with a customer, respect his or her point of view or need and provide the best possible service. In return, the customer will probably respect and appreciate you and your efforts. A variation of an old adage may help put this concept into perspective: *The customer may not always be right, but he or she is still the customer.*

If you lose sight of the fact that it is the customer who supports the organization, pays your salary, provides for your benefits, and gives you a job, you may want to examine why you are working in your current position. By acknowledging the value of your customers and affording them the respect and service they deserve, you can greatly improve your chances of having a satisfied customer. Some easy ways to show respect to customers include the following:

- When addressing the customer, use his or her last name and title. (If you are on the telephone, write down the customer's name along with other pertinent information so that you do not forget.)
- Stop talking when the customer begins to speak.
- Take time to address the customer's questions or concerns.
- Do not get into arguments with customers. If disagreements arise that you cannot handle calmly and professionally, refer the issue to a coworker or supervisor.
- Return calls or e-mail messages within reasonable amounts of time.
- Show up on time for scheduled meetings.
- Do what you promised to do, and do it right the first time, within the agreed-upon time frame.
- Tell customers that you value them and appreciate their business.

ELICIT CUSTOMER INPUT

Some organizations actually encourage rewarding customers who complain. Complaints provide feedback that can enable service providers and organizations to rapidly shift resources to fix things that are not working well in an effort to satisfy the customer. By taking the time to ask for customer input and actually listening to what he or she has to say, and then acting appropriately upon those comments, you can solidify a bond and further enhance the customer's level of trust in you. If you think about it, this makes sense. You cannot fix what you do not know is broken.

Many times, service providers do not take the time to ask for feedback because they are afraid that it may not be good. In other instances, they simply do not think of asking for customer input or care to do so. To increase your own effectiveness and that of your organization, actively and regularly seek input from your customers. No one knows better than the customer what he or she likes or needs. Take the time to ask the customer, and then listen and act upon what you are told. By asking customers questions, you give them an opportunity to express interest, concerns, emotion, and even complaints. There are many ways of gathering this information (e.g., customer satisfaction cards, written surveys, and service follow-up telephone calls; see Figure 10.2). The key is to somehow ask the customer, "How well did we do in meeting your needs?" or "What do you think?" If this is not a normal procedure in your place of business, you should consider bringing the idea up at a staff meeting. It will take extra effort on the part of the customer service employees, but the effort will be well-rewarded in the goodwill it will elicit from your customer base.

FIGURE 10.2 Customer Information-Gathering Techniques

There are many ways to gather information about customer satisfaction levels. Some of the more common include the following:

- *Customer comment cards* are simple 5 × 7 inch (approximately) card stock questionnaires that quickly gather customer reactions to their service experiences. These cards are commonly found on restaurant tables and at point-of-sale locations (e.g., cash registers). They typically consist of four or five closed-end questions that can be answered with yes/no or short answers and have a space for general comments.

- *Toll-free numbers* are often used to obtain customer opinions after a service encounter. Customers are provided a toll-free number on their sales receipt and encouraged to call within 24 hours. As a reward, they are often given discount coupons, bonus frequent guest/user points, or other small incentives.

- *Verbal comments* can be elicited from customers and logged in by service providers. By asking customers for feedback on their experiences and paying heed to them, immediate service adjustments can be made.

- *Follow-up telephone surveys* can be done by employees or consultants using a written list of questions. The key is to be brief, not impose on customers, and ask questions that will gather pertinent information (e.g., open-end questions).

- *Service contact surveys* that are mailed or e-mailed (with permission) to people who have contacted an organization to get information, make a purchase, or use a service can gather more in-depth information.

- *Automated surveys* that can be sent to targeted customers and taken through a link to a website following transactions or events in order to get their opinion. The Internet offers a variety of websites that provide survey services. Some are even free (e.g., www.surveymonkey.com).

- *Exit interviews* conducted by greeters, hosts, or hostesses as customers leave a facility. These are typically one or two quick questions (e.g., "How did you enjoy your stay?" "Were you able to find everything you needed?" or "What can we do to make your next visit more pleasurable?"). The key is to log in responses for future reference.

- *Shopper/customer surveys* that can yield a wealth of information. These are typically longer and more detailed than a comment card. They can be given to a customer as he or she leaves or can be sent to customers later (get names and addresses from checks written). Offer discount coupons or other incentives for returned surveys and provide self-addressed, stamped envelopes.

- *Focus groups* of six to eight internal or external customers can be formed to do in-depth, face-to-face or online (chat) surveys. Often organizations conducting these provide snacks and gifts (e.g., $50) for each participant. Ask open-end questions related to the organization and products and services provided. Often, trained marketing or other facilitators are used to conduct such sessions. They also analyze responses and provide reports to management along with recommendations for improvement.

- *Sales and service records* can provide a wealth of information. They can reflect whether customers are returning and what products and services are being used most, and can show patterns of purchases.

Customer Service Success Tip

Many organizations encourage employees to ask for customer input at the cash register or the end of the service experience. For example, "Did you find everything you were looking for?" or "Was everything satisfactory today?" If you are going to ask these questions, be prepared to deal with situations in which their response is negative (e.g. "No, I could not find..." "No, you did not have..." or "Not really, my food was cold/not good").

To prepare to deal with such instances, speak with your supervisor in advance to ask what your level of authority is to compensate a dissatisfied or disappointed customer and have responses ready for your customer(s). For example, you might be able to offer a discount coupon for a future visit or be able to take the customer's name and contact information and save it in the computer or a book by the register so that a notification can be sent when an item arrives. Often service providers ask these questions and when told of dissatisfaction, they simply state, "Oh, I am sorry about that." Then continue to process a payment or package items into a bag as if nothing happened. This is poor service. If you are going to raise a customer's expectations that you might be able to remedy a problem identified through your question, then be prepared to do so.

KNOWLEDGE CHECK

1. Why is trust so important to the customer–provider relationship?
2. How do recalls impact customer trust in an organization or industry?
3. What are some strategies that you can use to build customer trust?
4. What are some typical strategies that can be used to gather customer information?

LO 10-3 The Importance of Customer Relationship Management

CONCEPT Long-term relationships are the ones that sustain organizations.

Why bother building relationships with customers? The answer would seem obvious—so that you can stay in business. However, when you examine the question further, you may find that there are more reasons than you think. This is where the

customer relationship management (CRM) Concept of identifying customer needs; understanding and influencing customer behavior through ongoing communication strategies in an effort to acquire, retain, and satisfy the customer.

customer relationships Ongoing friendships with customers focused on making them feel comfortable with an organization and its service providers and enhancing customer loyalty.

customer relationship management (CRM) concept comes in. There are actually a number of components in the CRM process:

- Operational (involving sales and service representatives)
- Relational/Collaborative (involving interaction with customers through such means as e-mail)
- Technological Web pages and automated voice response (AVR) systems
- Analytical (involving analyzing customer data for efforts like marketing and financial forecasting)

Through CRM, organizations and employees get to better know their customers and project needs that can be satisfied through appropriate products and services.

At one point in history, business owners knew their customers personally. This is because in many instances their customers were also neighbors. They knew their customers' families, religious affiliations, and what was happening in their lives. That was then, and this is now. Our current society is more mobile; people live in large metropolitan areas where relationships are distant, and families live miles apart from one another in many instances. In many instances, people do not even know who lives next door to them. Large multinational organizations provide the products and services once provided by the neighborhood store. However, all this does not mean that a positive customer–provider relationship can no longer exist.

Additionally, with B2B (business-to-business), customers are often companies. This makes managing **customer relationships** more difficult because of the number of contacts you might have in an organization and the varying requirements or needs of each might have. Also, much of business-to-business service is delivered through technology. Numerous service organizations use CRM software to better keep track of customer needs, access multiple sources of customer information (e.g., credit reports, past contacts, and voice and e-mail messages), and record service provided. CRM is a crucial element of customer loyalty.

Typically, many service providers look at customer interactions from a short-term perspective. They figure that a customer calls or comes in (or they go to the customer), they provide service, and then the customer (or the service provider) goes away. This is a short-sighted viewpoint in that it does not consider the long-term implications. This is not the way to gain and sustain customer loyalty.

A more customer-focused approach is to view customers from a relationship standpoint. That does not mean that you have to become intimate friends with all your customers; it simply means that you should strive to employ as many of the positive relationship-building skills that you have learned as possible. By treating both internal and external customers in a manner that leads them to believe that you care for them and have their best interests at heart, you can start to generate reciprocal feelings. Using the interpersonal communication skills that you have learned throughout this book and through other sources is a great way to begin doing this.

People usually gravitate toward organizations and people with whom they have developed rapport, respect, and trust, and who treat them as if they are valued as a person. Relationships are de-

©Joey Foley/Getty Images

Relationships are a crucial part of customer service. By working to build trust and getting to know customer needs, service providers increase their effectiveness. *What techniques do you use to build rapport and trust with customers?*

veloped and enhanced through one-on-one human interaction. This does not mean that people who provide service via technology cannot develop relationships. Those relationships develop on a different level, using the nonverbal skills.

Trending NOW

Some organizations are starting to revert to a service strategy used by organizations up through the middle of the twentieth century–expedited or local home and office delivery of products. Some examples of this trend include the following:

Walgreen's Drugs delivers drugs prescribed for patients being discharged from a hospital to their hospital room on the date of discharge to eliminate their need to stop by a drug store on the way home.

Safeway, groceriesexpress.com, Amazon Fresh, and other grocery stores now offer local food delivery to customers, as their predecessors from decades ago once did.

Boise Milk has delivered milk since 2006 and has now expanded into fresh fruits, produce, and other farm products.

The U.S. Postal Service now offers special delivery of Express Mail to customers seven days a week.

Crystal Springs makes home and office deliveries of bottled water, coffee, teas, and breakroom products.

Doctors and veterinarians around the United States are slowly bringing back the "house call" service from the early days of the country in order to address the needs of patients who are older or who have more debilitating conditions. In some instances, these "visits" are via Skype or other electronic format.

Remember that long-term customer relationships (**customer retention**) are the ones that sustain organizations. In many organizations, particularly those that have contractual customers (e.g., members or subscribers), the **churn rate** is often an indicator of customer dissatisfaction, better targeted marketing and sales efforts or better or cheaper pricing by competitors, or factors related to service provider relationships with customers. No matter the cause, the issue is that organizations that have an ongoing high churn rate are doomed to failure.

The days of a customer adopting one product or company for life are long gone. With easy access and global competitiveness, customers are often swayed by advertising and a chance at a "better deal." Quality levels and features between competing brands and organizations are often comparable. The thing that separates most competitors is their level of service. It is not unusual for customers to switch back and forth between products or organizations simply because of pricing. This practice is sometimes referred to as service **churn**.

Every employee should work to reduce churn. Research on customer churn by Frederick Reinheld of Bain & Company "shows that increasing customer retention rates by 5% increases profits by 25% to 95%."[7]

Seeking out new or replacement customers through advertising and other means is a very costly proposition. According to a 2014 article in the Harvard Business Review, "acquiring a new customer is five to 25 times more expensive than retaining an existing one."[8] This is because in addition to having to find new customers, you and your organization have to educate and win them over. You have to prove yourself to newly acquired customers. More than likely, new customers are also going to be more apprehensive, skeptical, and critical than customers who have previous experience with your organization. For these reasons, it is imperative that you and every other member of your organization work to build and strengthen customer relationships and develop loyalty on the part of those customers with whom you have an existing relationship.

customer retention The ongoing effort by an organization to meet customer needs and desires in an effort to build a long-term relationship and keep the customer for life.

churn rate Refers to the number of customers who leave a supplier during a given time period.

churn The process of a customer switching between products or companies, often simply to get a better price, contract, rebate, or warranty.

Many organizations and industries seem to forget the value of fostering solid long-term customer relationships. They often treat existing customers poorly or not as well as newly acquired ones. You can find examples of this in the following:

- High maintenance and transaction fees charged for checking accounts by financial institutions
- High fees charged by hotels for local calls
- Escalating fees charged by airlines for ticket changes, baggage, seat assignments, snacks/food, and priority boarding
- Inability for existing cell phone or cable customers locked into contracts to get the same deals as new customers
- Fees by doctors' and dentists' offices regardless of the reason for patient appointment cancellations
- Restocking fees charged by many online retailers for returned items
- Charges at gas stations for vehicle air and water
- Fees charged to access Internet connections in hotel rooms

customer loyalty program An incentive program offered by an organization to reward customers for spending money and purchasing products and services.

Major organizations spend millions of dollars on **customer loyalty programs**. Unfortunately, small businesses cannot compete on those levels. What they can do is train all employees to build relationships on an interpersonal level and to take every opportunity to reinforce the value of customers when they interact with them. What this means is that just because a company does not have deep pockets or large staff resources, they can still strive to gain and retain customers the old-fashioned way... through building strong personal relationships with them.

A study on loyalty related to small and medium-sized enterprises (SMEs) by Barclays Bank found that

> ...the majority of consumers (58%) believe that small independent retailers are in a better or the same position to engender loyalty among their current customers than large, corporate brands—and it's the personal touches which count the most. Nearly two thirds (60%) of consumers said they are always, often or sometimes willing to pay more for a similar product from a small, independent retailer compared to a cheaper product from a large, corporate retailer. It is up to SMEs to convert these sales via customer loyalty.[9]

BENEFITS OF CUSTOMER RELATIONSHIP MANAGEMENT

When organizations attain a high degree of brand recognition and a reputation for providing quality products and services at a competitive price, while going above and beyond their customers' expectations, they are typically rewarded with customer loyalty and repeat and referral business.

According to a J.D. Powers and Associates North American Hotel Guest Satisfaction Index Study[BL26], "Hotels that proactively meet guest needs have the ability to create a positive guest experience ... While service recovery is extremely important in the hotel industry, it's most effective when the entire guest experience is a positive one. Hotel staff members need to maintain a proper balance between proactively addressing needs and responding to problems effectively. Doing so can help guests feel good about their selection of the hotel brand and the likelihood they will return for another stay or recommend it to others ... Staff interactions with guests have a great impact on mitigating problems. There is a 50 percent reduction in the average number

FIGURE 10.3
Loyalty Equation

Effective product/service delivery
+ Proactive relationship building
+ Elimination of dissatisfiers
+ Resolution of problems
+ Follow-up
= Customer satisfaction and loyalty

of problems experienced when staff members greet guests with a smile 'all the time,' compared to when guests are only greeted with a smile 'sometimes'."[10]

Other direct benefits of going above customer expectations include the following:

- Less need to obtain new customers through marketing because current customers are aware of offerings and take advantage of them

- Reduced marketing costs because direct mail, follow-up, and other customer recruitment activities are reduced

- Increased return on investment (ROI) because marketing can target specific customer needs

- Enhanced customer loyalty due to pricing and product service offerings that meet current customer needs

- Elevated profitability resulting from increased sales, customer referrals, and longer customer retention during life cycles

- Targeted marketing based on statistics on which customers buy more and on high-ticket item sales

By providing excellent customer service and dealing with dissatisfaction as soon as you identify it, you can help ensure that customers remain loyal and keep coming back. Figure 10.3 shows an equation that conveys the loyalty concept.

Traditionally, customers will remain loyal to a product, service, or organization that they believe meets their needs. Even when there is an actual or perceived breakdown in quality, many customers will return to an organization that they believe sincerely attempts to solve a problem or make restitution for an error. According to CX Solutions (formerly **Technical Assistance Research Program [TARP] Worldwide**; not associated with the U.S. federal government's Troubled Asset Relief Program), many organizations have found that, when complaints were acted upon and resolved quickly, most customers returned to the organization (see Figure 10.4).

The bottom line is that you and other employees must realize that customer service is everyone's business and that relationships are the basis of that business.

Technical Assistance Research Program (TARP) Worldwide An Arlington, Virginia–based firm specializing in customer service research studies for call centers and many other industries.

 WORK IT OUT 10.4

Personal Customer Relationship Experiences

Think about a service provider with whom you deal frequently and have established a better-than-average customer–provider relationship. Perhaps you have been dealing with the organization for a long period of time or visit frequently. Reflect on the relationship and make a list of positive customer service behaviors exhibited by this person. Then review the list and make it a personal goal to replicate as many of these behaviors as possible when dealing with your own customers.

FIGURE 10.4

The Importance of Customer Loyalty

For almost three decades, the research firm TARP has conducted various studies to determine the effects of customer service. The research has revealed the following:

- It will cost an organization at least five times more to acquire a new customer than it will to keep an existing one.
- On average, 50 percent of consumers will complain about a problem to a frontline person. In business-to-business environments, this figure jumps to 75 percent.
- For small-ticket items, 96 percent of consumers do not complain or they complain to the retailer from whom they bought an item. For large-ticket items, 50 percent complain to frontline employees, and 5 to 10 percent escalate the problem to local managers or corporate headquarters.
- At least 50 percent of your customers who experience problems will not complain or contact your organization for help; they will simply go elsewhere.
- Customers who are dissatisfied will tell as many as 16 friends about a negative experience with your organization.
- The average business loses 10 to 15 percent of its customers per year because of bad service.

Source: CX Solutions (formerly Technical Assistance Research Program [TARP]), 1100 Wilson Boulevard, Suite 950, Arlington, Virginia 22209. http://www.cxsolutions.com/

KNOWLEDGE CHECK

1. What does customer relationship management (CRM) involve?
2. What is meant by churn rate?

LO 10-4 The Role of Channel Partner Relationships on Customer Loyalty

CONCEPT   **Relationship with channel partners is a key component for managing customer loyalty.**

channel partner Relationship of two organizations through which partners are able to build a larger and stronger competitive presence in the marketplace.

A key component of managing customer loyalty is effectively managing **channel partner** relationships. Such partners can help organizations gain access to new business opportunities at lower costs, without having to merge or acquire more assets and employees. The result can be reduced retail and service pricing. Partnering with complementary organizations provides a more competitive posture for an organization. In addition, the relationship potentially attracts and holds customers because of lowered pricing and enhanced product and service availability. Through such relationships, organizations are able to build a larger and stronger competitive presence in the marketplace, which can help enhance customer trust and loyalty. This potentially occurs because customers view the organizations as a larger and stronger supplier or entity.

THREE TYPES OF CHANNEL PARTNERS

There are three types of typical channel partners with which your organization might have a relationship:

1. *Transactional or indirect.* These types of organizations provide a distribution outlet or link for your company's products and services. The challenge is that they maintain no specific loyalty and when the opportunity arises to obtain a newer product or service line, or one that is less expensive, they may move to other suppliers or vendors. Examples of transactional partners are online websites (e.g., amazon.com and overstock.com), retail stores, or service providers (e.g., plumber, laundry, pest control, masseuse/masseur, and car repair).

2. *Tactical.* This category of partners includes organizations intricately meshed with your company's internal operations. Examples of such arrangements include mobile phone service providers that use retail outlets (e.g., Best Buy or mall kiosks) that display and sell products. This strategy provides an inexpensive means for companies to extend their reach or presence in the marketplace. Operational costs are reduced and profits go up due to lowered overhead.

3. *Strategic.* The third type of channel partnership involves signing agreements through which one organization creates a long-term alliance with another organization to brand, develop, or produce each other's products or services. As example of this is code sharing that takes place between airlines. For example, two different airlines can sell seats on a single plane under their own individual flight numbers. Another benefit of such relationships is that when an airline overbooks a flight and passengers are bumped, they might be scheduled onto a partner airline flight going to the same destination. This can potentially reduce lost revenue when a passenger in a bumped situation requests a refund and moves to a competing airline to get to his or her destination.

KNOWLEDGE CHECK

1. What is a channel partner?
2. What are the three types of channel partners?

LO 10-5 Provider Characteristics Affecting Customer Loyalty

CONCEPT **Personal characteristics of a service provider may affect customer loyalty positively or negatively.**

Many of your personal characteristics affect your relationships with customers. In customer service, some circumstances are beyond your control; however, your personal characteristics are not. The following sections describe some of the most common qualities of service providers that affect customers.

RESPONSIVENESS

Customers typically like to feel that they are the most important person in the world when they encounter an organization (see Figure 10.5). This is a human need. If customers do not feel appreciated or welcome by you or another service provider, they will likely take their business elsewhere. However, they will often first complain to

FIGURE 10.5

Addressing Customer Needs

Everyone has needs that you must meet in some fashion. Here are six common customer needs, along with strategies to satisfy them. Keep in mind that no two customer interactions are exactly alike. As a result, you may find yourself using any of the strategies below (or others) to address a need that you identify for a given customer. The key is to remain flexible as you work with customers and adapt to their specific needs and requests.

Customer Need	Strategies for Satisfying the Need
To feel welcome	Use an enthusiastic greeting, smile, and the customer's name; thank the customer; be positive
To be understood	Listen actively, paraphrase, ask key questions, give positive feedback, empathize
To feel comfortable	Use an enthusiastic welcome, relieve anxiety through friendly communication, explain your actions calmly, ensure physical comfort (e.g., seats, refreshments)
To feel appreciated	Thank the customer, follow up, go beyond service expectations, provide "special" offers, remember special details about the customer (e.g., birthdays, favorite colors, facts about his or her families)
To feel important	Use the customer's name, personalize service, give special treatment when possible, elicit opinions, remember details about him or her (e.g., last purchase made, last visit, preferred styles or foods)
To be respected	Listen, do not interrupt, acknowledge the customer's emotions and concerns, take time to serve, ask advice, elicit feedback

management and will tell anyone who will listen about the poor quality of service they received. As you read in the TARP (CX Solutions) research summary, they may also tell up to 16 other people about their negative experience.

 WORK IT OUT 10.5

Personal Service Expectations

Think of expectations for treatment if you were a customer of the company for which you currently work. List behaviors that you would expect to encounter from customer service employees.

A simple way to demonstrate responsiveness is to attend to customer needs promptly. If you get an e-mail or voice mail message, respond to it immediately, if possible. If that is not possible, try to respond within four hours, or certainly within 24 hours. If you have face-to-face customer contact, greet customers quickly (within 10 to

15 seconds), even if you are busy with someone else. At the least, smile and gesture that you will be with them momentarily.

Once you do get to serve the customer, and before delivering service, greet the customer with a smile and start the interaction on a friendly note in one or more of the following ways:

Be enthusiastic. Use open body language, vocal cues, and gestures that you have read about previously in this book, coupled with some of the techniques described below to let your customers know that you are glad they have chosen you and/or your organization.

Use the customer's title and name. If you know the customer's name, use it. Remember, though, not to assume familiarity and start using the customer's first name unless given permission to do so.

Show appreciation. "Thank you for coming to (organization)." "It is nice to see you this morning." "You have been very patient while I assisted the previous customer. Thank you."

Engage in small talk. "What do you think of this terrible weather?" "Is this your first visit to our store?" "Did I see you in here last week?" (Say this only if you recognize the customer. If he or she answers yes, thank the person for returning to the store.)

Compliment. "You look like you are having a good day" (assuming the customer is smiling and does look happy). "That color really looks nice on you," "That is a beautiful necktie/dress," or other appropriate compliment. Just be careful that you do not come across as flirting and remember that in some cultures it may be inappropriate for people of the opposite sex to make such remarks.

ADAPTABILITY

In a continually evolving world, you will undoubtedly have many opportunities to deal with customers who have different beliefs, values, perceptions, needs, and expectations. You will also encounter people whose personality styles differ from yours. Each of these meetings will provide an opportunity for you to adapt your approach in dealing with others. By doing so, you can increase the likelihood of a successful interaction and a satisfied customer emerging from the interaction. It is smart of you to take measures to adapt your personality style to that of your customers in order to communicate with and serve them effectively. Keep in mind that you cannot change the customers; however, you can adapt to them and their approach to a situation.

Another, more subtle, way to show your ability to adapt relates to technology. By quickly learning and mastering new technology systems provided to you by the organization, you can respond faster and more efficiently to customer needs. This is especially true if many of your customers will likely be very technology-literate. If you cannot match their expectations, or at least demonstrate knowledge and effectiveness in using technology, you might frustrate them and drive them away. In turn, you might create negative word-of-mouth publicity about your organization and its employees.

> **Customer Service Success Tip**
>
> Listen to your customer and address his or her needs; do not just talk about yourself, your organization, products, and services. You can gain trust through use of positive relationship-building skills.

COMMUNICATION SKILLS

As you have read earlier in this book, your ability to obtain and give information; listen, write, and speak effectively; and deal with emotional situations are keys to successful customer service. By using a variety of effective interpersonal techniques, you

Customers have many choices for service. Each person in the organization must go out of his or her way to project a positive image and work to project a "can do" attitude with customers. *What do you do to show that you are worthy of your customers' patronage and support?*

©mangostock/AGE Fotostock RF

can determine customer needs. The most successful service providers are the ones who have learned to interact positively and build rapport with customers. To help ensure the most effective service possible, you should continually strive to improve your ability to interact and communicate with a variety of people. The better your skills are, the more likely you will be able to address different situations that arise in the workplace.

Trending NOW

Many marketers are using mobile applications to deliver coupons to customers in an effort to gain new customers and build brand loyalty. One estimate by Juniper Research projects that the number of mobile coupon users is projected to surpass 1 billion by 2019.[11]

WORK IT OUT 10.6

Passing Time

Partner with someone and try this experiment in order to better realize how customers and service providers might perceive the passing of time differently (e.g., while a customer is on hold). When your instructor says, "Go," mentally try to determine when 30 seconds have elapsed. When you believe 30 seconds have elapsed, say/shout "Now."

Afterward, you will participate in a discussion led by your instructor about perceptions about time and how yours and that of your customer can be significantly different depending on the situation.

DECISIVENESS

Decisiveness relates to being able and willing to make a decision and take necessary actions to fulfill customer needs. Taking a wait-and-see approach to customer service often leads to customer dissatisfaction. Just as you probably do, customers value their time. By causing customers to wait while you go to someone else for a decision or answer can be frustrating. Granted, such a situation is sometimes created by a manager's style that requires you to get certain approvals (e.g., for checks, returns or refunds, or discounts). However, these are internal issues that should be resolved before the customer encounters them. If you face such barriers, think of alternative ways of handling them, and then approach your supervisor with suggestions for improvement. Your ideas may make your life easier by reducing the chances of a frustrating and unproductive service encounter. They might also reduce customer churn.

Once you have supportive systems in place, gather information effectively by using the active listening techniques you read about earlier in this book. Then carefully and quickly analyze the situation and make a decision on how to best solve the problem.

ENTHUSIASM

As discussed earlier, attaining and maintaining a level of excitement about your customers, products, services, organization, and job that says, "I am happy to help you," is an important step toward establishing a relationship.

If you are enthusiastic about serving your customers, they will often respond by supporting you and the organization. People typically react positively to enthusiastic employees who appear to be enjoying themselves as they work. This does not mean that service providers should act unprofessionally or create an environment in which they have fun and detracts from customer service or attention to their customers. Find a good balance between fun and professionalism. Southwest Airlines has succeeded in finding the right mix. Employees dress casually, are recruited based on their personality, and often use jokes and games on flights to reduce some of the stress of air travel in a security-conscious industry. The company has been rewarded with continued corporate profits and awards while other airlines often report losses.

The long-term benefit is that if you and your organization can generate return customers through enthusiasm, the potential for organizational growth and prosperity exists. This in turn sets the stage for better benefits, salary, and workplace modifications that lead to higher employee enthusiasm. Once all the elements are connected, all contribute to successful customer service.

As a side note, many employees and employers are trying to find ways to make the workplace less stressful and more enjoyable for themselves and customers.

> **Customer Service Success Tip**
>
> Even if the organization for which you work does not have a conduct code, it is crucial that you and your peers guard against any words or actions that might raise scrutiny or customer skepticism.

ETHICAL BEHAVIOR

With a heightened incidence of actual or alleged corporate wrongdoing (e.g., Enron, Martha Stewart, and numerous politicians), customers have become wary of organizations, their leaders, and practices. Many organizations have formed ethics committees made up of employees from across their organization to deal with actual or perceived violations of ethical standards or organization codes. Many have adopted a **code of ethics** or codes of conduct that are shared with all employees, new and old, and to which they are held accountable. By having a written standard of conduct, organizations demonstrate to customers that they are concerned for

> **code of ethics** A set of standards, often developed by employees, that guide the conduct of all employees.

FIGURE 10.6 Examples of Ethical and Unethical Behavior

Some examples of ethical behavior follow:

- A company voluntarily recalls a product that it discovers was defective or potentially dangerous before someone complains.
- Doctors prescribing less expensive drug alternatives even though they could get a bonus from manufacturers for name brand products.
- A manager notifies a customer when he or she finds out that an employee has lied to or deceived the customer.
- An employee reports a theft carried out by another employee.
- A truck driver tracks down the owner of a parked car at a mall to identify herself as the person who accidentally scraped a bumper while making a delivery.
- A cab driver finds a wallet containing hundreds of dollars in his taxi and turns it in to his dispatcher.
- A law enforcement officer reports one of his own traffic violations to the police chief even though no one witnessed it.

Some examples of unethical behavior follow:

- Providing or substituting an inferior or more expensive product for an advertised name brand item.
- A doctor conducting unnecessary procedures or prescribing drugs because manufacturers provide kickbacks to the practice based on volume.
- Providing inferior or nonstandard parts or repairs on a service call but charging for factory parts.
- Manufacturers knowingly failing to alert the public or recall defective products that could cause injury to customers.
- Misleading a customer about coverage on an extended home warranty in order to sell a policy and make a commission.
- Failing to adhere to local, state, or federal regulations (e.g., dumping hazardous waste, such as petroleum or pesticide products, in unauthorized areas or collecting sales taxes but failing to report the taxes).
- Lying to a patient about why he or she has to wait so long before being seen by a technician, nurse, or doctor (e.g., the medical professional came in late or returned late from lunch).
- Promising a customer a delivery on a specific date when that is not realistic and the employee knows it.
- A realtor failing to tell a potential homebuyer about structural damage or other defects in a house.
- A lawn service company using chemicals that are hazardous to the environment in violation of regulations because they are cheaper that those approved by the government.

their welfare. They also demonstrate that they have the intention of operating in an ethical manner. This effort can ease customer trepidation or concerns that employees will take advantage of them. (See Figure 10.6 for examples of both ethical and unethical behavior.)

Establishing (and maintaining) high legal, social, and ethical standards in all interactions with customers is imperative. Failure to do so can lead to loss of reputation and business, and/or legal liability. While it is not always easy to take an ethical approach to getting wrong or illegal behavior corrected, it is the morally right thing to do. There will certainly be instances where you or another person brings improper behavior to someone's attention, which then results in personal loss and consequences (e.g., lost employment and income, having to testify in a court case against a coworker or supervisor for illegal activity, or feeling like an outcast from others). Even so, there is the personal satisfaction of doing the right thing and, often, there are financial rewards for your positive behavior. Still, monitoring and helping correct improper behavior is a personal choice based on your values and beliefs. You cannot control how other people act, but you can control how you act.

Ethical Dilemma 10.2

Your goal is to one day become a licensed real estate broker; however, with recent changes in the economy, you have decided to get a job in a related profession that provides a more stable income and benefits. To help position yourself for future opportunities in the field while you gain more knowledge and experience about how the profession works, you recently took a job as a professional assistant in a large real estate company.

From your previous research and a course you took at the local community college, you know that there are numerous federal laws pertaining to the real estate profession. One of them is the requirement to disclose known information about any potentially hazardous situations that exist related to a listed property (e.g., the presence of lead-based paint or asbestos).

You recently overheard two senior agents discussing a potential deal in which someone is interested in buying a retail property that has been on the market for some time. The potential buyers want to use the building for a child care facility. Apparently, it is an older building built in the late 1960s and the interior was repainted several times in the past. Somehow, one of the agents found out that the original lead-based paint was only covered over and not removed.

Coincidentally, you know one of the women interested in the building. Her children go to school with your son.

1. What are the ethical issues in this situation? Explain.
2. Should you say anything to anyone in the office? Explain.
3. Should you say anything to the potential buyer? Explain.
4. If you do not say anything, is there any potential liability? Explain.
5. If you do say something to the other agents, your boss, or the potential buyer, what are the potential repercussions for you?

INITIATIVE

Taking an action related to your job or customer service without having to receive instructions from others is a sign of initiative. Such actions also help to ensure that you identify and meet the needs of your customer in a timely fashion. Too many service providers take the "It is not my job" or "I cannot do that" approach to dealing with customer situations. This can lead to customer dissatisfaction because the provider seems to be lazy or uncaring. To counter such impressions, you should take responsibility when a problem arises. By building a strong knowledge base (as described in the next section) and using the skills discussed in this book, you will have the tools you need to deal effectively with various situations without having to turn to others for assistance. This can expedite service and enhance your reputation in the eyes of your customers, peers, and supervisors.

Initiative does not only apply to external customer situations. What you do around your boss and coworkers (internal customers) also sends powerful messages about you. For example, if you work in a retail store and walk down an aisle and you see a piece of trash on the floor or an item placed in the wrong location, you should take the time to pick it up and put it where it belongs. This sends a message of personal responsibility and the initiative to care about the image presented to external customers. By such a small act, you potentially prevent an external customer from developing a negative impression about your organization and its employees. Such opinions might ultimately affect sales and revenue levels. You also potentially gain the respect and appreciation of other employees because you have helped create a more professional work environment. Simple actions like those that you just read about often lead to career opportunities, raises, and other potential benefits.

KNOWLEDGE

Your customers expect you to know about your business organization. With all the products and service variations available to customers, the high level of technology, deregulation of industries, and innovations coming on the market daily, customers depend on service providers to educate and guide them in making purchases and decisions. Taking time to learn about policies, procedures, resources, products, services, and other information can help you provide total customer satisfaction in an efficient and timely manner.

If the organization for which you work does not provide training or resources, take the initiative to ask supervisors or team leaders for materials and information. Also, develop a network with other employees throughout the organization and use that network to gain access to information. Networking examples include the following:

- Attend general training sessions through organizations involved in your particular product or service.
- Locate mentors or other individuals who can help with your career development through service organizations like SCORE, the Small Business Administration, Rotary Club, or other fraternal organizations.
- Networking with others in your line of work or industry outside of your company can also help in many ways.
- Joining an organization whose membership includes people who do the same job in other companies can give you different perspectives and add to your knowledge base. It can also provide you with future resources and job search assistance.

By taking a proactive approach to learning and career development, you, your organization, and your customers will ultimately benefit from your initiatives.

PERCEPTIVENESS

Recognizing the need to pay close attention to verbal and nonverbal cues, cultural factors, and the feelings or concerns of others is important. By staying focused on customers and the signals they send, you can often recognize hesitancy, interest in a product or adamant rejection, irritation, anxiety, and a multitude of other unspoken messages. Once you have identified customers' signals, you can react appropriately and address their needs.

One way you can address customer needs is to anticipate them, depending on where you work. Suppose that a customer makes a comment like, "Man, is it hot outside. My lips are parched." You might offer a cold drink or direct the customer to a cafeteria or

⚙ WORK IT OUT 10.7

Preparing for Contingencies

Take a few minutes to think about a situation in your organization (or one that you have visited) in which a system did not function as it should (e.g., computer crashed, cash register stopped working, website went offline, telephones went dead, products did not arrive from a supplier as expected). What did you (or the service provider) do or say immediately to inform the customer of the situation? How was the problem resolved? How long did it take to fix the issue? If customers were inconvenienced, was anything done to compensate them? What could you, or the service provider, have done differently to better resolve the situation?

Discuss your answers with others and get their thoughts on how they would have felt if they were the customer in the situation you identified. Would your actions (or those of the service provider) have satisfied them?

soft drink machine. You might offer a blanket to a family member staying with someone in the emergency room in the middle of the night when it is very cold. Alternatively, you might offer a chair to someone who is accompanying a customer while he or she shops and tries on clothing. Such small gestures show that you are astute in noticing their needs and nonverbal cues. Remember, sometimes the little things mean a lot. Moreover, in all of these examples, by taking care of the customer's basic needs, you might encourage him or her to shop longer.

PLANNING ABILITY

Planning is a crucial skill to possess when operating in today's fast-paced, changing customer service environment, especially in technology-based environments. To

©stevecoleimages/iStock/Getty Images RF

Organizations usually provide training for new employees to increase their knowledge and effectiveness in interacting with customers. *What training do you think would be useful to you in a new position in customer service?*

FIGURE 10.7

Planning Process Model

Set a goal → Examine and evaluate → Identify alternatives → Select best alternatives → Create implementation plan

prepare for all types of customer situations, you and your organization must have a strategy. This often involves assessing various factors related to your organization, industry, products, services, policies and procedures, resources, and customer base. Remember that a systemic breakdown on your part or that of your organization is not the responsibility or problem of your customers. In fact, most do not care about your issues; they just want fast, efficient, quality service. If you and your organization fail to provide it, they may take their business elsewhere. By being proactive and thinking about such factors, you will be able to provide better service to your customers.

In addition, you should consider alternative strategies for dealing with unusual situations (**contingency plans**). Such alternatives are helpful when things do not go as originally planned (e.g., a computer database fails, service is not delivered as promised, or products that were ordered from another organization for a customer do not arrive as promised).

Figure 10.7 shows the **planning process model**, the basic steps of which are the following:

1. *Set a goal*. In a customer service situation, the obvious goal is to prevent problems from occurring. You also want to successfully address customers' needs, have them leave the service experience satisfied, spread positive word-of-mouth advertising, and return in the future.

2. *Examine and evaluate the situation*. In this phase of planning, you should look at all possible factors that could affect a customer interaction (e.g., the environment, policies, procedures, your skills and authority level, management support, and the customer). Keep these factors in mind, as you work with your peers and supervisor or team leader to establish criteria for selecting acceptable actions. For example, it might be acceptable to use voice mail if you are dealing with a customer; however, it is not proper to forward incoming messages to voice mail so that you can meet with a peer on a nonwork-related issue.

3. *Identify alternatives*. Meet with peers and supervisors or team leaders to develop a list of alternatives for dealing with various customer situations. Consider the advantages and disadvantages of each option.

4. *Select the best alternatives*. After reviewing all the options, select the one (or more) that best addresses the targeted goal of providing quality service to customers. Do not forget to measure this choice against the criteria you established earlier.

5. *Create an implementation plan*. Working with peers and supervisors or team leaders, decide which resources (human and otherwise) you will need to deliver effective service. Also, develop a system for evaluating success. For example, a customer wants two items, but you have only one in stock. You apologize for not being able to fulfill the customer's needs. Is this "success"? Or, would you be successful if, in

contingency plans Backup systems or procedures that are implemented when regular ones break down or fail to function as intended.

planning process model Five-step process for creating contingency or backup plans to better serve customers when problems arise or things do not go as expected.

Street Talk

A simple technique to ensure you are looking through the lens of the customer is to first identify with their emotions, and then meet their needs. For example, you might say, "I can see you are upset; let me see what I can do to take care of this problem" or "I can hear you are frustrated. Let me review the situation and see what I can do to help you." By identifying with the customer's emotions first, you let him or her feel valued versus feeling as if he or she is processed as just another transaction.

SOURCE: TERI YANOVICH, *President, T. A. Yanovich, Inc*

addition to the apology, you called other stores, located another item, and had it delivered to the customer's house at no cost?

PROBLEM-SOLVING ABILITY

If a customer has a problem, you have a problem. Remembering this simple concept can go a long way in reminding you of your purpose for being a service provider. Your primary job function is to address the needs of your customer. To do this when a customer is dissatisfied or has a concern, you should take responsibility for the problem instead of trying to place blame and defer the issue to someone else. What or who created the problem (e.g., the weather, you, the customer, or the manufacturer) does not matter. Your goal is to identify and implement appropriate solutions to the extent of your authorized authority. Otherwise, you should seek assistance from the appropriate person according to your organization's policy. To accomplish sound problem solving, you will need a process for gathering and analyzing information. As with the planning process discussed earlier, you should take some specific steps to find a solution to a customer's problem. These steps are described in the following sections.

Problem resolution is not difficult if you approach it systematically. If you have planned earlier and know what options are available and what authority you have, it becomes much easier.

PROFESSIONALISM

As you have read in previous chapters, projecting a positive personal image—through manner of dress, knowledge, appearance of your work area, and your mental attitude—is a crucial element in communicating an "I care" image to customers and potential customers. By paying close attention to such factors, you are better positioned to establish and maintain a strong customer relationship. This is especially true where attitude is concerned. Attitude can mean success or failure when dealing with customers. You can communicate it through the various verbal and nonverbal cues you have read about in other chapters.

KNOWLEDGE CHECK

1. List some of the common qualities of service providers that affect customers.

2. What are six common customer needs?

3. What is a code of ethics and what role does it play in building a stronger customer–provider relationship?

4. What is the risk of an organization failing to demonstrate high ethical standards?

5. Describe the five-step planning process model and why each step is important in delivering quality customer service.

Trending NOW

Eight Trends in Customer Expectations

1. **24/7/365 mentality.** Today's customers expect that they can get what they want, how they want it and when they want it 24 hours a day, seven days a week, and 365 days a year. When service and product providers are not available or cannot meet this expectation, customers simply go to a competitor who can.

2. **Efficiency in service.** With the advances of technology, customers do not expect inconvenience or to have to repeat steps when receiving service. This means that when they enter their credit card and personal information onto a computer screen or an automated phone system when ordering or calling with questions or problems, they do not want to have to completely reenter or repeat their information.

3. **Prompt response.** The days of accepting "Someone will get back to you within 24 hours" are over. Customers see progressive companies using multichannel service response systems (e.g., online FAQ, customer care center 24/7/365, access through mobile technology, automated voice response systems, e-mail, and chats) to ensure availability and response to customer needs, wants, and expectations. They expect all companies to follow a similar model.

4. **Human interaction.** Automated response might be acceptable in some situations if it provides the information or satisfies customer needs. However, efficient human contact is typically the preferred means of response. The key is that the humans involved need to be well trained, competent and knowledgeable, not scripted, and fluent in the native language of the majority of company's customers.

5. **Service effectiveness over fluff.** Incentive programs are nice, but what typically keeps customers coming back and enhances customer loyalty is that the organization provides timely, effective, efficient, and friendly customer service. Meeting the needs wants, and expectations of a diverse customer base will often win out of a free refill, discount off your next purchase, or buy 10, get one free.

6. **Low tolerance for errors.** In a world where companies like FedEx promised "When it Absolutely, Positively has to be there overnight," (FedEx's ad campaign) computers have spell-check to help catch errors, and many companies have unconditional guarantees to make it right when something goes wrong, customers are not as likely to accept excuses. They expect companies to live up to their promises and what they put on their websites. They also expect that all employees are empowered to make decisions and fix problems without having to get their supervisor.

7. **Free shipping.** For years, leading companies like Zappos, Amazon, L.L. Bean, and Lands' End have been offering free shipping, and in some cases free return shipping. This can result in big savings if someone orders from a company regularly or places large orders.

8. **Follow-through on commitments.** While not new, this expectation is magnified by the availability of technology. With all the channels of communication in existence today, many customers see little reason that companies cannot deliver as promised, provide information to them in a preferred format, and continue to update them regularly on the status of orders or problem resolution efforts. Employees must be trained to reach out and stay in touch with customers in order to maintain customer loyalty and achieve customer satisfaction.

LO 10-6 Making the Customer Number One

CONCEPT Make a good first impression by establishing rapport; then identify and satisfy your customers' needs. Follow up to obtain repeat business.

Most people like to feel that they are important and valued. By recognizing and acting on that fact, you can go a long way toward providing solid customer service, reducing churn, and building a strong relationship with customers. By being an "I care" person, you can generate much goodwill while meeting customer needs.

Every time you encounter a customer in person, through technology, or over the phone, you have an opportunity to provide excellent service. Some companies call a

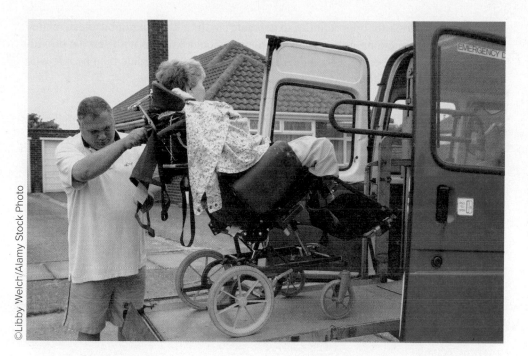

©Libby Welch/Alamy Stock Photo

You win customer loyalty by providing extra service to the customer. Organizations must assess individual needs and determine how to meet those needs better than the competition does. In this case, customers who have mobility impairments or limitations will keep coming back to this establishment because they have provided transportation for those with disabilities. *How can you provide extra service for customers with special needs?*

service encounter the **moment of truth** or refer to them as **contact points**, in which the customer comes into contact with some facet of the organization. At this point you and other service providers have an opportunity to deliver "knock your socks off" service, as Kristin Anderson and Ron Zemke discussed in several of their books on customer service. Each customer encounter moves through the following stages, although sometimes the order varies. At each step, you have another opportunity to provide excellent customer service.

moment of truth A phrase popularized by Scandinavian Airlines System President Jan Carlzon in his popular 1987 book of the same name. It is defined as any instance when a customer initially contacts any organizational element or representative.

contact points Instances in which a customer connects with a service provider or some other aspect of an organization.

☼ WORK IT OUT 10.8

Personal Customer Experiences

Reflect on a recent interaction you had with an internal or external customer as a provider (over the telephone, in person, via e-mail, or through any other means). Immediately after that interaction, if someone had handed the customer a piece of paper and asked him or her to write down impressions of the treatment received from you, what would he or she likely have said? Why do you believe the customer would have said this?

Note: If you do not deal with customers, think of a situation that you recently experienced as a customer and answer the questions based on your experience. Record your perspective of what your customer's comments would have been, along with anything you could have done differently to improve the situation. Be as objective as you can.

ESTABLISH RAPPORT

Customers react to and deal effectively with employees whom they perceive as likable, helpful, and effective. Throughout your interaction, continue to be helpful, smile, listen, use the customer's name frequently, and attend to the customer's needs or concerns. Also, look for opportunities to generate small talk about nonbusiness-related matters. When something goes wrong, people who feel a kinship with service providers typically give higher ratings on the relationship-rating point scale than people who do not feel this connection.

⚙ **WORK IT OUT 10.9**

Strategies for Making Customers Number One

On a sheet of paper, list each of the initiatives for making customers no. 1 that you just read. Then, develop an action plan for addressing each of them in your customer contacts. Be specific about exactly what you will do or say to address each strategy. Use the following initiatives and specify your actions and the expected customer response.

Make positive initial contact.

Establish rapport.

Identify and satisfy customer needs quickly.

Exceed expectations.

Follow up.

Encourage customers to return.

IDENTIFY AND SATISFY CUSTOMER NEEDS QUICKLY

Use the questioning, listening, observing, and feedback skills outlined in this book to focus on issues of concern to the customer. By effectively gathering information, you can then move to the next phase of customer service.

EXCEED EXPECTATIONS

Customers typically expect that, if they pay a certain price for a product or service, they will receive a specific quality and quantity in return; this is not an unusual expectation. The average customer looks for value.

Street Talk

When guests see you smiling and being steadfast while they are waiting, they are much more likely to be patient and can tolerate that pain of waiting. When the guests see you are not smiling and are being slow, their level of tolerance declines and you will be critiqued on every step of service delivered to them, even if you get their order right.

SOURCE: KELLY YUEN, *Store Manager, Dunkin Donuts/Baskin Robbins*

With the Internet and global competition, many products and services are only a mouse click away. If you and your organization fail to deliver as promised or expected, customers may simply go away or move on to another website in search of competitively priced, quality products and services. Today's customers tend to be better-educated consumers who recognize that if they cannot fulfill their needs in one place, they can easily access the same or similar products and services on the Internet or by visiting a competitor. Therefore, you need to exceed a customer's expectations.

Many terms are used to describe the concept of exceeding expectations—knock-their-socks-off service, positive memorable customer experiences, E-plus service, customer delight, dazzling service, fabled service, stellar customer service, and five-diamond or five-star service. All these phrases have in common the concept mentioned before of going above and beyond customer expectations—*under*promise and *over*deliver. By going out of your way not only to satisfy customers but also to "wow" them by doing, saying, or offering the unexpected related to high-quality service delivery, you can exceed expectations. The result could be the reward of continuing patronage or loyalty from the customer.

Examples

Here are two examples of unexpected service or going the extra mile and exceeding customer expectations. The author recently bought flooring tiles from a home product warehouse and took them home. Upon opening the box, he discovered that several tiles were broken. After he called the store to complain, an employee delivered the replacement tiles and assisted the customer in showing him how to properly lay them.

Another example occurred when the author purchased gift cards from five different restaurant chains for special occasions. Each chain rewards customers for their loyalty and encourages them to return. Brio Tuscan Grille, Longhorn Steakhouse, Logan's Steakhouse, Olive Garden, and Outback Steakhouse are all nationally known restaurant chains that give a free $10 gift card each time a customer purchases a $50 gift card around the end-of-year holiday season. This provides an instant reward, encourages future purchases, and helps get customers into the restaurants, where they are likely to bring others along and spend additional money.

FOLLOW UP

Service professionals regrettably often overlook this important element of the service process, although it can be one of the most crucial aspects in establishing long-term relationships. Follow-through is a major factor in obtaining repeat business. After you have satisfied a customer's needs, follow up with the customer on his or her next visit or via mail, e-mail, or telephone to ensure that he or she was satisfied. For external customers, you can couple this follow-up with a small thank-you card, coupons for discounts on future purchases, small presents, or any other incentive to reward their patronage. You can follow up with internal customers by using voice mail or e-mail messages, leaving Post-it® notes on their desks, inviting them for coffee in the cafeteria, or any other of a number of ways. The prime objective is to let them know that you have not forgotten them and appreciate their business and support.

> **Customer Service Success Tip**
>
> Smile, remind the customer you are available to help in the future, give an opportunity for last-minute questions, and invite the customer to return. Just as with your initial impression, you need to close on a high note.

KNOWLEDGE CHECK

1. What is a moment of truth with a customer?
2. How can exceeding customer expectations be beneficial to an organization?

LO 10-7 Enhancing Customer Satisfaction as a Strategy for Retaining Customers

CONCEPT Do the unexpected; deal with one customer at a time; handle complaints efficiently. These are just some of the things you can do to enhance customer satisfaction.

Keeping customers can be difficult in a competitive, global marketplace because so many companies have joined in the race for customers. By providing a personal, professional strategy, you can help ensure that customers return. This is because building good relationships in order to increase customer satisfaction is valuable—it can lead to repeat business—the key to keeping a business productive and profitable. Customers like doing business with those who understand them and their needs and go out of their way to deliver timely and quality services and products at a fair price. This can lead to satisfaction and that is a big factor for many customers in remaining loyal to a brand or organization. In your organization, your efforts could be a deciding factor in customer ratings for the quality of services rendered. The following are tips that can help provide quality service to customers.

PAY ATTENTION

As you listen, focus all your attention on the customer so that you can identify and address his or her needs. If you are serving in person, use positive nonverbal cues (e.g., face the customer, smile, use open body gestures, make eye contact, stop doing other things, and focus attention on the customer) and language. Ask open-end questions to determine the customer's needs. Also, use the active listening techniques to ensure that you get all the information you need to address the customer's needs or concerns properly.

Getting customers to visit or contact your organization is just the first step in the customer–provider relationship. Each person must strive to make the experience a positively memorable one so that he or she continues to return and tells others about the great service that he or she received. *What is your role in creating memorable experiences that help retain customers?*

©Fotosearch/Getty Images RF

DEAL WITH ONE CUSTOMER AT A TIME

You cannot effectively handle two people (on the phone or in person) simultaneously. When more than one call or customer comes in at the same time, seek assistance or ask one customer either if he or she could wait or if you might get back to him or her later. Then, give personalized attention to the other customer.

KNOW YOUR CUSTOMERS

This is crucial with long-term customers, but it is also important with everyone. You may see or talk to hundreds of customers a week; however, each customer has only one or two contacts with you. Although you might not recall the name of everyone you speak with during a day, your customers will likely remember what you said or agreed upon previously, and expect you to do the same. For that reason, use notes or your computer to keep a record of conversations with customers. You and other employees can review or refer to these notes in subsequent encounters. This avoids having customers repeat themselves, and they will feel "special" because you remembered them. Many professionals use database management programs or contact software (e.g., ACT or Maximizer) or customer contact management systems to log and catalog contacts and customers, as well as to keep detailed notes on each contact with a customer. Consider such programs to be your electronic "cheat sheet" to help you remember important details about all your customers, clients, or patients (e.g., spouse names, favorite colors, birthdays, sizes, last purchase, prior conversations, and other valuable information).

GIVE CUSTOMERS SPECIAL TREATMENT

As you read earlier, you should try to occasionally take the time for a little small talk with customers. This will help you learn about them and what they consider important (potential needs). Occasionally, paying them compliments also helps (e.g., "That is an attractive tie" or "That perfume is very pleasing").

SERVICE EACH CUSTOMER ADEQUATELY

Take the necessary time to handle your customer's questions, complaints, or needs. If you have a number of customers on the phone or in person, service one at a time and either ask to get back to the others or get help from a coworker, if possible. You might also suggest alternative information resources to customers, such as fax-on-demand or your website, online information system, or interactive voice response. This may satisfy them and help reduce the calls or visits from customers because they can now get the information they need from alternative sources.

DO THE UNEXPECTED

Do not just provide service; provide exceptional service. Provide additional information, offer suggestions that will aid the customer, send articles that may be of interest, follow up transactions with calls or letters to make sure that needs were met, or send cards for special occasions and to thank customers. These little things can mean a lot and make the difference between a rating of Average or Exemplary on the relationship-rating point scale.

Example: Give 'Em the Extra Pickle!

Bob Farrell, founder of Farrell's Ice Cream Parlor restaurants, provided an example of unexpected service when he reportedly responded to a customer complaint a

Consumer behavior and the manner in which service providers are addressing it have changed in recent years. Because of the rise of technology, today's shoppers no longer use just the traditional methods to access the products and services they seek. Organizations have moved from simple brick-and-mortar and telephone support to an **omnichannel** approach. This concept thoroughly integrates various forms of static and mobile technologies and service strategies into the traditional sales and service model. In such environments, service providers in stores, on the phone, or via chat can instantly access prior customer contact and purchase information. They can also access inventory and sales figures so that they are more knowledgeable when dealing with customers. This allows for more effective service without the need for the customer to repeat or provide information each time they reach out to the organization.

Companies that offer multiple options to help consumers meet needs, wants, and expectations can enhance satisfaction and build customer loyalty. This can lead to reduced customer churn and increased organizational revenue.

omnichannel An approach to sales and service that integrates desktop, mobile, and telephone technology with traditional face-to-face access in order to provide a seamless service experience for customers.

number of years ago. Farrell received a letter from a regular customer of many years. The customer had been ordering hamburgers with an extra pickle since he started patronizing Farrell's. At some point, the man went to Farrell's and ordered a hamburger but a new server told him that the extra pickle would cost an additional 25 cents. When the man protested and stated that he had been a loyal customer for years, the server conferred with her manager and happily reported that the extra pickle would cost only 5 cents. At that point the man left and wrote Farrell, who wrote back enclosing a free coupon, apologizing, and inviting the customer back.

The lesson here is that when you have a loyal customer whom you might lose because of enforcement of a trivial policy, you should be flexible. When policies inhibit good service and negatively affect customer relationships, you should point them out to management so that modification or elimination can be considered.

> **Customer Service Success** Tip
>
> Treat all customers as if they are crucial to the organization—they are! Do whatever is possible and reasonable to maintain a strong customer–provider relationship and keep the customer returning and recommending that others should do likewise. Whether someone is a new or existing customer should make no difference.

HANDLE COMPLAINTS EFFECTIVELY

Treat complaints as opportunities to redeem missed service expectations, and handle them effectively. Acknowledge any error on your part and do everything possible to resolve the problem quickly and to the customer's satisfaction. Thank the customer for bringing his or her concerns to your attention. Share the situation in staff meetings so that other employees can also learn from the situation.

SELL BENEFITS, NOT FEATURES

An effective approach to increasing sales used by most salespeople is to focus on describing how a customer benefits from a product or service rather than what it does. A feature differs from a benefit in that it is a descriptive aspect of a product or service (e.g., has a shorter turn radius, has 27 options, comes in five different colors, has a remote control, and uses less energy than competing models). Benefits help paint an image of how he or she will gain something (e.g., time, money, reduced stress, better efficiency, or whatever) by using the product or service.

Show each customer how your product, service, or information addresses his or her needs. What benefit will result? Stress that although other organizations may offer similar products and services, yours fit their needs best (if they do), and how. If your product or service does not fit their needs, admit it and offer any available alternatives (such as referral to a competitor). Your customers will appreciate your honesty, and even if you cannot help them, they will probably return in the future because you are trusted.

KNOW YOUR COMPETITION

Stay abreast of what other, similar organizations are offering in order to counter comments about them. This does not mean that you should criticize or belittle your competitors or their products and services. The latter behavior is unprofessional and unethical and will likely cause the customer to lose respect for you. In addition, when respect goes, trust goes.

Staying aware of the competition has the additional benefit of helping you be sure that you can describe and offer the products, services, and features of your organization that are comparable to those offered by others.

For example, the Marriott hotel chain recognized a need to compete with cheaper reservation rates offered on the Internet. Marriott announced its "Look No Further Best Rate Guarantee" that matched reservation rates for the same hotel, room type, and reservation dates at all its hotels (excluding Ritz-Carlton) no matter where the customer found them. The chain states as part of its guarantee, "If the lower rate you found qualifies, we will adjust your room rate to reflect that rate, and give you an additional 25% off the lower rate."[12] The hotel chain did this to remain competitive and fill rooms.

COST OF DISSATISFIED CUSTOMERS

There are many researches that have been designed to try to determine the **cost of dissatisfied customers**. Too often, service providers look at the loss of a sale when a customer is dissatisfied as a single event. However, as you saw in the last section, one dissatisfied customer can cost your organization a lot.

To get an idea of what one negative customer experience can cost your organization over a 10-year period, consider the following example.

cost of dissatisfied customers
Phrase that refers to any formula used to calculate the cost of acquiring a new customer or replacing a current one as a result of having a dissatisfied customer leave an organization.

Example

Ms. Ling comes in to return a product that she paid $22 for over a month ago. She explains that the product did not fit her needs and that she had been meaning to return it since the date she purchased it but kept forgetting. She also explains that she comes in at least once a week to make purchases. Your company has a three-day return policy, your manager is out to lunch, and you do not have the authority to override the policy. Ms. Ling is in a hurry and is upset by your inability to resolve the issue. She leaves after saying, "You just lost a good customer!"

Let's assume that Ms. Ling spends at least $22 a week in your store and calculate the potential loss to your organization.

22×52 (number of weeks in a year) $= \$1,144$

10 (number of years as a customer) $\times \$1,144 = \$11,440$

16 (number of people statistically told of her negative experience) $\times \$11,440 = \$183,040$

These numbers are the bad news. The good news is that you and every other employee in your organization can reduce a large percentage of customer defections by providing quality service.

KNOWLEDGE CHECK

1. What are some tips that a service provider might follow to enhance customer satisfaction?

LO 10-8 Strive for Quality

CONCEPT   **A customer's perception of quality service is often one of the prime reasons for his or her return.**

A final strategy for helping to increase customer loyalty relates to the quality of service you and your organization provide. So much is written these days about quality—how to measure it and its significance—that there is a temptation to think of it as a fad. In the areas of customer service and customer retention, thinking this way could be disastrous. A customer's perception of quality service is often one of the prime reasons for his or her return.

Terms such as **total quality management (TQM) and continuous quality improvement (CQI)** are used in many industries and by manufacturers to label the goal of improvement. Quality service involves efforts and activities done well and that meet or exceed customer needs and expectations. In an effort to achieve quality service, many organizations go to great lengths to test and measure the level of service provided to customers.

On a personal level, you can strive for quality service by working to achieve an Exemplary rating on the relationship-rating point scale. Your organization's ability to deliver quality service depends on you and the others who provide frontline service to customers. If you do not adopt a professional attitude and continually strive to improve your knowledge, skills, and efforts in dealing with customers, failure and customer dissatisfaction can result.

total quality management (TQM) and continuous quality improvement (CQI) Systematic approaches to identifying and quantifying best practices in an organization and/or industry in order to make improvements in effectiveness and efficiency.

Small Business Perspective

The world is rapidly changing. If you examine various reports by the U.S. Bureau of Labor Statistics, the United States and other countries are experiencing a shortage of skilled workers. With many aging and experienced employees leaving the workforce, small businesses are now competing, more than ever, with larger ones for qualified employees. This challenge is exacerbated by a declining pool of younger workers. In the past, immigrants were recruited to fill positions; however, with most developed nations striving to fill their own labor pools, getting qualified employees from other countries has become more of a challenge. To offset this trend, many entrepreneurs are setting up home offices and operating their own "one-person" operation. According to the U.S. Census, small businesses without payroll now make up over 70 percent of America's 27 million companies, with annual sales of $887 billion.

Like most organizations at the end of the first decade of the twenty-first century, the small business sector was hit hard financially. In addition, small businesses have to face competition and strive to maintain customer loyalty on three fronts. First, they have to compete effectively with local small business competitors. Secondly, they have to stave off competition from large chain stores and organizations that maintain a local presence and have large advertising budgets. Finally, they must compete with similar organizations worldwide on the Internet.

Building and maintaining customer loyalty is no easy task for small business owners, who typically have limited financial and human resources. Not only must they be concerned with the day-to-day business operations, but they also must continually monitor competitive practices and trends in society that might affect their financial bottom line. Without the buying power of larger organizations, they often struggle to maintain a profitable business model while looking for ways to continue to maintain or grow their business. Rising product and distribution costs, fees from banks and credit card processing companies, insurance, state and local taxes, employee expenses, and myriad other expenses work to eat away profit margins. These are major reasons why entrepreneurs and small business owners need to focus so heavily on customer loyalty. Those who take a reactive "next" approach to dealing with customers, where they wait for someone to click on their website or walk through the door, are doomed to failure. Successful businesspeople continually look for new and innovative approaches to serving their customers. This includes using an integrated approach to doing business (e.g., face-to-face, telephone, computers, and other available technology). Customers expect that anyone providing products and services will be competitive and prepared to match the service and delivery systems of others in their industry. Those organizations that cannot meet these standards are typically the ones that close their doors.

The cost of getting new customers versus maintaining current ones has traditionally been higher. According to CX Solutions (formerly TARP Worldwide), "the real ratio of cost to win a new customer vs. retaining a current customer varies from 2 to 1 to 20 to 1 (this depends on the size and value of the customer to the company/industry); and that it costs five times as much to win a new customer as to keep a current customer. This formed the basis for establishing many of the customer service 800 numbers in the early 1980s."[13]

A prudent business strategy for any size business is to keep the customers you have and try to bring in new ones with low- or no-cost initiatives (e.g., referral programs, incentives, discount coupons, brand recognition, and positive word-of-mouth publicity). Typically, some of the factors that can help sustain a loyal customer population for retail organizations include the following:

- Service representatives who are knowledgeable and helpful, have excellent communication skills, and care about their job and customers
- Service and assistance that is readily available and easily accessible 24/7/365 in a variety of formats (e.g., telephone, Internet, computer, and face-to-face)
- Unique products that differentiate from competitors
- Creation of a one-stop shopping experience where customers can obtain multiple types of products and services at one location

- High-quality products that require lower levels of maintenance and follow-up service
- A flexible, "no-hassle" return or exchange policy

Service organizations should also be concerned about customer loyalty. Some factors that can assist in enhancing customer satisfaction and retention include the following:

- Make staff members feel appreciated and valued. Employees who are happy with their job and supervisors are likely to be more customer-centric and take ownership for customer satisfaction and retention.
- Staff who are experienced, knowledgeable, trustworthy, and reliable and possess a "can-do" attitude.
- The ability of service representatives to create a true partnership with clients. The success of the customer should be a prime consideration, as opposed to just fulfilling the requirements of a contract or project.
- The ability of employees to see beyond the obvious and come up with customized, unique strategies and interventions to address client needs. Using a "cookie cutter" or "one-size-fits-all" approach to service never works.
- Treating customers like people, especially when dealing with them through technology. It is too easy for service representatives to forget remain personal when they cannot see a customer.

Impact on Service

Based on personal experience and what you just read, answer the following questions:

1. How well do small businesses deliver quality service and retain customers?
2. What factors have you seen small businesses faced with in the past couple of years?
3. What technology have you witnessed small business owners using to gain and retain customers?
4. Are there issues related to customer service and retention that small businesses face more than large ones? Explain.

▦|SMARTBOOK™ **Use SmartBook to help you read, study, and retain what you have learned. Access SmartBook in your Instructor's Connect course, or go to connect.mheducation. com for help.**

Key Terms

channel partner

churn

churn rate

code of ethics

contact points

contingency plans

cost of dissatisfied customers

customer loyalty

customer loyalty program

customer relationship management (CRM)

customer relationships

customer retention

customer satisfaction

moment of truth

omnichannel

planning process model

Technical Assistance Research Program (TARP) Worldwide

total quality management (TQM) and continuous quality improvement (CQI)

touch point

trust

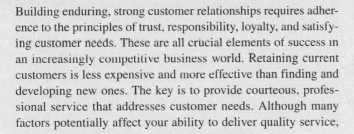

Summary

Building enduring, strong customer relationships requires adherence to the principles of trust, responsibility, loyalty, and satisfying customer needs. These are all crucial elements of success in an increasingly competitive business world. Retaining current customers is less expensive and more effective than finding and developing new ones. The key is to provide courteous, professional service that addresses customer needs. Although many factors potentially affect your ability to deliver quality service, you can apply specific methods and strategies to keep your customers coming back.

Too often, customer service representatives lose sight of the fact that they are the organization and that their actions determine the outcome of any customer–provider interaction. By employing the strategies outlined in this chapter, and those you read about previously, you can do much to ensure customer satisfaction and organizational success.

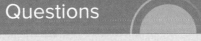

Review Questions

1. How can you build customer trust?

2. What are some key reasons why customers remain loyal to a product, a service, or an organization?

3. What are some of the provider characteristics that affect customer loyalty?

4. What are the steps in the planning process model? Describe.

5. What are six common customer needs?

6. What are ways for service providers to take responsibility for customer relations?

7. What are some techniques for making the customer feel that he or she is No. 1?

Search It Out

1. **Search the Internet for Information on Customer Loyalty**

   Search the Internet for additional information related to customer loyalty. Select one of the following projects:

   a. Go to the websites of organizations that deal with customers and service. Identify research data, articles, bibliographies, and other reference sources (e.g., videotapes) related to customer loyalty and create a bibliography similar to the one at the end of this book. Here are a few resource sites to get you started:

   Association of Customer Contact Professionals— www.associationccp.com

   International Customer Service Association— www.icsatoday.org

   North American Customer Service Management Association—www.internationalcustomerserviceassociation .com

   National Customer Service Association—www.nationalcsa.com

   Society of Consumer Affairs Professionals—www .SOCAP.com

   Customer Service Professionals Network—www .mycspn.com

   Customer Experience Professionals Association—www. cxpa.org www.amazon.com www.barnesandnoble.com

   b. Go to various search engines to locate information and articles on *customer loyalty*. To find information, enter terms related to concepts covered in this chapter or locate websites dealing with such issues. Here are a few to get you started:

   Customer loyalty
   Customer satisfaction
   Customer retention
   Customer Service Review magazine
   Total quality management in customer service
   Cost of customer service

2. **Additional Resources**

   Visit the author's Customer Service Skills blog at www. customerserviceskillsbook.com.

   Search Ted Talks for videos on customer service topics discussed in this chapter. Here is a starting point—https:// binged.it/2gs2Z10.

   Visit youtube.com and search for videos on the topics addressed in this chapter (e.g., customer loyalty and customer retention).

Collaborative Learning Activities

Building Loyalty

Here are four options for activities that you and others can use to reinforce the concepts of building loyalty that you read about in this chapter.

1. Working with a partner, think of times when you have both been frustrated or dissatisfied with service received from a provider. Make a list of characteristics the service provider(s) exhibited that had a negative impact on you. Once you have a list, discuss the items on the list, and then honestly say whether either (or both) of you exhibit any of these negative behaviors when dealing with others. For the ones to which you answered yes, jointly develop a list of strategies to improve each behavior.

2. Take a field trip around your town. Walk through and/or past as many establishments as possible. Look for examples of actions that organizations are doing to encourage and discourage customer loyalty. List the examples on a sheet of paper and be prepared to discuss them in groups assigned by your instructor when you return to class. Some examples of encouragement might be free samples of a product being distributed at a food court, discount coupons, acceptance of competitor coupons, or free refills on drinks. Negative examples might be signs that say "Restrooms for customers only" or "No change given," and policies that allow discounts only on certain days and no refunds on purchases (exchanges only).

3. Do a survey of at least 20 people of different age groups and cultural and ethnic backgrounds. Ask the following questions related to customer retention and loyalty, and then report your findings in class:

   - What is the most important thing that a service provider can do to get you to return to a store, organization, or website?

   - When shopping for a product or service, what referral source do you value most when making a buying decision (e.g., website, consumer article or media channel, newspaper, family member, or friend)?

   - If you are trying to decide where to purchase a product or service and the only two differentiators are slightly higher cost and a better approach to service, which would you choose?

   - If you could choose between buying an identical product locally or on the Internet, which source are you more likely to select?

4. Make a list of three companies or organizations to which you are a loyal consumer or member. What does each of these companies do in the way of product and service offerings that encourages you to continue to use or associate with them? Form a small group with other learners and share your responses.

Face to Face

Assessing the Need for Reorganization at Get Away

Background

After over nine years in business, the Get Away travel agency in Des Moines, Iowa, is feeling the pinch of competition. During the past 14 months, the owners, Marsha Henry and Consuela (Connie) Gomez, have seen business profits dwindle by 18 percent. Employee attrition was also over 50 percent in the past six months. Neither Marsha nor Connie can figure out what has happened. Although travel reservationists have had to deal with airline fee caps, customers making more reservations on the Internet, and the fact that many industry travel providers are cutting back, competing agencies do not seem to be suffering as much as Get Away. The problem is especially worrisome because Marsha and Connie recently took out a second mortgage on their office building so that they could put more money into promotion and customer acquisition efforts. The more efforts they make at gaining exposure, the more customers they lose, it seems. Recently, they lost a major corporate client that accounted for over $100,000 in business a year. Out of desperation, they have decided to hire you, a seasoned travel agency manager, to try to stop their descent and turn the operation around.

Your Role

As the new manager at Get Away, you have been given the authority to do whatever is necessary to salvage the agency. By agreement with Marsha and Connie, they are delaying the announcement of your hiring to other agency employees. Your goal is to objectively assess the operation by acting as a customer.

Your first contact with the agency came on Thursday morning, when you placed a phone call to the office at 9:00 a.m. posing as a customer. The phone rang 12 times and was curtly answered with, "Hello. Please hold (click)." After nearly five minutes, an agent, Sue, came on the line and stated, "Sorry for the wait; we're swamped. Can I get your name and number and call you right back?" Two-and-a-half hours later, you got a call from Tom. He said that Sue had gone home for the day because she was sick, and he was doing her callbacks. Sue would follow up when she came in the next day. You had asked a friend to make a similar call yesterday (Wednesday), and she had similar results.

On Thursday afternoon, you stopped by the office at 1:55 p.m. Of four agents who should have been there, only Claudia was present. Apparently, Tom and Sue were still at lunch. Two customers were waiting as you arrived. Aisha greeted you with a small smile and asked you to "take a number and have a seat." You looked around the office and saw desks piled high with materials, an overflowing trash can, and an empty coffeepot in the waiting area bearing the sign "Please have a cup on us." In talking to your fellow "customers," you learned that one had been

there for over 45 minutes. Both were irritated at having to wait, and, eventually, one left. You left after 30 minutes and passed Tom and Sue, who came in laughing. You thought you detected an odor of alcohol on Tom. Neither acknowledged you. From the office, you proceeded to a meeting with Marsha and Connie.

Critical Thinking Questions

1. What impressions of the travel agency did you have as a result of your initial phone call?

2. How did your office visit affect you?

3. What will you tell Marsha and Connie about employee professionalism?

4. What customer needs are being overlooked in this scenario?

5. In what ways can this situation be improved?

Planning to Serve

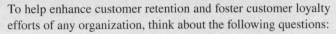

To help enhance customer retention and foster customer loyalty efforts of any organization, think about the following questions:

1. What are some strategies that can be used to show customers that their business is valued?

2. What obstacles exist to customer loyalty and how might they be removed?

3. What are some of the things that positively impact customer loyalty in many organizations?

4. What are some things that differentiate organizations and that can be accentuated to build customer retention and loyalty?

5. When a customer becomes dissatisfied, what can be done to appease and retain that customer's business?

6. What is the most difficult aspect of customer retention in your mind? Explain.

Quick Preview Answers

1. T   3. T   5. T   7. T   9. T   11. T
2. F   4. T   6. F   8. T   10. F   12. T

Ethical Dilemma Summary

Ethical Dilemma 10.1 Possible Answers

1. What would you say or do to the pharmacist?

   Because of the serious nature of this incident, you should not become part of a potentially litigious and health-threatening situation. Tell the pharmacist that you do not feel comfortable not telling the patient the truth and ask him to handle it himself.

2. Should you notify anyone else about the incident? Explain.

   Because of the serious nature of this event, you should definitely report it to the store manager and, depending

on the reaction that you get, you may want to consider whether this organization is really somewhere that you want to continue working. If the situation is not properly resolved with the disciplining and/or removal of the pharmacist, there are going to be major legal and other problems in the future. If it is not handled at a local level, you can always contact the regional store manager and, if necessary, corporate headquarters. If all else fails, each state has governmental agencies that license and oversee pharmacies and pharmacists. You can report the incident to them for investigation.

3. What do you do or say to the patient? Explain.

   In the immediate instance, you should probably defer discussion of the matter and explain that the pharmacist or someone else will be right with the customer.

4. What are the ethical issues here and how would you deal with them?

   This is certainly a very awkward, sensitive, and serious issue with which to deal. If you fail to share with the pharmacist your concerns and feelings about the way the situation is being handled, it will possibly be repeated, and potentially have serious medical repercussions or worse. The pharmacist is not only acting unprofessionally, unethically, and potentially illegally, he is also potentially putting himself and the organization in a litigious situation and endangering the lives of patients. Granted, this may have been a legitimate mistake on the part of the pharmacist; however, that does not make it any less serious.

   On the other hand, if you refuse to do as the pharmacist tells you, your job and future opportunities might be in jeopardy. This could be a reality; however, remember that federal law protects whistleblowers from retaliation. Also, you have an option of going to the store manager to discuss the issue. The bottom line is that this is a very serious medical issue.

5. How do such instances potentially affect customer loyalty?

   There have been many media reports of similar incidents in recent years and, as a result, consumers are very skeptical and leery about going to pharmacies. Typically, when these cases arise, there is an exodus from the involved pharmacies to their competitors. The old adage of "buyer beware" is certainly the watchword for many patients these days. Also, there are many watchdog groups monitoring such cases.

Ethical Dilemma 10.2 Possible Answers

1. Should you say anything to anyone in the office? Explain.

   In a situation where you are the "new kid on the block," it is likely that your inclination is to keep your mouth shut, especially since you do not yet have a strong rapport with co-workers. In such situations, most people would not feel comfortable approaching anyone to share their views. However, if you fail to say something to the agents or your supervisor, there is a chance that federal Environmental Protection Agency (EPA) guidelines are going to be violated and children are going to be put in potential physical danger. This is based on research that shows young children assimilate almost 50 percent of any lead that they might ingest (e.g., from eating paint chips they find on the floor). This can lead to mental and physical medical conditions.

You could try approaching the agents casually (in the break room) and sharing some interesting "research" that you read (go online in advance to read about the EPA rulings) about the effect of lead-based paint in buildings. Ask them how agents normally handle situations where they know about such paint in properties that are listed. This can put the agents on notice without accusing them and might even result in your finding that they were not aware of the EPA guidelines.

Another alternative would be to approach your supervisor and let him or her know that you have heard of a property the agency has listed that might violate EPA guidelines for lead-based paint and ask what types of disclosures agents have to warn potential buyers about. Again, you could do this in a nonaccusatory fashion.

If neither of these approaches has any direct corrective impact, you have a number of additional options. Some of these include the following:

- Confronting the agents about the conversation that you overheard and ask them to inform the potential buyer
- Telling your supervisor of the conversation and asking him or her to speak to the agents
- Telling the potential buyer of the situation
- Reporting the incident to the EPA if a sale is made and no legal disclosure was done
- Quitting your job and saying nothing

2. Should you say anything to the potential buyer? Explain.

   Before approaching a customer, you should always try to resolve the issue internally within the organization at the lowest possible level.

3. If you do not say anything, is there any potential legal liability? Explain.

   If a sale is made and legal disclosure is not made as required by law, the organization and agents could be held legally and potentially civilly liable.

4. If you do say something to either the agents, your boss, or the potential buyer, what are the potential repercussions for you?

   There are a number of potential results if you speak up:

- You might be thanked for bringing the issue to the attention of the agents, boss, or buyer.
- You might also be ostracized by your peers for intervening.
- You might be fired by your boss, if he or she is aware of the practice and wants to keep the illegal activity under wraps.

GLOSSARY

A

acculturated   The cultural and psychological changes that often occur as a person or group of people are integrated into another culture or country and adopt the habits and beliefs of their new environment.

acronym   Words formed by the initial letters of other words and pronounced as a word, such as NASA (**N**ational **A**eronautics and **S**pace **A**dministration).

Albrecht, K., & Zemke, R.,   Service America!: Doing Business in the New Economy. New York: McGraw-Hill, 2002.

Americans with Disabilities Act of 1990 (ADA)   A U.S. federal act signed into law in July 1990 guaranteeing people with disabilities equal access to workplace and public opportunities.

angry customers   Customers who become emotional because either their needs are not met or they are dissatisfied with the services or products purchased from an organization.

appearance and grooming   Nonverbal characteristics exhibited by service providers that can send a variety of messages that range from being a professional to having a negative attitude.

applications or apps   Software that can process information and perform various tasks on smartphones, tablets or electronic devices, and computers using Internet wireless (Wi-Fi) and wired connections.

articulation, enunciation, or pronunciation   Refers to the manner or clarity in which verbal messages are delivered.

artificial intelligence (AI)   Computer systems that perform tasks normally requiring human intelligence.

assertiveness   Involves projecting a presence that is assured, confident, and capable without seeming to be aggressive or arrogant.

attending   The phase of the listening process in which a listener focuses attention on a specific sound or message being received from the environment.

attitudes   Emotional responses to people, ideas, and objects. They are based on values, differ between individuals and cultures, and affect the way people deal with various issues and situations.

automated attendant systems   Provide callers with a menu of options from which they can select by pressing a key on their telephone keypad.

automated computer telephone interview   A voice recognition computer mechanism that queries survey respondents with questions and stores their responses. Depending upon answers received, the system can branch and follow scripted prompts.

automatic call distribution (ACD) systems   Telecommunications system used by many companies in their call centers and customer care facilities to capture incoming calls and route them to available service providers.

automatic number identification (ANI) systems   A form of caller identification system similar to home telephone caller ID systems. ANI allows incoming customers to be identified on a computer screen with background information so that they can be routed to an appropriate service representative for assistance.

B

baby boomer   A term applied to anyone born between 1946 and 1964. People in this age group are called "boomers."

behavioral styles   Descriptive term that identifies categories of human behavior identified by behavioral researchers. Many of the models used to group behaviors date back to those identified by Carl Jung.

beliefs   Perceptions or assumptions that individuals or cultures maintain. These perceptions are based on past experiences, memories, and interpretations and influence how people act and interact with certain individuals or groups.

biases   Beliefs or opinions that a person has about an individual or group. Often based on unreasonable distortions or prejudice.

blind transfer   The practice of transferring an incoming caller to another telephone number and hanging up once someone answers without announcing who is calling.

bloggers   Individuals who write content that is posted on blogs on the World Wide Web.

blogs or web logs   Online journals or diaries that allow people to add content. Many organizational websites use them to post "what's new" sections and to receive feedback (good and bad) from customers and website visitors.

body language   Nonverbal communication cues that send powerful messages through gestures, vocal qualities, manner of dress, grooming, and many other cues.

broadband Internet access   Refers to a very fast connection to the Internet that is made possible by technology that can communicate up to 40 times the amount of data or information possible with the old phone dial-up Internet connections. With broadband, users can download images, video clips, and music; send e-mail; and perform other functions at a much faster speed.

business-to-business (B2B)   Refers to business-to-business customer service.

C

channel   Term used to describe the method through which people communicate messages. Examples are face-to-face, telephone, e-mail, written correspondence, and facsimile.

channel partner   Relationship of two organizations through which the partners are able to build a larger and stronger competitive presence in the marketplace.

chat support   An online support system that provides customers with access to a "real person" to get answers and help resolve issues. By going to an organization's website that has chat capability, a customer can avoid having to navigate a cumbersome toll-free phone system that often requires him or her to sit on hold for endless amounts of time waiting for a service representative to become available.

Chicano culture   Refers primarily to people with a heritage based in Mexico.

churn   The process of a customer switching between products or companies, often simply to get a better price, rebate, or warranty.

churn rate   Refers to the number of customers who leave a supplier during a given time period.

circadian rhythm   The physiological 24-hour cycle associated with the earth's rotation that affects metabolic and sleep patterns in humans as day displaces night.

closed-end questions Inquiries that typically start with a verb and solicit short, one-syllable answers (e.g., yes, no, one word, or a number) and can be used for such purposes as clarifying, verifying information already given, controlling conversation, or affirming something.

cloud computing Technology that allows for remote storage of a user's data that can then be accessed through a web browser using a mobile application on the user's tablet, mobile device (e.g., smartphone), laptop computer, or desktop computer. The term relates to storing information "off in the electronic clouds" rather than on a user's storage device.

clusters Groupings of nonverbal behaviors that indicate a possible negative intent (e.g., crossed arms, closed body posturing, frowning, or turning away) while other behaviors (smiling, open gestures with arms and hands, and friendly touching) indicate positive message intent.

Coca-Cola, "Mission, Vision and Values," www.coca-colacompany.com/our-company/mission-vision-values.

code of ethics A set of standards, often developed by employers, that guide the conduct of all employees.

collective cultures Members of a group sharing common interests and values. They see themselves as an interdependent unit and conform and cooperate for the good of the group.

comprehending or assigning meaning The phase of the listening process in which the brain attempts to match a received sound or message with other information stored in the brain in order to recognize or extract meaning from it or assign meaning to it.

computer telephony integration (CTI) A system that integrates a representative's computer and phone to facilitate the automatic retrieval of customer records and other information needed to satisfy a customer's needs and requests.

concept of time Term used to describe how certain societies view time as either polychronic or monochronic.

conflict Involves incompatible or opposing views and can result when a customer's needs, desires, or demands do not match service provider or organizational policies, procedures, and abilities.

conflict resolution style The manner in which a person handles conflict. People typically use one of five approaches to resolving conflict: avoidance, compromise, competition, accommodation, or collaboration.

congruence In communication, this relates to ensuring that verbal messages sent match or are in agreement with the nonverbal cues used.

contact points Instances in which a customer connects with a service provider or some other aspect of an organization.

contingency plans Backup systems or procedures that are implemented when regular ones break down or fail to function as intended.

cost of dissatisfied customers Phrase that refers to any formula used to calculate the cost of acquiring a new customer or replacing a current one as a result of having a dissatisfied customer leave an organization.

cottage industries Term adopted in the early days of customer service when many people started small businesses in their homes or cottages and bartered products or services with neighbors.

cultural diversity The different racial, ethnic, and socioeconomic varieties, based on factors such as values, beliefs, and experiences, that are present in people grouped together in a given situation, group, or organization.

customer-centric A term used to describe service providers and organizations that put their customers first and spend time, effort, and money identifying and focusing on the needs of current and potential customers. Efforts are focused on building long-term relationships and customer loyalty rather than simply selling a product or service and moving on to the next customer.

customer defection Customers often take their business to competitors when they feel that their needs or wants are not met or if they encounter breakdown in customer service or poor-quality products.

customer expectations The perceptions that customers have when they contact an organization or service provider about the kind, level, and quality of products and services they should receive.

customer-focused organization A company that spends energy and effort on satisfying internal and external customers by first identifying customer needs, and then establishing policies, procedures, and management and reward systems to support excellence in service delivery.

customer-friendly systems Refers to the processes in an organization that make service seamless to customers by ensuring that things work properly and the customer is satisfied.

customer loyalty Term used to describe the tendency of customers to return to a product or organization regularly because of the service and satisfaction they receive.

customer loyalty program An incentive program offered by an organization to reward customers for spending money and purchasing products and services.

customer needs Motivators or drivers that cause customers to seek out specific types of products or services. These may be marketing-driven by advertising they have seen or may tie directly to Dr. Abraham Maslow's hierarchy of needs theory.

customer relationship management (CRM) Concept of identifying customer needs: understanding and influencing customer behavior through ongoing communication strategies in an effort to acquire, retain, and satisfy the customer. The ultimate goal is customer loyalty.

customer relationship management (CRM) software Software designed for use by organizations to assist their marketing, sales, and service professionals to better manage their relationship with current and potential customers by providing a database function for storage and retrieval of information about customers, products, and services.

customer relationships Ongoing friendships with customers focused on making them feel comfortable with an organization and its service providers and on enhancing customer loyalty.

customer retention The ongoing effort by an organization to meet customer needs and desires in an effort to build long-term relationships and keep them for life.

customer satisfaction The feeling of a person whose needs have been met by an organization.

customer service The ability of knowledgeable, capable, and enthusiastic employees to deliver products and services to their internal and external customers in a manner that satisfies identified and unidentified needs and ultimately results in positive word-of-mouth publicity and return business.

customer service environment An environment made up of and influenced by various elements of an organization. Examples are delivery systems, human resources, service, products, and organizational culture.

customers with disabilities Descriptive phrase that refers to anyone with a physical or mental disability.

D

data mining The process of searching through social media data to identify trends and potential customer bases by extracting information offered by social media participants.

decisive style One of four behavior style groupings characterized by a direct, no-nonsense approach to people and situations.

decoding The stage in the interpersonal communication process in which messages received are analyzed by a receiver in an effort to determine the sender's intent.

deliverables Products or services provided by an organization.

delivery system The method(s) used by an organization to provide services and products to its customers.

demand curve   Graphic representations of expected behavior in the real world that economists and business people can use to predict coming trends or shifts in consumer needs, wants, or expectations.

demanding or domineering customers   Customers who have definite ideas about what they want and are unwilling to compromise or accept alternatives.

deregulation   Occurs when governments remove legislative or regulatory guidelines that inhibit and control an industry (e.g., transportation, natural gas, and telecommunications).

difficult customers   People who challenge a service provider's ability to deliver service and who require special skills and patience.

disaster preparedness   A process through which an organization creates an active plan to contain the effects of a disastrous event in order to minimize injury and loss of life and property.

disparate treatment   Term meaning deliberate discrimination against a person based on his or her age, race, sex, ethnicity, or ability level.

dissatisfied customer   Someone who does not (or perceives that he or she does not) receive promised or quality products or services.

diversity   The characteristics, values, beliefs, and factors that make people different, yet similar.

downsizing   Term applied to the situation in which employees are terminated or empty positions are left unfilled once someone leaves an organization.

E

electronic commerce or e-commerce   Refers to the entire spectrum of companies that market products and services on the Internet and through other technology and the process of accessing them by consumers.

electronic mail (e-mail)   System used to transmit messages around the Internet. This technology is being replaced with instant messaging (IM) in some call centers as many younger consumers embrace it as a primary form of communication.

emoticons (emotional icons)   Humorous characters that send visual messages such as smiling or frowning. They are created with various strokes of the computer keyboard characters and symbols.

emotional messages of color   Research-based use of color to send nonverbal messages through advertisements and other elements of the organization.

emotion-reducing model   Process for reducing customer emotion in situations when frustration or anger exists.

employee assistance program (EAP)   Benefit package, offered to employees by many organizations, that provides services to help employees deal with personal problems that might adversely affect their work performance (e.g., legal, financial, behavioral, and mental counseling services).

employee expectations   Perceptions about positive and negative aspects of the workplace.

employee roles   Task assignments that service providers assume.

empowerment   The word used to describe the giving of decision-making and problem-resolution authority to lower-level employees in an organization. This precludes having to get permission from higher levels in order to take an action or serve a customer.

encoding   The stage in the interpersonal communication process in which the sender decides what message will be sent and how it will be transmitted along with considerations about the receiver.

environmental cues   Any aspect of the workplace with which a customer comes into contact. Such things as the general appearance of an area, clutter, unsightly or offensive items, or general disorganization contribute to the perception of an environment.

ethical behavior   Acting in a manner that sends a message of positive morality and good values when confronted with a customer situation or problem.

ethics   The term comes from the Greek word *ethos*, meaning character. Ethics involves right and wrong or good and evil and is illustrated by the way one responds to situations or acts.

etiquette and manners   Includes the acceptable rules, manners, and ceremonies for an organization, profession, or society.

expectations of privacy   The belief that personal information provided to an organization will be safeguarded against inappropriate or unauthorized use or dissemination.

expressive style   One of four behavior groups, characterized as being people-oriented, fun-loving, upbeat, and extroverted.

external customers   Those people outside the organization who purchase or lease products and services. This group includes vendors, suppliers, people on the telephone, and others not from the organization.

external obstacles   Factors outside an organization or the sphere of one's influence that can cause challenges in delivering service.

F

face   Refers to the important concept of esteem in many Asian cultures. In such cultures, one tries not to cause embarrassment or otherwise create a situation in which someone looks bad in the eyes of others.

Facebook   A social networking site founded in 2004 by Mark Zuckerburg and his college roommates as a social networking tool for students at Harvard University. It quickly expanded to other major educational institutions and then to the world. It is open for use by anyone over the age of 13 to share information, send messages, and network socially.

facsimile (fax) machine   Equipment that converts printed words and graphics into electronic signals and allows them to be transmitted across telephone lines, and then reassembled on the receiving end into a facsimile of the words and graphics.

faulty assumptions   Service provider projections made about underlying customer message meanings based on past experiences.

fax-on-demand   Technology that allows information, such as a form, stored in a computer to be requested electronically via a telephone and transmitted to a customer.

fee-based 900 number   A premium telephone number provided by organizations and individuals that, when called, can provide information and services that are billed back to the caller's local telephone bill.

feedback   The stage of the interpersonal communication process in which a receiver responds to a sender's message.

feel, felt, found technique   A process for expressing empathy and concern for someone and for helping him or her understand that you can relate to his or her situation.

filters   Psychological barriers in the form of personal experiences, lessons learned, societal beliefs, and values through which people process and compare information received to determine its significance.

foreign-born people   Refers to people not born in a given country.

form of address   Title used to address people. Examples are Mister, Miss, and Doctor.

G

gender communication   Term used to refer to communication between males and females.

gender roles   Behaviors attributed to or assigned by societal norms.

global terms   Potentially inflammatory words or phrases used in conversation. They tend to inappropriately generalize behavior or group people or incidents together (e.g., always, never, everyone, everything, all the time).

globalization The term applied to an ongoing trend of information, knowledge, and resource sharing around the world. As a result of a more mobile society and easier access to transportation and technology, more people are traveling and accessing products and services from international sources than ever before.

H

hearing A passive physiological process of gathering sound waves and transmitting them to the brain for analysis. It is the first phase of the listening process.

hearing disabilities Conditions in which the ability to hear is diminished below established auditory standards.

help desk Term used to describe a service provider trained and assigned to assist customers with questions, problems, or suggestions.

Hispanic culture Refers to people who were born in Mexico, Puerto Rico, Cuba, or Central or South America.

homesourcing The practice of bringing jobs formerly outsourced to organizations in other countries back to a company's home country.

human resources Refers to the employees of an organization.

hygiene The healthy maintenance of the body through such practices as bathing regularly, washing hair, brushing teeth, cleaning fingernails, and using commercial products to eliminate or mask odors.

I

"I" or "we" messages Messages that are potentially less offensive than the word "you," which is like nonverbal finger-pointing when emotions are high.

impact of culture Refers to the outcome of people from various countries or backgrounds coming into contact with one another and potentially experiencing misunderstandings or relationship breakdowns.

inclusive The concept of ensuring that people of all races, genders, and religious and ethnic backgrounds, as well as a multitude of other diverse factors, are included in communications and activities in the workplace.

indecisive customers People who have difficulty making a decision or making a selection when given choices of products or services.

individualistic cultures Groups in which members value themselves as individuals who are separate from their group and are responsible for their own destiny.

inflection This voice quality is also called pitch and adds vocal variety and punctuation to verbal messages.

information overload Refers to having too many messages coming together and causing confusion, frustration, or an inability to act.

inquisitive style One of four behavioral groups, characterized by being introverted, task-focused, and detail-oriented.

insourcing The opposite of outsourcing, this occurs when organizations decide to have internal employees assume functions and perform work instead of contracting out to third parties or outsourcing it.

instant messaging Refers to a form of Internet communication where users can transmit text messages or chat in real time via the Internet to one or more people. More advanced forms allow voice calling, video chat, and hyperlinks to various media.

intelligent callback technology Technology that gathers information from the customer and tells the customer when he or she can expect a callback.

interactive kiosks or digital displays Computer terminals that have customized software and hardware and are set up in a public area where users can touch a screen display to access applications for information, commerce, education, or entertainment. Many organizations are now using these in lobbies to allow self-service to customers. You may have seen these at airline check-ins, in banks (ATMs), or in theme parks or other entertainment venues.

interactive voice response (IVR) system Technology that allows customers to call an organization to get information from recorded messages or a computer by keying a series of numbers on the telephone keypad in response to questions or prompts.

interferences Noises that can interfere with messages being effectively communicated between two people.

internal customers People within the organization who either require support and service or provide information, products, and services to service providers. Such customers include peers, coworkers, bosses, subordinates, and people from other areas of the organization.

Internet callback technology Technology that allows someone browsing the Internet to key a prompt on a website and have a service representative call a phone number provided. These systems allow someone browsing the Internet to click on words or phrases (e.g., *Call me*), enter his or her phone number, and continue browsing. This triggers a predictive dialing system and assigns an agent to handle the call when it rings at the customer's end.

Internet telephony Technology that allows people to talk to one another via the Internet as if they were on a regular telephone.

interpersonal relationship Focuses on the need for service providers to build strong bonds with customers.

interpersonal skills The skills used by people to relate to and communicate effectively with others. Examples are verbal and nonverbal communication skills and the ability to build trust, empathy, and compassion.

L

lag time The term applied to the difference in the rate at which the human brain can receive and process information and at which most adults speak.

Latino culture Refers to people of Hispanic descent.

learning organizations A term used by Peter Senge in his book *The Fifth Discipline* to describe organizations that value knowledge, education, and employee training. They also learn from their competition, industry trends, and other sources and develop systems to support continued growth and development in order to remain competitive.

listening An active, learned process consisting of four phases: receiving/ hearing the message, attending, comprehending/assigning meaning, and responding.

listening gap The difference in the speed at which the brain can comprehend communication and the speed at which the average adult speaks in the United States.

M

malapropism The unintentional misuse or distortion of a word or phrase that sounds somewhat like the one intended but with a different context. This often has humorous results.

media blending Technology that allows agents to communicate with a customer over a telephone line at the same time information is displayed over the Internet to the customer. As with Internet telephony, this technology has not yet been taken to its full potential.

memory The ability to gain, store, retain, and recall information in the brain for later application. Short-term memory stores small bits of information (seven items, plus or minus two) for approximately 20 seconds while long-term memory can store much larger quantities of information for potentially unlimited duration.

mentors Individuals who dedicate time and effort to befriend and assist others. In an organization, they are typically people with a lot of knowledge, experience, skills, and initiative and have a large personal and professional network established.

message A communication delivered through speech or signals, or in writing.

miscellaneous cues Refers to factors used to send messages that impact a customer's perception or feelings about a service provider or organization. Examples are personal habits, etiquette, and manners.

mission The direction or focus of an organization that supports day-to-day interactions with customers.

mission statement An organization's mission statement that defines its purpose or objectives and *how* it will attain them. It is committed to writing and publicly shared with employees and customers.

mobility or motion impairments Physical limitations that some people have, requiring accommodation or special consideration to allow access to products or services.

modesty Refers to the way that cultures view propriety of dress and conduct.

moment of truth A phrase popularized by Scandinavian Airlines System President Jan Carlzon in his popular 1987 book of the same name. It is defined as any instance when a customer comes into contact with any element or representative of an organization.

monochronic Refers to the perception of time as being a central focus with deadlines being a crucial element of societal norms.

N

namaste Traditional greeting gesture in India (pronounced NAH-mes-tay) that is performed with a slight bow and by placing the palms and fingers of both hands together as in a prayer position in the center of the chest.

needs Motivators or drivers that cause customers to seek out specific types of products or services. These may be marketing-driven, may be based on advertising they have seen, or may tie directly to Abraham Maslow's hierarchy of needs theory.

networking The active process of building relationships and sharing resources.

noise Refers to physiological or psychological factors (physical characteristics, level of attention, message clarity, loudness of message, or environmental factors) that interfere with the accurate reception of information. It can also include environmental factors (e.g., external sounds or room acoustics) that inhibit communication and listening.

nonverbal feedback Messages sent to someone through other than spoken means. Examples are gestures, appearance, and facial expressions.

nonverbal messages Consist of such things as movements, gestures, body positions, vocal qualities, and a variety of unspoken signals sent by people, often in conjunction with verbal messages.

North American Free Trade Agreement (NAFTA) A trade agreement entered into by the United States, Canada, and Mexico to help, among other things, eliminate barriers to trade, promote conditions of fair trade across borders, increase investment opportunities, and promote and protect intellectual property rights.

O

objections Reasons given by customers for not wanting to purchase a product or service during an interaction with a salesperson or service provider (e.g., "I don't need one," "I can't afford it," or "I already have one").

offshoring Refers to the relocation of business services from one country to another (e.g., services, production, and manufacturing).

omnichannel An approach to sales and service that integrates desktop, mobile, and telephone technology with traditional face-to-face access in order to provide a seamless service experience for customers.

online information fulfillment system Technology that allows a customer to access an organization's website and click on desired information without having to interact with a service provider.

open-end questions Typically start with words like who, when, what, how, and why and are used to engage others in conversation or to gain input and ideas.

organizational culture Includes an element of an organization that a customer encounters.

outsourcing Refers to the practice of contracting with third-party companies or vendors outside the organization (often in another country) to deliver products and services to customers or produce products.

ownership of property Refers to how people of a given culture view property.

P

paralanguage Consists of voice qualities (e.g., pitch, rate, tone, or other vocal qualities) or noises and vocalizations (e.g., "Hmmm" or "Ahhh") made as someone speaks that let a speaker know that his or her message is being listened to and followed.

paraphrase The practice of a message receiver giving back in his or her own words what he or she believes a sender said.

pauses A verbal technique of delaying response in order to allow time to process information received, think of a response, or gain attention.

perception checking The process of clarifying a nonverbal cue that was received by stating what behavior was observed, giving one or two possible interpretations, and then asking the message sender for clarification.

perceptions How someone views an item, situation, or others.

personal obstacles Individual factors that can limit performance or success in life. Examples are disabilities, lack of education, attitude, and biases.

pet peeves Refer to factors, people, or situations that personally irritate or frustrate a service provider and that, left unchecked, can create a breakdown in effective service.

Pinterest A pin- or corkboard type of social media forum where users can share photos and images on various themes or interests.

pitch Refers to the change in tone (highness or lowness) of the voice as one speaks. This quality is also called inflection and adds vocal variety and punctuation to verbal messages.

planning process model Five-step process for creating contingency or backup plans to better serve customers when problems arise or things do not go as expected.

Platinum Rule Term coined by speaker and author Tony Alessandra related to going beyond the step of treating customers the way you want to be treated, to the next level of treating them the way they would like to be treated.

podcasts or podcasting A word that is a derivative of Apple® Computer's iPod® media player and the term broadcasting. Through podcasts, websites can offer direct download or streaming of their content (e.g., music or video files) to customers or website users.

polychronic Refers to the perception of time as a fluid commodity that does not interfere with relationships and elements of happiness.

posts Articles or other content published on blogs for site visitors to read, comment on, share, or download.

posture Refers to how one sits or stands in order to project various nonverbal messages.

predictive dialing system   System that automatically places outgoing calls and delivers incoming calls to the next available agent. This system is often used in outbound (telemarketing/call center) operations. Because of numerous abuses, the government is continually restricting its use.

primary behavior pattern   Refers to a person's preferred style of dealing with others.

problem solving   The system of identifying issues, determining alternatives for dealing with them, and then selecting and monitoring a strategy for resolution.

problem-solving model   The process used by a service provider to assist customers in determining and selecting appropriate solutions to their issues, concerns, or needs.

process improvement   Refers to the process of continually evaluating products and services to ensure that maximum effectiveness, efficiency, and potential are being obtained from them.

product   Something produced or an output by an individual or organization. In the service environment, products are created to satisfy customer needs or wants.

prohibitions   Local, state, or federal regulations that prevent a service provider from satisfying a customer's request even though the provider would normally do so.

protégé   Typically less experienced recipients of the efforts of mentors.

proxemics   Relates to the invisible barrier surrounding people in which they feel comfortable interacting with others. This zone varies depending on the level of relationship a person has with someone else.

psychological distracters   Refers to mental factors that can cause a shift in focus in interacting with others. Examples are state of health and personal issues.

pupilometrics   The study of pupil reaction to stimuli.

Q

QR code (Quick Response code)   Similar in concept to the standard bar code that appears on retail products, this code can allow access to virtually any type of stored information about products, services, or organizations.

R

rapport   The silent bond built between two people as a result of sharing common interests and issues and demonstrating a win-win, I care attitude.

rate of speech   Refers to the number of words spoken per minute. Some research studies have found that the average rate of speech for adults in Western cultures is approximately 125–150 words per minute (wpm).

rational style   One of four behavioral groups, characterized by being quiet, reflective, task-focused, and systematic.

Real-Time IM Relay for Customers with Hearing and Speech Loss   AT&T instant messaging system that allows people with hearing loss who have signed up for AT&T's free Relay Service to receive real-time instant messages from callers.

receiver   One of the two primary elements of a two-way conversation. Gathers the sender's message and decides how to react to it.

recognition   A process that occurs in thinking when a previously experienced pattern, event, process, image, or object that is stored in memory is encountered again.

relationship-rating point scale   The mental rating system that customers apply to service and service providers. Ratings range from exemplary to unsatisfactory, with an average rating being assigned when service occurs as expected.

relationship-rating points   Values mentally assigned by customers to a service provider and his or her organization. They are based on a number of factors starting with initial impressions and subsequently by the quality and level of service provided.

respect for elders   A value held by people from many cultures.

responding   Refers to sending back verbal and nonverbal messages to a message originator.

robocall   A term used to describe a type of automated phone auto-dialer that delivers a personalized, prerecorded message to recipients. Often these callers are scammers who offer fraudulent offers to unsuspecting recipients in an effort to get them to send money or to extract personal information from them. They are robotic in nature, thus the name. These calls are illegal to individuals on the Do Not Call Registry unless the caller falls into certain categories (e.g., political organizations or emergency agencies).

rude or inconsiderate customers   People who seem to take pleasure in being obstinate and contrary when dealing with service providers and who seem to have their own agenda without concern for the feelings of others.

RUMBA   An acronym for five criteria—realistic, understandable, measurable, believable, and attainable—used to establish and measure employee performance goals.

S

screen pop-ups   Used in conjunction with ANI and IVR systems to identify callers. As a call is received and dispatched to an agent, the system provides information about the caller that "pops" onto the agent's screen before he or she answers the telephone (e.g., order information, membership data, service history, contact history).

seamless service   Service that is done in a manner that seems effortless and natural to the customer. Processes and systems are fully functional, effective, and efficient. Service representatives are well-trained and proficient in delivering service, and there is no inconvenience to the customer.

semantics   The scientific study of relationships between signs, symbols, and words and their meaning. The way words are used or stressed often affects their perceived meaning.

sender   One of the two primary elements of a two-way conversation. Originates messages to a receiver.

service breakdowns   Situations when customers have expectations of a certain type or level of product or service that are not met by a service provider.

service culture   A service environment made up of various factors, including the values, beliefs, norms, rituals, and practices of a group or organization.

service delivery systems   The mechanisms or strategies used by an organization to provide service to customers.

service economy   A term used to describe the trend in which businesses have shifted from primarily production and manufacturing to more service delivery. As part of this evolution, many organizations have developed specifically to provide services to customers.

service industry   A term used to describe businesses and organizations that are engaged primarily in service delivery. *Service sector* is a more accurate term because many organizations provide some form of service to their customers even though they are primarily engaged in research, development, and manufacture of products.

service measurement   Techniques used by organizations to determine how customers perceive the value of services and products received.

service options Alternatives offered by service providers when an original request by a customer cannot be honored because of such restrictions as governmental statutory regulations, nonavailability of products, or inability to perform as requested.

service philosophy The approach that an organization takes to providing service and addressing the needs of customers.

service recovery The process of correcting something that has gone wrong involving provision of a product or service to a customer. The concept involves not only replacing defective products, but also going the extra step of providing compensation for the customer's inconvenience.

service sector Refers to organizations and individuals involved in delivering service as a primary product.

silence Technique used to gain attention when speaking, to allow thought, or to process information received.

Skype Refers to a software application that is a division of Microsoft® and provides free or paid service that allows people to connect with other Skype subscribers anywhere in the world with voice, video, or text messages.

Small Business Administration (SBA) U.S. governmental agency established to assist small business owners.

small talk Dialogue used to enhance relationships, show civility, and build rapport.

smartphones Mobile telephones that are built with a mobile operating system similar to a computer that allows them to perform a myriad of functions using what are called applications or apps.

social media Websites through which users come together as "communities" of friends, relatives, and like-minded individuals for social networking and microblogging (blogging) and to share ideas, content (e.g., videos or images), and personal and other information. Examples of social media include Facebook, Twitter, Tumblr, Instagram, Pinterest, LinkedIn, Google Plus, Dribble, and Reddit.

spamming or spam An abusive use of various electronic messaging systems and technology to send unsolicited and indiscriminant bulk messages to people (also used with instant messaging, web search engines, blogs, and other formats).

spatial cues Nonverbal messages sent on the basis of how close or far someone stands from another person.

speech or voice recognition The ability of a machine or software program to identify words and phrases in spoken language and convert them to a machine-readable format that can respond to vocal prompts and branch to optional responses.

stereotype Generalization made about an individual or group and not based on reality. Similar people are often lumped together for ease in categorizing them.

strategies for preventing dissatisfaction Techniques used to prevent a breakdown in needs fulfillment when you are dealing with customers.

T

tablet A personal computer (PC) that is a hybrid between a notebook or laptop computer and a personal digital assistant (PDA) and has a flat-screen viewing panel. Users can navigate the functions on a tablet by using a plastic-tipped stylus to tap icons or swiping and tapping on the screen with their finger.

talkative customers Customers exhibiting extroverted behavior who are very people-oriented.

Technical Assistance Research Program (TARP) Worldwide An Arlington, Virginia–based firm specializing in customer service research studies for call centers and many other industries.

Telecommunications Relay Service (TRS) Through such services, specially trained operators act as intermediaries between people who are

deaf, hard-of-hearing, speech disabled, or deaf and blind and standard telephone users.

telecommuting A trend seen in many congested metropolitan areas and government offices. To reduce traffic and pollution and to save resources (e.g., rent, telephone, and technology systems), many organizations allow employees to set up home offices and from there electronically communicate and forward information to their corporate offices.

Telephone Typewriter system (TTY) A typewriter-like device used by people with hearing disabilities for typing messages back and forth via telephone lines. (Also known as a Telecommunications Device for the Deaf [TDD].)

telework Similar to telecommuting (working from home rather than going to a designated workplace), this term applies to people who work in an office, but also conduct work from a remote location.

text messaging or texting The process of someone typing and sending a brief electronic message to another person over a phone network using a mobile phone or fixed or portable device.

thought speed The rate at which the human brain processes information.

time allocation Amount of attention given to a person or project.

total quality management (TQM) and continuous quality improvement (CQI) A systematic approach to identifying and quantifying best practices in an organization and/or industry in order to make improvements in effectiveness and efficiency.

touch point Any instance in which a service provider or organization (e.g., face-to-face, in writing, through technology) comes in contact with a customer; it is an opportunity to influence customer loyalty and enhance the customer relationship.

trust Key element in cementing interpersonal relationships.

tweets Messages limited to 140 characters sent via Twitter to other mobile equipment and computer users.

Twitter An online social networking service and microblogging service that enables its users to send and read text-based messages.

two-way communication An active process in which two individuals apply all the elements of interpersonal communication (e.g., listening, feedback, positive language) in order to effectively exchange information and ideas.

U

underpromise and overdeliver A service strategy in which service providers strive for excellent customer service and satisfaction by doing more than they say they will for the customer or exceeding customer expectations.

V

values Long-term appraisals of the worth of an idea, person, place, thing, or practice held by individuals, groups, or cultures. These affect attitudes and behavior.

verbal feedback The response given to a sender's message that allows both the sender and the receiver to know that a message was received correctly.

verbal fillers Verbal sounds, words, or utterances that break silence but add little to a conversation. Examples are uh, um, ah, and you know.

vision disabilities Conditions resulting from reduced or lost visual acuity or ability.

vision statement A vision statement communicates an organization's values and purpose and explains *what* the organization wants to be.

vocal cues Qualities of the voice that send powerful nonverbal messages. Examples are rate, pitch, volume, and tone.

Voice over Internet Protocol (VoIP) Technologies, methodologies, and transmission techniques involved in the delivery of voice and image communication via the Internet.

voice quality Refers to the sound of one's voice. Terms often attributed to voice quality are raspy, nasal, hoarse, and gravelly.

voice response unit (VRU) System that allows customers to call 24 hours a day, seven days a week by keying a series of numbers on the telephone keypad to get information or answers to questions.

volume Refers to loudness or softness of the voice when speaking.

W

wai Traditional gesture in Thailand (pronounced "why") used in conjunction with a slight bow as a greeting and to say "thank you" or "sorry." It is executed by placing the palms and fingers of both hands together as in a prayer position in the center of the chest. Holding them higher in relation to the face is an indication of more respect or reverence to the other person.

wants Things that customers typically desire but do not necessarily need.

websites A series of electronic "pages" that are hosted on a web server and provide vital organizational, product, and service information and multiple ways for consumers to get in touch with key company representatives via the Internet.

what customers want Things that customers typically desire but do not necessarily need.

Wi-Fi Technology that enables electronic devices such as smartphones, computers, and tablets to send and receive data wirelessly (using radio waves) over a computer network.

wiki A website that allows nontechnical personnel to create and edit website pages using any web browser and without complex programming knowledge. These interactive websites allow where users are freedom to in adding, modifying, or deleting information. Because of the casual and flexible nature of such sites, many people, especially educators, do not consider them a valid resource.

win-win situation An outcome to a disagreement in which both parties walk away feeling that they got what they wanted or needed.

Y

younger customers Subjective term referring to anyone younger than the service provider. Sometimes used to describe members of generation X (born to baby boomers) or later.

YouTube The largest video-sharing website on the Internet where users can upload, share, and view videos.

NOTES

Chapter 1

1. Source: Johnston, Louis D., "History Lessons: Understanding the Decline in Manufacturing, Minn Post, February 22, 2012,
2. Source: Bureau of Labor Statistics, Occupational Outlook Handbook, Customer Services Representatives, Summary.
3. Source: Bureau of Labor Statistics, Employment Projections: 2014-24 Summary http://www.bls.gov/news.release/ecopro.nr0.htm.
4. "Latest Telecommuting Statistics, Global Workplace Analytics," pp. 1–23, http://globalworkplaceanalytics.com/telecommuting -statistics.
5. Source: United States Department of Labor, Bureau of Labor Statistics, "Labor Force Projections to 2022: The Labor Force Participation Rate Continues to Fall."
6. Source: Colby, Sandra L. and Ortman, Jennifer M., "Projections of the Size and Composition of the U.S. Population: 2014 to 2060, Population Estimates and Projections," U.S. Census Bureau, March 2015.
7. "Internet Usage Statistics," pp. 1–32, http://www.internetworldstats .com/stats.htm.
8. U.S. Census Bureau, Current Population Survey, "Computer and Internet Access in the United States," October 2012, pp. 1–32, http://www .census.gov/topics/population/computer-internet.html.
9. Chad Brooks, "Technology Firms Outsourcing More Jobs Than Ever," *Business News Daily*, March 22, 2013, pp. 1–35, www.businessnewsdaily .com/4191-more-tech-firms-outsourcing-jobs.html.
10. Bureau of Labor Statistics, "A Century of Change: the U.S. labor force, 1950–2050," pp. 1–39, http://www.bls.gov/opub/mlr/2002/05/art2full .pdf.
11. United States Department of Labor, Bureau of Labor Statistics, "Labor Force Projections to 2022: The Labor Force Rate Continues to Fall," pp. 1–40, http://www.bls.gov/opub/mlr/2013/article/labor-force-projections-to-2022-the-labor-force-participation-rate-continues-to-fall.htm.
12. U.S. Census Bureau, U.S. Department of Commerce, "Quarterly Retail E-Commerce Sales 2nd Quarter 2016," August 16, 2016, pp. 1–41, https://www.census.gov/retail/mrts/www/data/pdf/ec_current.pdf.
13. Source: Fairchild, Caroline, "Recession Generation Opts to Rent Not Buy Houses to Cars," Bloomberg.com, August 7, 2012.
14. Bureau of Labor Statistics, U.S. Department of Labor, "Employee Tenure Summary," news release, September 22, 2016, pp. 1–52, http ://www.bls.gov/news.release/tenure.nr0.htm.
15. "Small Business: Small Business Is BIG!," U.S. Small Business Administration, pp. 1–56, www.sba.gov/managing-business/running-business/energy-efficiency/sustainable-business-practices/small-business-trends.
16. National Women's Business Council, "Women-Owned Businesses, NWBC Analysis of 2012 Survey of Business Owners," pp. 1–57, https://www.nwbc.gov/sites/default/files/FS_Women-Owned_Busi-nesses.pdf.

Chapter 3

1. Bureau of Labor Statistics, "Customer Service Representatives," *Occupational Outlook Handbook*, http://www.bls.gov/ooh/Office-and -Administrative-Support/Customer-service-representatives.htm.
2. U.S. Small Business Administration, "Small Business Trends," https ://www.sba.gov/managing-business/running-business/energy-efficiency /sustainable-business-practices/small-business-trends.

Chapter 4

1. About American Express, http://about.americanexpress.com/oc /whoweare/.
2. American Express 2015 Annual Report, http://ir.americanexpress.com /Cache/1500081626.PDF?O=PDF&T=&Y=&D=&FID=150008162 6&iid=102700.
3. Julius Fast, *Body Language* (New York: Pocket Books, 1960).
4. National Geographic Society, www.nationalgeographic.com.

Chapter 5

1. National Sleep Foundation, "Inside Your Bedroom: Use Your Senses," https://sleepfoundation.org/bedroom/.
2. Source: "Insufficient Sleep Is a Public Health Epidemic," Centers for Disease Control and Prevention. www.cdc.gov/features/dssleep/.
3. Source: "How Much Sleep Do Adults Need?" National Sleep Foundation. www.sleepfoundation.org/article/white-papers/how-much-sleep-do-adults-need

Chapter 6

1. Desmond Morris, *Bodytalk: The Meaning of Human Gestures* (New York: Crown Trade Paperbacks, 1994), pp. 118–19, 130–31.
2. Ibid., p. 142.

Chapter 7

1. Coca-Cola, "Mission, Vision and Values," www.coca-colacompany .com/our-company/mission-vision-values.

Chapter 8

1. Subway Our People, Our Communities, http://www.subway.com/en-us /aboutus/socialresponsibility/ourpeopleourcommunities#Diversity.
2. Tony Alessandra and Michael J. O'Connor, *The Platinum Rule* (New York: Warner Books, 1996).
3. American Indian Policy Center, www.airpi.org/research/tdlead.html.
4. Chickasaw Nation, www.chickasaw.net/site06/heritage/250_965.htm.
5. 10 Most Spoken Languages in 2016, http://speaklikenative.com /the-most-spoken-languages-in-the-world.
6. Bureau of Labor Statistics, U.S. Department of Labor, "Labor Force Characteristics of Foreign-Born Workers Summary," May 22, 2013, www.bls.gov/news.release/forbrn.nr0.htm.
7. National Geographic Society, http://www.nationalgeographic.com /magazines/l/multisubs/navH.html.
8. Disabled World, "Disability Statistics: Facts on Disabilities and Disability Issues," https://www.disabled-world.com/disability/statistics/.
9. Centers for Disease Control and Prevention, "Disability and Functioning (Noninstitutionalized Adults 18 Years and Over)," https://www .cdc.gov/nchs/fastats/disability.htm.
10. National Federation of the Blind, "Statistical Facts about Blindness in the United States," https://nfb.org/blindness-statistics.
11. The Mobility Resource, "Statistics about People with Disabilities," https://www.themobilityresource.com/about-us/media-room/mobility-statistics.
12. S. L. Coby and J. M. Ortman, "Projections of the Size and Composition of the U.S. Population: 2014-2060," March 2015, http://www .census.gov/content/dam/Census/library/publications/2015/demo/p25 -1143.pdf.

Chapter 9

1. J. Manyika and C. Roxburgh, "The Great Transformer: The Impact of the Internet on Economic Growth and Prosperity,", http://www.mckinsey.com/industries/high-tech/our-insights/the-great-transformer.

2. "ICT Facts and Figures 2016," http://www.itu.int/en/ITU-D/Statistics/Documents/facts/ICTFactsFigures2016.pdf.

3. "Nielsen, Millennials at the Mall: What Factors Drive Young Consumers' Retail Decisions," http://www.nielsen.com/us/en/insights/news/2015/millennials-at-the-mall-what-factors-drive-young-consumers-retail-decisions.html.

4. http://www.pewinternetorg/2014/04/03/older-adults-and-technology-use.

5. http://www.census.gov/retail/mrts/www/data/pdf/ec_current.pdf.

6. "Inquisitr, Black Friday Sales Figures: 2016 Online Sales Hit New Record with $3.34 billion in Purchases," http://www.inquisitr.com/3748502/black-friday-sales-figures-2016-online-sales-hit-new-record-with-3-34-billion-in-purchases.

7. K. Leggett, "Forrester's Top 15 Trends for Customer Service in 2013," January 14, 2013, http://www.blog.forresters.com/kate_leggett/13-01-14-forresters_top_15_trends_for_customer_service_in_2013.

8. "Top 5 Reasons Why People Follow Your Brand on Social Media," http://www.volusion.com/ecommerce-blog/articles/top-5-reasons-why-people-follow-your-brand-on-social-media-two-minutes-tuesdays.

9. "Nielsen Survey: Social Media Sucking up Most of Our Time," http://www.pcworld.com/article/2019194/nielsen-survey-social-media-sucking-up-most-of-our-time.html.

10. "Pinterest Statistics That Marketers Can't Ignore," http://www.sproutsocial.com/insights/pinterest-statistics.

11. J. Jargon, "Retailers Wage War Against Long Lines," *The Wall Street Journal*, May 1, 2013, http://online.wsj.com/article/SB10001424127887323798104578453293807869744.html.

Chapter 10

1. "Why Costco Is Crushing Walmart-Owned Sam's Club," www.huffingtonpost.com/2014/05/16/sams-club-vs-costco_n_5332306.html.

2. "Customer Service and Business Results: A Survey of Customer Service from Mid-size Companies," White Paper, April 2013, Dimensional Research, https://d16cvnquvjw7pr.cloudfront.net/resources/whitepapers/Zendesk_WP_Customer_Service_and_Business_Results.pdf.

3. C. Barton, J. Fromm, and C. Egan, "The Millennial Consumer: Debunking Stereotypes," The Boston Consulting Group, April 2012, p. 6, www.brandchannel.com/images/papers/536_BCG_The_Millennial_Consumer_Apr_2012%20(3)_tcm80-103894.pdf.

4. Source: Barton, C., Fromm, J. and Egan, C., "The Millennial Consumer: Debunking Stereotypes," The Boston Consulting Group, April 2012, p. 6, www.brandchannel.com/images/papers/536_BCG_The_Millennial_Consumer_Apr_2012%20(3)_tcm80-103894 .pdf.

5. "*Deepwater Horizon* Oil Spill," http://en.wikipedia.org/wiki/Deepwater_Horizon_oil_spill.

6. A. McInnes, "Customers' Problems Are Companies' Loyalty Opportunities," Forrester Blogs, December 6, 2012, http://blogs.forrester.com/andrew_mcinnes/10-12-06-customers_problems_are_companies_loyalty_building_opportunities.

7. Source: Gallo, Amy, "The Value of Keeping the Right Customers," Harvard Business Review, October 29, 2014.

8. A. Gallo, "The Value of Keeping the Right Customers," *Harvard Business Review*, October 29, 2014, www.hbr.org/2014/10/the-value-of-keeping-the-right-customers.

9. D. Hunter, "Customer Loyalty Boosts Small Business Profitability," May 30, 2013, www.freshbusinessthinking.com/news.php?CID=0&NID=18475&PGID=1#.UaeKlbnD-Uk.

10. J.D. Power and Associates, "2015 North America Hotel Guest Satisfaction Index Study," www.jdpower.com/pressrelease/2015-north-american-hotel-guest-satisfaction-index-study.

11. S. Smith, "Press Release: Mobile Coupon Users to Pass 1 Billion by 2019" July 29, 2014, http://juniperresearch.com/press-release/coupons-pr1.

12. Marriott, "Frequently Asked Questions," www.marriott.com/help/rates-faq.

13. TARP Worldwide, "Customer Mine Blog," November 9, 2008, http://blog.tarp.com/?m=20081109.

BIBLIOGRAPHY

Aguilar, Leslie; and Linda Stokes. *Multicultural Customer Service: Providing Outstanding Service across Cultures.* New York: McGraw-Hill/Irwin, 1996.

Albrecht, K., & Zemke, R., Service America!: Doing Business in the New Economy. New York: McGraw-Hill, 2002.

Alessandra, Tony; and Michael J. O'Connor. *The Platinum Rule: Discover the Four Basic Business Personalities and How They Can Lead You to Success.* New York: Grand Central Publishing, 2008.

Andersen, Peter A. *The Complete Idiot's Guide to Body Language.* New York: Penguin Group, 2004.

Anderson, Kristin; and Carol Kerr. *Customer Relationship Management.* New York: McGraw-Hill, 2002.

Anderson, Kristin; and Ron Zemke. *Knock Their Socks Off Answers.* New York: AMACOM, 1995.

Axtell, Roger E. *Gestures: The Do's and Taboos of Body Language around the World.* New York: Wiley, 1991.

Barlow, Janelle; and Paul Stewart. *Branded Customer Service: The New Competitive Edge.* San Francisco, CA: Berrett-Koehler, 2006.

Berman, Jillian, "Why Costco Is Crushing Walmart-Owned Sam's Club" Huffington Post, May 16, 2014.

Bureau of Labor Statistics, U.S. Department of Labor, "Employee Tenure Summary," news release, September 22, 2016.

Bosworth, Michael T.; and John R. Holland. *Customer Centric Selling.* New York: McGraw-Hill, 2004.

Bowden, Mark. *Winning Body Language: Control Conversation, Command Attention, and Convey the Right Message—Without Saying a Word.* New York: McGraw-Hill, 2010.

Bowman, Judith. *Don't Take the Last Donut: New Rules of Business Etiquette.* Franklin Lakes, NJ: Career Press, 2007.

Burgoon, Judie K.; Laura K. Guerrero; and Kory Floyd. *Nonverbal Communication.* Upper Saddle River, NJ: Pearson, 2009.

Bureau of Labor Statistics, U.S. Department of Labor, "Employee Tenure Summary," news release, September 22, 2016.

Calero, Henry H. *The Power of Nonverbal Communication: How You Act Is More Important Than What You Say.* Los Angeles, CA: Silver Lake Publishing, 2005.

Capodagli, Bill; and Lynn Jackson. *The Disney Way: Harnessing the Management Secrets of Disney in Your Company.* New York: McGraw-Hill, 2007.

Coca-Cola, "Mission, Vision and Values," www.coca-colacompany .com/our-company/mission-vision-values.

Disney Institute. *Be Our Guest: Perfecting the Art of Customer Service.* New York: Disney Editions, 2001.

Evensen, Renée. *Customer Service Training 101: Quick and Easy Steps That Get Results.* 2nd ed. New York: AMACOM, 2010.

Ford, Lisa; David McNair; and Bill Perry. *Exceptional Customer Service: Going Beyond Your Good Service to Exceed the Customer's Expectation.* Avon, MA: Adams Media, 2001.

Gee, Val; and Jeff Gee. *Super Service: Seven Keys to Delivering Great Customer Service.* New York: McGraw-Hill, 1999.

Greenberg, Paul. *CRM at the Speed of Light.* 4th ed. New York: McGraw-Hill, 2009.

Gudykunst, William B. *Bridging Differences: Effective Intergroup Communication.* 4th ed. Thousand Oaks, CA: Sage, 2003.

Gundling, Ernest; and Anita Zanchettin. *Global Diversity: Winning Customers and Engaging Employees within World Markets.* Boston, MA: Nicholas Brealey International, 2007.

Hicks, Rick; and Kathy Hicks. *Boomers, Xers, and Other Strangers: Understanding the Generational Differences That Divide Us.* Wheaton, IL: Tyn Dale, 1999.

Karp, Hank; Connie Fuller; and Danilo Sirias. *Bridging the Boomer Xer Gap.* Palo Alto, CA: Davies-Black, 2002.

Kelleher, B., Employee Engagement For Dummies. New York, NY: John Wiley & Sons, 2013.

Lebon, Paul. *Escape Voicemail Hell: Boost Your Productivity by Making Voicemail Work for You.* Highland Village, TX: Parleau, 2000.

Leland, Karen; and Keith Bailey. *Customer Service for Dummies.* 3rd ed. New York: Wiley, 2007.

Lucas, Robert W. *How to Be a Great Call Center Representative.* Watertown, MA: American Management Association, 2001.

Lucas, Robert W. *Please Every Customer: Delivering Stellar Customer Service across Cultures.* New York: McGraw-Hill Professional, 2011.

National Restaurant Association. *Customer Service Competency Guide.* Upper Saddle River, NJ: Prentice Hall, 2007.

Pease, Allan; and Barbara Pease. *The Definitive Book of Body Language.* New York: Bantam Dell, 2004.

Quinlan, Kathryn A. *Customer Service Representative.* Mankato, MN: Capstone Press, 1999.

Remland, Martin S. *Nonverbal Communication in Everyday Life.* 3rd ed. Boston, MA: Houghton Mifflin, 2008.

Richardson, Will. *Blogs, Wikis, Podcasts and Other Powerful Tools for Classrooms.* Thousand Oaks, CA: Corwin Press, 2006.

Satterwhite, Marilyn; and Judith Olson-Sutton. *Business Communication at Work.* New York: Glencoe/McGraw-Hill, 2000.

Solomon, Charlene M.; and Michael S. Schell. *Managing across Cultures: The Seven Keys to Doing Business with a Global Mindset.* New York: McGraw-Hill, 2009.

Solomon, Micah. *High-Tech High-Touch Customer Service: Inspire Timeless Loyalty in the Demanding New World of Social Commerce.* New York: AMACOM, 2012.

Sterne, Jim. *Customer Service on the Internet: Building Relationships, Increasing Loyalty, and Staying Competitive.* 2nd ed. New York: Wiley, 2000.

Stinnett, Bill. *Think Like Your Customer: A Winning Strategy to Maximize Sales by Understanding How and Why Your Customers Buy.* New York: McGraw-Hill, 2005.

Timm, Paul R.; and Christopher G. Jones. *Technology and Customer Service: Profitable Relationship Building.* Upper Saddle River, NJ: Pearson Education, 2005.

Toister, Jeff. *Service Failure: The Real Reasons Employees Struggle with Customer Service and What You Can Do about It.* New York: AMACOM, 2012.

Trompenaars, Fons; and Charles Hampden-Turner. *Riding the Waves of Culture: Understanding Diversity in Global Business.* 2nd ed. New York: McGraw-Hill, 1998.

Wainwright, Gordon R. *Teach Yourself Body Language.* Chicago, IL: Contemporary Books, 2003.

Wolvin, Andrew D. *Listening and Human Communication in the 21st Century.* Chichester, West Sussex, United Kingdom: Wiley-Blackwell, 2010.

Zemke, Ron; and Chip Bell. *Service Magic: The Art of Amazing Your Customers.* Dearborn, MI: Dearborn Trade Publishing, 2003.

Zemke, Ron; Claire Raines; and Bob Filipczak. *Generations at Work: Managing the Clash of Veterans, Boomers, Xers, and Nexters in Your Workplace.* New York: AMACOM, 2000.

Zimmerman, Scott; Ronald Finklestein; and Tony Alessandra. *The Platinum Rule for Small Business Mastery.* New York: Morgan James Publishing, 2007.

INDEX

A

Accessories, personal, 148–149
Acculturated, 297
ACD system. *See* Automatic call distribution (ACD) system
ACSI. *See* American Customer Satisfaction Index (ACSI)
Active listening, 114. *See also* Listening
ADA Amendments Act of 2008, 313
Adaptability, 411
Address, forms of, 299–301
Advertising
  cars as billboards, 148
  function of, 74
Aggressiveness, 124–127
Albertson's, 84
American Customer Satisfaction Index (ACSI), 393
Angry customers, 251–253
ANI system. *See* Automatic number identification (ANI) system
Answering machines/services, 373–375
Apologies, 277
Appearance/grooming
  clothing and accessories and, 148–149
  hygiene and, 147
  as nonverbal communication, 146–149
Applications (apps), 412
Articulation, 144–145
Assertiveness
  examples of, 122
  explanation of, 122
  methods to demonstrate, 124
  when dealing with demanding or domineering customers and, 248–249
Assigning meaning, 177
Assistance, offering, 165
Attending, 177
Attention span, 104
Attentiveness, 180
Attitude, 53
  explanation of, 304
  toward conflict, 303–304
Automated attendants, 338
Automated computer telephone interviews, 339
Automated surveys, 402
Automatic call distribution (ACD) system, 339–340
Automatic number identification (ANI) system, 339
Avoid criticism, 200

B

B2B. *See* Business-to-business (B2B)
Behavioral styles
  aggressive, 122
  communication based on, 156, 220–223
  cultural awareness and, 229–231
  decisive, 218–219
  explanation of, 191, 211
  expressive, 219
  identification of, 212–219
  inquisitive, 217–218

  nonverbal communication and, 224
  perceptions and stereotypes and, 233–235
  problem solving, 223
  process improvement and, 228–229
  questioning approaches and, 231
  rational, 216–217
  from small business perspective, 235–236
Beliefs. *See also* Values
  explanation of, 295
Best Buy, 21
Biases
  explanation of, 181–182
  against older individuals, 327
Blame, avoiding, 109
Bloggers, 354
Body language. *See also* Nonverbal communication
  assertive and nonassertive, 122–124
  eye contact as, 118, 138–139
  facial expressions as, 118–119, 139–140
  gender and, 155–157
  gestures as, 141–142
  head nodding as, 140–141
  management of, 130
  posture as, 140
Body Language (Fast), 137
BP. *See* British Petroleum (BP)
Brand loyalty, 389–391
Brewer, Rosalind, 387
British Petroleum (BP), 397
Broadband Internet access, 16
Brotman, Jeffrey, 387
Business-to-business (B2B), 25

C

Call centers
  technology in, 338–345
  trends in, 336
Call waiting, 373
Candler, Asa, 241
CCOs. *See* Chief customer officers (CCOs)
Channel partners, 408–409
Channels, 101–105
Charpentier, Patricia, 416
Chief customer officers (CCOs), 12
Churn, 405
Churn rate, 405
Circadian rhythm, 183–184
Closed-ended questions
  explanation of, 198–199
  for talkative customers, 263
Closure, 199
Clothing, 148–149
Clusters, of nonverbal behavior, 161
Coca-Cola, 241
Code of ethics, 413
Collective cultures, 304
Color
  emotions and, 153
  as nonverbal cue, 153–154

Commitment
    demonstration of, 83–84
    honoring, 260
Communication. *See also* Listening; Nonverbal communication
    aggressive manner of, 124–129
    assertive manner of, 122–123
    conflict and, 103
    with customers, 104–105
    for customers with language differences and, 307–312
    dealing assertively with, 122–124
    elements of positive, 122
    importance of effective, 98–100
    model, interpersonal, 101–105
    negative, 119–122
    of organizational culture and vision, 61
    on personal level, 111
    providing feedback to, 111–119
    skills, and customer loyalty, 411–412
    skills for telephone, 367–368
    two-way, 100–101
Compassion, 280
Compensation
    for inconvenience or loss, 280
    as motivator, 66
Competition, 427
Complacency, 69–70, 257
Complaints, 74, 426. *See also* Service breakdowns
Comprehending, 177
Computer telephony integration (CTI), 340
Computer use, 350. *See also* Technology
Conflict, attitude toward, 303–304
Consumer behavior, trends in, 32–33
Contact points, 421
Contingency plans, 418
Continuous quality improvement (CQI), 428
Costco, 387–388
Cost of dissatisfied customers, 427
Cottage industries, 9
Coupons, 412
Courtesy, 86, 163, 319
CQI. *See* Continuous quality improvement (CQI)
CTI. *See* Computer telephony integration (CTI)
Cultural diversity. *See also* Diversity
    among customers, 305
    attitude toward conflict and, 303–304
    awareness of, 97
    with customers having language differences, 307–312
    distance and, 157
    explanation of, 294
    forms of address and, 299–301
    gender, 303
    gender roles and, 303
    interpersonal relationships and, 301
    language differences and, 307–312
    modesty and, 298
    nonverbal communication and, 157
    privacy expectations and, 298–299
    property ownership and, 305
    respect for elders and, 301
    values and, 28–30, 296–306
Cultural values, 296–306
Culture. *See also* Organizational culture; Service culture
    explanation of, 53–55
Customer-centered approach, 110
Customer-centric organizations, 53
Customer comment cards, 79, 402
Customer defection, 257–258
Customer-focused behavior
    courtesy as, 163
    function of, 163–166
    strategies for, 160–161, 263–271
Customer-focused organizations, 6–7
Customer focus groups, 79

Customer-friendly systems, 73
Customer loyalty
    adaptability and, 411
    admitting errors or lack of knowledge to promote, 396–398
    and brand loyalty, 389–391
    business approach and, 229
    channel partners in, 408–409
    communication skills and, 411–412
    customer as number one and, 420–423
    decisiveness and, 413
    display of care and concern to build, 395
    effective communication and, 395
    eliciting customer input to promote, 401–403
    enthusiasm and, 413
    ethical behavior and, 413–415
    examples of, 390
    explanation of, 389–390
    fairness and, 396
    and follow up, 423
    importance of, 407–408
    initiative and, 415–416
    keeping an open mind to promote, 400
    keeping your word to promote, 398–399
    knowledge and, 416
    offering individualized service to promote, 400–401
    perceptiveness and, 416–417
    personalized approach for, 399
    planning ability and, 417–419
    problem-solving ability and, 419
    professionalism and, 419
    provider characteristics affecting, 409–419
    providing peace of mind to promote, 399
    responsiveness and, 409–411
    showing respect to promote, 401
    in small businesses, 428–430
    trusting customers to promote, 398
Customer loyalty programs, 406
Customer relationship management (CRM)
    benefits of, 406–407
    explanation of, 7, 404
    function of, 404–405
    software, 340–341
Customer relationships
    built on customer needs, 422
    communication interactions for positive, 104–105, 256
    cultural awareness as element of, 326–327
    explanation of, 404
    importance of, 405–406
    trust in, 83
Customer retention, 405
Customers
    agreeing with, 115
    angry, 251–253
    bonding with, 229
    communication with, 99
    cost of dissatisfied, 427
    creating partnership with, 85
    customer expectations and, 244
    dealing assertively with, 122–124
    demanding or domineering customers and, 248–249
    demonstrating empathy with, 87
    difficult, 246–255
    eliciting input from, 401–403
    expectations following service breakdown, 244
    expectations of, 34–35, 109–114
    external, 36–37
    focus on, 7, 99
    forms of address for, 299–301
    getting approval from, 115
    handling, 425
    indecisive, 249–250
    information-gathering with, 196–199
    internal, 37–39

Customers (*continued*)
    knowledge of, 44, 425
    language differences and, 307–312
    needs of, 73, 79, 196, 410, 422
    as number one, 420–423
    preparing for positive interactions with, 105–107
    rapport with, 116, 421–422
    rude or inconsiderate, 253 254
    staying connected with, 263
    strategies to exhibit importance of, 98
    talkative, 254–255
    trust your, 398
    working with, 84
    younger, 319–321
Customer satisfaction
    explanation of, 393
    methods to gather information on, 401–403
    paying attention, 424
    quality and, 428
    as strategy to retain customers, 33, 424–428
Customer satisfaction surveys, 79
Customer service. *See also* Service culture
    changing values and, 28–30
    deregulation and, 27
    e-commerce and, 32–33
    economy and, 13–19
    forms of address and, 299–301
    gender roles and, 303
    geopolitical changes and, 27–28
    global economic shifts and, 20–22
    historical background of, 47
    increase in white-collar workers and, 19
    individualized, 400–401
    interpersonal relationships and, 301
    older workers in labor force and, 31–32
    population and labor force shifts and, 22–24
    privacy expectations and, 298–299
    role of technology in, 30, 333–335
    service sector growth and, 12–13
    societal factors affecting, 19
    striving for improvement in, 68–69
    telephone use in, 371–373
Customer service environment
    customers and, 36
    deliverables and, 42–43
    delivery systems and, 43
    human resources and, 39–42
    organizational culture and, 39
    service and, 43
    service environment, 36–39
Customer service personnel. *See also* Employee roles; Employees
    competencies of, 42
    customer pet peeves of, 106–107
    quality of, 34–35
    roles and expectations of, 57
    telecommuting by, 16
    titles and functions of, 40–41
    verbal communication skills of, 110
Customers with disabilities
    explanation of, 191
    hearing, 314–315
    mobility or motion impairments, 316–317
    vision, 315–316

D

Decisiveness, 413
Decisive style
    communication with people having, 216–217
    explanation of, 218–219
    to handle service breakdowns, 283
    problem-solving using, 223

Decoding, 102–103
Defection, customer, 257–258
Deregulation, 27
Difficult customers, 246–255
Direct contact, 75
Direct questions, 200–201
Disaster planning initiatives, 281–283
Discrimination, 306
Disney, Walt, 391
Disparate treatment, 234
Dissatisfied customers, 251
    strategies to prevent, 263–271
Distance, as nonverbal cue, 149
Diversity. *See also* Cultural diversity
    age and, 296
    communication and, 297
    disabilities and, 312–317
    explanation of, 294
    small business perspective on, 324
Domineering customers, 248–249
Downsizing, 17, 62
Drucker, Peter F., 134

E

EAPs. *See* Employee assistance programs
E-commerce, growth in, 32–33
Economy
    consumer mindset and, 33–34
    globalization of, 25–27
    impact on jobs, 13–19
    projections for U.S., 23
Electronic mail (e-mail), 341
Emotion-reducing model, 255–256
Emotions
    color and, 153
    listening to identify, 118
    methods to handle, 255–257
Empathy, 87, 194, 271
Employee assistance programs (EAPs), 184
Employee exit interviews, 79
Employee focus groups, 78
Employee opinion surveys, 78
Employee recognition, 67
Employee roles
    establishment of, 59, 62
    explanation of, 57
    in large organizations, 61
    in nonprofit organizations, 62–63
    in small organizations, 88
Employees. *See also* Customer service
    personnel
    attracting and keeping qualified, 43
    empowerment of, 55, 71
    motivation of, 66–68
Empowerment, employees, 55, 71
Encoding, 102
Enthusiasm, 413
Enthusiastic service, 87
Environment, for communication, 101
Environmental cues, 150–151
Erin Brockovich, 82
Ethical behavior
    customer loyalty and, 413–415
    demonstration of, 81
    examples of, 414
Ethics, 81
Etiquette, as nonverbal cue, 153
European Union (EU), formation of, 20
Exit interviews, 402
Expectations
    of customers, 34–35, 109–114

of employees, 55, 57
of privacy, 298–299
Expedia, 336
Expressive style. *See also* Behavioral styles
  communication with people having, 216–217
  explanation of, 218–219
  to handle service breakdowns, 283
  problem-solving using, 223
External customers, 36–37
External obstacles, to listening, 187–190
Eyebrow raising, 160
Eye contact
  cultural diversity and, 157
  as nonverbal behavior, 163
  use of, 118

F

Face, loss of, 302, 304
Facial expressions, 139–140
Facsimile (fax) machine, 341
Fairness, 396
Fast, Julius, 137
Faulty assumptions, 186
Fax-on-demand, 341
Fee-based 900 numbers, 337
Feedback
  clarifying, 162
  customer, 116
  explanation of, 103
  nonverbal, 118–119
  social media and technology and, 190
  tips for providing, 117
  verbal, 118
Feel, felt, found technique, 87
Fidgeting, 159
Filters, 103
Finger-pointing, 141, 159
Flexible time, 67
Focus groups, 403
  customer, 79
  employee, 78
Follow-through, 152–153
Follow-up telephone surveys, 402
Foreign-born people, 307. *See also* Cultural diversity
Forms of address, 299–301
Forrester Research, Inc., 398

G

Gender, communication and, 155–157
Gender roles, 303
Generation X, 319
Generation Y, 319
Geopolitical changes, 27–28
Gestures, 141–142
Globalization
  cultural and language variations and, 103
  economic change and, 20–21
Global terms, 120
GoToMeeting, 17

H

Hand gestures, 142
Handshakes, 159
Harper, Jennifer, 162
Head nodding, 140–141
Health, listening and, 184
Hearing, 176

disabilities, 314–315
loss, 184–185
Help desks, 337. *See also* Call centers
Hinkle, Anne, 338
Hispanics
  forms of address and, 299–301
  in labor force, 42
Homesourcing, 262
The Huffington Post, 387
Human resources, 39–42
Humor, 310
Hygiene, 147

I

ICCSO. *See* International Council of Customer Service
  Organizations (ICCSO)
"I" messages, 111–112
Impact of culture, 157–158. *See also* Cultural diversity
Implied messages, 176
Indecisive customers, 249–250
Indirect contact, 75
Individualistic cultures, 304
Inflection, 143
Information-gathering techniques
  closed-end questions as, 198–199
  function of, 196–199
  open-end questions as, 196–198
Information overload, 187
Initiative, 415–416
Inquisitive style. *See also* Behavioral styles
  to handle service breakdowns, 283
Insourcing, 26–27
Instant messaging, 16, 341
Intelligent callback technology, 341
Interactive kiosks or digital displays, 342
Interactive voice response (IVR) system, 342
Interferences, 145
Internal customers, 37–39
  building relationships with, 261
  examples of, 38
  explanation of, 37–39
  working with, 258–262
International Council of Customer Service Organizations (ICCSO), 11
Internet. *See also* Websites
  statistics for use of, 346
  technological change and, 11, 19, 338
  telecommuting and, 16
Internet callback technology, 342
Internet telephony, 342
Interpersonal communication model
  channel and, 101–105
  decoding and, 102–103
  encoding and, 102
  feedback and, 103
  filters and, 103
  message and, 102
  receiver and, 102
  sender and, 101–102
Interpersonal relationships, 301
Intimate distance, 149
ISO 900, 11
ISO 10002:2004, 11
IVR system. *See* Interactive voice response (IVR) system

J

Jobs
  distribution of, 16–17
  quality of, 17–18
  quantity of newly created, 13–16

Johnson & Johnson, 397
Jung, Carl, 212

K

Knowledge
    admitting lack of, 396–398
    of competition, 427
    of customers, 44, 425
    of organization, 83
    product and service, 232, 416

L

Labor force
    ethnic and racial diversity in, 30
    Foreign-born individuals in, 307
    hispanics in, 42
    older workers in, 31–32
    projections for U.S., 22
    shifts in, 22–24
    women in, 30
Lag time, 186
Language. *See also* Communication
    assertive and nonassertive, 122–124, 123
    avoiding negative, 119–122
    customer-centric, 110
    "I" messages and "we" messages and, 111–112
    positive phrasing in, 112–113
    relationship-building, 119
    specific, 113
Leadership, 56
Learning organizations, 44
Listening. *See also* Communication
    active, 114, 192–194
    characteristics of good, 179–181
    for emotional responses, 99
    explanation of, 175
    external obstacles to, 187–190
    hearing and, 176
    hearing loss and, 184–185
    importance of, 37, 174–175
    indicators of poor, 185
    information-gathering techniques for, 196
    levels of, 185–186
    obstacles to effective, 187–190
    personal obstacles to, 181–185
    process of, 203
    question guidelines and, 200–202
    research on, 203
    from small business perspective, 201–202
    strategies to improve, 191–195
    thought speed and, 186
    willingness to, 194
Listening gap, 186
Listening self-assessment, 178
Loss of face, 304

M

MagicBands, 391
Malapropism, 145
Management inspections, 79
Management reports, 79
Management support, 55, 68–71
Manners, 153
Marriott hotel chain, 427
Massen, Sharon, 101
Media blending, 342
Mentors, 69
Meriwether Lewis Elementary School, 336

Messages. *See also* Communication; Nonverbal communication
    explanation of, 102
    hearing and receiving, 176–177
    "I" and "we,," 111–112
    implied, 176
    nonverbal, 137
Millennials, 390
Miscellaneous cues, 151–158
Mission, 55–57
Mission statements, 56
Mobile applications, 412
Mobility or motion impairments, 316–317
Modesty, 298
Moment of truth, 421
Monochronic time, 304
Motion impairments, 316–317
Motivation, rewards as, 55, 66–67
Mystery shoppers, 79

N

NAFTA. *See* North American Free Trade Agreement (NAFTA)
Namaste, 300
National Retail Federation, 387
National Sleep Foundation, 182
Needs
    customer, 243, 410, 422
    customers, 73, 79
    of customers, 196
    dealing with unmet, 258
    of younger customers, 319–321
Negative communication, 119–122. *See also* Communication
Networking, 18
Nichols, Ralph, 172
Noise, 103, 189
Nonverbal communication. *See also* Communication
    appearance and grooming as, 146–149
    behavioral styles and, 224
    body language as, 118–129, 138–142
    clusters of, 161
    color as, 153–154
    customer-focused behavior and, 163–166
    environmental cues as, 150–151
    etiquette and manners as, 153
    explanation of, 137
    eye contact as, 118, 138–139
    facial expressions as, 118–119, 139–140
    follow-through as, 152–153
    gender and, 155–157
    gestures as, 141–142
    head nodding as, 140–141
    negative, 158
    perception of, 121
    personal habits as, 151
    positive, 161
    posture as, 140
    in small businesses, 166
    spatial cues as, 149–150
    strategies to improve, 160–161
    time allocation and attention as, 152
    vocal cues as, 143–145
Nonverbal feedback, 118–119
North American Free Trade Agreement (NAFTA), 27
Note-taking, 194

O

Obama, Barack, 34, 336
Objections, 197
Objectivity, 181
Office politics, 262

Offshoring
  explanation of, 26
  function of, 76–77
  recession and, 262
Older individuals
  as customers, 317–319
  in labor force, 31–32
  respect for, 301
Oliver-Knappe, Stacey, 232, 298, 396
Online information fulfillment systems, 342–343
On-site management visits, 79
Open-ended questions
  for dissatisfied or angry customers, 251–253
  explanation of, 196–198
  to gather information, 196–199
Open mindedness, 400
Opinion surveys, employee, 78
Organizational culture. *See also* Service culture
  explanation of, 39
  mission or philosophy and, 55–57
  policies and procedures and, 63–65
  products and services and, 65–66
  social media and, 72
  training programs and, 71, 72
Organizations. *See also* Small businesses
  customer-centric, 53
  customer-focused, 6
  employee empowerment in, 71
  employee roles and expectations in, 55, 57
  employee roles in large, 60–61
  employee roles in nonprofit, 62–63
  employee roles in small, 62
  learning, 44
  policies and procedures of, 63–65
  separating average from excellent, 85–86
  vision of, 55
Outsourcing
  explanation of, 26
  function of, 76–77
  positive and negative aspects of, 77
  technology and, 26

P

Pacific Gas & Electric (PG&E), 82
Paralanguage, 141
Paraphrases, 102
Patience, 87, 180
Pauses, as vocal cue, 145
Peering over eyeglasses, 160
Pemberton, John, 241
Perceptions
  checking your, 121, 161–162
  explanation of, 232–234
  factors affecting, 233
  stereotypes and, 232–234
Perceptiveness, 416–417
Performance appraisals, 56
Permission, 115
Personal distance, 149
Personal habits, 151
Personal identification number (PIN), 391
Personal obstacles, to listening, 181–185
Pet peeves, 106–107
Petrovich, Tony, 314
Physical barriers, 189
PIN. *See* Personal identification number (PIN)
Pitch, 143
PLAN acronym (positive communication)
  addressing customer's expectations positively and, 104–105
  explanation of, 104
  letting customers know they are importance and, 112

  nurturing continuing relationship and, 114–117
  preparing for positive customer interactions and, 105–107
Planning process model, 418
Platinum Rule, 294
Polychronic time, 304
Population, 22–24
Posts, 354
Posture, 140
Predictive dialing systems, 343
Preoccupation, 184
Price Club, 387
PriceCostco company, 387
Priceline, 336
Privacy, 298–299
Problems, resolution of, 74
Problem solving
  behavioral styles for, 223
  customer loyalty and, 419
  explanation of, 272
  strategies for, 275–281
Problem-solving model
  explanation of, 272
  steps in, 272
Process improvement, 228–229
Products
  knowledge of, 231, 416
  organizational culture and, 65–66
Professionalism, 87, 419
Profit and loss statements, 79
Prohibitions, 277
Property ownership, 306
Protégé, 69
Provider-centered approach, 110
Proxemics, 149
Psychological distracters, 182
Pupilometrics, 138

Q

QR code (Quick Response code), 334
Quality
  customer satisfaction and, 428
  expectations of, 19–20
Questions
  closed-ended, 198–199
  for customers with language differences and, 307–312
  direct, 200–201
  guidelines for, 200–202
  open-end, 196–198
  positively phrased, 112–113, 200

R

Rapport, 116, 421–422
Rational style. *See also* Behavioral styles
  communication with people having, 216–217
  to handle service breakdowns, 283
  problem-solving using, 223
Real-Time IM Relay for Customers with Hearing and Speech Loss, 315
Recalls, 394
Receiver, 102
Recession of 2007
  economic effects of, 17
  reversal of offshoring due to, 262
Recognition, customer expectations for, 86
Recovery Act, 25
Refreshments, 165
Relationship-building methods
  cultural awareness and, 223–232
  discovering customer need as, 229, 422
  focusing on improvement as, 228–229

Relationship-building methods (*continued*)
    making customers feel special as, 229
    saying "yes" as, 226
    seeking opportunities for service as, 227–228
    when responding to customer problems, 226
Relationships
    gender and, 155–157
    interpersonal, 301
    methods to nurture, 114–117
    words and phrases that build, 105
Resources, sharing of, 84
Respect, 264–266, 317, 401
Responding, 177
Responsibility, 396–397
Responsiveness, 409–411
Return policies, 63
Rewards, 66–67
Richard, Wendy, 276, 401
Ross, George, 208
Ross, Joel, 240
RUMBA (Realistic, Understandable, Measurable, Believable, Attainable), 57–63
Rush Hour (film), 309

S

Sales and service records, 403
Sarcasm, 310
SBA. *See* Small Business Administration (SBA)
Screen pop-ups, 343
Seamless service, 228
Self-assessment
    behavioral style, 212
    listening, 178
Self-service, trends in, 85
Semantics, 145
Senge, Peter, 44
Service breakdowns
    adapting proactive approach to, 261
    building professional reputation following, 261
    customer defection following, 257–258
    customer expectations and, 244
    demanding or domineering customers and, 248–249
    difficult customers and, 246–255
    disaster planning initiatives for, 281–282
    dissatisfied and angry customers and, 251–253
    emotion-reducing model to deal with, 255–257
    examples of, 243
    indecisive customers and, 249–251
    internal customers and, 258–262
    meeting commitments following, 261
    preventing dissatisfaction following, 263–271
    problem-solving process following, 272–275
    rude or inconsiderate customers and, 253–254
    service-recovery strategy following, 275–281
    small business perspective on, 283
    staying connected following, 263
    talkative customers and, 254–255
Service contact surveys, 402
Service culture. *See also* Customer service;
    Organizational culture
    components of excellent, 85
    customer loyalty as element of, 53
    elements of, 91
    employee empowerment and, 71
    employee roles and expectations and, 57
    management support and, 68–70
    motivators and rewards and, 66–67
    products and services and, 65–67
    service delivery systems in, 74–77
    service measurement and, 78–89
    service philosophy or mission and, 55–57

    strategies to promote positive, 72–73
    system components in, 74
    that provides what customers wants, 75
    training and, 71
Service delivery systems
    customer service environment and, 43
    direct or indirect, 75–76
    explanation of, 74–77
    third-party, 76–77
Service economy
    explanation of, 11
    shift to, 11–13
Service industry, 6
Service jobs
    distribution of, 16–17
    quality of, 17–18
    quantity of newly created, 13–16
Service measurement
    explanation of, 78–89
    tools for, 78–89
Service options, 277
Service philosophy, 55–57
Service recovery
    explanation of, 44
    strategies for, 275–281
Services
    customer expectations regarding, 87
    enthusiastic, 87
    expectation of quality of, 34–35
    knowledge of, 416
    organizational culture and, 90–91
    providing follow up to, 84
    seamless, 228
    seeking opportunities for service as, 227–228
    skill improvement for, 83
    strategy for, 72–73
Service sector
    explanation of, 8
    growth of, 12–13
Shaw, Charles, 209
Shopper/customer surveys, 402–403
Silence, 145
Sinegal, James, 387
Skype, 16
Small Business Administration (SBA), 282
Small businesses
    customer loyalty in, 428–430
    customer service in, 16, 62
    growth in, 62
    listening skills in, 201
    service recovery in, 283
    technology use in, 355
Small talk, 111
Smartphones, 352–353
Smiling, 143
Social distance, 149
Social media, 16
    customer feedback and, 190
    function of, 16–17
    organizational culture and, 72
Social networking, 18
Spatial cues, 149–150
Speakerphones, 189
Speech- or voice-recognition, 343
Speech rate, 144
Sperry and Hutchinson (S&H) Green Stamps program, 391
Standard English, 309
Standing up, 164
Stereotypes
    diversity and, 295
    explanation of, 232–234
Succession planning, 69, 77
Suppliers, 84

T

Tablets, 352–353
Talkative customers, 263
TDD. *See* Telecommunications device for the deaf (TDD)
Technical Assistance Research Program (TARP) Worldwide, 407, 429
Technology
    advantages and disadvantages of, 355–360
    attention span and, 104
    communication skills and, 367–368
    customer contact/call centers, 337–345
    customer feedback and, 190, 349
    customer issues related to, 357–358
    employee issues related to, 356–357
    etiquette for use of, 361–365
    increased efficiency in, 24–27
    role in customer service, 333–335
    telecommuting and, 16
    trends in, 336
Telecommunications device for the deaf (TDD), 315
Telecommunications Relay Service (TRS), 314
Telecommuting
    advantages of, 26
    trends in, 16
Telephone communication
    advantages of, 99, 355–360
    creating positive image through, 369–371
    effective use of, 99, 371–373
    message taking and, 375–376
    overview of, 349
    strategies for, 376
    transferring and holding calls and, 371
    voice mail and answering machines or services and, 373–375
Telephone ringing, 188
Telephone tag, 375
Telephone typewriter system (TTY), 315, 344
Telework, 16
Texting, 353
Text messaging, 353
The Fifth Discipline, 44
The Insider (film), 82
Third-party delivery
    benefits and drawbacks of, 76–77
    function of, 77
Thought speed, 186
Time, concept of, 304–305
Time allocation, 152
Time off, 67
Toll-free numbers, 402
Total quality management (TQM), 428
Touch point, 389
TQM. *See* Total quality management (TQM)
Trade agreements, effects of, 27
Trader Joe's, 209
Training programs, 72
Travelocity, 336
TRS. *See* Telecommunications Relay Service (TRS)
Trust
    and customer loyalty, 389–391
    explanation of, 83, 392
    strategies to build, 395–403
TTY. *See* Telephone typewriter (TTY)
Two-way communication, 100–101. *See also* Communication

U

Understanding, 179
Unprofessional handshake, 158–159

U.S. Bureau of Labor Statistics, 40
U.S. Census Bureau, 292

V

Values. *See also* Beliefs; Cultural values
    explanation of, 295
    impact of, 28–30, 296–306
Vendors, treatment of, 84
Verbal comments, 402
Verbal cues, behavioral style and, 220
Verbal feedback, 118
Vision disabilities, 315–316
Vision statements, 56
Vocal cues
    articulation as, 144–145
    explanation of, 143
    gender and, 155–157
    pauses as, 145
    semantics as, 145
    silence as, 145
Voice mail, 373–375
Voice over Internet Protocol (VoIP), 344–345
Voice quality, 144
Voice response unit (VRU), 342
VoIP. *See* Voice over Internet Protocol (VoIP)
Volume, 143
VRU. *See* Voice response unit (VRU)

W

Wai, 299
Wait-time reduction, 165
Walk-through audits, 79
Walt Disney World, 391
Wants, customer, 243
Warner, Doug, 330
Websites. *See also* Internet
    up-to-date and easy to navigate, 75
"We" messages, 111–112
White-collar workers, 19
Wi-Fi, 353
Win-win solutions, 126
Women
    in labor force, 30
    nodding of head and, 140–141
Woodruff, Robert, 241
Work distance, 149
Workforce. *See* Labor force
Workplace. *See also* Labor force
    good-neighbor policy in, 261–262
    office politics in, 262

Y

Yanovich, Teri, 265, 418
Younger customers, 319–321

Z

Zappos.com, 5
Zero tolerance policy, 306